The United States and Japan

Cooperative Leadership for Peace and Global Prosperity

The Atlantic Council
of the United States

UNIVERSITY
PRESS OF
AMERICA

Lanham • New York • London

Copyright © 1990 by
University Press of America®, Inc.
4720 Boston Way
Lanham, Maryland 20706

3 Henrietta Street
London WC2E 8LU England

Co-published by arrangement with
The Atlantic Council of the United States

Library of Congress Cataloging-in-Publication Data

The United States and Japan : cooperative leadership for
peace and global prosperity /
the Atlantic Council of the United States.
p.   cm.
"Co-published by arrangement with the
Atlantic Council of the United States"—T.p. verso.
Includes bibliographical references (p.   ).
1. Economic assistance, American—Developing countries.
2. Economic assistance, Japanese—Developing countries.
3. United States—Foreign economic relations—Japan.
4. Japan—Foreign economic relations—United States.
5. International cooperation.
I. Atlantic Council of the United States.
HC60.U645   1990   337.52073—dc20   89–25090 CIP

ISBN 0–8191–7712–1 (alk. paper)
ISBN 0–8191–7713–X (pbk. : alk. paper)

 TM The paper used in this publication meets the minimum requirements of
American National Standard for Information Sciences—Permanence
of Paper for Printed Library Materials, ANSI Z39.48–1984.

TABLE OF CONTENTS

FOREWORD

Increased opportunities for political and economic cooperation between the United States and Japan led to the initiation of this bilateral policy program on United States and Japan cooperative leadership for peace and global prosperity. A Committee of Six, co-chaired by Ambassador U. Alexis Johnson and Ambassador Yoshio Okawara, and including General Andrew J. Goodpaster, Takashi Hosomi, Kiichi Saeki, and Paul A. Volcker, initiated the project, under the cosponsorship of the Atlantic Council, the Bretton Woods Committee, and the Japan Center for International Exchange. In order to explore new avenues for U.S.–Japan cooperation on global issues, particularly those associated with the developing world, they commissioned research on economic and politico-security relations and conducted extensive consultations with a wide range of U.S. and Japanese policy-makers and private sector leaders.

The objective of the project was twofold: (a) to promote a clear understanding of U.S. and Japanese shared responsibilities for global prosperity and security, particularly with regard to Third World economic development and stability; and (b) to develop a broad vision of cooperation and mutually agreed policy recommendations to guide both governments in addressing international economic coordination, environmental protection and improvement, energy supply and use, trade, foreign investment, multilateral lending, Third World indebtedness, growth prospects and enhanced security.

The work was accomplished through a combination of commissioned background working papers and meetings and plenaries in the United States and Japan:

The first bilateral meeting of the project's principals and senior advisers at Princeton University in November 1988 was focused on an extensive and candid discussion of the four commissioned working papers which now form Chapters II thru V of the present book.

A second joint session in Tokyo (February 1989) combined a bilateral executive meeting with a plenary meeting including an expanded group of senior Japanese participants from government and the private sector.

A U.S. delegation meeting in Washington (March 1989) brought together the U.S. principals with a broadly-based group of political and corporate leaders to elicit their views on the development of U.S.–Japanese cooperation.

The consultative first phase of the project concluded with a combination of meetings in Washington in April 1989:

— A joint plenary session at the Department of State, bringing together the project principals with some thirty leaders and experts from the U.S. public and private sectors to offer their own views on how the U.S.–Japan relationship may best be improved and how the two nations together may best assure adequate and sustained growth and security in the developing world. The U.S. Ambassador–Designate to Japan, Michael Armacost, addressed the participants at lunch.

— An executive session during which the U.S. and Japanese principals amended and agreed upon the final text of the "Group of Six Report" (Chapter I of the present book).

— A press conference at the National Press club to release the report.

— A luncheon during which the senior members of the project briefed Secretary of Commerce Robert A. Mosbacher and U.S. Trade Representative Carla Hills on the findings and recommendations.

— Separate briefings were also held by the "Group of Six" for Secretary of State James A. Baker at the State Department, and for the House Subcommittee on Asian and Pacific Affairs chaired by Congressman Stephen Solarz.

On behalf of the Atlantic Council and the Bretton Woods Committee, we want to thank the organizations that have provided the financial support enabling us to undertake and to complete this valuable work: the United States–Japan Foundation, the American Express Company, and the Boeing Company. Warm thanks are also due to the other participants in this project, who devoted considerable time and thoughtful analysis. It is an excellent and welcome example of a bilateral tradition of sharing ideas, experience, and wisdom—a tradition from which both nations have drawn great benefit.

U. Alexis Johnson   **Yoshio Okawara**

Working Group Members

The Committee of Six

Yoshio Okawara
Project Co-Chairman
Former Japanese Ambassador to the United States and Australia.

U. Alexis Johnson
Project Co-Chairman
Vice Chairman, Atlantic Council; former U.S. Ambassador to Japan and Thailand, and former Under Secretary of State.

Kiichi Saeki
Project Vice-Chairman (Security Issues—Japan)
Former Chairman, Nomura Research Institute, and senior official of the Japanese Defense Agency.

Andrew J. Goodpaster
Project Vice-Chairman (Security Issues—U.S.)
Chairman, Atlantic Council; former Supreme Allied Commander, Europe.

Takashi Hosomi
Project Vice-Chairman (Economic Issues—Japan)
Former Chairman, Overseas Economic Cooperation Fund of Japan, and Vice Minister of Finance.

Paul A. Volcker
Project Vice-Chairman (Economic Issues—U.S.)
Co-Chairman, Bretton Woods Committee; former Chairman, Federal Reserve Board, and Under Secretary of the Treasury.

Working Paper Authors

Susumu Awanohara
Japanese author of Security paper
Research Fellow, East–West Center (Hawaii), on leave from The Far Eastern Economic Review.

Makoto Sakurai
Japanese author of Economics paper
Senior Economist, Research Institute of Overseas Development, The Export–Import Bank of Japan.

Philip H. Trezise
U.S. author of Economics paper
Senior Fellow, Brookings Institution; former Assistant Secretary of State and Ambassador to the OECD.

Roy A. Werner
U.S. author of Security paper
Senior Research Fellow, Atlantic Council; former Principal Deputy Assistant Secretary of the Army, and Staff Member, East Asian and Pacific Affairs Subcommittee, U.S. Senate.

Rapporteur

Charles E. Morrison, Coordinator, International Relations Program, East–West Center (Hawaii), and Senior Research Associate, Japan Center for International Exchange.

Project Coordinators

Tadashi Yamamoto, President, Japan Center for International Exchange.

Joseph W. Harned, Executive Vice President, Atlantic Council.

James C. Orr, Executive Director, Bretton Woods Committee.

Advisers and Staff

Ronald Aqua, Program Director, United States–Japan Foundation.

Frank Ballance, Consultant, Bretton Woods Committee.

Kent E. Calder, Assistant Professor, Woodrow Wilson School, Princeton University.

John H. Costello, Executive Director, Citizens Network for Foreign Affairs.

Job L. Dittberner, Vice President, Programs and Projects, Atlantic Council.

Hiroshi Peter Kamura, U.S. Representative, Japan Center for International Exchange.

Eliane Lomax, Assistant Director, Programs and Projects, Atlantic Council.

Ellen Scholl, Assistant, Programs and Projects, Atlantic Council

Abby Sutherland, Deputy Director, Bretton Woods Committee.

Mariko Tomita, Program Officer, Japan Center for International Exchange.

CHAPTER I

Joint Policy Paper

A. Cooperative Leadership

Cooperation between the United States and Japan is indispensable to the global economy and western security. The United States remains, in military, political, and economic terms, a superpower. No single country, not even Japan, can in the foreseeable future assume the role of international leadership now required of the United States. Japan, however, is the leading economy in the dynamic East Asian region, and the world's second largest economy. The effective management of global issues requires a close working relationship among all the major industrial economies led by the United States, but the cooperation and supporting role of Japan is more important than that of any other country.

The most urgent task in U.S.–Japan relations is to develop an enhanced cooperative relationship—one based on common objectives and a more equitable sharing of policy-making responsibilities as well as the financial and political costs associated with international leadership.

The leaders of both countries are committed to such a relationship, but it takes time to instill new habits of consultation, influence-sharing, and responsibility-sharing. They need to become an established part of the normal political and bureaucratic process on international issues. Most importantly, the Congress, the Diet, and the publics of the two countries need to appreciate and support the policies and appropriations required for a strong association based on shared leadership.

Americans too often focus on the costs they want Japan to assume, but fail to genuinely accept a larger Japanese role in setting the objectives and strategies. Japanese too often discuss their international role in the narrow terms of meeting specific demands from various parties in the United States rather than in the broader terms of maintaining global economic, political, and security systems vital to both countries. The consequence of these outlooks is an often unhealthy degree of wrangling over the terms of cooperation.

In an era when much of the public discussion of U.S.–Japanese relations is dominated by economic competition, it is essential to bear in mind that the two nations share common values and have similar concerns with respect to world problems. Their security and economic interests are inextricably intertwined. Both countries require an international environment supportive of market-based economic activity, government based on the consent of the governed, and peace among nations. A worldwide process of economic integration has established an interdependent relationship between the U.S. economy, the Japanese economy, and the world economy: Neither Japan nor the United States alone can continue to prosper unless both prosper, nor can the industrialized nations prosper unless economic growth is widely shared and sustained in the developing world as well.

B. The Development Challenge

There are vast differences in the economic conditions of today's developing countries. A few, mostly East Asian newly industrializing economies, are growing so rapidly that they are closing the income gap between themselves and the developed countries. Others, including most developing countries in Latin America, have attained middle income levels and have made significant progress in developing their industrial and human infrastructure, but growth has stagnated or deteriorated during the 1980s because of high levels of debt servicing relative to foreign exchange earnings. In still others, including most of the countries of Sub-Saharan Africa, incomes are at low levels and economic development is lagging badly.

These different problems require varied policies from the United States, Japan, and other advanced countries. Open access to markets and investment capital are especially important to the rapidly growing industrializing economies, new approaches to the debt problem are critical for Latin America, and a combination of aid, trade, and human resource development programs is needed for the least developed. It should be emphasized that economic advance in all developing countries basically rests on their own efforts. Numerous examples, especially in East Asia, point to the importance of market forces, entrepreneurial activity, and private foreign investment. But developed country policies are crucial in maintaining international trade and monetary regimes that encourage the free flow of goods, services and capital.

The economic challenges that face Japan and the United States fall into several principal areas: maintaining growth in the developed world, strengthening the world trading system, encouraging the flow of investment capital, developing more effective approaches to the international debt crisis, and enhancing the effectiveness of official development assistance (ODA).

1. Growth in the Developed Countries

A prime objective for Japan, the United States, and other advanced countries must be to maintain the pace of their own economic growth. The primary risk of recession lies in the imbalances in savings, spending, and trade that emerged earlier in this decade stemming from the divergent economic policies of Japan, the United States, and the major economies of Western Europe, especially West Germany.

Rectifying these imbalances is a matter of utmost importance. If financial markets regard progress as too slow, there will be a continuing risk that financial instability could precipitate a major recession. Even if that danger is avoided, the large imbalances threaten to undercut prospects for growth and could provoke strong political reactions.

Critical elements of the adjustment process were implicit in the Plaza Hotel accord of September 1985: the lowering of the U.S. fiscal deficit, the stimulation of domestic demand in Japan and other large surplus countries, and exchange rates that facilitate the correction of trade imbalances. This has demanded a high degree of cooperation among governments as well as politically courageous economic policy actions.

In the United States, the twin fiscal and current account deficits have been reduced. The former has fallen from a peak of $220 billion in FY86 to $155 billion in FY88, although some increase is likely in the current year. The current account deficit has dropped from $154 billion in 1987 to $135 billion in 1988. This performance, however, has been below U.S. targets and is insufficient. Furthermore, the signs are that the progress made so far is coming to a halt. A new sense of urgency and a fresh policy impetus are needed.

In Japan, the general direction in which public policy should move was established by the 1986 Maekawa Commission. The relaxation of the long-standing fiscal austerity program and additional public works expenditures helped increase domestic demand and sparked an expansion of growth and imports in 1987 and 1988. However, this performance primarily reflects exchange rate appreciation rather than change in policy fundamentals. Sustained attention to reducing Japan's large surpluses is required.

The large external imbalances reflect national macroeconomic policies in the two countries in the first half of the 1980s that went in different directions. While precise coordination of macro-economic policies is not realistic at the present time, concrete and meaningful policy consultation between the two nations and their major economic partners and increased attention to the external ramifications of national economic policies are urgently needed. Japan and the United States should work particularly hard within the framework of the G-7 to achieve closer coordination of their macro-economic policies with each other and those of other major industrial nations. In particular, close coordination among central bankers is needed.

2. The International Trading System

A second fundamental objective of Japan and the United States should be to strengthen the international trading system. Trade is a powerful force for raising productivity and thereby real incomes. The drift toward protectionism in recent years threatens the economic prospects of developed and developing countries alike.

We attach great importance to a successful conclusion to the current Uruguay Round of GATT negotiations. The agenda for this Round offers the best hope for assuring and improving Third World nations' access to export markets, not just in the developed countries but also in trade with each other. Understandings have now been reached on negotiating guidelines for all items on the ambitious GATT agenda. Lengthy bargaining undoubtedly will be required to reach a successful conclusion on the most controversial subjects, in particular, agricultural trade which has always been the key to a successful Uruguay Round outcome. We urge our two governments to work closely together to bring about a multilateral agricultural trade agreement that will reduce and eventually eliminate trade barriers and other market distortions. We recognize that achieving this objective will require politically difficult decisions in both our countries but we urge that changes be made gradually so as to avoid distress to farmers or upheavals in rural society.

Some have urged that Japan and the United States initiate discussions leading toward a bilateral free trade agreement as a way of reducing trade tensions between them. We do not believe that such an agreement would be desirable. An exclusive free trade arrangement between the world's two largest national economies would undermine the multilateral trading system and entail a damaging amount of discrimination against the trade of others, particularly that of the developing countries. We believe the priority objective of the U.S. and Japanese governments should be an all-out effort to ensure the success of the Uruguay Round.

There are, however, important opportunities for enhanced U.S.–Japan cooperation that will reinforce the GATT–based, multilateral trading system. For example, our governments might begin consultations with a view toward reaching specific understandings between themselves and with other interested countries that would not discriminate against third countries and would strengthen the international economic system. Examples might be: implementing agreements on trade in certain service sectors consistent with the framework agreement on services now being negotiated in GATT and greater harmonization of regulations in securitities markets. Agreements in these areas could be designed to encourage participation by other countries.

Clearly case–by–case bilateral trade issues between Japan and the United States are a principal source of tension in the relationship and create an atmosphere that could jeopardize the two countries' ability to work constructively together on global issues. Japan and the U.S. should make their best efforts to address such issues and move aggressively ahead in discussions to resolve them. Efforts to address bilateral trade issues must be taken within the framework of the overriding principle of preserving and sustaining the friendship and cooperation between the two countries.

3. Direct Foreign Investment

Private direct foreign investment (DFI) is a source of capital, technology, and management skills, and can thus play a vital role in the development process. While the rapidly growing Asian developing economies continue to attract substantial foreign investments, the debt-burdened Latin American countries and the least developed countries are of less interest to private investors in Japan and the United States. Internal reforms in developing countries are necessary conditions for stimulating greater flows of private investments, including the repatriation of funds invested overseas, to developing countries. The newly created Multilateral Investment Guarantee Agency (MIGA), an affiliate of the World Bank, can play a helpful role not simply by guaranteeing investments against the political risk of appropriation, but also by providing advice on how to create a more favorable investment climate.

The United States is the world's largest provider of direct investment funds and also the largest recipient. American direct investment abroad exceeds foreign direct investment in the United States. Nevertheless, the rapid growth of foreign investment in the United States has raised concerns about excessive foreign ownership of American assets and stimulated proposals that would restrict new investments. Such restrictions would foster a climate of less openness around the world, harmful to the interests of all free economies, and should be strongly resisted. It would be counter-productive for the United States, working against the need to enhance investment and productivity.

The volume of foreign direct investment in Japan is small relative to the size of the economy. As a part of its international economic leadership role, and particularly at a time when Japan itself is investing heavily abroad, Japan should strive to improve the receptivity of its society to foreign investment. Such efforts will help blunt negative reactions to Japanese investment overseas.

Japan plays a particularly important role as an investor in developing Asian countries, which brings with it a responsibility to ensure that government-sponsored aid and investment programs are not used unfairly in competition with local investors and other foreign investors.

4. International Debt Crisis

Earlier cooperative responses to the international debt crisis by debtor and creditor nations alike have succeeded in substantially defusing its threat to the international financial system and inducing constructive economic changes in a number of borrowing countries. However, with real incomes stagnating and even declining, with inflationary pressures acute, and with the flow of new private credit largely ended, it has become apparent that a fresh impetus and new initiatives are necessary to restore and sustain growth in Latin America, the Philippines and elsewhere. What is at stake is not only economic performance but also political and social stability. While the United States, for political as well as economic reasons, has the largest direct stake, Japanese direct financial and political interests are also large. An adequate response to the crisis by the world community will be dependent upon the leadership of these two countries.

A broad consensus is developing that agreements between borrowers and lenders to reduce outstanding debt and/or interest payments will be necessary for a number of indebted countries to relieve external financial pressures and to better assure necessary resources for growth. The recent initiatives by Secretary Brady, building in substantial part on earlier suggestions by Minister Miyazawa, have helped importantly to define the nature of such approaches. Specifically, when flows of new money are not adequate, lending banks are encouraged to provide debt relief in the form of reduced principal or reduced interest rates. Such programs would, as in the past, be developed case–by–case, and be dependent upon strong efforts by the borrowing countries to sustain and reinforce needed policy reforms. In such circumstances, creditor countries would stand ready, collectively through the international financial institutions or individually, to provide some support for the renegotiated loans.

To be successful, this approach will continue to require an exceptional degree of international and public–private cooperation. The international financial institutions will necessarily be required to assume an even stronger leadership role.

Japan, by virtue of its strong internal growth over recent years and huge international surplus, is in a particularly strategic position to support this necessary effort financially. Part of that support logically would take the form of providing a substantially increased proportion of the financial resources available to the IMF, World Bank, and the regional development banks, a process that has already started. The U.S., and other members, at the same time will need to recognize that increased financial contributions justify larger voting rights in those organizations.

At the same time, Japan is in a position to provide substantial funds bilaterally to developing countries through its Export–Import Bank or other institutions both for new lending in support of development programs or to help support bank debt or interest-rate reduction efforts undertaken in conjunction with strong policy reform efforts. Other nations, including the United States, should participate in these efforts in the common interest. However, given the size of its external surplus and in the larger context of its appropriate international responsibilities, we believe a special effort by Japan, extending beyond the $4.5 billion promised over three years, will be required to assure the success of the international effort.

5. Development Assistance

The United States and Japan are the largest contributors to multilateral assistance institutions and the largest bilateral aid donors. While the U.S. bilateral program has decreased from its peak in 1985, the Japanese aid program has grown rapidly in recent years, especially in dollar terms. Both countries, however, are substantially below the OECD average in their contribution of official development assistance (ODA) relative to their GNPS, and Japan's ODA is offered on the least generous terms of all OECD donors, when measured by the ratio of grants to loans.

Increasing aid volume is an important goal, but improving the quality of aid is equally valuable. Japan has increased the volume of its aid substantially, making it the world's largest ODA donor country. It should make greater efforts to increase the grant share of its ODA and give added stress to programs that strengthen developing country ability to achieve self-sustaining growth. These include structural reform, support for indigenous private sector development, human resource development, and technical assistance. Japan should also strengthen its assistance to developing countries outside Asia, where 70 percent of Japanese bilateral ODA is concentrated. The United States should review its Economic Support Funds program to improve its actual economic development impact, and it should reduce the protectionist constraints in its ODA.

There are numerous opportunities for closer cooperation between the United States and Japan in the planning and administering of aid programs and projects. Japan has strong expertise in government-private sector partnerships that may be very beneficial to some developing countries and provide a model as U.S. foreign assistance programs are reassessed. The United States has a wealth of expertise based on over 40 years of on–the–ground experience, especially in Latin America and Africa, where Japanese expertise is limited. We urge the two governments to actively explore means through which Japan might be able to better tap into U.S. expertise in the field.

C. Physical Resources: Energy and the Environment

Energy development and environmental protection remain high priorities in the developing world. Most developing countries cannot meet current energy needs from domestic sources, and expect consumption to grow rapidly with development. Imported energy is often a significant drain on foreign exchange. The development of domestic energy supplies, where economical, can reduce these costs and stimulate the local economies.

A combination of actions on the part of the United States, Japan, the developing countries, and international institutions can facilitate further investment in energy. Developing countries should encourage investment by allowing greater equity ownership by private enterprise and by restructuring domestic energy policies to enhance the operation of free markets. On their part, private investors must recognize the interests of developing countries in the acquisition of technologies and the development of technical and managerial skills. We believe mutually advantageous agreements can be worked out. As a start in this direction, we urge that individual developing countries undertake systematic reviews of their national energy policies with the participation of energy investment teams from the private sectors in the developed countries and international organization experts.

Environmental degradation is an increasingly serious problem globally and in the developing world. Sound economic development requires increasing the productive use of natural resources to support growing populations and expand economic output. When natural resources are over-used so that a sustainable resource base is not maintained, longer-term growth and standards of living are jeopardized. The rapid disappearance of tropical forests, salinization of irrigated agricultural lands, and serious river and ocean pollution as a result of the dumping of untreated waste are examples of problems common to much of the developing world. These are problems of urgent international concern. As illustrated by the concern over global warming, they have global implications and require global solutions.

A sound environmental program requires a better understanding of the longer-term costs of degradation, appropriate legal regimes to ensure the sustainable use of resources, and the enforcement of these legal regimes. The United States and Japan should share leadership in developing international environmental standards and new environmentally sound technologies. We endorse the concept of a new "environmental fund" to promote research on the productive and environmentally sound use of developing nations' resources.

D. Human Resources Development

Improving standards of education and the acquisition of technological skills is important to the development process. Although developing countries are improving their own educational institutions, many of their higher level civil servants, managers, scientists, and other professionals are educated abroad. The United States has traditionally hosted a large number of foreign students in its institutions of higher education, while Japan's foreign student population, especially from Asian developing countries, is rising but is still small. Japan needs to increase its efforts to make its educational system more open to foreign students, while the United States should continue to maintain quality institutions of higher education open to the world. The development of science and technology adds to the human knowledge base that underlies economic growth. Advances in medical science, biotechnology, new materials and other scientific frontiers is of direct importance to developing as well as developed nations. It is important to the Japanese, U.S., and world economies that scientific and technological information be able to move across political boundaries with as few encumbrances as possible, except where restrictions are clearly required for national security reasons. The sale of technology by a U.S. firm, for example, benefits the U.S. balance of payments, rewards the firm's investment in that technology, provides the capital and incentive for that firm to stay on the cutting edge of technology, and often results in feedback from the buyer that improves the technology or its applications. Governments should be wary of imposing restrictions that interfere with the free operation of the market in scientific and technological information. The United States and Japan currently provide highly asymmetrical contributions to the world stock of scientific and technological knowledge. In the United States, much greater effort is placed on government supported research in the basic sciences, while a much greater share of the Japanese effort is in private sector applied research and commercial application. The research that results from the former is generally broadly accessible, but the latter tends to be commercial property. As Japan has reached the forefront of technology, it should be contributing more to the basic stock of world scientific knowledge, while the United States can no longer afford its relative neglect of private sector R and D. Discussions have begun within the scientific communities on the two sides on strengthening the japanese contribution to basic science and improving mutual and asymmetrical access to research results. We endorse these efforts.

E. Security Issues

The relatively weak economic and political structures of most developing countries make them vulnerable to internal social and political turmoil and external threats. Virtually all the conflicts since World War II have involved developing countries, with considerable costs to the developed world. Japan and the United States, therefore, should make it a priority to create political and security conditions that are conducive to a stable international order and to the peaceful settlement of international disputes.

There are a number of interrelated dimensions to these challenges. Clearly one is to maintain the nuclear and conventional deterrents and defense forces that protect the free world from potential aggression. Another task is to help developing countries strengthen their economies, thus enhancing national integration and internal stability. We have already discussed the main elements of this task.

This is an era of change and hope in international relations. We welcome the declared policy of the Soviet Union to reduce its offensive capabilities and work with our countries and other countries to foster regional stability. We hope that the Soviet Union will take further concrete steps, including unilateral measures to reduce its excessive military forces in the region. At the same time, significant actual reduction will probably come as a consequence of a long process of painstaking negotiations. Free countries need to remain strong and cautious, but ready to grasp opportunities to reduce military burdens where acceptable agreements can be reached. The United States and Japan have learned in the course of recent negotiations that close consultation and coordination on arms control issues helps bring favorable results. Such consultations and coordination should be continued as an integral part of an effort to broaden and deepen the East–West dialogue.

The Soviet Union has suggested an assessment of the military balance in the Asia–Pacific region. We should welcome an assessment that takes into account the respective geopolitical positions of the nations of the region. Such an assessment could provide a base from which regional arms limitations discussions could proceed.

The share of Japanese national income devoted to defense is less than a third that of the United States. This disparity causes some in the United States to suggest that Japan should make a much greater defense effort. We believe, however, that an extraordinary increase (for example, to 23 percent of GNP as suggested by some members of the U.S. Congress) cannot be justified by the security threats in the region and would provoke alarm in other Asian countries. As such, it would be undesirable and counter-productive.

As a matter of Constitutional prohibition reinforced by the political reality of strong pacifist sentiments, Japan cannot be expected to contribute to the collective military security of its region other than through strictly self-defense efforts. The United States, in the size of its absolute and relative defense expenditures and in the scope of its security commitments, will continue to bear a much greater defense burden than Japan. Japan in turn should bear a larger relative aid and economic burden, which also contributes to common security interests.

There are other means through which Japan can contribute more fully to the common security. It can assume a larger share of its own defense requirements without acquiring offensive military capabilities. We endorse continued expansion of joint planning and defense exercises, as the Japanese emphasis on surveillance capabilities within the framework of the 1960 Mutual Security Treaty and the 1978 Guidelines for U.S.–Japan Defense Cooperation. Although Japan currently contributes more than any other U.S. ally to the cost of U.S. forces based in its country, about $2.5 billion in FY88, it can more fully contribute to these costs. Bilateral cooperation on defense technologies should be continued and strengthened.

We welcome Japan's expanded role in supporting international peacekeeping activities and believe that it can be further developed, particularly as the role of the United Nations is enhanced in a period of reduced superpower tensions.

It should be noted that Japan is also increasing its diplomatic efforts with respect to conflicts in the developing world. As Japan's economic assistance and interaction with the Third World has grown, so too has its potential influence. Japan's leading financial role in a multilateral aid package for the Philippines that should help Filipino efforts to stabilize and develop their country and increase the likelihood of a continuation of strong Philippine participation in free world security is illustrative of this important Japanese role.

F. The Need for Leadership

The prosperity and security of both Japan and the United States depend heavily on the free world's international trade, financial, and security systems. The leadership of both countries in protecting these systems is indispensable to their survival. Neither the United States nor Japan has any sensible alternative to cooperative global leadership because not to do so entails serious risks to the prosperity and freedom of both.

It is a role of national leadership, including the heads of government, other executive officers of government, the members of the Congress and the Diet, and other persons influential in policy making, to appreciate this imperative and to keep it foremost in mind as the two countries deal with specific problems. Above all, the new relationship, whether dealing with bilateral or global issues such as those involving developing countries, must be informed by a shared vision of common interests and goals.

CHAPTER II

U.S.–Japan Economic Issues   *by Philip H. Trezise*

A. The Imperative of Cooperation

The United States and Japan together account for roughly a third of the world's production of goods and services and 45 percent of world trade. If the European Community is added, the figures become more than one half and three quarters.

These impressive numbers tell us that economic events in the OECD countries cannot fail to influence the course of economic events elsewhere. This is most certainly true of the developing countries or, to use the term, the Third World. More specifically, they argue that the most important contribution that the most economically advanced nations can make to economic progress in the Third World is to maintain steady economic growth at home. Put in the negative, any serious and extended economic downturn in the OECD countries will be bound to worsen—in some cases, critically—the outlook for economic and political advance in the developing countries.

Of course this is no more than to say that the United States and Japan will do best for the world economy, and its political health as well, if they can manage their own economies sensibly. They would wish to do that anyway. But in a world of interdependent nations, successful economic management will rest both on decisions made at home and decisions made elsewhere.

This would be true even if economic choices made by national governments in the 1980s had not contributed to the extreme imbalances that now characterize the world economic scene. As matters stand, if the imbalances remain or widen, the risks of panic and economic slump will grow. Policies to narrow and eliminate them will carry their own risks, with deflation or inflation threatening a recession that no one can afford. The requirements for consultation, cooperation, coordination are, if anything, greater than at any time in the past.

Cooperation between the United States and Japan thus should be willed by fundamental national interests. Indeed, Tokyo and

15

Washington have recognized as much, and to an increasing degree. Since 1985 we have had the Plaza Hotel and the Louvre accords, the opening of the Uruguay Round, and a $75 billion capital increase for the World Bank as major examples of multilateral agreements in which the United States and Japan have been principal actors. Meanwhile, American–Japanese consultation and negotiation has been virtually constant on economic issues that are nominally bilateral but which necessarily impinge on the economic interests of outsiders. There is no way, in short, for the United States and Japan to seek common ground in their economic relations without consequences for the rest of the world. The nature of those consequences is what may be in question.

The particular U.S.–Japan decision-making areas of most direct concern to the developing nations can be listed as trade, debt, aid, and investment. These are examined in the pages that follow.

B. Trade

The U.S. trade bill. The United States now has a new and sweeping trade law, the Omnibus Trade and Competitiveness Act of 1988. Its substance reflects Congressional and no doubt popular belief that the size and persistence of the U.S. trade deficit can be traced in some significant part to trade policies at home and abroad. The intent of the law is to make possible more vigorous attacks on perceived trade restrictions elsewhere and more certain resort to retaliatory import restrictions by the United States if the foreign restrictions are not suitably modified.

This law does not mandate restrictions or protectionism. The president will continue to have discretion in applying its provisions. It can be expected that President Bush, like all of his recent predecessors, brings a bias in favor of free trade to his office. In that sense, little has changed. But the Omnibus Act requires a series of reports on unfair foreign barriers to American exports. Once these reports are received, the president will be faced with the need to decide what action is to be taken. The law's language makes it clear that his responsibility is to negotiate away the offending foreign barriers or, failing that, respond with corresponding U.S. import restrictions. Since the U.S. definition of unfairness in some cases may be unilateral, the Act has a very sizable potential for causing international friction. If attempts are made to apply it extensively it could also accelerate the drift toward protectionism, not only in the United States but also, because of the likelihood of retaliatory measures, among our trading partners as well.

These dangers will be lessened if the U.S. external trade balance continues to improve, for that will give the president the basis for caution. So will progress toward the resolution of outstanding trade issues, especially those involving agriculture. As a practical matter, that means progress in the Uruguay Round. That round is a prime locus for U.S.–Japan cooperation for mutual benefit and for the benefit of the developing countries.

Contrary to the appearance of a negotiating deadlock, the December, 1988, mid-term review of the Uruguay Round demonstrated an impressive amount of positive achievement. Agreement was registered in a number of major areas, either in the form of a framework or a rule for concluding the negotiation or in a substantially completed text of a new or revised GATT section or article. These include:

—Trade in services
—Tariff reductions (a 30 percent overall target)
—Dispute settlement
—Trade related investment measures
—Trade in tropical products
—Functioning of the GATT system
—Subsidies and countervailing measures.

In April the other major issues were cleared for substantive negotiation:

—Trade in textiles
—Trade related aspects of intellectual property rights
—Safeguards (the GATT escape clause)
—Agricultural trade

Each of these is important in its own right.

The largest part of international trade in textiles has been conducted under rules contrary to the GATT for nearly three decades. The Multifibre Agreement, or MFA, is discriminatory against Third World suppliers and is fundamentally protectionist.

Property rights in the form of copyrights, trademarks, and patents are widely violated, while the present GATT provides grossly inadequate protection.

The GATT escape clause, Article 19, has been regularly evaded by "voluntary" restraints on exports, orderly marketing agreements, and industry–to–industry deals.

International discipline over trade in agricultural goods has been eroded. Earlier negotiations have failed to check the erosion, much less to reach agreement on effective GATT rules for this major sector of world trade. Another failure would threaten to torpedo the Uruguay Round and to call into question the survival of the GATT as a useful institution.

Hard work is ahead, therefore, despite the genuine advances that have been made. American and Japanese decisions over the next two years could be crucial to an outcome that could either help set the stage for a decade of expanding international trade and broad based economic growth or else signal a likely retreat from free trade. These decisions need not be in accord with all the positions taken by some of the leading developing countries. The central objective, rather, should be to strengthen the structure of multilateral trade. Such a result will benefit all the GATT Contracting Parties and most certainly the developing countries.

The most difficult issues: Agriculture. At the heart of the agricultural trade problem are domestic subsidies to farmers. The costs of these policies in the OECD countries are estimated to be $140 billion per year.

These expenditures cannot be made without restrictions on trade in agricultural goods. When governments guarantee agricultural prices above market levels, as is done in the United States, the European Community, and Japan, imports must be held in check to protect national budgets. Moreover, price guarantees tend to stimulate production beyond domestic requirements. An increasingly frequent response is to subsidize export sales. This is a major direct cause for the political tensions associated with international trade in farm products.

A trade negotiation then becomes a forum—and the only practicable one—for attacking the domestic policies that are the source of the agricultural issue. If progress toward freeing agricultural trade is to be made, the subsidy issue cannot be avoided. The United States negotiators in the Uruguay Round have therefore proposed the phased elimination of subsidies that can be demonstrated to distort trade flows. This proposal would require significant changes in farm policies in the U.S. as well as in other nations. Neither the EC nor Japan have been ready to agree to an end to domestic farm subsidies at some definite date.

If there is to be a compromise, its terms will still have to include commitments to reduce subsidies sufficiently to allow substantially increased flows of trade. Realistically, this means that the United States, the EC, Japan, and others will be required to begin a process that will lead to more open markets for products that are now protected—among them, the grains, certainly including rice, oil seeds, sugar, and dairy products. The challenge will be not only to the Community and Japan but to virtually all the developed country participants in the Uruguay Round, most importantly, the United States.

Safeguards. Among the weaknesses of the GATT is the observance given to Article 19, the "escape" or safeguard clause. The purpose of Article 19 was to make available temporary relief from unforeseen and politically unacceptable levels of particular imports. In practice, the obligation to follow the Article's procedures has frequently been disregarded in favor of extra–GATT import restrictions. All Contracting Parties have agreed that a move to a less capricious system is important to the future of the GATT.[1]

In the Tokyo Round, reform was blocked by the EC's insistence that the basic GATT precept of non-discriminatory treatment be relaxed in safeguard clause cases. The EC approach met general opposition. Attempts to find a compromise were unsuccessful and so the issue has been carried over into the Uruguay Round.

To break the non-discrimination rule would be a major departure from GATT principle and practice. It would be seen by the developing countries as a blow to their interests, and with reason. If the EC does not modify its position, an impasse is all but assured.

A possible route to compromise might be found in the Article 19 provision which calls for either the payment of compensation or the acceptance of retaliatory restrictions by the party making a claim to safeguard import relief. The provision is intended, of course, to deter governments from resorting to Article 19. In many instances, unfortunately, the choice has been to seek understandings that are outside the GATT and largely beyond any international discipline rather than to risk having to make compensatory concessions or accepting balancing restrictions on one's own exports.

Thus a sensible bargain would be to reject the EC demand for selective import restraints but to provide that a Contracting Party would not be liable to compensation or retaliation if the other requirements of a new safeguard clause were being or had been met. One of those requirements would doubtless be a time limit that would assure that the permitted import restrictions would be temporary, not permanent.

The United States and Japan have been parties to a number of the important instances in which Article 19 has been avoided by the negotiation of special escape arrangements. In addition to their concern for strengthening the GATT, the two nations should have a common interest in a safeguard clause that would reduce the incentive to turn to extra–GATT solutions. If a compromise is to be shaped on safeguards, they are in best position to cooperate in bringing it off.

Textiles. The Uruguay Round agenda speaks cautiously about formulating for textiles "modalities that would permit the eventual integration of this sector into the GATT." Caution is advisable, for the textile lobbies in the industrial countries have impressive powers of resistance to liberalization. Nor is it evident that every one of the developing countries with export capabilities would wish to overturn quickly the present structure of assured market shares in the form of quota rights. If reform is to be negotiated it will have to be for a credibly long period for adjustment. Even then many difficulties about procedure can be foreseen.

Difficulties aside, a good faith negotiation has been promised to the developing countries. If that cannot be delivered, demands for trade liberalization from these countries cannot fail to lose force— and the North–South division in the GATT to widen.

Probably the most feasible method of textile liberalization would be a progressive enlargement of import quotas over a five or ten year period. Provisions could be made for GATT approved temporary tariff increases to deal with special problems as quotas are liberalized. At the end of the liberalization period textiles would be left with tariff protection only and that protection would itself be open to reduction through the normal GATT bargaining process.

Japan was the first of the textile suppliers to have quotas imposed on its exports. It is still subject to quota restrictions.

C. Foreign Direct Investment

The United States has long been a proponent of foreign direct investment as an important means of transferring capital, as well as management skills and technology, to developing countries. Throughout most of the postwar period the United States has been the principal supplier of capital worldwide; only in recent years have other countries come to rival the U.S. position as the leading investor nation. The Reagan administration has been an evangelist for a greater private sector role in development, although the focus has probably been more on internal LDC policy reform than foreign investment.

While U.S. government policy has consistently favored foreign direct investment (FDI) through the creation of the Overseas Private Investment Corporation (OPIC), a public corporation to insure American investments abroad, and recently the establishment of the World Bank's multilateral investment insurance subsidiary (MIGA), a multilateral investment insurance agency under the World Bank umbrella, there has been an undercurrent of opposition in the political system. This has come chiefly from organized labor, which argues that American jobs are being exported as a result of production shifts abroad via investments insured by OPIC and now MIGA. The OPIC law specifically forbids the issuance of investment insurance for production directly shifted overseas.

There was substantial Congressional opposition to MIGA, from unionized and textile oriented constituencies. The *MIGA authorization was recently passed by Congress, with a limited base of corporate support. Japan, in contrast, was the first major industrial nation to ratify MIGA.

Somewhat inconsistently, organized labor and its supporters also express concern over increased foreign investment in the United States. Attention has focused particularly on Japanese investment, because of its visibility and concentration in a limited number of sectors and real estate markets. Japanese automotive investment has tended to establish new facilities in non-union areas such as Kentucky and Tennessee, in part to escape union in job classification rigidities. Foreign investment promises to become a more contentious political topic in the United States, and we can expect further calls to restrict FDI.

Several issues concerning FDI are stated below. There is some variance between studies of FDI and conventional wisdom on the subject. These differences underscore the proposition that simply urging greater foreign direct investment in developing countries without a closer examination of the circumstances has little value.

1. The United States is still the largest foreign investor, its stock of FDI growing more rapidly than Japan's. Japan's total stock of FDI was worth about $58 billion at the end of 1986, according to JETRO. The United Kingdom, West Germany, the Netherlands all had larger amounts, and the United States topped the list with FDI of about $260 billion ($309 billion in 1987). (*The Economist*, Feb. 20, 1988, p. 75). Three-quarters of the increase in U.S. FDI, or $35.7 billion in 1987, came from the reinvestment of earnings, reflecting a long established pattern of foreign operations. Another set of calculations in a study published by the Royal Institute of International Affairs in London figured new American FDI at $25.3 billion in 1986, Japan's at $14.5 billion, Britain's at $16 billion.

2. American FDI exceeds foreign FDI in the United States, $309 billion to $262 billion in 1987. Since the mid–1980s American foreign direct investment has risen, even as the dollar's value has fallen. Much of the explanation lies in the reinvestment of overseas earnings, with a double benefit from higher profits in dollar terms and a larger percentage of the profits being reinvested.

3. Foreign direct investment by American companies has been growing consistently faster over the past 20 years than the American economy. Large American companies have shown a continuous tendency to invest internationally in a search for technology, market access, and a rationalization of worldwide production. For example, Ford has decided to realign its worldwide operations so that the European division will be responsible for designing small cars, while the American division designs the large ones. American investment has gone where the markets are, primarily Europe and Japan. Investment in Mexico fell 17 percent between 1980 and 1987, despite the growth of the maquiladora program built on cheap Mexican labor.

4. Japan's FDI is growing rapidly. Recent Japanese FDI appears to have had two primary motivations: establishment of manufacturing facilities in its major markets in response to protectionist pressures, or search for lower wage production sites for manufactures. One long-term motivation has been to secure adequate supplies of raw materials for Japanese industry. Most of Japanese FDI in the

1970s went to other Asian countries—Indonesia to secure raw materials and gain access to its protected market; Hong Kong to take advantage of low wages. In the 1980s Japanese FDI in the United States and Europe has exceeded that going to Asia.

5. A shift in Japanese FDI strategy is apparent in Asia. Japanese companies are shifting their cheap assembly work away from the Newly Industrializing Countries, NICs, where high labor costs are cited as the main complaint by Japanese firms. Wages in South Korea rose by an annual average of 12 percent in real terms between 1977 and 1986. Production is now shifting to China and the ASEAN countries. The process is perhaps most clearly visible in Thailand, where Japanese FDI doubled from $124 million in 1986 to $250 million in 1987, and is thought to have surpassed that mark for the first nine months of 1988. A second Japanese concern is the appreciation of the NICs' currencies against the dollar, eroding their competitiveness.

6. Two general complaints are voiced on Japanese FDI. The first is that Japanese FDI is not balanced by FDI in Japan, which as of March 1987 was merely $7 billion, almost half of it from the United States. There are signs of increasing foreign investment in Japan, made more difficult however by the high value of the yen. The "reciprocity" issue could come to haunt Japan in the investment area, much as it has in traded goods and services.

7. The second complaint is over Japanese reluctance to transfer high technology with the direct investment. China and other Asian countries have expressed concern over this issue.

8. Although there is renewed interest in FDI as a source of capital for developing countries, its importance in the total picture has declined. In the 1960s and early 1970s FDI constituted about 25 percent of foreign capital flows. With the huge increase in commercial lending in the mid to late 1970s, its share declined to about ten percent. Direct investment capital flows to LDCs fell from about $15 billion in 1981 to $10 billion in 1983, and have remained at that level since. Foreign investors are not particularly interested in developing countries, except those in East Asia. While there is more interest in developing countries in attracting foreign investment, many of these countries have not yet undertaken the thoroughgoing reforms necessary to attract foreign investors.

9. The most often cited LDC success stories, the Asian NICS, do not support the proposition that FDI was crucial to their develop-

ment success. In fact, Latin America depended much more on FDI, while U.S. bilateral aid was crucial for Korea and Taiwan. Private capital was dominant in Latin America in the 1950s and 1960s, while public capital with softer terms was more important in Asia. Public capital gave greater control over the economy to governments in Korea and Taiwan, which intervened in shaping their economies to perhaps a greater extent than in Latin America. These tendencies are still present in Asia, and the Asian Development Bank is noticeably less concerned with distinctions between the public and private sectors than was, say, the Reagan administration.

According to Barbara Stallings of the University of Wisconsin, who has compared the experience of Korea and Taiwan vs. Brazil and Mexico regarding the role of foreign capital in development, "choice of development strategy goes a long way towards defining the requirements for foreign capital, both type and amount." A strong Latin American emphasis on import substitution, especially a heavy industry orientation in the 1970s, resulted in large capital demands, first from foreign investors and then from banks. In contrast, Asian NICs initially at least followed a less capital intensive, export oriented strategy.

In the late 1970s all four countries shifted to foreign borrowing to some degree, Taiwan the least, but with substantial differences in their ability to service their loans. According to Stallings:

"The high level of export revenue in the East Asian countries meant that debt service was not an insurmountable problem, while Latin America's greater import substitution emphasis exacerbated payments difficulties, once international conditions turned negative. Debt service ratios summarize the difference. Debt service as a share of export revenues in 1982 was 5.9 percent in Taiwan, 13.1 percent in Korea, 33.9 percent in Mexico, and 43.0 percent in Brazil."

The Asian countries had less need for foreign capital over time, and greater ability to control it. East Asian experts therefore tend to view foreign investment more favorably than their counterparts in Latin America, ironically because it played a less crucial role in their economies. It is wrong, however, to believe that the same policy advice can work in both regions; East Asian policies cannot be adopted wholesale in the very different historical-structural circumstances of Latin America.

Among the issues over which the United States and Japan might quarrel, FDI surely ought to be far down the list. We are the two largest direct investors in the world. Our private business sectors have proved to be venturesome and competent in establishing themselves in a wide variety of economic and political environments. Their foreign investments have in the main been profitable, which is to say that they have used their own and local resources efficiently. Countries host to our multinational firms have demonstrably benefited, as have the owners of the firms. Our joint interest is in promoting the conditions under which FDI can make its optimum contribution to world economic welfare. That interest extends to flows of direct investment between the United States and Japan. For the United States, as the world's preeminent borrower, FDI brings not only capital, which must be borrowed in some form anyway, but also adds technology and management skills to the nation's stock of productive resources. Japan, though now a large creditor, nevertheless stands similarly to benefit from flows of FDI into its private business and industrial sectors.

The third world debt problem gives special importance to greater openings for flows of FDI. While direct investment alone cannot be expected to provide all the necessary foreign resources, flows of new FDI can play a highly constructive role in fostering the economic growth that must in the end be the means to a resolution of the debt issue.

Direct investment is of course a voluntary decision by a firm or an individual willing to put resources at risk in the expectation of a return at least as great as from other available investment opportunities. Where governments attach burdensome conditions, FDI is certain to be inhibited in greater or less degree. It is desirable, therefore, to seek wider international agreement on standards for the treatment of FDI by host governments.

The Uruguay Round agenda includes a direct investment section, focussing primarily on so-called performance requirements such as minimum local content rules or mandatory levels of exports to be achieved. These are important constraints on FDI and the effort to bring them under GATT discipline deserves support. A further step would be to make national treatment of foreign investment the norm for GATT countries; that is, foreign businesses would be accorded treatment the same as that given domestic businesses unless specific exceptions have been made under agreed guidelines.

American and Japanese negotiators should have no difficulty in concerting on these Uruguay Round objectives for FDI. Beyond that, the two governments could make mutual gains and set a helpful example by updating the direct investment terms of their own 1953–vintage Friendship, Commerce, & Navigation Treaty. The treaty provides national treatment, subject to listed exceptions, for one another's direct investors. It does not deal with two latter-day troublesome questions: national security exceptions and registration requirements.

The right to declare this or that economic sector out of bounds for national security reasons can hardly be denied to sovereign governments. These have been instances, however, where investment decisions made in good faith have been overturned as risks to U.S. security with limited opportunity for the parties directly at interest to question the decisions. At a minimum, a new agreement should establish standards and procedures, as open as possible, for national security findings.

Both Japan and the United States require fairly extensive information from would-be direct investors. These data are then aggregated and made public without identifying individuals or firms. Legislation pending in the U.S. Congress would remove this assurance of confidentiality of personal and proprietary information. It is not likely that the present proposal will become law but the issue is one that should be resolved. A bilateral agreement could identify the kinds of information to be supplied and the manner in which it is to be treated, on a reciprocal basis.

The United States, for its part, was instrumental in creating the existing system of controls on the textile trade. It would be appropriate for the two to be leaders in looking for a way to redeem the implicit Uruguay Round promise of textile liberalization.

Intellectual property rights. The differing positions on this subject relate primarily to the precise character of the property rights that are to be protected. Articles 9 and 20 of the GATT allow Contracting Parties to take national measures to protect trademarks, patents, and copyrights. These provisions do not·define the norms or standards that apply to these property rights. That responsibility rests principally with the World Intellectual Property Organization, WIPO.

In the Uruguay Round the developed country group has proposed to write into the GATT more comprehensive and substantive standards for patents and copyrights and then to agree on multilateral action against violations. A number of developing countries, led by India, have objected to the idea of a GATT role in defining intellectual property rights. Their position, however, appears to accept the desirability of a GATT enforcement code.

Despite these differences, intellectual property is not basically a North–South issue. Some developing country negotiators accept the U.S.–Japan–EC approach. An eventual compromise may be to modify somewhat the specifics in the debate about defining standards if agreement can be reached on GATT enforcement provisions.

D. The Debt Problem

U.S. and Japanese mutuality of interests. Among the most important initiatives which the United States and Japan could advance to assist middle income developing countries is a debt strategy that would help to restore robust growth in countries most heavily burdened with debt service obligations.

The United States and Japan share most of the same interests with respect to these countries,[1] including desires for geopolitical stability, growth in trade and other commercial relations, and the need to ensure the soundness of the international and domestic financial and banking systems.

The Scope of the Problem. The debt problem is still very much with us. World Bank analysis shows the total external debt of the developing countries at $1.2 trillion, about half again as large as it was in 1982. All but ten percent is sovereign debt, that is, debt guaranteed by the borrowing government. The growth of debt by seven percent a year since 1982 has been somewhat less than half the rate of the preceding six years, when private lending to these countries soared.

About four-fifths of the total is long-term, of which 60 percent is owed to private lenders, 25 percent to governments of industrial countries, and 15 percent to the World Bank and the regional development banks.

However, the size of the total debt overstates the problem, or at least the threat it poses to the international financial system. Some ten percent is short-term trade finance, which should be self-liquidating and normally rolls over without much difficulty. Another five percent is owed by the debt-distressed sub-Saharan African countries, predominantly to industrial country governments and to the multilateral financial institutions. Private banks are minor participants. There is clear international recognition that these countries require concessional capital to support policy reform and a breakout from economic decline.[2] About one-third of the debt is owed by the countries that as a group still show tolerable debt-service ratios. Interest payments average seven percent of exports of goods and services, and net new lending (disbursements less repayments of principal) equals some 90 percent of interest payments. This describes a fairly manageable debt picture.

A large component of the debt owed by Poland, Hungary, and Romania has been supplied or guaranteed by industrial countries. In general, three-fifths of long-term debt supplied to countries in this group has come from official rather than private sources. A number of these countries have had to negotiate multilateral debt relief agreements since 1982, but the total debt rescheduled has been fairly small and much of it involved negotiations with industrial governments. Collapse of commodity prices or a sharp increase in interest rates or another setback for the international economy could add dangerously to debt-servicing difficulties, but on the whole these countries have kept clear of trouble.

The heart of the debt problem is found in the middle income countries most deeply in debt. A few key ratios show why the debt position of the group is much more difficult than that of other developing countries. Interest payments in 1985 – 1987 averaged 25 percent of exports of goods and services, more than three times as high as the ratio for other debtors. Net inflows of capital were equal to only one-fourth of interest payments. From the perspective of the private commercial banks, the debt problem is centered in these countries; private banks are the creditors for three-fourths of the total debt of the group.

The Growth–Oriented Strategy. Since 1985, the industrial countries whose private banks hold the bulk of their relevant third world debt have had a strategy based on the proposition that economic growth will be the answer to the problem. That is to say, growth will eventually bring debt/GNP and debt/export ratios down to economically tolerable numbers, as indeed has already been the case in several only recently heavily debt-burdened nations. The strategy's formula has been: domestic economic reforms to clear away unnecessary obstacles to growth; these reforms to be developed as appropriate with advice and financial assistance from the IMF; new voluntary lending by the private banks to help debtor countries through the period of transition to renewed full credit worthiness; increased lending by the World Bank, including loans to assist economic reform programs; steady economic performance and more open, or at least not more restricted, markets in the industrial countries.

Experience so far leaves the underlying rationale for the growth oriented strategy intact. There is no real alternative. Unless the debtor countries can raise levels of output and thus generate the resources both to service debt and provide for higher standards of living, the choice will be to default and to face a period, perhaps lengthy, in which access to world capital markets will be largely foreclosed. However, and despite the genuine successes that have been achieved, the strategy has been in trouble. By the end of 1988, revisions clearly were needed, primarily because new lending on the part of the private banks had never materialized on the scale expected under the Baker plan.

A recent World Bank study, based on a country–by–country analysis, provides a useful, quantitative perspective. The Bank estimates that most of the heavily indebted countries could achieve four to five percent annual growth over the next three years under these conditions:

(a) adoption of "significant though realistic policy improvements in many countries and sustained good policies in others";
(b) economic growth of two to two and one-half percent a year in the industrial countries and avoidance of an interest rate shock; and
(c) net capital inflows sufficient to finance an average current account deficit for the group on the order of $14 billion to $15 billion a year and additions to reserves of $2 billion a year. Even with four to five percent growth rates, the debt overhang would remain a serious problem. Nonetheless, the heavily indebted countries would experience an increase of one to two percent a year in per capita incomes and show steady improvement in debt-servicing ratios.

Net new lending in adequate volume by the commercial banks is not a realistic prospect. In launching the growth-oriented debt strategy in 1985, then Secretary of the U.S. Treasury Baker set a goal of $7 billion of new commercial bank lending per year. In fact, however, average net private lending in 1985 – 1987, fell sharply to $3 billion a year, equal to only 15 percent of interest payments due on outstanding loans. Flows in 1988 probably were negative. In the three years following the onset of the debt crisis, 1982 – 1984, net new private lending to the highly indebted countries averaged $18 billion a year, equal to 90 percent of interest payments. Also by contrast, net lending from public sources (World Bank, regional development banks, IMF, and industrial country governments) has held up fully since 1982 and amounted to 50 percent more than interest payments on their outstanding loans.

The immediate problem is thus one of coping with cash flow—that is, scaling down the outflow of funds on debt service account. It should be recognized that debt principal reduction—or interest rate reduction—can match new lending dollar for dollar. The change in U.S. policy announced in March of this year in effect accepted the reality that debt reduction would have to substitute in large part for new private lending.

The revised strategy. The decision to give an official blessing to debt reduction—the essence of the "Brady Plan"—was not a repudiation of the predecessor Baker plan. Growth remains the central objective; economic reform or structural adjustment on the part of the debtors is still considered the key to growth and restored credit worthiness. The approach continues to be case by case; there is still no all-embracing formula for dealing with the variety of economic and political situations among the debtor countries. Debt reduction, for that matter, had already been recognized as one of the means to ameliorate the debt problem; debt-equity swaps and other methods of bringing down debt servicing costs have been encouraged by creditor governments and the international financial institutions.

Now, however, relief via reduction of debt servicing costs has been moved to the center of the stage. The IMF and the World Bank are expected to provide incentives—some form of guarantees—to induce private banks to write down the face value of their loans or to lower the rate of interest on outstanding loans—or, in some cases, both. Japan's commitment of $4.5 billion of Export–Import Bank loans will help to support debtors undertaking structural reforms and thus qualifying for debt relief.

This new emphasis in debt strategy could evoke worrisome responses from both debtors and creditors. Debtor governments may choose to interpret the new approach as justifying claims to unduly large writedowns of outstanding loans, while the creditor banks could decide to defer their concessions until the form and size of the incentives are considered satisfactory. Then too, the funds expected to be available from the IMF and the World Bank, together with Japan's commitment, will be somewhat less than $30 billion over three years. This is by no means an irrelevant amount, even though the pertinent stock of debt is in-the order of $280$300 billion, but it will need to be used to optimum effect if real progress on the debt problem is to be made. Finally, political developments in the debtor countries could complicate, or make easier, this or any effort to resolve the debt problem in a broadly equitable and beneficial manner.

Thus the new or revised strategy, though it is an almost inescapable response to the realities of the debt situation, does not assure the desired results. If anything, its successful implementation will require more intensive consultation and cooperation among governments and with the international financial institutions and the private banks than in the past. After experience under the Brady plan it may well be that further adjustments in debt strategy will be necessary. In all this, the United States and Japan will have to be principal actors. The initial pledge of new Export–Import Bank lending was heartening evidence of Japan's intention to play an important part. It is prudent to expect, however, that further contributions will be necessary, and over a significant period of time.

E. Foreign Assistance

The Reagan years saw a substantial increase in U.S. foreign assistance in the first term, peaking in 1985 at about $20 billion, and a steady decline in the second term to a current level just under $14 billion. In constant dollars overall aid appropriations are now slightly below the levels at the end of the Carter administration. There have been significant shifts in emphasis in the aims and types of aid in the past eight years.

The security related portion of the aid budget grew more rapidly than the development assistance portion, especially up to 1985. From 1981 – 1985 the total foreign aid program in current dollars grew by 50 percent, but security assistance accounted for the lion's share of the growth: 68 percent, in contrast to the growth of development assistance by only 18 percent. Despite the fact that budget cuts since 1985 have fallen more heavily on the security programs, the overall balance has shifted by several percentage points to the security side. Two-thirds of the total aid program is security related; one-third is bilateral and multilateral development assistance, including food aid.

The strong initial Reagan administration bias in favor of bilateral aid and against the multilateral institutions was softened under Treasury Secretary Baker. In 1987 – 1988 the Administration managed to secure approval for three important pieces of multilateral legislation: authorizations for the International Development Association, the Multilateral Investment Guarantee Agency, and the General Capital Increase (GCI) for the World Bank. (Congressional Democrats tried unsuccessfully to tie the GCI to some Administration consideration of debt relief.) All three items of legislation were passed in a "package" form that obviated the need for direct consideration on the floor of the House and Senate, where they would have been likely to lose. The real level of multilateral assistance has declined substantially since the Carter administration.

There are, in effect, two American bilateral aid programs that live in uneasy antagonism within the same legislation. Security related assistance is comprised of the Economic Support Fund (ESF), a bilateral economic assistance program associated with short-term political or strategic objectives, and military assistance, made up of three programs: Foreign Military Sales (FMS) credits, Military Assistance Program (MAP), and International Military Education and Training (IMET).

Development assistance is the second major program, with about one-third of the total budget. This is made up of bilateral development assistance, normally in project form, food aid (PL-480), and multilateral assistance. Each set of programs has its Congressional supporters and public advocates. The liberals, mostly but not exclusively Democrats, normally argue for the development related programs; the conservatives and the Administration for the security related programs. The final appropriation levels tend to be a compromise between these competing forces, with the Reagan administration, particularly in the first term, tipping the balance to the security side. This balance of power is not expected to change appreciably with a new administration, except that the pressure to cut the foreign aid budget will probably increase.

Several characteristics of security assistance, especially ESF, are worth noting. Israel and Egypt are the top recipients of ESF, as they are of military assistance. Indeed, there are close parallels between the two programs. ESF and military aid are targeted to particular countries by Congressional "earmarking". Ninety-four percent of ESF moneys and 99 percent of military aid are earmarked by countries. This leaves virtually nothing for non-earmarked countries. Sixty percent of ESF is in the form of cash transfers, in which Israel bulks large. Thirty two percent is in project form. There is very little economic accountability in the cash transfer portion, and thus its development impact is questioned by many American religious and humanitarian organizations which follow the aid budget. ESF programs, with a handful of exceptions, are aimed at higher income developing countries. As a result, U.S. aid is skewed to the higher income developing countries. Only .04 percent of ESF goes to the poorest countries.

Another way of looking at U.S. aid programs is to examine the geographical concentration. Just as Japanese aid is focused on Asia, U.S. aid is concentrated on the Middle East and to a lesser extent on the NATO countries. Less than 40 percent of the U.S. aid program goes to Israel and Egypt, and this part is remarkably stable at about $5 billion per year. This is also the most politically popular aspect of aid, and will almost certainly be impervious to budget cuts. Another $1 billion is provided annually for economic and military assistance to four NATO countries: Portugal, Spain, Greece, and Turkey. The other big concentration of security assistance is in the four countries of Central America: El Salvador, Costa Rica, Honduras, and Guatemala. They received a total of almost $600 million in 1988. The large Latin American debtor countries do not receive bilateral U.S. assistance, but since 1982 Mexico has benefited from special rescue packages heavily backed by the U.S. Treasury.

The U.S. development assistance program has also undergone some shifts in priorities during the Reagan years. The early attempts to promote a conservative ideological agenda faded, except perhaps in the Administration's opposition to abortion in any population planning programs. AID announced a "Blueprint for Development" in 1981, which stressed four pillars: economic policy dialogue, institutional development, technology transfer, and support for the private sector. These themes have also been taken up in multilateral institutions, and the private sector emphasis has struck a responsive chord in many developing countries, as the evidence of the poor performance of excessively intrusive policies has become clear. Other important themes include the need for family planning, environmental protection, and energy conservation. At the end of the Reagan administration the development assistance programs are more notable for their continuity than change. Nevertheless, U.S. development assistance is now so small a fraction that it must be concentrated on special areas of comparative advantage or in pilot programs to test new ideas.

There is little doubt that the United States has made a major contribution to development thinking and progress, although it has had its fair share of fads and quick fixes. Large scale, capital intensive projects have disappeared from the AID portfolio, except for a handful in Egypt. The U.S. aid program has been more interventionist and people oriented than those of other donors, with a vast network of overseas AID offices more appropriate to the heyday of U.S. leadership. Japan, with a bilateral program now rivaling the U.S. in magnitude, has just 35 staff members in developing countries! It is not clear what a declining U.S. aid program in real terms will mean for U.S. leadership, but most likely the result will be increasing difficulty in impressing its views on other donors and recipients. There may be good and bad in this, but the world would certainly be worse off if centralized, government-dominated economies did prove to be the wave of the future.

Finally, it should be said that there is little political/policy coherence in the U.S. aid program. Congress has added more money for the programs with the fewest restrictions (ESF), and has added numerous development assistance objectives without increasing the funding. As Joel Johnson, formerly of the Senate Foreign Relations Committee staff, wrote recently: "When Congress has acted, it has increasingly provided more guidance where there are no resources, and resources where there is no guidance, except to designate country recipients."

A Congressional panel chaired by Representative Lee Hamilton (D–Indiana), a respected foreign affairs expert, has been soliciting views in order to rewrite the foreign assistance legislation, an effort last undertaken in 1973. It is not clear at this point whether such an effort will be successful. The same contradictions and divisions of opinion remain in Congress and in public attitudes. The religious and humanitarian community wants a pure development aid program unsullied by politics; the conservatives believe in a more security oriented program. Budget stringency puts any substantial increase in funding out of the question.

As has been remarked, Japan's aid program differs most remarkably from that of the United States in that the permanent staff stationed abroad is so minuscule. Whether this is in all respects a shortcoming may be debatable, but it may be partly responsible for the noticeable lag between appropriations of aid monies and their disbursement.

In any case, Japan's Official Development Assistance (ODA) has grown steadily in volume over the years. During the current fiscal year, the ODA budget (bilateral grants, grants to multilateral agencies, and loans net of repayments) in U.S. dollar terms may be $10 billion (at 135 yen =$1.00) which would make Japan the foremost national aid donor. ODA has been largely spared from Japan's budget austerity during the 1980s. As a share of GNP it has settled at about .031 percent, less than half way to the OECD–wide goal of .07 percent but well ahead of the United States (in the order of .02 percent). The grant share, considered to be one index of ODA's relative utility to the recipients, has been regularly expanded. It now accounts for more than 50 percent of expected net disbursements, but is still below that of most other donors.

Japan's aid traditionally has gone in main part to Asian countries. The Asian share is not likely to change significantly in 1989 unless Japan's three year commitment of $4.5 billion to the Brady debt relief plan results in early large loans to Latin America.

Coordination of development aid policy is conducted primarily through the OECD's Development Assistance Committee. Bilateral cooperation between the United States and Japan at the operating level offers opportunities for strengthening aid programs. The United States has both the most extensive experience with development aid programs and the largest staff of aid officials. Japan's experience is more limited, geographically and otherwise, and it has few career people in the field of aid policy and administration. Experiments with joint planning and implementing of aid programs conceivably could go so far as the co-opting of U.S. aid personnel for service on Japanese financed projects.

CHAPTER III

Japan–U.S. Economic Cooperation for the
Developing Countries   *by Makoto Sakurai*

In the years since the United Nations declared the 1960s a "Decade of Development," the developing nations have invested heavily in the effort to build up their economies. A number of them, including the four newly industrialized economies (NIEs) of Asia (South Korea, Hong Kong, Taiwan, and Singapore) and some of the ASEAN countries, performed admirably in this endeavor and have made great strides. But for many, the results have been far from satisfactory, and population pressures and poverty remain major concerns. With the advent of the 1980s, the problem of accumulating debt among the Latin American nations has become especially acute and their heavy burden of borrowing is a major destabilizing factor in the international monetary system.

The industrialized nations must assist the developing countries in extricating themselves from these difficulties, and the roles and responsibilities they carry in this regard will make all the difference. Interdependence in the international economy is more complex than ever and resource-poor countries like Japan are as much a part of the global web as resource-rich countries like the United States. It hardly need be said that the global economic and financial systems function most smoothly when the developing nations' programs of economic development are going well. Because Japan and the United States have such large economies and because they maintain very close relationships with the developing nations, the impact of their economic policies is especially great as far as these countries are concerned.

Both Japan and the United States have faced major economic issues beginning in the mid-1980s. Since the end of the Pacific War, Japan and the United States have maintained very close political and economic ties. But as the scale of the Japanese economy began to expand in the latter half of the 1970s, Japan's role and responsibilities in its bilateral relationship with the United States began to grow. With the changing nature of that relationship, friction has developed in several areas, in certain cases calling ultimately for fundamental restructuring in the economies of both countries. In recent years, this situation has generated heated international discussion. An additional issue for both nations that has generated much recent discussion is their role and responsibility vis–à–vis the world economy.

For a long time, Japan's official development assistance was criticized for its inadequate quality and quantity, uneven distribution, and bias for bilateral aid. This situation has been largely remedied with major changes adopted in ODA policy. Structural adjustment of the domestic economy in keeping with the recommendations for shifting the emphasis from exports to domestic demand contained in the 1986 Maekawa Report is in the process of transforming the economic scene as well. The rapid rise in the value of the yen against the U.S. dollar since September 1985 has served to propel these reforms and steady progress is being made in the recycling of the surplus in Japan's balance of payments for the benefit of the developing countries.

While Japan is assuming a more responsible role in the world economy, there is still room for Japan to play a larger part in the promotion of economic growth in the developing nations, particularly in cooperation and through coordination with the United States. Despite great efforts, the developing nations remain burdened by debt; indeed, their plight has become even more severe. In this paper, I shall consider how Japan and the United States can cooperate in promoting economic development, Japan's role in that endeavor in particular, from the viewpoint of policy.

A. Economic Problems of Developing Countries

1. Developing Economies

Poverty and debt. The typical characteristics of developing countries are low per capita income, high population growth, low savings, and a small proportion of investment vis–à–vis the gross domestic product. But the term "developing country" is extremely broad, embracing a large number of countries at various stages of economic development. The NIEs, for example, have a relatively high per capita income, and exports account for a large proportion of their gross domestic product, bringing them closer to the advanced economies. On the other hand, a large group of LDCs suffer from serious poverty and overpopulation.

Closer examination reveals marked regional characteristics. Many of the developing nations on the African continent, for example, have very low per capital income levels, and though they receive a certain amount of official economic assistance from other countries, there is very little inflow of funds via private financial markets or in the form of direct investment from the private sector.

In Asia, on the other hand, are a number of the world's newly industrialized economies where economic performance and high export rates have in some cases boosted per capita income over the $3,000 mark. The NIEs are both stimulated by large amounts of private-sector funds and the recipients of considerable private direct investment. Most recently, some Asian NIEs have reported surplus of current account balances for the first time and have even become creditor nations in terms of cash flow. The ASEAN countries, whose recent economic performance follows close behind that of the NIEs, also owe more of their success to the influx of private funds and private-sector direct investment than to official development assistance. The nations of South Asia have not fared so well; their per capita income is relatively low and they still depend heavily on ODA. Nevertheless, India and Pakistan have recently begun to draw attention in the private investment market, and Asia as a whole is benefiting from a steady flow of funds from the industrialized countries.

In Latin America, as compared to Africa and Asia, there are far more countries where the per capita income exceeds $1,000. These middle-income nations have a long history of economic development, many of them with industrialization programs dating back to the 1930s. By the 1960s and 1970s, they had achieved a certain degree of economic growth, but their industrialization and development strategies were directed mainly at promotion of import replacement industries. Even when attempts were made to switch over to export-based economic strategies, they usually failed.

In 1982, Mexico's debt burden had grown to crisis proportions, and with only a few exceptions, the other countries of Latin America have encountered the same problem. They have since adopted very stiff economic readjustment programs, and per capita figures for real economic growth have plummeted, dropping in some cases to zero or even below. This was also partly due to the growth of population. Tight policies will likely, if only temporarily, create massive unemployment and invite the accompanying risk of political instability. Even when these countries manage to reduce the balance of payment deficits and their economic growth can get back on track, real wages are also likely to drop. This is because they attempt to rehabilitate their economies through vigorous adoption of export-oriented economic development strategies.

Particular attention should be paid to the possible repercussions of restrictive economic policies on domestic politics and international relations. Generally, strict retrenchment policies are difficult to maintain under a democratic political system. Such policies may cause political instability at home as well as having unfavorable effects on other countries. Increases in unemployment, the lag in recovery of real wages and other problems as the result of economic readjustment are thus unavoidable. Theoretically, they are natural consequences, but these problems must be resolved somehow if economic growth is to be sustained over the long term.

The debt issue is of most immediate concern to the debtor nations and their creditors—primarily the banks and other private financial institutions of the industrialized countries—and such international financial organizations as the International Monetary Fund (IMF), World Bank, Inter-American Development Bank (IDB), and Asian Development Bank (ADB). Among these, it is the private financial institutions of the industrialized countries that are most affected by the debt issue; they can influence the debt issue most, as well.

Poverty, combined with population growth and food shortages, is the most basic issue confronting the developing nations today. The acuteness of poverty is evident in the statistics for population distribution in terms of per capita income. According to the World Bank's *World Development Report 1988*, the combined populations of the developing countries in 1986 totalled 3.76 billion. Of this figure, 2.49 billion, or 66 percent, lived in low per capita income (U.S.$450 and below) countries. Even the middle-income countries suffer from latent unemployment and the unequal distribution of wealth.

To date, official economic assistance from Japan, the United States, and the other industrialized countries has been primarily directed at meeting basic human needs and building infrastructure in the attempt to alleviate poverty. This is likely to continue to be the major focus for ODA and is certain to be emphasized in cooperative efforts among the industrialized countries.

The debt issue also entails a flow of funds from the industrialized countries just as in the case of ODA for fighting poverty, but the countries involved and the problems to be grappled with are quite different. The debt issue concerns mainly the middle-income countries of Latin America, but–because of the far-reaching effects on the international financial system, as well as on what Japan and the United States must do for the world economy in the immediate future, it should be given more priority than the poverty issue in the short and medium term.

Economic Development and Environmental Issues. Certainly one of the most pressing issues in economic development is protection of the environment. Up until now, environmental destruction and related problems have been considered the trade off for economic development, but experience is showing that we would be wise to try to eliminate such negative trade-offs by devising appropriate technologies and carefully reconsidering the fundamental premises of economic development.

Not all the environmental problems of the developing countries are caused by economic development: desertification, for example, does not in most cases stem from development-related causes. The environmental problems encountered as a result of economic development in the Amazon region, however, show a direct cause–and–effect relationship. These experiences will surely be carefully considered in future development planning and in cooperation by the industrialized nations. Cooperation and coordination with regard to common concerns of this kind will be relatively easy to achieve between the United States and Japan.

2. Japan, the United States, and the Developing Economies

Economic Relations. Economic relations between the industrialized and developing nations coalesce in two areas: transactions in goods and services through trade, and capital transfer (economic assistance, grants and loans, and direct investment). In addition, there is a certain degree of labor mobility from some of the developing countries to a number of the industrialized countries, but this is a relatively minor issue as far as economic relations go.

There are also regional differences. The United States' ties with developing countries concentrate in Latin America; those of Japan with its neighbors in Asia, and those of Europe with African and Middle Eastern nations. Nevertheless, patterns of trade, finance, and investment relations are quite similar regardless of region or source of cooperation. In the past, there was a tendency in the area of trade, for the developing countries to export primary products to the industrialized countries, which in turn exported capital goods. From the beginning of the 1970s, however, some of the developing countries began to export industrial products (labor intensive goods) to the industrialized nations. Today the amount of exports of this kind from the NIEs, in particular, are considerable.

A massive amount of capital has been transferred from the industrialized to the developing countries in the form of loans, direct investment, and economic assistance over the years, but since the beginning of the 1980s, a remarkable change has taken place in the flow of funds. The World Bank's World Debt Tables 1988 show minus values for net transfer from the industrialized to developing nations in the latter half of the 1980s. This indicates the extremely abnormal situation in which funds are actually flowing from the developing to the industrialized countries. The outflow from the Latin American countries began in the mid-1980s, a sign of the seriousness of the debt burden in that part of the world. The reversal in the direction of net transfer and the marked disparities between regions have a significant effect on the economies of the industrialized countries.

Japanese and American Relations with the Developing Countries. As noted, Japanese and American economic relations with developing nations are focused on different regions, the former mainly in Latin America and the latter mainly in East and Southeast Asia. The conspicuous difference in performance between these two regions since the beginning of the 1980s is having a considerable impact upon Japan and the United States.

U.S. exports to Latin America, particularly of capital goods, have slackened with the adoption by countries in the region of strict economic adjustment policies and their shifting orientation to exports for the sake of reconstruction. The United States' huge trade deficit today is aggravated in part by its trade with Latin America.

U.S. direct investment in Latin America came to a near standstill beginning in the early 1980s, but its trade with and investment in Asia have greatly expanded, clearly due to the favorable economic performance of Asian developing countries. This has led to a corresponding expansion of the U.S. trade deficit with Asian NIEs and the ASEAN countries, and since the latter half of 1986, adjustments have been made in the dollar's exchange rate with the currencies of these nations. This trend seems likely to continue.

Japan's trade with the Asian developing countries has been characterized by import of primary industrial goods and export of capital goods. Since the end of the 1960s, the Asian NIEs have followed export-oriented economic development strategies and their exports to the industrialized countries have expanded from labor intensive consumer products to intermediate goods and consumer durables. Their biggest customer has been the United States.

From the perspective of the Asian NIEs, Japan has functioned as the supplier of capital goods while the United States has served as a major market. Japan did not become a major customer for Asian industrial goods until the mid-1980s. The rising value of the yen since September 1985, however, has contributed to an increase in Japan's imports of parts and finished products, raising the percentage of manufactured/processed goods imports (the ratio of the dollar-based value of manufactured/processed goods to the value of all imports) from 31.0 percent in 1985 to 44.1 percent in 1987 (*Trade Statistics*, Ministry of Finance). As these figures indicate, Japan's role vis-à-vis the Asian developing nations is changing radically.

Economic assistance is another important dimension of economic relations between the developing nations and Japan and the United States respectively. Japanese ODA has been directed primarily at Asian countries and put to use in building infrastructure. Whereas Japan provides financial assistance in response to requests by recipient countries, the United States has traditionally directed its aid to developing countries, using ODA as a means of facilitating democracy, furthering human rights and maintaining global security. Japanese ODA has been criticized as being insufficient quantitatively and inappropriate qualitatively, but in recent years there has been a significant increase as far as quantity is concerned. This is clear from the table below.

Still, there is a great deal more Japan can do to improve the quality of its official development assistance, for example, in the area of untied grants. In 1986, the grant element in ODA accounted for 81.7 percent for Japan, 96.8 percent for the United States, 88.9 percent for West Germany, 89.1 percent for France and 100 percent for the United Kingdom. Japan is expected to continue to increase its ODA and make qualitative improvements. In June 1988, the Japanese government announced that it would provide a total of $50 billion in ODA over the succeeding five years (1988 – 1992), doubling the amount for the past five years.

Table 1

Official Development Assistance vis-à-vis GNP
($ billion; figures in parentheses indicate ratio to GNP)

	1985	1986	1987
Japan	3.8	5.6	7.4
	(0.29)	(0.29)	(0.31)
United States	9.4	9.5	8.8
	(0.24)	(0.23)	(0.20)
West Germany	2.9	3.8	4.4
	(0.47)	(0.43)	(0.39)
France	4.0	5.1	6.6
	(0.78)	(0.70)	(0.51)
Britain	1.5	1.7	1.9
	(0.33)	(0.31)	(0.28)

B. The Debt Problem

1. Statement of the Problem

Regional Disparities. At present, the foreign debt crisis is most acute among Latin American countries. Nations in Asia, Africa, and the Middle East confront the same problem, but in its scale, seriousness, and impact the crisis in Latin America goes far beyond that in any other region.

The reasons for the debt crisis are various. The drop in prices of primary products is one, high interest rates is another; but these are external causes whose impact is felt as much by the debtor nations of Asia and other regions as by Latin American countries. The plight of Latin America stems from specific causes, which I shall discuss in more detail.

Latin American Debt. Patterns of economic development in Latin American countries differ clearly from those of other parts of the world. For a long time, dependence on trade was relatively low considering the size of the economies involved, and growth was propelled largely through development of import-replacement industries. Today, of course, all Latin American countries have shifted to export-oriented or export-promotion strategies in economic development, but compared to Asian countries, the value of their exports vis–à–vis the gross domestic product (GDP) remains far smaller.

Table 2

Exports vis–à–vis GDP (1986)

Brazil	7.5%	South Korea	32.2%
Mexico	9.4	Thailand	22.0
Argentina	6.7	Malaysia	39.1
Colombia	13.1	Philippines	17.7
Venezuela	19.2	Indonesia	17.8

Source: World Bank. *World Development Report 1988.*

The ratio of exports to GDP in the Latin American countries in 1986 was small, only Venezuela showing figures comparable to those of the Philippines or Indonesia. For Brazil, Mexico, and Argentina, the ratio is still only a single-digit figure. It is easy to understand why countries with such low export ratios would experience greater difficulty in repaying debts. It is also easy to see that switching over from import replacement industries to export orientation is no simple task. Reliance on import replacement industries had led to poor investment efficiency in Latin America, the increments of capital-output ratio (ICOR) for the period from the latter half of the seventies through the early eighties running between factors of seven and nine for many of the Latin American countries as opposed to the three–to–five level for Asian countries during the corresponding period.

Current Situation and Prospects. Since 1982, a concerted effort has been made to alleviate the crisis situation through measures on the part of debtor countries themselves to restructure their economies, through rescheduling of repayment, and through increased financing for balance of payments improvement (in the heavily indebted developing countries) by such international organs as the IMF and the World Bank. Notwithstanding, the problems seem to grow even more intransigent; there is not even a fair prospect for their resolution at the present time.

Japan's economic ties with Latin American countries in terms of both trade and capital investment are weaker than those of the United States. They have focused largely on financial relations. Japanese private corporations and institutions, even more than the public sector, can be expected to make a major contribution to the economic restructuring efforts of the Latin American countries, helping to promote the growth of their export industries and the privatization of government enterprises and public corporations. Indeed, from now on, coordination and cooperation not only between Japan and the United States but between public- and private-sector organizations within Japan will be crucial in expanded efforts to meet Latin America's needs.

2. Toward a Solution

The Drawbacks of Current Responses. The debt issue involves three sides: the Latin American borrowers, the private financial institutions of the industrialized countries who are the lenders, and the governments of the industrialized countries. International organizations such as the IMF and the IBRD also play significant roles. The basic question at this point is how the three principals will decide to distribute the burden among themselves. The private financial institutions that have been doing the lending are not, of course, prepared to take the drastic step of cancelling the debts altogether. The debtor nations, for their part, can probably not go much further in tightening their belts or in restructuring their economies. Internal political factors make it exceedingly difficult to prolong such policies. The governments of the industrialized countries, for their part, have pressing domestic problems to deal with.

The United States, for example, is so burdened by its fiscal deficit that it has to limit the amount of economic aid it extends, and its current account deficits have turned it into a debtor nation importing foreign capital. Japan enjoys a surplus in its balance of payments, but this surplus is accumulated primarily in the private sector and the public sector has only limited financial leeway.

Given the lack of room to maneuver on the part of all three major parties in the debt problem, it is not easy to come up with a solution that is satisfactory to all. Thus far, two basic measures have been implemented. The first has been the rescheduling of debt payments and supply of new funds. The provision of new money under IMF and IBRD initiatives is designed to provide the conditions for structural adjustment in the areas of macro-economic policy and relevant institutional reforms and pricing policy. The structural adjustment loans (SAL) and sector adjustment loans (SECAL) offered by the World Bank are no longer temporary devices, but are becoming firmly established practices. They are further evidence that the solution to the debt problem is a long way off.

A second resolution of the debt problem utilizes the market mechanism. In this approach, known as the debt-equity swap, a market price (at a discount) is set for each country's credits extended to the debtor. The discount price naturally reflects the gravity of the debt crisis in the countries concerned. In actuality, the debts are so large that debt-equity swap can cover only a small percentage of the outstanding debts. As it is, the two formulas for solution outlined here are clearly reaching the limits of their effectiveness.

Limitations of Proposed Solutions. A number of ideas have been put forth for solution of the debt crisis ever since its gravity became evident in 1982. Two of the most important are the Baker Plan and the Bradley Plan.

In October 1985, then Treasury Secretary James Baker proposed that efforts should be directed at promoting growth in the debtor nations thereby improving their capacity to repay their loans. The way to achieve this, he argued, was to increase funding for development through international financial institutions while at the same time persuading private financial institutions to pour in an additional $20 billion in new money. Baker made further proposals in 1987 for specific steps to be taken in a so-called menu approach. By that time, the net transfer of funds from industrialized to developing countries had fallen to minus figures, creating a situation that hardly accorded with Baker's scenario.

The plan advocated by Senator Bill Bradley (D., N.J.), is also aimed at promoting the growth of debtor nations, but its approach is to exempt them from a part of the principal and interest. Among many other plans proposed is one calling for establishment of a new international institution charged with purchasing bonds issued by the debtor nations.

None of these proposals has yet to be actually applied, the major reason being that no concrete plan has been devised to provide the necessary financing. Even if such a plan were drawn up, however, it is unlikely that either the United States Congress or the Japanese government would be able to secure appropriate funds for the reasons I have already explained.

C. Japan's Role and Burden Sharing with the U.S.

1. Japanese and U.S. Roles

Japan and the United States must come up with a well–thought–out action program for the stability of the world economy and its expanding equilibrium, not just for the benefit of the developing countries, but for the entire global economic system. And to do this, they need to cooperate and share the burden of initial costs.

Any program of action to rescue the poverty-stricken and debt ridden developing nations must rest on three principles:

1. The bearing of initial costs by the governments and financial institutions of the industrialized countries
2. A long-term outlook
3. Strong political determination to execute the program.

Basic agreement on these three principles between Japan and the United States would mark a significant step forward in resolving the dilemma of the developing countries. Before such an agreement can be reached, however, there is a need to clarify exactly what Japan's role should be and to determine how much of the responsibility it can shoulder.

2. Japan's Response

The Maekawa Reports. Any future role to be played by Japan can be better understood if we first look at what Japan has done so far. Two important expressions of Japan's intentions regarding the imbalance of its current accounts are the April 1986 "Maekawa Report" and the May 1987 "New Maekawa Report." These two reports state that in order for Japan to reduce its massive trade surplus, it needs to:

1. Expand domestic demand;
2. Increase its imports of finished products and processed goods;
3. Increase its direct investment overseas;

4. Transform its industrial structure from an export-oriented to a domestic–demand–led structure.

The reports further urge that Japan participate actively in the Uruguay Round of multilateral trade negotiations for the maintenance and strengthening of the free trade system, implement qualitative and quantitative improvement of its ODA programs, increase its financial cooperation and trade with the developing countries, and improve the flow of funds for more effective results. Judging from the policy developments that have taken place since these recommendations were made, the Maekawa reports can be said to have played a significant role in shaping recent Japanese policy. The rapid rise in the value of the yen since September 1985 has, of course, played an equally important part.

The Recycling Plan and Its Drawbacks. The plan to recycle Japan's trade surplus to the developing countries was part of the emergency economic measures announced in May 1987 and is currently being implemented. According to this plan $30 billion in trade surplus funds (including the earlier planned $10 billion) is to be recycled to the developing countries over the three-year period from 1987 to 1989. The breakdown of the additional $20 billion: $8 billion to be channeled, as contribution or investment, to the World Bank and the IMF, $9 billion to be allotted by the Export–Import Bank of Japan and the Overseas Economic Cooperation Fund (OECF), and $3 billion to be supplied by the Export–Import Bank of Japan in the form of direct financing to the developing countries.

A major problem in implementing this recycling plan is that Japan has accumulated little know-how in this area, partly because of its lack of experience with SAL and SECAL, and other systems, for example. The recycling is expected to grow, and in order for it to be effective, Japan should endeavor to acquire the required know-how and put sufficient human resources into it.

Japan's Future Role. As I have shown, Japanese cooperation in the economic reconstruction and development of developing nations has been considered mainly in terms of what can be offered by the public sector. The role of the Japanese public sector will surely continue to be important in such efforts as the opening of Japan's markets, its own economic restructuring, and fund recycling. But the private sector can be expected to play an equally significant role through overseas direct investment and the promotion of the developing countries' export industries as long as there is some kind of guarantee system to cover the risks involved. The trade expansion that the developing countries have long asked for and considered even more helpful than financial aid is another area in which the private sector can contribute.

3. Burden Sharing between Japan and the United States

America's Global Economic Roles and Woes. The American economy is the largest and the most influential in the world. Yet since the beginning of this decade it has struggled with twin deficits (budget and trade) and since 1985 the dollar devalued steeply against the major world currencies. At the same time Japan's current account surplus has grown to the extent that the imbalance between the two countries has led to considerable friction.

What the American economy has to do now, both for its own survival and for the stability of the world economy, are to mend its twin deficits and stabilize the dollar. Too rapid a correction of the twin deficits, however, would have a drastic deflationary effect on the world economy as a whole and exert a negative impact upon the developing countries struggling to rise out of poverty and free themselves from their accumulative debts. If these negative effects are to be effectively countered, careful coordination of macro-economic measures must be achieved between the United States and Japan as well as among all of the industrialized countries. In this process, the United States will have to work to solve its own current account imbalance even as it fulfills its obligation to stabilize the world economy.

Japan's Future Role and New Responsibilities. Knowing the tasks and role of the U.S. economy, it is possible to define what role Japan should play and what new tasks it will come to grips with. If the U.S. role in aiding the developing countries is vital to stabilization of the world economy, then what Japan must do is to join the United States in the effort to foster expanding equilibrium while at the same time reducing its current account surplus. By performing that role well, the Japanese economy will help to stabilize the dollar and meet the needs of the developing countries.

In actual fact, Japan has been playing this role for some time, but sufficient effort was not made within the public or private sector to articulate Japan's role in the international context. Fortunately, Japanese are rapidly awakening to the need for their country to assume greater responsibility and greater efforts are being made to translate this consciousness into realistic proposals. This new awareness is reflected in the so-called Miyazawa Plan for solving the debt issue presented by Finance Minister Kiichi Miyazawa at the 1988 general meetings of the World Bank and IMF. The plan calls for further recycling of funds and sharing of the debt burden among the principals involved.

To date, Japan's strongest economic bonds with the developing countries have been with the countries of Asia. Henceforth the United States can be expected to forge equally strong ties with Asia while Japan directs more of its recycled funds and economic exchange in the private sector to the developing countries of Latin America. Correction of the U.S.–Japan trade imbalance should open up the possibility of increased exports from the Latin American countries to the United States, and Japan's recycling of its trade surplus should make possible an expansion of U.S. exports to the developing countries. In any event, Japan's future in the international community will be defined by its sharing of responsibilities with the United States and by the demands made upon it by the world economy.

CHAPTER IV

America and Japan in a World of
Multipolar Tensions   *by Roy A. Werner*

Introduction

We are in an era of transition; the international system is in flux. These changes are seen in domestic reforms in communist states, in growing macroeconomic imbalances in savings and investment levels that have led to volatile exchange rate swings altering national purchasing power among nations, unprecedented levels of debt, and threats of increasing protectionism. These economic difficulties for many of the world's 170 nations are new challenges, which added to the problems of the past and present, confront the security and well-being of nations. This web of economic and political independencies in the next decade will demand skillful management by national leaders.

A period of such change and challenge carries special dangers of instability, and the constant possibility of resort to force. Nowhere are such instabilities more evident than in the developing world. "Latin America officials are now warning that ... falling living standards are breeding a hopelessness that is beginning to translate into ominous political decay."[1] Within a short time after this warning more than three hundred Venezuelan citizens died in riots and Argentina had to impose martial law. It is our view that American and Japanese interests are so intertwined in the developing world that they warrant special study at this time. Our aim is to (i) examine the security interests of the U.S. and Japan and (ii) to provide policy recommendations based upon this analysis, which we believe warrant the consideration of our governments and people. This essay examines the interaction of security and economics in the hope of eventual generalization about the process of creating a more stable and peaceful international system.

Security is a subjective concept. Attempts at conceptualization are generally inadequate[2], but every discerning visitor can to some degree gauge the presence or absence of threats and fear. Without security it would be difficult to enjoy such values as liberty, justice, democracy, and economic well-being. Some observers have been surprised by the recent wave of democratization by several states. But market economics which necessitate competition, are quite conducive to democracy. Hence, markets and democracy have thus developed in tandem in several Pacific area nations. Indeed, in a fundamental sense, "security" is simply the safeguarding of such values and institutions against force or the threat of force. When these values are at risk, either internationally or internally, security interests are created to which governments must respond. Nations, great and small, seek a world free from want and fear, with the liberty to pursue their interests without the threat of force being used against them. Indeed, it is impossible to maintain commerce and, therefore, peace and prosperity in a warring world.

In the Sovereign territory of Japan and the United States, internal risks are not an immediate concern. But, in many of the developing states, internal security issues are vital and overwhelming. Yet the costs of security are staggering. Developing nations face especially tough choices between economics and defense. Yet all states, including the superpowers, need to find effective means of providing security at the lowest possible cost.

It is necessary to begin with how and why threat perceptions differ. What do these differences mean for regional and global stability? No Asian state, including Japan, fully shares American threat perceptions regarding the Soviet Union. The superpower balance is seen as only peripheral to the more immediate problems of nation building and economic development to which they give priority. Many Asians believe that protectionism is their greatest threat, and that internal insurgencies and regional wars are decidedly secondary.

1. Economics and Security

The linkage between economics and security is becoming increasingly obvious and offers a useful starting point for our analysis. Recognizing that security demands the retention of effective military forces, we must seek to deal with the causes of conflict rather than belatedly treating the symptoms through warfare. To this end, we must identify the ways and degree in which Japan and the United States can act in line with their respective interests by responding to changes in the developing world. Where interests exist which justify action, we should anticipate and act before conditions adversely affect the security and growth prospects of the developing states.

American and Japanese interests are not always the same; diverging policies are sometimes inescapable. Further, as the world's banker, Japan's leverage is growing. Yet, old habits die hard. As David Hale wrote in the *London Times*, "The U.S. is a debtor nation with the habits of a creditor nation; Germany and Japan are creditor nations with the habits of debtor nations."[3] Fortunately, Japanese and American basic values and security interests in the developing world strongly coincide and offer the possibility of a mutually satisfactory approach.

2. Anticipatory Security

Strategically a concept of "anticipatory security," designed to lessen the odds of conflict, provides an attractive policy for both countries. This approach is one of anticipating security problems and acting to forestall military action primarily through economic and political means. In effect, anticipatory security is an essential element of crisis prevention, a different segment of deterrence. Such actions can be taken at a much lower cost than conflict itself would involve. Of course, consideration of the evolution towards democracy is an important factor. Otherwise, such a concept is merely a recipe for stability, even of an authoritarian variety. A clear example is the curtailment of aid taken by Japan (the largest donor), Germany and the United States towards the repressive military regime which now rules Burma and has yet to permit free elections.

This broad concept of security, going beyond the purely military aspects, is appropriate for both countries. Liddell Hart said "there has been a very natural tendency to lose sight of the basic national objective, and identify it with the military aim."[4] Indeed, when there is no obvious external military threat, as in the case of Australia, Indonesia, and many Pacific island-states, the dominant national security concerns are basically economic issues, linked in some cases with internal instability. Most developing states fear internal threats, sometimes linked with external ideological or ethnic forces, that may endanger a regime more than the nation itself.

Given the "unity" of economic development and security for the developing nations, it is convenient to make assessments in these areas as part of the economic segment of this study. Nevertheless, it should not be forgotten that many developing nations lie at the very edge of disintegration. While economic progress may not be a sufficient condition for political and security success, it surely is a *necessary* one. Many historical examples make it clear that economic failure is an open invitation for conflict and despotic rule.[5]

The security policies of all states, great and small, must respond to their needs within the international system. Maintaining security has become more complex and difficult as interdependence has multiplied vulnerabilities. In conducting this study of suitable security roles for the United States and Japan, and in addressing the security issues affecting developing nations, we have no thought of imposing our views on others, as arrogating to ourselves responsibilities and decision that will and must be made by others. Ours is a more limited purpose: to define for ourselves the things we can and should do, and the contributions that we, in our respective ways, can make to a more favorable international environment from which all may benefit.

In our still anarchical world, national security cannot be attained individually by any nation, however powerful, in isolation. We utilize alliances and the cooperation of like-minded nations to deter conflict and participate in the global economy. To lessen risks, we seize opportunities to create a more favorable security environment, to protect what each nation might call its "national valuables." But what is to be done? How shall the responsibility be divided? What is the magnitude of effort required?

B. Risks and Threats

1. Japan and the United States

From the standpoint of Japan and the United States, the risks and threats that affect security and well-being are threefold. A further variable is the state of American-Japanese relations in each of these cases.

The first is directly military in form, centering principally on the massive military power and international policies of the Soviet Union. A generally stable military balance between East and West has been achieved and maintained. Recent shifts of Soviet policy are to be welcomed, especially the INF Treaty, in that they portend a possible lessening of international tensions and a lowering of the military confrontation of the past forty years. Nevertheless, it is necessary to wait to see these changes realized in practice—specifically, in reduced "invasion capabilities" (especially in Central Europe), in carefully negotiated arms reductions and the adoption of less threatening military postures. Likewise return of the Japanese Northern Territories seized by the USSR in the final days of WW II is desirable. Soviet willingness to return these islands is uncertain. Soviet policy apparently intends to preserve their access through the Kuriles chain given surveillance and interdiction difficulties in those waters. Further, the Soviets see the Seihan rail tunnel as militarily significant given the enhanced reinforcement capability it provides to Hokkaido.[6] Assuming no shocking new policies, the U.S.-Japanese Security Treaty is therefore likely to remain in force and serve both parties well.

Second, the potential for violence arising from other sources seems certain to continue. Islamic fundamentalism, the Arab-Israeli dispute, tribal rivalry in Africa, the problem of South Africa, unstable regimes in Central and South America, and the continuing strife in Cambodia, Korea, or the Philippines could flare quickly. Prolonged instability might even lead to a conventional force buildup by Japan if American-Japanese ties are broken and discarded. As in the case of the oil embargoes of the 1970s, these events could impact directly on important trade and commerce. Moreover, if the increasing Soviet activity throughout the Pacific Basic should attempt to exploit these disputes, or encourage the use of force to seize power, the finely balanced, but vulnerable economic life of the industrial democracies, could be placed in jeopardy. In any such contingency joint consultations are likely and will determine the future courses which each nation will take according to national priorities.

The third danger is that security relations between America and Japan may erode given the economic and trade frictions between them. This is the most unsettling possibility. Japan has followed basic economic principles in rebuilding its economy.[7] As an economic superpower, Japan has moved to center stage. The relatively enhanced position of Japan however raises concern elsewhere. Deteriorating public opinion polls of Japanese-American friendship in both countries, coupled with massive U.S. bilateral trade imbalances and Japanese unease over the "Super 301" trade rules and fears of racism, clarify the danger. The recent FSX debate is but the latest example. The growing domestic perception of the U. S. as a less competent bully is clearly harmful to mutual relations. Nevertheless the fact remains that no bilateral relationship in global history is as significant. No national economies have been so intertwined yet remain so crucial to global economic prosperity. Although the adjustment costs for all will be significant, we remain convinced that the American-Japanese relationship is growing ever closer through cross investments, common geostrategic views, mutual understanding, and that the difficulties of the moment will be overcome.

2. The Developing Nations

Unlike the advanced democracies, developing states face the potentially explosive problems of economic privation.

More than five billion people live on the earth. Some one billion people live in absolute poverty, barely eking out a subsistence existence. The poorest countries, such as Bangladesh and Ethiopia, have the smallest per capita GNP, generally have the lowest economic growth rates, and the least hope for future improvement. More brutally, they have the worst life expectancy, the lowest adult literacy rates, and the largest percentage of citizens employed in agriculture work. Finally, it has been the poorer nations where conflicts have broken out repeatedly since 1945.

An Economic Perspective On the World

GNP per capita	Nations	Population	Average GNP per capita
$400 or less.	35	2.318 B	$ 280
$401-1,635	47	672.2 M	$ 780
$1,636-4,300	21	472.3 M	$ 2,050
$ 4,300+	48	776.1 M	$11,630
No data	33		

Source: World Bank 1985 data.

In addition to curbing violence, a peaceful and developing world represents trade and marketing opportunities for everyone. Thus a common issue on the global agenda is how to help foster development.

C. Security Interests and Requirements—A Comprehensive, Anticipatory Strategy

1. Sustained Security for Japan and the United States

The main lines of security strategy needed to cope with the risks and threats likely to confront our countries, as briefly outlined above, are readily apparent. For the military threat, the requirements are twofold, and by now, quite familiar: First, to maintain a rough military equilibrium vis-à-vis the Soviet Union that will continue to deter thoughts of aggression and exert a force toward strategic stability. The potential threat posed by the Soviet military machine is the reason that alliance cohesion and cooperation between friendly nations is so important. Second, through arms reductions and confidence building measures, to make the role of military force in international affairs less active, less intense and less dangerous. Reducing the capabilities for sudden or surprise attack in great force, and making military power more an element of stability and order rather than elements of instability and disorder, are important objectives.

2. Enhanced Security for Developing Countries

For developing states who often face economic deprivation, denial of human rights, internal disorder, and hostile neighbors—a multi pronged effort is required. Troubled states need both economic and military assistance. Often they need both simultaneously. The "chicken or egg" argument about which comes first is an abstract illusion for either political or military leaders. It is difficult to achieve economic development if a nation is torn apart by violence. Thus, military assistance is a legitimate need, but must remain subject to overall political and socioeconomic objectives. The actual specifics in an nation will vary, but progress can be measured by three criteria:

a. Economic activity and growth that raises living standards for the people measured by income distribution which lessens huge gulfs and helps bring about a sense of social equality.
b. Pattern of political development that responds to the will of the governed, free from tyranny of any form.

c. A sense of security arising from civil liberties and safeguards from violence and the threat or use of force against either individuals or groups.[8]

Clearly these conditions are not enjoyed by many states. As pointed out earlier, starvation, economic stagnation, dictatorial regimes of the right or left, terrorism, and armed confrontations can be found around the globe. Such order and freedom as does exist, could lapse if the present military equilibrium were to be threatened or destabilized. Likewise, economic distress and factional strife could lead to forceful seizures of power. In particular, attention must be paid to the consequences of environmental damage, especially deforestation, deteriorating quality of soils, air and water, all factors that threaten health and economic growth prospects. Little study has been made of the effect of such international forces upon nation building. Clearly the global economic system affects the domestic political economy. Likewise foreign states may either help or hinder the transition to a prosperous democratic state through their interactions with domestic leaders, grants, specific policies, even war which can transform the society.

Conflict, of course, is more than a clash of arms. Indeed, the roots of conflict are most apt to be found in the underlying social, economic, ideological, and political factors that lead to resort to force.

Economic conditions thus, are a significant factor in the calculus of revolution or stability. The Reagan Administration's Commission on Security and Economic Assistance reported that "economic growth and rising standards of living are vital to internal stability and external defense. Threats to stability impede economic development and prosperity."[9] Earlier, the Carter Administration made a similar point:

Many of the serious international crises of the postwar era have arisen, not from ... great global issues, but from regional threats and instabilities. Because the U.S. cannot escape worldwide involvement, our security and our defense needs are a function of these developments and of the success of our foreign policy in dealing with them.[10]

There is, of course, no automatic or assured relationship between economic development and political stability. For example, India has been democratic and stable for three decades, but only recently did it begin to achieve notable economic gain. Meanwhile, South Korea has progressed rapidly in economic terms since 1961, but has only recently begun to acquire more democratic institutions and practices amidst turbulent political times. Yet, the complexity of these issues and the need to take a longer-term view, to take account of the historical and often distinctive base from which each country begins (especially former colonies), bedevils theoretical understanding.

Increasingly a number of developing states have reached the socioeconomic criteria that seems to be a pre-condition for democratic institutions: industrialization, per capita income, literacy, mass communications, urbanization.[11] Of course, economic progress does not inevitably lead to democracy. Instead of freedom, it may strengthen the hand of repression by making a regime more resilient as was the case with South Korea during President Park's tenure which ended in 1979.

Yet, crisis conditions of whatever origin could, of course, damage the international order from which both Japan, the United States, and others derive many benefits. Although quantitative precision is far from assured, it is possible through country and area studies to identify the major efforts that ought to be pursued and to calculate the order of magnitude efforts required in both military and economic spheres. In particular the legitimacy and effectiveness of the government must be included in assessing the state of security.

Different types of vulnerabilities may exists, but a government lacking the support of its people is already on a crisis slide.

D. Sharing Leadership and Responsibilities

Developing nations lack the investment necessary to create productive assets for economic growth. Moreover, the debt crisis of the past eight years has further intensified this shortfall with growth declining on a per capita basis in many nations.

Today, American military and economic assistance are limited by tightening budget constraints. Yet Japan has an extraordinary propensity to save with totals amounting to more than $1 billion daily. These two truths could provide an avenue of global benefit.

Yet a serious issue is the asymmetric roles of Japan and the U.S. in international affairs. Admittedly Americans are wary of being only a "global policeman" while the Japanese are perceived as a "sugar-daddy" dispensing economic aid. What we are proposing, and which we believe the objective conditions dictate, is a merging of these tasks designed ultimately to benefit all. The United States will take by far the larger responsibility for defense—counterbalancing the Soviet military threat and posture, maintaining an essential contribution to stable regional security, and providing at least limited military aid to help countries with their local and internal security. Japan, beyond its provisions for self-defense, and greater assistance to the United States forces in Japan, will put emphasis on financial and economic assistance.

There is, of course, real concern in the United States that this division will give Japan great commercial advantages over the United States. It may be expected that many countries will take the U.S. contribution to a state of stable security for granted. Other states may even resent some of the military activities of the United States that are essential to mutual security, but impinge on local emotions (such as nuclear weapons presence and movement), or bases on their territories. Meanwhile, Japan receives the appreciation—and the entree—that comes from the dispensation of largess. The issue cannot be wished away, since it comes from the realities of Japan's extraordinary economic power and progress. It will call for wise leadership, effective diplomacy, and careful attention to public understanding on the part of both nations.

1. The Japanese Position

Japan has the lowest relative defense burden among the OECD nations. This reflects past history, the evolution of Self Defense Forces (SDF), and the Mutual Security Treaty between the U.S. and Japan. The chart in the appendix provides a historical record of Japanese defense spending since 1955. But Japanese security requirements are uniquely different. Given their non-nuclear principles, Article 9 of the Constitution,[12] and the perceptions of Asian neighbors, a sizeable Japanese military buildup is out of the question—regardless of U.S. pressure. The Japanese have no desire to become a regional military power and therefore are not acquiring power projection capabilities. Rather, Japan is better suited and able to assist global security through the provision of aid, expansion of imports, and helping others to achieve political stability and economic progress.

A "re-militarized Japan" would be seen as a threat by many Asian states.[13] It is because the growth of Japanese Self-Defense Forces has occurred within the context of the U.S.-Japanese relationship, that other nations are comfortable with that growth. Expansion of Japanese forces will force other nations to distort their economic planning by allocating even more resources toward defense. The cumulative effect of such decisions, over time, will be to halt economic expansion.

American and Japanese defense cooperation is already widely practiced. The "take-off" point was a 1978 agreement on "Guidelines for U.S.-Japan Defense Cooperation. Joint staff planning became commonplace along with combined exercises involving the forces of both nations. The issue of technology was partially resolved in 1983 with a Joint Memorandum of Understanding permitting transfers of dual-use technology. In 1988 Japan paid about $2.5 billion (about 45 percent) of the cost of maintaining U.S. forces in Japan, including foregone taxes. In 1989, labor cost reimbursement to the U.S. rose by 29.5 percent) from 1988 to $419 million. Contributions for facilities increased by 14.4 percent to $783 million.

One of the bedeviling problems for all alliances is the calculation of defense efforts by the percentage of GNP. This is inherently an imprecise and faulty assessment since it ignores the nature of threats, appropriate force structures, and is compounded by the "indexing problem" since each currency buys differing amounts of resources in individual economies. Equally difficult to measure are the economic opportunity costs incurred by defense spending. Although subjective, it is reasonably clear that the difference between a 6.7 percent of GNP (U.S.) and a 1.5 percent of GNP (Japan, including pensions per NATO definitions) permits greater industrial and economic investments by the Japanese. Thus, recent Japanese initiatives to extend substantially greater economic assistance to developing nations is a welcome recognition of greater Japanese participation in the international system.

The simplistic statement that the United States defends Japan while incurring significant trade deficits obscures the reality of international security and the earlier Japanese deficits. Certainly a neutral or hostile Japan would exacerbate rather than lessen American security concerns. Indeed, the Japanese financing of one-third of the U.S. debt can logically be considered an important security contribution. As the world moves into global competitiveness, the issue of sharing the security burden will increasingly sharpen. The task for American and Japanese officials is to decide how we are to value the Japanese contributions?

Why should Japan accept a broader global role? Both domestic and international reasons support Japanese promotion of international stability through democratization and economic development. The official Japanese phrase, "Japan's responsibilities as a surplus nation," and the Foreign Ministry's recent "Bluebook" recognize the political significance of a wider global role. Indeed, the Japanese concept of "comprehensive security" readily incorporates such an expansion of aid, investment, and trade. Finally, we know that trade (and the investment to create markets) rank alongside of political change as the crucial elements of rapid economic growth.[14]

2. The American Position

The United States maintains sizeable military forces around the globe. We have already made that investment. However, the pressure of budget and trade deficits and the "earmarking" of economic and security assistance funds for particular nations have resulted in substantial reductions in American aid. Hegemony on the credit card will no longer be tolerated by other states. Our dual roles as the world's largest debtor and as the benign guarantor of peace are in direct conflict. These facts and the cost of future military modernization will require the United States to develop an unprecedented cooperative and shared approach to regional and global issues.

Reality will require two of the most dissimilar nations, Japan and the United States, to find ways that minimize force structure costs and asymmetries in global responsibilities. Thus, an essential objective of American foreign policy must be to expand Japan's political relationships to avoid a reliance on military might. This is also critical in easing the fears of Asian states with memories of Japanese militarism earlier this century.

At the same time, the U.S. is at a moment of truth when a choice must be made between some of its geopolitical commitments and its budgetary capabilities. Anticipatory security is the appropriate solution. Forced choices such as rapid withdrawals, will only alarm others and lead to global insecurity. The American market and defense umbrella are essential for Japanese prosperity and security. Japanese capital and expanded developmental assistance are essential for U.S. prosperity and security. These trade-offs offer a mutually beneficial avenue for both countries. Japanese wealth grew through their efficiency and the open world trading system. Now Japan must begin to match her economic superpower status with commensurate actions to help safeguard the international system.

The United States led the world into unprecedented prosperity. But the costs of safeguarding that economic progress through nearly five decades have grown too large. The U.S. must find alternative approaches to security while regaining economic competitiveness. Joint actions must begin to formally resolve these issues or the structural imbalances of the 1990s will lead to economic and political instability, even war.

3. Comprehensive Security

Comprehensive security is a Japanese term used to denote the integration of multiple factors in preserving security. Economics, ultimately the sinew of national power, is the driving element in this notion.

The primacy of internal development, both socially and economically, for the developing nations is clear. Ultimately, aid will be insufficient to meet capital needs. Thus, private investment and trade are essential to expand resources and enhance the feeling of security. A broader definition that includes non-military contributions to security must, therefore, include expanded and targeted overseas development aid, technology transfers, and human skill training. The joint Japanese-American proposals offered herein could serve as an example for other states to formulate a framework for their own policies and actions.

The Japanese concept of "comprehensive security"[15] is a useful recognition of these broader aspects of security as we pursue a peaceful and prosperous world. The desirable solution to joint Japanese-American security responsibilities is fourfold. First, expansion of Japanese payments to help defer the high cost of stationing and maintaining U.S. forces in Japan (this may require renegotiation of the Status of Forces Agreement between both nations), while modernizing existing Japanese Self-Defense Forces levels to emphasize long-range surveillance, target acquisition, greater C^3I readiness and war reserve stocks, and integrated defense planning. Second, utilize expanded Japanese aid to help stabilize nations threatened by economic and political instability. Third, retention of the American military and naval presence as a guarantor of relative peace. Fourth, explicit understandings between Japanese and American governments that trade and security issues are significant, but different, policy components. Agreement between the two governments on these two points will operationalize anticipatory security and help to create strategic stability through the extension of comprehensive security.

These policies reflect our traditional interest in fostering an international order that encourages democratic institutions, economic development, and self-determination throughout the world. In effect, we are confronted by a means-end issue that must be solved by new concepts.

E. The Components of Comprehensive Security

1. The Economic Components

Given the globalization of capital markets, the economic and financial policies of the United States and Japan which represent more than one-third of global wealth are most significant. For the world at large, for the long-term security and for the cooperative political relationship so greatly in the interest of each country, healthy economic and financial systems are imperative. Within the developing world, and between that world and the industrial democracies, many problems of a different order must be addressed and are dealt with in the accompanying economic paper. Our focus is on the interrelationship between economic growth and security.

Governmental elites do not need to be told that the opportunity costs of defense spending are high. But decision-makers will not hesitate to spend funds to insure survival and retention of office. It is precisely this reality that makes outside aid helpful. Added resources cannot guarantee greater spending on development rather than defense, but the absence of such aid can ensure that defense spending may continue to receive the highest priority given the complex interactions between threat perceptions, elite decisions, and national needs.

Economic security for developing states means coping with the ever expanding "debt bomb" while sustaining and enhancing the quality of life for their peoples. Thus, a substantial infusion of capital into poorer states, is needed to stimulate purchasing power, permit debt repayments, and provide markets for the more developed states. Too few Americans recognize that U.S. exports to developing states have risen at a faster growth rate than exports to advanced states.

Developing states naturally see global events as significant when they affect either economic development or national survival. The concept of power is being steadily and rapidly enlarged to include the financial, economic, and monetary instruments that are increasingly affecting daily lives everywhere.[16] Conversely, Burma today shows that more isolated states are still subject to the monopoly of military power. Nations face the paradox that unprecedented growth and prosperity are making war less, not more "affordable."

Structural changes occurring in the global economic system, and likely to continue, are linking nations in ways that compel greater cooperation to safeguard domestic economies. The more advanced technologies maintain some advantage over those less advanced, although investment by the more advanced to take advantage of lower cost labor or new material supplies may steadily narrow the gap. Trade and financial flows illustrate the ongoing "dependence" of many developing states.[17]

The economic growth of East Asian states seems likely to shift the global strategic focus and the center of global economic activity by the year 2000. Even a unified Europe may not have the GNP value of the major Asian actors (China, Japan, South Korean, and Taiwan). The three largest GNP states in 2010 may be the United States, China (despite a lower per capita GNP), and Japan. If however reforms within the Soviet Union were to succeed, the USSR could compete for a spot in the top three. Conversely, if modernization should fail in the PRC, China would not be among the three wealthiest states. Results suggest that the initiative and dynamism of capitalism evokes the most successful forms of economic development. Effective development combines wise policies[18] to create self-generating economic growth. The developing nations recognize that aid, essential as it is in many cases, will not alone give assurance of economic growth. Rather, assistance must be combined with national policies, trade, comparative advantages, and managerial skills to secure economic growth, and the prerequisites for domestic tranquility.

A crucial question is whether there are unique cultural aspects to these societies which treasure hard work, diligence, savings, and educational advancement that are essential to success, or whether others can achieve economic success working from different backgrounds?[19] The state itself can be a key variable in ensuring development through wise policies dealing with land reform, extension of credit, agricultural and industrial policies, and labor conditions. What seems clear is that, at the early stages of development that exist in many countries, considerable diversity must be anticipated—and accepted—in order to provide maximum opportunity.

One major "lesson" of success is that labor-intensive export led to higher growth rates than import substitution. That strategy, however, may encounter intensifying global and sectorial competition, possibly shrinking markets, and widening economic disputes. If so, the future of developing nations will become a major policy issue for Japan, the United States, and other industrial democracies. The issue is the widening gap that now exists between rich and poor nations.

Development and Violence. The consequences of these economic decisions, and resulting conditions, can generate security or insecurity, affect how national elites behave, and may, even on occasion, lead to conflict.

We are faced with the need for a definition of success from the standpoint of the interests of our two countries. One element is surely the absence of violence, but this leaves the question why peace and stability were not achieved in Nicaragua or Iran, but were successful in South Korea and Taiwan. The evidence suggests the importance of leadership and sound policies as key variables. Since one common factor was a large amount of American assistance over the years, clearly the import of capital is not the sole key to spurring economic growth.[20] There is considerable evidence of violence caused by the rising but unfulfilled expectations of development.[21] Relative deprivation seems to be a key factor in violence as indicated by conflicts within developing nations since 1945. This issue will become steadily more serious with the costly acquisition of increasingly destructive military technology by developing states.

Nations modernizing seem inevitably to encounter turbulent social environments in which violence can occur. Political and social modernization does not always occur simultaneously with economic development. This "modernization lag" in which political development seems to follow economic development means that internal violence may occur. Moreover such change (as the PRC and South Korea reveal) is disruptive of social conditions. It is necessary to recognize that development in and of itself is no guarantee of political stability. Even as a precursor of instability,[22] however, the long-term need for development seems such as to make it a trauma that must be borne.

The basis for aid is that the opportunity cost of the capital loaned or given to developing states will be outweighed by the later benefits achieved by all. The costs of restricted markets, raw materials access, and economic stagnation for the industrial nations is conceptually clear. What has been lacking is the importance of "anticipatory security" as a justification to skeptical leaders for increased aid. In this regard, a historical cost-benefit analysis focused on post World War II Europe might suggest that following independence and modernization, the combination of economic growth and stable deterrence has proved to be the recipe for peace.

Underdevelopment. It remains essential to examine the cause and remedy for underdevelopment. The so-called "South" averaged two percent less than the "North" (four percent to six percent) during the period 1960 to 1980. In the year 2000, over ninety percent of the world population of 5 billion will be found in developing nations, and will include hordes of young job seekers along with legions of elderly.

The seriousness of these issues may be seen in the malnutrition and sometimes even widespread famine that persist even though global food supplies have grown faster than population during the last three decades. The effect is reduced life expectancy, suscep-tibility to diseases, and lower productivity. For the nations chroni-cally dependent upon outside food assistance to feed their popula-tions, economic development focusing on agricultural productivity must be coupled with continuing food assistance. The American PL 480 program of surplus food distribution (which might be partly paid for by the Japanese) represents a viable policy option. Assistance in analyzing the impact of such food transfers upon domestic economics by such organs as the World Bank would be valuable in assuring that wise use is made of such programs while promoting expanded domestic food production.[23]

Assistance to enable entrepreneurs to learn the skills necessary to contribute to development is a further valuable option. The most successful assistance program per dollar spent, "Trickle Up," won the United Nations Bradford Morse Award for innovation.[24] The teaching of small entrepreneurs is a viable way to privatize the economy and build infrastructure, thus benefiting all through job creation, growth, and skill enhancement. "For the Goliaths of rural development like the World Bank, UNDP, USAID, etc., the Trickle Up approach appears to be a viable and self-sustaining strategy which could pull the poorest of the poor out of the doldrums of poverty, the clouds of powerlessness, the crippling lack of self confidence, ignorance and economic backwardness."[25] Japanese business leaders have established a $1 billion "Japan International Development Organization" to aid export industries in developing nations. The objective is to steer half of these exports to Japan, thereby further opening Japan's domestic market. Admittedly such investments may benefit Japanese business, but more importantly, they expand markets for developing nations and help to generate economic growth.

Developing nations require more capital than is forthcoming from domestic sources. Thus, official development assistance (ODA) is crucial.[26] The most startling change in the last three decades has been the decline of total ODA as a percentage of GNP. For example, both the United States and Japan remain well below the suggested United Nations target of 0.7 percent ratio between ODA and GNP.

Japan began raising its ODA in the 1970s and ODA is now five times greater than in 1977. During the same ten-year period, the U.S. aid contribution rose 1.9 times from a higher base.

U.S./JAPANESE ODA

(millions of $)

	1983	1984	1985	1986	1987
Japan CY$	3.76	4.31	3.79	5.63	7.45
%GNP	0.32	0.35	0.29	0.29	0.31
U. S. CY$	8.08	8.71	9.40	9.56	8.77
%GNP	0.24	0.24	0.24	0.23	0.20

The June 1988 announcement of a $50 billion commitment spread over five years show the Japanese desire to help others. Japan is the world's largest aid donor due to the rapid appreciation of the yen. Now under the new policies of the "Medium Term Target," grants will be expanded, technical cooperation increased, and the geographic diversity of recipients increased.

Responding to complainants about the quality of Japanese aid, the new plan contains a $30 billion recycling fund that is not formally tied to the purchase of Japanese goods and services. But Japanese insistence on "feasibility studies" means that Japanese firms suggest projects and set specifications which create an "incumbency" position. Further, the DAC definition of "tied loans" stipulates that if any portion of a loan is "tied," then the entire loan is considered tied.

An example is the rapidly expanding PRC market. With their typical skill, the Japanese have created an integrated market entry position combining trade, concessional aid, commercial loans and increasingly direct investment. Since 1982, the PRC has been the largest single recipient of Japanese development assistance. From 1979 to date, Japan has provided about $7.2 billion in aid and loans with recent commitments for another $6.8 billion for 1990-1995 (includes both Japan Eximbank and Overseas Economic Cooperation Fund). The United States is conspicuous in Chinese eyes by the absence of aid. The major U.S. activity is about $314 million in trade financing since 1980 by the American Eximbank and more than $3 billion in investment.

These initiatives raise the specter of Japanese dominance in the Chinese or other Asian markets, but the national differences in China mirror a continuing insensitivity to competing in global markets by American firms and government. Almost alone among nations, the U.S. utilizes the bulk of its economic aid for humanitarian rather than business development purposes. In an era of rising global competition, this practice cannot continue unabated. Either other nations must shift towards humanitarian aid (as the Japanese are proposing) or the United States must utilize aid to achieve greater market penetration. Global market share in numerous industries (automobiles, consumer electronics, semiconductors), could be significantly increased, for example, if the Japanese utilize comparative advantages in China for essentially commercial purposes. Likewise, the NIEs would also suffer economically. Finally, as the events of

1985-86 suggest, too much dominance in the Chinese market may create an anti-Japanese backlash by the Chinese people.

Both Japan and the United States must adjust their policies to avoid a potentially bitter dispute over ODA and global business practices. A trade financial program needs to be established to enable American firms to compete on an equal basis with Japanese and European competitors. Without such a program for U.S. goods and services, American firms will supply an ever dwindling share of the global market. Further, the comparatively small AID sponsored "Trade and Development Program" must be greatly enlarged to enable funding of feasibility studies for large-scale infrastructure projects and more equal competition with other national suppliers. While strict reciprocity in trade matters is undesirable and unworkable, the principal of reciprocal market access must become a reality.

From a global perspective the Japanese should move beyond their technically "untied" aid to fund more "human needs" and diversify further into Africa and Latin America, ideally through multilateral agencies. Presently, about 65 percent of Japanese aid goes to Asian nations. This geographical focus, combined with business development practices, may create a yen-denominated market closed to other competitors. Given the potential harm to free trade, reciprocal market access must be preserved if we are all to prosper and to strengthen peaceful political ties.

The assumption that the U.S. is merely shifting the aid burden to Japan would be equally damaging to the U.S. image and commercial market development. Therefore, Americans must also increase their aid. Such assistance may differ from Japanese forms, to include military articles and training, but must be obvious. In 1957, the U.S. economic development program (Point IV) and security assistance were formally separated into different accounts. This dichotomy saw bilateral humanitarian aid peak in 1970 (excluding PL 480) and security assistance peak during the Reagan years. Earlier during the Carter term, multilateral assistance was increased. In effect, both the U.S. and Japan must jointly move forward to renew aid designed to create self-sufficiency and thus sustain economic growth.

Increasingly, economic growth has become the basis of political legitimacy and societal mobilization. Moreover, a growing economy helps to alleviate domestic political problems. Finally, the economic destiny of any state is no longer determined by itself, but by the collective community.

The common security challenges of national growth to political stability and security faced by America, Japan, and the developing nations will demand joint policy coordination. The growth in economic and security interdependence is perhaps the most significant international reality of this century. Yet, accelerating interdependence can create both conflict as well as cooperation. The actions proposed here could lessen vulnerabilities for all nations, thereby encouraging continued economic growth. The key to progress and collective economic security will be political decision.

2. The Military Component

Military resolution is seldom the most effective, and never the cheapest, means of settling disputes. Yet, the military component nevertheless remains vitally important and essential. For this reason, the U.S. maintains a strong global presence based upon deterring major war together with a capability to act against other challenges to peace and stable security, from which the whole world greatly benefits. This effort costs Americans $300 billion annually. Japan has a military force equal to those of many NATO states and is the world's third largest military spender at about $31 billion per year. She continues to modernize her Self Defense Forces, stressing surveillance and air defense. Further the Japanese contribute more than $2.5 billion annually (calculated to include foregone outlays such as tax collections) for support of U.S. forces stationed in Japan.

In broad terms, military requirements respond to the multiple, constantly evolving conditions that affect the security of individual nations and groups of nations. So long as grievances exist in political systems and the threat of violence remains endemic in society, military security must be central to the concerns of every state. Indeed, perceptions of military strength are a critical element in any confrontation. Deterrence of actual attack is a top-priority aim, with the military serving as an insurance policy.

Likewise, in today's world, arms control has become significant in stabilizing the military balance, thereby helping to lessen political tensions and urgencies. Crisis prevention is an important contribution to anticipatory security and hence to crisis management. The anticipation and prevention of crises—and their avoidance through timely economic development and the strengthening of orderly democratic processes—thus advance the same security objective that the military forces are intended to serve.

Defense forces to deter the use or threat of force against us, together with actions to avert crises before they impact on our security and well-being, must be designed to meet any contingencies. The actual defense planning, including, in particular, the determination of force size and composition, as well as deployments and readiness posture, is an increasingly complex and demanding process involving many conflicting assessments. One of the most fundamental issues is the type of conflict deemed to threaten the state, and how severe and immediate the threats are, and what priority should be given to meeting them. Responses to these questions drive the strategy, budget, and eventually the force mix.

A state without defenses could not expect long to survive, though none acting alone can afford the theoretically optimum force. As we look to the future, it seems likely that this interdependence will grow and that the "Correlation of Forces" between East and West will have to take account of not only global, but also regional and local military forces and their supporting establishments if stable security and a peaceful international order are to be maintained.

The military component of comprehensive security thus includes traditional elements such as an adequate defense and collective security, in addition to non-military actions such as arms control to reduce or contain the actual or potential threat. Cooperation along these lines hold the promise of strategic stability with reduced overall costs and burdens along with increased benefits for all—notably including a reduced likelihood of levels of violence, coercion or conflict that could be harmful to the interests of the United States and Japan, as well as those of other nations that might be involved.

The objective of anticipatory, comprehensive and international security as herein proposed, is to make violence a last resort. For many developing states, however, the notion of a "permanent revolution" is likely to be attractive so long as governments fail to establish sustainable economic growth and legitimacy. An imprecise, but suggestive study, shows a decline incidence of coups according to the stage of development (measured by per capital GNP).[27]

Until the starvation, overpopulation, and similar problems that exist today are ameliorated, tensions will exist which may be controllable only through the presence and if necessary the actual use of military forces. Such forces of reasonable size in Third World countries thus are an inherent part of comprehensive security, and defense budgets an indicator of governmental needs. In this regard, the steady and timely support of military forces appropriate in size, composition, and mission may be a measure of true economy and foresight. Examples abound where the breakdown of constitutional order, civil war or local conflict is devastating the country and leaving vast numbers of its citizens starving, homeless, and impoverished. A classic example of coping with insurgency is to be found in the Magsaysay Administration in the Philippines in the 1950s, which successfully fought off the communist Huks rebellion. The essential point is clear. Deterring war or insurgency is easier than fighting insurgents or hostile forces.

With regard to the military component of security, the key issue is to maximize the diverse resources and talents of our two nations in order to help make this a more secure world. There is much that each can appropriately do toward meeting the principal requirements outlined earlier:

— maintaining together with other like-minded countries, a rough military equilibrium vis-à-vis the Soviet Union itself while seeking to lessen the military confrontation and to eventually reduce force levels. The Japanese Self Defense Forces are capable professional organizations. Future emphasis should be placed on further enhancements of C^3I readiness and training, expanded war reserve materials, and air defense improvements to enhance self defense capabilities. Japanese restraint in arming, maintenance of security relations with the U.S., and transfer of resources into global development and strategic stability pursuits may well be the best example for developing nations.

— helping to maintain regional and local security environments that will discourage, and hopefully deter, armed conflict between nations, with emphasis for the U.S. and Japan upon those areas where our respective high-priority interests are involved, notably sources of oil, food, and raw materials, as well as important channels of trade

— supporting individual countries (and regional groupings) in their individual and joint efforts to establish and strengthen those internal security conditions essential to the building of democratic institutions and the achievement of sustainable economic growth.

The United States bears by far the heaviest responsibilities worldwide, but especially in the Pacific area, and for this purpose maintains, at a heavy cost, the impressive array of air, ground, and naval forces prepared for conventional or nuclear war. Japanese Self-Defense Forces are professionally skilled, though limited in size, and constitutionally committed only to a conventional defense of the home islands. While there is no immediate basis for force reductions of substantial size, the new policies being put forward within the Soviet Union do offer some prospect that, if converted into tangible restructuring, such reduction may become possible in the future. In the meantime, the present force balance seems to offer a basis for confidence that stable security can be maintained, although the increases in Soviet military activities in the Pacific during recent years means that this balance must be continually reevaluated.

Japan will need to maintain and modernize her Self-Defense Forces, but without expansion of the SDF. Rather, supportive actions such as the suggested aid program, technology transfer in accordance with existing documents, and continued joint defense planning seem the most appropriate Japanese policies. The judicious aggregation of American and Japanese capabilities can make the whole both stronger and safer.

In helping to maintain a secure environment throughout the region, the United States must accept the continued burden of guarantor of peace and stability, especially as it pertains to military and naval strength. The forces which serve to balance Soviet (and North Korea) military deployments provide the principal basis for carrying out this task, though added attention to the needs of low-intensity conflict have been repeatedly recognized. Fortunately, some significant steps are being taken, though much more needs to be done. Of even more concern than the state of military planning and the adequacy and appropriateness of military forces is the lack of consensus on policy at high governmental level, notably and most sharply as between the U.S. Executive Branch and the U.S. Congress. It seems possible, however, that recent favorable developments in Afghanistan and Angola, together with possible policy changes in the Soviet Union, may enable the new Administration in the United States to find more common ground with the Congress.

Even so, possibilities of conflict will not be lacking. The continuing Arab-Israeli dispute, the strife in Ethiopia, the drug traffic and violence, as well as continuing armed struggle in countries of Central America continue to deny the achievement of the secure international environment we seek.

For the third military task—supporting countries in their efforts to establish domestic security, the resources are severely strained. Once funds are set aside for the major outlays (for Israel, Egypt, the Philippines, Pakistan and Turkey), little is left. In recent years, U.S. military aid has followed the pattern shown in the tables on the following page. The projected FY90 security assistance budget is $5 billion (FMS financing, IMET, MAP, and FMS credits).

Given the substantial opportunity costs, care must be taken in shaping U. S. military assistance to recipients regarding the type, scale, and possible uses of equipment. Recipient states must carefully weigh funds spent on buying armaments against other needs to avoid an over-investment in defense that may stifle economic development.

Increasingly expensive and sophisticated weapons exacerbate economic costs, make conflict more deadly, and generate potentially significant political and social costs. We thus urge continuation of a carefully monitored program to help secure the goals outlined in this study. Ultimately such assistance may be essential to promoting both the political and economic stability of legitimate democratic governments.

The meager resources available in this area, unless significantly augmented, put added stress on the importance of assistance in other areas—economic in particular—to forestall the possibilities of social and political violence. It remains an area worthy of increased, judiciously planned support. Comprehensive security cannot be attained without the latent threat of military force. Yet, paradoxically, its true goal—the avoidance of war—is best served by a political democratization and expanded economic aid.

3. The International Security Component

Any nation, regardless or economic or military strength, may be threatened. Moreover, these threats range from terrorism, nuclear war, insurgencies, to economic coercion and indifference to national disasters. Thus, it is in the interest of every state to seek a just and lasting peaceful order, accompanied by appropriate security.

But how is security to be achieved? The more open the international system, the greater the vulnerability. Interdependence therefore poses significant challenges to all states. A complex, interactive web has been created which necessities continued attention to issues of energy security, adequate food, trade and the balance of payments, environmental damage, alongside of military and economic security.

The consequences of these trends suggest only three options. First, a passive, rudderless acceptance—an unlikely policy for any nation. Second, an aggressive set of policies designed to promote self-interest which will, inevitably run the risk of conflict. Third, and the preferred option, to seek joint remedies to the many problems of interdependence. It is in that spirit that these recommendations are made, recognizing that global peace and stability requires anticipating the problem, utilizing the tools of comprehensive security to help redress the problem, and working to maintain a harmonious and just international system. This challenge will continue to hold center stage in the global theater for the coming decades.

F. Conclusions

The major objective of both the U.S. and Japan should be to utilize their unique capabilities to contribute towards greater regional and global economic growth, strategic stability, and democratization. This is best accomplished through the mutual commitment to security cooperation within the context of the Mutual Security Treaty and coordinated aid activities. Further, the United States should regard Japanese undertakings along these lines as a security contribution included in the calculations of the GNP percent. The concepts of anticipatory and comprehensive security offer a basis for realizing these goals in practice and for determining longer-term U.S. and Japanese security strategy.

Other conclusions arising from this analysis are:

1. Security Related Factors:

— If successful, this collaborative model of expanded assistance and security for the developing nations offers a means towards those elusive goals of peace and prosperity for all. There is no simple dichotomy between economics and security, especially in the developing world. Although this collaborative effort is in its infancy, it is responsive to the needs of developing nations and recognizes the economic pluralism of the 1990s. Ultimately it recognizes our joint strengths—open democratic political systems, strong economics, diligent hard working peoples, and a commitment to human rights.

— We should seek an equitable balance between the efforts of the United States and Japan, with those of the U.S. giving primary (though not exclusive) priority to the military aspects of security, and those of Japan giving priority to economic aid, while maintaining defense commitments generally at the current level. In this respect, further Japanese contributions towards American expenses in Japan should be considered.

— We welcome the recent Japanese offers to participate in United Nations Peacekeeping Operations, as a positive indication of Japan's commitment to fulfill her international responsibilities and a strengthening of the United Nations system.

2. Development Aid Factors

— National leaders must focus their efforts on achieving desirable economic outcomes. Recent market oriented initiatives by several nations are commendable. Economic growth must coincide with the resolution of social and ethnic tensions if stability and legitimacy are to be "won" by governments.

— The American and Japanese economies are so intertwined that any bilateral disruption will harm the financial and economic health of both nations and endanger global prosperity. Japan is the premier creditor nation. America remains the premier market. The financing of investment in the developing nations will be crucial to maintaining global economic growth. For example, expanded Japanese assistance to Latin American nations would probably increase U.S. exports. thereby helping to curb macroeconomic imbalances. Further, the expansion of domestic demand in Germany and Japan will add to this momentum.

— The policy focus of Japanese overseas aid should emphasize areas outside of Asia, in order to reflect Japan's global role and ease concerns over Japan's gaining undue economic advantage within Asia. Consideration should be given to increased multilateral funding, to include "feasibility studies," thus lessening the informal ties to Japanese goods and services. While it is clear that the U.S. and Japan must play a leading role, our two countries should press the other industrial democracies, to shoulder an appropriate part of the burden. Additionally, as Japan is now doing, increased imports from developing nations are desirable.

— A joint operation whereby Japanese ODA partly pays for expanded U.S. PL 480 and Commodity Credit Corporation food distribution is worthy of consideration by both nations.

— A greater role for Japan in the global financial institutions seems warranted. Further, since governmental aid to poorer nations is relatively small compared to the capital flows, trade, investments, and financial flows from business and the private non-profit sector, both governments should encourage continued activities of this nature under market conditions. These activities facilitate capital inflows, employment, and integration into the global economy.

— As American and Japanese officials consider joint aid decisions, consideration ought to be given to particular world-wide humanitarian aid projects that synergistically combine each nation's skills.

Examples include the emerging frontier between artificial intelligence and brain research and critical environmental problems such as the greenhouse effect which transcend all national boundaries. In many ways, and despite our differences, we live in a global village.

Finally, we urge both governments to educate their citizens regarding the inescapable economic and security linkages that already exist between our two societies. The argument made here is direct: encouragement of the non-military aspects of ensuring security in developing nations through a collaborative by the American and Japanese governments and peoples. What we seek is an international community built upon peace and stability, not war and upheaval. Mutual consultations, not violence, is the path towards revitalizing the global economy and promoting democracy. Acting together our two nations can make a valuable contribution to global economics and peace.

JAPANESE DEFENSE SPENDING

Year	Defense Budget in Trillions of Yen	Defense Budget As % of GNP	Increase Above Past year	Defense As % of Total Budget
1955	.1	1.78 %	3.3 %	13.61 %
1965	.3	1.07 %	9.6 %	8.24 %
1975	1.3	0.84 %	21.4 %	6.23 %
1980	2.2	0.90 %	6.5 %	5.24 %
1981	2.4	0.91 %	7.6 %	5.13 %
1982	2.5	0.93 %	7.8 %	5.21 %
1983	2.7	0.98 %	6.5 %	5.47 %
1984	2.9	0.99 %	6.6 %	5.80 %
1985	3.1	0.997 %	6.9 %	5.98 %
1986	3.3	0.993 %	6.6 %	6.18 %
1987	3.5	1.004 %	5.2 %	6.50 %
1988	3.7	1.013 %	5.2 %	6.53 %
1989	3.9*	1.006 %	5.9 %	6.50 %

*Calculated at ¥127 = $1.00, or $30.9 billion.
N.B.: The Japanese fiscal year begins in April.

CHAPTER V

Security Burden Sharing—
a Japanese View   *by Susumu Awanohara*

A. INTRODUCTION

With its emergence as an economic superpower, what international roles Japan will play has become a burning question. There is
already broad agreement that Japan has important economic contributions to make and its recent attempts to play a greater political
role have by and large been accepted by the international community as natural, given Japan's economic position.

Opinion is sharply divided, however, on whether Japan should
also take on a greater security role outside its territorial boundaries.
On the one hand, the United States, cognizant of its own relative
economic decline and Japan's rise, and increasingly impatient with
Japan's defense "free ride," has intensified pressure on Tokyo to
increase its "burden sharing" in the security of Japan as well as that
of the "free world". In general, on the other hand, having suffered
greatly the last time the Japanese offered their political/security
leadership in the region, Asians generally are still not keen to see
Japan play a major political role. Many Asians are loath to let Japan
play a military role.

Taking the U.S. defense umbrella for granted, the Japanese had
until recently found it convenient to be disqualified as a political or
military power and concentrate on economic growth, an endeavor
at which they proved more adept than most had imagined possible.
For a long time, the Japanese had limited their regional/ international
role to the economic sphere, while engaging in a low-posture
reactive diplomacy and a defense-only security policy. Such a
Japanese attitude is no longer tenable.

The thrust of the U.S.-Japan Leadership Project is on the two
countries sharing responsibilities with respect to developing
countries. At least for the time being, the developing countries,
particularly those in Japan's neighborhood, are likely to reject Japan
playing a positive regional or international military role on their
behalf. Thus military burden sharing will remain a bilateral U.S.–

Japan issue, largely irrelevant in the discussion of how the two powers should cooperate with the developing world. However, Japan may be able to play a security role, in the region and more globally, if security is interpreted widely to have economic and political, as well as military, dimensions. Through economic and political efforts in security burden sharing with the U.S., Japan may be able to enhance the security of developing countries and hence, of the Western alliance.

This paper has two objectives. The first is to examine the state of U.S.–Japan security (including military, political and economic) burden sharing. The second objective is to explore how Japan and the U.S. can in the future work out a formula for sharing security responsibilities which is desirable, or at least satisfying, to the two countries and at the same time helps, or at least does not threaten, developing countries.

Section B examines salient American attitudes towards Japan's contribution to common security. It is argued there that the Americans will, in the main, shift between two options, demanding a straight buildup of Japan's military capability and accepting a division of labor between the two countries and allowing Japan to contribute in non-military ways. Section C is an examination of Japanese attitudes towards defense, which, it is maintained, will vacillate between two positions, advocating a moderate-paced military buildup, always taking into account domestic and external political constraints, and pushing for a faster military buildup to meet perceived serious threats from the North. Section D identifies specific areas in which security burden sharing between the U.S. and Japan actually takes place and discusses some of the outstanding issues and problems in each area. The growing difficulty of sharing military technology—as illustrated by the protracted controversy over Japan's choice of its next-generation support fighter aircraft—is a central concern of this section.

Section F speculates on the future of U.S.–Japan security burden sharing, by exploring factors which may influence the U.S. and Japanese choice of options. This section also examines the possible combinations of U.S. and Japanese options and what the combinations imply. In Section F we examine East Asian fears and suspicions of Japan's "resurgent militarism" and consider how, to forestall this spectre, the region's countries might try to secure the least threatening combination of options in the U.S. and Japan. Finally, Section G lists a few areas where the Japanese need to deepen thought and work towards consensus before they can find a formula for sharing security responsibilities which they and others can support positively, not one they are forced into by pressures and circumstances.

B. The U.S. Pressure: From "Straight Buildup" To "Division of Labor"

U.S. pressure on allies, including Japan, to take on greater burdens of common security is not new. What is new this time is the dramatic shift in the background against which the bargaining takes place. America today is the world' s biggest debtor nation and Japan the biggest creditor nation. This change was to a large extent the result of U.S. defense buildup in the 1980s and the concurrent surge in American imports, coming from Japan and other East Asian economies, among other sources. Many Americans have asked why the U.S. must continue to defend Japan, or more pointedly, why Americans must risk their lives to secure passage of mostly Japanese oil in the Persian Gulf when the Japanese themselves are not helping themselves.

The Americans seem determined not to let the Japanese get off easily this time. Recent improvements in U.S. relations with the Soviet Union have not yet softened the U.S. attitude towards Japan on the burden sharing issue. But there is a dilemma for the U.S. On the one hand, many Americans feel the U.S. has been too sensitive to supposedly unique Japanese sensibilities flowing from experiences of the last world war, in which they caused a great deal of suffering in much of Asia and became the first victims of nuclear assault. On the other hand, the Americans are realizing how strongly the feeling against Japanese militarism still runs in Asia. Fear of revived Japanese militarism is not negligible in the U.S. itself.

While there was a whole spectrum of opinion both within the U.S. Congress and in the Reagan Administration, and indeed outside the government, it is safe to say that Congress has tended to want Japan to stop making excuses and increase its military burden sharing, while the administration has tended to acknowledge Japanese efforts in this area and be more open about allowing Japan to share the burden in non-military ways. The Bush Administration should not differ greatly from the Reagan Administration on this point.

Congress' position is reflected in some of its proposals, notably a resolution passed in June 1987 (House Resolution #1777) that called on Japan to spend at least three percent of its GNP on defense. More recently, the interim report of the House Armed Services Committee on burden sharing confirmed the idea that "Japan's defense contributions and capabilities are inadequate given its tremendous economic strength"—although the report, despite its sharp tenor against Japan, showed understanding of domestic Japanese constraints and Asian fear of a major Japanese military buildup and clearly accepted the validity of non-military contributions.[1] While "Congressional pressures" may often originate from just a handful of specific individuals and lack in direct policy significance, they are nonetheless taken seriously as they reflect and further influence public opinion.

By contrast, the administration took the position that Japan is doing more in the military area than is often given credit for and should not be pushed beyond reason. Then Assistant Secretary of Defense Richard Armitage, in his often quoted statement of March 1988, articulated this position. He criticized the house resolution calling for a three percent defense spending by Japan when, in his view, Japan had already acquired considerable capability for only one percent and could acquire quite enough for less than two percent. "What would the additional funds be used for? A nuclear capability? Offensive projection forces? Some...... speak of carrier task forces and long-range missiles.... Is that what Congress wants? Would that enhance stability in East Asia?" Armitage challenged.[2]

Still more cautionary voices are heard, among others, former Secretary of State Henry Kissinger who warns: "As Japan's military capacity grows, and as America emphasizes burden sharing, the price Tokyo is prepared to pay for U.S. military protection is bound to decline."[3] Here Japan's quest for autonomous defense, dreaded in East Asia, is clearly implied.

A U.S. scholar, Mike Mochizuki, recently identified four American schools of thought concerning the U.S. Far East policy and its alliance with Japan.[4] Two of these are extreme and lack policy significance. By emphasizing the relative decline of U.S. economic power, the first school argues for an American military disengagement from East Asia and the assumption of primary responsibility for regional security by Japan. The other extreme view rejects the notion of American decline and supports a continued U.S. military buildup without much reliance on allies' burden sharing.

The remaining two views are more in the main stream, both advocating closer cooperation with Japan, but with different emphases. Those who supported the Reagan administration's policies have advocated both a decisive Japanese military buildup and greater U.S.–Japanese cooperation in a joint deterrence strategy. We may call this the "straight buildup approach." Those critical of American pressures on Japan to increase its defense capabilities have stressed domestic and Asian constraints against a larger military role for Japan. Consequently they have taken what is described as a "division of labor approach" to security cooperation; while the U.S. would continue to provide most of the military requirements for regional security, Japan should share the burden by continuing to expand non-military contributions, notably foreign aid, according to this school.

This division of labor approach—positively recognizing Japan's nonmilitary efforts as compensating, to an extent, for purely military efforts—is not entirely new but contains novel elements. Strong Asian reactions against Japan's buildup had an impact on Washington. The Reagan administration was surprised to learn of these reactions when President Suharto of Indonesia and President Ferdinand Marcos of the Philippines visited Washington in close succession in late 1982 and expressed grave concern about U.S. efforts to strengthen Japan militarily.[5] Another new factor may be behind the current U.S. willingness to accept Tokyo's non-military efforts as compensation. This factor is America's realization that Japan's military buildup has gained great momentum and that Japan has—as epitomized in the controversy over who will design and manufacture the FSX, Japan's next-generation support fighter planes—begun challenging the U.S. in the vital areas of defense technology.[6]

In all likelihood the Bush Administration, like Reagan's, will "[encourage] Japan both to continue the steady progress it is making in its defense efforts, and to build upon its strategically oriented economic aid program,"[7] while laying emphasis either on the former or the latter (that is, moving between the straight buildup and the division of labor approaches).

C. The Japanese Response: The Rise of "Military Realism"

For reasons of history, the Japanese have generally not tried to conceptualize precisely what their fair and just share of the defense burden would be, considering the nature of the threat they face and given the stakes the U.S. and Japan have in the security of Japan and the region. Rather they have started with the American demands, taking them as more or less reasonable or anyway immutable, and tried to reconcile them with various domestic constraints, often using the latter to drive a bargain with the Americans.

Even so, Japanese attitudes towards defense have undergone a significant change over time. The fervent pacifism of the early post-war period gradually gave way to "political realism," which acknowledges the need for building up Japan's military capabilities, up to a point and within the framework of the U.S.–Japan security treaty, but still relies heavily on U.S. protection and attempts to minimize Japan's own defense outlays. By the late 1970s, this political realism was being challenged by "military realism," which holds that irrespective of the popular sentiments and political constraints, Japan faces real military problems which must be countered militarily.[8] The two "realisms" have competed for ascendancy and are likely to continue to do so. Obviously the categories, political and military realisms, introduced by Mochizuki, are only approximations—ideal types extracted through his study of Japanese opinions on defense. There are no organizations calling themselves by these names and within their realms, the two realisms contain diverse elements which could be classified further into sub-categories. As always in these exercises, some opinion formers are difficult to classify into one group or the other, and many change positions over time as external circumstances or they themselves change. Despite all this, the categories are accepted, sometimes grudgingly, by many principals in the Japanese defense debate—one strong indication of their analytical utility.

In many ways, political realism is a new name for what others have variously referred to as "the Yoshida School," "the Yoshida Doctrine" (after the eminent early post-war prime minister Shigeru Yoshida) or simply "the conservative mainstream." Yoshida argued that Japan should rely on the U.S. for defense and export market. While supporting the development of the Self Defense Forces (SDFs), he strongly resisted U.S. pressures for Japan's major rearmament, citing Japan's weak economy, the "peace constitution," Japanese psychological aversion to the military and likely reactions from Japan's neighbors.

Unlike the political realists, the military realists begin their analysis by assessing the military environment and developing a strategy to meet the likely threats. The military realists do not restrict their policy recommendations to those which would fall within the domestic political constraints. They develop war scenarios and work out what capabilities Japan needs to deny or repel enemy (read Soviet) attacks. The military realists are convinced that Japan needs both a major buildup of conventional forces and deepened cooperation with the U.S. forces. The loss of clear U.S. military superiority in Asia and the rapid Soviet buildup in the Far East were crucially important in the rise of military realism.

Aside from the political and military realists, Mochizuki sees two less influential groups on the Left and the Right, the "unarmed neutralists" and the "Japanese gaullists." While these groups are opposites in many ways, they share a desire for autonomy—a contrast with the political and military realists' commitment to alliance with the U.S.[9] The unarmed neutralists have, perhaps ironically, come to champion the war-renouncing Constitution handed down by the Americans. They have refused to believe that Japan faces a military threat from the Soviet Union and have kept vigil against moves to revise the Constitution or any of the other self-imposed restraints on Japan's defense. As we shall see, they have not been very successful.

The Japanese gaullists not only fear the Soviets but also doubt the U.S. commitment to defend Japan and are therefore for independent defense, ultimately. They have clamored to remove Japan's self-imposed constraints on defense policy such as the one percent of GNP defense spending limit, ban on weapons exports, the three non-nuclear principles and above all, the Constitution, which denies Japan the right of belligerency. Some so-called gaullists defy the terminology, however, saying they are pro-American and against a nuclear option for Japan.

The military realists have accused the political realists of hiding behind uninformed domestic constraints, and in return the political realists criticize the military realists of ignoring non-military factors of security, emphasizing too much the enemy's capabilities and not enough its intentions and going too readily for more guns rather than butter. The political realists have also warned the Americans that there were "hidden gaullists" among the military realists, whose pro-Americanism was mere expediency. But given the U.S. penchant for the straight buildup approach until recently, the Americans generally welcomed the rise of military realism, with only minor concern for the Japanese impulse towards autonomous security.

Yasuhiro Nakasone's accession to power in 1982 epitomized the rise of military realism. Even before Nakasone took over, the Japanese were speeding up their defense buildup in compliance with U.S. demands. Nakasone accelerated the pace. In beefing up defense, the Japanese have made some significant modifications to their basic defense stance, which are enumerated below.

As a result, Japan today is more clearly committed to the U.S.–Japan alliance and is more inclined to counter military threats militarily. The Americans have generally welcomed these changes, only wanting more. But there is a feeling among political realists as well as unarmed neutralists that Japan has moved too quickly towards buildup, often overcompensating the U.S. for troubles in the bilateral trade area, and become too deeply involved with U.S. global strategy.[10]

1. Redrawing of the Defense Perimeter

It was Nakasone's predecessor, Zenko Suzuki, who in 1981 declared that Japan would expand its defense perimeter to cover sea lanes out to 1,000 nautical miles. The Japanese government had long taken the position that the country's right of self defense was not necessarily confined to the geographic scope of the Japanese territorial land, sea and airspace. Whereas in 1969, the government said that the right of self defense extended to "surrounding" open sea and air, in later statements even this vague delimitation was withdrawn, although the government declared instead that the defense perimeter did not extend to the territory of other countries.[11] Suzuki's pronouncement for the first time put a concrete figure on the defense perimeter. It is debatable whether 1,000 nautical miles is sufficient or otherwise from a strategic point of view, but Japan's neighbors certainly felt that it was an awfully long distance. On encountering such a reaction, the Japanese pledged that the distance will be measured from Tokyo Bay, not from anywhere on the main Japanese islands.

Apart from sea lane defense, Tokyo's eagerness to acquire off-shore air defense capability, with backing of such new weaponry as over–the–horizon radars and Aegis missile ships; its decision in 1982 to include mid-air refueling facilities in purchasing F-15 fighters (whereas it had excluded such facilities in purchasing F-4 fighters in 1968) ; and Nakasone's statement in 1987 that it would not be unconstitutional for Tokyo to send minesweepers to the Persian Gulf, are also seen as demonstrating Japan's tendency to redefine—and expand—the area to which its right of self defense applies.

2. Relaxation of the Arms Export Ban

In 1983 Nakasone partially lifted the ban on the export of weapons and military technology by legalizing defense technology transfers to the U.S..

The "three principles on arms export" of 1967 had banned arms export to communist countries, countries under United Nations sanctions and to countries that are at (or are likely to become involved in) war. An even stricter guideline of 1976 practically banned all arms and military technology export. In justifying the new move, Nakasone's chief cabinet secretary said that Japan had benefitted from transfer of U.S. defense technologies in building up its defense capability, and that given the recent advance of Japanese technology, "it has become extremely important for Japan to recipro-cate."[12]

The relaxation of the ban paved the way for the subsequent Japanese decisions to participate in Strategic Defense Initiative (SDI) research and to develop the FSX support fighter jointly with the Americans.

3. Breach of the One Percent GNP Ceiling on Defense Spending

Arguably the least significant in substance but symbolically the most important among the Japanese defense constraints, this limit was breached in the fiscal year (FY) 1987 budget following a great deal of debate in the mid 1980s. The unarmed neutralists and many political realists wanted to keep the one percent limit while the military realists and the gaullists stressed that the limit had no meaning. The one percent limit was set in 1976, a week after the unveiling of Japan's first coherent defense doctrine, the National

Defense Program Outline, which did not address the question of cost.[13] During the ten years in which it was effective, the one percent limit became the battle line between those who wanted a more rapid Japanese buildup (and the removal of the limit) and those who desired a slower or no buildup (and the preservation of the limit). The Americans supported the former group while Asians generally supported the latter group.

Nakasone made a frontal attack to break through the one percent limit in the summer of 1985 when he tried to have it nullified explicitly. Resistance was great, including from his seniors within the LDP who belonged to the "conservative mainstream," and the attempt failed. But at about the same time, Nakasone was able to ensure in a more indirect way that the limit will be breached in the near future when he pushed the Mid-Term Defense Program for FY 1986 - 1990, costings 18.4 trillion in 1985 prices, through the Diet. It was clear that given the slow GNP growth rate prevailing, the annual defense budget would exceed one percent of the total budget some time during the five program years. The one percent limit was broken by a small margin in the FY 1987 budget and was officially revoked, although the government said it would "continue to respect the spirit of the 1976..... decision which called for moderate defense buildup efforts."[14]

4. Toward Collective Defense?

Japan has voluntarily denied itself the right of collective defense (that is, the right to use force to stop an armed assault on an ally). It accords itself only the right of its own self defense. This makes the U.S.–Japan security treaty a non-reciprocal arrangement in which the U.S. would defend Japan if the latter is attacked but Japan will not do the same for the U.S. A more reciprocal arrangement is desired by some in both Japan and the U.S.

Although legitimizing collective defense would be extremely difficult politically, some of Nakasone's statements (such as that the security of the West is indivisible and must be approached on a global basis) reflect such a desire. In 1983 the government took the position that the SDFs are able to come to the aid of U.S. naval vessels on the high seas if these vessels are engaged in operations directly related to Japan's security. Here, Japanese support for U.S. ships was still justified as an act of individual self defense, not of collective self defense. Earlier debates had acknowledged that there were gray areas between individual self defense and collective self defense. The government's interpretation in 1983 reduced the gray areas by widening the scope of individual self defense, rather than openly legitimizing collective self defense.[15] The joint U.S.–Japan study on "facilitative assistance to be extended to the U.S. Forces by Japan in the Far East in the case of situations outside Japan which will have an important influence on the security of Japan," started in 1982, is likely to contain other extensions to the definition of individual self defense.[16]

5. Revision of the National Defense Program Outline

In a crucial passage, the National Defense Program Outline states that "Japan will repel limited and small scale aggression, in principle, without external assistance." It adds: "In cases where the unassisted repelling of aggression is not feasible,.... Japan will continue an unyielding resistance by mobilizing all available forces until such time as cooperation from the United States is introduced, thus rebuffing such aggression."[17]

The Outline is considered to be post-war Japan's first defense doctrine. Before the Outline, all Japan had were the "peace constitution," the Basic Policy of National Defense, and the U.S.–Japan security treaty—all three being abstract—and the four defense buildup plans (for the years 1958 – 1976) which were essentially shopping lists of desired weapons. The outline for the first time defined the nature of the threat faced by Japan and spelled out ways in which this threat would be met.

But the document has become increasingly unpopular among the military realists, as well as the Americans. The Outline is seen by military realists to have been a rationalization for the prevailing force levels and an attempt to win domestic public support for defense— and as such, useful and justified. But it predated, and is incongruous with, (1) the 1978 Guidelines for Japan–U.S. Defense Cooperation which accelerated bilateral cooperative efforts; (2) the massive Soviet buildup of forces in the Far East; and (3) Japan's new commitment to take on offshore sea and air defense, the military realists argue. They also maintain that the very premise of the Japanese deterring small scale attacks by themselves but relying on the U.S. for bigger attacks is flawed because, as in Western Europe, the reality is that the Japanese and U.S. forces will fight together from the start against aggression of any scale. The realists add that instead of fearing embroilment in a U.S.–Soviet conflict, Japan should make far greater efforts than are called for in the outline to secure maximum U.S. participation and reinforcement in case of an enemy attack on Japan.[18]

After the one percent limit was lifted, the 1976 Outline has become the major bone of contention between those who want to keep it and those who think the document has outlived its usefulness. Many political realists belong to the former group while the military realists tend to be in the latter.

D. Areas of Burden Sharing

We now turn to specific areas in which U.S.–Japan security burden sharing actually occurs. There is today a desire on both sides to see a voluntary and harmonious sharing of responsibility, not burden sharing which results from arm-twisting of one by the other. But at least until now the pattern has been for the U.S. to state what was expected of Japan in each of these burden sharing areas and for Japan to comply, satisfactorily or otherwise. In each area, there are outstanding issues and problems.

1. Japan's Own Defense and U.S.–Japan Defense Cooperation

Formally Japan's task under the U.S.–Japan security agreement is to defend its homeland and surrounding waters and, in times of crises, to prevent the use of the three vital straits around Japan. Naturally, the U.S. wants Japan to acquire capabilities necessary to carry out these "roles and missions." Opinion is divided on whether force levels planned in the current Mid-Term Defense Plan is enough to carry out such tasks, but attainment of levels specified in the 1976 Outline (and updated in 1981) has been considered an immediate and minimum objective by the Americans. According to the latest defense white paper, *The Defense of Japan 1988,* Outline levels will be attained in most areas by the end of FY 1990, except in the numbers of Maritime and Air SDFs' combat aircraft.

What sort of buildup is envisaged beyond FY 1990? The Americans have been more forthcoming on this point than the Japanese. In a typical U.S. statement, former Deputy Defense Secretary, William Howard Taft, said: "The anti-submarine aircraft, naval vessels and interceptor aircraft the Japan Defense Agency is now acquiring make it far more difficult for the Soviets to plan operations approaching Japanese territory. Acquiring longer-range early warning aircraft and surveillance systems, such as an over-the-horizon radar, would extend Japan's security perimeter even farther. Still other measures—hardening Japanese bases and providing greater sustainability for the SDFs and upgrading communications between U.S. and Japanese forces—would further deter Soviet aggression."[19] The U.S., however, does not want Japan to obtain offensive capabilities.[20]

In the area of defense cooperation, the "Guidelines for U.S.–Japan Defense Cooperation" of 1978 is the key instrument, for the first time assigning specific roles to the three SDFs in case of an armed attack on Japan. It has led to a host of joint studies on defense cooperation (which are all classified) as well as to larger, more frequent and more elaborate joint exercises, including those involving all three forces of the two countries, both to the distress of their critics.[21]

2. Japanese Support for U.S. Forces, Japan

The Japanese feel they have made major efforts to reduce the costs to the U.S. of maintaining forces in Japan, by providing facilities and paying for a growing proportion of the labor costs. To compensate for the sharp appreciation of the yen in the mid 1970s, the Japanese started a "facilities improvement program" in FY 1979, undertaking reconstruction of old U.S. facilities and building of new ones at their expense. Similarly, measures were taken to raise the amount of money that Tokyo pays to the Japanese who work for U.S. Forces, Japan (USFJ). More recently, in view of another round of sharp appreciation of the yen, Tokyo has made further concessions to pay up to 100 percent of the base workers' bonuses and allowances. The U.S. must still pay their basic salaries.

All in all the Japanese are now paying more than 40 percent of the $6 billion a year that the Americans spend on USFJ. That, according to one calculation, comes to roughly $45,000 per U.S. serviceman stationed in Japan—higher than in any other country where the U.S. has bases. The U.S. government says it appreciates this (although a recent congressional study complained that the figure was overstated). It wants Tokyo to do more, such as start paying the workers' basic wages, USFJ's utilities bills and repair costs.

The Japanese are saying this would be difficult, legally and financially. To pay more for USFJ may require a revision of the existing

Status of Forces Agreement, which could touch off an unwanted new debate on foreign bases, some officials say. Financially, it would reduce the amount left over for the SDFs as spending for USFJ must come out of the total defense budget.

3. Cooperation in Military Technology

Sharing of military technology has become the single most contentious area of burden sharing. Serious mismanagement in this area can damage the bilateral relationship and even threaten the U.S.–Japan alliance, as the recent FSX controversy suggested.

Americans have long wanted the Japanese to make the exchange of military technology a two-way affair. The framework for this was established through a 1983 agreement allowing the Japanese to transfer defense technology to the U.S. Two items of technology concerning ship conversion and ship building (belonging to Ishikawajima-Harima Heavy Industries) have since been transferred. A third, a keiko SAM technology involving the Japan Defense Agency and Toshiba, was agreed on but has been stalled after the Toshiba scandal (in which Toshiba Machine, a subsidiary of the giant Japanese manufacturer, was caught illegally selling sensitive technology to the Soviets). It has been reported that the U.S. is interested in a number of additional Japanese technologies, including micro- and milli-wave technology, optical electronic engineering, optical fibers and micro electronics but transfer negotiations have not progressed.[22]

In 1986 Tokyo decided that the Japanese private sector can participate in SDI research but, justified or not, many Japanese industrialists, suddenly smug and jealous of their technology, are worried about loss of freedom and commercial advantage.[23] Popular science writers warn of the U.S. in future trying to restrict widely applied and hence relatively low-cost Japanese civilian technologies just because they have potential military applications.[24]

The Toshiba scandal incited Japan's techno-nationalism. Although few Japanese disputed that Toshiba Machine was in the wrong, it was felt that the group was being punished, many said excessively, for a reason; the scandal was exposed just as the FSX fighter aircraft controversy was heating up in 1987. Friction in the defense technology field arose again over the Japanese purchase of the U.S. guided-missile destroyer weapons system known as Aegis. Some of the same members of the U.S. Congress who have criticized Japan for not spending enough on defense opposed selling this technology to Japan, citing the sensitive defense technology involved or arguing that the U.S. should force Japan to buy not only the Aegis system but also the hull to put it in. [25]

But the FSX proved to be the most intractable problem of all. Japanese engineers have dreamed of once again developing serious and wholly home-grown aircraft and saw an opportunity for a leap forward in the SDFs' next generation support fighter. In the background was Japanese defense establishment's growing resentment at what it sees as U.S. attempts to arrest the erosion of its defense technological superiority, restricting technology transfers to Japan and yet discouraging Japan from developing its own weapons systems. Growing confidence in their dual-use technology prompted the Japanese to defy the U.S. which, of course, wanted Japan to buy U.S.–manufactured aircraft off the shelf, arguing that they are better and cheaper and that the purchase of them would help balance bilateral trade and ensure interoperability of the U.S. and Japanese forces.

The compromise solution—joint development—was not satisfying to either party. The fact that the FSX joint development agreement, reached towards the end of the Reagan Administration, left some crucial details to be worked out later allowed some U.S. Congressmen and even Bush Administration officials to complain that U.S. trade and industrial interests were about to be sacrificed for diplomatic and strategic ones, in the name of a good overall relationship. Most of the U.S. media opposed the agreement. A review of the agreement was thus forced and Tokyo was compelled to make concessions.

In Japan, too, the FSX incident fueled nationalism. In essence, the U.S. was seen to be barring Japanese entry into a new field (aviation industry) for the first time; the U.S. had never done this, for TV sets, cars, machine tools or even semi-conductors. And irrespective of the substance of the controversy, in terms of procedure, the image of an overbearing U.S. unilaterally revoking a government–to–government agreement to get a better deal was particularly damaging to the bilateral relationship. It made a lot of pro-American Japanese in the political center, who are neither technonationalists nor defense-nationalists, sympathize with those who are. It is hoped that U.S.–Japan leadership would avoid testing how many more similar incidents would undo the U.S.–Japan alliance.

4. Peacekeeping Efforts

Japan clearly bans dispatch of SDFs to exercise the use of force in other countries' territorial land, sea and air. But after it was severely criticized in the U.S. for only offering money and not "blood" for the policing of the Persian Gulf in 1987, the Japanese decided it was time for Japan to offer some "sweat" in addition to money.[26]

Prime Minister Noboru Takeshita made Japan's "contribution to peace" the "first pillar" of his three-point International Cooperation Initiative, thereby opening a new era of Tokyo's activism in international conflict resolution.[27] Tokyo has now dispatched a civilian to join the UN cease-fire observation team in Afghanistan. In the Iran–Iraq war settlement, a civilian each has been sent to join the UN military observation groups (UNIMOG) in these two countries. As Namibia gains independence from South Africa in the course of the withdrawal of Cuban troops from Angola, it will need to conduct a national plebiscite under UN supervision, for which Japan plans to send about thirty civilians. Japan is also seeking a significant role, financially and in terms of manpower, in the event of a Cambodian settlement.

To support such new efforts and to justify them, the UN Bureau of the Foreign Ministry has begun a study to establish how the personnel should be recruited, what status and treatment they should be accorded and whether changes in law would be required.

Whether or not dispatch of civilians would lead to that of uniformed personnel is a moot point at this time. But there are some among the policy elite who believe it should and see the dispatch of civilians as a preparatory step, to be followed by that of doctors and medical personnel, from the SDFs as well as other public agencies and the private sector, and eventually by dispatch of uniformed personnel.

5. Diplomatic Efforts—Political Burden Sharing

Diplomatic efforts are not an area that the Americans have stressed in recent bilateral talks on security burden sharing. This reflects satisfaction on the U.S. part since Japan has become a more willing alliance partner and there are few serious differences of view between the two countries on diplomatic issues at the moment. But diplomacy is an area in which the Japanese, for their own reasons, are wanting to become far more active. Eventually dissonances may develop, making mutual accommodation necessary.

Japan has at least two official faces externally—one for the U.S. and the West, and another for the world at large, but directed mainly at the developing world. With the first, Japan wants to appear a committed and occasionally tough ally. With the latter, it wants to project the image of a nation which may be low-key but is peace-loving, constructive and reliable. Nakasone's declaration that Japan is an "unsinkable aircraft carrier" of the Western alliance typified the desire to present the first face and was indeed much applauded in Washington, but caused shudders elsewhere. His lackluster attempts to mediate between Iran and Iraq and Takeshita's promotion of international cultural exchanges have been more Japan's attempts to win acceptance by a broader audience.

Japan has not been entirely successful in projecting either image; the world sees a third Japanese face—that of a one-dimensional mercantilist nation which, for better or worse, shuns abstract principles and lacks a sense of its place and responsibilities in the world. This image results from the international behavior of the Japanese and cannot be expunged without a basic change in the behavior, which cannot be expected in the short term.

Meanwhile, the Japanese will need some deft diplomatic footwork to use the two official faces to their advantage. Becoming a better ally of the U.S. can alienate non-allies and will at times force some tough choices on Japan. On the other hand, Japanese policies aimed at the world at large are likely to be more effective if they are seen to be independent of Washington's wishes. The U.S. may welcome Japanese success in these policies where it suits U.S. interests, but it may not consider such policies as contributions to U.S.–Japan or Western security. Obviously the U.S. will oppose Japanese policies directed at the wider world if they are seen to conflict with Japan's alliance position.

6. Aid Efforts—Economic Burden Sharing

Economic aid is crucial in the U.S.–Japan sharing of responsibilities with respect to developing countries—the primary theme of the U.S.–Japan Leadership Project—as it is the form of Japanese contribution the developing countries are most likely to welcome and accept. Aid is also crucial in the debate on U.S.–Japan security burden sharing.

Reluctant to commit itself to a drastic defense buildup, the Japanese have argued for Washington's benefit that their aid was at least in part a contribution to regional and global security, as well as to the welfare of the recipient countries per se. And the U.S. is increasingly tending to agree that Japanese aid, or *strategic* aid as the U.S. defines it, at least, compensates in some general way for what is considered a slow defense buildup, although it can never be a full substitute for buildup.[28] Many Americans have proposed that Japan raise its total defense and aid expenditure to this or that level. There was, for example, a congressional resolution that Japan should raise its total defense and aid contribution to three percent of its GNP without specified breakdowns. Other suggestions have come with the breakdowns. Zbigniew Brezezinski, for example, wants a four percent of GNP contribution to security from Japan, of which 1.5 percent will go to defense and 2.5 percent to strategic aid.[29]

But such proposals are not taken seriously in Japan. For one thing, Japanese officials are convinced that not all Japanese aid will be considered a contribution by the Americans; Japanese aid to China— now Japan's biggest bilateral aid—is looked on with suspicion as intended largely to promote Japanese commercial interests in that country, to the exclusion of the U.S. and other countries. More fundamentally, in the continuing absence of a solid consensus about threat, need for self defense, alliance with the U.S. or responsibility for system maintenance, the Japanese do not readily accept the Western practice, derived from the theory of public/collective goods, of regarding defense expenditure, along with aid, as "a contribution." This is made difficult by the Japanese relinquishment of the right of collective defense. In fact, to many Japanese (and Asians, incidentally) , attaching positive values to Japanese defense buildup and mixing it with economic aid seems strange, even outrageous.[30]

Turning to the actual record, aid, like defense, has been a favored item in the Japanese national budget. Tokyo has recently set yet another target for aid, this time to double concessional official development assistance (ODA) to U.S.$ 50 billion over the coming five-year period. Criticisms of Japanese aid persist—that it is small as a proportion of GNP and has a low grant element, that it is excessively concentrated on large-scale infrastructure development and neglects human resources development, that it continues to be tied to Japanese exports despite vaunted "untying" efforts, or that Japan's aid machinery is increasingly inadequate to handle huge amounts of funds now being disbursed. But the fact is that Japan has been the biggest ODA donor in Asia since 1977 and is now emerging as the No. 1 in the world.

Japan has also responded to U.S. calls for "strategic aid" at least since the mid-1960s when it was pressured to provide aid to Indonesia's newlyestablished pro–U.S. "New Order" regime, although much of this can be considered to have been in Japan's own interest. More recently Japan has channelled aid, at U.S. pressure, to such countries as Turkey, Pakistan, Jamaica, Sudan and Somalia (countries in which Japan would not otherwise have taken great interest) as well as to Thailand and the Philippines, which are of vital importance to both Japan and the U.S.

One looming problem is that the U.S. and Japan may disagree as to which potential aid recipients are strategic and how to go about helping them. In the case of the Philippines—a crucial test case today—some Japanese aid officials resented the U.S. proposal of a "Mini Marshall Plan" for the country, which they felt was ill-advisedly linked (at least at the time of the proposal) with the then ongoing U.S.–Philippine bases negotiations and which put an American face to largely Japanese-financed aid which was forthcoming anyway, without the new packaging.

Until now, the Americans more or less took Japan's acceptance of their aid priorities for granted and Japan has had little input in setting them. It was simply expected to put up the money, and did. The danger now is that Japan will increasingly demand sharing the power as well as the burden in maintaining security while the U.S., used to calling all the shots, will resist—as has happened at some multilateral organizations, notably the IMF and the World Bank. In extreme cases Japan may refuse to provide the aid desired by the Americans. Thus there could be dissonances even if both the U.S. and Japan agree that the Japanese should emphasize aid, not military buildup, in sharing the security burden.

E. Probable Future Outcomes

We are now ready to speculate on what future scenarios of U.S.–Japan security burden sharing are probable. In this section, we shall attempt to answer two questions. First, what forces would cause the U.S. or Japan to choose a certain option? Secondly, what combinations of such options in the two countries are possible and what do they imply? The analysis is based on earlier-introduced ideal-types and is necessarily highly speculative; there is no pretense here at capturing all the nuances of reality or at being exhaustive. The hope is that the analysis simplifies without distorting excessively.

1. Determinants of Respective Options

We argued earlier that the U.S. is likely to emphasize either division of labor (DOL) with Japan or Japan's straight buildup (SB) while Japan is likely to tilt towards either political realism (PR) or military realism (MR). We posit here that while SB and MR call for Japan's greater military efforts, DOL and PR call for more non-military efforts, particularly aid.

There are more extreme impulses in both countries: in the U.S., an impulse to reassert hegemony or to withdraw altogether from Asia; and in Japan, hankerings for unarmed neutrality or for independent defense. These impulses will have an influence on what course is chosen but are not likely to prevail as policy in the near future.

What factors will determine which way the two countries will go? In the U.S. case, who is in the White House or Congress may influence the choice of direction and likewise in Japan, who is prime minister may make a difference, as was particularly the case with Nakasone. But in both countries, international circumstances— economic, political and strategic—are likely to be more important than the ideas and personalities of the leadership in shaping policies. In the following, we shall sketch how external factors may impinge on choice of courses.

Economic Factors. The external position of the U.S. economy will be crucial. If U.S. economic difficulties become more serious, particularly if U.S.–Japan bilateral economic imbalances increase and bilateral tension mounts, U.S. demands for reciprocity in trade and for greater Japanese burden sharing are likely to intensify generally. In burden sharing, the emphasis is more likely to be on SB than on DOL, because SB tends to be seen as pure cost to Japan whereas DOL may be deemed to bring too many benefits, as well as costs, to Japan. Similar emphasis on SB may result if the Bush Administration must after all resort to painful tax increases and/or further drastic cuts in defense spending to balance the budget. In raising taxes, Bush will be compelled to convince Congress and taxpayers that he is making sure that the allies are also paying their fair shares for common defense. If the defense spending cuts are in areas where Japan would be affected, Bush would advise the Japanese to do all they can to minimize the adverse effects through more or less direct replacement.

Japan, for its part, may move towards MR when the U.S. is having economic difficulties and bilateral economic relations are strained because of a desire to placate the U.S.; up to a point, defense spending is more likely to pacify Washington than aid. Other things being equal, tax increases and/or defense spending cuts in the U.S.—which most educated Japanese have come to consider essential to the health of the world economy—would be welcomed in Japan and may help the position of MR; military realists will be able to make the case that Japan's defense buildup is essential, indirectly, to world economic health. As in the past, the hidden gaullists will welcome new U.S. pressures for a Japanese buildup and join forces with the military realists, but with the gaullists' own ultimate objective of achieving autonomous defense. Even when economic problems are pushing the U.S. towards SB, however, it is possible that Japan will insist on PR lines, promising to expend more non-military efforts.

If the U.S. external economic position should improve significantly, and particularly if it happens not as a result of painful measures such as tax hikes or large defense spending cuts but through improved U.S. competitiveness and boosted exports, the U.S. could ease its pressure on Japan generally and in the area of burden sharing be more inclined to let Japan choose its own method of contribution, including aid. Other things being equal, DOL is the more likely option for Washington than SB when U.S. economic conditions are good. Responding, Japan is likely to tend toward PR, since politically aid is so much easier for Tokyo to increase than defense spending, and since aid outlays generally benefit a far larger number of Japanese businesses than does defense spending.

Political–Strategic Factors. Significant improvement in super-power relations—as exemplified by the INF agreement and talks on strategic arms reduction—may not necessarily lead to a U.S. inclination towards DOL vis–à–vis Japan. That is a possibility but the U.S. may still want Japan's SB if the U.S., for economic reasons, wishes to build down its own forces more quickly than the improving super-power relations warrant and wants Japan to offset this.

U.S. military leaders have said they are waiting to see what Soviet leader Mikhail Gorbachev does, not what he says. If indeed Moscow should freeze or build down forces in Soviet Asia as well as in Eastern Europe, it is more likely that the U.S. will adopt a DOL position towards Japan, once Japan has acquired enough capabilities to fulfill its current roles and missions.

The Japanese are divided on how to respond to improvement in superpower relations; unarmed neutralists and some political realists say Japan's buildup is no longer urgent, while military realists and gaullists insist that strategic arms reduction, weakening the U.S. nuclear umbrella covering Japan, makes the latter's conventional buildup all the more essential. It is not clear which of the two tendencies, PR and MR, would prevail but the Soviets will have to major conciliatory moves to soften the Japanese attitude towards them. A Soviet forces freeze or build-down in Asia, in addition to better super-power relations, should favor PR over MR. A further Soviet peace offensive, particularly if it includes some breakthrough in the intractable territorial issue, would also boost PR.

If, as a result of failure of Soviet reforms or for other reasons, superpower relations deteriorate significantly, the U.S. will probably push Japan towards SB again and Japan in turn will respond by adopting MR—up to a point. But if fear of war mounts beyond some threshold, and moreover, if there is doubt about U.S. commitment to defend Japan at the risk of nuclear confrontation with the Soviets, Japan may veer towards PR—or even towards unarmed neutralism or gaullism. Such impulses toward autonomy were already noticeable in the early Reagan years when the U.S. took a particularly hard line against Moscow, but they are not likely to dominate Japanese policy except under extreme circumstances where U.S.–Japan relations are also severely damaged.

Below the superpower level, regional developments, particularly China's attitude and policies, could influence the Japanese course. Given history, most Japanese are resigned to Asia's obsessional fear of their "resurgent militarism" but beyond a certain point, Asian accusations can give rise to emotional Japanese reactions. There is already considerable irritation in Japan, especially among military realists and gaullists, at China's "interference" on such matters as revision of Japanese history textbooks and political leaders' visits to Tokyo's Yasukuni Shrine (where the war dead including war criminals are honored) and its "hypocrisy" in condemning Japan's "resurgent militarism" while itself nurturing a nuclear strike capability and exporting weapons to raise hard currency. It is not inconceivable that Japan would choose MR over PR because of a perceived threat from China.

A case in which the U.S. responds to the situation in Japan, rather than vice versa, is conceivable. As Japan becomes stronger militarily, albeit as a conventional power, and increasingly challenges the U.S. in the field of military technology, the Americans may grow wary and shift increasingly towards the DOL approach to slow Japan down. A nationalistic Japanese reaction, namely insistence on MR or even gaullism, cannot be ruled out.

2. Combinations of Options

If it is true that the U.S. will emphasize either DOL or SB while Japan tilts towards either PR or MR, four basic combinations of U.S. and Japanese attitudes are possible. Combination 1 links DOL in the and PR in Japan; combination 2, DOL and MR; combination 3, SB and PR; and combination 4, SB and MR. Japan veering towards autonomy (unarmed neutralism or gaullism) cannot be ruled out but unarmed neutralists and gaullists are more likely to exert influence through combining forces with other groups.

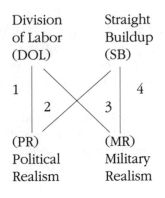

U.S.	Division of Labor (DOL)	Straight Buildup (SB)
	1	4
	2	3
JAPAN	(PR) Political Realism	(MR) Military Realism

Option combinations	Japanese Policy emphasis	Outcome
1.U.S. DOL/ J. PR	aid > > defence	A. buildup decelerates
2.U.S. DOL/J. MR	aid > defence or aid < defence	B. buildup slowed/ J. resentment C. buildup despite U.S./ U.S. resentment
3. U.S. SB/ J. PR	aid < defence or aid > defence	D. reluctant buildup/ J. resentment E. aid despite U.S./ U.S. resentment
4. U.S. SB/ J. MR	aid << defence	F. buildup accelerates

We sense that combinations 1 and 4, in which the two sides agree as to the relative importance of Japan's military and non-military (aid) efforts, are more probable than combinations 2 and 3, in which the two sides disagree, given Japan's reactive diplomacy. Combinations 2 and 3 are not ruled out, however. They could result, for example, when desire for autonomy is on the rise in Japan, or more specifically, when political realists are under pressure from the unarmed neutralists or conversely, military realists are under pressure from the gaullists to resist U.S. demands for further defense buildup or closer joint action. Unarmed neutralism could conceivably regain strength if, for example, U.S.–Japan relations are severely strained or Soviet–Japan relations improve markedly. Recent events have shown that gaullism is being boosted by the rising techno-nationalism in the Japanese defense establishment. Indeed there is a danger that techno-nationalism will become the vehicle for an aggressive nationalism.

In combinations 1 and 4, there is agreement between the U.S. and Japan, and Japan's defense build up will clearly decelerate (outcome A) or accelerate (outcome F) accordingly. With disagreement on whether to emphasize buildup or aid, combinations 2 and 3 are more unstable in the sense that the outcome is not obvious and that whichever side prevails, the other side will resent it. Resentment may accumulate on both sides if negotiations are bitter and outcome not clear-cut. Thus if in combination 2, the U.S. prevails and the buildup slows (outcome B) , the Japanese will resent this, and if Japan prevails (outcome C), the U.S. may become apprehensive about a fasterthan-desired Japanese buildup. Similarly if in combination 3, the U.S. prevails and the Japanese are compelled to accelerate buildup (outcome D), the Japanese will be unhappy, and if the Japanese prevail (outcome E), the Americans are likely to step up criticism of Japan's defense "free ride." or if, as is more likely in the real world, neither side wins completely in combinations 2 and 3, the outcomes will be a mix of B and C or of D and E, and there will be frustrations on both sides.

Something like combination 3 (SB and PR) obtained for some years before Nakasone took over with a mix of outcomes D and E—that is, the Japanese reluctantly built up their defence forces, and the Americans thought that the Japanese were using aid as an excuse for not doing enough in the defense area. combination 4 (SB and MR) obtained during much of the Nakasone years, when both sides agreed that the emphasis must be on military rather than nonmilitary efforts.

Takeshita more clearly than Nakasone hailed from the conservative mainstream and was hence expected to be more of a political realist, but he was not in office long enough to make a clear choice between PR and MR. If the new prime minister decided to shift Tokyo's emphasis from MR to PR, and if President Bush continues to stress SB, we may return to combination 3 of the pre-Nakasone period. There will be more Japan bashing on the "free ride" grounds, more half-hearted Japanese buildup as well as increased Japanese aid, which the U.S. will be disinclined to consider as a contribution. If Bush places priority on DOL over SB while Japan reverts to PR, combination 1 will result, with Japan emphasizing aid and its defense buildup experiencing a slow-down.

However, if, as is more likely, MR continues to be more prominent than PR in Japan and if the Bush administration continues to stress SB, that is, if combination 4 persists, the relatively rapid buildup which we saw at the height of the "Ron-Yasu" leadership will go on. Combination 2 (DOL and MR) will obtain if the U.S. wants Japan to give precedence to aid and Japan insists on emphasizing military buildup. This will be a new combination. Resentment could rise on both sides, particularly if U.S. desire for DOL is a result not of improved U.S. external economic position but of a rising apprehension at Japanese military and technological might.

F. Neighbors' Fears

Japan's neighbors have feared its rearmament and U.S.–Japan disagreements on security matters. To many Asians, the ascendant military realists in Tokyo appear arrogant and aggressive, having abandoned the post-war Japanese contrition and desire to atone. But in a sense, this is natural given the military realists' conviction that military reality surrounding Japan must be assessed and dealt with militarily, abstracted from history and politics. The shrill assertions of the Japanese gaullists are similar in spirit to those of the prewar ultra-nationalists. Together, the military realists and the gaullists can indeed project the image of a "resurgent militarism." In addition, Asian observers are often frustrated to find that many Japanese policy makers, the political realists among them, are ignorant about things military and do not realize how powerful Japan has already grown as a conventional military power.

Applying the analysis of the previous section, we can argue that of the four combinations of U.S. and Japanese options, only the first (with outcome A) is desirable from the point of view of Japan's neighbors, which want to prevent or at least slow down Japan's military buildup and make sure that the U.S. stays in the region to restrain Japan. All other combinations have negative implications. Combination 4 (with outcome F, or accelerated buildup) is frightening to many Asians. Combinations 2 and 3 (with outcome B or C or B/C mix, and outcome D or E or D/E mix, respectively) are also fraught with problems. If it has to be a choice between combinations 2 and 3, Asians would probably prefer combination 3, in which the Americans are pressing for Japanese military buildup and the Japanese are reluctant, to combination 2, where the Japanese themselves are eager for buildup but Americans have misgivings about it. Outcomes B and E, in which aid is emphasized over defense, are better than outcomes C and D, where defense takes precedence, but Japanese resentment in B at U.S. restraint should be worrying. Along with outcome F (fast buildup flowing from combination 4), outcome C must be the most negative for Asians. In C, Japan goes for military buildup despite U.S. misgivings or opposition. And whereas in F, Japan at least will be acting within the U.S.–Japan security arrangement, C contains seeds of Japan going it alone.

Late in 1987 Singapore's Prime Minister Lee Kuan Yew spoke for much of East Asia when he made Japan's continued low defense posture and reliance on the U.S.–Japan security treaty a condition for his optimism about the region's future.[31] He added: "It could be disastrous if the Japanese decided that their economic-security relationship with the U.S. was no longer valid and that they must build up their own defense." Lee stressed that Japan should play an economic role, relocating industries to the region and importing more from it. In the following, we shall examine some of East Asia's specific complaints and worries about Japan.

Having expressed mixed views about Japan's buildup, China has become its most vehement opponent. The Chinese used to attack Japan's "resurgent militarism" before normalization of diplomatic relations with Tokyo in 1972. Then in the remainder of the 1970s, the Chinese wanted an alignment of nations against the Soviet Union, which they regarded as the most imminent threat to China, and were seemingly not averse to seeing Japan build up its military capabilities against the Soviet threat.

The Sino–Soviet thaw and developments inside Japan produced a clearly different Chinese attitude by the mid-1980s. The Chinese saw that Japan's GNP was growing very large and that the country was developing its technological prowess while abandoning its defense-only stance. Most disturbingly, the Japanese appeared to be deviating from their pledge at the time of normalization to reflect deeply on history. Furthermore, the Japanese were seen by some Chinese to be abandoning their position that Peking is the sole legitimate government of China. It is said that Peking is seriously worried about Japan's links, existing and potential, with Taiwan. Aside from the close Japan–Taiwan economic links, the general Taiwanization of the Taiwan elites (diluting the mainlanders' dominance) and the supposed Taiwanese fondness for Japan could become obstacles to reunification, the Chinese apparently fear. As was earlier suggested, mutual recriminations between China and Japan about each other's defense policy could lead to an arms race between the two.

At the popular level South Koreans harbor much the same suspicion and hostility towards Japan as the Chinese do. The image of a militarily humiliated Japan dominating South Korea economically and becoming once more a major military power evokes strong negative emotions in South Koreans.[32] But in contrast with the

Chinese case, South Korea's recent economic performance outshining Japan's and the fact that both South Korea and Japan are allies of the U.S. seem to moderate South Korean feelings about Japan. Further, the South Korean realization that their image and standing in Japan is undergoing vast improvement, unthinkable a generation ago, must also mellow the South Korean sentiment.

It is increasingly obvious to the South Koreans that their economic relationship with Japan is becoming more equal. Many see the bilateral trade balance—chronically in favor of Japan and a rallying point of South Korean resentment against the Japanese—reversing itself in South Korea's favor in the not too distant future. In the area of security, South Korea has insisted that its security is vital to Japanese security and that therefore Japan should help it defend itself against North Korea—but economically, without any arms or men. The Japanese quietly agree but prefer to state that its economic aid is purely economic. Defense cooperation between Seoul and Tokyo is slowly developing, through exchange of officers and intelligence but the Soviet anxiety over an "Eastern NATO"—a U.S.–Japan–South Korea alliance—is premature.

In Southeast Asia suspicion and hostility towards Japan have been attenuated by time and circumstances. Generally the ASEAN countries have come to think that economic ties with Japan are vital to their economies and hence, to their security, even though many still think the ties are lop-sided and Japan takes far too much of the accrued benefits. ASEAN's fear of China as a potential economic competitor and regional hegemon and its greater familiarity with Japan seem to make the regional grouping relatively relaxed about Japan's defense policy.

Although most of ASEAN is not ready to let the Japanese play an explicit military role regionally, some experts there see Japan playing supportive security roles. According to a Malaysian specialist, for example, Japan can first help increase national resilience of the regional states through aid. It can also seek to sustain a U.S. presence, especially in the Philippines, by supporting and indirectly contributing to a compensation package for the U.S. bases there. Thirdly, Japan should provide security assistance to coastal states to ensure the safety and security of maritime transportation in the region. Finally, Japan should seek to develop regular consultations with the countries in the region on political and security matters.[33] Some ASEAN military leaders have gone further to explore the possibility of obtaining military assistance from Japan. The Indonesians have asked about Japanese weapons and the Thais about the Japanese sharing costs incurred by ASEAN in preventing the expansion of the communist Indochinese states.[34]

Having been identified by Japan as its main threat and justification for a military buildup, the Soviet Union has unsurprisingly viewed Japan's buildup in an entirely negative light. But whereas Moscow's past style was to castigate, intimidate—verbally and physically—and harden the Japanese, Gorbachev's new diplomacy finally seems to be catching up even in the relatively low-priority Moscow–Tokyo relations. In his Krasnoyarsk speech of September, 1988, Gorbachev used sweet reason to appeal to Japan. He said: "The Soviet people ..... are worried by the stubborn buildup of [Japan's] military potential within the framework of "burden sharing" with the United States." He then asked why Japan, which has advanced to the status of "great power" without relying on militarism, should now "discredit this unique experience which is so instructive to the whole of mankind? Why burden..... the unusual vigor of Japan's economic presence almost everywhere in the world by historical associations of prewar and war time?"[35] Gorbachev then went on to propose regional consultations on freezing naval forces and lowering military confrontation.

How can Japan's neighbors obtain the best results for themselves with respect to Japanese security policy? What leverage do these countries have to pressure Japan to give precedence to PR rather than MR and the U.S. to stress DOL rather than SB? As we have seen, Moscow may try making some real concessions to soften Japanese attitudes, or threaten Japan with danger of nuclear war to drive a wedge between it and the U.S. For now, it is suggesting a less drastic path of confidence building.

Other neighbors with less leverage will have to decide on the optimal level of pressure to apply to Japan. Mild protestations may be ignored; firmness, sometimes even a "shokku" (shock) or two, may be required. Collective appeal particularly in the case of ASEAN may prove effective. But too much pressure can backfire, making many Japanese feel victimized and self-righteous. Excessive pressure was exemplified by Peking's attacks on the Japanese courts for an allegedly pro–Taiwan and anti-Peking ruling in a case involving a dormitory for Chinese students. The attacks on the courts were taken as attacks on the hard-won separation of powers, thus alienating the normally pro–Peking liberal press as well as the general populace. Applying the right amount of pressure on Japan would require disaggregation of Japanese polity and society to find potential allies who share the outsider's views on issues at hand.

Asian countries have appealed with the U.S. not to prod Japan to become a major military power. The U.S. has not reversed its policy. But it will take Asian feelings into consideration when pushing for Japan's military buildup while at the same time trying to assuage Asian fears and demanding that Japan itself help in this regard.[36] Asking the U.S. to adopt DOL, not SB, implies that Japan's neighbors should think of ways to win an American commitment to stay in the region as a military power. Indeed, most regional countries prefer this scenario to another major power (be it the Soviet Union, Japan or China) filling the vacuum after a U.S. build-down in Asia.

Economically, complying positively with U.S. market opening demands may help to an extent—although the regional countries have become accustomed to unreciprocal relations with the U.S. which favor them and may worry that the U.S. would anyway squander the marginal economic gains thus obtained, without setting its economic house in order. Militarily, there is not much the regional countries can do to induce the U.S. to stay on in the region. In fact, the dilemma is that the more self-sufficient the regional countries become in defense, the more likely is the U.S. to reduce its presence.

Telling the U.S. it is appreciated and wanted cannot do any harm but politically, this is not easy. The idea was tried—and failed—when Manila elicited ASEAN's open endorsement of the U.S. bases in the Philippines in late 1987 because some heads of government, committed to non-alignment, did not wish to go on record giving such an endorsement. Similar attempts no doubt will be made when bases negotiations begin again, for the period beyond 1991.

G. Need For More Thought, and Communication

We have established what formulas for U.S.–Japan security burden sharing Japan's neighbors will dread or, *faute de mieux*, welcome. Not surprisingly, the least threatening combination of options for much of Asia is one in which the U.S. continues to take on the bulk of the military burden and Japan contributes in non-military ways. We have not answered the more difficult question as to what formula would be desirable from a joint U.S.–Japanese point of view. As Armitage has pointed out, "Governments of free peoples will not sustain any major investment of resources [in common security] unless the benefit to them is well-understood."[37] But coming to such an understanding is a daunting task. Polls show that many Americans regard the U.S.–Japan security relationship as more beneficial to Japan, while the Japanese think the opposite.[38] Within Japan, variance of opinion on the benefits of burden sharing is still so great that forcing the issue can prove divisive and counter-productive.

Nonetheless, there is urgent need for Japanese rethinking about defense, aid and national priorities. Given that Japan has indeed become a major military power whose capabilities can theoretically be directed at all neighboring countries, and given that Japan's current defense doctrine has been superseded by practice in certain crucial respects, there is a strong argument for reassessing and revising the official defense doctrine. And above all the Japanese must make their defense policy transparent. Wishing to preserve the current doctrine to check Japan's further military buildup, some are reluctant to review the current doctrine. Meanwhile, some pro-defense groups also fear the high political cost of reopening a national debate and doubt the utility of a new doctrine which at any rate can never be 100 percent honest or transparent. But neighbors' "uncertainty and concern that ..... Japan may build up its military capability without a clear strategy and become a military power without knowing what the power is to be used for"[39] must be assuaged.

A debate on aid is necessary at a time when Tokyo's ODA outlays are increasing rapidly but there is no consensus on their objectives. Tokyo has explained to the recipients that the objectives of Japanese aid are economic and humanitarian, and to the U.S. that the aid sometimes has strategic aims and payoffs. However, Japanese officials are quietly resisting radical politicization of aid. Among the Japanese public there is tacit understanding that aid as "cost" or "dues" enhances Japan's national economic interest as well as some corporate interests. Some Japanese are beginning to ask whether Japan, in giving aid, should not also assert more forcefully than in the past how the recipients should spend it. Some argue that Japanese aid is crucially lacking in political philosophy while others say the absence of high-flown idealism is a strength, not a weakness.

√ theory of aid, attempting to synthesize the above disparate
ιents, is called for.
√inally, in order to have a meaningful debate on defense or aid,
ιe Japanese must attempt to establish their national priorities in
today's international context, asking who they want to be and how
they intend to help shape the world—not just how they will react to
the world. The fact is that recent developments have made the
Japanese more than normally self conscious and there is already
considerable debate over "whither Japan?" Some political realists
maintain that Japan can and should on principle remain a "merchant
state," refusing a military buildup. There is also the view that by
renouncing things military, Japan has become the hub and inspiration of a new and superior Asian–Pacific civilization. Military realists
cite history to debunk such "delusions." One military realist argues
that Japan can best achieve its objectives of prosperity, freedom and
security for its people by playing second fiddle to the U.S.—a view
the gaullists will not accept.

The problem is that most of the debate has so far remained
internal. Internationalizing this debate would help the Japanese
understand how they are seen by the rest of the world and what the
world expects of them. it would also inform the world of the evolving
Japanese self-images, aspirations and intentions—which are, increasingly, a legitimate world concern given Japan's growing power
and influence.

Given our meager powers of articulation, we Japanese may find
the dialectic cumbersome and frustrating. But it is an essential
process if we are to become trusted citizens of the world.

ENDNOTES

Chapter II

1. The 17 heavily-indebted middle income countries include Argentina, Bolivia, Brazil, Chile, Colombia, Costa Rica, Ecuador, Ivory Coast, Jamaica, Mexico, Morocco, Nigeria, Peru, Philippines, Uruguay, Venezuela, and Yugoslavia.
2. Important steps have been taken to supply that capital, specifically, the replenishment of the International Development Association (IDA), the new financing of the IMF Structural Adjustment Facility, and the World Bank Special Action Program in Africa.

Chapter IV

1. Alan Riding, "Latins Want Bush to Help On Debts: See Falling Living Standards as a Threat to Democracy," *New York Times*, Nov. 29, 1988, pp. 1 and 14.
2. Perhaps the best is an early examination by Arnold Wolfers, "National Security as an Ambiguous Symbol," in *Discord and Collaboration* (Baltimore: John Hopkins Press, 1962) pp. 147-165.
3. The publication date is Dec. 5, 1986. I am indebted to former Japanese Foreign Minister Saburo Okita for this incisive summary of the macroeconomic problems. See his "East Asia and the Global Economy," a paper prepared for the Pacific Forum (Hawaii) in November, 1988, p. 5.
4. H. Liddell Hart, Strategy, 2nd edition. (New York: Praeger, 1967) p. 351. See also Edward Azar and Chung-in Moon, "Third World National Security: Toward A New Conceptual Framework," *International Interactions*, v. 2, n. 2 (1984).
5. For an argument that it is indeed the key to security, see Robert McNamara, *The Essence of Security* (New York: Harper & Row, 1968) p. 123. "For, in the end, poverty and social injustice may endanger our security as much as any military threat."
6. Col. V. Rodin, "The Seihan Submarine Rail Tunnel," *Zarubezhnoye Voyennoye* (Moscow), no. 3, March, 1988, pp. 73-74.
7. Until the Lyndon Johnson presidency (1963-68), Japan was the largest borrower from the World Bank. Today, Japan is the biggest national aid donor in the world, a testimony to the skills and diligence of the Japanese people.

, restates the "guiding principle of democracy" in the excellent work *ansitions From Authoritarian Rule* (Baltimore: The Johns Hopkins *niversity* Press, 1986) by Guillermo O'Donnelll and Philip C. Schmitter. In their analyses of Europe and Latin America cases, liberalization usually precedes democratic institutions. What is needed for theoretical insight is to blend their assessment of political change with equally incisive examination of economic development in the same nations. What are the conditions which lead to "pacts" among competiting leadership groups that foster national development and democracy?

9. *Report of the Commission on Security and Economic Assistance.* Informally known as the Carlucci Commission. (Washington, D.C.: U.S. Government Printing Office, Nov. 1983) p. 2.

10. Secretary of Defense Harold Brown, *Fiscal Year 1980 Department of Defense Annual Report.*

11. See the path-breaking work of Seymour Martin Lipset, "Some Social Requisites of Democracy: Economic Development and Political Legitimation," *American Political Science Review*, v. 53 (1959), pp. 69 - 105.

12. Interpreted as permitting only "self defense" forces.

13. A recent example is Jusuf Wanadi, "Armed, Yes, But Must It Be To the Teeth," *Far Eastern Economic Review*, July 14, 1988, pp. 32-33. Wanadi is a noted Indonesian analyst and government official.

14. Lloyd G. Reynolds, "The Spread of Economic Growth to the Third World, 1850-1980," *Journal of Economic Literature*, v. 21 (Sept., 1983) pp. 963-966.

15. The report was delivered to the government in 1980. A stimulating American review is to be found in Robert Barnett, *Beyond War* (New York: Pergamon-Brassey, 1984).

16. Private capital flows, corporation transfers, and technology transfers are both larger, and in many ways, more critical than governmental capital flows. Yet, these are much harder to track.

17. Although a vast and controversial literature exists on this point, a useful overview is the single issue of *International Organization*, v. 32 (Winter, 1978).

18. For a stimulating overview, see the version of a Noble Laureate speech printed by Theodore W. Schultz, "The Economics of Being Poor," *Journal of Political Economy*, (Aug., 1980). His conclusions provide further empirical evidence that rational economic policies are more significant than aid in achieving economic "takeoff."

19. See Robert Cassen, *Does Aid Work? Report to an Intergovernmental Task Force* (A World Bank task force, 1986) which notes distinct differences between results in Asian and Africa. The crucial finding is the need for better coordination (economic planning) at the national level. Culture may however provide a "comparative advantage," insufficient to ensure development, but clearly an important asset. See also: Peter Berger, "An East Asian Development Model," *The Economic News*, Sept. 17-23, 1984, Taipei, Taiwan; G. S. Becker, *Human Capital: A Theoretical and Empirical Analysis, With Special Reference to Education* (New York: Columbia University Press, 1964); and Edward F. Dension, "Education, Economic Growth and Gaps in Information," *Journal of Political Economy*, v. 70, n. 5 (Oct., 1962).

20. Simon Kuznets, *Postwar Economic Growth*. (Cambridge: Harvard University Press, 1964), pg. 41, clearly shows that the direct impact of capital is a necessary but not sufficient condition for per capita income growth. Later Guillermo O'Donnell, argued that such capital investment was dependent upon a "good" investment climate which requires stability in his work *Modernization and Bureaucratic Authoritarianism* (Berkeley: Institute of International Relations, 1973).

21. The concept of relative deprivation is explained in Ted Gurr, *Why Men Rebel* (Princeton: Princeton University Press, 1970) and James Davies, "Toward a Theory of Revolution," *American Sociological Review*, v. 27, n. 1 (February 1962). Further discussion includes: Peter A. Lupsha, "Explanation of Political Violence," *Politics and Society*, v. 2, n. 1 (Fall 1971); B. N. Gorfman and E. N. Muller, "The Strange Case of Relative Gratification and the Potential for Political Violence: The V-Curve Hypothesis," *American Political Science Review*, v. 67 (June 1973), especially the "Tocqueville Paradox" on p. 537. This paradox means that those perceiving a positive change in their well-being are more, not less, prone to violence.

22. Mancur Olson, Jr., "Rapid Growth as a Destabilizing Force," *The Journal of Economic History*, December 1963.

23. See both James Bovard, "Free Food Bankrupts Foreign Farmers," *The Wall Street Journal*, July 2, 1984, p. 18 and Sudhir Sen, "Farewell to Foreign Aid," *World View*, July, 1982, p. 8. The latter piece is an economic argument downplaying moral issues.

24. The co-directors are Glenn and Mildred Leet, 54 Riverside Drive, New York, N.Y., 10024. African businesses rose from 1 in 1981 to 2,779 by June 1988. Equally relevant is the conclusion that recipients can calculate the economic advantages regardless of literacy. Lloyd G. Reynolds, "The Spread of Economic Growth to the Third World: 1850-1980," *Journal of Economic Literature*, v. 21 (September 1983) pp. 947-950.

25. Dr. Ajaga Nji, "Small is Possible and Efficient: An Empirical Verification of the Impact of Size on the Utilization of Local Resources in Rural Development Projects in Cameroon," cited in *op cit.*, *Newsletter*, v. 8, n. 3 (15 Sept. 1988) pp. 2-3.

26. These funds are coordinated through the Development Assistance Committee (DAC) of the 24-nation Organization for Economic Cooperation and Development (OECD). More than 67 percent of all ODA is provided through the DAC.

27. Hopkins, "Civil-Military Relations in Developing Countries," *British Journal of Sociology*, v. 17, n. 2 (June 1966) p. 175.

Chapter V

1. Report of the Defense Burden Sharing Panel of the Committee on Armed Services, House of Representatives, 100th Congress, August 1988. See especially the report's six-point "Interim Conclusions and Recommendations," pp. 8 - 9.

2. Richard Armitage, testimony before Senate panel, USIS distribution, March 21, 1988.

3. Henry Kissinger, "A Memo to the Next President" in *Newsweek*, September 19, 1988.

4. Mike Mochizuki, "The U.S.–Japanese Alliance in Transition," a paper presented at the Conference on U.S.–Japanese Relations, Maui, Hawaii, August 1988.

5. Charles Morrison, "Japan and the ASEAN Countries: The Evolution of Japan's Regional Role," in *The Political Economy of Japan, Volume 2, The Changing International Context*, Takashi Inoguchi and Daniel I. Okimoto eds., Stanford, Stanford University Press, 1988. p. 425.

6. Takashi Obata, "Japanese Defense Technology and the FS-X Controversy," (a working paper), Stanford, Center for International Security and Arms Control, 1988. p.2.

7. Richard Armitage, op. cit.

8. For the original definitions of political realism and military realism, see Mike Mochizuki, "Japan's Search for strategy," in *International Security*, Volume 8, No. 3. Winter 1983/84, and Yonosuke Nagai, *Gendai to Senryaku*, (Tokyo: Bungei Shunju, 1985). See also Mike Mochizuki "The U.S.–Japanese Alliance in Transition."

9. Mike Mochizuki, "Japan's Search for Strategy." See also Yonosuke Nagai, "Boei ronso no zahyojiku," and "Anzen hosho to kokumin keizai," in his *Gendai to Senryaku*, (Tokyo, Bungei Shunju, 1985).

10. Susumu Awanohara, "A Yen to Contribute" in *Far Eastern Economic Review*, March 28, 1988. pp. 34 - 36.

11. The government's position on defense perimeter was stated in the Diet on December 29, 1969, April 17 and October 3 1981. The first said the perimeter extended to "surrounding open seas and air" but the other did not. See *Boei Handobukku 63 nen ban*, Tokyo, Asagumo Shimbunsha, 1988. pp.379 - 80.
12. Statement of Chief Cabinet Secretary on Transfer of Military Technologies to the United States, Tokyo, January 14, 1983.
13. "Concerning the Defense Buildup for the Time Being," a Cabinet decision, November 1976, in *Defense of Japan 1987*, p.153.
14. See Ushio Shiota, "Ichi paasento waku kekkai no 500 nichi (500 days to the collapse of the one percent limit)" in *Chuo Koron*, April 1987. pp. 140 - 55.
15. Masashi Nishihara, *Senryaku kenkyu no shikaku*, Tokyo, Ningen no kagaku sha, 1988, p. 236.
16. The study is mentioned in Muthiah Alagappa, "Japan's Political and Security Role in the Asia–Pacific Region," Contemporary Southeast Asia, Volume 10, Number 1, June 1988.
17. National Defense Program Outline, October 29, 1976.
18. Some of these criticisms against the Outline are found in recent writings of Seizaburo Sato, "Naze, soshite donoyona gunjiryoku ka (Why and what sort of military power does Japan need?)," in *Chuo Koron*, December 1985; Hisahiko Okazaki, "Magarikado ni kita nichibei domei (Japan–U.S. alliance at a crossroads)," in *Bungei Shunju*, July 1988; and Masashi Nishihara, *Senryaku kenkyu no Shikaku* (Points of view of strategic studies), (Tokyo, Ningen no kagakusha, 1988).
19. William Howard Taft, Remarks to the Japan National Press Club, Tokyo, May 12, 1988.
20. Richard Armitage, op. cit.
21. See for example Kiyofuku Chuma, "Nichibei anpo taisei o minaosu (Reassessing the Japan–U.S. security system)," in *Nichibei shinjidai* (New era of Japan–U.S. relations), Tokyo, Osaka shoseki, 1988, pp. 124 - 27.
22. Chuma, ibid.
23. See for example "Nihon no senzai gunji gijutsu (Japan's potential military technology)" in *Voice*, September 1987, in which technology levels of Japan, the U.S. and the Soviet Union in key defense areas are compared, with Japan looking strong indeed.
24. Cited in Susumu Awanohara, op. cit.
25. Gaston Sigur, a speech at the School of Advanced International Studies of Johns Hopkins University, March 6, 1988.

26. The expressions "money," "blood" and "sweat" were actually used by Tokyo policy elites. This is hinted at in, for example, "Kokusai kyoryoku koso no imisuru mono (The meaning of the International Cooperation Initiative)," an interview with Shoichi Kuriyama, *Sekai no Ugoki* (World Developments), Tokyo, Gaimusho, August 1988.
27. Noboru Takeshita, a dinner speech for the Japan–America Society of Chicago, June 22, 1988.
28. Frank Carlucci, to the Japan National Press Club, June 6, 1988.
29. Zbigniew Brzezinski in an interview with Masataka Kosaka, *Asuteion*, Fall 1987.
30. For example, Isamu Miyazaki, a prominent private-sector economist formerly of the Economic Planning Agency, warned against "an automatic application of [the] argument [that military cooperation constitutes a form of international contribution] to promote further military buildup of Japan" at the 1988 annual Trilateral commission meeting in Tokyo.
31. Lee Kuan Yew, "The Asia–Pacific Region: Present Trends, Future Consequences," at the International Herald Tribune Conference "Pacific 2000: Global Challenge," in Singapore, November 1987.
32. See, for example, Edward Olsen, *U.S.–Japan strategic Reciprocity*, (Standord, Hoover Institution Press, 1985).
33. Muthiah Alagappa, "Japan's Political and Security Role in the Asia–Pacific Region," in *Contemporary Southeast Asia*, Vol. 10; No. 1, (Singapore, Institute of Southeast Asian Studies, June 1988.) p. 41. The author is associated with the Malaysian Institute of Strategic and International Studies, which is close to the government.
34. Prasert Chittiwatanapung, "Japan's Role in the Asia–Pacific Region: Political Dimension," unpublished paper.
35. Gorbachov, Mikhail, the Krasnoyarsk speech, September, 1988.
36. See House Armed Services Committee interim report.
37. Richard Armitage, before the Senate panel, May 26, 1988.
38. See for example, *Challenges and Opportunities in United States–Japan Relations*, A Report Submitted to the President of the United States and the Prime Minister of Japan by the United States–Japan Advisory Commission, September 1984. p. 13.
39. Jusuf Wanandi, "Japan's International and Regional Role: An Indonesian Perception," a paper presented at the Thirteenth Indonesia–Japan Conference, Bali, June 1988.

APPENDIX

THE ATLANTIC COUNCIL OF THE UNITED STATES

Founded in 1961. The Atlantic Council of the United States is the national center for education and for the formulation of policy recommendations on the problems and opportunities shared by the developed democracies. The Council is national in scope, rigorously bipartisan in orientation, and actively centrist and consensus-building in nature.

For over a quarter century, the Atlantic Council has focused on: strengthening Western cohesion through our Atlantic and Pacific alliances; improving our long-term relations with the USSR while enhancing our collective ability to resist the Soviet Union's attempts to extend its influence through military means or intimidation; exploring the interrelationships of previously segregated "Atlantic" and "Pacific" issues; integrating the traditionally fragmented aspects of our international economic and national security policies; and serving as a catalyst for better understanding and communication by bringing together the younger "successor generation" leaders from the public and private sectors of Western Europe, North America, East Asia and the Pacific.

THE BRETTON WOODS COMMITTEE

The Bretton Woods Committee is a bipartisan group organized to increase public understanding of the World Bank, the International Monetary Fund, and the regional development institutions. The Committee represents more than three hundred regional leaders throughout the United States including business representatives, educators, association executives, and former members of government.

The Committee believes that effective U.S. policy toward the international financial institutions requires the understanding and support of the American public. To this end, the Bretton Woods

Committee engages in a variety of activities in the field of public education.

The Committee is also engaged in the study of the future role of the Bretton Woods institutions in the international economic system and shares its conclusions with Congress, the Administration, the management of the international institutions and foreign officials.

THE JAPAN CENTER FOR INTERNATIONAL EXCHANGE

Founded in 1971, the Japan Center for International Exchange (JCIE) is an independent, non-profit, and nonpartisan organization dedicated to strengthening Japan's role in international affairs. JCIE believes that Japan faces a major challenge in augmenting its positive contributions to the international community, in keeping with its position as the world's second largest industrial democracy. Operating in a country where policy-making has traditionally been dominated by the government bureaucracy. JCIE has played an important role in broadening debate on Japan's international responsibilities by engaging Japanese from different sectors in privately sponsored programs of exchange, research, and discussion with their foreign counterparts.

JCIE creates opportunities for informed policy discussion; it does not take policy positions. JCIE receives no government subsidies; funding comes from private foundation grants, corporate contributions, and contracts.

PARTICIPANTS IN MEETINGS AND PLENARIES*

Anthony Albrecht
Councillor, Atlantic Council; former Deputy Assistant Secretary of
   State, East Asia Bureau
Madeleine Albright
Director, Atlantic Council; Professor of International Affairs,
   Georgetown University
Lamar Alexander
President, University of Tennessee
Michael Armacost
U.S. Ambassador to Japan
Anne C. Bader
Director of Development, Atlantic Council
Joseph Barr
Former Secretary of the Treasury
Joseph Berghold
Executive Vice President, *NVRyan
John Block
President, National American Wholesale Grocers Association
William Breer
Director, Office of Japanese Affairs, Department of State
John L. Caldwell
President, U.S. Trading & Investment Company
William Clark, Jr.
Acting Assistant Secretary of State for East Asian and Pacific Affairs
Paul Cook
Center for Strategic International Studies
Kenneth S. Courtis
Vice President, Deutsche Bank Capital Markets (Asia)
Mark Curtis
Chairman, Education Committee, Atlantic Council
Henry H. Fowler
Former Secretary of the Treasury

---

*These participants are in addition to the Working Group Members (listed on pages ix-xi).

Takehiko Kiyohara
Chairman of the Editorial Board, *The Sankei Shimbun*
Akira Kojima
Editorial Writer, *Japan Economic Journal*
Michihiko Kunihiro
Deputy Minister for Foreign Affairs
Takakazu Kuriyama
Vice Minister for Foreign Affairs
Sol Linowitz
Director, Atlantic Council; Senior Partner, Coudert Brothers
Haruo Maekawa
Chairman, Kokusai Denshin Denwa Company Ltd.; former Governor, Bank of Japan
Koichiro Matsuura
Director General, Economic Cooperation Bureau, Ministry of Foreign Affairs
Yukio Matsuyama
Chairman of the Editorial Board, *The Asahi Shimbun*
James McDivitt
Senior Vice President, Rockwell International
David McGiffert
Partner, Covington & Burling
Patrick Mulloy
Senior Counsel, Committee on Banking, Housing and Urban Affairs, U.S. Congress
Masashi Nishihara
Professor of International Relations, National Defense Academy
Shijuro Ogata
Deputy Governor, The Japan Development Bank
Ryoji Onodera
Director General for International Affairs, Defense Agency
Henry Owen
The Consultants International Group, Inc.
Jacques J. Reinstein
Director, Atlantic Council
Eugene Rotberg
Executive Vice President, Merrill Lynch Company; former Treasurer of the World Bank
Robert Seal
Director, International Affairs, The Boeing Company

William Sherman
Johns Hopkins Strategic and International Studies Institute
Motoo Shiina
Member of the Diet (LDP)
Atsushi Shimokobe
President, National Institute for Research Advancement (NIRA)
Lindley Sloan
Executive Director, Japan-U.S. Friendship Commission
Lee Smith
Executive Director, Industrial Cooperation Council, State of New York
Shigetami Sunada
Member of the Diet (LDP); Chairman, Special
nal Economic Cooperation, LDP
Naomichi Suzuki
Director"General, International Trade Policy Bureau, Ministry of International Trade and Industry
Nobuyuki Takaki
Editorial Writer, The *Mainichi Shimbun*
Tatou Takahama
Political Writer, *The Yomiuri Shimbun*
Makoto Utsumi
Director"General, International Finance Bureau, Ministry of Finance
Alfred D. Wilhelm
Former Army Attaché, U. S. Embassy, Beijing
William Woodward
Councillor, Atlantic Council
Shinichi Yamamoto
Visiting Researcher, Brookings Institution
Kensuko Yanagiya
President, Japan International Cooperation Agency

de Gruyter Studies in Organization

An international series by internationally known authors presenting current fields of research in organization.

Organizing and organizations are substantial pre-requisites for the viability and future developments of society. Their study and comprehension are indispensable to the quality of human life. Therefore, the series aims to:

– offer to the specialist work material in form of the most important and current problems, methods and results;
– give interested readers access to different subject areas;
– provide aids for decisions on contemporary problems and stimulate ideas.

The series will include monographs, collections of contributed papers, and handbooks.

de Gruyter Studies in Organization 7

Organizing Industrial Development

Editor
Rolf Wolff
Professor für Betriebswirtschaftslehre
Nordische Universität in Flensburg
Fakultät Wirtschaftswissenschaften
2390 Flensburg
Bundesrepublik Deutschland

This book is dedicated to *Walter Goldberg*

Library of Congress Cataloging in Publication Data

Organizing industrial development.
  (De Gruyter studies in organization ; 7)
  Bibliography: p.
  Includes index.
  1. Organization.   2. Industrial management.
  3. Industry and state.   I. Wolff, Rolf, 1953-   ;
  II. Series.
  HD31.0783   1986   338.9   86-24074
  ISBN 0-89925-168-4 (U.S.)

CIP-Kurztitelaufnahme der Deutschen Bibliothek

Organizing industrial development / ed.: Rolf Wolff. – Berlin ;
New York : de Gruyter, 1986
  (De Gruyter studies in organization ; 7)
  ISBN 3-11-010669-8
NE: Wolff, Rolf [Hrsg.]; GT

Organizing Industrial Development

Editor: Rolf Wolff

Walter de Gruyter · Berlin · New York 1986

Preface

We are always being told what exciting times we live in – but are we perhaps trying to give ourselves courage? The information society is beginning to reveal its contours, and we are facing problems which appear insoluble. The idea of "complexity" has become a euphemism for the uncertainty felt by anyone considering the sheer volume of the problems awaiting solution. One of the instruments of problemsolving, and at the core of all change, is the organization. Organizations mediate between individuals, between different spheres of society, between the private and public sectors, between nations and between continents. We are living in an organized world; we spend most of our everyday lives in organizations of various types, organizing and "reproducing" our society. Organization research thus throws light on many different aspects of the social world.

A good deal of organization theory focuses upon the understanding of economic organizations. Over the last ten years this field has expanded considerably, not only as regards methodology but also in the choice of topics and objects of study. The rediscovery of institutionalism, for example, promises exciting developments. Profound changes in the traditional boundaries between economics, politics, public-sector organizations and special-interest organizations are affecting this whole field of research, which in turn also affects these boundaries in a process of continual mutual influence.

The scientific society is itself an organization, depending on people capable of creating stimulating environments for research, of bringing together persons of an enthusiastic and curious cast of mind. A great deal of credit is generally given to the results and achievements of individual researchers, whilst little attention is paid to those who play a crucial part in organizing and networking research. When one person combines within himself both the scientific and the organizing capacities, the outcome is bound to be extraordinary. This book is dedicated to one of these rare personalities – Walter Goldberg, who over the last thirty years has contributed so much to the development of our field. We are all indebted to him in a great variety of ways. The following contributions and their focus on the future are therefore an expression of our shared hope that this co-operation will long endure.

Generous financial aid has been provided for this project by the Gothenburg Business School Foundation and this is gratefully acknowledged. The Science Center in Berlin offered a relaxed working atmosphere over a period of several weeks. Special thanks are due to Barbara Czarniawska for writing Walter

Goldberg's biography, and to Nancy Adler, our own English-language adviser. And finally our thanks are due to David Hickson for his invaluable help and encouragement.

Rolf Wolff   Stockholm, November 1985

Contents

"What Moses meant when he spoke to the King of Edom was, "We will not drink from the well that we have with us, and we will not eat the manna that has been given us. You won't be able to complain that we were nothing but trouble to you, because we will bring you business".

Tanhuma (ed. by Solomon Buber)
on Numbers, portion, p. 61b

1. Introduction: Organization Theory – A Contribution to our Understanding of the Visible Hand

Rolf Wolff

The problem of industrial development falls within the domains of several scientific disciplines. Neo-classical economics focuses on aggregate levels in the economic system, emphasizing the rationality of optimization and favoring the theory of the "Invisible Hand". According to these theories the market is perfect and free, if all transactions are performed without any transaction costs. Information is freely available, and information search can be calculated in terms of its costs and benefits, decision-making is rational, alternative buyers and sellers are always available, and so on. Economists have themselves challenged some of the major assumptions of Neo-classical theory (Thurow, 1983). But the main challenges have been imposed on economics from "outside", from business administration theory, organization theory, and decision-making theory. Whereas economists tend to describe the world in terms of what "ought to be", business administration and organization theory capture the world "as it is". The problems of strategic behavior and decision-making in industrial organizations bring simplifications such as "utility maximization" and "rational behavior" up against the facts of real life. Economic behavior as described by economists in terms of optimization, allows for a description of the real world in elegant formal mathematical models and theories. Economic behavior described in terms of quasi-rational behavior and bounded rationality, leaves the organization theorists still facing the complexity of everyday business life.

There are some interesting developments which should be mentioned within Neo-classical theory itself. The outstanding work of Nelson and Winter (1982) illustrates some potential interdisciplinary and boundary-transcending approaches to explaining economic change. They combine Schumpeterian institutionalism with microeconomic knowledge and theories of decision-making in business firms. This kind of approach extends the analysis of the economic system "in isolation". The role of bounded rationality in decision-making, and the role of industrial politics, are taken into account in developing an evolutionary approach to economic change.

The market and hierarchies approach as developed by Coase (1937, 1972) and by Williamson (1975), also combines organization theory with microeconomic theory. The question as to what business firms actually do, has been the core problem in all "visible hand" theories. Coase started to answer this question by first asking why a firm exists at all, "since this gives us a clue as to the direction in which to look in order to uncover what determines what a firm does" (1972: 63).

Nevertheless it represents a formal model for evaluating the cost of different institutional alternatives. This approach to behavior still draws on the notion of rational or quasi-rational economic calculations. The way in which industry is organized is thus dependent on the relation between the cost of undertaking transactions on the market and the cost of organizing the same operations within the firm that can perform the task at the lowest cost. How this calculation is carried out and by whom, and how this particular activity relates to other activities, is not explained. "About all we know is that the working out of these interrelationships leads to a situation in which visible organizations are small in relation to the economic system of which they are a part" (Coase, 1972: 64).

Williamson (1975: 1–19) refers to his mode of inquiry as a "new institutional economics" approach. Finding received Neo-classical economics too abstract, Williamson tries to forge a synthesis that complements rather than replaces it. American institutionalists claim that they have specialized in historical-empirical studies and that they support democratic economic planning as opposed to the Neo-classicists who support the free-market paradigm (Dugger, 1983: 95). Given this paradigmatic differentiation between institutionalism and transaction theories, the "new institutionalism" is not institutionalist at all. "Instead, it is a more realistic and sophisticated Neo-classicism" (Dugger, 1983: 96).

Does institutionalism explain the blank areas on the map? Over the last few years institutionalism has re-emerged at least in Scandinavia as a way of describing and analysing economic processes in a broader frame of reference and in a historical perspective. But the use made of the term "institutionalism" is specific and draws upon different theoretical traditions. Sjöstrand (1985) attempts to combine institutionalism, microeconomic theory and organization theory. March and Olsen (1983) elaborate the inconsistencies of the new institutionalism as it appears in the political sciences. Hernes (1977), in a series of studies of power in Norwegian society, investigates institutionalism from a sociological point of view. He defines institutions as rational contexts for allocating and distributing resources in society. For this purpose different institutional alternatives are developed in certain historical situations. The confusion in the applications of the term "institutionalism" derives partly from the different starting-points of the authors concerned. But it also stems from a historical gap which has existed for the last 40 years. Institutionalism in the Schumpeterian tradition has a very strong history in Scandinavia. Myrdal (1978) and Dahmén (1950), starting from an institutional and thus a historically oriented tradition, had a great impact on developments in this field in Scandinavia. But the tradition was almost forgotten during the 1970s, and we should now ask ourselves whether these researches have something to tell us today.

The renaissance of institutionalism and the challenge to formal economic theories brings us back to the fundamental questions of all economic research: what is to be produced, in what ways, under what conditions, for whom, what kind of relationships and institutional settings are involved, etc. The market and hierarchies approach supplies two institutional explanatory alternatives. Ouchi (1980) introduced clans as a further alternative. Sjöstrand extends the number of institutional alternatives to include three more forms: federations, movements and circles (1985: 16).

Whatever the approach or methodology, the transcending factor is organization. Schumpeter introduced the idea that "companies are regarded as drops in the ocean" (1928: 479). The "ocean" is the market and the notion of the "invisible guiding hand" seems to provide an excuse for the lack of any explanation of empirical phenomena in economic theory. On industrial markets, for example, where buyer and seller are both companies, we now know that relationships between these companies are often organized *not* via the market (i.e. via the price-system) but are influenced by factors such as mutual confidence in the other party's ability to solve the technical problems involved, confidence in the establishment of long-lasting relationship that will provide both parties with the necessary development resources, etc. (Hägg and Johansson, 1982). The investment share is thus not only a function of revenues and estimated market potentials but also a consequence of decision-making processes in the networks of which the firms form a part. Further, at least in Europe, the problem of resource employment is no longer defined simply by the demands of the market (as expressed in enforced cost reductions), but is being solved by complicated negotiations between special-interest groups (e.g. unions) and political systems (e.g. municipalities and governments).

The emergence of the information society affects the organization of industry and its relationship with other economic sectors. All these changes are interrelated, and the diversity of economic research may perhaps provide us with as many sensible explanations as there are problems.

The contributions in this book raise a great many crucial questions about the wide range of industrial change. The methodological starting-points and theoretical interests vary. They represent psychological, managerial, philosophical, organizational, industrial-organizationist and sociological views and interpretations. They all share an interest in economic organizations and their evolution.

The book is divided into four parts. Part I discusses some general problems of industrial development and the way in which it is organized. Part II is concerned with an understanding of the role of economics and politics and the relationship between them, in organizing industrial development. All the contributions in this part draw upon empirical research. Part III takes up different strategies for industrial development and discusses some of the related problems. Part IV addresses problems connected with the design and control of decision-making, and some of the related question of rationality and efficiency. Organizational action and theories of choice are discussed on a normative and to some extent also an explanatory methodological basis. The philosophy of organizational design and its role in evolutionary change is investigated.

The organizing of industry is the key interest in macro- and microeconomics and business administration. The variety of microeconomic-oriented industrial economists is great, and they could perhaps provide the necessary explanatory bridge between macroeconomic processes and developments at the corporate level. The concept of strategic behavior represents one possible connection between industrial economics and business administration (Scherer, 1984: 15). Business administration and organization theory generate the rich empirical information available to us about actual strategic behavior and decision-making in business. In the first contribution to this book Frederic Scherer addresses the world's productivity-growth slump from an industrial econo-mist's point of view. His paper analyses trends in productivity growth in the industrialized countries and focuses in greater detail a possible cause of falling growth rates, namely a decline in research, development, and inventive activity. For all the seven countries, except Japan, for which data were analysed, there was an absolute decline in patenting activity prior to 1973. For all but Sweden, there was a clear decline in the growth rate of real research and investment in development. Possible reasons for this retrogression in R&D and patenting activity are explored.

Rolf Lundin examines the concept of organizational economy and argues that it provides us with relevant and useful approaches. The organizational econ-omy is characterized by various kinds of systematic phenomena: coalitions provide actors and organizations with better control possibilities, large invest-ment projects can become institutionalized and specific roles emerge which are described by the concepts of "representative man" and "enterprising man". The discussion refers to empirical studies conducted in Scandinavia.

Ilan Vertinsky uses analogies from ecological studies of resilient animal populations in order to explore patterns of decision-making and control processes in the Japanese economy. The focus of this contribution is the study of industrial decision-making and the formulation of public policy in Japan. His model posits ecologically sound relationships between the myopic search for individual efficiency through competition and the long-term collective quest for resilience. The paper investigates patterns of decision-making and organization (1) within firms, (2) within the industrial groups, (3) within the public sector, and (4) in the linkages between the public and private sectors. Evidence is provided that confirms the existence of dual control systems similar to the one found in the animal studies that balance the competing demands of the individual short-term pursuit of efficiency and the collective maintenance of resilience. The two control systems were found at every level of the industrial decision-making and public-policy processes.

Despite some misgivings most societies recognize the company as an instrument for the pursuit of business. It is a piece of society and is therefore regulated by social and legal norms. The big corporation, however, represents a much larger chunk, and the whole question of regulation and control thus becomes vitally important. But "it" – the big corporation – is by no means a clearcut of definitive entity. On the contrary it is a rather fluid phenomenon composed of numerous firms and legal units and governed by certain controlling interests (the "sway group" in the terminology of Stymme, 1970: 29). Bengt Sandkull re-examines the role of the corporation in society, and its relation to society, in order to discuss ways in which it might be controlled, and by whom. In addressing this question he discusses production (the labor process), human communication and power systems in society. To exemplify the labor process he chooses the car industry, because of its all-pervading impact on society.

What are the mechanisms which cause clashes between our standards and our frames of reference? How do they interfere with development and the organization of development? Sten Jönsson examines accounting practices and their consequences for what is perceived as normal or deviant. Standards are powerful tools. Justified by efficiency, standards can be used to establish monopolies as well as professions or departments. The most threatening thing about standards, however, may be that they provide a vehicle for domination that is essentially unintended. Conceptual standards determine in some way what can and cannot be said. They define the terms in which their own functionality may be discussed. And what is the consequence? Accounting systems that everybody complains about but nobody thinks we can change!

Part II of the book takes up one of the most important problems of contemporary societies: the relationships between the private and public sectors. This relationship is encumbered by a number of controversial myths. One of the myths concerns the differences or similarities between the two sectors as regards efficiency and effectiveness. The private sector is often taken as the positive example of effective organization, and its solutions are compared with those of the public sector. Another common myth refers to the hierarcical relationship between "public" and "private". In fact this is two myths: either people see the public sector as controlling the private, or vice versa. In complex industrial societies the relationship is much more intricate and complex than either of the myths suggest. Much empirical research is needed to throw light on the processes and patterns that actually constitute the relationship and to distinguish ideal models from *de facto* functioning. David Hickson and associates investigate whether or not management action is affected by government and public agencies. They look beyond the abstractions of state and economy, and try to discover whether major strategic decisions are affected. They also examine possible differences between organizations. The results of their research were an unanticipated by-product of the Bradford studies of strategic decision-making in organizations. The authors describe the influence on strategic decisions exerted by government departments and public agencies, as experienced by the top managers and administrators interviewed.

A prominent theme in the current economic debate is industrial policy. Much of this discussion is dominated by various normative stances. In Sweden and probably elsewhere these normative biases have influenced a great deal of research. Wolff and Brunsson have therefore approached the question of industrial policy from more general systemic frames of reference. Industrial policy exemplifies the mutual dependence between politics and economics. Wolff, starting from a structural analysis of the actor systems of industrial policy – politics, the public administration, industry – examines the internal properties of each actor system and its couplings with the other systems. Society's functional differentiation is taken as the basis for an analysis of the interdependencies between industrial-policy actors. Brunsson focuses upon the leading role of the politicians in industrial policy, as the Swedish debate is largely based on this bias. He challenges the assumption that the state controls, or at least strives to control, large parts of societal development, in this case the industrial sector. Both contributions build on empirical research.

Högberg, Norbäck and Stenberg describe some empirical studies of government policies for technological development in Remote Sensing and Bioenergy. They present an interorganizational framework in order to analyse innovative processes in different industrial sectors. The four main actors involved are public agencies which administer government policy instruments, researchers, business firms and public agencies and other institutions using new technology. Both sectors are described as policy sectors, which means that "market forces" (business firms and researchers) are unlikely to become successful innovators without the political support of the public sector (public agencies which administer government policies and public agencies using the technologies).

This part concludes with a discussion of politics as an essential ingredient in business strategy. Larsson examines the interplay between business environments and strategy development. The behavior of managers in strategy development is usually referred to in terms of the structure of the decision-making process. Uncertainty-reduction and commitment-creation are described in existing theory as ingredients in rational or quasi-rational strategy formulation. The question of decision rationality in integrative strategy development is discussed. The strategic action environment in which managers work is described in terms of handling shifts in the process and of adapting arguments, problem-demarcation and stakeholder-support to the needs of the particular situation.

Part III investigates particular aspects of industrial development and looks also beyond industrial society. There are reliable signals that industrial society is changing. What directions these changes may take is far from clear. At the corporate level a stronger interconnectedness between firms can be discerned. People in organizations are also pressing more strongly for healthy, meaningful and rewarding jobs. The tendency towards quality, service, productivity and the use of new technology in organizations calls for commitment and motivation on the part of those involved in developing these areas. Over the last few years a great deal has been published on the subject of leadership, and this can be seen at least partly as an answer to these new needs in organizations. Management, as consisting mainly of planning and control, is distinguished from leadership, which focuses on the internal and external political function of the top of any organization. On a basis of empirical research Anders Edström investigated the interrelation between changes in business conditions and their consequences for the leadership of real-life business organizations.

The development of a new product line or the revision of an existing line of business are difficult undertakings requiring an exceptional amount of motivation and creativity, as well as the co-operation and trust of the people involved. Corporate innovation processes often fail because of external factors, but more often they fail because of internal obstacles such as lack of support, insufficient preparation, or plain error. Gerhard Mensch's article focuses on the internal risks of failure ("internal uncertainties") resulting from disturbances in human relations and organizational behavior. The author introduces the concept of the favorable positioning of the firm, and postulates that other things being equal a firm's favorable position tends to deteriorate naturally as its technology base gets older (Wolff's Law of Progress). Corporate innovation processes take time. Hence, the preconditions for the success of any single

innovation within the firm may deteriorate faster than organized innovative
activity can progress. For many firms this reported failure to seize the market
opportunities eventually leads to an unmanageable and irreversible situation
("shake-out"). This article highlights the findings of an extensive, exploratory,
"clinical" field study of innovation processes in small, medium, and medium-
large industrial firms in Berlin.

Economic stagnation has its own dynamic features. Decline and stagnation are
organizational phenomena which have still been largely disregarded in research, although there is an intimate relation between the different business
developmental phases. One aspect of decline and stagnation concerns the
process by which products are "disinvested". Product disinvestment is an
important element in the life cycle of a product, and it has been neglected in
both theoretical and empirical research. The bias towards growth has simply
been too strong. Sternhufvud and Wolff investigate obstacles to the disinvestment decision and to the implementation of product disinvestment, and on a
basis of some empirical case studies they suggest prescriptive devices for
organizing this difficult process.

Herbert Simon discusses ways of understanding and developing the new
advances in electronic communication. He advocates a shift from the common
focus on the availability of information to a focus on the capacity for attending
to information. He asks whether the workplaces of the future will be more, or
less, congenial to human beings than workplaces are today. His third question
concerns the impact of the new information technology on the distribution of
power in organizations.

It is widely recognized today that economic developments in the northern
hemisphere are closely interrelated with developments in the South. The
current debate about ways in which the less developed or "underdeveloped"
countries should be helped and given aid of different types, raises the whole
question of the context of development and of reasonable forms of cooperation. Organization theory seems to have almost totally ignored the
contributions that it could perhaps make to the solution of these problems. We
can learn a great deal both from Bob Geldof's Life-Aid Project, and from the
contemporary organization of development projects – often unsuccessful not
only in the short but also, and even more, in the long run. Bo Hedberg starts
by discussing ways in which information technology could help the developing
countries, and considers the opportunities for decentralization which it can
open up. Can information technology perhaps provide developing countries
with the necessary infrastructure to solve their own problems in their own
culture- und ecology-bounded way?

In conclusion Part IV takes up some major issues of organizations research.
The concepts of decision-making in organizational choice, organizational

action and control are discussed. Our "theories-in-use" about decision-making, acting and control are biased as much by rational as by cultural features. An awareness of these biases and assumptions will help us towards a better design in our organizations.

Herbert Simon, James G. March and others revolutionized organization theory in the late 1950s by introducing the concept of bounded rationality. The challenge to the classical model continued during the 1960s with the introduction of the "garbage-can" model, largely based on research results from studies of Norwegian educational organizations and computer simulation. During the 1970s the topic was pursued by the next generation of researchers. While most of these work in the USA (William H. Starbuck, John W. Meyer, Brian Rowan, W. Richard Scott and others), there is also in increasing number of Swedish researchers who have recently launched the concept of action rationality to replace that of decision rationality. Czarniawska and Wolff discuss the empirical basis of Scandinavian organization studies, their culture-bound generality and their relevance to other cultural contexts. Their paper is a plea for greater awareness of the cultural dependence of all research concerned with social realities. It is also a plea for more comparative studies.

James March's article summarizes some recent work on the role of decision-making in theories of choice. Behavioral research on the way in which decisions are made in organizations contrast the theoretical concepts of decision-making implicit in theories of choice. Prescriptions based solely on theoretical models and disregarding the learning and imagination of the decision-makers thus fail in their purpose. The clues provided, which are supposed to help us to think about decision processes in organizations, do no more than offer a few fixed points in an otherwise confusing and complex organized world.

Czarniawska/Wolff and March discuss theories of decision-making and action in organizations in a general way. Monthoux then presents an action frame of reference developed in a socialist-economic context. He starts from a technical definition of action, as typical of capitalist societies. We might expect to find this narrow definition ("what is worth doing is simply what pays best, and what pays best is what is valued most highly") transcended in socialistic contexts, for ideological reasons at least. According to Monthoux this definition of action is taken for granted in capitalist societies, whereas socialism does at least provide an opportunity for an immanent critique of the concept. He introduces us to the praxeology of the Polish philosopher Tadeusz Kotarbinsky.

The question of control is one of the prominent themes in current organization theory. In his contribution Richard Cyert confronts the simple Neo-classical model of organization control determined by the decision rule about marginal costs equalling marginal revenues, with decision-making processes as they actually occur in individual firms. Firms establish targets and then adopt a control approach to attain the targets. In a sense the optimal control techniques replace profit maximization as the objective of the firm.

The organizations of today are badly designed. Big improvements could be made to minimize the harm which organizations inflict on their members and on society. Nystrom and Starbuck's contribution can therefore be regarded as a milestone on the way to a Theory of Organizational Harm. Their article raises a lot of urgent questions about the relationship between organization theory and praxis. It suggests a program for research, but primarily it offers advice about a more appropriate research praxis.

These varied contributions provide an overview of the concerns of organization theory today. They do not give many ready-made answers, but they raise a lot of questions and should therefore encourage a more fruitful approach to the problems of the real world and the future. About this (research) future Hegel declares:

'... this new world is perfectly realised just as little as the newborn child ... A building is not finished when its foundation is laid ... In the same way science, the crowning glory of a spiritual world, is not found complete in its initial stages'. (Hegel, G. W. F., The Phenomenology of Mind, London 1931: 75/6).

References

Coase, R. H. (1937) The Nature of the Firm. *Economia* 4, pp. 386–405.
– (1972) Industrial Organization: A Proposal for Research. *Policy Issues and Research Opportunities in Industrial Organization*. Victor R. Fuchs (Ed.), New York: National Bureau of Economic Research, pp. 59–73.
Dahmén, E. (1950) Entrepreneurial Activity in Swedish Industry in the Period 1919–1939, Vol. I, Stockholm.
Dugger, W. M. (1983) The Transaction Cost Analysis of Oliver E. Williamson: A New Synthesis. *Journal of Economic Issues,* Vol. XVII, No. 1, March, pp. 95–114.
Hägg, I., Johanson, J. (1982) Företag i nätverk. Stockholm.
Hernes, G. (1977) Mot en institusjonell Økonomi. *Forhandlingsøkonomi og blandingsadministrasjon.* Gudmund Hernes (Ed.), Bergen–Oslo–Tromsø, pp. 196–242.
March, J. G., Olsen, J. P. (1984) The New Institutionalism: Organizational Factors in Political Life. *The American Political Science Review,* Vol. 78, pp. 734–749.
Myrdal, G. (1978) Institutional Economics. *Journal of Economic Issues,* 4, pp. 771–783.
Nelson, R. R., Winter, S. G. (1982) An Evolutionary Theory of Economic Change. Cambridge Mass.
Ouchi, W. (1980) Markets, Bureaucracies, Clans. *Administrative Science Quaterly,* 1.

Scherer, F. M. (1984) On the Current State of Knowledge in Industrial Economics. International Institute of Management IIM, Berlin, 24.

Schumpeter, J. (1928) Unternehmer. *Handwörterbuch der Staatswissenschaften.* L. Elster, A. Weber, F. Wieser (Eds.), Jena, pp. 476–485.

Sjöstrand, S.-E. (1985) Samhällsorganisation (The Organization of Society – Towards an Institutional Micro-Economic Theory). Lund.

Thurow, L. C. (1983) Dangerous Currents. The State of Economics. New York.

Part I. Industrial Dynamics – Some General Problems

The World Productivity Growth Slump

Frederic M. Scherer[1])

This paper addresses what I consider to be the most important economic problem facing the Western industrialized world – the productivity growth slump that has been evident since the early 1970s. (I exclude a more important problem, the arms race, as non-economic and largely unrelated.) I confront the productivity problem, long a concern of Walter Goldberg, with some apprehension. A considerable portion of my research has been focused on the U.S. manifestations, yet I, like other scholars, cannot pretend to understand fully what happened even in my own homeland. About European conditions and European data I know even less. Nevertheless, the problem is so important that it justifies the risk of falling into error.

Consider the experience of the United States. During the 1970s, aggregate productivity growth fell sharply. Had output per hour of work continued to grow through the 1970s at its 1960s trend rate, private sector output in 1983, assuming the same level of employment, would have been 31 percent higher than it actually was. Thirty-one percent! How much could have been accomplished with an increment to GNP of that size!

The first question that arose as I began to probe beyond U.S. borders was, how comparable has the experience been in other nations? Tables 1 and 2 provide some evidence for twelve industrialized nations. In nearly every case, there is evidence of a decline, often sharp, during the mid- to late-1970s. In manufacturing, for which the productivity statistics are probably more reliable than for overall GDP, and which historically has been one of the most dynamic sectors, the slump is somewhat less dramatic but still unmistakeable. For GDP the simple average decline from 1961–68 to 1973–79 is 2.33 percentage points, which in six years compounds to an output shortfall of 15 percent.

It was said in 1984 that productivity growth was resuming, at least in many nations, as the industrialized nations began to pull out of an exceptionally severe recession, and that things would soon be back to normal. One hopes so. But there are grounds for skepticism. It is well known that productivity rises as the economy emerges from recession, and resources that were underemployed

---

[1]) An earlier version of this paper was presented as keynote lecture at the Fontainebleau meetings of the European Association for Research in Industrial Economics in August 1984. The paper was written while the author was visiting scholar at the International Institute of Management, Berlin.

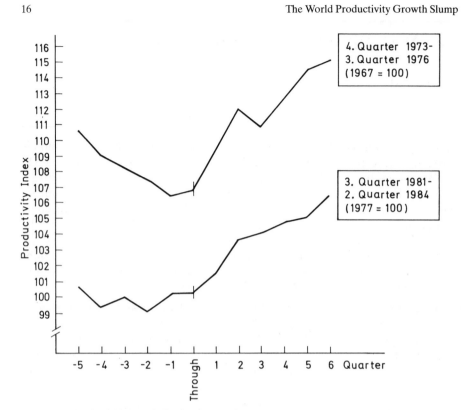

Figure 1:   Productivity Levels During two Major U.S. Recessions
Sources: U.S. Economic Report of the President, Appendix B Tables, various years.

during the slump become more fully employed without a commensurate increase in new hires. Figure 1 plots indices of output per employee hour in the U.S. private non-farm business sector for the twelve quarters surrounding the two most severe postwar recessions – one with a trough in March 1975, and the more recent recession with a trough in November 1982. Both curves exhibit strong recoveries in labor productivity, but the more recent post-trough six quarter growth was at an annualized rate of only 4.0 percent, compared to 5.2 percent for the mid-1970s recovery. Mitigating a pessimistic conclusion may be the differing pre-trough experiences, with much more productivity decline during the 1974–75 downturn. This undoubtedly reflected the sudden and largely unexpected character of that downturn, whereas 1981–82 was the partly anticipated second "dip" of an unusual "double-dip" recession which had already occasioned considerable slack-cutting. Still the data scarcely provide much support for the view that 1983–84, coming after four years of near-zero productivity growth, foreshadowed a new productivity growth boom.

Some Explanations

My use of 1973 as a dividing-point year follows what has become standard practice, at least in the United States. Although there are defensible grounds for the choice, it may also hide some information. It is difficult to be certain about when productivity growth rates turned downward, in part because 1973 was a year of unprecedented synchronized world-wide boom, during which output per worker might be expected to be abnormally high even for a peak year. Despite this, the data on GDP/employee (Table 1) reveal a modest 0.36 percentage point slackening of average growth rates from 1961–68 to 1968–73. When a computation is done for 1968–72 only, the decline widens to 0.45 percentage points. For five Table 2 nations on which comparable annual data on manufacturing sector productivity were available, the average productivity growth rates were 5.76% for 1960–68, 5.51% for 1968–73, and 5.37% for 1968–72. It cannot be ruled out that a decline was underway before 1973.

Late 1973 was, of course, when the first great OPEC price shock struck the world economy. It is reasonable to suppose that OPEC's actions contributed significantly to the decline of productivity growth. The large price increases of 1973–74 and 1979–80 drained from most industrialized nations funds that could not be respent immediately, providing one of the few clear examples in history of how income redistribution occasioned by monopoly pricing can trigger an

Table 1: Annual Growth Rate of Real Gross Domestic Product per Person Employed, Twelve Nations, Three Periods*

	1961–68 %	1968–73 %	1973–79 %
Canada	2.72	2.68	0.48
United States	2.58	1.48	0.36
Belgium	3.91	4.42	2.39
Denmark	3.36	3.12	1.35
France	4.68	4.68	2.83
West Germany	4.08	4.19	3.11
Italy	6.02	4.78	1.60
Netherlands	3.95	4.68	2.29
Norway	3.79	2.18	2.71
Sweden	3.66	2.83	0.61
United Kingdom	2.81	3.05	1.28
Japan	8.40	7.46	2.90
Simple Average	4.16	3.80	1.83

* Sources: Computed by the author from four OECD publications: *National Accounts: 1961–1978* (Paris: 1980); *National Accounts: 1964–1981* (Paris: 1983); *Labour Force Statistics: 1957–1968* (Paris: 1970); and *Labour Force Statistics: 1968–1979* (Paris: 1981).

Table 2:   Annual Growth Rate per Hour of Employment in Manufacturing, Twelve Nations, 1960–73 vs. 1973–82*

	1960–73 %	1973–82 %
Canada	4.5	1.6
United States	3.0	1.7
Belgium	7.0	6.0
Denmark	6.4	4.1
France	6.7	4.5
West Germany	5.7	3.6
Italy	6.9	3.7
Netherlands	7.6	4.8
Norway	4.5	2.0
Sweden	6.6	2.2
United Kingdom	4.4	1.8
Japan	10.7	7.2
Simple Average	6.2	3.6

* Source: Donato Alvarez, Brian Cooper (1984), Productivity Trends in Manufacturing in the U.S. and 11 Other Countries. *Monthly Labor Review* (U.S. Bureau of Labor Statistics), p. 53.

underconsumption recession. The price increases also forced governments to adopt, with varying alacrity, anti-inflationary measures. The combination of purchasing power leakages and deliberate macroeconomic brake-treading led to two world-wide recessions, and recession, we know, is detrimental to productivity growth. Also, the stop-and-go character of compensatory macro policies may have increased business planning uncertainties and spread to most industrialized nations what once was considered a peculiarly "British sickness".

Some economists, such as Hudson and Jorgenson (1978), have argued that the OPEC shocks had their main negative impact on productivity by biasing new capital investment in energy-saving directions. Since, they claim, energy-using technologies tend to be capital-intensive, the bias has ultimately been labor-using, implying reduced labor productivity. This seems implausible, in part because it is hard to find actual micro-examples of such substitution. It is at least as likely that in energy-intensive industries such as steel, petrochemicals and electricity generation, high energy prices have induced scale-up and other investments in newer technology that are *both* energy-saving *and* labor-saving. Also, as Denison has observed (1979: 141–142), the share of energy among all factor inputs appears too small to be responsible for much of the measured productivity growth decline unless improbably high substitution elasticities are assumed.

Dozens of other explanations have been proposed: e.g. demographics, the "modern kids don't want to work" hypothesis, the spread of an economy driven "underground" by high taxes, systematic productivity measurement error, declining investment (debatable for the United States), Mancur Olson's (1982) arterioschlerosis theory, the stifling effects and resource reallocations associated with government regulation, growing worker alienation (Weiskopf et al., 1983), merger mania, and much else. I agree with Denison (1979: 145) that there may be some validity in most conjectures, and that "it is possible, perhaps even probable, that everything went wrong at once among the determinants." Yet one would like more insight as to why the 1970s were the period in which everything happened to go wrong, and why everything went wrong *everywhere* – i.e. in most or all of the industrialized nations, with their widely varying demographics, institutions, tax structures, etc. If OPEC's actions are not of sufficient weight to carry the full explanatory burden, what other properly timed shock might have contributed?

R&D, Technological Change, and Productivity

When I began thinking about this paper, I had an answer for the United States but scarcely a clue (except for some provocative tabulations by Robert Evenson, 1984) for other nations. My research (Scherer, 1984, Chapters 15 and 16) and others' has shown that industrial research and development (R&D) has a powerful impact on productivity growth. In 1970 – well before the OPEC crisis – something went wrong with R&D in the United States. Company-financed R&D, which had been growing at 6.4 percent per year in real (i.e. GNP-deflator-adjusted) terms during the 1960s, peaked in 1969 and then declined for two years – an event unprecedented in post World War II history. In 1972 growth resumed, but at a much slower rate, at least until the late 1970s. Had the 1960s growth rate persisted, real R&D in 1981 would have been 38 percent higher than its actually recorded value. Foreshadowing the slowdown of R&D growth, real industrial basic research spending (which comprised only 3 to 4 percent of all industrial R&D) peaked in 1966 and did not attain its 1966 peak *level* again until 1979. At the time of the overall R&D spending peak, the U.S. Patent Office's applications backlog had been reduced to approximately two years. Two years after the R&D peak, the number of invention patents issued to U.S. corporations, which had been growing at 4.3 percent per annum during the 1950s and 1960s, peaked in 1971 and then declined by 27 percent from 1971 to 1978. Thus, the evidence of a pre-OPEC slowdown in invention and innovation is unmistakeable.

We know that R&D drives productivity growth only with a lag, although we know little about the exact lag structure. That the R&D slowdown had something to do with the U.S. productivity growth slump seems certain. My own research (Scherer, 1984: Chapter 16), which has taken into account more inter-industry spillovers than others' and shows higher social rates of return on R&D, suggests that the R&D growth slump explains only a part of the U.S. productivity growth slump. My best estimate of the impact is a retardation of annual productivity growth ranging between 0.2 and 0.4 percentage points. This estimate is subject to substantial statistical error and possibly to systematic bias – downward if the R&D cutbacks were triggered by a depletion of the pool of technological opportunities, upward if the cutbacks were induced by decreasing appropriability of the returns to R&D (Scherer, 1984: 290–291). There is much to be done toward understanding these important relationships better.

At this point, my work on R&D ended and I began research on whether "merger mania" might have been partly responsible for America's productivity growth problems. It is premature to report confident answers. But the invitation to write this paper spurred me to reconsider the R&D – productivity growth question from a broader, trans-national perspective. It seemed clear that the productivity growth slump was world-wide. Was it possible that changes in R&D had a causal role outside the United States? Or at least, was the decline in industrial R&D growth observed for the United States evident also in other nations?

As an old patent hand, I turned first to the data on patents applied for, and issued to, domestic residents of seven representative industrialized nations. Applications data are preferred over issues data because issues can vary from year to year for administrative reasons and because the average lag from application to issue is variable and sometimes quite long – as long as six years for Japan. Nevertheless, both sets of data are summarized in Table 3.[1]) The results are striking and surprising, at least to me. In seven of the thirteen cases (excluding the U.K. issues, for which data were unavailable), average patenting peaked in the 1963–68 period – long before the 1973 OPEC shock. In four instances, average patenting peaked in the 1969–73 period, which might be consistent with the hypothesis that demand-pull deficiencies resulting from the OPEC shock depressed subsequent activity. However, in each of those four cases, the single-year peak (or for Swiss applications, two-year peak) occurred *before* 1973, indicating the onset of decline before the OPEC shock. Indeed, in eleven of the thirteen cases, the peak occurred before 1973. Only Japan is the exception, with both applications and issued patents growing erratically but

---

[1]) The applications series is terminated in 1977 and the issues series in 1978 because after that, domestic patenting activity may have been affected by the availability of Europatents. The first Europatent applications were accepted in June 1978, and the first grants were made in January 1980.

Table 3: Trends in Patenting, Seven Nations, 1963–78*

Nations	Average Number of Patent Applications Filed by Nationals per Year			Average Number of Patents Issued per Year to Nationals			Peak Year	
	1963–68	1969–73	1973–77	1963–68	1969–73	1973–78	Applications	Issues
USA	67,470	70,234	64,112	46,289	51,294	44,754	1970	1971
France	17,061	14,061	12,025	14,451	10,821	7,822	1968	1968
West Germany	35,054	31,735	30,511	10,992	9,393	10,332	1965	1966
Sweden	4,740	4,484	4,287	1,720	2,245	1,857	1967	1970
Switzerland	5,520	5,915	5,616	4,646	4,156	3,494	1971–72	1966
United Kingdom	24,980	24,542	21,075	n.a.	10,000	8,626	1968	?
Japan	61,004	94,523	132,095	16,277	25,005	36,205	1968	

* Source: World Intellectual Property Organization, *Industrial Property*, Annual Statistical Reports. Data for East Germany were separated from those of West Germany using the *Statistisches Jahrbuch der Bundesrepublik*. Checks in other nations' statistical abstracts revealed the WIPO compendium to be generally accurate.

persistently – applications at an average rate of 6.6 percent per year and issues at 6.2 percent per year.

For the United States, as noted before, there is distinct evidence that the turning point in patenting followed with the correct lag from a change in company-financed R&D expenditures. For other nations, consistent data in the detail I would have desired were not available. The best I could do was to use the summary graphs on deflated industrial R&D expenditures (company- and government-financed) presented (without appropriate splicing) in two OECD publications (1979, 1984). For all seven nations (including the United States), the 1967–78 trend was generally upward, as expected. The question with which I confronted the data was therefore: was there evidence of a turning point, after which the growth of real R&D expenditures slackened for more than a year? The answer is, such turning points did materialize for every nation but Sweden, which experienced fairly smooth growth and only faint traces of retardation. The pre-retardation peak years, with a recapitulation of the patent application peak years, were as follows for the other six nations:

	Last Year Prior to R&D Retardation	Patent Application Peak Year
United States	1969	1970
France	1972	1968
West Germany	1971	1965
Switzerland	1969	1971–72
United Kingdom	1969	1968
Japan	1970,73	none

Two observations are warranted. First, there is further evidence that something happened to shock industrial R&D negatively before the OPEC shock of late 1973. The disparate timing of the R&D retardation points is not associated in any obvious way with business cycle movements. Second, although the patent and R&D turning points are seldom far apart in time, the lags are in the wrong direction for France, Germany, and the U.K. Despite strong growth on both variables, Japan's behavior conformed more closely to the expected lag structure. The first noticeable R&D slowdown, after a growth rate of 19 percent per annum over 1967–70, was followed by a fall in patent applications during 1971 and a resurgence only to 1970 levels in 1972. A second R&D slowdown beginning in 1974 was followed by stagnant patent application activity from 1975 through 1977, after which growth resumed. Overall, Japan achieved a much reduced but respectable 4 percent average real industrial R&D growth rate from 1970 through 1978.

One further point deserves mention. Following the declines in industrial R&D growth rates during the early 1970s, there was an acceleration in most nations' spending later in the 1970s. For the United States, the resurgence began in 1976. Between 1975 and 1983, real U.S. company-financed R&D grew at an average rate of 6.3 percent – nearly as rapidly as during the 1960s (U.S. National Science Foundation, 1984). For Japan, Germany and France, the upsurges came later, usually in 1979, and their persistence is not yet clear.

What Went Wrong With R&D?

The evidence I have been able to assemble suggests strongly that something happened to R&D during the late 1960s or early 1970s that preceded the OPEC price shock and that almost surely contributed to the world-wide productivity growth slump. It is important to recognize that it may not be necessary for R&D actually to decline in real terms to cause a productivity rate decline. When one considers what we know quantitatively about economic growth in the leading industrialized nations over the past two centuries, one is struck by the fact that while output per labor hour has been growing at approximately two percent per year, the amount of effort devoted to science and engineering has been growing at four to six percent. There may be a "law of nature" requiring some such disparity of growth rates (Scherer, 1984: 258–259). The absolute fall in patenting with slower real R&D growth rates would be consistent with such a law. That is, as technology advances, it may on average (but with important exceptions) become more and more costly to keep adding equivalent inventions at the same proportional rate.

The question remains, why did R&D growth rates slacken? And why have they accelerated again during the late 1970s?

One possible explanation, which I shall rule out immediately, at least for the United States, is that R&D growth was curbed by supply-side resource constraints, e.g., by the limited availability of scientists and engineers. It is true that in the United States, enrollments in many fields of engineering and natural science stagnated during the 1970s. But the reason is almost surely that young would-be professionals saw engineers being laid off and anticipated better career opportunities in business, law, medicine, and the like than in industrial R&D (or teaching). Renewed R&D growth in the late 1970s brought the expected supply-side increases in technical education enrollments. We must look therefore to the demand side.

Again for the United States, there is a simple demand-side explanation. There is evidence from two quite different but rich data sets that the profitability of industrial R&D was severely depressed during the mid-1970s, and was probably also depressed during the early 1970s. See Ravenscraft (1983), and

Ravenscraft and Scherer (1982). Firms responded by pruning their R&D portfolios, and either because they overshot or because other conditions changed, profitability seems to have risen during the late 1970s, inducing a resurgence of R&D spending.

Nevertheless, we are compelled to carry the argument one step farther and ask, why did the profitability of R&D fall? Here we can only speculate. There are two main possibilities.

One is that by the end of the 1960s, we had through development "fished out" the pool of technological opportunities more rapidly than it could be replenished through advances in science and new technical breakthroughs. Recognizing that there are clear exceptions such as computers and microelectronics, I find this hypothesis plausible for at least the United States.[2]) During the 1930s and World War II, there was very little new civilian sector "fishing." Following the War, there was an explosion of private-sector industrial R&D activity and investment in the new products and processes it generated. With rapid exploitation of the opportunities, diminishing returns eventually set in with respect to the development of further advances, the diffusion through new capital investment of frontier technology, and the feedback through demand-pull from capital investment to incentives for investing in improvement R&D. In other words, the world may since the late 1960s have been experiencing a Schumpeter-Kondratief downturn. To distinguish the point I am making from the argument that the macroeconomy experiences "long waves" of some regular periodicity, I hasten to add that it may be the *first* such clearly evident Schumpeter-Kondratief downturn.

Why the same phenomena should hold almost simultaneously in other nations generally considered to lag the United States technologically (at least during the 1960s) is not clear. One might have supposed that with a greater distance to travel to reach the applications frontier, they would at least have had more incentive to sustain adaptive R&D through the investment demand-pull feedback mechanism. But if the unexploited technological possibilities simply weren't attractive, this mechanism would be thwarted. In such a case, one would see also in Europe a slowdown of R&D and a retardation of productivity growth. But with still-unexploited possibilities for diffusion, the (reduced) European productivity growth *rate* would remain higher than that of the United States (which was nearer, but by no means at, the frontier). This is pretty much what the available evidence shows.[3])

---

[2]) For a further development of this argument, see my 1977 paper reproduced in Scherer (1984: Chapter 14).

[3]) Added support comes from Kontorovich (1984). Soviet Union enterprises are required to plan and report ex post on the savings they have achieved by introducing new methods of production. Using aggregations of those reports, Kontorovich shows that the gains from innovation have been secularly declining.

This explanation leaves two puzzles unresolved. First, why have the Japanese maintained such a high rate of productivity growth, patenting growth, and (less clearly) real R&D growth while the activities of other nations were stagnating? That the Japanese started farther from the frontier than others is a plausible answer for the 1960s, but for the 1970s it can no longer be accepted, since the Japanese were at the frontier in many areas of technology and were continuing to advance rapidly. Second, why has there been an acceleration of real R&D growth rates in the later 1970s, led, it would appear, by the frontier-straddling United States?

One possibility is that the pool of unexploited technological possibilities had somehow become replenished, and that the Japanese were fortunate in maintaining their R&D momentum, rather than having to rebuild it, as conditions became more propitious. This hypothesis cannot be ruled out, although subjecting it to empirical verification will be extraordinarily difficult.

Another possibility is even more speculative. Is it conceivable that the Japanese were not only the odd men out, but also an important *cause* of the R&D behavior observed in America and Europe? The Japanese rise to technological leadership, accompanied by vigorous export activity, was both swift and largely unexpected. It struck hard at the sales and profitability of frontier Western enterprises, perhaps first in the United States and then in Europe. As theoretical work on the dynamics of research and development rivalry has shown (Kamien, Schwartz, 1982: Chapter 4, 5; Scherer, 1984: Chapter 5, 6), established firms can react to a new technological challenge in either of two ways. They can turn submissive, reducing the intensity of their R&D efforts, or they can intensify their efforts to retain or regain market leadership. The more of an unassailable lead the innovative rival has, e.g., because its advances were unanticipated or because it has unusual strengths, the more likely a submissive reaction is. In view of this, the initial reaction of Western enterprises to unanticipated Japanese advances already well underway may have been submissive. But as the continuing Japanese rivalry at the frontier became anticipated, and as Western firms realized that they either had to mount a strenuous technological effort or be relegated permanently to a secondary position, R&D efforts accelerated. This explanation is consistent with anecdotal evidence on the behavior of U.S. and European companies.[4]) It is also possible that the slackening of European patenting during the mid- and late-1960s represented a submissive reaction not to Japanese inroads, but to "le Défi Américain" as U.S. firms came to hold what Servan-Schreiber (1967: 63, 65, 101) characterized as "overwhelming" leadership in research and development.

---

[4]) See e.g. Industry Takes Dominant Science Role. *New York Times,* July 17, 1984, p. C1; and Europe's Technology Revival. *New York Times,* May 21, 1984, p. D1.

Conclusion

Much of what I have said here is highly speculative, intended more to stimulate than to be a definitive statement on recent events. Yet if there is even a grain of validity to my speculations, there is considerable work of a microeconomic character to be done toward illuminating the sources of the world productivity growth slump. One cause was almost surely a retardation of industrial research, development, and invention. My calculations suggest that it was not a preponderant cause, at least in the United States, but the estimates are subject to considerable uncertainty and could stand further refinement. It is possible that our theories of research and development rivalry can help explain why the growth rates of R&D and patenting declined. Here linkages between industrial R&D data and international trade flow data are required. Microeconomic analysis is also needed to determine how productivity has been affected by government regulation, mergers, and "paper entrepreneurship." And detailed work must occur to improve the quality of our output measures, e.g., by developing better hedonic price indices for technologically advanced products. There is much to be done. Productivity growth questions are too important to leave to the macroeconomists.

References

Denison, E. F. (1979) *Accounting for Slower Economic Growth.* Washington: Brookings Institution.

Evenson, R. E. (1984) International Invention: Implications for Technology Market Analysis. *Patents, R&D and Productivity.* Zvi Griliches (Ed.), National Bureau of Economic Research Conference Report, Chicago: University of Chicago Press, pp. 89–122.

Europe's Technology Revival (1984) *New York Times,* May, 21, p. D1.

Hudson, E. A., Jorgenson, D. W. (1978) Energy Policy and U.S. Economic Growth. *American Economic Review,* Vol. 68, pp. 118–123.

Industry Takes Dominant Science Role (1984) *New York Times,* July 17, p. C1.

Kamien, M., Schwartz, N. L. (1982) *Market Structure and Innovation.* Cambridge: Cambridge University Press.

Kontorovich, V. (1984) Technological Progress and the Soviet Productivity Slowdown. Draft Manuscript, Pennsylvania: University of Pennsylvania.

Olson, M. (1982) *The Rise and Decline of Nations.* New Haven: Yale University Press.

Organization for Economic Cooperation and Development (1979) *Trends in Industrial R&D: 1967–1975.* Paris.

– (1984) *OECD Science and Technology Indicators: Resources Devoted to R&D.* Paris.

Ravenscraft, D. (1983) Structure-Profit Relationships at the Line of Business and Industry Level. *Review of Economics and Statistics,* Vol. 65, pp. 22–31.

Ravenscraft, D., Scherer, F. M. (1982) The Lag Structure of Returns to R&D. *Applied Economics,* Vol. 14, pp. 603–620.

Scherer, F. M. (1984) *Innovation and Growth: Schumpeterian Perspectives.* Cambridge: MIT Press.

Servan-Schreiber, J. J. (1968) *The American Challenge.* New York: Atheneum.

U.S. National Science Foundation (1984) *Science Resources Studies Highlights,* NSF 84–329.

Weiskopf, T., Bowles, S., Gordon, D. M. (1983) Hearts and Minds: A Social Model of U.S. Productivity Growth. *Brookings Papers on Economic Activity,* No. 2, pp. 381–450.

Organizational Economy –
The Politics of Unanimity and Suppressed
Competition

Rolf A. Lundin

The Organizational Economy

Our point of departure in the following argument is the presumed existence of something we can call the organizational economy. In describing the structures and processes involved, we deliberately try to avoid the traditional terminology. But this does not mean that we want to come up with unique terms. Rather, the idea is that a different language sometimes evokes different thoughts and feelings, whereas a traditional vocabulary tends to chain our mental acitivities to traditional insights and ways of describing the world around us.

However, that is not the same thing as saying that the ideas proposed are void of empirical evidence. In fact several empirical studies have been made, which describe the outlines of the organizational economy. A Norwegian contribution, a report on power in Norway,[1] disentangled many relevant points. This work focused on the role of negotiations rather than the market as a basis for relations in the economic system, and in light of this surveyed the power conditions affecting private and public organizations in Norwegian society. More specifically, data on the organizations of trade and industry, on multinationals, on the mass media, and on civil servants in the public administration were all extensively reported.

In Sweden several empirical studies have been devoted to one of the major features of the present situation, i.e. the overlapping of "public" and "private". These studies encompass the implementation of public policy in the economic domain (the downturn of the 1970s precipitated vigorous governmental action in several areas), as well as local responses to crises in industry. In both these instances the interface between public and private seems to be changing.[2]

---

[1] The report actually consists of more than 100 reports, books and articles. A summary was published as an Norwegian official report (NOU, 1982: 3).

[2] Several studies of this question have been made in Scandinavia. Two of these are Leif Lindmark (1983) *Strukturomvandling och industristöd* (Industrial change and government support). Malmö: Liber, and (1984) *Kommunal näringspolitik. Omfattning och erfarenheter* (Local Government Industrial Policy in Sweden: Scope and Experiences). Stockholm: SIND, 1984: 8.

There is no coherent or commonly accepted theory of the organizational economy. Thus the fragmentary version that follows should be regarded as personal to myself, in the sense that I have made no attempt to incorporate more than a few of the many studies relevant to the subject. There are two important characteristics of the organizational economy:

1. The abundance of organizations. Society is thoroughly "organizationalized" in that the number of organizations is overwhelming, and that the organizations embrace almost all aspects of life. Most organizations depend on others for their very existence, while some organizations are also diametrically opposed to one another.
2. The overlapping between private and public. The sectors are intertwined to such a degree that it is no longer possible to distinguish clearly between them. Further, in practice the integration appears both natural and necessary. There is certainly nothing unnatural in co-operation between private and public interests. In fact in many instances it is a necessity.

Neither of these two characteristics is new, but in present-day society they seem to affect the functioning of the economy more profoundly than they have done before. In economic behavior it is possible to discern a set of systemic phenomena and behaviors related to the abundance of organizations and to the integration of public and private interests.

Some Systemic Phenomena

In illustration, three phenomena will be introduced and described in this section: coalitions between actors and organizations, the institutionalization of projects, and the erasing of corporate boundaries. This list is by no means exhaustive, but it is probably enough to illustrate the point that the organizational economy has a bearing on system behavior.

Coalitions

The lone wolf does not enjoy a strong position in the organizational economy. Actors without a foothold in some appropriate organization find it increasingly difficult to exert any influence on economic activities. Conversely, belonging to an organization grants liberty to the actor, especially if he is able to exert influence on intraorganizational activities. Ties with an organization are useful when it comes to affecting and controlling developments and events involving other organizations and other people. In order to augment the control possibilities even further, it can be useful and appropriate to form a coalition, especially if interests overlap.

The need for coalitions has developed and is still developing in various ways. One major factor in Western countries is related to the problems of unemployment. In Sweden this kind of problem has been most obvious at the local level, where actors and organizations of various types have been activated. In connection with unemployment, coalitions have become a popular problem-solving instrument. Unemployment has been defined as unacceptably high, and has become the subject of close discussion between local government politicians and employers. Coalitions have been formed of actors and organizations with an interest in ways of solving employment problems. Politicians are motivated by their responsibility for employment and tax revenue. Employers are motivated by their need to promote the interests of the industrialist group and by the opportunities for utilizing recent commitments to the employment question, or for exploiting the business climate and entrepreneurship. In general the structure of business is changing. Risk-taking is no longer the sole responsibility of companies, but factories and machinery are quite often owned by the community at large. (One might argue that the meaning of "infrastructure" is changing as a result of public involvement in business crises.) Joint ventures are one of the possible outcomes of such coalitions.

Not only politicians and employers become involved in coalitions. In many communities special officials are appointed to organize co-operation between public agencies and employers. The financial managers of local government are also often deeply involved in questions connected with local trade and industry. Public officials regard this involvement as a way of fulfilling their tasks as civil servants.

Further, union representatives often take part in coalitions. In one sense the traditional antagonism between employers and unions is breaking up. More often than not unions are heavily involved in ventures of the kind mentioned here. In these endeavors employers and unions act side by side to further the common cause.

In the Norwegian report mentioned above, coalitions based on various interests of this kind have been dubbed "iron triangles". The examples cited there are at the national level, but to extend the metaphor to our present case it seems appropriate to speak of "iron squares" as there are four parties involved: politicians, employers, civil servants and union representatives.

The type of coalition we have been discussing up to now is initiated by a crisis and by a general concern for increasing local unemployment. The coalition draws its strength from the fact that the problem is a serious one. The actors involved find themselves exposed to very strong demands for concrete action. The perception of crisis provides an impulse for action – a "push effect".

A coalition may also have its main origin in the perception of possibilities. The exploitation of government support is such an initiating factor. Here it is appropriate to speak of a "pull effect", where a vision provides the main motive power. Sometimes work groups are formed to investigate the possibilities of attracting financial support from the government for various projects. Sometimes these work groups achieve almost permanent status and their membership is formalized. In this way a more stable organization comes into being. The concept of the "boundary organization"[3]) has been used to stress the interorganizational and stabilizing functions of these organizations. The boundary organization represents a superstructure in the organizational world, in the sense that several other organizations are linked together by the boundary organization. Dual membership is its linchpin.

Beside these kinds of coalitions, several pseudo-coalitions[4]) have also appeared. It has become fashionable to organize in response to real or imagined threats against local trade and industry. Boundary organizations have been formed even where the prospects of obtaining government support are nil, and "iron squares" have been established where local employment is not a serious problem.

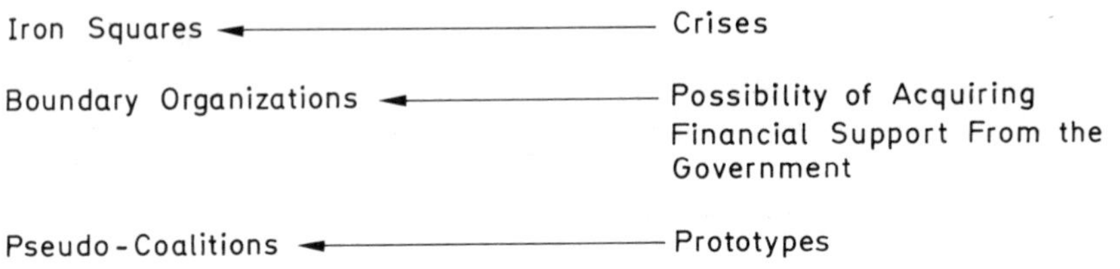

Iron Squares ◄──────────────── Crises

Boundary Organizations ◄─────────── Possibility of Acquiring
                                    Financial Support From the
                                    Government

Pseudo-Coalitions ◄──────────── Prototypes

Figure 1:   Examples of Coalitions and Their Main Driving-Forces

One conspicuous fact about these kinds of coalition is their inconspicuousness. Their deliberations are not public, and in general there is good reason for suspecting that horse-trading is a natural ingredient in the way they work.

---

[3]) Karelmo, P. (1983) Organisationsteoretiska perspektiv på förmedling av industri- och region-alpolitik: Gränsorganisationer i fokus (Organization Theory Perspectives on Industrial and Regional Policy: Boundary Organizations in Focus). Unpublished manuscript, University of Umeå.
[4]) Karelmo, P. (1982) Näringspolitiska myndigheter och organisationer i Norrbotten (Organizations and Authorities Related to Industrial Policy in the Province of Norrbotten). Unpublished manuscript, University of Umeå.

Institutionalized Projects

Projects of the investment type can become "institutions"[5]) when they are launched in several organizations at once. The foundation for the institutionalization is laid when a project's initiators try to promote wide support for it. Arguments are evolved in such a way that the usefulness of the project becomes evident simultaneously to members of several other organizations.

The plastic bike – Itera – may serve as a well-known example of an institutionalized project. Originally the plastic bike was a fairly simple invention: some engineers constructed a bicycle that would not rust. Eventually the production of the bicycle became the hope of a small crisis-stricken town in Northern Sweden, with the introduction of a technology new to that part of the country. Without going into details we need merely state that several organizations became involved in the project: the Ministry for Industry, the local government of the town, various industrial companies, marketing people who launched a worldwide campaign, and so on.

As a result of this introduction process, the project is almost automatically guaranteed survival as a solution-in-principle. A solid foothold in several organizations means that the project is developed and becomes firmly entrenched right across the board. Arguments are evolved gradually in these organizations, so that the main ideas of the project survive even if the project itself comes under attack elsewhere. The initial character of a solution-in-principle promotes its survival among the individual people who come into contact with it and who participate in the work involved. Arguments often develop differently and even disparately, but the label of the project survives as a common denominator. Thus the project becomes an institution in the minds of the actors concerned. It is in itself a subject of discussion, and its mere existence as a matter of common importance affects the main actors in their dealings with other matters as well.

An institutionalized project is strongly resistant to any negative information about its own general usefulness. Support for the project in the shape of positive arguments is developed and internalized as part of the institutionalization process. Negative evidence even seems to strengthen the project, since it serves to mobilize the support. Nor does hard data affect it; economic data can easily be dismissed on grounds of uncertainty of alleged errors in the evaluation base. Confusion about what are the "correct" yardsticks can always be used as an excuse for not taking negative information into account.

Thus it seems virtually impossible to dispose of a project by using expert judgment. The issue has to be resolved by a political decision in some suitable

---

[5]) Brunsson, N. (1983) Projektinstitutionalisering – Ett fall (Institutionalized Projects – A Case Study). Unpublished manuscript, Stockholm School of Economics.

form. But the kind of arguments that have been developed as part of the project survive the decision, and can be repeated under other circumstances – something that further stresses the importance and vitality of the project.

Referring again to the plastic bike case, we could say that the project died in the sense that production of the bicycle was discontinued. But several of the arguments developed in connection with the project still linger on locally and could easily be revived.

In simple form the arguments regarding institutionalization can be illustrated as follows:

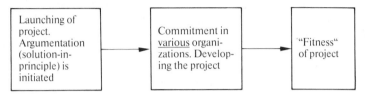

Figure 2:   Institutionalization of Projects

Coalitions and institutionalized projects have several points of contact. They can carry over into each other or they can occur in intermediate forms, thus vitalizing the project even more. But the institutionalization of a project can spring from a more direct source than a coalition. Sometimes the initiator plays an important role in deciding the success of a project, in which case he is putting his personal reputation on the block. A coalition never has a strong initiator of this kind. More often than not the event, or the project initiating the formation of a coalition, is objectified.

Thus the main difference is that coalitions seem to be based on exchange. A coalition stays alive as long as the members expect there to be future exchanges of a positive nature, otherwise it is discontinued. The institutionalized project, on the other hand, may "move" or change in terms of its concepts and/or its constituent groups. The conception of the plastic bike certainly changed over time, as did the various special interest groups involved in the project.

Erasing Corporate Boundaries

There is constant controversy among organization theorists about organizational boundaries. What should be regarded as part of the organization, and what should be counted as its environment? Today the pattern of contacts that most companies command is so extensive and detailed, that to use it as a practical definition of corporate boundaries hardly seems very useful. And since no particular contacts will do, this approach fails to solve the theoretical problem.

Moreover, the network approach is characterized by the idea of the company at the center, and this creates a perspective "from within". If on the other hand we assume a viewpoint from the outside, and look at corporate issues and actions connected with what is normally called the environment, then clearly the environment is being mapped into the company. The environment has of course become integrated with the company in various ways; very few questions are purely internal any longer. In a broad sense then, co-operation with the environment is necessary in almost all instances.

Legislation regulates many areas of company activities: working-life aspects are affected and environmental considerations set limits on production processes. Consumerism and competition are also regulated. And both national and local governments have adopted new means of control, such as support for investment, which make it possible for them to exert considerable influence on corporate decisions.

The press and the mass media in general have penetrated the corporate world more noticeably than before. The decisions and actions of entrepreneurs are made visible to a wide range of people who can be activated to intervene. This is especially true of the officials and local politicians working on the problems of unemployment.

In addition to all this, the business leader usually has roles in other companies as well as his own, perhaps as a member of other boards, and in the business community at large. Loyalty is not only a question of loyalty between a specific company and a business leader. Some business analysts still look upon this as a natural relationship, but it is easy to refute them on empirical grounds at least in present-day Sweden.

Coalitions and institutionalized projects also add to the picture of the blurred company boundaries. In fact it would be easy to argue that the organization pattern of business life as a whole has little in common today with the descriptions of traditional economic theory. Institutionalized projects, coalitions, interlocking directorates, technological imperatives and similar factors all serve to link companies together in strong dependence relationships. As a result the company is no longer such an independent unit as it once was. In fact it could be regarded simply as a convenient construct for taxation purposes.

But although company boundaries are fuzzy, the companies themselves are important ingredients of the organizational economy. The fuzziness means that company behavior is less predictable on a basis of what is being done at any one moment. Institutionalized projects and coalitions sometimes serve to break up the unity of the corporate organization. Simple postulates about the guiding-lines for corporate action seem more useless than ever. All this serves to blur the edges even more, and so we can see that the systemic phenomena described here are not really independent of one another. Nor of course is the list complete; but it suffices to make the point and to illustrate the scope available for the character roles in the organizational economy.

Character Roles in the Organizational Economy

The most important element in a society is, by definition, people – all of whom play a variety of roles in their own immediate environment, such as the family. If we look specifically at the organizational economy, we find two roles that seem particularly interesting:

"Representative man" and "Enterprising man"

As the number of organizations has increased, so has the number of people representing them. Enterprising man does not necessarily have a specific organizational seat. But his behavior and activities seem specifically designed for the organized economy, which suggests that he is not an entrepreneur in the traditional sense.

"Representative Man"

The multiplicity and complexity of the organization world is impressive. Moreover, organizations make a major impact on most citizens and other organizations. The everyday experience of virtually every citizens in a modern society includes encounters with the organization world. The news media devote a substantial amount of time and space to issues connected with national organizations such as unions, employer associations, political parties etc, and the most important representatives of these organizations are almost guaranteed public attention for their doings and sayings. The idea that representatives are important people is thus reinforced.

Organizations cannot generally be personified in the manner that is sometimes adopted in organization studies, especially when it comes to relations with the environment. Rather, organizations impose their will on others through their representatives, who negotiate and act in the name of the organization. Thus we have an even more complex system of representatives to cope with, and one that is extremely difficult to oversee.

Representatives spend most of their time monitoring various matters of interest to their organizations.[6] Surveillance is their most important task.

---

[6] Cf. Jansson, B., Jönsson, S. (1978) Social Accounting in Sweden. Unpublished manuscript, University of Göteborg.

They generally have various sanctions at their disposal, if their surveillance exposes activities in the environment that are unfavorable to their organization. Representative men thus constitute "linchpins" in the economy.

Some important mechanisms or factors should be considered here, as we ask ourselves: how does the representative get his mandate?, and what issues should he keep an eye on? Compared with politicians, who have a wide range of responsibilities and problems to attend to, the representative usually only has to watch over a few questions or activities only, or certain aspects of different issues. He also memorizes and carefully records the way these issues develop over time. The sequence of events bearing upon relevant issues has implications for his discretion.

This question of relevant issues also has implications for bargaining. The representative can hardly bargain away the main areas for which he is responsible, or disregard previous handling of the relevant issues. However, since he is interested in relatively few questions, his position actually makes it easy for him to embark on horse-trading; he can take the opportunity to support other actors in cases where the interests of this own organization are not very important. This favorable horse-trading position could well be the major source of his influence over others.

Freedom of action is another important factor. In general it seems that the authority of most representatives is on the decline. The trend (at least in legislation in Sweden) is to strip individual people of authority and responsibility. Collective bodies such as company boards are becoming more powerful in relation to the company president for instance.

This means that the representative is becoming less of a representative and more of a feeler for his organization. His mandate does not extend to making decisions on behalf of the organization. His position helps to prolong the decision-making processes. He can be informed, but he will normally remain uncommitted to a specific course of action.

The way the representative understands his job has various consequences. The following figure illustrates one example. It should be understood that representatives predominantly choose, or are confined to, left-column behavior.

Strong commitment behavior on the part of representatives should be expected only for that limited range of issues which the representative has to monitor for his organization. The main task of the representative is surveillance and negotiation on behalf of his organization. He is a negotiator, whereas enterprising man is an entrepreneur.

	Base	*Commitment*
implies that the representative	is informed in advance about a measure to be taken	is supporting the measure in public
implies that the issue	has not acquired new evidence	is being developed as part of the argumentation, and is elaborated
implies that afterwards the representative	may criticize the "solution" (I was informed, but. . .)	has some difficulty in changing his mind
implies that the group of interested persons	consists of few people people	involves a wide range of persons

Figure 3:   Differences Between Base and Commitment[7])

"Enterprising Man"

In the organizational economy another type of actor has also emerged. Enterprising man bases his activities on a solid foundation of knowledge about the functioning of the organizational economy. He utilizes his position in a net of contacts with other actors and organizations and his knowledge of the rules and legislation in the economic field, to get things done. This kind of actor tends towards pragmatism and action.

The role can be played by people in various positions. One is the business leader[8]) who functions as an entrepreneur in the organizational economy, while exploiting the opportunities for making a living that the organizational economy provides. This type of business leader does not necessarily base his position on knowledge of markets or production. Neither does he have to possess superior skills when it comes to working with people in an organization. Rather, the business leader might utilize the company's position for creating employment. In this type of endeavor, his contacts with government play an important role, and negotiating favorable conditions for the activities of the company is an important task. He also has to maintain a network of contacts[9]) with officials, politicians and other business leaders. Such a network of contacts make it possible for him to support his own actions by "pulling

---

[7]) Adapted from Svante Leijon, Rolf A. Lundin and Ulf Persson (1984) Förvaltandets förändring (Public Administration Change). Lund: Doxa

[8]) Cf. Hägg, B. (1984) Inventions and New Ventures in Development Companies. University of Linköping. See also Wåhlin, N. (1984) Småföretagsgruppen ur ett management perspektiv (A Managerial Perspective on the Small Company Group). Unpublished manuscript, University of Umeå.

[9]) Cf. Olofsson, Ch. (1983) *De regionala utvecklingsbolagen – Instrument för industriell utveckling?* (Regional Development Companies – Instruments for Industrial Development?). Stockholm: SIND, 1983: 4.

several strings" simultaneously. At the same time he has to keep up with developments in a centralistic perspective. Information about future legislation which has a bearing on his company is of the utmost importance. By keeping himself informed he not only maintains a base for local activities, but he also remains fairly independent of the local scene. In other words he is a cosmopolitan rather than a local actor.

The same type of actor can be found in the public sector. Politicians and civil servants can both play the part of the enterprising man in specific contexts. Enterprising man takes on the entrepreneurial job of getting things done. The difference compared with the traditional idea of the entrepreneur is that the organizational economy is a major source of the work and of the restrictions on it.

A successful enterprising man regards coalitions as a way of effecting action in a frozen organization world. Coalitions and institutionalized projects are among the weapons of the enterprising man.

The differences between representative man and enterprising man can be summarized as follows.

	"Representative man"	"Enterprising man"
Basis for activities	Organization	Knowledge and will to change and develop
Activities	Surveillance, negotiation	Action, entrepreneurial ventures
Motivation	Task description, external source	Achievement motive internal source
Basis for evaluation	Success or failure in surveillance as determined by the organization	Successful or unsuccessful projects

Figure 4:   Some Differences Between Character Roles

The roles contain a dualism similar to that in the famous Wildavsky[10]) model of the budget process (cf. guardians and advocates). Bargaining can be seen as a way of stalling action. We could perhaps speak of the Janus face of the organizational economy; bargaining is generally opposed to action.

---

[10]) Wildavsky, A. (1975) *Budgeting*. Boston: Little, Brown and Company.

The Politics of Unanimity and Suppressed Competition

It is always hazardous to describe an area of research as new.[11]) This is particularly true of the social sciences, where no research issues or findings are ever as obviously "new" as the X-ray, penicillin, or the combustion engine. The social sciences have generally developed in a less revolutionary way. Over the last half century ideas and results have been added to the body of knowledge in a smooth and continuous flow. Societal changes and theoretical advances have frequently exhibited their mutual dependence: theory has presented evidence of societal dynamics, and real-world practices have adapted themselves to the theory.

At present societal changes appear to be so extensive that any marginal adjustment of research perspectives seem inappropriate. We can take the example of politics and business, both of which are experiencing change in the organizational economy. Because of crises in the business world, a deep concern for unemployment becomes imperative to politicians. Rather than insisting stubbornly on party differences, politicians unite to fight for a common cause. Instead of exposing conflict, they advocate action. There is a general tendency for politicians to leave the representative category and to move instead into the enterprising class. The suppression of fierce business competition becomes a way of achieving a shared goal. Iron squares provide a strong safeguard against disruptive competition that might jeopardize employment.

---

[11]) The arguments presented here have been adapted from Carin Holmquist, Rolf A. Lundin and Elisabeth Sundin (1984) *Förhandla mer – räkna mindre* (More Negotiations – Fewer Calculations). Stockholm: Liber.

Economic Growth and Decision-Making in Japan: The Duality of Visible and Invisible Guiding Hands*

Ilan Vertinsky

Introduction

In the 1960s Japan fuelled its high rate of economic growth with inexpensive and plentiful oil. It entered the 1970s with the consumption of oil increasing at an annual rate of 15%. Thus, at the start of a decade characterized by "limits to growth", without any significant endowments of natural resources, Japan was perhaps the most vulnerable to an energy shortage among the industrialized countries. The first oil crisis led to a fundamental readjustment in Japan's industrial structure. In fact, this threat was turned into an opportunity. When the second oil crisis of 1979 hit in the wake of the Iranian revolution, Japan prospered. It increased its industrial production by 10% during the second half of 1979 while breaking the positive income elasticity mould, reducing oil consumption by 2.8%.

The 1980s have so far been characterized by an intense competition for technological leadership. Japan, which in the past was almost completely dependent on technology importation, entered the 1980s set to win the race. An examination of patent applications as a crude yardstick for technological development reveals a significant change in Japan's role in technology markets. Applications for patent rights in Japan more than doubled between 1966 and 1980 from 8600 to 191 00. The number of patent applications in the United States increased only slightly in that time from 89 000 to 104 000, while in West Germany it declined from 57 000 in 1966 to 49 000 in 1980. Japanese applications for foreign patent rights more than tripled during the same period from 10 000 to 35 000, while those filed by the U.S. and Western European applicants decreases (Asai, 1983: 31).

The success and resilience of Japan is rather surprising and has caused the attention of both scholars and practioners to focus upon how the Japanese organize, manage and decide. The quest for what makes Japan so successful

*) Partial support for research leading to this paper was received gratefully from the Center for International Business Studies at U.B.C.

has tended to highlight the differences between what was perceived as "Japanese style or attributes" and styles and attributes which characterize other systems. Nakane (1964), for example, in comparing Japan to India, found many parallels between these two systems inspite of the fact that ohne was characterized by economic failure while the other achieved extraordinary economic success. Nakane observed, however, that while both societies are characterized by a vertical social structure of the family and the community, this structure is transferred in Japan in a modified form to the school and work place in a way which promotes the achievement of their objectives. This is not the case in India. Other differences between Japan and India are more pronounced: cultural, linguistic and ethnic diversity in India versus homogeneity in Japan, and a tendency for precise problem definition and conflict articulation in India versus conflict avoidance and ambiguous problem definition in Japan. Glazer (1967: 87), commenting upon Nakane's work, asks: "Can the specific differences in social structure and values explain the differences in economic outcome?" He suggests that the suspicion cannot be ignored that if it were India that had proved to be an economic success and Japan an economic failure, the ingenious social scientist also could have explained these outcomes by the same differences. After all, a rigid hierarchy is rarely associated with modernization, ethnic and cultural diversity in many situations was considered a source of economic growth and enrichment, and certainly, ambiguity in problem definition does not appear to be a source of effective decision-making. The dangers of undisciplined induction from what could be spurious associations are only several of many constraints upon the distillation of normative management principles from the Japanese experience. Perhaps a more difficult constraint to overcome is the intellectual treatment of rationality under uncertainty. We lack a prior normative model of what should constitute appropriate behavior under uncertainty.

The difficulty that the hindsight assessor faces is the need to evaluate the effectiveness of decision processes, not only with respect to what happened but also with respect to what could have happened. To distil the lessons from Japan's economic experience in the postwar period, we therefore chose to employ in this paper an ecological model which was derived from our biological research concerning the means by which some primitive animals cope successfully with uncertainty. In particular we have studied animals which appear to lack internal resources (appropriate physical adaptations) to cope with harsh and volatile environments. The indentification of common principles of behavior in resilient populations at different poles of the evolutionary scale is used to identify behavioral principles which contribute to fitness in the Darwinian sense. In the first section we outline the model which articulates relationships between an ecologically sound choice of behaviors and feedback from highly uncertain environments and the relationships of collective benefits and competition between individuals. We then explore the extent to which similar attributes are present in choice mechanisms and economic decision processes employed by businesses and public organizations in Japan. The paper concludes with an analysis of the potential risks which lie in possible changes in decision structures which may be induced by the explosive growth in information processing and computational capabilities in Japan.

Coping With Uncertainty: Behavior of Some Successful Populations in Highly Variable Environments

Two approaches can be identified to the problem of coping with an uncertain environment: (a) choice of behavior based on *prediction*, and (b) behavior motivated by a quest for *resilience*. Successful behavior based on prediction requires accurate identification of the crucial problem posed by a particular habitat not only at a given time, but also in all future times. Knowledge of the future permits investment in permanent structures which reduce the costs of coping with particular anticipated threats or permits exploitation of opportunities. Behavior based on prediction, however, makes a population vulnerable to surprises (failure of the prediction). Resilience, on the other hand, allows for surprises by maintaining sufficiently flexible response systems to exploit opportunities, buffer threats, and spread risks. Neither approach can work for long by itself. Since organisms have only limited capacities to collect and process information, tactics for dealing solely with predictable contingencies must fail. Similarly, there are limits to flexibility, beyond which the costs of responding to repeated surprises become prohibitive (Rollo et al., 1983: 150). Clearly, to succeed in an uncertain complex environment (and over evolutionary times all environments are complex and uncertain), an animal must mix and balance these approaches. Our research focused upon the relationship between environmental variability and the use of feedback information. We chose, as a subject of research, animals whose success appears surprising in view of an apparently maladapted physiology. For example, we chose to investigate three species of terrestrial slugs. These animals occupy a wide range of comparatively hostile environments. They not only survive but are abundant in dry places from which they should be barred by their constant need for moisture (e.g. see Machin (1975), Denny (1980)). We also studied orchard mites exposed to extreme fluctuations in temperatures, predators and food supplies, and yet despite high threats of disaster, seem to proliferate. Finally we investigated behavior of tent-caterpillars that maintain stable large populations in areas with high climatic variability (see e.g. Thompson et al.,

1976, 1979). The major finding of our studies revealed that the complex pattern of animal activities can be produced by a few simple behavioral rules. These rules control switching between preprogrammed behaviors and competitive behaviors which respond to direct feedback from the environment (and forecasts based upon the feedback). The switching rules are triggered by three classes of variables: (a) biological time, (b) the internal state of the animal, and (c) external stimuli related to a myopic need hierarchy (e.g. hunger, sex drive, temperature, moisture). These classes of variables can be viewed respectively as (a) feedforward of the cumulated experience of the species coded as response to a biological clock, (b) the assessment of internal buffers and reserves of an individual, and (c) information about the current external environment. Comparison of behaviors of members of the same species living in different environments revealed that minor adjustments to switching rules in response to the type of environmental variability and the degree of risks experienced, resulted in successful adaptations.

For example, in environments where conditions changed rapidly, the window of activity was regulated more strictly by clocks (the Circadian rhythms) than was that of animals living in more stable environments. It was observed that a sensitive response to feedback which also involves a lag period may actually be counter-productive, especially when conditions are changing rapidly ("doing the right thing too late"), (Rollo et al., 1983: 332). An analysis of the costs and benefits to individuals of choices, given alternative weights to feedback and feedforward information, revealed that myopic optimization in response to feedback yields higher expected net benefits than behavior that placed a higher weight on activities regulated by the Circadian rhythm, for example. However, when a collective point of view was taken, the regulation of behavior by variables not related to the immediate environment was beneficial. Often such induced behavior resulted in a diversification of the portfolio of activities. The interplay between a myopic sensitive response to feedback from the environment and the regulation of activities by variables changing at qualitatively different rates produced a smooth activity pattern consisting of many small changes. Thus our biological studies portray an ecological concept of successful behavior under uncertainty: the achievement of balance in the role of feedback and feedforward upon behavior or, alternatively stated, the balance between a competitive myopic individual search for efficiency and a collective search for resilience. This concept provides the lens from which we will view economic policy and decision-making in Japan.

Decision Processes in the Economic Domain in Japan: In Search of Basic Attributes

In this section we explore whether the basic structure of behavior controls under uncertainty found in successful primitive populations has a counterpart in regulating economic behavior in Japan – a society richly endowed with skills and knowledge. We first investigate internal decision processes in Japanese companies and the structure of inter-company interactions. We then explore the structure of government decision processes in economic matters and the role played by the government in guiding the economy.

The Behavior of the Japanese Company: Employment Patterns (Reward Systems) and Internal Decision Structures

Any analysis of the behavior of Japanese companies must first recognize the basic fact of dualism in Japan's industrial structure (Dore, 1943). Dualism here refers to the "coexistence within the Japanese economy of large firms, engaged in capital-intensive modern industries, achieving high productivity and paying high wages; and small firms, sometimes in traditional industries, using less capital, achieving lower productivity, and paying lower wages" (Clark, 1979: 44).

The large firms provide the economic leadership, while the smaller firms respond to opportunities created by the large firms (e.g. subcontracting) or filling niches in the production process abandoned by the larger firms. Our analysis, therefore, centers upon the internal organization and decision processes of the larger firms.

The employment patterns of the large firms in Japan are characterized by the ideal (not necessarily the practice) of 'life employment' with associated structures of rewards and promotion which are linked partly to age and length of service, and partly to collective and individual performance. The career path which involves a lengthy socialization process relies on shared goals and shared responsibilities among company executives in the development of strategic decisions. Clark observes that: "New recruits have to earn their way into the organization. They have to live in the organization for a long time to learn the implicit and idiosyncratic interdependency among various tasks and sub-units" (p. 25).

Reward systems in the Japanese company continue to reinforce the duality of competition and cooperation throughout the career of the employee, i.e. rewards for individual performance and initiative within constraints of the accepted organizational procedures ensuring the predominance of the collective point of view. The impact of the reward system and the socialization process of balancing myopic or individualistic tendencies of decision-makers with concern for long term and collective goals, is further reinforced by the structure of prevailing decision processes.

The decision structure in Japanese companies is characterized by two attributes:

(1) a hierarchy with limited individual authority to make independent decisions; and

(2) collective decision-making in strategic matters.

The decision structure of the Japanese firms often severely limits the authority of the manager. Companies prepare charts setting out how much expenditure a man in each standard rank may authorize without resorting to collective decision processes. "The financial limits are frequently very low ... It is not only these formal restrictions that limit the freedom of the Japanese middle manager to run 'his' part of the organization as he likes – and in Japanese a singular possessive pronoun would not be used. Informally, too, his decisions are subject to what might in the West be thought of as interference from superiors and colleagues in other departments, who may casually suggest improvements to his unit, or comment on the way he is handling a problem, with less diffidence or fear of trespass than they would in the West" (Clark, 1979: 132–133).

The narrow span of discretion ensures that adaptive responses to feedback from the immediate environment will consist of many small steps. Information about the environment, however, would be transmitted through informal channels and shared. Significant strategic moves require experience pooling through collective decision-making. The typical instrument for collective decision-making is the circulation of the ringi – a proposal. A formal system requires circulation of a proposal both horizontally and up the hierarchy for comment and approval. All those who are consulted attach their comments to the proposal. When the decision reaches the top level of the organization it provides a record of opinions. Since the proposal is successively modified on its way to the top until it gets the approval of those consulted, by the time it is presented for decision it is rarely rejected (see e.g. Yshino, 1968). This formal means for modification of individual responses to their immediate environment is further reinforced by the Japanese culture (Hajime, 1981). One can find the principles of collective decision formalized already in the Constitution of Prince Shotoku (574–622 A.D.). He wrote, "Decisions on important matters should generally not be made by one person alone. They should be discussed with many others. But small matters are of less importance, and it is unnecessary to consult many persons concerning them. In the case of weighty matters, you must be fearful lest there be faults. You should arrange matters in consultations with many persons, so as to arrive at the right conclusion"

(Prince Shotoku's constitution article 17, translated by Hajime 1981: 146). The collectivistic tradition in decision-making, however, is meshed with the centralization of formal authority (Dore, 1973). It is the president, typically unconstrained by constitutional limitations to his power who is a source of absolute authority. In times of serious crisis or in facing great opportunities this authority can be exercised. In these circumstances the 'ringi' serve as a means of cooperation and information sharing. They are initiated formally by lower levels of the hierarchy at the instigation of the top levels.

To conclude, marginal operational adjustments can be made quickly and with low transaction costs. These may involve decisions that in the West would be thought delicate and to require much deliberation, such as decisions about changes in work allocation.

Indeed a sequence of many marginal adaptations in response to changing micro-environments may produce qualitatively significant adjustments in the overall posture of the firm. These adjustments would tend to produce smooth transitions.

When significant initiatives are considered they are subjected to lengthy decision processes and involve a significant amount of information pooling. They tend to invoke a collective, long-term corporate perspective. A major discontinuity in the environment which requires a swift realignment of corporate resources, however, can lead to the exercise of formal authority vested at the top level of the organization.

The Role of Inter-Company Linkages: The Duality of Cooperation and Competition

The behavior of the Japanese firm is influenced to a larger degree than its counterpart in the West by its links to other firms and its industrial context. Clark (1979) identified four characteristic tendencies of the company in Japan: (1) the company in Japan tends to be a clearly defined cell of industrial and commercial activity; (2) Its activities are narrowly specialized; (3) It has a clearly recognizable standing in a hierarchy in the industry, a standing related to size, and it searches to improve the standing; (4) The company is associated with other companies in some form of group.

The first three characteristics enhance myopic competition and consequently a sensitive response to the immediate environment. The fourth characteristic provides a mechanism for the balancing component of behavioral control – a collective core inducing cooperation.

The types of groups which tie companies are diverse and their collective cores are typically fuzzy and serve a variety of functions.

The atomistic definition of a company as a community, manifested for example in the existence of company-wide unions rather than functional unions cutting across the industry, permits the efficient mobilization of resources for successful competitive behavior. The narrow product specialization and range of recognized company competencies provide a focal definition of rivals and a framework for intense competition. The clear performance scoring system (i.e., the industrial hierarchy) provides an effective mechanism for feedback and learning from experience. The collective element in the industrial structure manifests itself in complex overlapping groupings of companies. The most significant grouping is the Kieretsu. There are three types of groups within this particular grouping: (1) the descendents of the prewar Zaibatsu; (2) the bank groups and (3) constellation of subsidiaries and subcontractors formed around the nucleus of a large manufacturer. The prewar Zaibatsu were giant combines organized around a family-owned holding company. The holding company, through interlocking directorships, controlled the combine. The modern groups emerged after the dissolution of the old combines by the Occupation authorities through an exchange of shares and directors and the establishment of presidents' clubs. The diversity of group styles and the persistence of the group principle led Wallich and Wallich (1976: 204) to observe that "since the phenomenon appears to repeat itself under very different circumstances, one is bound to conclude that in the Japanese environment the group principle offers important advantages". The density of connections of the postwar organization was much looser, reflecting a new focal role, that of information sharing and the preservation of a potential infra-structure for cooperation. It is important to note that even before the War the duality of individual competitive and collective orientations was maintained within the combines. Firms showed preference for other members of the group but bought from outsiders if they could get a better deal. The modern Zaibatsu companies preserve the duality though the share of buying from outside companies has increased substantially. In crisis situations, modern Zaibatsu have proved that, in spite of their lack of cohesion, they tend to rally and support a company temporarily stricken (see e.g. Clark, 1979: 76). The bank groups are somewhat less cohesive than the modern Zaibatsu, but provide a similar infra-structure for cooperation and information sharing. The division of labor in bank groups is less distinct and they may have some duplication and overlap in function among member companies.

In contrast, the third type of industrial grouping presents the most clear example of industrial specialization and gradation (Clark, 1979: 80). The dominant firm presents a core which, while cultivating its constellation of affiliates in the long run, exploits their dependence and weakness to obtain a realignment of posture in the short run.

The three types of groupings provide for a diversified continuum of mechanisms to achieve the balance between individual, myopic competition sensitive to environmental changes and the long term oriented collective control of behavior.

Other types of groups are the industrial associations. Samuels (1983: 499) observes: "these varied industry associations function much like the industry associations in other nations. They represent a central clearinghouse of technique and commercial data for their membership. The Japan Light Metal Association, for example, has a publications list that includes over fifty journals, newsletters, statistical abstracts, and technical handbooks designed to keep its members abreast of the development of the aluminun industry worldwide. These associations host symposia and workshops, and otherwise provide innumerable opportunities for members to meet and know each other." Industry associations serve, not only as a means for information generation and sharing, but provide, during periods of crisis, the framework for an articulation of collective goals aimed at the development of long-term opportunities. They also provide a basis for risk reduction through risk sharing, which the development of long-term options requires. Ouchi (1984) describes the role of the powerful network of private trade associations as part of what he terms a powerful social memory which restricts selfish behavior and encourages long-term oriented teamwork within the framework of competition.

One type of privately initiated industrial grouping which receives government sanction is a group of rival companies formed to promote collective long-term R & D objectives which myopic competition would preclude. Under 1962 legislation, companies may join with rival companies to form a Technical Research Association (TRA) for sharing the costs of R & D. Once they agree on an R & D plan and form the association, the Minister of International Trade and industry (MITI) is virtually obliged to recognize the association. Once recognized, the TRA becomes eligible for significant government assistance. One of the aspects of TRA's which is of particular interest is their limited life. Sometimes, after a few years of existence, they are disbanded. Each company goes its own way with a share of the techniques developed and reverts to compete fiercely against recent partners (MacDowall, 1984: 12).

The government also reinforces the collective element in the behavior of the private companies by endorsing privately-run discussion councils and managing a variety of advisory commissions (shingkai). These provide the most important forms in which all interested parties in a major policy area are formally brought together to hammer out an acceptable program. "An advisory commission report will never have the force of law, nor will it literally reflect the full context of the negotiations and agreement reached by the parties involved; but because it involves a process of widespread and authoritative consultation, it will often be acted upon by legislators and industry representatives" (Samuels, 1983: 500–501).

The Role and Impact of Government: How a Balance Between Collective Long-Term and Short-Term Competitive Forces is Maintained

Governments are the formal instruments through which collective concerns can be addressed. Krasner (1978) has suggested that government can achieve one of three qualitatively different levels of control over economic behavior. The most forceful government can change the behavior of private economic agents as well as the structure of the economy itself. A weaker government can resist private demands but is unable to transform the behavior of private economic agents. The weakest government becomes an instrument of private sector pressure groups. Japan, however, appears to defy this hierarchy of intervention capabilities. Samuels (1983: 49), on analysing Japan's post-war energy policy, observes for example that "transwar Japanese energy policy seems neither a story of a dominant state nor one of a state captive to private interests. Nor even does it seem one of an impartial 'broker' state. It is one of an activist state, a 'player' with comprehensive visions and a role, but with capabilities that do not seem consistent with general characterizations that posit Japan should necessarily resemble France more than the United States."

Johnson (1983) observed that even during the war, the Zaibatsu managed to resist attempts by the government to achieve full control of production and distribution. Samuels concludes, on the basis of his and Johnson's studies, that "It is hard to come away from these studies with any impression about state autonomy short of its very existence. State and private interests clashed often and with such widespread effects that any imputation of the Japanese state as a passive institution *sans* autonomous (even if often uncoordinated and hopelessly unachievable) goals and visions for the nation is inconceivable. The state seems an autonomous player, but its role is clearly limited by historically determined configurations of the negotiated market economy. Secondly, these studies suggest it is at least debatable whether or not the transwar Japanese state enjoyed a capacity to see these visions through their attainment. While the Japanese state may have a strategic position in these negotiations, one is struck as much by the constraints upon the Japanese state as by its unfettered prerogatives."

Our own study (Nemetz et al., 1985) of Japan's energy strategy and Vogel's (1979) analysis of MITI's influence support the proposition of a system of checks and balances based on the dual orientation of economic behavior controls. While swift and radical intervention is taken in a crisis to secure the collective survival, it is the market which ultimately prevails. When a crisis dissolves and market forces dominate, government policy retreats to a subsidiary role of keeping options open, disseminating information, and ensuring a smoother transition to the new state dictated by the market. Transition-rationalization cartels are major examples of the facilitative mechanisms encouraged by the government (see e.g. Caves and Vekusa, 1976).

The history of the car industry in Japan provides an excellent illustration of this interplay between government policies and market forces. "In 1952, the government did succeed in curbing automobile imports under a strict quota system. Those import controls, which continued until October 1965, did help Japan's automobile industry stand on its own feet. But when MITI tried in 1955 to shape the development of the auto industry directly with a plan to build a "national car" it went too far. The plan sought to have a single company mass produce an ultra small popular car that was both inexpensive and exportable. MITI proposed to grant the manufacturer of such a car financial aid and legal protection in a bid to increase employment, improve technical know-how, and lay the groundwork for an automobile export industry. However by the time MITI introduced this grand scheme, consumer choices were already influencing corporate strategy. The forces of the marketplace ultimately led Japan's auto makers into a growth pattern totally different from what MITI had in mind" (Tsuruta, 1983: 45).

How is the balance between the collective control and individual competition maintained? An important observation that our biological studies yielded was the fact that the adaptation necessary for collective survival was obtained by flexible behavioral mechanisms rather than by an expensive investment in physiological or morphological adaptations. An analysis of the role of the Japanese government in the economy reflects a similar pattern of flexible exercises of controls and influence upon the private sector, rather than the strengthening of a permanent public sector infra-structure and its share in the economy. Lida (1981) provides some numerical comparisons which lend support to this observation. The number of public employees per thousand employed (in 1976) was 99 in Japan. It was 205 in the U.S., 239 in the U.K., 205 in West Germany and 172 in France (these numbers alter somewhat if defense is excluded but Japan still possesses the lowest ratio of 93 versus 150–179 for the others). When general government expenditures to GNP were compared, Japan ranked lowest (1977) with 20.5%. The U.S.A. government spent (in 1978) 34.0% of the GNP, U.K. 43.9%, West Germany 44.6% and France 44.0%. If we exclude government capital formation and social security transfers and assess the proportion of GNP the government consumes, Japan's government presents a lean posture with 9.6% versus 18.3% for the U.S.A., 20.8% for the U.K., 20.0% for West Germany and 14.8% for France.

The constraints of size on the public sector are reinforced by the maintenance of internal competition and overlapping responsibilities within the bureaucracy. For example, the Machinery and Information Industries Bureau of MITI, in charge of information-processing industries, semi-conductors, space, hardware and patents, shares responsibilities in promoting the information industry – the targeted industry for the 80s and 90s, with many other government agencies. "The Ministry of Education (MOE) has responsibility for university based R & D, copyrights and education; the Ministry of Health and Welfare (MHW) for biotechnology, medical equipment and pharmaceuticals; the Ministry of Finance (MOF) for information based financial services, electronic banking and automatic funds transfer; the Science and Technology Agency (STA) for space satellites; the Ministry of Post and Telecommunications (MPT) for telecommunications (Rapp, 1984: 46). The internal competition and diversity within the government not only provide for checks and balances, constraining the control of the government over economic behavior, but also ensure that the influence of collective controls maintains diversified investment options." It appears that, even in an institutional structure aimed at the articulation of a collective point of view, the duality of competition and cooperation in Japan is maintained and produces high-quality decisions. Samuels (1981: 163), for example, examining the politics of alternative energy R & D in Japan concludes: "We have scratched consensus and found conflict, and we have scratched conflict and found consensus. To disengage the two would be both to denude the issue and delude the reader. We are therefore left with the paradox that conflict and consensus in the Japanese policy context, far from being antithetical, seem perfectly compatible; indeed, they seem to be mutually reinforcing. If the politics of alternative energy R & D in Japan is any guide, Japan is neither a monolith of rapturous harmony, nor a pit of contentious and self-destructive discord. In itself this is hardly striking, but upon examination of the quality of accommodation reached even on bitterly contested issues, one cannot help being optimistic about Japan's energy future."

Government and Industry

We have already pointed out the pivotal role that the advisory committees to the government play in producing what Ouchi (1984) described as a social memory so complete and so powerful that both the selfish and cooperative will be remembered and repaid – social memory which is needed to attain teamwork and competition simultaneously. Another function that the collective element in controlling system behavior must attain is the provision of a long-term framework for competition. The government agencies and their advisory committees have performed this role by issuing plans and forecasts. Johnson (1983: 38), commenting on the meaning of planning in the context of industrial policy observed that by planning one means consistent, long-term government policies that are known and publicized, so that private sectors in the economy know what the government is going to do and adjust to it. "The Japanese government's industrial policy is published. Any citizen can buy it at the corner newstand. What is called the Economic Planning Agency in Japan is, in fact, an Economic Propaganda Agency, a hortatory body if you will" (see also Caves and Vekusa (1976) for similar role definition). Plans and forecasts issued by the government and the advisory committees aim to draw attention to problem areas and opportunities. These documents often create "anchors" for other forecasts by providing a reference point. A complex and sensitive signalling system has evolved around the issuance of plans and forecasts to provide a structure for subtle negotiation and coordination which is necessary in an otherwise highly competitive market environment. Our own study of Japan's energy policy (Nemetz et al., 1985) describes the highly ritualized and coordinated signalling system which evolved around MITI's long-term energy forecast. This system maintains a pragmatic flexibility rarely found in Western planning and forecasting efforts. Indeed the publication of the forecasts triggers a sequence of publications of alternative forecasts by different industrial associations. The timing of public releases of the various projections and the forms of commentary appear to provide meaningful signals to the various actors in the energy field. The efforts of the bureaucracy to coordinate, however, do not result in a loss of information from the system. The maintenance of alternative sources of information seems to be an important objective of the bureaucracy. Indeed, the goal of the government's own planning-oriented research contracts are not to increase control over information-generation; rather, it is aimed at maintaining the diversity of independent information sources. Thus, instead of pooling collective information resources and processing the information to generate, perhaps, a more perfect and consistent "prediction", the design of the collective core aims at achieving resilience through the maintenance of diversity.

This objective characterizes the employment of another important instrument through which the government and the industry pool resources to pursue long-term collective goals: the hybrid combination of public and private enterprises known as the "third sector" (Johnson, 1978). These companies utilize private sector technological and managerial expertise and government and university research capabilities and are jointly funded by private and public sector capital. These types of companies are used typically to develop and maintain long-term technological options and complement the research and development work of other government and privately funded research efforts.

Perhaps the most attended example of the application of such a joint venture instrument is the Fifth Generation Computer Project. This project has a 10-year horizon. It joins the government electrotechnical laboratory with all the major computer makers in Japan in an effort to develop an intelligent computer (Feigenbaum and McCorduck, 1983). The Institute for New Generation Computer Technologies was opened with staff seconded from eight firms that make up the consortium and the two national laboratories which participate in the project – NTT's Musashino Laboratory and MITI's Electrotechnical laboratory. The researchers were seconded for three years. In this case the joint venture arose from a collective, long-term search for opportunities. In other cases third sector companies were established in response to a crisis already experienced or expected. The New Energy Development Organization, for example, was a collective joint private-public sector company which was established in response to the energy crises and with a view to expanding Japan's energy options to meet another future possible energy crisis. These joint projects are often characterized by constant conflict and tend to have a limited life-span.

Conclusion and Prognosis

"A system . . . that at every point in time fully utilizes its possibilities to its best advantage may yet in the long run be inferior to a system that does so at no given point in time, because the latter's failure to do so may be a condition for the level or speed of long-run performance" (Schumpeter, 1975: 83). Japan's economic history appears to confirm this observation. In a world characterized by uncertainty and sharp discontinuities, the short-term efficiency obtained by competitive markets may threaten long-term survival. Increased powers of "prediction" tend to lead to a higher degree of uniformity of responses to a changing environment and therefore increase the vulnerability of the system as a whole to low-probability risks. Furthermore, increased power of prediction intensifies the gap between what is desirable from a collective point of view and what is desirable from an individual point of view. Indeed, a sacrifice of short-term efficiency or tampering with the individual pursuit of maximum net benefits can be beneficial only if it increases the resilience of the system as a whole. Inefficiency in itself increases vulnerability of the system and dominant centralized collective controls may decrease resilience.

Johnson (1983) has described how the American economic managerial paradigm is based on the assumption that long-run optimal policy merely consists of sequences of short-run optimal policies. The Japanese paradigm that emerges from our analysis is one based on duality, a system of competitive myopic maximization within a guiding framework oriented to a collective long-term resilience. This duality is similar to the one that our biological studies of successful primitive populations living in highly uncertain environments seemed to indicate. The managerial paradigm based on this duality appears to be embedded in every level of the industrial decision process. We have identified it in the decision structure of the firm and we have then observed similar principles of design in the behavior of different groups of firms. Even within the government, an instrument for the articulation of collective controls, we found the duality of fierce myopic competition between different bureaucracies and the pursuit of long-term collective goals. Finally we have found the duality in the relationship of the public and private sectors.

The major functions of the collective element in controlling system behavior (that emerged both in our animal studies and in analysing the economic system of Japan) is the maintenance and generation of information, options and diversity within a system. The secret of success in all the systems we studied appears to be the preservation of a balance between the two control systems. An example which illustrates this principle was provided by Dr. Lindsay, a noted fish biologist from IARE: 95% of the individuals in a salmon population return to the specific place from which they originate and to which they have adapted over generations. About 5% stray to other streams on their return from the ocean. Clearly, for an individual to return to the stream from which it originates, constitutes an optimal behavior. It is the strays, however, that provide the population with resilience. Most salmon today, in Canadian and U.S. streams are descendants of strays. If, however, the percentage of strays was to increase significantly, the mortality among individuals would increase, and the population might not survive the expensive attempt at diversification. If no fish strayed, rare catastrophic events such as a stream blockage would wipe out the population.

In Japan we have observed a similar relationship between the two control systems. Market competitive responses dominate, but the "social memory" ensures diversification and option-generation. In the future, however, threats to this dual system could emerge. Evolutionary selective processes ensure the balance of "prediction" and "resilience" through genetic programming in the primitive population. In human populations, however, as information-processing, computation capacities and knowledge increases, so does the capacity for "prediction". Almost "perfect" prediction may lead to overconfidence and a complete reliance on the prediction. The temptations to reduce investment in resilience are likely to grow.

In the West the Greco-Judeo traditions, with their normative emphasis upon consistency and certainty, reinforce the tendency to rely on "prediction". Indeed, "the usual tests and language habits of (the Western) culture tend to promote confusions between certainty and belief. They encourage the vice of acting and speaking as though we were certain when we are only fairly sure" (Savage, 1971: 800). In contrast, Japan's culture emphasizes harmony and tolerance of contradiction. Its language permits or even encourages ambiguity. Thus the duality of management based on prediction and the quest for resilience, may survive the threat of overconfident but uncertain knowledge.

References

Asai, T. (1983) R & D in Japan. *Journal of Japanese Trade and Industry,* May/June, pp. 31–33.

Caves, R. E., Vekusa, M. (1976) *Industrial Organization in Japan.* Washington, D.C.: The Brookings Institute.

Clark, R. (1979) *The Japanese Company.* New Haven, Conn.: York University Press.

Denny, M. (1980) Locomotion: The Cost of Gastropod Crawling. *Science,* 208, pp. 1288–1290.

Dore, R. (1973) The Origins of National Diversity in Industrial Relations. *British Factory-Japanese Factory,* Berkeley: University of California Press.

Feigenbaum, E., McCorduck, P. (1983) *The Fifth Generation: Artificial Intelligence and Japan's Computer Challenge to the World.* Reading, MA: Addison-Wesley.

Glazer, N. (1976) Social and Cultural Factors in Japanese Economic Growth. *Asia's New Giant: How the Japanese Economy Works.* H. Patrick and J. Rosovsky (Eds.), Washington, D.C.: The Brookings Institution.

Hajime, N. (1981) Basic Features of the Legal, Political and Economic Thought of Japan. *The Japanese Mind.* C. A. Moore (Ed.), Honolulu: The University Press of Hawaii, pp. 143–164.

Johnson, C. (1983) Interview, Close Up. *Journal of Japanese Trade and Industry,* May/June, pp. 37–40.

– (1978) *Japan's Public Policy Companies.* Washington, D.C.: American Enterprise Institute for Public Policy Research.

– (1982) *MITI and the Japanese Miracle: The Growth of Industrial Policy 1925–1975.* Stanford, CA: Stanford University Press.

Krasner, S. D. (1978) *Defending the National Interest: Raw Materials Investments and U.S. Foreign Policy.* Princeton, MA: Princeton University Press.

Lida, T. (1981) What is Unique About the Japanese Economy. *The Oriental Economist,* July, 44, pp. 8–11.

MacDowell, J. (1984) Management for Innovation in Japan. Ottawa: Ministry of State for Science and Technology.

Nagai, Y. (1983) Inspite of' or 'Because Of'? Japan's Success and Japanese Culture. *Speaking of Japan,* 36, pp. 7–11.

Nakane, C. (1964) Logic and Smile When Japanese Meet Indians. *Japan Quarterly,* 11, pp. 434–38.

Nemetz, P. N., Vertinsky, I., Vertinsky, P. (1985), Japan's Energy Strategy at the Crossroads. *Pacific Affairs* Winter, pp. 553–576.

Ouchi, W. G. (1984) *The M-Form Society: How American Teamwork Can Recapture the Competitive Edge.* Reading, MA: Addison-Wesley Co.

Rapp, W. V. (1984) Unbundling Japan Inc. *Creative Computing Focus on Japan,* Vol. 10, No. 8, pp. 43–48.

Rollo, C. D., Vertinksy, I. B., Wellington, W. G., Kanetkar, V. K. (1983) Alternative Risk-Taking Styles: The Case of Time Budgeting of Terrestrial Gastropods. *Researches of Population Ecology,* 25, pp. 321–335.

Samuels, R. J. (1981) The Politics of Alternative Energy Research and Development in

Japan. *The Politics of Japan's Energy Strategy.* R. P. Morse (Ed.), Berkely, CA: University of California, Institute of East Asian Studies.

– (1983) State Enterprise, State Strength, and Energy Policy in Transwar Japan. Working Paper, MIT EL 83–010, MIT, Boston, Mass.

Schumpeter, J. A. (1975) *Capitalism, Socialism and Democracy.* New York: Harper & Row.

Savage, L. J. (1971) Elicitation of Personal Prohabilities and Expectations. *Journal of the American Statistical Association,* 60, pp. 738–801.

Thompson, W. A., Cameron, P. J., Wellington, W. G., Vertinksy, I. B. (1976) Degrees of Heterogeneity and the Survival of an Insect Population. *Researches on Population Ecology,* 18, pp. 1–13.

Thompson, W. A., Vertinsky, I. B., Wellington, W. G. (1974) The Dynamics of Outbreaks: Further Simulation Experiments With the Western Tent Caterpillar. *Researches on Population Ecology,* 20, pp. 188–200.

Tsurumi, Y. (1984) *Sogoshosha.* Montreal: I.R.P.P.

Tsuruta, T. (1983) Thy Myth of Japan Inc. *Technology Review,* Vol. 86, No. 5, p. 45.

Vogel, E. (1979) *Japan As Number 1, Lessons for America.* New York: Harpen Colophon Books.

Wallich, H., Wallich, M. (1976) Banking and Finance. *Asia's New Giant: How the Japanese Economy Works.* H. Patrick and H. Rosovsky (Eds.), Washington, D.C.: The Brookings Institution.

Yoshino, M. Y. (1968) *Japan's Managerial System: Adaptations and Innovations.* Cambridge, Mass.: M.I.T. Press.

Industry, Government and the Public – The Public Role of Big Corporations

Bengt Sandkull

In this recent book on power Henry Mintzberg (1983) discusses power relationships between industry and society, mainly in a North American perspective. In this paper I will address the same issue, but I will take the analysis a step further and argue that the large Swedish corporations are at present enjoying a historic opportunity to improve the social relations of production in a way that may lead to new conformations in society as a whole.

The Issue

Before the advent of the large corporation in the nineteenth century, and before legal incorporation with share ownership and limited liability, a firm was an enterprise closely associated with its founder-owners. No single firm was particularly important to society as a whole. It was the joint-stock company that signalled a new development.

The laws governing incorporation that were introduced in Europe and the United States made it possible for anybody able to raise capital to start a company – even for some risky venture – with only limited liability attached. The freedom to trade in stock together with the intricate mesh of banks and trust companies made the joint-stock company a very flexible legal form of association. But as a result of the incorporation laws, a corporation came to be regarded as a legal person – a legal status that was granted as a matter of course, although it gave the stock capital itself the necessary legitimation to the property rights for the whole product of the firm (Ellerman, 1980). Giving companies rights superior to those of people meant that the ownership of stock became an instrument for controlling a firm.

This form of ownership of firms was not and is not simply a legal fiction, as Mintzberg would have us believe (Mintzberg, 1983: 526), but a device that gave capital predominance over labour. According to the employment contract, free citizens had to forego some of their civil rights, i.e. the results of their work (for a recent discussion of this see Ellerman, 1980). This deprivation, and the idea that the price of labour should be set on a market, turned labour into a commodity. Among economists there was much scepticism about the joint-stock companies. Adam Smith doubted whether they would be able to attract leaders who were not either corrupt or lazy (Guillet de Monthoux, 1983: 297). According to Gustav Schmoller the solution was to find good leaders – not money-makers as in the United States, but eminent leaders able to satisfy the ethical controls imposed by the public. Managed by good leaders, companies could be transformed into obedient instruments (Schmoller, 1904, according to Guillet de Monthoux, 1983: 298–299).

Despite some misgivings most societies recognize the company as an instrument for the pursuit of business. It is a bit of society and is therefore regulated by social and legal norms. The big corporation, however, represents a much larger chunk, and the whole question of regulation and control thus becomes vitally important. "We need it subjected to a variety of controlling forces" is the stance taken by Mintzberg (op. cit. 647), and he discusses a range of positions with regard to control, from nationalization to a complete absence of restriction. But "it" – the big corporation – is by no means a clearcut or definite entity. On the contrary it is a rather fluid phenomenon composed of numerous firms and legal units and governed by certain controlling interests (the "sway group" in the terminology of Stymne, 1970: 29). A re-examination of the role of the corporation in society, and its relation to society, is necessary before we can discuss ways in which it might be controlled, and by whom. In addressing this question I shall discuss production (the labour process), human communication and power systems in society. To exemplify the labour process I have chosen the car industry, because of its all-pervading impact on society. An emergent core industry such as the car industry has an extensive impact on society, both economically and technically.

Industry (both manufacturing and service) employs people in the labour process and converts their labour into products. The value added is realized through the market mechanisms in the form of profit which can be used to improve the labour process further. This "improvement" usually takes the form of efficiency measures aimed at reducing the labour cost per item, and it affects the relations between labour and capital.

As Habermas pointed out, we should be concerned not only with rational and purposeful systems but also with social norms and language, i.e. the social interaction systems that guide human communication and action. According to Goonatilake (1982) the highest degree of alienation was to be found in the car industry, because the level of mechanization was high and work operations were broken down into their simplest elements. The assembly line enforces a uniform pace that most workers find distressing. The worker response to this is absenteeism, high turnover, negligence and even sabotage. The social relations in the car industry articulated the antagonism between management and labour. In connection with the large-scale transfers of people from less-industrialized areas to the growth poles, there were also big changes in social norms and human communications (changes that have been only partially documented, for example by Ahrne, 1981; Andersson, 1982; Himmelstrand, 1981). The attempts to apply the ideas of the sociotechnical systems in the 1960s and 1970s should be considered in light of this background.

An industrial society represents an institutional order which imposes rules and regulations, or systems of power, on all members of the society. The big corporations are among the societal institutions constituting the systems of power which introduce and systematically legitimize distorted communications in society (Schroyer, 1973: 155). Ideologies and myths about the society are important in this context. Their importance at the organizational and corporate levels has recently been recognized anew by some management researchers (Jönsson and Lundin, 1979), but their significance in the context of power and control has not yet been fully examined.

In Sweden one pervasive myth concerns the "Swedish model" which is based on the idea that only a Social Democratic government can guarantee the welfare state. The free market economy is another myth so deeply entrenched in ideology, that its position as the most rational form of industrial society is regarded as being beyond argument.

The Genesis of the Industrial Society

Much of Swedish industry originated in metalworking traditions going far back to medieval times. Wherever people discovered natural resources (ore, forest, and water) they established "works", very often in partnership. Much later new owners transformed the surviving works into "company-town" industries. The crown also established metalworking factories. The tools for the mechanization of farming at the end of the nineteenth century were largely provided locally by village smithies. Many of these started to grow, and some became industrial names known all over the world.

The tradition of the metalworks, based on respect for trade and craft skills, survived until very recently in Sweden, in many places well into the 1950s and 1960s. Volvo started in 1926/27 in this tradition (Ellegård, 1983). Although Swedish industry in general was late in following the practices of American industry, during the 1930s Volvo pioneered the organization of manufacturing operations in machine groups and introduced the conveyor belt into its assembly work. During the 1950s MTM methods were introduced, but only after lengthy labour disputes (Hermele, 1982).

During the 1960s Volvo's production was far smaller than what was regarded by industrial economists internationally as the viable minimum. But from the start Volvo had created a system embracing all its major suppliers, which offset its competitors' alleged economies of scale. The Volvo management succeeded in running the whole supply system in a way that combined efficiency with flexibility. The general idea of managing a supply system is also characteristic of the Japanese car manufacturers, especially Toyota (Sugimori et al, 1977). Despite its small size the Volvo Corporation was competitive, compared with much larger European and American car manufacturers.

The other aspect of Volvo's success was its repercussions on the Swedish economy. Together with its suppliers Volvo became a prominent local employer in many towns and other communities. In 1976 Volvo and the other Swedish car manufacturer Saab-Scania together employed about 67 000 people directly and indirectly in Sweden (Hermele, 1982: 10). After the decision to enter the North American market in the 1960s, Volvo also became one of the major earners of foreign currency. Saab-Scania and Volvo together generate about 12 per cent of total Swedish exports (ibid: 69).

Given the successes of the Volvo group there is every reason to transfer the famous slogan "What is good for General Motors is good for America" to the Swedish scene: "What is good for Volvo is good for Sweden". This point is further underlined in that Volvo became the symbol of Swedish quality, which for many years was the hallmark of Sweden's export goods. Volvo's top executives were also skilful in their dealings with the Swedish government, heeding the principles of the welfare state and complying with the rules of the game according to the Swedish model.

The Response to Worker Unrest

Although Volvo had become firmly entrenched in the Scientific Management tradition, at the beginning of the 1970s its new executives responded to new demands from the workers for a voice in decision-making and for less degrading conditions of work. The high labour turnover in the old plants and later the large stocks of unsold cars highlighted the need for cooperation on the part of the workers. The previous concentration on maximizing production capacity was no longer paramount, and the production flow came into focus instead. The importance of the workers' consent to the production process was thus recognized in a new way, and a good deal of experimentation with new forms of organization followed.

Although it is the best known, the Kalmar plant does not in fact constitute the most advanced solution in the Volvo Group. In retrospect we can see that the Kalmar plant and the other new plants in the Volvo Group primarily represented a great achievement in production technology and much improved working conditions. The MTM methods still reigned, and opportunities for good work and worker participation remained meagre; but the Volvo management is eager to foster more involvement, or at least a sense of involvement (Auguren et al, 1984; Jönsson, 1981). Somebody at one of these plants once said to a visitor: "We have created a setting for worker participation in shop-floor management, but our administrative routines which are based on scientific management are formidable obstacles to a new philosophy. In that language, worker participation does not exist."

The Kalmar plant did not bring the expected breakthrough in worker-management relations, and ten years later one of the main innovations – dock assembly – was abandoned in favour of a modified assembly line using an invisible conveyor belt. It is still the workers who have to adapt to the technology. But the new thinking and the rhetoric involved have had repercussions both on production technology and on labour relations in the whole Volvo Group.

In continuing to refine its labour process, the Volvo management has favoured the increased mechanization of production in combination with schemes for inculcating greater loyalty and more responsibility into the workforce. The strategy for transforming assembly work into craftmanship still seems to belong to the realm of rhetoric (Jönsson, 1981: 30; cf. the opposite development at Kalmar (1984) *Ny Teknik*, p. 6). Today Volvo's management is even more convinced that efficiency must be combined with human concern, as exemplified by the changes in the Volvo Components Corporation. The solutions introduced there are extremely ambitious, but so far they have failed to break away from the old tradition of submission, or even to recognize it. However that may be, Volvo's approach to the question of consent is in sharp contrast to the mainstream mode which still resembles a "war on labor" (Goldman and Van Houten, 1980).

For 50 years the industrialist Marcus Wallenberg dominated Swedish industry. He was respected by the Social Democratic government because he always tried to promote Sweden's economy, and because he was concerned with industry and not only with profit and financial manipulations. Several industries in the Wallenberg empire faced increasing competition during the 1970s. The problems were countered by intensified rationalization and mergers, and already before his death the empire was beginning to fall apart.

The Volvo Group seems to be gradually replacing the Wallenberg empire as the major industrial setup in Sweden. The car industry is still its main driving-force. Wallenberg believed in strong owner influence and detested situations like that at Volvo, where the wide spread of share ownership meant that no special group of shareholders could acquire influence over company policy, which could instead be dictated by management. In 1978, however, Wallenberg managed to mobilize strong enough opposition to out-vote a top-management initiative involving a proposed agreement with Norwegian interests, which would have bought a substantial portion of the shares. But since this defeat the Volvo management has been able to strengthen its position further by engaging in cross-ownership together with a few other industrial groups which are also free of dominating shareholder factions. In effect management has used cross-ownership and shareholder proxies as a means of bypassing the ownership rights of the stockholders.

The Swedish Model

Whereas Marcus Wallenberg barely tolerated the modern welfare state, the Volvo management took a much more positive attitude towards the Swedish model.

It was during the 1950s that the Swedish model as such came into being, although the label was invented much later. The model was based on the principles of bargaining agreed to by the parties on the labour market in 1938, and the government's strict adherence to the principles of the market economy, i.e. manpower is a commodity and capital resources are allocated according to market values, with the two important exceptions of the agricultural and building sectors. According to my interpretation the following elements were fundamental to the Swedish model.

1. A division of work between industry and government. Industry was allowed to keep its responsibility for industrial policy, while the labour government assumed the role of arbitrator, urging industry to increase its efficiency. The centralized wage negotiations and the rigorous minimum-wage policy forced the less efficient parts of industry to become more efficient or to go out of business.
2. A deal between the government and the labour unions. The unions got a social security safety net, which as well as providing for labour's basic rights also reduced labour's character as a commodity on the market. In exchange the unions had to accept big structural changes that resulted in closedowns and unemployment.
3. A tacit contract between labour and industry. The unions expected industry to guarantee full employment and annual wage increases. On the other hand they had to accept management's prerogatives, in particular as regards mechanization and rationalization.

Cracks in the Swedish Model

The model worked very well for quite a long time. Swedish industry became famous for its quality, and exports increased steadily. Industry expanded, and despite mechanization had some difficulty in recruiting people. When the largely non-industrial northern regions had been tapped of their manpower reserves, the recruiting teams went to Yugoslavia, Greece and Turkey. To check any unlimited import of guest workers, industry was obliged to treat their foreign recruits on an equal footing with their domestic workforce and to provide them with courses in the Swedish language.

This period also saw a great deal of activity in the struggle for women's liberation. With the support of officially adopted programmes for sex equality, women were encouraged to take employment. To facilitate their participation in the workforce, the municipal authorities were urged to build enough day-care centres and to give support to other child-care facilities. The right to part-time work while their children are small and an extension of paid maternity leave were other measures directed at women.

As a consequence of this the public sector expanded and reinforced the building boom which had been initiated by the "million houses programme" of 1965 (see Brodén, 1976). The influx of labour to the industrialized urban centres from the peripheral regions had caused severe housing problems and had been holding back industrial growth. The rationalization process in industry was accompanied by concentration, and vast industrial groups were formed by mergers and takeovers. The accompanying building boom brought a similar development in the building and construction industry.

The municipal administration underwent rationalization which reduced the number of local government units from about 2700 to 260. In a similar vein the school district boundaries were redrawn. A new uniform curriculum was introduced to enable schools to give children an education corresponding to industry's needs. A government agency – the National School Board – was created to supervise the schools.

The period up to the end of the 1960s witnessed a major transformation of Sweden. No longer a mainly rural country where most people worked in small plants producing primarily for domestic consumption, Sweden became a country fully integrated into the global economy, most of whose industrial workers were accounted for by the big leading industries exporting 80–90 per cent of their production. At the same time the system of public welfare tended to replace many of the traditional family bonds involving the care of the elderly, the children and the sick.

The Collapse of the Swedish Model

The 1970s opened with the convulsions of growth and the protests of those exposed to exploitation. The miners' protest is the best known example. In 1969 the miners in the state-owned iron-ore mines in Kiruna (LKAB) came out on unofficial strike. Their main grievance concerned the health hazards of working underground. The workers were no longer satisfied with the annual wage increases; they also wanted to be able to influence their working conditions, including the organization of the work. The strike was a direct blow aimed at the leadership of the labour movement including the Social Democratic government. When it was finally settled, the workers had got rid of the piece-rate system imposed by production management to pace their work, in exchange for monthly salaries conditional upon the achievement of production targets (see Kronlund, 1973).

Strikes by the miners and other discontented workers, protests against the piece-rate system and reactions to the neglect of working conditions were signals to which the labour movement slowly responded. In 1974 the old Work Environment Act of 1949 was brought up to date. It was amended in 1978 to include social and psychological aspects of work, and in effect treating work organization as part of general working conditions. The workers were also granted the right to participate in the design of their work environment.

The Security of Employment Act also came into effect in 1974. Swedish employers had previously enjoyed the unrestricted right to dismiss people without having to give any reason. According to the new act the employer must state objective grounds for dismissal.

The demand for influence was satisfied in part in 1973 when the employees in any company with a workforce of more than 100, were given the right to appoint two representatives to the board, in the Act on Employee Representation on Boards. But the unions wanted to refute the employers' exclusive rights to govern and to distribute jobs. This resulted in the 1977 Act on the Joint Regulation of Working Life (MBL), which establishes the local union's right to be consulted in negotiations before any decisions affecting the company or the production system are taken. The union may call for negotiations on almost any issue. The act also requires the employer to keep the unions informed on the current economic status of the company.

These amendments to the Swedish model were initiated unilaterally, and imposed by way of legislation. Industry has only partly heeded them, as it had advocated local agreements instead. Industry has been somewhat reluctant to improve the work environment and has almost completely neglected its non-physical aspects.

As a result of government intervention Sweden has been simultaneously experiencing a long period of industrial growth, the rapid emergence of a welfare state, and steady growth in private incomes. All went well so long as growth propelled the model. But once growth stopped, it became painfully obvious that the Swedish model was dependent on externally induced growth.

Structural Contradictions

The evolution of modern capitalism has led in Sweden as in other advanced countries to a number of new problems. Industry has experienced a falling rate of profit in manufacturing and the rate of investment has declined (Dahmén, 1977; Söderström, 1984). Many businessmen have turned to financial transactions, thus contributing to the inflationary economy. The ordinary man faces the threat of unemployment, degradation of the content of his work, inflation that undermines apparent wage increases, and further pollution of his living environment. Successive Swedish government have attacked these problems without very much success.

The economic policy pursued by the Social Democratic party with a view to maintaining the viability of the Swedish model has created its own contradictions, in addition to those that anyway bedevil modern capitalism. The problems of inflationary wage drift and of union wage rivalry made themselves felt already in the middle of the 1960s. The "million-houses programme" with its immediate effect on local government expenditure and taxes, was one of the obvious stimuli behind the inflationary wage drift. The building sector attracted a great deal of capital, some of it speculative. The economy received an inflationary boost, the effects of which have since resulted in a marked increase in building costs and tenant rents.

The Swedish Trade Union Confederation (LO) has also had difficulty in maintaining a wage policy based on its tradition of solidarity. The export industries were willing to pay more to their workers than other industries, because of their favourable market situation. The public sector employees, whose pay has traditionally been lower than industry's, wanted to catch up. All this made it very difficult for LO to prevent wage rivalry among its member unions. Most of industry could show good profits and gave way fairly readily to the demands, thus also giving itself good reason to step up investment in labour-saving equipment. The rapid advance of the public-sector unions in LO and of the white-collar unions in government and industry outside LO, has aggravated the problem. LO has never since been able to regain its undisputed leadership in wage-setting.

Government Industrial Policy

The accelerating pace of structural change has led to an increase in plant closures. The social cost of the structural changes is rising, and to a great extent it is those directly affected who have to bear it. As the economic gains from the structural changes started to level off at the same time, the outcome has tended to be more inequality rather than less.

In order to stimulate more venture investment, the Swedish Investment Bank was established. It made financial commitments to a number of small companies, but most of its capital became tied up in helping the victims of structural change. It soon became heavily involved in the textile industry, where several failing companies were forced to merge. The Investment Bank now occupies a somewhat marginal position, and has proved unable to fulfil its expected role of providing a major impetus to industrial investment.

The government's new industrial policy also concerned itself with research and development. The Swedish National Development Board was established to make more efficient use of government money, and it was made responsible for technical research and development up to the prototype stage. As well as assisting industry, the Board was to act as an agent of socially useful technical research for which there was no ready-made market. An evaluation of the Board ten years after its start revealed that very few projects had been able to move beyond the prototype stage, and that resource allocation was governed exclusively by market values.

Altogether implementation of the new industrial policy has had little positive effect on industry. It has increased government expenditure and created a state apparatus which has made it possible for the government to intervene on a case-by-case basis, in particular when employment was at issue.

Because of the structural changes the outcome of state intervention has become less predictable. It became clear that the government's capacity to steer industry in the interests of the labour movement was inadequate. Leading members of the labour movement have failed to recognize that Sweden has reached the limits of Keynesian political economy, and that the prerequisites of industry have changed. During the 1960s and 1970s Swedish industry became fully integrated in the global economy. As a consequence of rationalizations affecting both products and manufacturing arrangements, most people are now employed in companies belonging to vast industrial groups. In the Social Democratic market economy these large companies have become islands of planning exempt from the dictates of the market.

Industry's increasing dependence on the state for infrastructure, regulation and planning has not changed the power of capital. Decision-making is still in the hands of those controlling the corporations. In a desperate search for ways of managing a reluctant industrial sector in the alleged interests of labour, the labour movement latched firmly on to the idea of collective wage-earner funds (Meidner, 1978). By controlling capital, labour would be able – it was claimed – to exert ownership rights and to influence the allocation of capital resources to productive investments in a way that would not increase economic inequality. The ideal of full employment would thus be secured. The labour movement began to regard collective funds as a cure for all ills. The apparent contradictions of the union/owner role did not deter the labour movement from forcing through a proposal based on this idea (see Albrecht and Deutsch, 1983; Sandkull, 1984). The establishment of five regional funds in 1984 was a token measure of little economic weight but great symbolical importance. The debate that preceded the bill and the protests that have followed it have helped to distort human communication in society even more.

Attempts to Salvage the Swedish Model

The success of the initial growth period in Sweden, when industry made possible a better standard of living, resulted in affluence for most of the population. It is one of the ironies of history that this affluence now threatens to jeopardize that mainstay of capitalism (including trade unionism), the money incentive. Quite suddenly a lot of people began to feel that the qualitative aspects of life mattered more to them than any further increases in private consumption. Many of them also became critical of poor working conditions and their subordination at their place of work. They discovered that their living conditions outside the workplace had deteriorated as a result of the industrial exploitation of land and water, and of poor planning in new housing areas and the destruction of the older parts of the cities.

The Social Democratic government has often demonstrated its lukewarm interest in questions of the quality of life apart from its purely material aspects. It has seldom hesitated to destroy some part of a valuable living environment, if jobs could be saved. The government's predilection for solutions involving centralization, bureaucratization and environmental destruction has reduced even many blue-collar workers' faith in the Social Democratic politicians. The new labour legislation has ensnared many unions in interpretations of the law and has widened the gap between the leader and the rank-and-file members. Union leadership has become a new career.

There appear to have been major structural changes in values as well as in material conditions. Several studies suggest that the work ethos has lost much of its hold on young people (for example Ahrne, 1981; Himmelstrand, 1981). They realize that modern society offers too few jobs in which personal skills are important. They would "rather go fishing", if they can get the money. That is the snag: as neither industry nor government can any longer provide enough jobs for the young, they have to resort to other ways of getting money.

As soon as growth ceased, the state's fiscal crisis quickly snowballed. The new Liberal-Conservative government which succeeded the Social Democrats in 1976 continued the previous economic policy more or less unchanged when it came up against the effects of the recession in the international economy.

When leading industrialists recognized what was happening and found that the non-socialist government was incapable of decision-making, they launched a campaign to restore the value of the money incentive and to reduce the social cost of labour. The wage policy based on solidarity should be scrapped, so that wages could be paid according to the value of the labour to each particular industry. The regulations reducing the commodity element in labour should be relaxed. The deficit in government spending must be reduced by cutting the welfare budget and applying fees to previously subsidized public goods.

When two of the government parties made an agreement with the Social Democratic party about a tax reform in order to break out of the impasse, the Conservatives withdrew. The other two parties remained in power on their own, and belatedly presented a plan for tightening the budget and bringing the Swedish economy into balance. They were attacked from two quarters. Freed from the responsibility of government, the Conservative party demanded much tougher cuts, while the Social Democratic party bitterly opposed any cuts at all in welfare spending. The Centre-Liberal government fell easy prey to the Social Democratic attack in the election campaign, and at the next elections in 1982 the Social Democratic party regained power after a campaign promise to restore the golden days at almost no sacrifice to the common people.

Once in power, the new Social Democratic government shocked the nation with a 16 per cent devaluation of the Swedish Krona. The Social Democratic leadership still thinks it can pursue a modified Keynesian economic policy and it has consequently launched ambitious research programmes on production and information technology, and is supporting the application of micropro-cessors and automated equipment in industry.

Towards a new Swedish Model?

A now retired but much respected economist, Eric Dahmén (1982), who differs from the otherwise somewhat homogeneous band of Swedish economists, assumes a different perspective altogether. He accuses present-day economists of lacking any understanding of the peculiarities of Sweden's economic history. He concludes that the country's economic progress during the 150 years up to the 1960s was mainly the result of good luck. It cannot be ascribed to any superior economic insight on the part of the politicians or their economic advisers, nor to the leading businessmen; Marcus Wallenberg is a possible exception.

The present serious situation, he claims, has come about because of a failure to make quick adjustments to changing conditions in the world economy. The economists' suggested solutions for rescuing our ailing economy fail to take this basic aspect into account.

The Swedish model has generated a unique and in many ways very efficient structure for collaboration between labour and capital. But the same structure has raised an enormous barrier to changes in policy or attempts at making basic structural changes in the economy. The shipbuilding industry is a case in point (in Sweden as elsewhere). Neither the industry itself nor its unions nor the government took any precautions when the industry expanded during the 1960s to become second only to Japan in the world. When the market collapsed, the owners of the shipyards more or less abandoned them. The government had to bail out the owners, because for political reasons it was impossible suddenly to lay off all their employees. The government created the Swedish Shipyard Corporation to assume responsibility for this sector, but its executives were quite unprepared to produce the new thinking necessary to make productive use of the competence and knowhow that had accumulated in the shipyards over the years. The unions were anxious as usual to save jobs by any means, but for a long time they had no serious alternative to political lobbying.

The hegemony of neo-classical and Keynesian economics in Sweden has made it very difficult to discuss any other ideas about conditions in the world economy. Since the mid-1960s the world economy has undergone major structural changes, described among others by Frank (1981). Even if we only accept part of Frank's analysis, the facts are there. It is also quite obvious that a large part of Swedish industry is closely connected with international structures.

All the industrialized countries in the OECD, and a few others, are setting their hopes on high technology. Competition is, and will be, fierce. Huge sums are being invested in this field, but for some countries the gains will be dearly bought. Sweden has already had spectacular failures in the fields of nuclear energy and computer technology (Annerstedt, 1970). The present stakes in arms and space technology, for example, ought to be guided by some kind of industrial strategy and not only by optimism. But there is no such strategy.

Confusion in interpretating the economic situation is compounded by a deterioration in the political dialogue. Prevailing ideologies and myths have long defied any reasoned critique of their own validity.

Despite prevailing references to the "information society", the car industry still represents the backbone of the Swedish economy. This was recently demonstrated by Volvo's agreement with the government for locating a new plant in a town suffering from the collapse of one of the large remaining shipyards. And only 20 km away the other Swedish car manufacturer has a plant which has generated 1700 new jobs in two years and whose management predicts a further increase of 1000 workers during the next two years.

The management of the Volvo Group seems to be among the few who understand Sweden's close connection with the global economy, and recognize that a strategy for economic renewal has to be drawn up together with other leading European industrialists.

The extensive unemployment in Europe, particularly among the young, is an expressive indicator of an ailing economy. It can be eased to some extent by relief work programmes – improvements in the infrastructure – but more radical measures such as reducing working hours are called for.

Despite unemployment many industries have difficulty in recruiting young people. Industry needs skilled and loyal workers, but is not very willing to provide initial conditions likely to produce skilled and loyal workers later on. Very often newly recruited employees resign after a couple of months, without any immediate prospects of a new job, because of frustrated hopes and the monotony of the job. The work organization in Swedish companies generally follows the old Taylorite prescriptions: the experts do the brain-work while the rank-and-file workers are supposed to do what the others put before them. In the Volvo Group, however, great efforts are being made to change this division of labour.

If industry is going to take a leading role in a new economic strategy, it has to come to grips with the old question of workers' rights. The solutions will have to acknowledge the inherent antagonism between capital's property rights and human labour, and go further than the Japanese solutions which are based on the legacy of feudalism (see Sandkull, 1985). The present chief executive of the Volvo Group may answer Maccoby's description of a "statesman" (Maccoby, 1981), provided he can generate processes that will start to liberate the workers from their commodity status and set off the kind of "good circles" of participation that were envisaged by Carole Pateman (1970: 43). The workers whould then feel encouraged to take part in open communications in the company; they would become creative participants in the labour process and not only passive operators or observers. "The industry of the future will need the whole man", as one prominent union leader put it recently.

Some steps in this direction have been taken by a few Swedish companies. The chief executive of one company in the Volvo Group who had to guarantee increasing productivity in a contract with a U.S. partner, did not want to sign until he had obtained the workers' promise of complying. He discussed the matter in 50 groups altogether, each group consisting of about 50 employees. Each meeting lasted two hours. Only then was he prepared to sign the contract, which he did three weeks later – convinced that the promise could be fulfilled. This episode is now quoted as a curiosity, because a system of regular open communication has not yet been developed in this company.

In practice the Volvo management has eliminated the control attaching to share ownership. It can itself largely choose the board to which it is supposed to be responsible. What is lacking is any suitable mechanism for making executives accountable to the workers as well. The Group's corporate committee – the Group Works Council – perhaps provides the embryo of such a system. The committee is advisory. It provides the corporate executives with an efficient forum for information and discussion with the 16 union representatives, who are spokesmen for all the Volvo employees in Sweden.

Instead of seeing Sweden become socialized, which hardly anybody believes would be to the country's advantage, perhaps we will witness a Volvo-fication. A new Swedish model could be created, based on full participation and open communication. Such a change would genuinely transform the social relations of production, and would establish a basis for the necessary control of big corporations by the people who work in them. A new Swedish model along these lines would also reduce the importance of hierarchy in favour of markets and networks as the mechanisms of control.

References

Ahrne, G. (1981) *Vardagsverklighet och struktur.* Göteborg: Korpen.
Albrecht, S. L., Deutsch, S. (1983) The Challenge of Economic Democracy: The Case of Sweden. *Economic and Industrial Democracy,* 4, pp. 287–320.
Andersson, L.-G. (1982) *Arbete och kommunikation på Volvo. Inst. för lingvistik.* Stockholm *(Arbete och språkmiljö, rapport nr 3).*
Annerstedt, J. (1970) *Datorer och politik.* Lund: Zenith.
Agurén, S. et al (1984) Volvo Kalmar Revisited – Ten Years of Experience. *Utvecklings-rådet,* Stockholm.

Brodén, P. (1976) Turbulence and Organizational Change. Dissertation, University of Linköping, Linköping.

Dahmén, E. (1977) *Balans- och utvecklingsproblem i svensk ekonomi. Skandinaviska Enskilda Banken Kvartalstidskrift,* pp. 3–10.

– (1982) *Veckans Affärer,* 26.

Ellegård, K. (1983) *Människa – Produktion. Tidsbilder av ett produktionssystem.* Dissertation, Department of Geography, Gothenburg.

Ellerman, D. P. (1980) Property and Production: An Introduction to the Labor Theory of Property. Working paper, Economics Department, Univ. of Mass. Boston MA.

Frank, A. G. (1981) Reflections of the World Economic Crisis. *Monthly Review Press,* New York and London.

Goldman, P., Van Houten, D. R. (1980) Uncertainty, Conflict, and Labor Relations in the Modern Firm II: The War on Labor. *Economic and Industrial Democracy,* 1, pp. 263–287.

Goonatilake, S. (1982) *Crippled Minds.* An Exploration into Colonial Culture. New Delhi: Lake House Bookshop, and Colombo: Vikas Publishing House.

Guillet de Monthoux, P. (1983) *Läran om företaget.* Stockholm: Norstedts.

Habermas, J. (1968) *Technik und Wissenschaft als 'Ideologie'.* Frankfurt am Main. In English (1971): *Towards a Rational Society.* Boston: Beacon Press.

Hermele, K. (1982) *Den drivande kraften, Bilindustrin som exempel.* Stockholm: Liber.

Himmelstrand, Ulf (1981) Beyond Welfare Capitalism. London: Heinemann.

Jönsson, B. (1981) Corporate Strategy for People at Work – The Volvo Experience. Paper presented at the International Conference on the Quality of Working Life in Toronto, Göteborg: Volvo.

Jönsson, S. A., Lundin, R. A. (1977) Myths and Wishful Thinking as Managerial Tools. *Prescriptive Models of Organizations.* Nystrom and Starbuck (Eds.), North-Holland/ TIMS Studies in the Management Sciences, Amsterdam: V. North-Holland Publ. Co.

Kronlund, J.(1973) Paysystem, Production and Safety. A Study in a Swedish Iron Ore Mine. Linköping: Department of Management and Economics, University of Linköping.

Maccoby, M. (1981) The Leader. A New Face for American Management. New York: Simon and Schuster.

Meidner, R. (1978) Employee Investment Funds: An Approach to Collective Capital Formation. London: Allen and Unwin.

Mintzberg, H. (1983) Power in and Around Organizations. Englewood Cliffs, NJ.: Prentice-Hall.

Ny Teknik (1984) p. 6.

Pateman, C. (1970) Participation and Democratic Theory. Cambridge: The University Press.

Sandkull, B. (1984) Using New Technology to Erode Economic and Industrial Democracy. *Economic Analysis and Workers' Management,* 18, pp. 287–296.

– (1985) Industrial Management, Production Technology, and Working Conditions in Japan and Sweden – A Cross-Cultural Comparison. *The Organization and Management in East Asia.* Clegg, Dunphy and Redding (Eds.), Hong Kong: The Centre of Asian Studies, Univ. of Hong Kong.

Schmoller, G. (1904) *Grundrisse der Allgemeinen Volkswirtschaftslehre.* Zweiter Teil, Leipzig: Duncker und Humblot.

Schroyer, T. (1973) *The Critique of Domination. The Origin and Development of Critical Theory.* New York: Braziller.

Stymne, B. (1970) Value Systems and Processes. A Systems Study of Effectiveness in Three Organizations, Lund: SIAR & Studentlitteratur.

Sugimori, Y. et al. (1977) Toyota Production System and Kan ban system – Materialization of Just-in-time and Respect-for-human System. *International of Production Research,* 14.

Söderström, H. T. (1984) *Den svenska ekonomins balansbrister ur finansiellt perspektiv. Skandinaviska Enskilda Banken Kvartalstidskrift,* pp. 42–53.

Mental Standardization and Industrial Development

Sten Jönsson

Abstract

Standards are powerful tools. Justified by efficiency, standards can be used to establish monopolies as well as professions or departments. The most threatening thing about standards, however, may be that they provide a vehicle of domination that in essence is unintentional. Conceptual standards in a way determine what can be said and what cannot be said. They define the terms on which their own functionality may be discussed. The consequence? Accounting systems that everybody complains about but nobody deems possible to change!

Introduction

In managerial accounting there is an ever-present preoccupation with the normal and deviations from the normal. In contrast to financial accounting where the design of reports is governed by numerous mandatory statements backed up by a professional body (the chartered accountants), managerial control systems can be designed to suit the preferences of the specific management of a single unique company. One would therefore expect to find tailormade systems reflecting the particular management style of a company, and a flexibility in design to anticipate future organizational and managerial changes.

Instead we find frequent complaints from managers about the counterproductive rigidity of management accounting systems, which do not provide decision-makers with the right information at the right time.

This is not because computer capacity or software packages prevent managers from registering, storing or reporting almost anything they like. Presentday software allows for extensive modelling of the processes to be controlled, and computers have a capacity to drown any decision-maker in information. No; it seems that managers tend to build conceptual prisons for themselves.

Theoretical Perspectives

This paper is being written at the start of a research program which is planned to continue for several years and which will deal with information support for decentralized economic responsibility in industrial production. Some preliminary studies have already been made and some literature surveyed. The working hypothesis is that we can improve our understanding of present problems by charting the way in which firms have arrived at current designs of management and cost-accounting systems.

It seems sensible first to present the theoretical perspective that has inspired the analysis to be reported below.

Three authors have been the most direct source of inspiration – Mitroff, Argyris and Foucault. Let me present the fragments of their writings that have provided the basis for the approach used here. My aim is not to supply a coherent framework, but rather to illustrate the angle from which the present material will be approached.

To illustrate the process of corporate policy-making Mitroff (1983) takes the case of a drug company in the USA facing low-price competition.

The company manufactures a pain-killer, which has a narcotic base and can thus be obtained only on prescription issued by a physician. Also available is a low-price generic brand substitute, and in some states pharmacists are required by law to inform patients of its existence. No doubt the competitor sees to it that physicians are also informed. This low-price drug is a threat to the whole company. What should be done? The CEO called in the whole management team to analyse the problem:

"A strange thing began to happen. The twelve executives split into three subfactions. This was not done out of any animosity among them, but because complex problems naturally suggest more than one best alternative. The groups began to coalesce around particular alternatives. Each group then proceeded to make the best, that is, strongest, case for its alternative to the exclusion of the other two.« (Mitroff, 1983: 15)

The three alternatives were 1) to lower the price 2) to raise the price, or 3) to ignore the competition.

The group that wanted to raise the price argued that an increase in price would be a signal to the market that there was a difference in quality between the two products. The group that suggested doing nothing about the price wanted to cut internal costs, and the group that called for a lower price obviously wanted to defend market shares.

The only legitimate way to defend a decision among highly qualified managers is to back it up with data. All three groups made extensive analyses of ex post data, and where possible collected new information. Each group reinterpreted common data to suit its own case, and new data were then collected to confirm it. "Hence, instead of data being used to test each alternative, believers in each alternative were procuring data that would confirm its validity." (Mitroff, 1983: 18).

The management group was not able to break out of the deadlock. Outside help was called in, and the solution was to analyse the assumptions that each group had made about important stakeholders in the situation and then to design a real-world test of these assumptions.

The moral of this case in the context of the present paper is that it is not possible to make decisions without also making assumptions about the part of the real world in which the decisions will be implemented. The rational decision models that we carry with us through life are not well-equipped with mechanisms for challenging their own adequacy. On the contrary the models tend to steer the data-gathering that we do to fit themselves. We are not very good at seeing the consequences of making assumptions that become self-evident or that we simply take for granted.

Questioning the self-evident is what Argyris calls "double-loop learning". Argyris (1982) also uses cases to illustrate the problem. One of the cases concerns the president of Davis College and the committee he appointed to prepare concrete recommendations for the future of the college. The recommendations presented by the committee were analysed by participants in an executive program, who found them "Vague – typical of committees with no specific goals", etc.

Argyris points out that the microtheory of management on which this kind of diagnosis is based is that "if you specify the job and reward fairly, employees will produce what you expect, if they do not, you have a right to question their actions or even punish them" (Argyris, 1982: 4).

This microtheory is part of life and is taken for granted. The rules and expectations embedded in it are the basis of order. But what if the faculty committee had realized that concrete and specific recommendations could pull the organization apart? Neither they nor the president would be able to deal effectively with the reactions. The consequences would be counterproductive to the established order. So the committee produced a vague set of recommendations, typical of a faculty committee.

Argyris maintains that distancing, undiscussability and counterproductive advice are predictable responses to problems like this. People seem to be programmed to act like the actors in the case, remaining blind to the paradox. Many recognize the paradox when it is pointed out to them, but they are doomed to repeat their automatic responses. People choose to deal with such difficulties by using games "whose primary features are that they are known to all players, they are undiscussable, and their undiscussability is undiscussable" (Argyris, 1982: 10).

Argyris illustrates this inability to break away from frames of reference and to learn new approaches in several cases, and he formulates conditions that facilitate double-loop learning.

The trick is to make ourselves aware of our theories-in-use – and that is no easy task, since our actions are learned through socialization and are therefore highly skilled. "The essential feature of highly skilled actions is that they can be performed without giving attention to the mental programs required to produce them" (Argyris, 1982: 474). This skillful action makes it possible to entertain disconnected "espoused theories", without noticing the discrepancy between these and the theories-in-use embedded in skillful action. In problematic situations people tend to behave in accordance with their theories-in-use, without being aware of it.

The thing to do then is to provide directly observable data which can be used to test/infere evaluations and attributions, and then to recognize that one is responsible for specific actions in a given situation but not solely for having been socialized into one's theory-in-use. In this way theories-in-use become discussable and amenable to redesign. Who is responsible for the socialization that produces theories-in-use, one might ask.

It is obviously no easy task to answer this question, since theories-in-use emerge as it were out of use itself. They are not imposed by some outside agent but are generated by action. Yet they are very powerful determinants of action. They are their own cause and are not therefore amenable to rational analysis. Gödel's theorem comes to mind, and his statement – in a slightly adapted version as spoken by myself – "All Swedes are liars".

An approach is needed to act as a can-opener to break the circularity. It seems that Foucault can provide one with his archeological approach to knowledge. "Archeological analysis involves comparison: comparison of one discursive practice with another and a discursive practice with the non-discursive practices (institutions, political events, economic and social processes) that surround it" (Sheridan, 1980: 105). Archeological analysis is also a description of change in which the focus is on the existence of rules of formation of discourse. "Discourse is not about objects: rather, discourse constitutes them."

A discourse is a limited space of communication not as extensive as a "science with its historical development". The analysis of discourse examines the conditions governing the production of statements; the group of rules that emerges characterizes a discursive practice. In this way Foucault avoids basing his analysis on an intuition of the intentions expressed by subjects. His analysis looks for the facts; statements accumulate, some are lost, some are reactivated. The analysis becomes archeological.

The driving-force is the will to knowledge (a term borrowed from Nietzsche) and the production of discourse also produces a kind of enslavement. The production of discourse is controlled by procedures of exclusion; one such procedure is prohibition (we are not free to speak of anything at any time); another is division and rejection (there is a definition of the madman, and he is not allowed to sign contracts), and the opposition between true and false: "True discourse, that which inspired respect and terror, that to which all had to submit because it held sway over all, was the discourse spoken by men as of right and in accordance with the required ritual" (Foucault, *L'Ordre du discours,* p. 17, quoted by Sheridan, 1980: 123).

Further, the highest truth resides not in what discourse was or in what it did, but in what it *said.* The discourse and its will to truth operates on a whole institutional base; the education system, the distribution of information through learned societies, libraries and so on. It becomes a subject for commentary; those who speak become rarefied through rituals of qualification and societies of discourse are formed. At the same time as discourse generates power to deal with some aspect of life, it also exerts power. A network of micropowers is at work, but since it is not a centralized, hierarchized organization of rules, it cannot be overthrown by revolutionary struggle aimed at the destruction of institutions or leaders. The struggle has to be localized.

In order to understand, we have a threefold task: "We have to question our will to truth, restore to discourse its character as event and abolish the sovreignty of the signifier." The methodological principles required are *reversal* ("What traditionally have been regarded as the sources of discourse – author, discipline, will to truth – must be seen as the negative action of segmentation and rarefraction of discourse" (Sheridan op. cit.: 128)), *discontinuity* (... "discourses must be treated as discontinuous practices that variously intersect, juxtapose and exclude one another" (Sheridan op. cit.: 128)), *specificity* ("discourse must be concieved as a violence we do to things or at least as a practice we impose on them, in which the events of discourse find their regularity" (Sheridan op. cit.: 128)), and *exteriority* ("not ... towards some inner core of meaning concealed within it but proceed from discourse, from its specific emergence and regularity, to its external conditions of possibility" (Sheridan op. cit.: 128)).

With the help of Sheridan (1980) I have come to the conclusion that intuitively Foucault seems to provide an approach that can help us to understand why the cost accounting discourse in Sweden is in its present state. It is not any specific method of data collection that comes to mind, but an approach to the whole complex of influences that appear to have been in play. It seems necessary to find a different perspective in order to understand the closely knit system of practices and rules that cost accounting comprises today. Kaplan (1982) points out the need for new approaches to academic managerial accounting and suggests that we start collecting our anecdotes from present-day corporations, instead of relying "on the experience of successful organizations 60 to 100 years ago" (p. 51). It is rather remarkable that an academic discipline should exhibit the behavior that Kaplan describes! Another phenomenon that we noted from the start in our hitherto modest fieldwork, is that even if cost accountants are very well-informed about the details of present procedures, they do not generally seem to know what problems the present procedures were invented to solve, and are thus ill-equipped to adapt the system to present needs. On arrival in the company they seem to be initiated into the inherited practices, and then remain constantly preoccupied with the application of those practices to emergent problems. The necessity for understanding the justification of the practices has been suppressed by the urgency of current problem-solving.

It is certainly not true that cost accountants are a special breed of human being. But cost accounting is a very powerful discourse. It seems as though it creates a "region of truth" about the organizational world. Yet there is some variety. National standards promulgated by men of authority provide a framework for debate, while company standards – sometimes also established through committee processes – aim more directly at concrete practices. Is there a relation between these two levels? Under what circumstances do standards change?

These issues need to be studied if we are to be better prepared to deal with current problems. The approach to be used is indicated by the perspective described above. The method will be to account for the historical development of the cost accounting discourse at the national level in Sweden since the First World War, and then to take a closer look at one of our major industrial companies.

However, first there ist the question of the origins of the authority of those standard-setters. Why have engineers dominated the stage in Sweden? Obviously in a short paper it is only possible to indicate a few ideas. There are movements in business life that bring new insights, which in turn affect practices. The Scientific Management movement was such an initiator of change.

There also appear to be culturally determined loci of institutionalized authority. At the turn of the century Sweden had age-old cultural links with Germany, where by way of the "Reichskuratorium für Wirtschaftlichkeit" founded in 1921, the state bureaucracy occupied the major institutional role. In the USA and the UK professional associations were more important.

And there was of course the initial historical situation in terms of the state of the art and general industrial development. In the following section I shall try to set the stage for die Swedish process by referring to certain issues and influences that seem relevant.

International Influences

Garner (1954) provides a survey of the early development of cost accounting in the English-speaking world which has been widely read. He found that the 19th century up to about 1885 deserved the label "the Dark Ages" (Garner, 1954: 68). Before 1900 it was mainly the English who contributed to the literature of the subject, but since the beginning of the present century the initiative seems to have passed to the USA.

On the wages and materials side there was a steady development without any dramatic leaps. The rapid price changes at the beginning of the 1920s, however, stimulated a debate on the use of replacement cost for raw materials. It also became customary to argue for the use of standard costs.

Accounting for overheads interested few authors before 1885, but Garke und Fells writing in 1887 distinguished between production and administrative overheads. The latter should be charged direct to the profit and loss account while the former should be allocated to the products concerned. By 1910 the general opinion was that sales and administration costs should not be included in the cost of production, since they did not contribute to the value of the product.

A new and interesting factor was introduced into the debate with the question of whether interest on capital employed in production should be counted as a cost, which meant that economic-theoretical thinking began to infiltrate the accounting debate. The inclusion of interest on borrowed capital is a natural consequence of its appearance in financial accounting as an expenditure to outside parties. But the inclusion of interest on equity capital called for justification in terms of opportunity cost.

Around the turn of the century this issue arrived to stay. A questionnaire sent to about 40 companies in the USA at the time (Garner, 1954: 146) showed that the majority regarded interest on employed capital as a cost. By about 1910 the general opinion on both sides of the Atlantic seems to have been that interest on employed capital should be included as a cost (Garner, 1954: 151). But then opinions started to change again. Dickinson maintained in 1911 that interest is part of profit allocation, and thus should not be counted as a cost. A number of accountants now appear to have entered the debate, which had previously been dominated by production engineers. Webner opposed Dickinson, maintaining that investment in buildings and equipment was obviously necessary to the production of the products sold; consequently interest was part of total production costs. During the war the debate continued. Church represented a change of opinion in 1917, declaring that whether or not interest is counted as a cost is of little consequence. Management should decide to do as they saw fit. In 1918 the American Institute of Accountants put the problem officially on its agenda, and the special committee came to the conclusion that interest should not be included in the cost of production. "The inclusion in production cost of interest on investment in unsound in theory and wrong, not to say absurd, in practice." (*American Institute of Accountants Yearbook*, 1918: 112).

Besides interest, the treatment of the cost of unused capacity was another major problem, resulting naturally from the ambition to allocate costs fairly.

An early proponent of an advanced line of argument on this issue was Church. He developed his "scientific production center" technique for the allocation of overheads at the beginning of the present century. Production centers can determine their production costs because they are billed for all services enjoyed. Church discusses overheads as costs for a number of specific "service factors" (space, power, machinery, storage, transport and other service factors).

He determines the standard cost of every service factor and the share of each production process in the different services. Only two problems then remain: to determine whether the standard was the correct one, and to decide how idle-running time should be treated. Church solved these problems by calculating the cost of a process hour (the rate) and then monitoring real cost per month and carrying unabsorbed burden over to the profit and loss account.

When Garner (1954) summarizes developments in the Anglo-Saxon world of cost accounting before 1925, these are this main points (p. 341f):

– cost accounting aroused little interest before 1885
– the English were in the lead up to 1900, whereupon the Americans took over
– overheads were hardly discussed at all before 1900
– "bad times" seem to generate innovations in cost accounting
– early developments were generated by engineers rather than accountants.

Institutionalization

First for purposes of comparison I will briefly describe the emergence of a British institutional basis for a cost accounting debate, before examining the German influence which seems to have had the most important impact on Swedish developments.

Britain

During the First World War the British government found it necessary to "interfere" with business in order to mobilize the resources necessary for the war (Crawford, 1984). The system of pricing embraced cost of production plus a reasonable profit. Obviously this system was not easy to supervise. Profiteering caused industrial unrest, and increased the demand for accountants. The supply was limited. A few months after the end of the war the Institute of Cost and Works Accountants (ICWA) was established. There was an economic boom up to 1920 followed by a severe depression in 1921, and industrial disputes. It was necessary to rationalize production. The first costing conference organized by the ICWA was entitled "The necessity of scientific costing". A special committee was formed in 1922 to deal with "the very important subject of nomenclature of costing terms" (Crawford, 1984: 42). At the conference frequent references were made to the success of the uniform system of the Federation of Master Printers which made it possible for individual firms to find out whether they were above or below average efficiency (ibid.: 43). Several speakers favored standardization of costing methods as well as terminology.

The German Connection

Ever since the Thirty Years War in the seventeenth century, the German influence on Swedish society has been considerable. It was to be expected that the foreign literature on cost accounting reaching Sweden at the beginning of this century would come mainly from Germany. This was partly due to the translations of German books made by the Industrial Bureau, a subsidiary of the Federation of Swedish Industries established in 1910, and partly to the establishment of the first Swedish business school in Stockholm in 1909. Its first professor of management was a German (Walb), although he was soon succeeded by a Swede (Oskar Sillén), who worked part-time for the Business school and part-time for the Industrial Bureau – which at the time was the center of the Scientific Management movement in Sweden. Sillén held a degree from a German business school, and when he was asked to join the Stockholm business school was actually working at the Berlin office of AB Separator whose chief engineer, E. A. Forsberg, was a leading proponent of scientific management and a part-time teacher at the Royal Institute of Technology. Forsberg was succeeded by T. Sällfors at the Institute of Technology in 1928, at which time Sällfors was head of the Industrial Bureau.

To students at the business schools it was Schmalenback and Schmid who relayed the gospel, while to practioners – in so far as the literature of the subject had any influence – it was the books translated by the Federation of Swedish Industries.

Schmalenbach wrote a paper about full cost calculation in 1899, published in book form in 1928. He declares that overheads can be covered only by receipts from customers. The burden should be borne by those who enjoy the benefits. The bookkeeper should thus allocate overheads in such a way that the origins of profits or losses can be traced. He discusses different bases for allocation, but does not mention interest on equity or on capital employed.

When the Federation of Swedish Industries published Calmes' book on *The Organization of Factories,* in 1911, the aim was "to spread an interest in organizational science and an understanding of the application of modern organization in business". "Organization", according to Calmes on the first page, means order, division of work an monitoring. He goes through the items indicated in the title, organization, bookkeeping and full cost calculation.

Sperlich (1917) presents his case through detailed case studies. He does not mention interest on capital. The concrete descriptions in his book suggest why such an idea never comes into the text. It seems that the first basis in bookkeeping makes an imputed cost like interest on equity an impossible accounting event.

In 1918, what is today called DIN (Deutsche Institut für Normung) was founded. The war had demonstrated the need for technical standardization.

Schmidt (1921) published his main contribution after the war. It refers to Schmalenbach and to society at large. The new element here is the idea of valuation at replacement cost. In Schmidt's view normal interest and a salary to the entrepreneur should be included in overheads. "Vieles spricht dafür, daß der Vermögensverbrauch das Verschenken von Kostenteilen schon beginnt wenn nicht mindestens der normale Zinssatz auf das Unternehmungskapital und ein Unternehmergehalt erzielt wird" (p. 116). The striving for standardization efforts intensified, and the first guidelines for full cost calculation were published in 1920 by the "Ausschuß für wirtschaftliche Fertigung" which was incorporated in the Reichskuratorium für Wirtschaftlichkeit in 1921. After Schmalenbach published his famous *Kontenrahmen* in 1927, the Reichskuratorium – which was the center for standardization work in Germany – started to produce "normal" charts of accounts for different industries with the help of a committee under Schmalenbach. The charts may not have had much effect on practice, but they provided the basis for the overall standard and compulsory chart of accounts promulgated in 1937 as part of the Nazi war effort (cf. ter Vehn, 1945).

The Swedish National Level

As we have seen Oskar Sillén was asked to succeed Ernst Walb as professor of management at the Stockholm School of Economics. He was not satisfied with the pay offered, nor did he consider the job security satisfactory, but it was possible to arrange a part-time job for him at the Industrial Bureau, and so he accepted the job in 1912. In 1913 he published a small booklet on the basic characteristics of industrial full-cost calculation (Sillén, 1913). In the preface he points out that practice varies and that his book by no means provides a general prescription for making industrial cost calculations. In fact it is not possible to provide a model that would be generally applicable. Many people do not realize this, which opens the market to irresponsible consultants. In the preface Sillén also thanks E. A. Forsberg, his former boss, for much valuable advice.

The need for full cost calculation, says Sillén, "has arisen during the last few decades as a result of the intensified competition between companies" (p. 7). If they had a reliable full cost accounting system, many companies would see the wisdom of cutting down their range of products. Sillén consistently maintains a relativist approach: there are different practices – one may suit some companies, another may suit others – and this attitude affects his treatment of capital costs. Some companies include only interest paid in their cost of capital, while some include interest on the necessary equity. Sillén does not take sides. In a concluding chapter he says that in the final analysis the cost of capital (including interest on equity) has to be covered by sales revenues, so the discussion is really about whether it should be considered as part of cost or part of profit. On the one hand two products made on different machines should be charged differently according to the cost of the machines; on the other, conformity with existing practices would best be achieved by including the cost of capital in general overheads.

Forsberg was a part-time teacher in industrial management at the Royal Institute of Technology, a scientific management enthusiast and a production engineer at AB Separator. In Forsberg (1916) he had wider aims than Sillén, and his approach was normative. He wanted to provide an overview of the basic principles of industrial management. Forsberg's book contains the first Swedish discussion of real time-and-motion studies.

Forsberg defines full cost as the price at which a product can be sold without profit or loss. However, this definition has to be modified somewhat, since "one of the most important aims of full cost calculation is to make comparisons between different production methods possible" (p. 14). Therefore a distinction should be made between production full cost and sales full cost. "Consequently we deduce that in no industrial firm should any cost of sales be included in full cost" (p. 15). Interest on loans as well as equity should be included. Uniform overhead charges as a percentage of wages is reprehensible.

Spreading the Word

The Industrial Bureau was started by the Federation of Swedish Industries in 1912 as a consulting firm specializing in industrial organization (de Geer, 1978: 104f). Oskar Sillén was appointed to be its CEO for the first 5 years.

Sillén soon started to concentrate on auditing and financial accounting; engineers took over cost accounting. The lodestar was Scientific Management, whose ideological center the Industrial Bureau (Industribyrån) soon became.

The Federation of Swedish Industries and the Swedish Association of Technologists provided the institutional setting for the development of costing standards, and it was in fact a debate at the Swedish Association of Technologists that lay behind the establishment of the Federation in 1910.

In April 1924 Olof Kärnekull of the Industrial Bureau wrote an article in Teknisk Tidskrift (The Technical Journal), in which he proposed that a new section for industrial organization and economy should be added to the Association, to provide a forum for the discussion of rationalization issues. Kärnekull was asked by the board to work out a program for the new section. The program was sent out for comments and met with resistance. The idea was shelved.

Things improved at the annual meeting of the Association in 1928. The agenda drawn up by the organizing committee was not kept; at the last minute a major discussion of the principles of full cost calculations and industrial bookkeeping had been substituted (de Geer, 1978: 189). This was occasioned by a letter from the Standardization Committee of Swedish Industries (SIS) asking for comments on a proposed standard for the terminology of full cost calculation (see below). In 1931 Kärnekull again proposed that a permanent section for industrial organization and economy should be established. This time he succeeded. The section was called Section I.

A prominent participant in the costing debate at the time was Nils Fredriksson. He was a senior officer on the Royal National School Board, in charge of the bureau for occupational training and chairman of one of the sections of the Association.

The major information channel for the Scientific Management movement was *Affärsekonomi,* a new journal started in 1928. Oskar Sillén was chairman of the editorial committee, Kärnekull was a member.

The Standardization Process Starts

On 5th February 1927 the Royal National School Board wrote to the Standardization Committee (SIS), calling for some action to achieve a uniform terminology of full-cost calculation to be used in schools. In March SIS appointed a special committee to work out a draft. Members of the committee were N. Fredriksson (who wrote the letter!?), T. Kristensson, R. Liljeblad, H. R. Schultz, and O. Sillén. One year later a proposal was presented for a "Uniform basic terminology for full-cost calculation". It closely resembled the German AWF-plan from 1920.

The procedure for full-cost calculation was divided into three steps; the determination of the cost elements (1), the allocation to cost centers (2), and the allocation to cost units. Overhead costs are defined as costs common to more than one cost unit, and are divided into material overheads, production overheads, and sales overheads. Concepts such as allocation base, burden variable and fixed costs, a priori calculus (estimate) and ex post calculus (costing), and prime costing were also suggested.

The proposal was greatly influenced by the terminology used by ASEA, a heavy manufacturing company with a very large product range. Two members of the committee, Liljeblad and Schultz, both engineers, represented ASEA.

There were critical voices, primarily from SKF the ball-bearing company in Göteborg. In May 1928 Forsberg stressed the relation between absorption costing and cost accounting in a speech given to the Swedish Association of Technologists (Forsberg, 1928). He described the standard cost accounting that SKF had used since 1918. Two cost calculations are compared on the production account – on the credit side the estimated normal (standard) cost and on the debit side the real acquisition costs and production costs with a deduction for unused capacity. He maintained that all costs should be evaluated at the historic rate, and that working hours provide a better basis for the allocation of overheads than wages. Furthermore, neither interest on employed capital, nor debt, nor equity should be included. He also suggested that some practising cost accountants should be brought on to the SIS committee, as this was not a task for engineers or academics.

The committee was enlarged to include among others E. Jacobsson of SKF, and in December 1929 a revised draft was presented. In its introduction the point was made that every cost estimate should be geared to the decision situation at hand (different costs for different purposes).

The concept of "cost element" is replaced by "type of cost", while the cost center and the cost unit are given less prominent treatment. The committee discussed estimates using historic cost, current cost, and replacement cost. The question of the inclusion of interest was postponed, until it could be discussed in connection with costing procedures. At this stage the issue was terminology. It was maintained that full cost consists of production costs, sales costs and administration costs.

Production costs consist of direct material, direct wages and production overheads. Cost calculations that serve different purposes are based on different assumptions regarding the selection and evaluation of resources. In March 1930 a new draft was sent out for comment. About 50 comments were received. Critical voices were heard from the SKF camp. A. Gabrielsson, an engineer, the CEO of Volvo and a former employee of SKF, delivered a speech at a meeting of the Swedish Association of Business Economists in April 1930, sharply criticizing the draft for failing to distinguish between cost accounting and cost estimates. Current costs, interest on employed capital etc. should not be part of cost accounting. The selection of the current prices and opportunity costs that are relevant in a decision situation should be made when the estimate is undertaken, and not according to some predetermined standard. In the discussion Liljeblad of ASEA was the main actor.

In February 1931 SIS presented another revised draft for terminology, and this was published as a provisional standard in June. The leaning towards ASEA praxis was still there. Some clarifications, e.g. that full cost means the inclusion of all costs up to the point when the product is delivered and paid for, had been added.

The committee says:

"It is obvious that a proposal for a general terminology will initially meet resistance from many parties. There are great difficulties involved in drafting a proposal that will satisfy all interested parties. The terms and definitions now presented, however, probably represent what is at present considered to be the generally accepted and from different viewpoints the most suitable practices. The committee itself has felt doubtful on several points, however, and is very well aware that justified objections can be raised against certain aspects of the draft. It therefore seems appropriate that the draft should be tested over a period before being promulgated as Swedish standard. It also seems appropriate that such promulgation be postponed until a proposal of norms for a uniform procedure for absorption costing has been worked out. The committee deems it most desirable that such norms should be worked out as soon as possible by a suitable body."

At the meeting of Section I (Industrial organization and economy) of the Swedish Association of Technologists in the spring of 1931, the need for uniform procedures for absorption costing was discussed. A resolution to approach SIS on the issue was adopted. SIS later passed the matter back to Section I, asking for an investigation of the measures that should be taken. Section I appointed a committee in February 1932 to plan and estimate the costs of working out such procedural norms. The members were: N. Fredriksson (chairman), E. Gillberg, R. Liljeblad, O. Kärnekull, E. Jacobsson with

H. R. Schultz and T. Sällfors as alternates. It was decided that the Swedish Association of Technologists, the Academy of Technology, SIS and the Federation of Swedish Industries should share the cost.

Liljeblad took the initiative by proposing that the full cost concept should be based on the sales price at which the firm can operate continually at normal use of capacity and without financial contributions from outside, but also without profit exceeding the payment of interest on the capital employed. This means that absorption costing should consist of a "normal" calculus using current costs.

Materials should be calculated at standard cost, as close to current cost as possible. The cost of fixed assets should be based on present values as regards age and condition. Interest should be included, and the rate should be the one at which the firm can borrow in the open market.

Enthusiasm on the part of SKF/Volvo to participate seems to have faded. Jacobsson, who was busy monitoring the compliance of the SKF subsidiaries with the SKF standards, resigned from the committee and was replaced by Thorelli of L. M. Ericsson.

The committee presented its "Proposal for uniform principles for absorption costing" in April 1934. The ASEA philosophy prevailed. In a memo to the committee Gabrielsson of Volvo presented his critique and proposed a compromise. He maintaned that two kinds of costing are needed simultaneously: absorption cost accounting and absorption cost calculation.

By absorption cost *accounting* he meant the costing which is built into the cost accounting system and conducted according to cost accounting principles and which results in real manufacturing costs. Absorption cost accounting should be organized in such a way that the resulting price of the finished goods does not contain any unrealized profit. Thus it should not contain cost of capital or present of future values of materials.

By absorption cost *calculation* he meant a separate cost estimate designed to provide a basis for the determination of sales price. The calculation will be different for different purposes. The selling price involving no loss of substance but also no return on capital is calculated by adding to the accounting cost of production a charge for sales and administrative overheads and a correction for present or future material prices. A charge for capital costs is also added, etc.

His main objection was that the committee had been biased towards cost calculation and had disregarded accounting principles. His suggestion was that the manufacturing cost should be based on accounting principles i.e. on historic costs. The principal issue, according to Gabrielsson, was whether greater priority should be given to Liljeblad's fear of faulty costing due to changing prices or to his own fear of subjective accounting. He referred to Anglo-Saxon auditing principles whereby every accounting transaction that generated income should be based on a real business transaction involving external parties. Liljeblad replied that cost accounting should be based on principles that give correct results even in times of radical price changes, and the use of current costs was based on ASEA's experience of such a complicated system of job orders that the method proposed by Gabrielsson would mean an enormous amount of work.

"Uniform principles for absorption costing" was promulgated as the Swedish standard in 1936. It was well-adapted to manufacturing industry, it was in fact the Association of Machinery Industry that was the first to promote it. Already by April 1937 the Association had appointed a committee to adapt the principles further to the needs of its members.

The first application to a specific industry occurred in 1939, when the principles were adopted by the foundries. In the introduction to the committee's report (1938: 7) we can read: "In no industry does the need for uniformity in cost calculation seems to be greater than in the foundry industry. Anybody who has had an opportunity to compare foundry tenders cannot have avoided being surprised by the huge differences in price between offers."

The Normal Chart of Accounts

In debate the main argument for uniform cost calculation practices seems to have been the elimination of "unhealthy competition".

Another argument for uniformity (besides the German standard chart of accounts of 1937) was now added: the need for the cost control of state contracts, and for general price control in wartime.

In our story the initiative now moves to the association of Machinery Industry (Mekan). In November 1940 Mekan's board (of which Nils Fredriksson was a member) appointed a committee for uniform accounting methods. The secretary to the committee was professor Robert Kristensson of the Royal Institute of Technology.

The committee wanted a standard chart of accounts for manufacturing industry that would be more flexible than the German standard as regards costing principles, cost control systems, valuation methods, accounting techniques and size. In December 1941 it produced a preliminary draft which was presented at a meeting organized by Section I of the Swedish Association of Technologists. The discussion led to revisions. In March 1943 it was decided to employ professor A. ter Vehn of the Göteborg Business School to produce a commentary on the proposed chart of accounts. (Since then this chart of accounts, which is excellent for teaching purposes, has been something of a trademark of the Göteborg Business School.) It is not possible to describe the system in any detail here. There were 10 classes of accounts with financial accounts in classes 0, 1, 8 and 9 and cost accounts in the remainder. It can be adapted to any kind of costing method. The normal chart of accounts quickly became generally accepted and widely used, and this completed the standardization process.

The post-war debate on uniform methods of cost calculation started on 27th October 1948, when the economist T. Palander presented a paper on the merits of uniform principles for cost calculation at a meeting organized by the Association of Business Administration (note: not engineers) (Affärsekonomi 1949, nos. 1, 3 and 13). Palander maintained that cost calculations were supposed to facilitate the choice between alternatives (decision-making) and that marginal cost was the proper basis for this. He used highly stylized formulations of types of production to prove his point, and he stimulated a good deal of debate. Liljeblad was the first to enter the fray. He maintained that firms are not as simple-minded as Palander seems to assume, nor are the extremely simplified examples that Palander used of any practical relevance. ASEA had 40 000 different products, and it is impossible to see how we should go about decreasing production of one to increase another.

This occasion was important perhaps not so much because of what was said that evening but because it marked the beginning of a new era, one in which managerial ideas rebelled against traditional absorption costing and the ASEA philosophy.

Soon after this a manager in the textile industry, Ericsson, wrote (Affärsekonomi 1950, nos. 1, 3 and 5) on the blessing of direct costing and pointed out that overheads are not covered until the product is sold. What about pricing then? Well, why not charge what the customer is willing to pay? Overheads should be monitored by way of budgetary control. The objectives of the accounting system should be set first, and the simplest possible solution should then be sought.

Liljeblad replied to this (Affärsekonomi 1950, no. 11), stating that the "Uniform principles ... are basically grounded on the ASEA experience." Later they were both the target of unfounded criticism: Palander was out of touch with reality and Ericsson's experience disastrous if applied to manufacturing industry in general. Market prices are determined by cost levels.

The debate continued and early in 1951 there was a new turn of events. A representative of a major steel company (Kling, in Affärsekonomi 1951, no. 7) joined Palander and Ericsson on the stage and pointed out that the decision situation ought to be determined before the choice of relevant costs can be made.

Ericsson and Liljeblad met in a further discussion on pricing, which was reported in Affärsekonomi. They did not manage to convince one another.

This was probably the last public appearance of Ragnar Liljeblad, who had been an authority on cost calculation for 20 years.

This marked the beginning of a switch to an almost exclusive focus on costing for optimal choices in various decision-making situations. Product costing was a hot issue for some time, but soon marketing, organization and management science took over the center of the stage.

The RP Project

In February 1973 a project concerned with the design of accounting systems was presented at Mekan. A working party consisting of representatives from several major firms had been set up to look into the structuring of data for accounting systems so as to promote greater flexibility in reporting. The multidimensional recording of transactions and database thinking had been under discussion for some time, and now the "RP project" was started. From 1975 this project began to generate output in the form of books, manuals, case studies and seminars. Today it is well-established as the way of dealing with accounting system design. Its terminology is accepted in practice and in educational courses in management accounting.

The accounting plan (in Swedish _Redovisningsplan_) is a plan for governing the activities of the accounting process. The following diagram illustrates its scope:

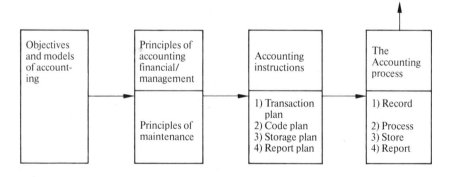

Principles are deduced from the objectives of the accounting system and the models used for management control. The accounting instructions, which could be said to be the core characteristic of the RP model defines what transaction are to be recorded in the system, what codes (mostly "labels" of accounts) that are used in the system, how information is stored and what reports are generated (standard and contingent). As can be seen from this very short presentation, the RP project provides not a standard for accounting but a terminology and to a certain extent a procedure for designing systems. Any control model and any computer program package can be fitted into this framework. The RP group has refrained from prescribing what accounting models should be used, and has worked instead on describing a number of cases. The aim is to show that different solutions to most problems are possible. However, no matter how ambitious a project plan may be to begin with, companies which have decided to revise their accounting systems often end up simply converting the old system to a new computer package. It seems well nigh impossible to generate enough impetus to be able to carry out major changes in those extremely complex and interconnected systems that we call management control systems. What happens? Which are the forces that block us on our way towards the completely flexible management information system of our dreams?

The Company Level

Towards the end of the 19th century several of Sweden's major manufacturing companies were founded, often based on inventions (Separator, AGA, Ericsson, ASEA, SKF). At the same time industry in general expanded and factories were organized for mass production. SKF was a breakaway from the textile company Gamlestaden, and it was based on the construction of a self-regulating ball-bearing invented by Sven Wingqvist. Operations started in 1907 and by 1913 annual production exceeded one million bearings. By 1917 factories had been acquired in the UK (1911), Germany (1914), the USA (1916) and France (1917), while the Göteborg factory had been expanded several times. SKF's strategy was to sell directly to the customer through its own agents, which meant that a strong marketing organization had to be set up.

During 1915 and for a year or two after that, Uno Forsberg and Björn Prytz were in the USA in connection with the takeover of the formerly German-owned factories in Philadelphia. There they came across new approaches to organization, technology and management accounting Forsberg wrote to his boss (Wingqvist) in May 1917. "It is to be expected that when this war is over there will be fierce competition on the world market in all industries especially in ours. As a consequence it will be of crucial importance that production is conducted in the most rational and efficient ways possible. There are primarily three things I have in mind concerning our organization in Göteborg which – at least when I left – were not up to the standard nowadays required, namely an efficient and carefully designed time-keeping system, a systematic and fully implemented routing system, and a reliable factory accounting system that not only records ingoing and outgoing materials but also keeps track of labour values, productive and non-productive, in a way that makes it possible to include a complete ingoing and outgoing balance."

He thus suggested that a time studies department should be set up and that production planning should be improved. He wanted to hire a time study and organization man and a factory accounting man, who were first to learn in the US factories and then to be placed in Göteborg. Wingqvist gave the go-ahead by telegram.

So they got started. Prytz succeeded Wingqvist as CEO in 1919 and specialized in administration, sales and finance, while Forsberg was responsible for production and technology. Walsh, Jacobsson and Stenberg were in charge of accounting. Jacobsson spent a couple of years at the plants in the USA (and Canada) in 1916–18, and Assar Gabrielsson worked on the sales side. In 1919 there was a reorganization which included a new department for "production planning". It planned the work and the material flow necessary for production. There were registers for machine capacities and the necessary parts for each typ of bearing. Thus the necessary conditions for establishing pre-calculated standard costs were there. A work and time study department had also been started the same year.

At this time SKF also switched to a consignment stock operation. This meant that the ball bearings remained the property of SKF until they were sold to the end user. Formerly the German producers had been the price-leaders; now SKF produced price-lists based on their own standard costs and took over the market leadership. But pricing had to be flexible; the price based on the standard costs was announced as a target price. SKF has always had separate responsibility for production and sales. The new price-lists also indicated transfer prices from production to sales.

To hold everything together, a new accounting system was introduced in 1920. It focussed on financial accounting and required uniform accounting principles throughout the SKF group. The internal audit scrutinized monthly reports, and central management received a much greater flow of data on operations.

The Chart of Accounts

The chart of accounts was described in what was called "the SKF bible". It continued to be used virtually unchanged until 1971. The basic structure of the cost accounting thus remained the same right through a very long period of dramatic industrial development. Maybe the system was flexible enough from the start to accommodate change. SKF is said to have been the first Swedish company to "computerize" its cost accounting (using punch-cards), and that this could be done without redesigning the system, but it is still difficult to explain how the system can have worked under such varying conditions over such a long period. We cannot be sure that the cost accounting practices were uniform among the SKF subsidiaries, but we know that young men were trained in the use of the "bible" at the Göteborg head office, and that they were then placed around the world to implement the Göteborg model. We also know that in 1928 people from SKF criticized the national terminology draft standard (Forsberg, 1928), adding that these things should not be developed exclusively by engineers and academics. As a result the group controller of SKF – Jacobsson – was appointed to an enlarged national committee. However, he soon resigned due to lack of time. And what made him so busy was his frequent journeys, visiting companies in the group to see that the SKF bible was being uniformly applied.

There were some changes in the costing system, generally concerning the calculation of overheads. From the start machine hours rather than labor was used as the base of allocation, since one man could sometimes run more than one machine. The changes were concerned mainly with the allocation of indirect overheads.

Towards the end of the 1950s a number of costing problems had been discovered. The reason was that at that time the European factories were producing most of the product line. When capacity use was low, factories would ask whether it would not be a good idea to produce a certain product in the factory that had the lowest cost. But when costs were examined more closely, it was found that they were not always comparable due to differences in accounting procedures.

It was then decided to set up a "cost committee", whose members should be chosen from the European factories. Its mission was to decide on the principles for cost calculation to be applied in the group as a whole. The first meeting was held in November 1959, and a 15-point agenda was drawn up. One point, for instance, concerned the allocation of "non-productive overheads". (After some discussion it was decided that the principle used by the Göteborg factory should be used.) Late in 1963 the cost committee issued a handbook "Principles for cost calculation in the SKF group". This ended the committee's first active phase.

It was re-activated in 1970. The problem now was to adapt cost calculations to the new strategy for meeting low-price competition. In order to counteract this mainly Japanese competition SKF had decided to rationalize its operations and to go in for longer runs. This meant a restructuring of production. Ball-bearing types should be produced in as few factories as possible and in longer runs. As well as the economies of scale due to the production-line system, this meant a marked increase in internal trade between factories and sales departments in the group. Overhead charges were split into several items, and machine hours as the basis for overhead charges was scrutinized.

In 1971 the chart of accounts was replaced by a system in which numbers only were used to classify accounts. This change was the result of growing complaints from the mid-1960s onwards that the old listing of accounts had become inappropriate as it cut through number series etc. These complaints were not very serious and there was no need for any radical change. The 1971 chart of accounts is still being used today.

Measuring Capacity

In a standard cost system the determination of capacity is of vital importance. At the cost committee meeting in 1959 it was found that the largest plants in Germany, France and England used "normal capacity" as a basis for their cost calculation, rather than the capacity actually used. Göteborg then started using "normal capacity" as well. Production statistics were used to determine which departments constituted the bottlenecks. A safety margin was deducted from the number of machine hours in such departments, to arrive at normal capacity. Now the capacity for each department or machine group was calculated separately. There was one safety margin for line production and another for batch production. In this way the importance of localizing bottlenecks was no longer particularly important, since all departments were continuously monitored. After some years it was noticed that variances in the production departments were too high. Continuing modernization and rationalization tended to generate overcapacity. Activity levels in the departments were then carefully checked, and if actual machine hours deviated too far from the standard assumption, then a number of machines were taken out of "active duty" and a new standard was established.

Standard cost has been a central issue all along. A mark-up on standard cost has been used to determine a normal price. Then there have also been rebates and so on, to accomodate to market conditions. Inventory valuation has been at standard cost, which has also been widely used in cost control.

When inflation and currency rates became more unstable, standards had to be adapted more frequently. Since 1976 SKF calculates an annual standard cost to include all costs up to delivery into the "Stock of Finished Goods". This value is modified in a number of ways. The effects of capacity-use were mentioned above. Interest on capital employed has never been officially considered as part of overheads at SKF; it has been regarded as part of the profit, and has thus not been included in the cost accounting (but naturally it has been added for pricing purposes). Now and then this point has been brought up for discussion. The last time it was seriously considered was in the early 1970s. Capital turnover was the issue; the sales side wanted some instrument for indicating the cost of the capital tied up by types of bearings and by customers.

Again, the cost committee decided that interest should not be included in the standard cost but should be kept separate. The reasons were:

- that it cannot be properly controlled by operation or by order
- there is no logical key to use as an allocation base
- standard costs are used for fiscal valuation of inventories
- the variance analysis would be more complicated if interest were charged to production orders.

Consequently capital employed is reported separately to the sales side.

From the start, depreciation for cost purposes has been based on historical costs. In 1975 the cost committee decided that there were strong reasons for switching to a replacement cost basis, and this was done.

The first budget for the Göteborg plant was made in 1957. It was a fixed annual budget. At about that time the Philadelphia plant used a flexible budget system, in which the rates were based on a certain percentage use of capacity – the same base as the one used for standard costing. In 1967 Göteborg produced its first flexible budget. Reporting against this budget occurred monthly, at first including controllable overheads only. Later all overheads were included. There is a disadvantage in using this approach: the allocation of overheads is carried out centrally, and it is the controller's office that largely determines how costs vary with use of capacity. To remedy this, and to make cost-center managers more aware of their responsibility for keeping overheads down, since 1977 the Göteborg plant has operated to a fixed annual budget and a quarterly operational plan. The latter is based on the concept of the flexible budget. Lately SKF has been moving towards a more pronounced "responsibility-center" approach.

Comment

There were two basic changes in the organization of the chart of accounts in SKF, in 1921 and 1971. In both cases the changes represented a kind of confirmation of the action taken to cope with increasing competition. Apart from this there were a great many changes in the cost-calculation and overhead-allocation schemes, apparently always in response to internal problems of fairness. It should be noted that a frequent argument in the national debate as well, was that the new standards would promote "fair competition".

It is obviously unwarranted to generalize here, but perhaps we might venture to suggest that there is a relation between system change and fairness of representation.

Men of action, whether at the company or the national level, are anxious that the outcome of their actions should be fairly represented by performance measures (ex ante or ex post). This goes for institutional rules as well as for intracompany competition. Change is initiated or accepted when representation is regarded as unfair. We might expect to hear arguments in terms of economic efficiency or decision-making relevance etc. in justification of change, and to some extent such arguments do occur at the national level, but it seems that the fairness arguments are the important ones when it comes to the initiation of change.

There appear to have been two schools of thought at the national level in the early days: the ASEA school which wanted to integrate calculation into the cost accounting, and the SKF school which wanted to keep calculation separate from accounting. That the former school is more compatible with the scientific management philosophy is obvious, and can be seen in the debate regarding the objectives of cost accounting. For instance, Forsberg's oral presentation of the SKF system in 1928 was followed by a discussion in which the first speaker was Liljeblad of ASEA. His main point was that it is meaningless to discuss principles of full cost calculation unless we have specified the purpose of the calculation – which in his view was to provide a basis for pricing and for the planning of efficient production. Forsberg had mentioned several possible purposes, and in replying to Liljeblad he stressed the need for reliability, meaning that cost accounting should be checked against standard cost accounting and closely linked to the general ledger in order to remove any arbitrariness. In a way the ASEA school stresses decision purposes, while the SKF school stresses that accounting figures should constitute a data base of facts that can be used for different purposes.

The scientific management engineer wants to establish a basis for rational discourse by establishing a rationality criterion. The cost accountant, always under pressure from different parties, likes to deal with verifiable fats. Both professions consequently demand standardization, but for different reasons. What become of the standardization process at the national level will then depend on which profession dominates the process. In Sweden it was the engineers who dominated, and the result was an approach geared to a full cost concept, that "normal sales/production volume makes continued business possible without the addition of external capital, but also without real profit in excess of interest on investment and, of course, adequate depreciation" (Liljeblad in Forsberg, 1928) – a rather abstract and general conceptual framework, giving little help to the cost accountant who is looking for ways of separating facts from fiction.

At the company level things are different, and the real situation intrudes on all abstract discourses. The company we have studied represents a comparatively simple production process characterized by line or mass production. The engineers were certainly strong, but commercial aspects were important and price was an important competitive factor. Accountants were involved at the company level, and they were influential. However, it must also be pointed out that we did not encounter any radical changes during the 50 years that we studied; in fact there was not very much change at all. If we call the core cost accounting system a secondary system, then change has taken place in primary systems dealing with inputs and outputs to the secondary system. The few changes that have taken place are easier to relate to changes in the external business environment than to changes in the "conceptual environment".

If we approach the material presented above in a Foucaultian spirit, we should note that there is no reference in the company standards to the debate at the national level, although some SKF representatives took part in the early national debate. The two sets of standards seem almost to have developed independently of each other, or at least in this case there was little influence from the national level to the company level. There may have been a strong influence from ASEA to the national level.

It might be suggested that when they are placed in an abstract setting such as a committee report, conceptual standards do not have the same power as when they are placed within a praxis. This means that it is action, rather than cognition or rational analysis, that provides fertile soil for the formation of concepts that will last. It also explains the fact that when changes occur in company standards, they seem to be triggered by external threats or expected threats to competitive capability rather than by the outcomes of debates between colleagues. Adjustments in company standards often seem to have been triggered by internal complaints that performance measures were not providing a fair representation of economic responsibility. Again, we have an action-related basis.

These observations highlight a more fundamental issue that deserves greater attention on the part of management accountants, both practitioners and academics. This is the question of whether learning is conceptual or associative, structuralist or data-driven.

If it is mainly structuralist, which means that a structure of concepts in the individual mind – what we could call a cognitive structure – helps the individual to filter relevant information from irrelevant and thus to perceive the situation through the conceptual glasses that he is wearing, then standards which are concepts will be very important to the company's ability to adapt to a changing environment. Unsuitable conceptual structures will delay action or lead to misjudgements. This would also mean (although now we are going beyond what is justified by the empirical material) that it is appropriate to discuss the evolution of cost accounting irrespective of the industrial reality in which it takes place, as cost accounting is a professional activity of ever increasing perfection and conceptual refinement. This is the approach adopted by Little-ton and Garner.

If on the other hand learning is associative or data-driven, it will start from experience; in this case concepts – in so far as they are used – will more closely resemble manifestations of the customary use of expressions for communication purposes than instruments of thought, and this means that "concepts" may survive for a very long time after losing their usefulness. They are not necessary to the conducting of daily business or the understanding of decision situations, but they may be used to convey formalistic messages in an important "conceptual" superstructure.

The problem, then, is that on a basis of the material presented here we can envisage two kinds of learning: one, concerned with how to conduct business efficiently, is associative; the other, concerned with ways of designing information systems and especially cost accounting systems, is structuralist. This would mean that cost accounting systems are doomed to permanent inadequacy due to their lack of adaptability. They are not normally of any use to managers in the conduct of business; they simply serve as disciplinary control frameworks.

However, there were some changes at the company level where real action sometimes breaks through the control framework to show deviations from the norm. Then there may be changes which improve the fairness in the representation of action. These changes can then be explained in terms of the current business situation, rather than as conceptual refinements in an evolving cost accounting system.

There are accounting research problems here that deserve attention.

References

Argyris, C. (1982) *Reasoning, Learning, and Action*. San Francisco: Jossey-Bass.

Calmes, A. (1911) *Fabriksorganisation – Organisation, bokföring och självkostnads-beräkning för industriella företag*. Sveriges Industriförbund.

Carlsson, J. (1929) *Industrins rationalisering – en praktisk handbook*. Stockholm.

Church, H. (1901) The Proper Distribution of Establishment Charges. *Engineering Magazine*.

– (1930) *Overhead Expenses*. New York: McGraw-Hill.

Crawford, A. (1984) *Cost Accounting, Work Control and the Development of Cost Accounting in Britain 1914–1925*. Dupl. paper presented at the EAA congress 1984 in St. Gallen.

Daudi, P. (1984) *Makt, diskurs och handling*. Lund: Studentlitterature.

Dickensson, A. L. (1911) The Economic Aspects of Cost Accounts. *Journal of Accountancy*.

Ericsson, T. (1950) De fasta kostnadernas behandling. *Affärsekonomi*, no 1, 3 and 5.
– (1950) "Kostnadsberäkning enligt tradition eller efter behov?" *Affärsekonomi*, no 17 and 19.
Ericsson T., Liljeblad, R. (1951) Prispolitik och kostnadsberäkning. *Affärsekonomi*, no 13 and 15.
Foucault, M. (1973) *The Order of Things. An Archeology of the Human Sciences.* New York: Randon House.
Forsberg, E. A. (1916) *Industriell ekonomi.* Stockholm.
Fredriksson, N. (1911) *Verkstadsorganisation vid blandad tillverkning.* Stockholm.
Garcke, E., Fells, J. M. (1983) *Factory Accounts, Their Principles and Practice.* London.
de Geer, H. (1978) *Rationaliseringsrörelsen i Sverige.* SNS Stockholm.
Guillet de Monthoux, P. (1981) *Doktor Kant och den ekonomiska rationaliseringen.* Göteborg: Korpen.
Handbok i industriell driftsekonomi och organisation. T. Sällfors (Ed.), Stockholm.
Johnson, H. T. (1981) Towards a New Understanding of Nineteenth-Century Cost Accounting. *Accounting Review*, pp. 510–518.
Kaplan, R. (1983) *The Evolution of Management Accounting.* Plenary Address AAA meeting.
Liljeblad, R. (1950) Kostnadsräkning och lönsamhetsanalys. *Affärsekonomi*, no 11.
– (1950) Svar på Ericssons svar. *Affärsekonomi*, no 19.
Mitroff, I. (1983) *Stakeholders in the Organizational Mind.* San Francisco: Jossey-Bass.
Schmalenbach, E. (1921) *Buchführung und Kalkulation im Fabriksgeschäft.* Leipzig: Gloeckner.
– (1927) *Der Kontenrahmen.* Leipzig: Gloeckner.
Schultz, H. R. (1923) Enhetlighet i industriell självkostnadsberökning. *Teknisk Tidskrift.*
Sekerholm, J. J. (1916) *Arbetets vetenskap.* Stockholm.
Sheridan, A. (1980) *Michel Foucault The Will to Truth.* London: Tavistock.
Självkostnadsberäkningar för järngjuterier (1939), Stockholm: Sveriges Maskinindustriförening.
Sperlich, A. (1917) *Unkostenkalkulation.* Leipzig.
Sällfors, T., Niechels, H. (1921) *Modern verkstadsorganisation enligt den vetenskapliga arbetsledningens principer.* Stockholm.
Webner, F. E. (1911) *Factory Costs.* New York: Ronald Press.
ter Vehn, A. (1945) *Mekanförbundets Normalkontoplan.* Sveriges Mekanförbund.

Part II. Industrial Development – Interrelations Between the Private and the Public Sector

Governmental Influence Upon Decision Making in Organizations in the Private and Public Sectors in Britain

David J. Hickson in association with Richard J. Butler, David Cray, Geoffrey R. Mallory and David C. Wilson

Introduction

The 20th century is remarkable for many things, not the least among them being the attempts by governments from East and West, from North and South, to control economies. Some succeed sometimes, some succeed hardly at all. In Europe, the sharpest divide is between the varieties of direct control practised in the East, and the varieties of indirect control practised in the West. But the aim of governments on both sides of this sad divide is to influence the managements of organizations.

Usually this is discussed in the West in terms of generalized policies such as taxation policy or export subsidies or market protectionism, and of generalized indicators such as inflation rates or balances of payments or government borrowing. Much less is known, often nothing is known, of how government influence – if any – is brought to bear. How is it done?

To go to the heart of the matter requires investigating whether or not managements are affected in what they do by government and its agencies. That means getting beneath the abstractions about state and economy to ask whether or not major strategic decisions by managers and administrators are influenced. And are these decisions influenced more in some organizations than in others, notably in the government's own public sector organizations as compared to the "free" enterprise private sector organizations? It is these critical decisions which in the aggregate determine what the condition of the economy shall be.

The Bradford studies of strategic decision-making in organizations were designed on a large scale to analyse types of decision process, and explain the differences between types by features of the decision and the organization. They include information on the influence exerted by all interests on each decision studied. These interests are both internal, such as the sales (and equivalent), finance, and research departments; and external such as suppliers or trade associations or trades unions (the influence of unions is analysed in detail in Wilson et al., 1982).

A quite unanticipated by-product of the research was information on the influence exerted on strategic decisions by government departments and agencies, as reported by the top managers and administrators who had experienced it. This paper examines that influence, based on extracts from the full accounts of the Bradford studies published elsewhere (Hickson et al., 1984, 1986).

Sample and Data Collection

A data base was built up of 150 cases of strategic decision-making obtained by interviewing, and six of the same cases traced by intensive case-study methods. Data collection, all in Britain, took place from 1974 to 1980, especially in the years 1977 to 1980. The decision-making processes described often reached back in their origins, and most were concluded by the time of the data collection, so that they occurred over periods from the mid 1960s to the late 1970s.

Organizations were first approached by a letter to the chief executive, supplemented by telephone calls as necessary. Of those approached, two thirds, that is 30 organizations, cooperated. They range in size from 100 to over 50 000 employees; there are 17 privately owned (manufacturers, financial institutions, road transport etc.), and 13 publicly (state) owned (health service districts, universities, utilities etc.); there are 11 manufacturing (metal components, glass, chemicals, breweries) and 19 service (banking, insurance, airways, local government etc.). Most were relatively prominent, a large proportion being national or international leaders in the private or public sectors and household names, which prevents publication of some details in case histories. They were taken from published directories with the aim of getting as even a coverage as possible over a selection matrix which offset private and public ownership categories against manufacturing and services categories to reflect as far as practicable the diversity of contemporary organizations. However, the resulting set of organizations depended upon personal managerial collaboration because those at the top who were centrally involved in cases of decision-making had to be willing to give considerable information about decisions that to them were still important and had occurred sufficiently recently to be readily recalled. They also had to be willing and able to give time to researchers. As in all this sort of research, any biases introduced by self-selection are beyond knowing.

In an initial interview the chief executive reviewed the history of the organization, its outputs and basic structure, and external relationships. He was asked to nominate major decisions involving more than just one department or section and with widespread effects, five of which were chosen to include when possible one each concerning inputs, outputs, core technology, personnel and reorganization, but there was no hard and fast sticking to these categories.

Centrally involved 'eye-witness' informants were then interviewed about each case, for example managing directors and function directors in firms, vice-chancellors and deans in universities, management team members in health districts, and chief officers in local government. Since what was wanted was information about *processes* of decision-making which take place at top managerial levels, middle management or lower employees or unions were not approached as they would know nothing first hand of the inner workings at this level. Interviewees were informants giving information about events, not respondents talking about themselves; each was interviewed at length, often more than once. There was an average of six informants per organization; in one third of the cases there were two or more informants but when the direct account was from one informant only, then as otherwise many interviews were joined by managerial colleagues who were asked to come in and add to what the informant(s) could say.

Each interview began with an historical narrative of the sequence of events as they unfolded. This was followed by numerous open-ended questions about particular aspects of the story which led the informant to elaborate on certain features of what had happened, seven of which were then in addition rated on five point scales (for example, of influence and of prevalence of delays). These ratings provided precise summings up, whilst the narrative notes gave them meaning.

In each of three organizations – a public utility, a university, and a private manufacturer – two cases were studied in far greater depth by intensive methods. Three were followed concurrently as they happened, and three were treated historically, by interviews, casual discussion, lunchtime contacts, and document searches throughout management across departments by a researcher who spent hours or days weekly in the organizations over two to three years. These six case studies are fully reported by Wilson (1980, 1982).

Governmental Influence

On the whole, government is surprisingly weak (see also Hickson et al., 1986). In Britain, its national departments and agencies, and also city and county local governments, average only a low place towards the bottom of five point influence rating scales running from 'little influence' to 'a very great deal'. Here is the symptom of government in a pluralistic society wrestling with a recalcitrant economy whose decision-makers do not leap to do its bidding. The influence it exerts on what they decide is on average less than that of most of their internal departments, implying that an organization's own interests are very much first among the considerations, governmental interests taking a back seat. Among the external pressures, the influence of customers or clients is again well ahead of governmental interests, implying that marketplace survival, success in the field of operation whatever it may be, takes priority over any governmental desires.

An efficient totalitarian government relying less on cajoling and more on force will be in a stronger position, of course, and organizational decision makers will find themselves much more hemmed in. A change in a society in that direction will slice away their alternatives as the giant Dutch firm Philips found under totalitarian German rule during the Second World War. Its alternatives in what it could make and what people it could employ were reduced until it was collaborating in military production and in using forced labour, whatever may have been intended to begin with (Teulings, 1982).

However, the normal Western European government relies on subsidies and regulations and propaganda and nationalization and the like. It may also sponsor work that has long-term indirect effects. In a leading private manufacturer which dominated its market, a decision was made to commit huge sums to the development and testing of a radical new product that could not have occurred but for government action years previously. A state research laboratory had been established where an employee, who incidentally was not British, found the solution to a technical problem that for decades had baffled researchers and firms throughout the world. The manufacturer bought the patent rights and decided to develop the product. Private enterprice exploited what public initiative had opened up.

This case was unusual. The 150 Bradford cases show that in Britain governmental influence is usually exerted through the appropriate channel among a set of channels evolved to connect government with particular sectors of activity. Strategic decisions in the health service are influenced by the Department of Health, in the universities by the University Grants Commission, in industry by the Department of Industry, and in public utilities by the Departments of Environment or Agriculture and by local governments with interests in the services provided. Intervention other than through these specialized channels is rare, and conspicuous personal moves by a Prime Minister such as those by James Callaghan who visited an American airline to support British airplane parts manufacturers are rarer still.

Though government in a state such as Britain does not have the influence to order everything to its own liking, it can still have fingers in a great many pies.

Influence from governmental sources was reported in as many as 40% of the decisions studied (60 out of 150). The first impression, therefore, is a weak but intensive influence. However this general impression is superficial and rather misleading. There are more subtle features which are more notable.

Since an ideological reason for state ownership is to subject organizations to greater governmental influence, differences would be anticipated between the decision-making of nationalized (state-owned) industries and services and those which are privately owned. Is decision-making a public industries and services beset – or maybe stimulated – by governmental influence, whereas private enterprise decision-making is blithely free of it?

Before the findings are examined, it must be remembered that the nationalized organizations depend on the state for their financing, a power base that is latent behind every decision made. It gives government an ultimate stranglehold. Government can sell off parts of them, or close parts of them down.

Thus though it is surprising it is not wholly surprising to find that the amount of governmental influence reported in the decision-making of the state-owned business organizations is no greater than in those that were private. If anything, it could have been less, though the difference if any appears negligible and nothing much should be read into it. The mean rating of the influences of national government departments, and of agencies such as the Health and Safety Executive and the Monopolies Commission, was 2.5 (on a 5 point scale) for 9 instances of influence in the decision-making of three state-owned organizations, against 3.0 for 17 instances in 13 privately owned organizations. The three public organizations were an autonomous division manufacturing products different to that of its parent corporation, a subsidiary company also making products different to those of a parent that had been reluctantly taken into a form of public ownership because of its economic difficulties, and a large service organization that was a household name in Britain and beyond. The 13 private organizations ranged from manufacturing to brewing and financial services.

The comparison is of the influence ratings of all reported instances of government department of governmental agency involvement in the decision-making in comparable business organizations. This excludes three private firms where there were no such involvements in any of their five cases of decision-making and therefore no ratings of governmental influence: it was not meaningful to equate no rating with nil rating numerically. Also excluded are eight non-commercial public services in health, education, the police, and local government; and two public utilities and an industrial research association.

However, although the *amount* of influence exerted by any one department or agency upon any *one* decision does not differ on average between public and private business, government influences a much *greater proportion* of the decisions of nationalized concerns. Switching from the influence of interest units to the number of decisions influenced (irrespective of amount exerted), fifteen cases of decisions were studied in the three state-owned organizations, five in each, and among these eight showed governmental influence, that is 53%. Eighty decisions were studied in 16 privately owned organizations (the 13 where governmental influence was reported, and 3 where there was none), only 15 of these decisions showing any governmental influence, that is 15/80 or 19%. Hence there was governmental influence on nearly three times the proportion of decisions in nationalized industries and services as in private business. Again caution must prevail, since the numbers in the nationalized industries are small, but the proportionate difference strongly supports the assumptions and periodic complaints of public sector managements that they encounter government at every turn whatever they do. *In nationalized businesses, government does not exert a greater amount of influence on any one decision, but it exerts influence on more decisions.*

A striking example of intrusive but ineffectual governmental influence in the public sector is two decisions that coincidentally were virtually the same and so make an apt comparison, one in a nationalized manufacturer and one in the leading private manufacturer that has been mentioned before. Each chose to cite a substantial new plant in Sweden and committed the required financial investment. The private firm went ahead with this major commitment which created employment in Sweden and not in Britain with no interference from government. From the British government that is, for the Swedish government was of course positively influential (ratings of 2 for Swedish national government and 5 for local government). Whereas the nationalized corporation was caught between two governments pulling in opposite directions. The Swedes were again very positive (with an influence rating of 4), but on the other side were the British Treasury and Department of Industry (both rated 5) striving to retain capital investment and employment in Britain. The state owned business had to contend with them whereas the private business did not. Yet the decision also shows that once the financing and terms of operation of nationalized organizations are arranged the British government influences but does not determine even their strategic moves, for in this case the investment went to Sweden despite the efforts of the Treasury and the Department of Industry to stop it. A similar case where the French government delayed but eventually did not stop foreign investment by the nationalized Elf oil corporation is reported by Bauer and Cohen (1983).

The obverse to this should not be missed. If government influences any one decision in a state business no more than in a private business, that also means there are times when it *can* influence a decision in a private business just as much! Private business cannot exclude government from its deliberations.

So public/private differences are relatively small. Indeed, they are by no means the feature of governmental influence. There is a much more vivid contrast which cuts across the decision-making of both. Governmental influence is far greater when its departments and agencies intervene or threaten to intervene specially, than when routine subsidies and regulations are applied in the ordinary way. This goes equally for the public and private sectors (see Table 1).

In the Table, the 9 instances reported of governmental interest units exerting influence in the decision making of state owned businesses are compared with the 17 instances in private businesses, both divided into instances of routine support and regulation versus particular interventions. If every decision in each organization was influenced by one governmental interest unit then, for example, the Table might show ten units influencing ten decisions in two organizations (all five cases studied in each of the organizations), and the entries would neatly correspond along the rows in an immediately self-evident way. As life is not so tidy, there is no such correspondence since first, not all decisions are influenced by a government department or agency, and second, some decisions are influenced by more than one such unit. So for example in the first row under the heading Routine Support and Regulation, there are *five instances of influence* (the Department of Trade influenced two decisions, and the Department of Industry, the Health and Safety Executive, and the National Enterprise Board influenced one each), which give a *mean of 1.2* (on a five point scale), in *five decisions* (here it does happen that each decision was influenced by one unit only) among the ten cases studied in *two state-owned* business organizations.

Comparing first these routine instances, the influence attributed to the five departments and agencies involved in the decision-making of the two state-owned businesses was weak, the mere 1.2 rating, and that of the 12 units involved in the larger number of decisions in nine private businesses was no higher than a mean of 2.4. It is again noticeable that when decisions are classified in this way, government may even have less overt influence in the decision-making of state organizations than in private business, if there is any material difference at all, but that is not the significant point. The conspicuous feature is the relatively low influence *irrespective of ownership* of the Department of Industry when giving grants towards new industrial and commercial developments, of the Department of Trade when a nationalized service it was concerned with purchased equipment abroad, of the Health and Safety Executive concerned with pollution, and of the National Enterprise Board which at the time held shares in firms on behalf of the state and in one case approved expansion in the firm's manufacturing capacity. All these are instances of relatively routine subsidizing and regulating of business. Whilst for state policy they are evidence that governmental action of this kind does have some effect, they show that it is far from decisive. It is merely a contributory level of state action.

Beyond it is a further and more vigorous level of action. The instances of particular intervention shown in the lower section of Table 1 average very high

Table 1:   Governmental Influence in Public and Private Business

Government Department or Agency influencing a decision	Influence Rating	Decisions Influenced	Organization
Overall Means			
State Owned Businesses:			
9 interest units	Mean 2.5	8 decisions	3 organizations
Private Businesses:			
17 interest units	Mean 3.0	15 decisions	13 organizations
Routine Support and Regulation			
State Owned Businesses:			
5 i. e. Departments of Trade (twice) and Industry, Health and Safety Executive, National Enterprise Board	Mean 1.2	5 decisions, i.e. new products and factories, massive re-equipment	2 organizations
Private Businesses:			
12 i.e. Departments of Industry (10 instances), Health and Safety Executive (twice)	Mean 2.4	11 decisions, i.e. new products, buildings and plant, and one factory closure	9 organizations
Particular Interventions			
State Owned Businesses:			
Specialist Ministry	5	Major reorganization by merger	Transport Service
Specialist Ministry	4	Reorganization of personnel	
Treasury	4	Siting of plant in Sweden	Manufacturer
Department of Industry	4		
	Mean 4.2		
Private Businesses:			
Treasury	5	Change in interest rates	Financial Institution
Department of Environment	5		
Department of Employment	5	Productivity agreement	Insurance Company
Arts Council	4	Budget and programme	Entertainment Service
Monopolies Commission	3	New credit service	Finance Company
	Mean 4.4		

influence indeed in both state and private businesses, the means being respectively 4.2 and 4.4. These are occasions when a department or agency deliberately influences a particular decision in a particular organization as far as it can. Among the state businesses, major reorganizations with repercussions beyond Britain were successfully influenced; and influential efforts were made to prevent investment in Sweden though these were unsuccessful, as already described. Among the private businesses, key interest rates were successfully influenced in the direction of government policy, and the Department of Employment influenced an unusual 'white-collar' productivity agreement in a world leader insurance company at a time when government was attempting to push such agreements in the direction it wanted. The Arts Council directly affected an entertainment organization's programme by the terms and size of its financial grant, and the threat of Monopolies Commission action constrained a finance company's move into a new credit service (Hickson et al., 1986).

The case of the unsuccessful effort to prevent a nationalized manufacturer investing in Sweden rather than in Britain shows that it is necessary to interpret these cases of high attributed influence in conjunction with the outcome of the decision-making. It is possible for a decision to go against highly influential government interests, either because they lack absolute power or because they come to accept or tolerate the opposite view. Influence on this scale appears to be of two kinds:

(a) *constraining*, where the influence of the government department or agency is taken into account in framing an alternative or alternatives acceptable to them, as for example with the insurance company's productivity agreement approved by the Department of Employment, and the entertainment organization's programme shaped to fit likely Arts Council financial support.

(b) *indicatory*, where their influence is exerted in favour of a specific alternative. Although they have a high probability that this alternative will be decided upon, they can be unsuccessful as they were over the Swedish investment.

However, it is clear that specific non-routine governmental interventions can and do have an effect; and that this can be just as great in the private sector as in the public sector. Though at first sight government looks weak and though its influence may at all times be outweighed by all the other influences upon a decision of which it is only one, it can be a force to be reckoned with when its departments and agencies intervene in particular situations.

From this comparison of public and private sectors three remarkable inferences can be drawn. First, government does not have any special ability to 'call the tune' for any one decision even in its own nationalized corporations, though it does influence a larger proportion of their decisions. Second, government influence does penetrate the privacy of private enterprise, albeit as a lesser influence among greater internal managerial influences. Third, government is most effective in this form of influence, both in public and private sector organizations, when its departments and agencies intervene in particular circumstances beyond the usual run of subsidizing and regulating.

References

Bauer, Michael, Cohen, E. (1983) The Iron Law of 'Private Governments' in the French Industrial System. Paper presented at the *6th EGOS Colloquium*, Florence.

Hickson, David J., Butler, Richard J., Cray, David, Mallory, Geoffrey R., Wilson, David C. (1984) Comparing one Hundred and Fifty Decision Processes. *Organizational Strategy and Change.* J. M. Pennings (Ed.), San Francisco: Jossey-Bass.

– (1986) Top Decisions: Strategic Decision Making in Organizations. Blackwells (Britain) and Jossey-Bass (USA).

Teulings, A. (1982) Interlocking Interests and Collaboration With the Enemy: Corporate Behaviour in the Second World War. *Organization Studies*, 3/2, pp. 99–119.

Wilson, David C. (1980) *Organizational Strategy.* PhD Thesis, University of Bradford, England.

Wilson, David C.., Butler, Richard J., Cray, David, Hickson, David J., Mallory, Geoffrey R. (1982) The Limits of Trade Union Power in Organizational Decision Making. *British Journal of Industrial Relations*, XX/3, pp. 322–341.

Industrial Policy –
Control and Dependence in a Systems Perspective

Rolf Wolff

Politics and Economics – Power and Efficiency

In everyday language and in theory we divide our societal system into two main spheres: politics and economics. Our theories are based on the assumption that these systems differ from one another in their tasks and their structures. The political system is concerned with immaterial values. An overall view of society guides political decisions and actions. Economics, on the other hand, belongs to the material world. It is determined by rational calculations and transactions. Individual profit ambitions dominate. The material system does not concern itself with the holistic view; it is the function of politics to guarantee this side of things. Politics is also supposed to endow what happens in society with meaning. Politics represents the immaterial or "spiritual" aspect, economics the material aspect or "nature".

The classic theme in political theory is power. The absolutist state, whose exercise of power certainly did not preclude its abuse, was much criticized. Democratic theory developed as a counter-theory to this power structure, and the welfare state with its concomitant theory stemming from the beginning of the present century, emerged as the next historical step. The influence of the working class on power generates a "claim" on the resources created by society as a whole. The capitalistic society is transformed into the welfare society. This means that the state becomes far more active in certain key areas of society, including the economic sphere. This historic shift is also the result of a theoretical reorientation. Power, from being primarily a political phenomenon, becomes an economic problem; the theoretical consequences of this are many. Above all the dividing-lines between scientific disciplines and the various issues at stake become increasingly sharp. Political theory is concerned with the power phenomenon in the economy, macro-economics and micro-economics with the problems of the efficient allocation of resources under conditions of scarcity. This theoretical segregation still persists today, although societal developments are prompting a holistic view of different problems and diverse subsystems. Thus a new degree of theoretical abstraction is called for (Luhmann, 1981), as well as a firm empirical foundation for our societal theories. Politics and economics are growing together – a process which has accelerated particularly since the Second World War, when the structures of the welfare state acquired a more lasting form. Each of the two spheres is heavily dependent on the other, even if voices in the public normative debate try to claim the contrary. Suggested solutions call for more, or for less, intervention by politicians in the economy. The authors of these solutions are generally actors in the system, and their bias in knowledge and theory is shaped by their roles within it. It is the function of research to provide a distanced and holistic view, and an understanding of the empirical processes that can be observed in society. Researchers must discover the theories of which the institutions are a manifestation, and chart the theories held by the different actors about their own particular social reality.

The inherent dialectic between politics and economics is particularly evident in industrial policy. With the help of various instruments, the state tries to influence industrial development. Companies and industries exploit the available means to hasten the process of structural change and renewal. In an economy such as the Swedish – in international terms a small one – industry is particularly vulnerable and to a great extent dependent on extensive resources. Because of the smal domestic market, Swedish companies are compelled to compete on the international market at an earlier stage than other companies. The success of this activity affects both society's prosperity and the legitimacy of its government. The more positive the economic development, the more stable the government's power base.

Thus industrial policy exemplifies the mutual dependence of politics and economics. These interdependencies will be examined in the following pages. I shall base my argument partly on my own empirical studies of industrial policy, and partly on a more general theoretical base regarding the way in which different organizations function. I shall examine what industrial policy is, and describe industrial policy in its economic-institutional context. I shall then discuss society's functional differentiation, and in particular the impact of this differentiation on the power phenomenon. Can industrial policy act as a control tool? In a concluding section I shall discuss the characteristics of the different subsystems, and the empirical knowledge that is available about them.

Industrial Policy and Institutional Economics

According to the official definition (Swedish Government Official Reports, 1981: 72) industrial policy has two aims: 1) to influence industrial development and the structural adaptation of industry, and 2) to reduce the social consequences arising in connection with structural change. The first of these represents "offensive" industrial policy and the second "defensive". While the focus of offensive industrial policy is long-term, defensive policy aims at reducing the short-term social consequences engendered by the processes of adapting to structural change. Further, a distinction is made between permanent and selective measures. During the 1970s the selective tools became increasingly important.

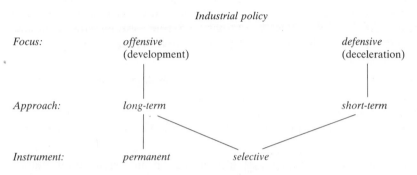

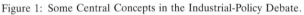

Figure 1: Some Central Concepts in the Industrial-Policy Debate.

Regardless of whether debaters are advocating offensive or defensive, long-term or short-term, permanent or selective types of aid, industrial policy has implications for society that are more farreaching than the debate would suggest. Industrial policy is after all an example of the way in which markets, politics and the public sector are merging with one another. Almost all types of company accept support of various kinds, regardless of whether they are making enormous profits (like the automobile industry), or whether (like the shipyards and the steel and mining industries) they are running at an enormous loss. Thus industrial policy is an example of a more general phenomenon: the institutional economy.

In economic theory the concept of the "institution" was taken up anew in the mid-1970s (Hernes, 1978; Williamson, 1975, 1981; Sjöstrand, 1985). The term is used in different ways, and the methodological starting-points in particular can differ. A feature common to all the approaches, however, is the new interest in allocation mechanisms other than markets. For example, Williamson (1981), building on Coase (1937, 1972), uses markets and hierarchies as two alternative allocation institutions in his transaction-cost approach:

"The study of transaction-cost-economizing in thus a comparative institutional undertaking which recognizes that there are a variety of distinguishable different transactions on the one hand and a variety of governance structures on the other." (1981: 1544)

Sjöstrand distinguishes between a number of different institutional ideal types and characterizes institutions:

"Institutions resemble a kind of infrastructure which facilitates or hampers exchanges or resource movements. They stem from ideas and notions – either individual or of a more collective type – and from material structures." (1983: 18)

Every society is made up of a number of institutional arrangements. Institutions discriminate between what is right and what is illegitimate. The market is an institution for allocating resources, and it is organized according to a variety of norms and rules. Economists have long limited their analyses to allocations that occur via markets. But the market itself is regulated by other institutions. Furthermore, alternative mechanisms for allocation also exist. Thus economic institutions can be defined as conditions and rule systems for economic transactions under conditions of scarcity. The market is thus a special case of an economic institution.

Since there are alternative allocation systems, economic theory must help to explain why and under what conditions the different alternatives are chosen. The transaction-cost approach can be regarded as a formal theoretical model only, which needs supporting and complementing with empirical investigations.

There are primarily three functional and interacting subsystems in an industrial-policy system: the political system, the public administration and industry. They are three different institutions, representing different rationality contexts (Hernes, 1978). By a rationality context is meant the specific norm structure of a system or subsystem that makes it function differently from other systems. The norm structure is a consequence of the societal function of the system. The function and the norm structure tell us what processes are possible or impossible in the respective subsystems. Politicians, for example, must follow certain basic democratic rules, regardless of the political area in which they are acting at the particular moment. The same applies to the bureaucracy. The companies also have certain legally established rules for their actions, supplemented by others of a company-specific and industry-specific nature. Thus, if we are to understand industrial policy, our analysis must start from these more general systems characters. As a subsequent step we should ask ourselves whether industrial policy is not itself accompanied by specific decisions and actions and system dependencies. But before embarking on this analysis, a more general discussion is needed of the functional differentiation to be found in our modern societies.

Society – A System Without a Power Center

Our modern Western social systems have developed hierarchically, with the state as the power center. In theory, the state used to control the other societal functions, among them the economy. Characteristic of modern society is its functional differentiation (Luhmann, 1981). Functional differentiation implies that society consists of several subsystems with different goals and tasks. Examples of functional subsystems in the welfare state are the political system, science, the economy, etc. Thus politics is one functional system among others. The traditional view of the state and society as two disparate systems is consequently misleading. The state does not stand outside society, but is a part of it. The state has a specific function for the totality. All the other subsystems represent "the environment" of the state, and vice versa. Thus a modern society is a system without a top or a center. There are probably several centers (The Norwegian Government Official Reports, 1982: 3). The complex welfare society is dependent on the fulfillment of a number of functions, and so functional dependencies are formed between subsystems. For these functions to be fulfilled, resources are required. Resources are limited, and control over resources is therefore a major factor of power and control in the system.

In political theory, the hierarchical view of society was and is the dominating one. In its normative aspect, this view evokes a call for the return of power to the central system. Against this view is the functional approach, whereby functional differentiation is seen as an evolutionary step. But functional differentiation has also had negative consequences, in particular the division of responsibility, and the limited attention that is concentrated on certain problems. In future there will perhaps be less functional differentiation, and the present integration of our societal subsystems can be regarded as the expression of an ongoing adjustment process.

Industrial Policy – A Political Instrument of Control?

In a system which has no "natural" power center one power base is the control of resources. An industrial-policy system consists of the three subsystems, politics (government, parliament and the Ministry for Industry), the public administration, and industry. Traditionally Swedish politics has maintained an active profile. "We should try to control events rather than letting ourselves be controlled, try to be longsighted rather than shortsighted, to be change-oriented and innovative rather than conservative and repetitive" (Ruin,

1983: 31). These norms have helped to shape politics in general and economic policy in particular, and in that area industrial policy most of all. In the general debate politics is allotted a controlling function. This was particularly evident in connection with industrial policy during its defensive period in the 1970s. The structural changes of the 1970s were very difficult to handle, and industrial policy was geared to defensive action. The extent of state-owned enterprise increased as a result of the enforced purchase of industries in crisis. Selective aid measures predominated, and on an average 4 per cent of GNP was spent on industrial-policy activities.

The express goal of industrial policy is to influence industrial developments in the country. Mainly as a result of the Boston Consulting Group report (1979) about how Sweden's industrial policy *should* be focused, the normative debate about the controlling role of industrial policy gathered momentum – although present knowledge about the functioning and the potential of industrial policy is pretty limited (Wolff, 1983). The normative debate can be said to have suppressed an interest in the fundamental questions that should be asked about industrial policy and that are still waiting for answers. These are:

1. What role do different actors play in the industrial policy system?
2. How do the different subsystems – politics, administration and industry – interact?
3. What are the implications of industrial policy for industrial development?
4. What instruments have what effects?

In the following section the structure, roles and existential conditions of the industrial policy system will be analysed. The analysis is supported by the results of empirical research on industrial policy, in so far as such are available.

Industrial Policy – Dependence and Control of Resources

Every system is dependent on resources for its survival. Resources are not created within the system, but in exchanges with the surrounding world. Thus every system is dependent on its environment. Since resources are limited, there will be competition to acquire them. This competition increases the uncertainty already linked with the creation and control of resources. Other organizations control the resources that any particular organization needs. This generates exchange relationships, which in turn reinforce the interdependence.

In order to reduce the uncertainty connected with the creation and maintenance of resources, formal and informal relationships with the surrounding world are built up. The more important these relationships to the survival of the organization, the stronger the tendency to make arrangements in the organization for handling them (Tolbert, 1983). Institutionalized dependence relationships reduce uncertainty. They are relatively easy to predict, whereas ad hoc relationships only increase the uncertainty.

Control of resources ensures the legitimacy upon which the organization depends. Every organization has a variety of stakeholders all making their different demands, which have to be balanced and fulfilled. This is partly made possible by the fact that systems/organizations have more than one goal, which means that different goals can be satisfied on different occasions. Thus at any one time the demands for efficiency are different for different stakeholders.

The need for resources involves the organization in dependence relationships and exchanges with the surrounding world. The effects of these dependencies on the organization will depend on the importance to the organization of the various exchange relationships, and on what other alternatives there are. For a market-based organization alternatives generally do exist. So long as the market generates sufficient resources to allow for freedom of action, alternative exchange relationships can be created. For a budget-based organization, such as a public agency, the situation is less flexible. The budget defines the frames and, thus, the dependence and flexibility of the agency visàvis the environment.

In an industrial-policy system consisting of the political system, the public administration and industry, functional dependencies will obtain. The policy is dependent on a positive development of industry. The industrial-policy administration receives its grants for action within the bounds of budgets established by the government. Industry's dependence relationships with the other systems, on the other hand, are less evident. And yet we know that even companies with enormous profits make substantial use of the subsidies available. But this does not in itself constitute dependence. Subsidies represent an exchange of resources, mostly without the politicians attaching any controlling conditions to them.

In the following pages I shall examine in greater depth the possible functional and resource-based dependencies in this system, i.e. between the three subsystems. The analysis must be based on empirical investigations of industrial policy. However, there are structures attaching to each of the subsystems regardless of industrial policy. Political systems, public agencies and companies possess general characteristics which are also active in industrial-policy contexts. Thus, every dependence relationship will be examined on a basis of general knowledge about this type of system, and these findings will be complemented by studies of industrial policy. In conclusion the results will be summarized in a descriptive model of industrial-policy systems.

Politics and Industrial Policy – Basic Characteristics of Political Systems

Political systems are open and self-referential (Luhmann, 1981). The openness refers to the system's functional dependence and exchanges with other subsystems in society. The state (government, the political system) has acquired an increasing number of tasks and demands which it has to satisfy. Most political actions, however, create new problems which were not foreseen when the actions were implemented. This creates complicated decision situations for the political system, and a high degree of dependence. The more satisfactorily the various demands are fulfilled, the longer the political system will survive. Because of the prevailing functional differentiation, many problems arise in other subsystems which the politicians have to deal with. The overloading which can result is handled by political systems, in that they are self-referential, i.e. the decisions and actions undertaken by political systems are geared to internal interpretations rather than standards in the environment. "All standards for politics are political standards and will be defined as such in the political communications process between political actors" (Luhmann, 1981: 61).

Essentially there are three dependence relationships handled by political systems: relations with the citizens, with the public agencies, and with specific societal subsystems. These relations are controlled by way of political programs and manifestos, personnel policy, and laws and ordinances regulating the administration's relations with its clients.

Is it reasonable to expect an introverted system to observe, interpret, analyse and solve problems arising in other subsystems in society? Is the system not dominated by its own internal problems, e.g. party rivalry? What can guarantee that the most urgent problems will be dealt with? Which problems are urgent? What our analysis has revealed is that many problems are structurally conditioned. The functional differentiation of modern societies leads to a fragmentation of the approach to problems, which in itself makes for many intractable difficulties. In economic theory "external effects" are an example of this. The political system has two main control tools with which it can try to solve these problems: laws and money. But a drawback of the economic system in this connection is that it has no power center. The economic system is much more heterogeneous than the political. The stakeholder organizations in the economy have no mandatory controls over their members. They can only make recommendations. The law is used by the political system as a direct or indirect means of control (Lindblom, 1977: 23). Indirect control may concern the frames, e.g. rules and regulations for the market system. An example of direct control based on law is the quota system for production capacity.

The effects of controls are uncertain. Companies are inventive; they find ways of getting round laws. Money as a means of control is even more uncertain; it is after all exchangeable, and it is not possible to check that a particular sum of money has been used for the purpose intended. Moreover, accounting systems provide an excellent opportunity for manipulating cash flows at will.

In order to handle these control problems – arising from the autonomy and absence of power centers in other subsystems, and the uncertain effects of different controls – bureaucracies are created. They are the agents of the political system, intended to improve the handling of problems and to relieve politicians of the details of everyday problem-solving. Thus bureaucracies are marginal organizations on the borders between the political system and other subsystems, as well as buffers to off-load some of the pressure. And in itself the existence of bureaucracies reinforces the dependence relationships between the systems:

"It is our impression that organizations are becoming more interconnected and that the cause of this increasing system connectedness is most often government action" (Pfeffer and Salancik, 1978: 70).

Thus the industrial-policy bureaucracy can be regarded as a buffer and a marginal organization between politics on the one hand and industry on the other.

Research on the Politics in Industrial Policy

Studies of the handling of selective aid by the government reveal the use of a special stereotype (Swedish Government Official Reports, 1981: 72). Vague goal formulations are common. To motivate the different actions, industrial-policy, business-cycle and structural reasons are all cited.

The material providing the base for decisions is often produced by the industries or companies themselves (Swedish Government Official Reports, 1981: 17, 18). There are no routines for handling questions of aid at the Ministry for Industry. Written material is not very extensive. Little attention is paid to long-term strategic goals; short-term considerations dominate (Henning, 1981).

In a study of a major politically initiated, industrial-policy program for a particular region in Sweden no trace could be found of any analysis of the problems. It proved difficult to define the role of the politicians on the basis of a problem-solving model. The results suggested instead that a good deal of the nature of politically based industrial policy can be defined in terms of a legitimation model (Brunsson and Wolff, 1984).

Investment is a driving-force in corporate development. Thus, within the framework of industrial policy, attempts are made to influence corporate investment behavior. A recent study of 30 large Swedish Corporations, suggests that the effects of investment aid are almost non-existent (Gandemo, 1982). In a few cases only the effect was to bring forward an investment that was anyway going to have been made later. But the aid resulted in no new investment.

A Modified View of Political Control via Industrial Policy

Politically initiated industrial-policy action is not always aimed at solving problems in industry or at controlling industry. At least some of the measures are intended to create legitimacy for the political system.

Problem-solving in the sense of changing the material conditions of industry is only one of the alternatives open to the political system. Other alternatives, which do not necessarily engender material change, are decisions and talk (Brunsson and Wolff, 1984).

Because of the openness of the political system, many of its decisions and actions are not consistent with one another. Goal formulations, decisions and actions may be contradictory or inconsistent, since they are needed for handling different or contradictory demands. In fact it may be helpful to formulate vague goals, to make decisions without action, to act without the actions necessarily agreeing with the decisions. In a legitimation context this is rational. In problem-solving terms vague goal formulations are often a prerequisite for broad political agreement (Brunsson, 1981; Saetren, 1983).

The effectiveness of the means of control – laws and money – appears to be limited. No current studies of Swedish industrial policy confirm that this policy in fact steers industrial development. The function of talk and communication as a means of control has been largely disregarded. In an earlier study (Brunsson and Wolff, 1984) it was noted that the creation of positive expectations was very important: politicians influence the expectations linked to various industrial-policy decisions, and the higher the expectations the greater will be the motivational effects of the action. Naturally, though, higher expectations also mean a greater risk of failure and the loss of political legitimation. However, failure becomes visible only after careful long-term evaluations of industrial-policy action, and at the present time no such evaluations are being made (Wolff, 1983). Perhaps the material effects are not so important to politicians; perhaps the time horizon is too long; perhaps they do not want to make evaluations because of the high expectations surrounding the original decisions.

In view of the nature of political systems, industrial policy can often be expected to have a legitimating function. As a result of the creation of a number of industrial-policy agencies (marginal organizations) with different goals, competences and tasks, Swedish industrial policy has acquired an extensive bureaucratic apparatus. Can this subsystem compensate for some of the weaknesses of politics in its control function? What is the nature of the dependence relationship between the industrial-policy agencies on the one hand and politics and industry on the other?

The Administration and Implementation of Industrial Policy – Fundamental Characteristics of Public Agencies

Public agencies are a manifestation of the varied undertakings of the welfare state. In a way they embody the areas of responsibility to which the political system gives priority. The concept of the "bureaucracy" is a metaphor, and many ideas have become attached to it. These ideas are often misconceptions about how bureaucracies (should) function. In the welfare state "bureaucracy" is often equated in everyday usage with inefficiency. But the kind of problems which are typical of public agencies, the continuous expansion of the bureaucracy, and the problems that face politicians when it comes to controlling the agencies, are all structurally conditioned. The functional differentiation which we mentioned above endows the agencies with a substantial role and considerable freedom in the welfare state.

In the everyday view, and also in political-science theory (above all in implementation research), the relation between politics and the administration is seen as a hierarchic one. The politicians make the decisions and the administration implements them. However, much of the way in which the public agencies work, is affected by the structure of politics. As a result of the introverted structure of politics, the administration acquires a considerable range of freedom, despite the controls available to the politicians. But the public agencies are also self-referential, and to a great extent they develop their own standards and patterns of action.

The freedom of the agencies depends on: 1) The political system is self-referential; politicians develop their own standards for handling problems; moreover, they are in latent competition with other politicians, which affects all kinds of orientations. 2) Thus to a great extent politicians are dependent on the agencies which free them from part of their load; this is why agencies are created; they take care of problem areas selected by the politicians – the selection process is thus a simple political function. 3) As a result of the creation of agencies with defined areas of responsibility, the political system is relieved of various kinds of detailed work. 4) This in turn means that decisions are prepared and handled within the agencies. Decisions grow up "from below", and politicians actually take decisions on actions prepared by the agencies. Thus the administration assumes an expert function visàvis the politicians. The politicians respond by creating political expert functions for every problem area, which exercise control over the recommendations of the agencies. 5) Budgets and grants are inadequate as far as control is concerned, as they only establish frames for the operations of the agencies. And in any case budgets grow up from below in the bureaucracy.

The bureaucracy learns these structural aspects of politics, and so does the political system. In the public agencies this leads to the development of operational standards and decisions of their own. In the political system it means learning to take vague and sometimes even contradictory decisions, so as to generate the greatest possible concensus around a decision. The more vague a decision, the more likely it is to be passed. Thus both systems increase their flexibility, and both gain from it (Baier, March and Saetren, 1982).

This means that as far as industrial policy is concerned, the public agencies must be regarded as occupying an important and initiatory role. The industrial-policy agencies can push their own ideas and programs, and their selection of problems and issues can greatly influence the orientation of industrial policy.

Research Findings on the Role of the Public Administration in Industrial Policy

There have been very few process studies of industrial policy in light of the relation between politics and the administration. In the study of a politically initiated program already quoted, (Brunsson and Wolff, 1984) the role of politics and the public administration was analysed. The government put considerable time pressure on the Ministry for Industry. The development program had to be produced within a few weeks. The administration investi-gated and proposed the measures that were to be supported. They also defined the cost frames. Implementation was handled by the relevant public agencies over a period of three years. No evaluation of the effects was made. Neither the politicians nor the bureaucrats initiated any evaluation of the program. To the politicians the program represented a good way of demonstrating their responsibility for the region in question, and the direction they wanted the action to take. Up to a point the agencies could push the issues and ideas which they believed in, as regards solutions to the different problems. As soon as the program had passed through the Riksdag, the politicians were relieved of the problem and could devote themselves to other matters – after all, the public administration had assumed responsibility.

In the difficult period of structural change in Sweden during the 1970s, companies turned increasingly to the government direct. Because of its open-ness, the government had to assume responsibility for many of the conse-quences of structural change. The growing number of state purchases of industries in crisis is an example of the trend. At the beginning of the 1970s, 85 per cent of industrial-policy resources were distributed through the industrial-policy agencies; by the middle of the 1970s, the equivalent figure was only 55 per cent. The other 45 per cent was allocated direct from the government. Since the beginning of the 1980s, however, a change can be glimpsed in this trend. The Ministry for Industry in particular, has reacquired an important buffer function, i.e. industry has to register its claims via the public agencies. Also, as a result of budgetary problems, attitudes have changed. The government has become increasingly unwilling to subsidize industries in crisis, which reinforces the buffer function of the agencies: claimants try as far as possible to avoid calling on politicians for direct aid.

The control of the state-owned companies has altered since 1982. During the 1970s the state had to go a long way towards covering the companies' losses, because of its direct responsibility as owner. But now the state-owned companies have been reconstructed, and during 1982–83 the state reduced its direct ownership of the largest companies e.g. in the steel industry. A new ministerial function was also established, exclusively for the state-owned companies. The companies are now controlled by means of policy and budget negotiations. Thus, the frames for these companies, organized as group enterprises, are established by the minister and corporate management in conjunction. The companies received their last subsidies in 1982–83, since when they have had to manage on their own; in other words they must generate their own resources via the market. Profitability has become the watchword, and rationalizations have been introduced. As a result of these structural arrangements, the government has been able to reduce its direct involvement in the state-owned companies. A new independent functional area of responsibility has been created. The government has been relieved of controlling the state-owned companies.

The Public Administration – An Active Participant in Industrial Policy

In Sweden there are a great many different industrial-policy agencies to take care of different tasks. The agencies are organized both regionally and functionally. Each time a new problem has arisen since the end of the 1960s, a new organization has been created. Technological development, new enterprise, risk capital, advice in various forms etc have been taken in hand by different agencies at the central and regional levels. The system has been growing continually, both in the number of organizations and the amount of capital invested in it. Differences in the way in which these organizations work confirms the degree of freedom which we have claimed for them. Their level of activity also varies; some are extremely active, cooperating with the companies as much as they possibly can.

At the present time we know little about the way the agencies work or about the effects of their efforts. They are still in many respects "black boxes", and penetrating studies are needed to improve our knowledge of their structure and effects.

Companies and Industrial Policy – Companies in an Institutional Economy

Companies differ very strikingly from the "firm" of microeconomic theory as described in textbooks and other standard works. For microeconomists and even for many organizational theorists the tension between the company and the market is the main subject of study. The company embraces planning, coordination and control. It is also a hierarchy. The market, on the other hand, is a distinct system of allocation, where the predominant organizational mechanism is assumed to be price. According to current economic theory, it is on the market that companies generate their resources for survival.

Over the last few decades organization theory has evolved as a market theory. The company used to be regarded in the first place as creating legitimacy for itself by way of its output on markets. It is on the market that the company finds the basis for its survival. This view of company and market as complementing one another, has been replaced by another, according to which companies and markets are regarded as alternative institutional arrangements. Companies are organizations that replace the market. With the help of rules and hierarchies they replace the price system and the uncertainty that the market represents (Arrow, 1969, 1974). In a perfectly functioning market system, there should not really be any companies at all. In such a conceptual microeconomic world, the existence of companies is an expression of the less-than-perfect functioning of the market.

Companies appear when it is more effective in terms of cost to organize transactions with the help of hierarchies (Commons, 1934; Coase, 1937; Williamson, 1975). Companies are cooperative systems in which people of different interests collaborate in order to satisfy their needs. Companies guarantee the cost and price advantages which this form of resource transaction implies. Thus the company is a special case in an institutional allocation theory.

A drawback of the microeconomic and the transaction-cost approach is that the analysis takes little account of the evolutionist element in the genesis of different institutional allocation alternatives. The economic rationality (efficiency) that imbues the transaction-cost approach and other theories, in fact restricts their explanatory value. There is no support for the claim that people form companies only to ensure cost advantages in certain transactions. The net advantage attending the formation of a company as opposed to relying on the market (or vice versa) can rarely if ever be calculated in exact amounts. Decision theory has shown that economic decision processes are very complicated and often anything but rational. I would claim that the formation of companies is often unplanned and economically irrational, but that it still yields a "net advantage" in the shape of social exchange. Cooperative effort attaches itself to ideas or utopias. Enterprise in this sense is driven by an entrepreneurial spirit free of economic calculation.

Up to now we have been discussing the formation of companies as against the market. But how do companies survive? According to microeconomic theory, companies which cannot generate resources via the market should be eliminated. In a market economy, the success of companies is determined by the market. The market is the ultimate tribunal. In a functionally differentiated society, embracing a variety of alternative economic institutions, the situation is different. In an institutionalized economy companies are not only dependent on other institutions apart from the market; they are also more dependent on one another (Hägg and Johansson, 1983). Furthermore, the market generates effects which it does not deal with itself. This, too, leads to the formation of new institutional arrangements, usually as a result of political intervention. Furthermore, companies are surrounded by an increasing number of stakeholders all with their different demands, and companies have to strike a balance between these interests just as the political system has to. Dependence relationships with the surrounding world are increasing. The legitimacy of what the company does, is a variable critical to its survival.

The legitimation function is thus crucial to companies in an institutionalized environment (Meyer and Rowan, 1983). The better a company manages to adapt to its institutionalized environment, the greater is its legitimacy. And the greater the legitimacy of a company, the more support and access to resources it will enjoy. But company thinking is geared to ideas of efficiency and productivity; resource transactions are to be carried out in the most effective way. Such claims to economic rationality may then come into conflict with the demands of the environment, and the resulting inconsistency is dealt with by a division of activities, whereby operational and legitimizing activities are kept apart. The company creates functions for handling environmental and stakeholder demands. There are thus two systems in every company: one, the operative system, can generate support and resources via the market, and the other, the legitimizing system (generally management), can create resources in other ways, for example via the political system or the public agencies. The more legitimate the demands appear, the more likely they are to be fulfilled. One claim to legitimacy is often based on the demand for the company's products, another may invoke the importance of the company's survival for maintaining a certain level of employment. The legitimacy bases for the company's two functional subsystems may differ, but should not do so. The advantage of the functional division is that a company creates formal legitimizing functions visàvis the environment, while the operative side remains responsible for meeting technological demands.

Industrial Policy – A Resource System for Companies

The market is the tribunal for the technological operations of the company. Companies sell their products successfully, and thus survive. If they do not sell, they disappear from the market. But in an institutionalized economy, where the political system assumes responsibility for external economic effects, and where – more importantly – it creates development resources by way of its industrial-policy actions, there is access to another allocation system. Companies design strategies for creating resources through this system. Successful companies can acquire an extra bonus from their efforts on this front regardless of their operating profit, and thus enjoy success in the operational and in the legitimizing systems. But many companies find themselves in difficulties on the operational side, and they design strategies for exploiting the industrial-policy resources as part of their struggle for survival. A common strategy during the 1970s was to create a situation in which politicians could not refuse to grant aid. The mobilization of popular support – the general public and the mass media – was an effective way of influencing the political system. Municipal politicans often acted as intermediaries between companies and government. Other strategies aim at creating a single alternative for political action. The steel crisis of the early 1970s had been foreseen by the companies in the industry long before it became a fact. Information was withheld, and once the crisis was upon them the government had no alternative but to grant aid for the sake of employment (Swedish Government Official Reports, 1981: 72).

To qualify for aid, companies have to present themselves simultaneously as a failure and as a success. The failure belongs to the past. It was caused by factors over which the company had no control: cost developments, the business cycle, international competition, etc. The success belongs to the future. Now we're going to get on. Now the company's going to survive and expand – always provided we get the support we're asking for. The success of these and similar strategies depends on the openness of the political system. It is much easier for companies to find out about the way the politicians function, than the other way round. To the politicians the companies are "black boxes", while the companies recognize all too well the vulnerability of the politicians – a strategic advantage that is exploited in the cause of their economic requirements. Finally, the industrial-policy system has expanded so much in the organizations and instruments that it commands, that it has not been possible to coordinate the various efforts. Wandén (1982) describes how companies exploit the system by applying for aid to several industrial-policy agencies simultaneously. They often succeed.

Dependencies and Control in Industrial Policy

We have investigated the structural conditions of the industrial-policy system and the problems attaching to it. The characteristics of the separate subsystems have been analysed and the dependence on other actor systems investigated. The hierarchic interpretation of the industrial policy debate – namely that politicians can and want to exert control – has been questioned. The industrial policy system is a system without a power center. The three actor systems that constitute the system are dependent upon one another. All three want to survive. With survival in mind dependence relationships are created, and attempts are made to control adequate resources. Because of its openness, and given the type of control it can exert, the political system has only a limited chance of controlling both the public agencies and industry. Instead, the political system depends on a public administration that possesses a high degree of freedom: because of the varied demands and interests that the politicians have to satisfy, the administration acting as a kind of marginal organization between politics and industry is growing in scope and importance. The industrial-policy administration is perhaps the most important actor in relation to industry.

All three of the systems discussed here are self-referential. The political system is influenced in the first place by political standards. To the politicians, companies represent "black boxes". Because the control exercised by the politicians is limited, the administration develops its own internal standards for decisions and action. This is reinforced by the vagueness of the political programs and decisions. Companies handle this institutionalization by separating their operational from their legitimizing activities. The market and the industrial-policy system represent allocation systems which can offer the resources necessary to survival.

All three systems are functionally dependent on one another. The politicians must deal with the problems that industry cannot solve. The politicians must provide industry with the legitimacy it needs for its operations. Conversely, the politicians are dependent on a surplus-generating and workplace-creating industry. The public agencies are controlled by their clients (the companies) and by the budget frames and policy decisions of the politicians.

Industrial-policy research must take account of the existing structural conditions and dependencies. In light of the structural conditions, any debate about the efficiency of industrial policy or the efficiency of particular instruments acquires a different focus. It is in the interaction between systems that industrial policy is created. Industrial policy is a result of structural problems in industry in particular and in the economy in general. And the system in its entirety is influenced by strong dependence on the surrounding world, which provides yet another reason for the politicians' involvement. If industrial policy did not have an important function in – and for – the system, it would not exist. The functional dependencies and the institutionalization in the worlds surrounding the systems are a condition of economic policy – but also a result of it.

The Whole – Responsibility and Meaning

Organizationally, the functionally differentiated society and the society with a single political power center are alternatives: a society that chooses and accepts the advantages attaching to a functionally differentiated system cannot also have a single center of political power, whereas the society that opts for the single political center of power must to without the benefits of functional differentiation. Thus hierarchy and functional differentiation represent mutually exclusive principles of organization. In contemporary political debate it is often claimed that politics should resume the central power that it is supposed to have enjoyed in earlier periods. Apart from the fact that this would mean risking the functional differentiation which makes the welfare state possible, it also assumes that single political power centers actually have existed in previous societies. And certainly in earlier societies politics has been described as a central power factor. But even in our own society certain theories assign to politics an important and central position of power. Both these descriptions of formal structures, however, represent 'ideal' models and provide only limited information about actual power conditions.

The premise underlying the theory of the welfare state is that the state assumes responsibility for everybody and everything. Against this, we have to set the politicians' limited opportunities for action – limitations depending on legal conditions and questions of capacity. The state has to restrict its own intervention in order to guarantee the democratic liberties of its citizens. The state is unable either quantitatively or qualitatively to supply solutions to the problems that arise. Moreover, state intervention in a society always creates new problems which cannot be planned or predicted.

The functional approach represents a radical view of society, in that it accepts the limited function, power and responsibility of the political machine. In a system whose only certain attribute is change, categories such as "progressive" and "conservative" are obsolete. The essential point is how we decide to handle change. And there is much to suggest that in this context a system of functional differentiation, with its decentralization of problem-solving, is superior to a hierarchic system with its centralized power.

"Meaning" is a scarce resource today. In a society lacking any generally accepted center, there is no given morality or given rules. The underlying theory of the welfare state cannot satisfy all needs if there is no meaning in society. Nor can any calls for a strong political center fill the vacuum.

In the next chapter we shall examine more closely the idea of the political system as power center.

References

Arrow, K. J. (1969) *The Organization of Economic Activity: Issues Pertinent to the Choice of Market Versus Non-Market Allocation in the Analysis and Evaluation of Public Expenditure: The PPB System.* Vol. 1, US Joint Committee, 91st Congress, 1st Session, US Government Printing Office, pp. 59–73.
– (1974) *The Limits of Organization.* New York: W. W. Norton & Co.
Baier, V. E., March, J. H., Saetren, H. (1982) *Implementation as a Doubtful Metaphor.* Working Paper, Stanford Graduate School of Business.
Boston Consulting Group (1979) *En ram för svensk industripolitik.* Stockholm: Liber.
Brunsson, N., et al. (1981) *Politik och administration.* Stockholm: Liber.
Brunsson, N., Wolff, R. (1984) *Industripolitisk rationalitet.* Stockholm: EFI.
Coase, R. H. (1937) The Nature of the Form. *Economica, N. S.,* 4, pp. 386–405.
– (1972) Industrial Organization: A Proposal for Research. *Policy Issues and Research Opportunities in Industrial Organization.* Victor R. Fuchs (Ed.), New York: National Bureau of Economic Research, distributed by Columbia University Press, New York and London, pp. 59–73.
Commons, J. R. (1934, 1951) *Institutional Economics, Its Place in Political Economy.* New York: Macmillan.
Gandemo, B. (1982) *Investeringar i företag.* The National Industrial Board, Stockholm, p. 17.
Henning, R. (1980) Politikernas informationsunderlag. *Att utveckla en långsiktig industripolitik.* The National Industrial Board, Stockholm, pp. 81–114.
Hernes, G. (1978) Mot en institusjonell økonomi. *Forhandlingsøkonomi og blandingsadministrasjon* G. Hernes (Ed.). Bergen: Universitetsforlaget, pp. 196–242.
Hägg, I., Johanson, J. (Eds.) 1982 *Företag i nätverk.* Stockholm: SNS.
Lindblom, Ch. E. (1977) *Politics and Markets. The World's Political-Economic System.* New York: Basic Books.
Luhmann, N. (1981) *Politische Theorie im Wohlfahrtsstaat.* München – Wien: Olzog Verlag.
Luhmann, N. (1984) *Soziale Systeme. Grundriß einer allgemeinen Theorie.* Frankfurt a. M.

Meyer, J. W., Rowan, B. (1983) Institutionalized Organizations: Formal Structure as Myth and Ceremony. *Organizational Environments. Ritual and Rationality.* J. W. Meyer and W. R. Scott (Ed.) Beverly Hills et al.: Sage Publications, pp. 21–44.

NOU (1982) The Norwegian Government Official Reports. *Maktutredningen.* Final report Oslo, p. 3.

Pfeffer, J., Salancik, G. R. (1978) *The External Control of Organizations. A Resource Dependence Perspective.* New York et al.: Harper & Row.

Ruin, O. (1983) *Svensk politisk stil: att komma överens och tänka efter före i land i olag.* Arvedson, Hägg and Rydén (Ed.), Stockholm: SNS, pp. 31–56.

Saetren, H. (1983) *Iverksettning av offentlig politik.* Bergen et al.: Universitetsforlaget.

Schneider, D. (1981) *Geschichte betriebswirtschaftlicher Theorie,* München: Oldenbourgh Verlag.

Schumpeter, J. (1911, 1952) *Die Theorie der wirtschaftlichen Entwicklung. Eine Untersuchung über Unternehmergewinn, Kapital, Kredit, Zins und den Konjunkturzyklus.* Berlin.

Sjöstrand, S.-E. (1984) *Samhällsorganisation. En ansats till en institutionell ekonomisk mikroteori.* Lund: Doxa.

The Swedish Government Official Reports (1981) SOU, *Att avveckla en kortsiktig stödpolitik.* Stockholm, p. 72.

Tolbert, P. S. (1985) Institutional Environments and Resource Dependence: Sources of Administrative Structure in Institutions of Higher Education. *Administrative Science Quarterly,* Vol. 30, No. 1, pp. 1–3.

Wandén, S. (1982) *Företagsstöd.* Stockholm: RRV.

Williamson, O. E. (1975) *Markets and Hierarchies: Anlysis and Antitrust Implications. A Study in the Economy of Internal Organization.* New York: Free Press.

– (1981) The Modern Corporation: Origins, Evolution, Attributes. *Journal of Economic Literature,* Vol. XIX, pp. 1537–1568.

Wolff, R. (1983) *Industripolitikens kunskapsbehov.* The National Industrial Board.

Industrial Policy as Implementation or Legitimation

Nils Brunsson

Society as Hierarchy

In the popular European political debate it is customary to regard the state as a controlling organ. It is assumed that the state controls or at least strives to control large sections of societal development. Society itself is often conceived as a hierarchy, in which the state constitutes the superordinate leadership unit – the same image that is generally used to describe the state's own vast organization, which is also assumed to be hierarchic, i.e. topped by the politicians who control the work of the ministries, which in turn control the various government offices and boards. Thus, ultimately, the state political system is perceived as controlling society as a whole – a vertical conception which generates a sense of order and meaning. As a result of this hierarchic view, the role of the state in society is discussed in terms borrowed from the world of the individual organization and its leadership. It is assumed that management, i.e. the political system, is willing and able to change the behavior of other subordinate actors on a basis of its own "goals", which bear upon the development of society as a whole. Political decisions are to be "implemented", thus leading to the fulfilment of the political goals. One of the major problems, however, is that this process is often obstructed, perhaps by an intractable and complicated administration or by opposition and reluctance from other groups of citizens.

Industrial policy is one of many areas in which the hierarchic metaphor recurs. It is assumed that the function of industrial policy is to influence the structure and development of industrial enterprises, to bring them more in line with political preferences regarding employment, expansion, level of technological development, export sales, etc. Such an ambition requires not only that the political system takes the initiative and actively controls the development of individual companies but also that it solves difficult problems – after all, it is rarely at all clear how the desired ends should be attained. Swedish industrial policy has triggered off a wide-ranging normative debate, including sharp criticism of the way the policy is conducted as well as many suggestions about what should be done instead.

According to the hierarchic metaphor industrial policy is something which the political system initiates and carries through. If we abandon this image it becomes more clearly evident that industrial policy calls for the participation of at least two parties, industry and the politicians. Industrial policy can be defined as the interaction between industry and politics. It is not immediately clear which of the two is most interested in industrial policy, which is most active, or which takes the most initiatives. Industry and politicians both conduct industrial policy. Firms often have strong reasons for joining up with the national politicians: the state has money; it is a source of finance which has often proved possible to tap when other sources have run dry. The state has also shown an ability to survive far exceeding that of business companies. In other words the interest of companies in industrial policy is not difficult to understand. The willingness of politicians to join up with corporate enterprise seems more difficult to explain. The hierarchic metaphor – that the role of the politicians is to govern and guide – offers an explanation, but a highly dubious one.

In the following pages I am going to raise sone doubts regarding the hierarchic metaphor in the sphere of industrial policy. The hierarchic metaphor pre-supposes that the state, with the politicians at its head, is *able* and *willing* to control. Both these assumptions will be called in question below.

Can the State Control Industry?

The hierarchic metaphor presupposes that the political system of the state can control industry, that the state has qualities and tools which make it able to steer individual companies in the direction it desires. In other words the interaction between state and industry should mean that the state can influence the behavior of companies in areas which it regards as important.

However, several empirical studies of industrial policy in Sweden have shown that the state's ability to exert control in individual cases is often very small. Neither the type nor the amount of investment undertaken by large Swedish corporations is affected by the substantial state aid which has been received. Rather, this aid tends to finance investments which were anyway going to be made (Gandemo, 1983). In making decisions about economic aid to individual companies in trouble during the 1970s, the state was in a weak bargaining position; it was "practically impossible to say no" (Swedish Government Official Reports, 1981: 72).

These results do not seem so surprising when we remember that politicians also have found it very difficult to control their own agencies. (Brunsson and Jönsson, 1976; Wiberg, 1985). A lot of problems arise when the politically composed units seek to influence the activities of the hierarchically ordered administrative units. The political units are built on different principles, and this greatly affects these difficulties in exerting control.

In the same way the state and the business firms represent different forms of organization. The state is a political organization in which the "management" at least has been composed specifically to reflect and express conflicting norms in its environment and it is important that these conflicts should be openly reported (Brunsson, 1986). Companies are more hierarchically organized, with greater emphasis on a homogeneous leadership which strives to promote co-ordinated action in its organization. Compared with the state, companies are also more closed and more anxious to conceal their internal conflicts from the outside world.

Political and hierarchic organizations have different types of organizational ideology, i.e. the views of the members about their organization and its situation are of a different character. Hierarchic organizations tend to have "strong" organizational ideologies. In hierarchic organizations there are powerful forces striving to inculcate in their members a common, consistent attitude towards crucial issues. The common organizational ideology is often also both precise and complex; the members have fairly exact and detailed knowledge about the area of operations of their organization. Political organizations, on the other hand, tend to have "weak" organizational ideologies, i.e. ideologies that are inconsistent, vague and simple. The definition of a political organization says that its leading members should have at least partly conflicting views about the situation of the organization and about what should be done. The management of a political organization is generally composed primarily on grounds of representativeness rather than of expertise.

A weak ideology is easy to change by disseminating another that is stronger (Brunsson, 1985). It is therefore relatively easy for hierarchic organizations to manipulate political ones. Political organizations find it easy to let Themselves be influenced; it could even be claimed that this is their central function. They are after all meant to represent the ideas obtaining in their environment.

Individual companies thus have an ideological advantage when they negotiate with the state. This is particularly evident when the bargaining involves large companies and a lot of money. Huge sums are often handled by the political leadership – the government and the parliament; the negotiations are not delegated to the public agencies which are more hierarchically organized and which therefore in principle have a stronger bargaining position. Large companies often possess a kind of monopoly of knowledge; many of the country's experts work within their area of production.

Yet another difficulty dogs the state and the political leadership when it comes to controlling business firms. This is the openness of the state system; virtually all companies and projects can call on the state to handle their problems. The state cannot avoid tackling problems; if it should try to do so, this is seen as the adoption of an active stance visàvis the demands in question. In Sweden the national politicians are regarded as ultimately responsible for almost everything, including the problems of the corporate sector. Unlike most organizations, the state can only answer "yes" or "no" to demands it receives from outside – neglecting the demands or to reject them on grounds that they fall outside the organization's responsibilities is simply not a practical possibility. The state has little control over its own agenda.

Because of this openness the political leadership is responsible for positive decisions to support corporate projects – but this is not all. Since even rejections are regarded as active decisions, the politicians are held responsible for these as well. In order to cope with saying "no", they need arguments which the surrounding world will regard as legitimate. Thus both acceptance and rejection have to be equally well motivated. Strong arguments in favour of approval are willingly supplied by the aid-seekers. But because of the companies' superior knowledge, it is often difficult for the state to find counterarguments which the applicants cannot refute. And without credible counterarguments, the state finds it difficult to justify its refusals.

The story of the BAS investment (Brunsson, 1983) illustrates the weakness of the state when it comes to controlling industry. BAS was one of Sweden's largest industrial investments of the 1970s. It commanded a huge amount of state aid, and resulted in total economic failure. The money invested was never recovered; the plant did not even cover its own running costs. The state provided economic aid in two rounds: on the first occasion the politicians responsible in the government were very dubious about whether the project could be profitable, and on the second occasion they were convinced that it was not profitable. On neither occasion, however, did the government see any possibility of refusing to support the project, and this for several reasons.

The government lacked legitimate arguments for a refusal. The BAS project was presented in such a way that it accorded well with the government's own proclaimed strategy, namely to invest in "futures" industries. According to the very complicated estimates produced by the project management, the project would be profitable. Although the government did not believe this, it could not prove that the estimates were wrong. These had been made by Sweden's leading experts in the relevant product area. No equivalent foreign experts were available, and would in any case have belonged to rival companies.

The government was approached at a late stage, when a great deal of money had already been spent, houses on a suitable piece of land had already been demolished, the project had gathered a good many supporters in the trade unions and the municipality, and expectations in the region were high – the project was expected to come off. Thus a lot of people already felt bound to the project, and were assuming it would be realized. In such a situation it was very difficult for the government to turn it down. And in fact the government realized a rejection on its part would probably be overturned in the parliament where there was much interest in supporting industrial expansion and little in protecting the national budget from major expenditure. In other words the state could not bring itself to say "no", although politicians and civil servants in the Government Office considered the project to be extremely doubtful or even downright unacceptable.

Approval was made easier because responsibility was dispersed among several organizations as well as being spread over a long period of time. The government's own decision was split between two occasions, and responsibility for each sub-decision was thus diluted. Several organizations had previously taken a number of positive subdecisions about the project, and they thus shared the responsibility for approval with the government.

The BAS project illustrates some of the difficulties facing the state when it comes to exerting control over business companies. These difficulties are a problem for the hierarchic metaphor – but are they actually a problem for the state and its leaders? Does the political system really want to control the business companies? This is the question I shall be addressing in the following section.

The Will to Control – Implementation or Legitimation?

The hierarchic metaphor presupposes not only that the political leadership of the state can control the business companies, but also that it *wants* to. The metaphor is closely associated with a belief that, unlike most other organizations, a political organization such as the state is geared primarily to influencing conditions outside its own boundaries. While industrial companies, for example, are assumed to be interested solely in their own wellbeing, the state and the municipalities are assumed to be working unselfishly for the welfare of other people. Moreover, the state in particular is credited with a notable inability to leave things alone; it is assumed to want to change a great variety of material conditions in its environment.

This assumption that political organizations are so very extrovert and change-oriented appears dubious to say the least. The idea seems to have been borrowed from the way political organizations talk about their role and their functions, rather than from any empirical studies of their actual situation. In fact it seems more probable that an organization which bases its legitimacy to such a great extent on reflecting the various ideas obtaining in its environment rather than on taking action, would generally have little real interest in changing its environment. And this applies particularly when changing or improving the environment meets with great or insuperable obstacles.

In this section I shall discuss some conceivable relations between the state and industry. Using a case study I shall illustrate the way in which these relations can work out in practice. I shall differentiate between two possible functions for the state's industrial policy – as implementation or legitimation. Viewed in light of the hierarchic metaphor, the main function lies in implementation. The state is supposed to make decisions about changes in society, and these decisions are also supposed to be carried out. A whole branch of research, implementation research, has developed around this approach concerned among other things to discover why so many powerful decisions made in various political assemblies fail to generate the relevant action or to attain the effects of which the decision-makers spoke. If instead the main function of the state is assumed to be legitimation, the perspective is almost the reverse: action by no means represents the only way of achieving legitimacy and it is not even certain that consistency between decision and action is desirable. Let us now examine the implementation and legitimation perspectives in greater detail.

Different Forms of Implementation and Legitimation

In an implementation perspective it is action and its effects that are the important result of politics. The political system is interested in the first instance in influencing other systems apart from its own. According to this view, the obstacles to action or to the realization of decisions lie outside the political system, in the state's own administrative apparatus or in the industrial system. The political system has firm intentions for the development of industry, and it strives to solve problems and to exert control.

Even if in practice industrial policy could be understood largely in an implementation perspective, it still does not need to possess all these attributes. Instead we could conceive of different forms of implementation policy, embodying different amounts of "implementation attributes". The most extreme form would then be *problem-solving*. Such a policy would mean that the political system tries to solve problems in the industrial system, i.e. the state is equipped not only with powerful intentions (which identify the important problems and possible solutions), but also with activities geared to discovering the best possible – or at least some acceptable – actions, which should then be carried out.

In a less extreme variant the political system aims not at problem-solving but at *control*. Even if the political system does not initiate action with a view to solving industrial problems, it may still want to help to determine what action is taken. The political system wants to control what happens, and it is active in taking the initiative.

In the mildest form of implementation policy the political system still expects to see that certain measures are taken, but it does not actively concern itself with controlling what these actions are. By making decisions, or in some other way, the political system *supports* certain actions. The actions need not be controlled by the political system; even less need they represent solutions to problems which the politicians themselves have put forward.

Thus we have three kinds of implementation policy – problem-solving, control and support. In all these, action is the essential result, but the political system's link with the action varies in its strength. In a legitimation perspective, on the other hand, actions taken or measures adopted are not the major result of the operations of the political system. Action is not an end; at most it is a means. The vital result is now legitimacy.

A legitimation policy involves activities on the part of the political system directed towards creating legitimacy for itself. The main strategy of the political organization for creating its own legitimacy is to reflect in its structure, its processes and its production the norms and values and interests that obtain in the environment. (Brunsson, 1986). This represents a *direct* way of creating legitimacy. But legitimacy can also be created indirectly, through the agency of the industrial system. This indirect aspect of legitimacy is connected with the question of the *responsibility* resting with the political system.

Increasingly often the political system is given responsibility for industrial problems. To be responsible for something means being regarded as a cause. If, for instance, the political system is responsible for the unsatisfactory state of industry, it means that the political system is regarded as having caused the situation or of being in a position to correct it (but of having chosen not to do so). This responsibility associates the political system with the industrial system, and means that the legitimacy of the political system becomes dependent on the legitimacy of the industrial system. If industry enjoys a high degree of legitimacy, there is no political problem; but if the industrial system is lumbered with qualities of a strongly negative kind and is thus low on legitimacy, then the political responsibility becomes problematic. In such a situation the political system can acquire legitimacy in two diametrically opposite ways: either by trying to dispose of its responsibility for the situation, or by accepting responsibility but endowing the situation with greater legitimacy.

If the political system disposes of its responsibility, then it detaches itself from the industrial system. We can call the rejection of responsibility the destabilizing line. Applied more extensively it means that the political system distances itself from major aspects of societal development, which can generate conflict and instability in the industrial system and perhaps in the long run in the political system too.

The assumption of responsibility can then be said to represent the stabilizing strategy. On the whole it has been the main strategy of political systems in many industrial countries since World War II, and it has led to what is sometimes called "overload", i.e. the political system has shouldered responsibility for almost everything from the state of the world economy and industrial development to the problems of the young and house-building technology.

If the political system adopts the responsibility-assuming strategy, it can increase its legitimacy by steering people's ideas about the industrial situation in a positive direction. This can in fact be done by attempting to influence the industrial system by implementing various measures. The strategy then consists of implementation by way of problem-solving, with all the difficulties that this can give rise to. But people's ideas about a situation can be changed, without there being any material alteration in the situation itself. Exerting influence exclusively on people's ideas in this way can be dubbed *situational legitimation*. Situational legitimation means that the political system is legitimized and at the same time its environment is affected, but this is influence of a different kind from the influence resulting from an implementation policy.

Tools

Three types of tool for creating legitimacy can be distinguished: talk, decisions and action. Talk is an important tool for political organizations. Using this tool people can describe situations as positive or negative, they can describe their own role, they can influence their responsibility or provide arguments for decisions and actions and situations, and much else besides. Decisions are generally seen as a choice between different action alternatives. A person who has made a decision has therefore also made a choice and has thus at least helped to cause an action or an event and to be regarded as a cause of something means being assigned responsibility for it. The decision process can be designed in such a way as to reinforce or weaken the decision-maker's responsibility and legitimacy. Different types of action, e.g. action initiated by different persons, can also affect legitimacy in different ways.

Talk and decisions are tools which the political system can also use when it comes to implementing action. In order to carry out an action it is often important to be able to describe and justify it, in a way that is appropriate to the person who is to perform is. The way in which decisions are made is also important; for instance, the decision process may aim to bind the implementor to the decision, and the decision can express the political system's commitment to the action, and its determination that the action really will be carried out.

And in fact the action itself can also be an instrument of implementation: recommendations that are differently designed may be more, or less, likely to be carried out. There may be a difference between suggestions that are vaguely or operationally defined, between proposals involving the payment of money for an operation or those that describe more directly how it should be carried out, between actions to be taken via the administration or direct by industry itself. Money payments to the public agencies with vague directives about what they are to be used for probably belong to those actions most likely to be performed, but they involve the least control and the least specific problem-solving.

To summarize: industrial policy can function either as a way of effecting the implementation of action in the industrial system, or as a means of legitimizing the political system. An implementation policy may concern problem-solving, control or simply support for action. The legitimation policy may concern direct legitimation, legitimation by influencing responsibility, or situational legitimation. The main tools available to the political system are talk, decisions and actions.

An Illustration

To illustrate this discussion of implementation and legitimation I shall briefly describe and analyse a case of state industrial policy – PLACE. PLACE was presented by one of the Scandinavian governments as their suggestion for saving jobs in a community suffering from severe unemployment. In the BAS case we could say that the state became a victim of an industrial policy conducted by companies and projects in the industrial system. In the PLACE case the initiative lay to a great extent with the state, and the opportunities for exerting control and steering events could therefore have been expected to be greater.

PLACE – A Description

PLACE is a municipality with high unemployment and extensive state-owned industry; it is also a big recipient of government industrial aid. On several occasions hopes of a more favorable situation for industry and more jobs have been dashed. The government presented a special bill for this community, including various decisions and actions which were to improve the situation there. It was estimated that the measures would cost several hundreds of million pounds. The idea was to restructure a state-owned company in the municipality, which would lead to more unemployment, and to introduce a whole series of aids to industry and new investment by the state. How had the government arrived at this comprehensive bill, incorporating decisions about so many measures that would cost so much money?

The story began several years earlier. First the trade unions in the municipality had produced a union program of action. A little later representatives for the community also raised the question within the government party and per-suaded the national party organization to adopt certain declarations about the necessity of tackling unemployment in the area. Representatives of the com-munity then presented the party board with further demands for action. The board decided that a plan of action should be drawn up.

A working group was appointed, including central and local representatives of the party. The central representatives were anxious that any recommendations made should be firmly rooted in the community – what everybody thinks must be important – and the local representatives were anxious that "the outsiders" should really face up to the problems and the demands that were being raised. Thus a common interest lay behind the way things were organized, whereby the group held discussions with various leading actors in the municipality and the trade unions, thus gathering together virtually all the suggestions that were being made in the community.

It was then a question of deciding which proposals should be included in the plan, and how they should be presented. The plan was to include only promises which would be kept. Where the technical problems connected with a proposal appeared insoluable or the decision base was inadequate in some other way, or where opinions were divided in the community, the approach was cautious and it might be suggested that a proposal be "investigated further" or it might be recognized as "important" without any promise being made for any definite action. It was often stated that things *"ought"* to be done rather than that they *"would"* be done. A great many concrete and often minor proposals were included in an appendix, and it was felt that this implied no promises about them. A provisional plan was sent out for comment by everyone who had been involved in making suggestions. As a result a great many "oughts" were altered to "will be". After this the plan was approved by the local section of the party, thus providing the basis for the party's election propaganda. The difference, compared with the other parties, was that a plan was being presented and not just a series of wishes – a plan which would be realised since it had been worked out together with the central party leader-ship.

The plan then formed the grounds on which a government bill could be based. After making a comprehensive technical examination of the realism, the cost and the possible employment effects of the different suggestions in the plan, the bill was written after barely a month, during which the possibility of implementing some of the measures was further discussed and negotiations were held between technical departments and the Ministry of Finance, and the details of the proposals were worked out. The state-owned enterprise and other organizations in the municipality were given another opportunity to submit demands. A further round of comments from the government departments generated several new suggestions about the arguments which would be used.

The final bill took up a little over half the 30 or so proposals originally included in the plan. It is difficult to say exactly what constitutes a proposal and just how each one was handled, but roughly speaking seven of the proposals were accepted in the bill, albeit often in a somewhat altered form. According to the same kind of assessment, six proposals were referred to new or ongoing investigations. All these proposals were among the more prominent in the plan. But more than half the proposals in the plan were not accepted. Some were rejected explicitly in the bill, but most were simply not mentioned. The proposals that were not mentioned had lacked active advocates either in the government departments or outside them. Nor had they been particularly prominent in the plan.

In presenting the bill, three things in particular were emphasized: that the measures were intended to deal with problems in the short and long term; that the costs amounted to several hundreds of million pounds; and that the bill agreed with the plan. In interviews in the mass media the prime minister emphasized the "democratic" aspects of the bill: the proposals had been worked out by the residents of the community themselves. Subsequent developments would depend on the people there, and not on centralized decisions in the capital city.

PLACE – Implementation Policy or Legitimation Policy?

How can we interpret the activities described above? To what extent can they be understood in terms of the model presented here: how far can they be interpreted as problem-solving, control or support?

Problem-Solving

There is nothing to suggest that the work on the PLACE bill had a problem-solving function. Problem-solving would have presupposed an analysis, in which the causes of the problems – in this case the longterm unemployment problem – would have been investigated. The actions to be taken would then have emerged from the analysis. Such an analysis was almost demonstratively avoided; gathering rather than analysis was the method for generating solutions. Furthermore, ideas were sought in the community, i.e. among those who had demonstrably *not* succeeded in solving the problems themselves. If a start had been made by analysing the problems, there might have been a risk of producing problems without solutions; now, instead, solutions were produced without problems. Nor did the time allowed really permit of any problem-solving: the plan was drawn up in a month and the bill was designed in a couple of months and actually written in a few days.

Nor were the criteria for the gathering of proposals based on any analysis of the problems. Suggestions were rejected or changed because they were too costly, because they didn't fit the present aid system, because they came within the brief of committees already sitting, because they largely competed with other communities, or because they were not realistic (e.g. industrial projects which were obviously not profitable). Predictions for future jobs were produced in a slapdash manner.

Nor did any of the actors interviewed claim to know how the problems of the community could be solved. They did not even believe they would be solved, particularly not as a result of the bill. The problems were formulated in terms that were vague or foggy; in the bill the emphasis was on the long-term employment effects while the proposals concerned short-term effects: and when the actors discussed the results of the bill they were more inclined to talk of "a new spirit" and better profitability in the state-owned enterprise.

Control

All the work on the bill seems incomprehensible if we assume that its function was to solve problems. It is also difficult to interpret it in terms of control, or even as an attempt at control. In presenting the bill the leading politicians emphasized that it was the community's own recommendations that were being supported, not their own. And this was of course absolutely correct, even if the recommendations had two sources. Most suggestions came from the plan, while recommendations for cutbacks in the state-owned company came from the company itself. Even regarding the state-owned company, the express policy was that the political system should not exert control: the company's goal was profitability, and the way this was attained was not a political question but something to be decided by the company board and corporate management.

The central politicians intentionally assumed the role of *defensive examiners* (Brunsson and Jönsson, 1979) visàvis proposals from the local politicians and trade unions and civil servants. Instead of taking the initiative themselves, they waited for proposals which they then examined and assessed. It was not the central politicians but the people in the community who took the initiative regarding the development plan. It was not the central politicians who made any suggestions for action; rather, they listened to proposals from the grassroots. They let themselves be influenced. On this basis they signed a text which contained among other things promises of future action and contributions to be made.

Defensive examiners presuppose suggestion-makers, and such were indeed mobilized. The procedure involved "soaking up" ideas – all the ideas that were floating about in the party and the trade union could be gathered up in this way. The result was that hardly any ideas that were abroad in the community were left untried. The plan did not contain a single original thought, as one opposition politician declared. But no-one had intended that it should.

The "control" consisted largely of the political system seeing that proposals were put forward, in an area where they wanted – or felt compelled – to do something. That was the function of the plan, and of the plans called for from the state enterprise in the area.

It can be said that it was the central politicians who let themselves be controlled. The central politicians exposed themselves to influence from local actors and from their own civil servants. They limited their own role to saying "yes" or "no" to proposals that were actively driven by local politicians or officials. Even the selection of proposals was made in collaboration with the proposers, and as we have seen it mainly followed criteria which had nothing to do with political will. The central politicians simply did not have to make up their minds about any proposals that lacked "drivers".

Support for Action

Thus work on the bill had nothing to do with problem-solving and very little with political control. And yet it could still have been implementation-oriented in that it would have supported certain actions which, while not qualifying as problem-solving or having very much to do with political initiative and will, were still intended to be carried out.

However, in the PLACE case there was little need for support for action, since the politicians possessed no problem-solving or control ambitions. Most of the measures had after all been suggested by various groups on the spot, thus enjoying strong support there from the start.

Further the politicians' support for many of the measures was rather vague. Most measures were so cautiously worded that it was not clear whether they were really to be implemented or not: they "ought to" be carried out, they were "urgent", or they should be "investigated further". Some proposals did not refer to concrete actions, but to some sort of "goal". Other proposals were non-operative, e.g. it was difficult to know exactly what should be done to "stimulate" or "support" some particular development. Finally, of course, a whole series of proposals was simply lodged in the appendix to the plan. In the case of a few measures only was any definite promise made.

The measures for which it was difficult to gain acceptance in the community, and which thus needed support if they were to be implemented, were the cutbacks in the state-owned company. These commanded support, but not in the plan. Instead, support and justification were to be found in the company's own plans. The main argument was that like other state-owned companies this one must be run on businesslike lines and must aim to be profitable. Any negative effects should be specially handled. The cutbacks were to be complemented by other positive measures. It is even possible to see the whole bill as compensating – and thus supporting – the reduction in the workforce of the state-owned enterprise. Action there, which could in fact have been suggested by one minister, was supported by the efforts of several ministers and departments.

Direct Political Legitimation

Thus it is rather difficult to find anything in the processes, the arguments or the proposals to suggest that work on the bill was particularly geared to an implementation policy. There are many more factors suggesting that its essential function was directly or indirectly to provide legitimation for the political system. Let us look first at direct ways of legitimizing the political system.

Political organizations create legitimacy for themselves mainly by reflection, i.e. they seek in some was to mirror or handle the interests or values of the environment in their organization or their operations. I have already mentioned three main tools for bringing this about: talk, decisions and action. In working on the bill, the central politicians used all three instruments.

The work was organized in three stages, corresponding to the three instruments. The plan represented the talk level: no decisions were made at that stage. The greater part of the text of the plan is devoted to enumerating the problems of the community and expressing a general wish that action should be looked into, considered, or taken. Every proposal which had some degree of attachment to the community was treated positively in the development plan. In some cases concrete and binding pledges were established. In other cases it was said that measures "ought to" be carried out, or investigated or considered, and yet other suggestions were assigned to the appendix to the plan – which really meant that the group had decided *not* to support them. All the proposals mentioned were of course already familiar and nobody expected the group to reject them in so many words. Thus the function of the text was not to support action. But nor can it be regarded as providing support for non-action; on the contrary it was emphasized that the community's problems were serious and something must be done to improve the situation. Rather, the function of this part of the process can be seen as a legitimation of the politicians, by reflecting attitudes and values in the relevant environment. The politicians did not say "no" to the proposals; instead they associated themselves with them, but without binding themselves in any way.

In the bill, which can be said to represent the decision level, the number of proposals had to be reduced: in a decision context any inconsistencies between different proposals become more obvious, and the link with implementation is stronger. The proposals had to be weeded out more severely; those that were loosely anchored in the community, or were subject to differences of opinion, were dropped. Negative decisions were not made unnecessarily; most of the proposals which did not lead to decisions were simply left unmentioned. But the number receiving affirmative decisions was still very high, and some proposals were counted twice. In several cases it was decided to reconsider proposals at some later date in connection with a different investigation.

Because of the time lag between plan and bill, between talking and deciding, it was possible to defend failures of consistency. And in any case, according to the actors, it was never intended that everything in the plan should be decided upon or implemented, particularly those proposals which came into the "ought to happen" category.

The proposals which were then carried out are the system's actions. And many of the proposals that were agreed upon were in fact realized. But we can also regard some parts of the process as actions. According to the prime minister the process had been "democratic" since everybody had been able to take part in the process and to influence it. The massive effort in itself should show that the political system cared, and that it was tackling the problems. In a five-line summary on the front page of the bill it was pointed out exactly how much the effort was costing; from a problem-solving point of view, costs should be kept as low as possible, but when it is a question of legitimation the reverse may be true.

The effects of all these legitimizing actions are naturally difficult to pinpoint. But many of the actors declared that they provided a high degree of legitimacy. For example they were believed to have contributed to the party's continuing election successes.

Influencing Responsibility

The main point of the bill was to express the responsibility of the local and central political systems for developments in the community, and the work on the bill was in itself further evidence of this responsibility. However, work on the bill was accompanied by a whole series of arguments indicating that the responsibility of the central politicians and the authorities was not unlimited, particularly not in a future perspective. It was after all proposals emanating from the community and not from the government which were now being decided. It was also firmly pointed out by the central politicians that this was the last time they would take action; after this the residents of the community were to manage on their own – the bill itself was making it possible for them to do so. Just because such vast sums of money were being invested now, the government had no responsibility for the future. In the same way it was pointed out that the state-owned enterprise had now been provided with the conditions needed for profitability; fulfilling the profitability goal was now the responsibility of corporate management, not of the government.

But the inclination to hive off responsibility was not total. In one case the political system decided to assume responsibility, namely when it came to maintaining one profitable state-owned company in the area. If this company had been sold to the municipality, the need for further subsidies would have disappeared altogether. But that proposal was rejected already before the plan was written. Perhaps this community and its problems provided an important arena for the political system, which the central politicians did not want to lose altogether?

Influencing the Legitimacy of the Situation

Some features in the process, the proposals and the arguments were functional for making the community feel more satisfied with its situation. The bill undeniably demonstrated that, despite the severity of the problems, the government was doing everything it possibly could. No suggestions that could be regarded as technically possible and that enjoyed widespread support in the community were actually rejected. Somebody cared, somebody wanted to help. The political system also tried to arouse expectations that things would be better in the future and the problems might perhaps be solved. This openly expressed belief in the future was in marked contrast to the great pessimism among the central politicians themselves as to whether the problems could ever really be solved.

Most of the politicians interviewed emphasized the importance of the policy in legitimizing the situation. When they were asked about the possible future effects of the bill, they said that certain effects could already be noted: they had enhanced people's way of thinking about and facing up to their situation although no concrete action had been taken as yet. The great importance of the plan and the bill was that a new spirit had arisen in the community, people had come to believe in the future with optimism, courage, self-esteem and determination. The "depression" and pessimism which had formerly prevailed was the main reason for composing the plan and the bill at all.

Giving legitimacy to the prevailing situation must have been an important task, in view of the predictions which the politicians actually made. Not one of them believed that the concrete problems of the community would really be resolved, despite the measures which were to be adopted. They did not expect the unemployment figures to fall; they believed they would remain the highest in the country.

If the impact on feelings in the community was really as great as the politicians claimed, it was quite remarkable: during the period when this change of heart was taking place, unemployment in the area actually increased as a result of cutbacks in the state-owned company.

A Summary

The result of the analysis is not particularly surprising. The process, the proposals and the arguments are all incomprehensible if we assume that their function was implementation in the sense of problem-solving and control. What actually happened has little in common with the picture conjured up by the implementation model, with the politicians trying to impose their ideas about what should be done on to a refractory environment. The whole thing becomes comprehensible only if we assume that support and legitimation were the prime goals. That the politicians had no problem-solving function is not surprising, since none of them had any idea how the community's problems could be solved and since they did not even believe that they could be solved. Perhaps it was just because the problem really was insoluble, that the politicians felt they ought or had to intervene. And since it was not possible to devote themselves to solving the problems, they naturally had little interest in exerting control either, restricting themselves mainly to what was feasible and desirable in the situation as it was, namely supporting the "necessary" cutbacks in the state-owned company and legitimizing the political system and the situation in the community.

The politicians' main function here was legitimation. And this also seems to have been what they intended and what they achieved. Nothing suggests that the process was irrational, i.e. that the actors were being forced into the various steps against their will or their sense of what was appropriate.

The Role of Politics

The PLACE case provides an illustration of the role of the state as legitimator: legitimizing both itself and its environment. Naturally the case does not reveal legitimation as the state's only function. But it does show that we cannot always assume the state to be aiming at implementation – solving problems, exerting control, or transforming decisions into action. The hierarchic metaphor is misleading not only in the cases described here, but in several other studies of state and political control as well (Swedish examples are Brunsson and Jönsson, 1979; Brunsson and Rombach, 1978; Olson, 1983;

Jacobsson, 1984; Wiberg, 1985). The political system, like the state as a whole, finds it difficult to control its environment; and as well as its environment it is concerned with its own position. Influencing the environment need not necessarily involve control; instead it can involve legitimation.

The fact that it is popular to talk about implementation, about the political system solving problems and exerting control, need not have much connection with things as they are. Rather, it may reflect myths about organizations – myths which are in fact extremely functional. Paradoxically, political organizations often try to establish their legitimacy by proclaiming their focus on problems and action and their lack of interest in their own legitimacy. Action is important, and action is motivated by problems (cf. Starbuck, 1983).

Industrial policy is obviously an area in which implementation is very difficult, a rational political system can be expected to avoid as far as possible a policy of implementation. Too little is known about the identity of the problems, their interconnectedness, their causes, and their possible solutions, to provide any basis for rational – as opposed to superstitious – problem-solving. It is difficult to know what industrial development would be appropriate. How, for example, should we balance an interest in job opportunities against an interest in a high level of technology? Nobody knows what causes industrial development, and we know even less about how political systems can stimulate it. Controlling industrial companies and steering their development is no easy matter. And this being so, it does not seem particularly rational to put the main emphasis on problem-solving and control. Rather, we should expect industrial policy to include a significant element of legitimation. A policy geared to making people "happier", to "increasing their welfare" or to "promoting their interests" for example, can be expected to contain a large measure of responsibility-assumption, in other words of legitimation strategy.

A high degree of legitimacy in the political system and in the situation is probably also important to the stability of the system. Attempts on the part of the political system to steer industry in a particular direction will have a destabilizing effect, while also reducing the political system's ability to reflect a variety of interests and values. This in turn makes it more difficult for it to create legitimacy in this way. Legitimacy then has to be based on action instead, i.e. on implementing actions that satisfy diverse interests and views. But if there is doubt about the efficacy of the actions of the politicians in this respect, then legitimation by reflection is better for the political system. Perhaps it is also better for the industrial system and the citizens?

Perhaps the role of politics in society often involves something far more important than controlling and redistributing material resources. Its task is perhaps rather to create wellbeing and happiness, in other words to exert an influence on ideology, and it may not always be necessary to proceed the long way via controlling material resources. In the PLACE case, for example, the politicians felt that the major effects arose from their talk and decisions, not from actions undertaken by the state.

A given situation can be legitimized by affecting the way people think about it. But it can also be legitimized by the assumption of responsibility. Man has a strong desire to explain events, both the good and the bad (Geertz, 1973). In a secularized culture such as our own, it is important to be able to explain things by reference to people: if people rather than chance or natural forces or social laws have caused an event, this also means that the event can be controlled. An illusion of explanation and control can help to reduce existential anxiety (van Gunsteren, 1976). Since assuming responsibility is to establish oneself as a cause of what has happened, one way of assuming responsibility is to make decisions. Decisions suggest a choice between alternatives, and in choosing a particular action you become at least part of its cause.

The political system sets great store by decisions, and politicians often claim openly to have influenced decisions. Furthermore they can make decisions about almost anything, not only the government's actions but also those of the citizens or of business firms. Politicians readily assume responsibility or have it assigned to them. For the people around them it is perhaps particularly important that they assume responsibility for situations perceived as negative or troublesome. That someone should bear the burden of our sins has been a central tenet of western Christian culture for almost 2000 years, and we can therefore assume that the idea will persist even if the sins are now borne by another. From this point of view our regular carping at the politicians and our criticisms of the state and its institutions in periods of economic decline, are something quite natural and serving a necessary function. Politics and the politicians are more important, more crucial, to our culture than the hierarchic metaphor implies.

Assuming responsibility and creating legitimacy are important political tasks. The way they are effected is by making decisions and claiming to exert control. But the means should not be unreflectingly interpreted as goals.

References

Brunsson, N. (1983) Projektinstitutionalisering – ett fall. Stockholm: EFI report.
Brunsson, N. (1985) *The Irrational Organization*. Chichester: John Wiley and Sons.
Brunsson, N., Jönsson, S. (1979) *Beslut och handling*. Stockholm: Liber.
Brunsson, N., Rombach, B. (1982) *Går det att spara?* Lund: Doxa.
Gandemo, B. (1983) *Investeringar i företag*. Stockholm: SIND.

Geertz, C. (1973) *The Interpretation of Cultures*. New York: Basic Books.

van Gunsteren, H. (1976) *The Quest for Control*. London: John Wiley and Sons.

Jacobsson, B. (1984) *Hur styrs förvaltningen?* Lund: Studentlitteratur.

Olson, O. (1983) *Ansvar och ändamål*. Lund: Doxa.

Starbuck, W. (1983) Organizations as Action Generators. *American Sociological Review*, 48, pp. 91–102.

Swedish Government Official Report (1981) Att avveckla en kortsiktig stödpolitik. Stockholm.

Wiberg, S. (1985) Bild och handling. Manuscript, Göteborg.

Innovation in Industrial Policy Sectors –
The Cases of Remote Sensing and Bioenergy

Bengt Högberg, Lars Erik Norbäck and Thomas Stenberg

Background

It seems to be generally held by researchers, practitioners and politicians in the field of industrial policy that (technological) innovations make a major contribution to economic growth. As a result, the interest in innovation – for instance, the assessment of the instruments of government policy – is liable to increase during periods of economic stagnation, as was the case in Europe during the late 1970s. Yet, there is no general theory of innovation available which can be used to guide government policies for technological development in specific industrial sectors.

"Today, obviously no valid innovation theory seems to be available, based on behavioural methods, except for very narrowly specified clusters of firms or cases. No generalization, however, is yet possible. Policy recommendations so far are feasible only in very limited and extremely well-specified cases. As the situation is not very different when it comes to the utilization of methods of economic research, it is today still hardly possible to base any policy proposal on solid scientific grounds. We are lacking a general theory of innovation and most likely will never be able to develop a singular general theory of innovation." (Goldberg, 1981: 39)

In this paper we will present not a general theory of innovation but an interorganizational framework, which can be used in tracing and analysing innovative processes in different industrial sectors. We will also apply this framework to two such sectors, in both of which four types of actors operate:

1. public agencies administering government policy instruments
2. researchers (inventors, idea-generators etc in universities or other research organizations)
3. business firms (transforming the inventions and ideas into products and bringing them to the marketplace)
4. public agencies or other types of institutions (users and customers of the new technologies/innovations).

The sectors have been chosen because they can be characterized as political economies (Benson, 1975: 4). In our present context this means that "market forces", i.e. actor groups 2 and 3 above, are unlikely to become successful innovators without political decisions in the public sector, i.e. actor groups 1 and 4. Thus we are discussing arenas, or networks, with interdependencies between profit and non-profit organizations when it comes to technological innovation. The concept of the policy sector can be useful here.

"The policy sector is a cluster or complex of organizations connected to each other by resource dependencies and distinguished from other clusters or complexes by breaks in the structure of resource dependencies." (Benson, 1981: 16)

Our two policy sectors are bioenergy (energy woods, forestry waste etc) and remote sensing (such as observation of the earth from satellites). The sectors differ in many respects although both have a "systems character". In fact, in line with a quasi-experimental tradition, we have sought policy sectors which are as hetereogeneous as possible, provided only that our four actors groups are involved. By comparing the two sectors we hope to explore the possibilities for public agencies to promote technological innovation processes.

An Interorganizational Approach to the Promotion of Industrial Development

An interorganizational approach to the development of new industries or of new products in existing industries is motivated by the fact that markets are imperfect, i.e. a (rapid) adjustment of products and services does not occur as predicted by micro-economic theory. Some support for the development of a framework can be found in theories of oligopolies and monopolistic markets. However, an interorganizational theory sees beyond profit maximization as the only or even the dominant behavioral assumption.

Some Structural Concepts for an Interorganizational Framework

To get a new product accepted and to make it profitable is often more than a question of offering a lower price or better functions. The product exists within a larger system of functional and organizational interconnectedness, consisting of its interface with other products and with other companies investing in the same or competing products. If this interconnectedness is strong, then even a small change in one subsystem could trigger off changes in other subsystems. Such triggers may be seen as threats or opportunities by those occupying established positions, thus evoking retaliation or support in the system. If on the other hand the interconnectedness is weak, then the adjustments required are probably less farreaching.

It has been argued that interconnectedness has been increasing as a result of the growing scarcity of resources, the concentration of industry, and government intervention (cf. Pfeffer and Salancik, 1978). This leads in turn to interdependencies between organizations. Interdependence is a source of uncertainty which organizations handle either by increasing their mutual interdependence or changing its composition. In this way an organization reduces other parties' alternatives or increases its own; it is a question of the creation of power.

Another source of uncertainty stems from the lack of information about the environment in which a production or service is to compete (cf. Aldrich and Mindlin, 1978) i.e. information about the structure of interdependencies in the system or network of organizations.

Attempts have been made in the fields of institutional economics and organization theory to explain why interorganizational arrangements – cooperation agreements or hierarchies – have been created by the organizations themselves instead of markets (Commons, 1934; Pfeffer and Salancik, 1978; Williamson, 1975). The two most important and partly overlapping explanations are based on the assumption that organizations give priority to the reduction of uncertainty, and in discussing the concept of transaction costs Williamson (1975, 1979, 1980) argued that under certain conditions markets will result in higher transaction costs compared to other alternatives.[1]) Transaction costs are a function of perceived uncertainty, of the frequency of the transactions, and of the extent to which transaction-specific investments are needed.

The organizations may create a system of regulations which partly replaces the market forces. This can be done by several equally strong partners, or by a single organization or leading actor, and the idea may be to control resources, to reduce uncertainty, to take advantage of economies of scale, and so forth.

In Table 1, four "ideal" structures are defined. The dual scheme is based on the type of functional interconnectedness and the distribution of power in the

Table 1:   Four Ideal Structures

		Power			
		Concentrated		Dispersed	
Functional interconnectedness	Strong	I	Dominated by a few actors. Other actors must adapt.	II	Cooperative measures are needed to handle interconnectedness
	Weak	III	Power is not required to manage interconnectedness	IV	A "perfect" market or "atomistic" structure

---

[1]) Williamson placed little confidence in intermediate forms between market and hierarchy, because they do not sufficiently reduce uncertainty and opportunism (cf. Williamson, 1975).

system. Naturally there are other complementary bases for classifying systems of organizations, e.g. the level of investment to achieve economies of scale, the munificence of resources, or the number of organizations in the system. We will introduce some of these variables in the following section.

Table 1 also specifies the type of regulation needed in order to manage interconnectedness, other things being equal. Box I represents a structure of strong interconnectedness, dominated by one or a few actors who can prescribe the rules to which other actors will have to adapt. Box II represents a situation in which interconnectedness can be handled either by way of cooperative regulation or a change in structure, perhaps towards the type of structure specified by Box I. When the degree of interconnectedness is low, then a concentration of power is either dysfunctional or it is motivated for other reasons such as economies of scale (Box III). Finally, Box IV represents a perfect market situation. We refrain from discussing the relative effectiveness of each type here.

A Life-Cycle Perspective

The above discussion is mainly concerned with existing structures. Our present purpose calls for an understanding of the way in which new business develops, based on an interorganizational framework. The role of interorganizational cooperation in new-product development has been studied by, for example, Aiken and Hage (1968) and Edström et al. (1984a and b). Development processes are often described in terms of life cycles (Abernathy and Utterback, 1975; Ford and Ryan, 1981; Kotler, 1967). Usually, however, life cycles refer to a single technology or product rather than to systems of products and actors and their structural interrelations as they develop over time. Over the whole life cycle the structure of the system will change. Thus the life cycle concept can be applied to different levels of analysis, i.e. to a technology, a product, or a branch of industry. Below we characterize a possible development pattern, in which different business concepts[2] compete in the market. The accumulated life cycle is then the sum of the sales of each concept.

During the life cycle, the tasks confronting the actors will vary. We distinguish four such tasks here:

- the basic development of a business concept
- the anchoring of the concept in the environment (Olofsson, 1969, 1979) and further systems-building around the concept
- the expansion of capacity
- the consolidation of competitive positions.

---

[2] A "business concept" is defined here as the combination of hardware and software as it is thought to serve the customer. The same product can be part of different business concepts in the hands of different companies.

The period prior to the market introduction of a new product is usually known as the technical development phase. But although technical development may well be given priority, action may also be taken in preparation for market introduction. In cases of strong interconnectedness, market introduction may be difficult if no attempt is made to anchor the business concept in the environment until the technical development phase is over.

During the market introduction phase the new concept is confronted by interdependencies and competition on the market. Technical adaptations requiring additional development resources may be needed. There are two dimensions to the environmental anchoring of the new business concept:

- the task of understanding the interconnectedness and power distribution in the network
- the task of adapting the embryonic business concept to these conditions and of establishing a position in the network.

The first of these at least is a learning process, which can be frustrating to the new entrant.

Let us assume that the new business concept represents a radical change in relation to the established concepts on the market. It might even represent the creation of a new industrial sector. The greater the incompatibility of the new concept with existing systems (i.e. the greater the adaptations required of others), and the stronger the interconnectedness and the more dispersed the power in the established networks, the more difficult it will be to anchor the new business concept in the environment.

The new business concept must overcome the uncertainty that potential customers will feel about its reliability and profitability. The first deliveries may be tailormade, and there may be little standardization to begin with. All these factors add to the transaction costs.

Several concepts may be competing and each concept may have a short life cycle, which creates further uncertainty among customers, suppliers and finance institutions.

The environmental anchoring and completion of a single business concept may call for systems-building at an industry level, i.e. for developing ways in which interconnectedness is to be regulated at an interorganizational level.

If the new concept manages to survive the introduction phase, it may move into a growth stage. The frequency of transactions grows, uncertainty is reduced and, depending on the demand/supply ratio, standardization increases. And so transaction costs fall. With growing experience, the relative cost advantages over competing concepts increases.

Excess demand will slow down the integration process, while a balanced development could lead to further integration and a refinement of the interorganizational structure. The power structure could become unstable because new entrants are attracted into it. During the growth stage priority is given to the expansion of capacity.

Maturity begins when the growth rate levels off. Competition increases, and price becomes an increasingly important means of competing. Companies invest in rationalization as well as in horizontal and vertical integration in order to consolidate their positions in the competition for scarce resources. If one or a few organizations dominate the industry, other organizations will try to differentiate their concepts in order to avoid direct cost-based competition. New business concepts may threaten the established companies, and a new process of development could then start.

Government Promotion of new Industries

There may be several reasons for government supporting new business concepts or new industries.

1. A new concept, although economically advantageous, may not be able to break through in a well-established industry dominated by a few powerful organizations.
2. A technology that looks interesting may need support during its infancy, until it can benefit from experience-curve and transaction-cost effects.
3. For social reasons a government might want to promote a concept – e.g. certain health-care products – for which there is no demand under "ordinary" market conditions.

In the first two examples government support will be of a temporary nature, while in the third case it may have to be permanent. The government can employ direct and indirect means. The former imply direct involvement by way of orders or government investment, while the latter are aimed at creating conditions beneficial to the desired development.

The government (or its agencies) can assume various roles in promoting new industries.

1. The "push role" whereby supply is promoted either by way of directives or by economic support e.g. tax subsidies to manufacturers.
2. The "pull role" whereby demand for the new product or services is supported.
3. The "project-leader role" whereby the government involves itself in the creation of the systems structure. The involvement can vary from indirect means such as the dissemination of information, to direct means such as acting as broker or creating a "leading actor".

The third role is the most farreaching, because the government does not rely on "manipulated" market forces alone. It also attempts to manipulate the interdependencies and the power structure of the system. The type of intervention should be adapted to the specific development situation, as discussed above. We have chosen two examples of situations in which the market forces were rather weak and, in one of the cases, the achievements of government research were to be launched on the market.

Data

Data for this study were collected over a three-year period 1981–1983, in the course of investigations for two public agencies involved in the evolution of industrial policies, namely the National Accounting and Audit Bureau and The National Agency for Research about Energy Production. However, we have not followed the traditional approach of evaluation research (e.g. Weiss, 1972; Rossi et al., 1979; Lind, 1979). There appear to be three different modes:

- efficiency measurement
- agency auditing, evaluating how agencies act in accordance with goals prescribed by higher authorities
- effectiveness measurement, i.e. evaluating the effects of steps undertaken (Lind, 1979: 19).

There are no clear borderlines between the three approaches. Besides, in a policy sector with many interdependent actors often pursuing diverging goals, it is not easy to separate the effects of the instruments of government policy. It may even be difficult to say whether the development pattern in the sector can be explained as the result of such instruments or as something that has emerged despite them.

We decided to start with a development process (innovations in a policy sector) which is subject to government policies. We have sought to describe the process, using the framework presented above. In this phase we also analysed the characteristics of the process, and the way in which such processes can be promoted by government policies. We then analysed the activities of the agencies. Did they promote or obstruct the development process? Have the agencies been capable and skilful enough to promote the process? Since resources are not free, it is important to evaluate the trade-off between the use of resources and the needs of the development process.

At the same time we also investigated the government goals for the policy sector concerned. We have regarded these as means and measures on an equal footing with the means and measures taken by the public agencies themselves. Thus we have not performed any agency audits, but have taken such goals for granted and have evaluated the way in which the agencies interpreted them and transformed them into action.

We collected different types of data from different types of actors. No interviews were held at the governmental goal-setting level. There we merely analysed official reports and documents. In public agencies (administering the instruments of government policy or using the new technologies/innovations), business firms and research-organizations interviews were held with leading decision-makers. Official and unofficial documents were also made available to us.

Our data-collecting and our analyses to trace the development processes were guided by questions concerning the history of different projects and activities, of contacts between actors, of obstacles and problems, and of leading actors (organizations as well as individual persons) and their function in the process. Our purpose was to create an image of the structure of the policy sector – of the relationships including the interdependencies between the actors, and of significant problems and actors during different periods – in order to create an image of the development process as well.

About 40 organizations and 70 people in these organizations were interviewed.

Remote Sensing

Background

Remote sensing is the recording, processing and analysis of electromagnetic radiation, with a view to obtaining information about the object analysed without actually coming into direct contact with it. Sensors are placed on platforms at varying distances from the object in question. The platforms may be mobile, e.g. satellites, aircraft, ships or ground vehicles, or they may be stationary, e.g. mountain peaks, watchtowers or tall buildings. Remote sensing can be done by passive sensors (e.g. TV cameras or microwave radiometers) that record reflected radiation or radiation from the object itself, or it can be done by active sensors (e.g. radar) that emit primary radiation towards the object, from which the reflected radiation can be recorded.

On 1 July 1972 the Swedish Board for Space Activities was established to administer Swedish space operations. Its principal task under royal jurisdiction, was "to be in charge of planning, policy-making, and the distribution of the funds allocated to space operations". (Govt. bill, 1972: 48: 33)

At the same time the governmental Swedish Space Corporation was established as the technical executive authority. "The tasks of the corporation are to manage the national program of rocket surveillance, to administer ESRANGE (a missile-launching station in the north of Sweden) to carry out investigations and office work for the Space Board, and to support the international marketing of Swedish space technology" (Govt. bill 1972: 48: 34). The focus on applications and industrial development is thus illustrated by this quotation. From the start it was assumed that the Corporation existed to carry out work for the Space Board.

In 1973 the Space Board drew up a 5-year plan for Swedish remote sensing. Contact was made and reinforced with companies, scientists and authorities. Systems analyses and experimental demonstrations were undertaken and prototypes were developed. During the period of 1976–81 priority was given to ocean surveillance (in particular checking for oil discharge, the monitoring of ocean ice) air pollution and vegetation.

During the 1970s the goal was to bridge the gap between a small number of initiated scientists and users who, because they lacked knowledge about the techniques, were inclined to be sceptical. The strategy was to demonstrate the usefulness of remote sensing within clearly defined areas, with users and Swedish companies sharing in the operative application of the techniques. To begin with the Space Board assumed the main financial responsibility for the development work, but the idea was to get the users and the participating companies to accept that responsibility later on.

The strategy for the continuing activities of the Board was set out in the 5-year plan for 1981–1986, in which priority was given to four programs:

– Applications in the form of a few clearly defined projects in cooperation with the users.
– Development of techniques and methods which are of interest in several areas of application but which cannot be developed within a specific application project.
– Informing and training potential users who are not actively participating in any project.
– Applied research with the intention of developing "new ideas".

Study of the Development Process at the Project Level

Four application projects were studied.

– *Airborne Ocean Surveillance.* The coastguard is the main user. He seeks to discover and determine the position of oil discharges, to identify the ships that discharged the oil, to determine the extent of the discharges, to transmit information from aircraft to ships and communications offices, and to collect evidence of the discharges. The Space Corporation has partly financed the development work, and has done some of the work; it has also acted as technical consultant and purchaser of radar equipment from a domestic company.

– *Monitoring of air pollution* by means of a mobile system. The National Nature Conservancy Board has acted as "substitute user" for all the interested parties in the field of industrial pollution, city environment, etc. where air pollution needs to be monitored. The Space Corporation has partly financed the development of a minibus equipped with laser radar, and has acted as customer to the group of scientists which developed the system.

– *Weather forecasting service.* This is a program whereby the Swedish Meteorological and Hydrological Institute seeks to improve its services, and to provide better products adapted to the needs of the clients. It calls for better short-term local forecasts and selective distribution to clients, and above all for modern techniques of observation, transmission, analysis, forecasting and presentation. A Swedish company has accepted responsibility for making systems specifications. The Space Corporation has participated in the earlier stages, and in areas where it possesses special knowledge.

– *Image data from remote sensing satellites.* In the early 1980s a new generation of remote sensing satellites with greater capacity was expected to be launched during the rest of the decade. There was already a receiving station in northern Sweden that was part of the collaborative European effort. It was planned to be enlarged to receive data from the new satellites. The Space Corporation would also develop techniques and systems for refining image data into special products for many users in different areas of application such as forestry and agriculture, map revision, area planning and water conservation, as well as for various applications in developing countries. The Space Corporation has formed an independent affiliate to take charge of this task.

The development of a commercial technology was in 1983 most advanced in the first two projects, but the Space Corporation has been unable to find a company willing to accept full marketing responsibility for any complete system. It has itself sold systems of ocean surveillance. Up to 1983 no company had been found that was willing to start manufacturing and marketing the air-pollution technology.

Two kinds of problems arise at the commercial stage. First, there is the problem of finding companies willing to develop, manufacture and market components and parts of systems (products). This is basically a question of market evaluation on the part of the companies. If there is any doubt about profitability on the market, it will be hard to get companies to invest during the earlier stages. Second, it is difficult to get users and manufacturers to cooperate on selling complete systems on the international market.

The two larger projects – weather forecasting and satellite image data – had in 1983 not produced any complete systems. There were, however, some partial systems both as prototypes and in operation. In the case of weather forecasting, a company prepared to accept systems responsibility had been found. In the case of image data, commercialization of the equipment was not particularly interesting; of greater interest was probably the commercialization of image products produced with the help of such equipment.

The Space Corporation has cooperated with centralized users, some of them already established and some set up for the purpose. This has meant, in terms of Table 1, that the Space Corporation has attempted to turn type II and type IV structures (dispersed power) into type I structures (concentrated power). This has been favourable to the development process, since the cost of the technical development and the demands for technical know-how would put too heavy a burden on any single regional or local user. It has been the strategy of the Space Corporation to concentrate in areas where appropriate users could be found, and to involve these users further in the early stages of the development work, in order to match needs and development problems as soon as possible to routine operational use.

The means used by the Space Corporation can be described as a combination of "push" and "project leadership". Normally, projects have been initiated by the Space Corporation, which to begin with produced the funds; the user has then been gradually involved to a greater extent, and has ultimately taken over responsibility for development.

In the case of satellite data, the Space Corporation has chosen to develop the receiving and processing resources itself. In other cases as well, the Space Corporation's own staff has developed the technology. However, the opinion of industry is that such development work ought to be assigned to industry, and that such a procedure would also prove advantageous at the commercialization stage. Apart from this there is general satisfaction with the actions of the Space Corporation.

Summary

The development process in the area of remote sensing can be characterized as follows.

1. There is a common ideology at the political level: Sweden, being a highly technological country, has to invest in an international technological breakthrough in this field. Remote sensing has long been "the technology of expectations", and technical developments have not been governed entirely by the demands of the users. On the contrary, the technical possibilities and expectations have created an awareness of what can be achieved with the new technology. The fact that the industrial-policy aspects of remote sensing have been emphasized all along is evidence of this.
2. There has also been agreement as to the need for a central authority, where execution has been kept apart from the allocation of funds and program

responsibility. This has been important to the way things have developed. The Space Corporation has acted as the driving-motor in the development process.

3. Among the many potential areas of application there has been a special interest in areas where powerful authorities are to be found, or can be created or simulated. This has generally meant direct control of specific projects, with the users becoming involved at an early stage and then gradually taking over responsibility for developments.

4. Points 1–3 above have created opportunities for forming social networks. Users, manufacturers and scientists have been brought into contact with one another in the different departments of the Space Board. Together with the Space Corporation they have also been in close contact with the Ministry of Industry. Relationships in the projects that we have studied were marked by mutual confidence and a low level of conflict.

5. The greatest difficulty has been to bridge the technology gap between a small number of scientists and other initiated individuals, and the users. Once the differences in culture (norms and values) have been overcome, once discussions have brought the demands and the technical possibilities into agreement with one another, then there has been no further obstacle to advancing towards the operational stage.

6. The method used is a combination of "push" and qualified "project leadership" (technical consulting, purchasing, technical systems specifications), while responsibility has been gradually transferred to the users as they become informed in the relevant area. Five-year plans have then been used for the Space Corporation's own activities and for the cooperation between the Corporation and the authorities.

7. The development process has been subject to the idea of evolution in stages, e.g. research – application – commercialization. For this reason the commercial aspects may have been introduced a little late. But there are two contradictory aims here, in that important public demands have to be met (for example supervision of oil discharge in coastal waters), while it is also necessary for technical development projects of this kind to require an "industrial policy profile".

Bioenergy

Background

Energy woods and forestry waste are not new as sources of energy. Recently, however, bioenergy has been expected to play an important role in reducing the dependency on oil, at least in the short run. With oil prices rising rapidly, there has been a natural increase in the number of forest-owners who abandoned oil for solid fuels. They had a supply of the raw material themselves, and when the government introduced energy-saving subsidies in the mid-1970s, investment in solid-fuel boilers began to increase. Similar developments in the use of bark, lye and forestry waste for energy purposes also started in the forest industry.

In these two cases the development process could be described as "natural", because it would have happened even without government support. But government support might have speeded up the process.

There is also a subsector consisting of municipalities and other organizations which do not have free access to forestry waste etc. In this case distribution systems and a market for biomass must develop. Our bioenergy case concerns developments in this subsector.

The development of a well-functioning bioenergy system does not involve any great basic research effort or applications building on very advanced technology. However, the technical problems involved are by no means trivial. The R & D problems have another dimension, concerned with developing integrated refinement chains.

The development of the bioenergy system in Sweden is described and summarized in Table 2 below.

Table 2: The Development of the Bioenergy System

Politics	Government support		Activities in the industry
1975 First energy bill. Little attention to R & D in bioenergy.	Several govt. support organizations are founded; each with its own responsibility.	Limited support activities for research on bioenergy. For- mally, however, bet- ter on the applied side.	Few projects Forest industry critical about use of heating purposes.
1976 Proposal for a new 3-year energy research programm		More money for R & D	Several projects initi- ated. At the start, fairly easy to borrow money.
1977/78 Govt. bill attaches more attention to R & D			More critics in the forest industry, due to change in policies.

Politics	Government support		Activities in the industry
1980			
National referendum on nuclear power.	Oil-conversion fund is founded and replaces some other funds.	More money for applications	Project investments are carried out. Consumption of bioenergy increases rapidly. However, technical problems in several projects.
1980/81			
New guidelines for energy support. Concentration of efforts proposed	Energy Research Commission proposed but decision postponed.	Support is narrowed to certain sectors of use.	Profitability uncertain in several cases. Difficulties in financing product- and systems applications.
1982/83			
	Energy Research Commission starts operating	Greater emphasis on systems – development	Attempts to "organize" the industry: Vertical and horizontal integration

Study of the Development Process at the Project Level

The following analysis of the development process is based upon an extension of a study made at the request of the National Agency for Research about Energy Production (Högberg and Swahn, 1983). Four municipalities and six companies were studied. The municipalities are primary users, i.e. they produce hot water from wood chips, wood pellets or wood powder. One of the municipalities is also involved in the production of pellets. Three of the four municipalities have been variously involved in development projects.

One of the companies is mainly concerned with manufacturing equipment. The other five companies refine and distribute the forest waste. Distributing companies have also been involved in development projects, mainly due to difficulties encountered in the handling of chips and other forms of biomass.

The projects were initiated between the end of 1977 and 1979. Operations started between the end of 1979 and 1980.

The following difficulties have been encountered at the company/project level in the course of introducing biomass.

1. Biomass was not easily accepted, because of resistance on the part of the forest industry. The positive effects in terms of increased employment and oil substitution were dismissed on the grounds that biomass was a threat to the provision of wood to the pulp industry, and thus also to export income. The government organizations were puzzled by the fact that biomass

appeared from the cost comparisons to be a competitive alternative, but it failed to penetrate the market accordingly.

The forest industry's activities probably affected the users' investments, and the chances of reaching agreement at the political level. Furthermore, competing energy-production systems were well-developed and dominated by strong organizations.

2. Technical development was not as easy as had been believed in the mid-1970s. Events in raw-materials handling, distribution and use all reveal technical problems. These are of two kinds:

 * the development of new products and systems
 * the modification of applied products and systems.

Since the bioenergy industry was young and lacked experience, development proceeded stepwise, in a kind of gradual lerning-by-doing process.

3. The lack of leading actors was another problem, partly connected with the technical developments. No actor was able to direct technical development and trade in general. Gradually one or two companies began to assume a "leading-actor" role by integrating horizontally and vertically. These organizations began to internalize certain functions and operations, and this reduced the uncertainty among customers and distributors.

4. In a new industry characterized by strong interconnectedness it is important that different levels in the refinement chain are developed simultaneously. During the initial stage, however, functions were divided among different actors, i.e. vertical integration was limited, although there was strong technical interconnectedness between the different levels in the refinement chain.

5. Profits in several projects were low. This naturally had serious complications for small companies with a weak debt-paying ability. Such companies found it difficult to handle adaptations and modifications. There was a great need for government support, in order to give the systems-building sufficient strength.

Government Roles

In the mid-1970s government support could be described as belonging to the "push" type. Subsidies were directed more towards technical development and less towards market introductions. During the later 1970s support shifted towards investors in heat-production units – a "pull" role. Neither of these development strategies was successful, because the technical interconnectedness could not be managed within the systems structures that evolved.

As a result the government also began to develop a "project-leader" role. As a prerequisite of support, the government required that a complete refinement chain be assured. The government also directed its support to leading actors, i.e. to companies which assumed this role for themselves.

Like the industry itself, the government support system consisted of a large number of organizations, none of which could take a "project-leader" role or could develop a total systems concept of support measures. In the early 1980s the support system was reorganized, whereby most organizations were merged into a state energy board.

A Comparative Analysis of the two Policy Sectors

The development processes in the two policy sectors – bioenergy and remote sensing – reveal similarities and dissimilarities which are important to an understanding of government policies for technological development. In both sectors public support played an important part. Without it, only marginal advances would have been possible. In both sectors developments were at an early phase which called for an "anchoring" of the projects in the environment and a further "systemsbuilding". Table 3 illustrates some properties of the two sectors.

Table 3:   Properties of Bioenergy and Remote Sensing

Description variables	Bioenergy	Remote sensing
Competition and power distribution	– Competing ideologies, opposing interests	– Common ideology
	– Substitute for existing systems with high technical and econom- ical standards as well as pow- erful actors	– New possibilities (no substitute)
	– Many actors with limited power	– Few actors, good interpersonal relations
	– Lack of natural leading actors	– Leading actors created by gov- ernment
Functional inter- connectedness	Strong interconnectedness	Strong interconnectedness
Technology	– Low technology ("trivial" prob- lems)	– High technology
	– Need for successive adaptations	– Clearly defined process with dis- tinct phases, such as R & D, ap- plications, commercialization
Potential profitability	– Low profitability	– High potential for profitability in many areas

The Development Processes

Remote sensing is a high-technology area. Its connection with the space research program also gives it high status. Bioenergy has less of this "glamour". Its technology is less advanced. Nevertheless technological development is necessary if bioenergy is to survive on its own without government subsidies.

Bioenergy is full of opposing interests. The opposition from the traditional forest industry has been a powerful obstacle. Politically, diverging opinions about the optimal use of forest raw materials for bioenergy purposes have emerged. To some extent these differences are in the nature of competing ideologies, since they are based on principles and opinions rather than on facts and figures.

The remote-sensing sector has a relatively homogeneous set of actors. As a high-tech country Sweden "must" invest in this new technology. In some instances, such as weather forecasting, remote sensing may be regarded as a substitute and thus as a threat to existing systems, but on the whole the new technology represents new possibilities.

In the bioenergy sector the new technology faces a tough task. It is supposed to (partly) replace oil as a fuel. This means that it has to fight a very sophisticated and efficient distribution system, as well as representing a different fuel technology and economy. Bioenergy is handicapped not only because of its early development phase, but also because the nature of the fuel causes problems in distribution and burning technology.

The bioenergy sector also has a lot of different actors (and functions) with opposing interests. This makes it difficult to comprehend and to cope with. There are many obstacles to the further development of bioenergy.

The remote-sensing sector is different. Here the Space Corporation is a natural (government-created) leading actor, possessing both competence and a general overview of the situation. In the bioenergy sector nobody fulfils this role. An attempt to create such an actor was made in 1983 when the Energy Board was established.

Technological development in the remote sensing area has followed the traditional pattern of R & D, application and commercialization, while the bioenergy sector provides an example of a trial-and-error process involving successive adaptations. Technological development has been guided by the problems arising in the different areas of application. There is little chance of government support for product modifications within the existing frames, partly because the "one-way" model of R & D, application and commercialization has guided government policies.

Government Efforts and Contributions

Government efforts and contributions in the two sectors are indicated in Table 4.

Table 4:   Government Efforts and Contributions

Description variables	Bioenergy	Remote sensing
Role played by govt. bodies	– Many bodies, none with a leading role	– Central bodies as project leaders; allocation of resources and operational project leadership separated from each other
	– Lack of public agencies acting as competent buyers. Central policy body created late in the process	– Public agencies (users) acting as buyers and also participating in the development process (especially in the application phase)
Compatibility of policies and efforts	– Efforts and contributions distributed according to different principles; (e.g. government departments v. sectorial bodies)	– Efforts and contributions distributed by leading actors
	– Changes in support conditions not always coordinated	– High degree of uniformity in treatment of support means
Dominating view of R & D and application	– Inadequate integration between R & D and applications, even if key actors have been working in several bodies	– Attempts to integrate R & D and applications facilitated by project leadership of central body

In the bioenergy sector the government's efforts and contributions were spread over several bodies, partly corresponding to the R & D-application phases and partly corresponding to producers and users. Thus, the complex structure at the microlevel was duplicated at the government support level. Although certain key individuals appeared to represent different bodies, and consultation between the different bodies was said to take place, the support system was still unable to identify R & D-needs or to initiate R & D and effectively transform it into commercial applications.

In the remote-sensing sector the government created a project-leader role to cope with the changeovers from one development phase to another. Our interviews stressed the importance of this function, while in the bioenergy sector the absence of such a function was regarded as a serious obstacle to development.

In both sectors the public bodies assumed that R & D, application, and commercialization can be regarded as three distinct steps. This may be more justifiable in remote sensing than in bioenergy. In the latter sector no natural users (public agencies or other institutions) exist which can act as competent buyers. In some projects, policy agencies have acted as acting or deputy buyers with some success.

In the remote-sensing sector natural public users did exist, or were created. They became actively involved in the application phase of the development process. Policy agencies adopted a deliberate strategy to get user competence involved at an early stage of development. In several cases, however, the technical competence of such users was relatively slight. Commercial issues beyond the first users had so far been given low priority.

Conclusions

In our opinion it is not possible to formulate any general theory of how public agencies can stimulate technological innovation. We suggest, rather, that a systematic frame of reference could appropriately be used, and we will present below some suggestions and tentative ideas which could form part of such a frame of reference.

A Process View

Technological innovation should be regarded as a process. Simple technical-development tasks often turn out to be far more complex than expected. Some of the major variables, such as power distribution and degree of interconnectedness, were described in the frame of reference.

In traditional planning a means-ends analysis is used. First, certain goals or targets are formulated. Then different means are chosen, based on judgements about the way in which these means will affect goal fulfilment. An important aspect of this is to identify relevant development obstacles. In this model the relationship between R & D, application, and commercialization must be made clear. It is evident that some goals or means cannot be formulated in advance, at least not in genuine development processes. Thus, with the "wrong" goals, or with ends that do not lead to goal fulfilment, the risk of failure is high. Investment in "wrong" means can be reviewed, but this takes time and energy, and the development process will loose momentum.

A process-oriented view, based on a genuine understanding of the nature of development processes, provides an alternative model. Here technical (and major technical-development) steps are undertaken as part of an effort to anchor the project in the environment (cf. Olofsson, 1969). According to this view operative public agencies will be given the opportunity to design their own means, and to adapt them to contingencies and deviations from expected courses of development. This is not the same as taking ad-hoc action. Rather, means should be related to an understanding of the nature of the development process. (Hirschman and Lindblom, 1962; Högberg, 1977; Jönsson, 1971; Normann, 1975).

In practice this could mean that a project application is divided into phases. The public agency can reserve resources for the project as a whole, but actually hand out funds for the first phase only. At the end of the first phase a new analysis is made and the means are adapted to the situation at hand. A common problem in our bioenergy case was that of obtaining additional funds because of unexpected events, especially if the funds for the original application had been reduced.

A process view calls for close contact between companies, institutions, and agencies in the sector. A company interested in a technological development project will certainly prefer public agency decisions allowing for a longer planning horizon than ad-hoc action would permit. Thus the adaptation of means must be regarded by the companies as ad-hoc.

A Balanced Development of the System

In the type of technological innovation described here it is important to evaluate, as early as possible, what kind of commercial rewards may be available for different actors. We learned from the bioenergy case that action must occur in all parts of the "system" if obstacles are not to arise.

Such stumbling-blocks may consist of operations or levels in the chain of refinement which are not profitable or which require heavy and risky investments that are beyond the means of the companies. Public agencies could then apply classic "push" or "pull" strategies. Thus imbalances of this kind can become constructive if interesting supply or demand markets are created (cf. Jönsson, 1971, 1973).

Sometimes the use of a project-leadership model can be productive. It can be restricted to crucial development blocks (Dahmén, 1950) or subsystems, which can be envisaged as subpolicy sectors consisting of the parts that are needed in order to bring a new technique into practical or operational use. The project leadership role may be required in systems characterized by strong interconnectedness, low profitability and dispersed power structures.

In the bioenergy and remote sensing sectors it is obvious that coordination in (local and central) systems is needed. It is thus vitally important for the public policy agencies to recognize that development problems often have to be solved across organization boundaries.

A Project-Leadership Role

A public agency which intends to assume a project-leadership role must have the right competence, including a process view, as a basis for its actions. Two problems of competence appear to be paramount; one concerns relations with the political decision-makers, and the other the skills and structure of the staff of the agency.

In the remote-sensing sector one agency acts as an incorporated company, undertaking projects on its own or in cooperation with others and subleasing projects to other organizations (universities, businesses etc). The legal status as a company enables the "agency" to act freely in recruiting and rewarding personnel, taking commercial risks etc, in a way that would be impossible for a true agency. At the same time the government retains control over the funds.

The actors at the political level can thus limit their activities to policy planning. With a competent project-leader organization at their disposal, they can keep in close contact with the operational level, provided that the contacts between the political and agency levels function well. The conditions for a process-planning view are then available. Naturally this does not mean that the political level should not make their own independent judgements of the results achieved.

In the bioenergy sector no project-leadership role was created. Instead individual officials tried to undertake the role. However important their efforts, they were not enough to coordinate the various agencies and their different means. Problems and issues will always fall between two chairs, especially if policies are based on public investigations and aggregated information. When the Energy Board was set up, this situation improved.

Coordination is Achieved by Individuals

Organizations do not interact, but individuals do. Civil servants can sometimes accept important coordination and driving tasks on an informal basis (Norbäck, 1978). Organization charts have little impact if they are manned by the wrong kind of people, even if the "infrastructure" is important to the recruiting of the right people.

Thus, to a great extent, coordination across organizational boundaries in development processes must take place by way of individuals. The coordinated decisions and activities are important. In order to improve coordination and mutual understanding, different mechanisms can be deliberately employed. Examples are:

– transfers of personnel and career patterns across the boundaries of agencies, companies, universities, etc

- cooptation/infiltration, i.e. adding new members to the decision bodies (boards, policy committees, reference groups, advisory committees, etc) of one's own or other organizations
- joint programs, perhaps for supportive functions such as EDP, health care, internal education etc, in order to increase the contact between organizations
- participation in trade associations or other voluntary organizations.

There are other alternatives as well. They all aim at establishing a system of regulations between organizations which are dependent on one another for their development. In sectors with strong interconnectedness and dispersed power (type II in Table I) this becomes extremely important.

The Not-Invented-Here Syndrome can be Overcome

Many members of the business community argue that public agencies should not carry out their own R & D, but that they should stimulate and support others to do so instead. This view is supported by the not-invented-here-syndrome (NIH), which implies that organizations do not feel motivated to realize ideas and proposals originating somewhere else. It is therefore important to engage the interest of users and producers as early as possible in the development process, in order to anchor the project adequately in the environment.

This view is contradictory to the idea that R & D and applications can be regarded as two separate steps which can be kept apart logically and organizationally.

Applications and/or R & D

In the remote-sensing sector applications gradually became more important (the Space Corporation). To begin with, many R & D proposals are generated. Some of these will be tested in different application areas. Skilled researchers or research directors are not usually skilled entrepreneurs capable of managing application projects. The influence of users and producers – important participants during the application phase – may grow too strong in the project-leader organization. R & D activities may be given too little priority. Project-leader organizations may thus be regarded as temporary organizations. Some departments may be detached and given new assignments. This calls for good relations with users and producers (networks). Sometimes it may be natural to transfer suitable people to the user or producer organizations.

Commercialization – The Role of Industry

Our cases show that government policies can induce industry to act in accordance with government ambitions, provided the projects are financed by public agencies. However, when it comes to commercialization – bringing the new technology to the marketplace – the willingness to participate often declines. Industry may regard it as unprofitable to take this step, if government subsidies are reduced or abolished.

One reason lies in the technology itself and in its application areas. Even if the technology can be advanced to the point where technical, operational and economic standards for the user are met, it is quite another matter to find a market for it. When the users are public agencies, central or local authorities, there may not even be any further domestic market after the first few prototypes. And if one of the problems in the development process had been to bridge the technology gap between opportunities (research results) and willingness to use the technology (technological competence), it will certainly not be easier to embark on the same process on foreign markets. It may be necessary for the producers and users to appear jointly on the foreign markets, and if the product has a systemic character – as is often the case – this is no easy matter (cf. Stenberg, 1982).

Another reason lies in the innovation policies of the companies. They often prefer to invest in areas where they can use their existing strengths (products, technologies, competences, markets, distribution channels, etc). The uncertainty is often very high in completely new areas (diversification). The market and profit potential must be extremely good, to compete with alternatives which reinforce the company's main product lines or use its existing investments.

The commercialization aspects are probably undervalued by policy agencies. There appear to be at least two reasons for this. First, commercialization is the last phase of development, and is thus regarded as a question for the distant future. Second, public agencies often fail to understand the business conditions and alternatives available to the companies. Consequently they do not pay enough attention to the companies' reasons for participating.

Alternatively, the public agencies may create the necessary organization themselves (development, production, marketing). This can be appropriate if

- the area is well-defined, the interdependencies are limited, and no natural organization exists (e.g. image data from remote-sensing satellites).
- the undertaking is huge and capital-intensive, such as a nuclear plant.

And, naturally, cooperation and joint efforts with the industry may be appropriate.

A Concluding Remark

In this study we have addressed the question of how public agencies can stimulate technological innovation in settings where research organizations, business firms and other public agencies (as users) also participate. This is a special case – and a special role for government policies – of the more general case of industrial innovation. Our limited empirical observations show clearly that the conditions affecting the agencies' performance of this role can vary very much in different sectors.

In our opinion it is not possible to formulate any general theory of the way in which this role should be played. Rather, we have suggested that a systematic frame of reference could be used. We have also presented some ideas which could form part of such a frame of reference.

References

Abernathy, William J., Utterback, J. M. (1975) A Dynamic Model of Process and Product Innovation. *Omega*, Vol. 3, no. 6.

Aiken, M., Hage, J. (1968) Organizational Interdependence and Intraorganizational Structure. *American Sociological Review*, 33, pp. 912–930.

Aldrich, H., Mindlin, S. (1978) Uncertainty and Dependence: Two Perspectives on Environments. *Organization and Environment*. Karpik (Ed.), Beverly Hills: Sage, pp. 149–170.

Benson, J. Kenneth (1975) The Interorganizational Network as a Political Economy. *Administrative Science Quarterly*, 20, pp. 229–249.

– (1981) *Network and Policy Sectors: A Framework for Extending Interorganizational Analysis*. Working paper, Columbia: Departments of Sociology and Rural Sociology, University of Missouri.

Commons, John R. (1934) *Institutional Economics*, Madison: University of Wisconsin Press.

Dahmén, Erik (1950) *Svensk industriell företagsverksamhet. Kausalanalys av den industriella utvecklingen 1919–1939*. Stockholm: IUI.

Edström, A., Högberg, B., Norbäck, L. E. (1984a) The Strategic Role of Interfirm Cooperation. *Mergers: Motives, Methods, and Modes*. Walter Goldberg (Ed.), Aldershof, Hampshire: Gower.

– (1984b) Alternative Explanations of Interfirm Cooperation. *Organization Studies*, 5, pp. 147–168.

Ford, D., Ryan, C. (1981) Taking Technology to Market. *Harvard Business Review*.

Goldberg, Walter (1981) Explorations Into the Instrumentality of Innovation Policies. *FE Report*, no. 196, University of Göteborg, Department of Business Administration.

Government bill (1972) Angående rymdverksamhet. 48.

Hirschman, A. O., Lindblom, C. E. (1962) Economic Development Research and Development, Policy Making: Some Converging Views. *Behavioral Science*, Vol. 7, pp. 211–222.

Högberg, Bengt (1977) Interfirm Cooperation and Strategic Development. Göteborg: *Business Administration Studies (BAS)*.

Högberg, B., Swahn, H. (1983) *Utvecklingsproblem i den svenska bioenergibranschen.* Report to the National Agency for Research about Energy Production.

Jönsson, Sten (1971) Om utvecklingsbolagens planeringsproblem. Göteborg: *Business Administration Studies (BAS)*.

– (1973) Decentralisering och utveckling. Göteborg: *Business Administration Studies (BAS)*.

Kotler, Philip (1967) *Marketing Management: Analysis, Planning and Control.* Englewood Cliffs: Prentice-Hall.

Lind, R. (1977) *Evaluation Research – En kort biografi.* Stockholm: Business Research Institute.

Norbäck, Lars Erik (1978) Relationer mellan samarbetande företag. (Relations between Cooperating Firms). Göteborg: *Business Administration Studies (BAS)*.

Normann, Richard (1975) *Skapande företagsledning.* Lund: Aldus.

Olofsson, Christer (1969) Produktutveckling – Miljöförankring. *SIAR Dokumentation AB* (SIAR-S-22), Mimeograph.

– (1979) *Företagets exploatering av sina marknadsrelationer. En studie av produktutveckling.* Linköping: Department of Management and Economics, Linköping University.

Rossi, P. H., Freeman, Howard E., Wright, Sonia R. (1977) *Evaluation: A Systematic Approach.* Beverly Hills: Sage.

Stenberg, Thomas (1982) Systemsamverkan en möjlighet för svensk industri? Göteborg: *Business Administration Studies (BAS)*.

Weiss, Carol H. (1972) *Evaluation Research: Methods of Assessing Program Effectiveness.* Englewood Cliffs: Prentice Hall.

Williamsson, Oliver E. (1975) *Markets and Hierarchies: Analysis and Antitrust Implications.* New York: The Free Press.

– (1979) Transaction and Economics: The Governance of Contractual Relations. *Journal of Law and Economics*, 22, pp. 233–261.

– (1980) *The Economics of Organization: The Transaction Cost Approach.* Working paper, University of Pennsylvania.

Politics in Business – The Interaction Between Environment and Strategy Formulation

Stig Larsson

Background and Approach to Politics in Strategic Action

Stakeholder Structure in Strategic Decision Situations

Any strategic development process will encounter a variety of obstacles liable to affect the projection of the strategy into the action environment. It is necessary for a manager to be able to handle these obstacles in order to exert some control over business areas or stakeholder relations and thus to be able to proceed. The obstacles could consist of environmental objections to planned factory facilities, trade union demands for measures to maintain employment in face of structural rationalization, or the need to acquire financial support for an investment from the government. Or, if the manager is himself regarded as one stakeholder among others, then it may also be a question of convincing supervisory boards etc of the need for a particular line of action.

We can look upon strategic integration as a process in which new dependencies are successively formed. These are critical to the strategy, and some form of decision is required to create the necessary freedom of action in the management role. Depending upon the particular situation and on management's competence, the handling of the decision will lead to an outcome which may or may not be favourable to the strategy.

As time passes business companies become surrounded by an ever-widening circle of stakeholders. The different special-interest groups among these can participate both formally and informally in the decisions. Thus each move into a new phase of strategic integration referred to below as "phase shifts", may involve a complicated political process, in which management's ability to act skilfully in a political context is put to the test.

In the relative tranquillity of an earlier growth climate, the possible influence on strategy of diverse stakeholders and interested parties was something of which managers could often remain blissfully unaware. In a far more pluralistic society, an awareness of the political basis of strategic control is an important factor that requires examination. At the same time pluralism creates uncertainty about the conditions for action, and it therefore also provides fertile soil for conscious political action.

Authorized Leadership

Formally speaking a chief executive is appointed by his board of directors, and he also reports to the board. In the real pluralistic world, however, a variety of informal coalitions are formed at various times. Thus in reality a strategy is dependent on the support of various stakeholders and on their sub-goals in the strategic concept. It is often a question here of short-term and specifically issue-oriented stakeholder groupings, whose function is determined not only by external conditions affecting the decision but also by the ability of different managers to mould and handle stakeholder relations. Thus in complex stakeholder structures highly skilled managers can be said to create their own action environment in a conformation of coalitions relevant to the situation and favourable to the strategy.

The strategy thus creates a dependence between the stakeholders and the company. This in turn calls for a capacity for steering and controlling relations so as to bring about the intended exchange, which for the manager means being able to convert stakeholder needs into a common approach to action. In individual cases and particular decision situations, this finds expression in the way an issue is composed – its form and its content.

In a process of legitimation the sub-goals of the parties involved can be summarized in strategic frameworks strong enough to carry action one step further. Thus in an open pluralistic system, which includes several well-equipped special-interest groups in conflict with one another, a manager shifts his point of support and protects his strategy by adapting his arguments and their factual content to the strategic needs of the specific situation.

As owner-power has grown weaker, the manager is better able to respond as a free agent and an advocate of strategic visions spanning a wider range. Thus, in the transition from a system of predominant ownerpower to a pluralistic environment for strategic development, the role of the leader has changed. Managers used to be regarded as agents of the owner, whose task it was to see to the administration of the business; they were not seen as independent beings with a stake in the strategy. If we do so regard them, however, then what we have is a management function of great potential influence with a strong political power base founded on professionalism.

As a result of his organizational leadership function, the manager commands greater knowledge of the company and can plan and initiate concrete action in quite a different way from a stakeholder located outside the organization. Inherent to the leader role is also a reserve of trust, which can be exploited in political action. A subject of some controversy at the present time is the possible threat to long-range corporate effectiveness resulting from crosswise ownership, whereby managers can operate as their own principals even in formal terms.

A Framework

In a graphic illustration strategic development can be described in terms of the development of commitment from a pluralistic stakeholder environment to the content of a leadership role. Conversely, the process can be described as a progression from reflection or reappraisal to change, in which the commitment affects the control, the dependence, and the action environment (Figure 1).

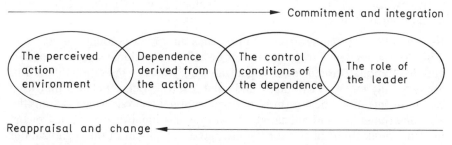

Figure 1:   The Connection Between Strategic Environment and the Leader Role.

In the discussion of politics and strategy it is not the nature of the descriptive structures which is of primary interest, but the tensions between them in a particular case or in a broader perspective. These tensions provide the impulse to a phase shift (see above p. 183) in the strategic process. Therefore, in the integrative progression from environment to role the following questions are important:

- How should we interpret the interaction between pluralism in the decision environment and the formulation and development of a particular case?
- How is a power base created or destroyed during a legitimation process, in terms of the interaction between internal conditions and the actors' perception of these conditions?
- How can we assess the leader role during an integrative process, in terms of the need to adapt to the control conditions?

Politics in Strategy – Approaches and Theories

Pluralism and Strategic Organizing

Danielsson (1978) claims that there is little point in considering the stakeholders of a company in a general and undifferentiated light. Instead we should look at their relationship with the company in the framework of a particular stated time and place. He also recommends us to adopt both a "inside perspective", in the stakeholder's relation to the company's goals, and a "outside perspective", in the company's role vis-à-vis the stakeholder's goals.

According to the prevalent bureaucratic image, the company is often conceived as a hierarchy enjoying common goals and neutralized from power struggles. If it is to function rationally, its values, routines and operations have to harmonize at different levels in the organization.

Benson (1982) discusses some approaches in organizational theory, and criticizes the tendency to cling to what he calls the "rational selection model" and the "rational structuring of organizations", whereby the rationality norms are generally taken as axiomatic and value-neutral. Benson claims that what we get in this theoretical form is an organizational analysis which is "unreflexive, instrumental, and alienated". Real organizational theorists must recognize the implications of this for the life and development of the organizations concerned.

Benson classifies developments in organizational theory in "schools", by reference to the classical questions of objectivity and rationality. From a *strictly value-neutral* conception, the focus has shifted to *myth-building* in the organization. Thus leadership and the leader's person have become directly linked to the organizational perspective. The analysis of myth-building can be extended to include the way the myth is created, what interests it represents, and how it is controlled – which brings us to a *political aspect of organizational life*. If the view is extended further, we leave the perspective from within and look at organizational actions instead from a common perspective with society as a whole. Benson calls this the *ecological perspective*.

It has been suggested that all the dynamic force in a social system is generated by opposing forces challenging the dominant points of view (Blau, 1964). Selznick (1957) claims that every shift of a decision from one level to another entails a political process. Normann (1975) doubts that prompt, major strategic reorientations can occur within the boundaries of a single power system without the agency of some external political process.

If these theoretical bases of organizational analysis are summarized in the context of describing the connection between the strategic environment and the dependence generated within it, we find that:

- An organizational analysis should be based on a specific perspective from which reality is being viewed. In interpreting different aspects of the organization's effectiveness, it is then important to measure the satisfaction of needs and goals in light of this chosen perspective.
- If we want to analyse strategic decision-making, then the relationship between action environment and dependence must be adapted to the time and space dimension required by each individual decision.

A politically charged strategic decision in its preparatory stage offers an organizational picture which is short-range and vague, compared with operative decisions in a stable environment that lends itself to long-term programming. Obviously different tools are needed for the analysis of such fundamentally different decisions.

Power and Control in a Legitimation Process

Burrell and Morgan (1978) make a comparison between uniform and pluralistic approaches, by reference to goals, conflicts and power. The authors conclude that:

- The pluralist view sees the organization as a network of interests. While the uniformist claims that everyone is working towards the same goal, the pluralist sees people as having different goals but working towards them by common means.
- The pluralist regards conflict as natural, unavoidable and not without constructive potential, while the uniformist defines conflict in terms of disturbance and threat.
- To the pluralist the organization is a political arena with several power centres, whereas the uniformist has a more neutral view of the power situation.

Wrong (1979) divides the concept of power into the possession of power and the exercise of power. The first attaches to a person's rank in the social system, while the second is concerned with the means which can be used to protect that rank in a decision situation. We can then identify rank by isolating the factors which need to be dominated in order to have a sufficient "power base" for action. The overt "exercise of power" can then be seen as the response to a failure to accomplish this domination. Clegg and Dunkerley (1979) put it as follows:

"It is only when control slips, taken-for-grantedness fails, routines lapse and problems appear that the overt exercise of power is necessary. Ant that is exerted in an attempt to re-assert control." (Clegg and Dunkerley, 1979: 481)

The handling of tension follows different patterns depending on the degree of control that can be exercised in the process. Simon and March (1958) list four theoretically distinct types of decision process: a) problem-solving, b) persuasion, c) compromise, and d) "politics". Pettigrew (1973) defines politics as a search for a fundamental rationality norm, which agrees with Simon and March's view.

I regard all four types of process as political means which can be chosen in different situations by the actors concerned, depending on what sort of coalition can be formed. Gamson (1956) defines a coalition as a "temporary, means-oriented alliance between parties who have separate goals". This definition calls to mind the need for openness and flexibility in the political process, since the norms of rationality must be adapted to the degree of integration in the process. The long-range administrative coalition that we are apt to regard as evidence of the company's existence in a given system, corresponds to this aim in the legitimation process.

Thus strategic visions, goals and perceptions of rationality should be viewed in relation to the control which management commands over the dependence relationship in the decision situation, in terms of knowledge, command of resources, and other important factors. When decisions have to be made in a climate of opposition, the generation of business ideas will call for an awareness of both goals and processes. We need a flexible vision if we are to control learning and not become locked into fixed positions too soon (Normann, 1975). In handling stakeholders this means keeping open the possibility of adjusting factual content, arguments and stakeholder coalitions, to strike a balance between the need to achieve a social contract and to maintain the freedom of action necessary to the particular situation.

The Politician

In most strategic situations the manager role is the bearer of the business company's strategic ideas, and it is crucial to an understanding of the company's strategic culture. The role concept can be defined as follows: "A role is a way of behavior associated with a defined position in a social system." (Selznik, 1957: 82). The issues in which the leader engages himself, the manner in which he deals with them and the results he achieves then reflect the role he has been given. In saying "has-been-given" I am basing my approach on Barnard's view of authority in leadership as deriving from the support of the stakeholders (Barnard, 1938).

Barnard describes the stakeholders as a "potentiality of assent", an idea which links up with the earlier discussion of the way in which coalitions are formed and how they lead to strategic integration. An informal social contract is established between the leader and those stakeholders who are interested in the strategy. They may tolerate, accept or actively support the action taken, just as they may also suspect, question and intervene against the strategy. To use a political term we can thus say that *a business leader acts on situation – related mandates from stakeholders.*

The mandate thus has the two sides which Katz and Kahn (1966) have identified as the "sent role" and the "received role". Between the business leader in an active strategic role on the one hand and a scrutinizing environment on the other, various degrees of freedom and tension will exist. The division of roles is tested in decision situations, and becomes embedded in the accumulated experience of these situations.

The organization has been described as a struggle between roles (Brunsson, 1981). In short-term political perspectives role-awareness is very important, and the role becomes a visible power base.

Empirical Background to the Analyses

During 1980–1982, I made three case studies on strategic decision processes in politically charged environments. The cases focussed on:

1. the strategic action environment, the exercise of power and the building-up of issues in strategic situations
2. the political process in a strategic issue, and
3. the authorization of strategic role-taking in a pluralistic stakeholder environment.

The findings from these studies are summarized below.

The Exercise of Power and the Building-up of Issues in a Strategic Decision Process

In this case study I tried to discover the factors which can be identified as particularly important to controlling a strategic process. In static terms influence can be seen as related to the control of critical resources, but in process terms it is more important to determine how control over these resources is acquired or lost.

The case describes how Cementa, the leading business in the cement manufacturing industry in Sweden, succeeded in gaining a national monopoly in its field by forming coalitions between business companies, government, central trade unions and others. The openness in particular decision situations created different conditions for political action.

Four sub-steps were presented in the analysis of the case, illustrating how Cementa's power base was built up in the course of the process:

- Cementa took and maintained the *initiative*.
- The company used its initiative for the purpose of *controlling the flow of information and the build-up of knowledge* in the process.
- The structural change was *planned in concrete action programmes* linked to the coalition conditions.
- Cementa *controlled the critical material resources* in terms of capital and organization.

The parts of the total process were linked together by the company identifying "issue boundaries" which would promote the interaction with other parties necessary to a constructive development. In the traditional view of the decision situation the problem is more or less given and efforts are concentrated on evaluating the best action alternative. In this politicized process it was rather the formulation of the issue that was the bearer of a coalition and which carried the process forward. In a negotiation situation, the function of the issue-formulation was to bring together different special interests in a solid – though to begin with fairly general – programme. In this pluralistic environment it was important to be well acquainted with possible coalition interfaces, and to be creative in formulating the problem. As the issue developed integratively, it naturally became necessary to be more concrete. In the case I exemplified this by dividing the process into four phases:

- the *search phase*, with great openness in both issues and vision
- the *establishing phase*, with a stronger vision and a concrete issue into which knowledge and information can be filtered for acceptance
- the *stabilizing phase*, during which the conditions are firmly incorporated into more concrete programmes in whose implementation the parties will be obliged to participate
- the *implementation phase*, in which an informal strategic coalition has been formed to back up action with support and resources.

Politicial Forces Challenging Established Strategy

The strategy is often based on well-founded, objective calculations and the company sees itself as an expert on the question of how the particular issue should be solved. Moreover, managers are often personally deeply committed to the strategy, so that if a strategic line of action is challenged by opposing forces it may be difficult for management to maintain the open attitude to the process which we referred to above.

The second case study concerned a company which hoped to build a chemical plant on a new industrial estate near a small town. This idea met with solid opposition from local environmentalists and set off an interesting political interaction. In this case the analysis concentrated on the way in which participants' perceptions of the case changed during the process. Project management had expert knowledge of this kind of manufacturing and therefore found it difficult to recognize that the character of the decision process changed when the environmental activists began to intensify their actions. From the company's point of view the activists' arguments and actions appeared irrelevant and subjective, and the altered decision conditions were perceived as disturbing and irrational. The gap between the company's ambitions and the real possibility of carrying out the project increased as the legal case progressed, but without having any effect on management's behaviour.

The environmentalist group adapted its arguments and actions accordingly as it gradually gained ground. Its expectations changed with its successes, and the new expectations generated new method of attack. The flexibility of the group's political concept gave them the final victory and the project was stopped.

This case shows how political action can both lead to and call for a reorientation in the perception of rationality, in a more or less conscious sequence of "expectation – evaluation of experience – new expectation". Project management had a stable picture of the problem, and even when the threat against their project intensified they never questioned the basic assumptions. Because of this inflexibility the company was vulnerable to political attacks. It might perhaps have been possible to reach a compromise solution with the environmentalists, or even to persuade them to agree to the plant. But as it turned out a clash of interests became an ideological conflict, in which the parties could no longer reach each other.

Authorized Leadership

The third case was concerned with the decision process for the planning and building of a new factory. It focussed on the relationship between the president and the board of directors, and the board's hesitation to authorize the strategic line of action followed by the president. While the decision process was under way various things happened: developments on the market were rather unfavourable, costs rose distressingly, and in addition plans were shelved for vital parts of the large industrial complex of which the planned factory was to be a part. But the president was strongly committed to the idea of a new factory, as time passed he came to identify himself increasingly with it. He therefore brushed aside any threats to the project. The board was much less bound to it, however, and began to dissociate itself from the whole idea. They showed this by failing to provide full funding, by calling for complementary investigations and new estimates, and postponing the question until this information was available. the confidence gap gradually grew so large that the board in principle disclaimed any responsibility for the project.

The analysis describes how the social contract concerning this project was built up during an initial phase, only to collapse later on. During the later stages of the project the board's attitude to the contract evolved through a) doubtful questioning, b) searching for ways out of the strategy and out of the personal commitment, c) open internal opposition and d) countermeasures and repudiation of both the strategy and the president. When the business leader realized that he was losing support, he reinforced his message instead of trying to adapt his arguments, or the factual content or the relations attaching to the process.

The president did not maintain sufficient distance from his leader role to be able to judge his own behaviour. Had he recognized that a legitimation process requires successive changes in the role, he would probably either have suspended the project or tried to make up for the board's weak support by activating some other more powerful stakeholders. There were strong forces which he could have done more to mobilize for the defence. These included local politicians, the trade unions and others who were more concerned about the positive effects which the project could have on the employment situation than about short-term profitability.

The role analysis showed that there would have been good reason to translate the ingredients of the power base into role characteristics, in a process aimed at authorizing leadership. The following figure shows how the different phases in the legitimation process call for role changes, and how important it is that people should be aware of these changes in the strategic actions (Figure 2).

Character of the manager	Search phase	Establishing phase	Stabilizing phase	Strategic coalition phase
The initiative?	Ideagenerator	Solutiondefiner	Modelbuilder	Ideadefender
The knowledge?	Visionary	Informationfilter	Propaganda-disseminator	Normsetter
The planning?	Relationseeker	Strategist	Budgeter	Controller
The resources?	Bidsubmitter	Contractwriter	Resourcecollector	Debtor

Figure 2:   Summary of Management Roles in a Legitimation Process.

Questions to the Manager

The legitimation process is an interaction between a) the commitment in the management role, b) the resources necessary for action, and c) the external support needed to acquire those resources.

The cases described above all exemplified situations in which the managers could have helped themselves by asking questions corresponding to the integration phases in the decision process (Figure 3).

	Search phase	Establishing phase	Stabilizing phase	Strategic coalition phase
A:	Motive for commitment?	Commitment demands?	Need for articulation of the issue?	Effectiveness of standards required?
B:	Resource requirements?	Adaptation of resource requirements to possible support?	Need for control of resources?	Need for "payback"?
C:	Need for external support?	Terms for coalition support?	Mobilization strength in the coalition?	Trust thresholds in implementation?

A = Commitment?
B = Resource requirement?
C = Support function?

Figure 3: Questions in the Managing of a Decision Process.

Managers often become firmly wedded mentally, socially and economically – to a particular line of action; what they need is something to help them to distance themselves from their commitment, to retain their ability to rethink and consider changes in the process. These questions represent such a tool and could also provide a means for describing organizations at specific stages in the development of a strategy.

Summary and Conclusions

What can we Learn From the Case Studies?

I have regarded the strategic issue as a product of the dependence-creating activities in which the company engages when seeking to integrate new resources, or to defend existing ones, in a prevailing stakeholder market. There are three basic strategic elements which can be varied in the pluralistic environment: *the contents* of the issue, *the arguments* in its favour, and *the configuration of the stakeholder set*. In a system which provides for active owner influence on the company, management's freedom to vary these elements is of course limited in certain vital respects.

The demarcation of the issue and the need for articulation depend on the trust that exists between the partners in a coalition. If a manager enjoys the confidence of his superiors, he will naturally be able to tackle more important and longer-term questions than if he lacked this trust. The content and formulation of an issue thus becomes a measure of the confidence and the mobilization strength of the coalition, which means that the issue itself reflects the temporal and spatial integration of the coalition at that particular time.

Similarly, the tension between different phases of integration is the bearer of the opposition. From a management point of view it is thus extremely important in a pluralistic action environment to recognize that the issue is the bearer of the coalition, and that control of the process depends on an ability to perceive critical boundaries to the issue in terms of factor variation and phases in the legitimation.

We have identified four ingredients in the power base for controlling the strategic issue: a) initiative, b) knowledge, c) planning, and d) the critical material resources. These factors which together constitute an entity in the power base can also be individually weighted in the different integration phases. The person who takes the initiative often gains a head start in the acquisition of knowledge about the particular problems; the possibility of planning builds on superiority in knowledge and the flow of information, and an offensive strategy cannot be based exclusively on command of the critical material resources without superior knowledge and control over the planning system.

Figure 4 summarizes the process conditions in terms of problem-solving, power base, and cooperation between the parties.

	Search phase	Establishing phase	Stabilizing phase	Strategic action phase
A: Focus on problem-solving	Identify problems and solutions	Define the issues	Channel the issues	Implement measures
B: Focus on power bases	Initiative and creativity	Knowledge-superiority and information-control	Planning opportunities	Control of recource use
C: Focus on joint action of outside parties	Search for coalition partners	Gaining acceptance for the issues in the coalition	Stabilizing coalition support	Defending the strategic coalition

Figure 4:   Generalized Control Conditions in Decision-Making.

If the leader achieves a balance between commitment and reappraisal he will be better able to learn and unlearn from behaviours adapted to the particular stage of development.

Freedom of Action and Decision Requirements in the Strategy

By his actions the manager attempts to acquire control over the critical resources which he feels he needs in order to run the company. The search process is channelled through a more or less reluctant environment. When he has achieved freedom of action in one respect, he is confronted by a new obstacle and a new decision situation.

Barnard (1938) claims that at any specific position in the strategy there are always critical factors, which we must learn to handle in order to move on. By learning to handle them we transform them into complementary factors in possible future action. If we approach the handling of stakeholders in the same way, we can identify *critical mandates* in different parts of the process.

In new situations the coalition has to be changed and its supporting function challenged. In any given mandate situation, only issues (or a phase in a specific issue) of a certain dignity and frequency can be channelled. Reducing a constraint requires a social investment requiring time and energy, and this must be weighed against the need for quick results. If confrontations are to be avoided, with opponents who are too strong, then it is a question of acting within a framework of conflict-solution methods which one is capable of handling.

In judging the rationality and effectiveness of a company, we often think in terms of internal administrative and operational criteria. Perhaps we distinguish between internal efficiency or "how" the task is handled, and external effectiveness or "what" is being dealt with (Norman, 1975). In a legitimation process for strategic action we can envisage an integration process, in which success is manifest in a drift from the question of "what" to the question of "how".

When we distinguish between "external" and "internal" management, it simply means that in a social context we see differences in the position of the authority in the role conditions in a given situation. Carlsson (1947) suggests that the company can be defined in different ways, depending on whether the focus is on social, technical, economic or legal forms. He regards the company in a social sense merely as an "action sphere" for an actor or an area of interest. Politics enters into strategy when by our actions we challenge the action spheres of other people.

References

Argyris, C. (1976) Single-Loop and Double-Loop in Research and Decision Making. *Administrative Science Quarterly*, Vol. 21, pp. 363–376.
Barnard, C. (1938) *The Functions of the Executive.* Press. Boston: Harvard University.

Benson, J. K. (1977) A Dialectical View. *Administrative Science Quarterly*, Vol. 22, pp. 1–21.
– (1982) *Paradigm and Praxis in Organizational Analysis*. Paper, Ohio: Ohio State University.
Berger, P. L., Luckman, Th. (1971) *The Social Construction of Reality*. Middlesex: Penguin.
Blau, P. (1964) *Exchange and Power in Social Life*. New York: Wiley.
Bower, J. (1970) *Managing the Resource Allocation Process*. Boston: Harvard University.
Brunsson, N. (1981) *Politik och administratim*. Stockholm: Liber.
Burrell, G., Morgan, G. (1979) *Sociological Paradigms and Organisational Analysis*. London: Heineman.
Carlsson, S. (1945) *Företagsledare och företagsledning*. Stockholm: Nordisk Rotogravy.
Chandler, M. (1962) *Strategy and Structure*. Cambridge, Mass.: MIT Press.
Clegg, S., Dunkerley, D. (1979) *Organization, Class and Control*. London: Routledge & Kegan.
Cyert, R. M., March, J. (1963) *A Behavioral Theory of the Firm*. Englewood Cliffs, N. J.: Prentice-Hall.
Danielsson, A. (1976) *Företagsekonomi – en översikt*. Lund: Studentlitteratur.
Easton, D. (1965) *A Systems Analysis of Political Life*. New York: Wiley.
Festinger, L. (1957) *A Theory of Cognitive Dissonance*. Evanston: Row Petersen.
Hedberg, B., Jönsson, S. (1977) Strategy Formulation as a Discontinuous Process. *International Studies of Management & Organization*, Vol. VII, No. 2, pp. 88–109.
Larsson, S. (1981) *Hällekis – en ort i avveckling och utveckling*. 38, Stockholm: Arbetslivscentrum.
– (1984) *Företagsledare som politiker*. Göteborg: BAS.
Lidén, L. (1973) *Makten över företaget*. SNS series "Studier och debatt", No. 1, Stockholm.
March, J., Simon, H. (1958) *Organizations*. New York: Wiley.
Mintzberg, H. (1983) *Power in and Around Organizations*. New York: Prentice-Hall.
Normann, R. (1975) *Skapande företagsledning*. Lund: Aldus.
Pettigrew, A. M. (1973) *The Politics of Organizational Decision Making*. London: Tavistock.
Pfeffer, J., Salanzik, D. (1978) *The External Control of Organizations. A Resource Dependence Perspective*. New York: Harper & Row.
Selznick, A. (1957) *Leadership in Administration: A Sociological Interpretation*. New York: Harper & Row.
Silverman, D. (1971) *The Theory of Organisations*. London: Heineman.
Thompson, J. (1967) *Organizations in Action*. New York: McGraw-Hill.
Tushman, M. (1979) A Political Approach to Organizations: A Review on Rationale. *The Academy of Management Review*, Vol. 2, No. 2.
Weick C. (1979) (1969) *The Social Psychology of Organizing*. Reading.
Wrong, D. (1979) *Power, Its Forms, Bases and Uses*. Oxford: Blackwell.

Part III. Strategies for Industrial Development

Leadership for new Business Conditions

Anders Edström

Introduction

Swedish industry is currently subject to major sources of changes. These driving-forces are so strong that many companies need to adopt new forms of leadership and organization in order to cope with the emerging conditions. The forces of change stem from developments on several fronts – market, technological, political and ideological. Such developments are not restricted to Sweden; they affect a large part of the industrial world. But any particular country the forces assume a specific interpretation and meaning, and they manifest themselves in conflicts and consequences conditioned by that country's culture and institutional arrangements. In this article we will examine the major forces behind the new industrial era and their consequences for leadership and organization in Sweden. I will refer to a case study concerned with the introduction of a new form of leadership and organization in a company, and will illustrate the dynamics of change thus revealed.

New Business Conditions

In the context of a short essay it is possible only to hint at some of the major developments which are profoundly affecting Swedish industry and society today. Changes at the societal level have been analysed by others, such as Bell (1973) and Toffler (1980). The aim of this essay is to present a middle-range description of the forces of change.

In many sectors of industry technology and competence are both on the increase, which means that customers have more suppliers to choose from. Steel production, shipyards, air transportation and automobile production all provide examples of how new international competitors can master the necessary technology and management competence in order to hold their own. The new industrial nations often possess good educational systems, which provide an important support system for industrial development.

At the same time many customers command smaller resources than before, as a result of stagnating world trade and economic growth (Sou, 1984: 4); they are thus motivated to choose more carefully among suppliers, and are open to new options. The same tendency is noticeable among public agencies, which are under pressure to provide more cost-effective service and administration. Public telephone and telecommunication companies, for example, are now more likely to change suppliers, if they believe they can get a better deal.

The spread of technology and competence combined with the scarcity of resources puts pressure on companies to develop some unique competence or position in the market-place which can help them to survive in a strongly competitive environment. Further, since companies are under pressure to develop an unique competence and a special position, customers satisfying their needs, both generally and more specifically. The focus on strategy, productivity, quality and service can be seen as a consequence of these market forces, although other factors must also come into the picture.

Technological advances, particularly in electronics, computers and telecommunications, allow for increased automation in the production processes and for greater flexibility in satisfying quality requirements or customer demands for special features or small batches at reasonable prices. Technological advances have also opened up new opportunities for coordination, planning and organization. There also seems to be a tendency for companies to develop networks of suppliers and contractors, to be able to strike a balance between the need for flexibility, low cost, and quality.

The focus on productivity, quality and service, and the use of new technology, calls for commitment and motivation on the part of many people throughout the organization, since improvements in these respects depend on the ingenuity, the competence and the motivation of the individuals actually doing the job or supplying the service. Central planning and coordination is inadequate when results depend upon the commitment of production workers, repairmen, inventory clerks, delivery personnel etc. Companies are increasingly dependent on the motivation and competence and potential of all their employees, which also means that responsibility and freedom in the workforce acquires a new importance.

Studies of attitudes to work (Zetterberg et al., 1983) indicate a growing concern for personal development and empathy, and an interest in the quality of life. People are more anxious to exert influence and take responsibility, and to play a more active role in their organizations. Individuals need to feel that they are contributing, and that others recognize their contribution.

In the political world the trends are less clear. There is a tendency towards deregulation and greater openness to competition and private initiative in some areas and in certain countries. At the same time, however, new regulations and restrictions on trade and business are also being imposed.

The changes mentioned above can lead to a new society – a post-industrial society (Bell, 1973), an information society (Toffler, 1980), or a techno-service society (Maccoby, 1985), depending on the particular point of view and the analysis in question. For our present purpose it is sufficient to note that for many companies the kind of forces described here imply a systemic change in business conditions, which requires a new business and management philosophy and a new role and identity for the firm. At the Swedish Council for Management and Work Life Issues, we are presently involved in the study of such changes, both successful and unsuccessful.

The changes referred to above have historical roots, and are not of course entively new. Also, some companies and sectors have gone further than others towards coping with the new conditions. Towards the end of the 1970s, however, the mutually reinforcing tendencies of several trends highlighted the forces of change more clearly than before.

Implications for Business and Management

The forces of change which we have briefly described above have important implications for business and management. They imply a new balance between the forces which impel development. An example can illustrate this. In air transportation, an area which we have been studying empirically, development received its first thrust from the exploitation of technological advances. As a result of these the airlines were able to reduce the cost per passenger-mile while simultaneously increasing the speed and range of their aircraft. By keeping up with technological progress and by developing operations and support systems accordingly, it was possible for air companies to grow by opening up new destinations, while also attracting new customers by reducing the real cost of air transport. In this sense we can say that air transportation was impelled by technological factors. The advances were so pronounced, that competitors had to emulate one another's moves. The technological innovations were easy to describe and demonstrate to the market; they were all related to the basic product, namely the transport of people from one point to another.

Technological developments slowed down at the beginning of the 1970s, and further advances could be achieved only at a rising cost per passenger-mile. Supersonic aircraft, which have not proved commercially viable, provide a striking example of this. Developments were further affected by the rising cost of fuel, stagnating real incomes for large groups of people, a decline in world trade and lower profits in many companies. In this kind of situation any potential improvement or alteration in product and service, will have to be weighed against the number of customers who will value the improvement enough to pay more for it. Such a situation enhances the power of the customer, and development ideas have to be sought on the market and tested against the market. Companies start building up their business in response to particular market segments. In this case business development is primarily market-inspired. Once we start looking at business from the customer's point of view, we become interested in the way customers weigh up different characteristics of the product and elements of service to arrive at an overall evaluation. There are generally a great many such aspects and elements, and the right balance needs to be struck. This calls for the development of peripheral services in addition to the basic service that was previously emphasized. Many service elements involve social interaction between customers and employees, and here the diverse priorities in different customer groups are an important factor. Business becomes localized in the sense that it is focused on particular customer groups, and that the customer's evaluation depends on the social interaction between himself and the company's employees. Where the quality of interaction becomes important in this way, we can say that business development is both market and service-inspired.

The situation varies somewhat in different industries. In telecommunications the impulse to business development comes from both technology and the market; features of the switching equipment, which determine the capacity and performance of a station in technological terms, and the various functions allowing for flexibility in meeting customer requirements, are both equally important. But the tendency is towards more market orientation, with increasing collaboration between company and customer on the development side and a greater emphasis on service. The technological advance which makes this dual focus possible, is the greater flexibility now available in the field of information and communications.

The implications for business seem to be that companies will increasingly have to build their uniqueness on customer segments and evaluations, rather than simply on technological and operational performance, because in the long run others are more likely to be able to match them on these fronts.

A change in the driving-forces behind business development also has implications for management. Greater emphasis on service and quality as well as on productivity to achieve uniqueness in relation to a particular market segment and/or customer group, requires flexibility in action combined with consistency and high quality in performance. I would argue that people are likely to act consistently and with high quality if they regard their work as meaningful and worthwhile, and if they recognize that other important actors see it in the same way. Work is meaningful to the individual if he understands how he can make a personal contribution to broader goals and objectives. Work is worthwhile if the individual sees the work and the goals it supports as consistent with his personal value system. In a business geared to market and service thinking, it becomes important to create conditions for meaningful and worthwhile work. People need to perform within broad guidelines, if consistent action, a sense of meaningfulness for the individual, and opportunities for personal contributions are to be realized. A shift towards delegation and greater freedom of action is called for. At the same time, however, goals and strategies are needed to guide the company as a whole towards a business position that is sufficiently unique to guarantee long-term survival. In the technologically inspired business there is a tendency towards more centralized decisions for the introduction of technological changes and more control over their implementation while technological development can blossom in a decentralized structure. In the market-inspired business the technological base is relatively stable.

The shift towards more market and customer input into business development, together with greater management emphasis on strategy, flexibility and meaningful and worthwhile jobs, involves a long process of change. Vision is not enough; an understanding of development on both the business and the management fronts is also needed. We suggest that such development must be participative, in the sense that different groups of people and types of competence have to interact in order to evolve a common base of meanings and values on which organizational action can build.

The Role of Leadership

The forces of change which are shaping new business conditions are also compelling companies to reconsider strategies, structures, systems, management and competence. In other words they call for what has become known as institutional leadership (Selznick, 1957). According to Selznick the institutional leader is concerned with the organization as a whole, and his tasks include the definition of the institutional mission and role, the institutional embodiment of purpose, the defense of institutional integrity and the ordering of internal conflict. Selznick contrasts the role of the institutional leader with the role of the administrative manager, who is concerned with the technical problem of achieving prescribed aims and goals.

In order to guide a company to a new level of development, a vision of a new role for the organization in its environment is needed. A vision is a means of expressing values and attitudes and knowledge and beliefs in a new way. It provides a reinterpretation and re-evaluation of the activities of the company. The really great leaders possess this creative ability to articulate visions. But if a vision is to catch on, it must appeal to the people in the organization in terms of their values and attitudes, and their knowledge and beliefs. If people have been given the opportunity to influence the vision, they are more likely to accept it.

A vision can be described in terms of the business and management philosophy of a company. The business philosophy describes the aspired role of the company in relation to its environment. The management philosophy refers to the desired conception of the managerial role in relation to the subordinates, and the main organizational arrangements.

In shaping a new identity for an organization, achieving the active participation of a large number of people seems to be the greatest challenge to the leadership. I suggest that a common vision, i.e. a common business and management philosophy, is created by active participation in action. It is in action that the reinterpretation and re-evaluation of the activities of the company are shaped and made explicit.

Business organizations are complex systems involving not only employees but also owners, customers, unions, public agencies, suppliers and others. Commitment and support from these stakeholders are essential to the survival of the firm. To motivate stakeholder participation requires effort, and also a vision which helps them to recognize the value of the context in which they are participating. Thus, in managing stakeholder relations attention has to be paid to structure, forms, strategy and competence. For instance, companies must consider their societal and union strategies. The vision of the company's role in its environment is still the guide to action.

I envisage that cooperation with unions will continue to be essential, but it needs to be developed in terms of active union participation in local development projects that have central support but are not subject to rigid constraints. In order to achieve this, the competence and resources of the unions need to be strengthened – a process in which business leadership should be willing to help, since it is in their own best interest. It is also in the interest of the unions, since they benefit from competitive and profitable companies.

In a similar vein, relations with public agencies and the bureaucracy need to evolve in a more flexible and mutually supportive direction, which in turn calls for more decentralization and adaptability. If decentralization is to work, clear goals and strategies are needed. In this sense the politicization of companies and public agencies is an obstacle to the development of Swedish society as a whole, and of business in particular. Clearer and better developed goals and strategies in companies hoping to improve their unique capabilities and thus to become competitive, need to be matched by clearer goals and strategies in the unions and the public administration. Only then does the development of industry become possible. What we ultimately need is a new vision for Sweden.

There are severe obstacles to active participation. Because of constraints on time, organization and competence, participation in specific decisions has to be limited. However, the essence of decision and action can be interpreted and communicated in many different forms, including myths, stories, etc. The symbolic perspective is thus important in the interpretation of history and the creation of the context for action. To simplify, we can distinguish between central and local levels of action in an organizational structure: central actions build up a context for local action. If a company is to adapt to new conditions, a new business and management philosophy has to be realized both centrally and locally.

Leaders

The leader is a symbol of the business and management philosophies of a company. But he can act as a symbol only if the values and attitudes embedded in the philosophies are consistent with his personality and character, and if the vision embodies important personal values and represents a significant challenge in terms of personal development. The leader realizes his own potential in working for the realization of the vision of the company. Thus the vision is internalized in the leader, making it possible for him to act consistently without generating uncertainty in others. A vision is needed to impel development, and the vision has to be expressed in strategies which provide guidelines for action.

The leader's values and attitudes, his knowledge and beliefs are being continually molded throughout his life. His competence in a broad sense depends on experiences which are relevant to his present job. Kotter (1982) found for instance that the most effective general managers seldom move to a different industry. Working in one industry, they accumulate experience and form contact and information networks which can serve them well in leading positions.

Studies of leaders, mainly entrepreneurs, indicate that leaders do not behave in the same way as managers (Zaleznik, 1977). Zaleznik claims that leaders shape ideas instead of responding to them, create excitement in work and relate to people in intuitive and empathetic ways, and their sense of self derives from a profound separateness. If this is generally the case, there may be problems when it comes to creating conditions for the active participation of others. This is probably the reason for observed entrepreneurial crises (Greiner, 1972), but if entrepreneurial leaders are able to overcome their separateness they will probably be able to avoid such crises (Hackman, 1984).

Maccoby's studies of leaders (1976, 1981) suggest that people who thrive on competition and change and on the challenge of the game of business, who want to influence change, to get results and to win are increasingly those best suited to contemporary conditions in the United States. Whether this type of leader, which Maccoby calls the gamesman, also fits Swedish conditions is something that calls for further study.

In general we in Sweden appear to need a different kind of leadership, whereby the administrative managers who have worked successfully during the 1960s and early 1970s should give way to leaders who can stimulate change and adaptation by articulating a new vision, a new business and management philosophy to guide action in more productive directions. In order to succeed, the business and management philosophies must appeal to a great many people in the company. The process of developing common meanings and values is thus particularly important.

The Dynamics of Business Development

The seeds of a new business and management philosophy already exist in many organizations confronted by the new conditions. Younger employees in particular aspire to more responsibility and more satisfying work than they are being given. People at lower levels in the organization want to be treated with dignity and to feel that their contribution is recognized. People who would like to produce high-quality work, feel that the work organization and the reward systems do not give them a fair chance to do so. Salesmen generally recognize the need for better adaptation to the market, and so on. Many of these people also have ideas about what could be done to improve the situation.

Unfortunately these seeds are often prevented from growing by an inability on the part of management to interpret the signals and to recognize their importance and their implications for change. The dominant coalition in most organizations will have gained its experience and had its values shaped under different conditions. And experience and values which have received reinforcement over a long period are difficult to alter.

When change signals are reinforced by the accounting system, revealing themselves in declining profitability, they often stimulate action. But the problem seems to be that the action thus generated stems from existing interpretations and power structures in the organization.

It is thus difficult to provide the right motives and values for change. It can also be difficult to persuade those with the greatest competence and strong values

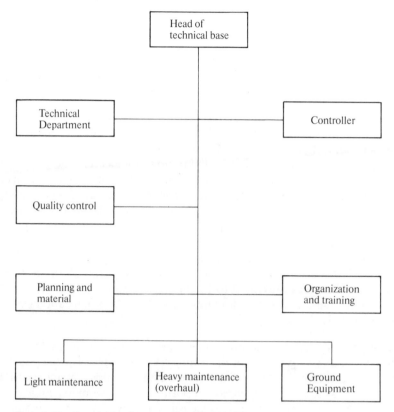

Figure 1: The Organization Structure of the Technical Base

to help to find a reasonable way of adapting to new conditions. This explains why organizations in crisis often reinforce previously successful strategies (Hedberg, 1981). What really seems to be needed is a new philosophy allowing people to reinterpret and re-evaluate the activities of the organization, in order to adapt to a new situation.

The SAS-Case

It seems that because of the strategic role which business occupies in the present economic situation, business organizations are the leading actors when it comes to developing Swedish society (Edström et al, 1985). New forms of leadership are emerging in response to the forces of change we have identified above. Some companies provide what we could call "learning cases" for Swedish industry. The development of the Scandinavian Airlines System is an example (Edström et al., 1984). Partly due to the wide publicity this case has received, it is looked upon as a source of ideas for development, particularly by other service organizations in the private and public sectors.

In 1979/80 after seventeen consecutive years showing a profit, SAS reported a loss. This was one of the main reasons for the appointment of a new general manager for SAS Airline, to achieve a turnaround in the airline business.

The first phase in the subsequent events in SAS consisted of business development. In the period November 1980 to February 1981 intensive consultations were held and studies made of the industry and its development, of the performance of SAS and its development, and of ideas for a new strategy for the company. It is difficult to assess how many people contributed at this early stage, but they certainly included people from many functions in the company and quite a few external consultants. The core group, however, was the new airline management which was appointed during November and December 1980. These were the pioneers of the airline's new direction – or at least this is how they saw themselves. The efforts of the core group, led by the new manager of SAS Airline, Jan Carlzon, resulted in a proposal for strategy and organization that was presented to the board in February 1981. The strategy found support among the board members, and a new organization came into effect on 1 April 1981.

To implement the strategy more than 100 projects were launched to improve primarily the service products of the airline. A key project was the punctuality campaign which within four months made SAS the most punctual airline in Europe. It was a project of major importance to customers, highly visible within the organization, and easy to measure. It served as a demonstration to others inside and outside the organization that the strategy was viable, and that management not only talked but acted as well. The punctuality project was followed by many others, to reinforce the first positive impression among those who had been doubtful at the start.

Strategy and action were supplemented by information. Major education and information projects were launched, to inform all personnel about the main ideas in the strategy. A series of big meetings was held for the personal presentation of the key ideas. Educational programs were designed for different levels of management, to create an understanding of strategy, organization, economic control and leadership. A lot of time and resources was devoted to informing people about the new strategy in SAS.

The business development of the company has continued; the profiles and strategies and the management of different businesses within the group, have become more clearly defined. The changes in the formal structure which have taken place since April 1981, have all been associated with the redefinition of business and strategies.

After the strategy-action-information sequence, attention turned to the management philosophy of the company. At first the focus was on top management and efforts were then made to get the ideas accepted in the rest of the organization. However, this last campaign has not been successful. The business philosophy of the company was created in the strategy-action-information sequence, by people directly involved in the strategic management of the company. For people at lower levels the philosophy needs to be adapted to other relevant situations. In other words it must be recreated in a new sequence of strategy-action-information at the local level.

The distinguishing feature of the first phase was close attention to the market and the needs of the customers. The result was redefinition of the different businesses involved such as airline, hotels and leisure, and the development of service chains and maintenance chains to meet customer demands. This has generated a good deal of vitality in top management and among those directly involved in customer service, while other groups in middle management and in the more indirect support functions such as heavy maintenance, and even the pilots, have felt left out.

The management philosophy which emerged during the first phase was based on the assumption that individuals want responsibility and that they can make a contribution, if given the chance. The philosophy has been to define responsibilities as clearly as possible in terms of goals and strategies, and then to give maximum freedom to realize the goals and strategies, providing support by way of information and complementary competence. There is no doubt that this philosophy has proved successful so far, but it has also turned out to be insufficient.

The role of leadership during the business development phase has been to evolve a new vision and new strategies for the company, to mobilize people in support of the new vision and strategies, and to make practical changes in the organization and the products in order to concretize the vision and strategies and demonstrate their feasibility. The leader has to articulate a new conception of the business, and values to support. In order to articulate something new, the leader has to break away from the past while also appealing to people in the existing organization. All this requires a modification of the power system.

The turnaround in SAS has meant taking a more precise view of the market and putting more emphasis on the market input into business development rather than on input based primarily on technology. It has meant emphasizing the importance of competitive service, in addition to the basic ingredients of safety, timetables, network and punctuality. Further, profit responsibility and the purchase of services and resources by the commercial division from the other supply or service divisions, have all been decentralized.

The Dynamics of Management Development

The development of a new business philosophy and a new strategy also involves certain changes in structure. These are needed to allow for responsibility for the emerging strategies, and to accommodate somewhat different management principles – in this case reflecting a shift in focus from central administration to the service chain towards the customer. The recurring problem here is that changes in dominating ideas and philosophy, and concrete changes in structure and products, call for changes in attitudes, working conditions, competence and behavior among the many people who have to develop the social system within which the new vision and strategies have to be realized. This is even more problematic when it is necessary to increase the responsibility and freedom of action of people at the bottom of the traditional hierarchy. A study of one of the technical bases in SAS Airline can provide some examples of the reinterpretation and re-evaluation of roles in an organization.

Figure 1 illustrates the key activities of the technical base.

As a result of the emphasis on service, punctuality and efficiency, there seems to be a slight shift from staff to line. Previously maintenance and overhaul was under strong central leadership. Most decisions were taken by the manager of the base and his staff. The maintenance departments reported not to the base manager direct, but to an intermediate production manager. The staff department managers generally hold university degrees, while the maintenance department managers have often started as mechanics and been promoted to higher positions, simultaneously complementing their theoretical base. This recruiting and promotion tradition has affected the nature of the leadership.

Staff roles are also changing now. The technical department is responsible for all design and specifications for aircraft maintenance and refitting. The quality control department checks that flight safety is not jeopardized. Both these departments are dependent on the aircraft manufacturers and the state aviation authorities for instructions and recommendations, and their traditional role has been to act as "instructors" telling the maintenance departments what to do. At present attempts are being made to establish a relationship that is both closer and more open, in which the work of the technical and quality control departments is explained to the maintenance people and discussed with them. The help of the technical department is also sought in checking errors or faults. So the new role which is emerging contains a greater emphasis on help, support and explanation, to complement the specifications. Similar demands are being made on the controller. Organization, training, planning and materials management have traditionally been the preserve of experts in the particular fields, working for the base manager and supporting the maintenance activities. Now we can see a gradual shift towards acting as a unit providing service to the maintenance departments, which are coming to be regarded increasingly as internal customers.

The base manager's role is becoming more strategic, with the emphasis on defining a new role for the base in relation to the other divisions, and particularly to the commercial division.

The changes described above have been appearing successively, as the vision for the base is discovered, as changes are made in recruitment, and as education and training progresses.

Management development is needed at all levels in the organization, from top management to shop floor. There is a difference, though, in that it is easier to accomplish personnel changes at top management level, particularly during a turnaround phase. At lower levels and particularly in a Scandinavian context it is necessary to act as though the crew were already on board. Our example from the technical base is from the middle management level.

The role of leadership in the management development phase is different, mainly because the development is local in character. To achieve the most effective results, the people and working conditions on the spot have to be taken into account. A leader is needed who cares about people and who can develop relationships based on openness and trust. This kind of leader will find satisfaction in seeing people develop and perform, without being personally on the stage himself. His role could be described as that of coach or developer.

Local management development needs central back-up. Special resources, support and guidance are required to achieve something new without compromising the overall vision and strategy. With central support, different experiences of local development can also be shared.

The leadership roles for business development and management development are determined by the need for a unique competence and strategy for the organization, and for greater responsibility, competence and freedom of action at the bottom of the traditional hierarchy. They are also affected by the time constraints – in turnaround situations the urgency to adapt is particularly great – and by the changes in dominant ideas, formal structures, products and technology in relation to competence attitudes and behaviour.

References

Bell, Daniel (1973) The Coming of Post-Industrial Society. New York: Basic Books.

Edström, A., Norbäck, L.-E., Rendahl, J.-E. (1984) Leadership and Corporate Development. The Case of the Scandinavian Airlines System. Unpublished manuscript.

Edström, Anders; Maccoby, Michael; Rendahl, Jan Erik; and Strömberg, Lennart; (1985) Ledare for Sverige (Leaders for Sweden). Lund: Liber.

Greiner, Larry (1972) Evolution and Revolution as Organizations Grow. *Harvard Business Review,* July–August, pp. 37–46.

Hackman, Richard (1984) The Transition That Hasn't Happened. *New Futures: The Challenge of Transition Management.* J. R. Kimberly and R. E. Quinn (Eds.), New York: Dow Jones-Irwin, pp. 29–59. Hedberg, Bo (1981) How Organizations Learn and Unlearn. In: P. Nyström and W. Starbuck (Eds.) *Handbook of Organizational Design,* Vol. 1, pp. 3–27.

Kotter, John (1982) *The General Managers.* New York: The Free Press.

Maccoby, Michael (1976) *The Gamesman.* New York: Simon and Schuster.

– (1981) *The Leader.* New York: Simon and Schuster.

– (1985) The Techno-Service-Society. Unpublished manuscript.

Toffler, Alvin (1980)*The Third Wave.* New York: William Morrow.

Zaleznik, Abraham (1977) Managers and Leaders. Are They Different? *Harvard Business Review,* May–June, pp. 67–78.

Zetterberg et al. (1983) *Det osynliga kontraktet.* (The Invisible Contract). Stockholm: SIFO.

Innovation Management in Diversified Corporations: Problems of Organization

Gerhard O. Mensch

Introduction

Developing a new product line or innovation within an ongoing business is a difficult undertaking. A company's innovation project may fail because of external factors, such as barriers to entry, market resistance, or technological superiority of rivals; but most often internal factors are at the root of the failure, notably if the process of innovation takes several years and involves a restructuring of the organization. This paper thus investigates the relationship between internal uncertainty, which is human-factor related, and the dynamic efficiency of the firm. In this paper, only qualitative considerations (taxonomies and ontological relations) are given to the interdependencies between internal uncertainty and dynamical efficiency; analytical results will be published elsewhere in a paper on the quantifiable relations within the framework of neoclassical disequilibrium theory of the firm.

In the classical theory of the firm, the entire firm acts like a homo economicus. By contrast, and according to more recent lines of thought often called neoclassical theory of the firm, a firm's total performance is the result of the various, varying internal interactions of individuals and groups within the firm who as members of the organization act as homo economicus (Alchian and Demsetz, 1973; Jensen and Meckling, 1976). This line of theorizing would not, however, explain the full extent of inefficiency (Leibenstein, 1979) that many firms so often get away within imperfectly competitive markets. The case studies from which we report here suggest that a vast amount of internal uncertainty results from micro-political interaction within the firm (March and Simon, 1958) and that the long-term behavior of the firm cannot be understood but by political-economic factors internal to the organization.

The interplay of internal factors comes into view much clearer under conditions of turbulence rather than stability. This article focuses upon the human resource side of corporate innovation processes and identifies internal causes of innovation failure. In essence, it is a combination of the leadership perspective and the human resource perspective of organizational restructuring in situations of disequilibrium and discontinuity.

It is the task of entrepreneurs and corporate leaders to position the firm in such a fashion that ongoing changes in customer needs, technology, and other market conditions work to the firm's advantage. This necessitates timely changes from unfavorable to favorable tendencies in the business and its environment.

This requirement is more easily formulated than fulfilled, as observed in our field study of the corporate innovation process in 118 small, medium and medium-large industrial firms in Berlin, with up to 250, 500 and 1,000 employees respectively. Over the last seven years, we have observed "in situ" the course of events of 64 innovation projects. By an innovation project we mean a case of new product development (new for the firm) not merely a case of product variation. A product innovation in this strict sense always involves new technology, and usually new marketing techniques (new for the firm).

On the average the cases of successful product innovation took four to five years from the inception of the product idea to its completion, defined either as a success, i.e., at least breaking even, or as a failure, i.e., abandonment of the project. The five year average lead time between inception and market introduction is consistent with the findings of Fernelius and Waldo (1980), based on their study of 78 cases of industrial innovation. It should be noted, however, that some new product developments took less than half that time to reach commercialization.

How do we distinguish between product innovation and product variation? Product variation occurs routinely in industrial firms as products pass through the four stages of their product life cycle. Product innovation involves the strategic selection of an unfamiliar market or market segment, thus the adoption of new marketing methodology, and the development or application of technology that is new – at least to the firm. In our field of study we had planned to study cases of new technology (new for the market), but it turned out that over a stretch of some years (the length of the innovation process) what was new for one firm had already been done by another firm.

In our study, we identified 64 cases of product innovation occurring simultaneously with a broad sample of product variation projects. At the time of this report, 15 of the product innovation projects had been successfully completed; one-third (21) had been terminated as failures, and 28 were still pending, either in process of shelved for future implementation.

Since innovation processes take so much time, they often die or are delayed for purely internal reasons. Hence, in dealing with the management of genuine uncertainty, the proof of having done things right or wrong ultimately rests with events that occur some years down the road. An observation we made in all firms, successful or not, is the lack of suitable evaluation standards, and, hence, the right incentives. It is just as inappropriate to measure managerial performance regarding ongoing innovation projects by short-term profitability as by long-term commercial success of an innovation. The first performance criterion is too restrictive, and the second is too permissive. Hence, in many cases, innovations management appeared rather "flabby" as compared to functional management.

Positioning the Firm

According to the theory of the firm, one would expect that what really matters in successfully managing industrial product innovation is developing a posture for the firm which encourages market participants to present previously unkown opportunities to the firm, and which forces these suppliers to assume the bulk of the risk. This stance is optimal as it is maximizing the chances of serendipity and reduces uncertainty. Such a favorable posture characterizes a dynamic equilibrium. A state which is achieved by barely one-fourth of the 118 corporations in our study.

Our study showed that at times of recessive structural change this position tends to deteriorate. Burns and Stalker (1961) observed similar tendencies, postulating that previously organic organizations under recessive conditions tend toward the mechanical.

Most firms have considerable difficulty positioning themselves well in the first place. The majority of firms pursue a product-market strategy which originally was formulated for the ongoing (old) line of products, which has become incongruent with developments in the firm's environment. Not only the firm's strategy, but also its organizational structure and work processes do not fully comply with external necessities.

Favorably positioned industrial firms have arranged their corporate structure, their backward linkages (purchasing) and forward linkages (marketing), as well as their work organization (production) in such a way that the opportunities for product and process improvement are obtained frequently and at relatively low cost. Concurrently, the market uncertainties and technological risks are at least partly carried by market participants, such as suppliers, or customers, or some other sector of the public.

Unfavorable positioning of the firm leads to increased uncertainties, a series of difficulties, the disturbance of the regular working processes, and sub-optimization of effort, i.e. filling one ditch today and creating several new ditches tomorrow. Hectic attempts to escape this vicious circle usually fail, due to fragmentation of managerial effort, ineffectiveness resulting from half-hearted attempts, and foot-dragging on the operative level of the hierarchy. People soon learn that a "wait and see" attitude is safest for them. Inaction and preservation of the status quo become rewarded activities among rank and file members of such business organizations. The impression we gained from our clinical research in the unfavorably positioned firms is that deterioration occurs faster than in the more favorably positioned firms.

As potential acquisition candidates, the balance sheet of such firms – a measure of the efficiency of both material and human capital – would reveal a bleak picture. Plant and machinery appear underutilized. Many of the staff's potential contributions are wasted, and the probability that the incumbent managers can both stabilize the existing line of business and develop additions or alternatives appears to be near zero.

Determining the Position of the Firm

Our clinical studies enable us to draw a set of inferences concerning developments which either place firms in a healthy, stable, profitable position, or permit them to slip into nearly unmanageable situations. In the latter, only drastic intervention (turnaround) can save the organization. The problem in turnaround situations is that new leadership has to stabilize floundering, old lines of business under worsening circumstances, while attempting to master the challenges of initiating a new line of business.

A collection of diagnostic findings are presented in condensed form in Graphs 2–4. These graphs are structured around significant diagnostic categories. How did deterioration in many industrial firms develop? What are easily recognizable indicators? What debilitating habits often lie behind them? Graphs 1 and 5 summarize our findings and sketch those relevant areas of sensitivity which have consistently risen in our studies as major trouble spots. These can be remedied effectively by relatively simple organizational intervention.

Adopting Marshall's idea of a "representative firm", we characterize the unhappy situation of a typical medium-large industrial corporation in the state of bad organizational health. Our firm is both differentiated enough to have malfunction spread over various departments, and is sufficiently diversified to have vested interests which cause coordination failures among the various divisions. From the clinical research perspective, we feel we learned most from observing the phenomena which occurred within the 22 medium-large firms in our study; larger firms have the same problems (but with more white noise), and smaller firms have them (but less traceable in small-groups interactions).

Basically, the difficulties developed because of a mismatch between inter-organizational needs (environmental change) and intra-organizational activities (lack of internal adaptation). As a result, the firm had to increase the productivity and profitability of its old product line plus initiate development of new product lines in the face of deteriorating performance. In this situation, the firm's organizational powers were handicapped by unsuitable strategy and structure. Given the present imperative for short-term survival and the necessity of restructuring for future survival, the firm is caught in a double-bind of conflicting priorities. These contradictory rationalities stifle both the process of strategy reformulation, and the efficient execution of intermediate plans.

Disappointing levels of sales, costs, and return on the firm's investments were the most apparent indicators of unfavorable developments. If such disappointments occurred, insiders usually acknowledged that these were inevitable as certain business parameters had been changing for some time to the firm's disadvantage, and corporate policy and practice had not been revised despite these warnings. Usually, insiders were quite aware of early signals of increasing internal stress and maladaptive performance. These signals manifested themselves, for example, in imbalances in the product mix, and in discrepancies among contributions of essential business functions, such as marketing, manufacturing, and research and development.

Such imbalances and latent conflicts nearly always resulted from some underlying unresolved problem which had some problematical issue-history. In the past, the persons involved hat learned to cope in some way. In the present, this coping mechanism had become a preprogrammed approach to resolving or avoiding the latent conflicts. This historically inherited, preconditioned response-pattern usually inhibited new forms of conflict resolution, freezing the creative energy of the persons involved.

Thus a protective shield was constructed around the behavioral cause of the present weakness. One can understand the issue-history of the conflict by tracing its causation in the market history and technological past of the corporation. A more refined diagnosis of the underlying critical behavioral issue can usually be obtained by an interaction analysis. For our purposes, a sketch of typical developments in organization and top personal suffices. The diagnosis, then, leads from the analysis of the issues to the recognition of problems. We identified 9 problems in Graphs 2–4.

How Deterioration Developed

Some typical developments are put into perspective in Graph 2. These tendencies have shaped the internal and external conditions of the old product line over the last three decades or so. In many branches of industry these tendencies coincide with the four phases of market evolution, which can be described as first, the phase of innovation (1945–55); second, rapid market growth (1956–66); third, maturation (1967–73); and fourth, saturation of demand (1973–82). Over the past thirty years, most markets for durable consumer goods and the capital goods to produce them have developed to a point where many potential buyers already possess an older version of some goods and, as product technology has been perfected, the incentive for switching from an older to a newer version of the goods has greatly diminished. Thus, these markets evolved from a stage of many relatively important innovations, and relatively few process innovations, to a stage with very few true product and process innovations.

Standardization tendencies, return-to-scale exploitation, and increasing industrial concentration characterize the phase transitions. Typical internal adjustment problems occur during the transitions, and a few characteristic modes of problem resolution emerge at the respective times.

Within our diversified and differentiated firm, these market phase transitions left their traces, especially with regard to two holistic features of the corporation: (1) its type and style of leadership, and (2) its form of organization. The situational logic, as it appeared to be under the respective circumstances, shaped the views of the dominant coalition and its priorities, in both the selection of top personnel and the selection of rules of conduct in accordance with the chosen organization structure. Typically, at points of phase tansition the personality of the chief executive selected in the process, plus the team that surrounded him, shifted from that of "dynamic entrepreneur" via "calculated risk-taker" and "careful controller" to a type which we may call "conservator" and "reformer", typically makes it to the top in times of decline. A related chain of structured changes first replaced the functional organization with a matrix organization, and then in recent years moved to some mixed form of organization. Each of these phase transitions were prompted by problems, and later created new problems as technology aged, market structure changed, and the organization adjusted to this change in the way chosen at those junctures. From the unfolding of this pattern wie can identify several core problems for particular consideration in the present stage.

1. The industrial firm in stagnant markets should stay alert to core problem one – the possibility of surprising product developments by its rivals. This is all the more so because of the fewer true product innovations which have occurred in this sub-branch of industry in recent years. This not only increases the probability of innovation, but potential customers may become more responsible. In turn, since mobility of demand may facilitate rapid shifts in market shares, potential competitors view this market turbulence as a splendid opportunity for forceful entry. This, incidentally, is consistent with the results from PIMS studies which discovered that returns on product quality improve-

ment were highest in relatively "quiet" markets (Strategic Planning Institute, 1977).

It is indeed somewhat paradoxical that in times of relatively fast changing, "young" markets, when product innovations occur in rapid succession, the firm suffers little harm if it skips a new product opportunity, as more are likely to come and take its place. If in "mature" markets a firm misses out on an infrequent opportunity, however, it loses not only this advantage but also some market share in its unimproved product line.

2. Core problem two concerns the particulars of the generational change in top management. More often than not, the incumbent directing manager has advanced to the top in recent years as a "careful controller" and/or "consolidator" of the old lines of business. He may be unprepared for the dual role he must now play in promoting the old lines ("conservator") and simultaneously developing alternative new lines ("reformer"). Furthermore, it has been said repeatedly by business leaders that the usual reward system based on short-term profit orientation discourages spending on long-range innovation projects. Thus, managers may be reluctant to promote those projects which require an extended payback period, and which may not achieve profitability until after the manager's tenure.

In addition, the matrix organization does not appear to be the best coordination system if the desired objective is to achieve creativity and entrepreneurial risk-taking. The institution of a matrix organization in most larger firms has resulted in a fragmentation of the marketing function.

In the 1960s and early 70s, many medium-large firms introduced the concept of product managers, thus imitating the large corporations precisely at the time when diversification was considered the non-plus ultra in market penetration. Because of the rapid profusion of product manager positions, many of which were staffed with newcomers, they were assigned a middle rank. Out of these positions one should not expect too much entrepreneurial initiative to emerge, especially if it involves planning and scheming that reach beyond the scope of the respective strategic business unit. Such initiatives easily provoke fire from other units. Also, many customers notably in the investment goods sector, perceive fragmentation of marketing as an ambiguous sales policy of the firm, especially if the main customer buys package deals.

3. The third core problem involves the willingness and ability to innovate. In the aforementioned situation, both qualities have become severely restricted during the deterioration of the firm's position. In previous years, cost control was the order of the day. Investment recommendations for exploring alternatives were frequently discouraged. Avoidance of "sticking your neck out" became acceptable behavior (the French refer to this as the "champignon effect"). As a consequence of this type of domestication, the unlearning of

risk-taking and the learning of protective schemes went hand in hand. As a result, many business leaders currently complain that personnel are reluctant to follow through with new product planning.

Our field studies yielded the following: personnel problems, such as adverse staff reactions, were often encountered when top managers made innovation-related demands, and were significantly related to the firm's inability to bring an innovation project to a definite end – either success or termination. Both success and failure were closely related to the frequency of complaints about this type of personnel problem.

Recognizable Indicators of Deterioration

In Graph 3 we exhibit some of the obvious indicators of the vulnerability of our representative industrial firm. Foremost is the slump in profitability, which is not just the result of a recession in the business cycle, but is predominantly due to recessive structural change in the market and the maladjustment of our firm. One ought not to address a short-term setback which the next upswing of the market cycle will surely straighten out, but rather address an existing crisis in the firm.

4. The fourth core problem frequently observed is the lack of convincing future business plan within most ailing enterprises. A medium-range concep-tion spanning two times the length of the business cycle does not exist, or if it does exist, people either seem not to believe in the plan or in the wigdom of carrying it out.

Several imbalances can be easily detected among the indicators of the organi-zation's deterioration. One such imbalance is in the product mix – notably the "hot" pursuit of business in certain lines of business and the "cold" pursuit in others. Strategic marketing theory which was invented at a time of secular boom, tells us that it should be this way. In practice, however, we observe a concentration of talent and financial backing on the side of so-called star and cash cow products, together with an underendowment of talent and resources in product areas in which the perceived attractiveness (both to the firm and the entrepreneurial talent) seems more a function of past prejudices than of analysis-based judgement of future market potential.

A second imbalance that results in missed opportunities involves the dispro-portionate influence of either the marketing group, production, or R & D personnel, or any other one of the three. Frequently two of these three functions form a coalition which relegates the third to an inferior position. Notably in firms with a generalist sales force, we often observed a coalition of production and development personnel which resisted product ideas brought in by sales persons. Furthermore, in firms that have long enjoyed superior returns to scale, or a relative calm in government regulated markets, or in selfregulated oligopolies, we frequently observed a coalition between marketing and manufacturing which frustrated suggestions offered by the research and development department. Under these circumstances R & D was often organizationally and locationally disjoined from the sales and production departments, and was subservient. R & D existed exclusively for the purpose of defending existing product lines, with an occasional sprinkling of loose-end research struggling along.

5. The fifth core problem is the chaos which develops when the said imbalances in product mix and managerial functions result in the stifling of badly needed contributions from some business area and/or some business function. According to the well-known law of the minimum factor, one would expect that some of the non-bottlenecks become either idle or chaotic in futile attempts to compensate for a lack in contribution. Indeed, as a consequence of the said imbalances, we observe that executives in the dominant coalition spent an enormous proportion of their time on seemingly subordinate problems which could easily be tracked-down to such inconsistencies.

6. Smoldering conflicts among professional groups in functional areas within the organization are a characterization of firms which are not optimally positioned. Goal conflicts have not been clarified, and zero-sum games continue to take their toll in productivity. In the majority of cases studied, the people involved frequently did not remember or care about the true historical reasons of the latent conflict. The propensity to act in a predetermined way had become an habitual factor. Stated simply, the sixth core problem is inefficiency due to friction, with fairly old sand hindering the spin of old and new wheels.

Habits Behind the Deterioration

From the discussion of the indicators and the historical causation of the firms' handicaps it should become obvious by now that we attribute most (about three-quarters) of the risks of failure of product innovation projects to internally determined factors (Graph 1). This direct observation result deviates considerably from the research findings obtained by other researchers through hindsight observations. *Ex post facto* reports are strongly biased toward blaming outside factors. However, if one directly observed the corporate innovation process *in situ* over the years, one will conclude that many so-called unforeseeable market changes, unfavorable consumers' reactions or technical failures can be attributed to a lack of inquiry, sloppy preparation, etc. and could have been avoided.

Graph 4 presents some of the frequent deficiencies in interaction within the organization; part of these deficiencies are plain coordination failures, part are more serious and deep-rooted than that. In innovating firms, contradictory rationalities disturbingly arise from the need to continue with the old product line and simultaneously develop an alternative or additional new line which does not immediately produce sufficient income. There exist "hot" and "cold" organizational units side by side, disturbing one another in very subtle ways. These disturbances in interaction are often preprogrammed and reinforced by historically developed habits. Calling them irrational imponderables, as is often done, does not do justice to qualms between, say, "technicians" and "sales people". Their persistence and their counterproductive effects indicate their more objective nature: the differences inherent in turning around an old business and creating a new one under the same roof. Clinical research reveals that objective determinants of polarized behavior inside the firms matter greatly, as intricate development projects which consume several years of subtle interaction go on simultaneously with "business as usual" in other divisions of the same firm.

7. As the seventh core problem then, we identified interface problems that exist between functional areas, such as marketing and development. This is particularly troublesome because these two areas also represent a line of segmentation among different types of professionals – business economists and industrial engineers, for example.

8. It has become customary in the world of the large corporations to say that the team approach is an important factor in high performance, and indeed it is. As an unintended consequence of this opinion, however, some subsidiary leadership functions, such as conflict resolution and performance control, are believed to be handled well by teamwork. In fact, this is frequently, but not consistently, the case. In dealing with uncertainty, teams may become divided over conflicting issues when several different innovative actions may become admissible at any point in time. Polarization within the team was frequently observed. On the one hand, an ambitious "dare devil" might lead the majority into a high risk decision or risky shift. This hit-and-run behavior was often facilitated or accompanied by idiosyncratic intervention from someone at the top.

Conversely, a cautious shift might lead the team toward a low level of initiative or effectiveness. This possibility was often connected with the superior's lack of control, or his lack of willingness to follow up when a task team or some member underperformed. Such mistakes probably were the principal reasons for the delay or failure of many new product developments (core problem eight).

9. Related to these mistakes are two managerial errors which we have often observed in cases of delay of ongoing innovation projects, notably in cases where the pressures from above and the needs of the situation prompted

questionable choices. For example, an impatient "reformer" type supervisor intervened too often with the planning, design or coordination work of his staff, thus discouraging people from finalizing their contributions. Or, the project team forfeited necessary "conservator" type of steering committee. When the firm expropriated the first returns of an innovation from the innovating unit it killed the motivation of entrepreneurial talent at work on some new product line. Core problem nine suggests that the allocation of funds to the innovation project, and the delegation of authority to the project manager, either may be insufficient, or insufficiently firm.

Conclusions

We have identified, by clinical research whithin small, medium and medium-large industrial firms, a set of nine core problems (or "clinical syndromes" in Roethlisberger's terminology). Our clinical research finding is that disturbed human relations within the firm, and resulting dysfunctional organizational behavior, seem to be especially damaging to the most vulnerable processes: to innovation processes within the corporation. These processes take several years of time, require initiative, creativity, and risk-taking, and are particularly sensitive to imbalances in differentiation and integration (Lawrence and Lorsch, 1969). Hence, many things can go wrong at the interface of elementary and institutional behaviors (Homans, 1961, 1974), and often do (Murphy's Law). Thus, a number of determinants of "internal risk of failure" (say, $x_1, \ldots, x_n$ and $n = 9$ in our study) appear together with failure (say, y_1 and y_2 for the failure of single innovation processes within the firm, and the failure of the firm, respectively).

Of course, these clinical syndromes are purely descriptive. Not being predictive or even prescriptive (these purposes we are pursuing currently in the "analytical phase" of the innovations research agenda), they cannot in general be applied directly by the knowledge user for his proactive purposes in innovations management, human resource management, and corporate policy making. Nevertheless, a few special results should be immediately useful. Upon careful reflection we have resolved that most so-called "external obstacles" to innovation can be traced to internal primary causes. About 75% of the "flop risk" of corporate innovation processes is internally generated. Hence, the found association of y_1 and $(x_1, \ldots, x_n)$ confirms the practitioners' view that the culture of the organization is more influential on the success of any single innovation project than is market resistance, and the larger the firm, the stronger this influence both in terms of facilitating and inhibiting innovation.

From this point of view, one would look for the manifestation of organization-cultural irrationality, its general cause, and the source of continued irrationality, see Graph 5. There are three major sources of internal uncertainty:

(1) The most potent source of conflict, distrust, and irrational behaviors seem to be that interface where external data (notably on customers' wants and needs) meets with internal data (notably the company's technical abilities for creating R & D results). Several researchers have found the interaction of marketers and technical people the most conflict-ridden. We found that a strong determinant of the dysfunctional behavior at this interfunctional boundary is the number of times any of the two groups has been burnt in the past by having created useless results when relying on the other group's data, which turned out to be wrong, or carelessly researched. Sealing this dominant source of irrationality would not only reduce the "internal uncertainty" for the ongoing innovation process but improve on the organizational culture in general.

(2) An honest conflict history revision, discussion of the underlying issues, and firm conflict resolution will restore a higher level of rationality by nourishing emotional reactions where and when cool-headed initiatives and creativity were required by the logic of the situation.

(3) Bringing the corporation back up to the full level of operative rationality will require a revision of the product/market strategies, in the strategic business units, and their consistencies with the corporate overal strategy. More often than not, this revision will reveal, in a phase I, that there is no strategy to be revised. Thus, in a phase II, a top-down corporate strategy formulation process and a bottom-up product/market strategies formulation process will be initiated. There is no better way of recognizing the best practice in the market, and the firm's actual and desired position visàvis this frontier, than this top-down-and-bottom-up process of strategies formulation. Again and again, we have heard managers of strategic business units disagreeing with the way top managers proceeded to classify the SBU as "dog", "cash cow", or "wildcat", when the criteria for such classification is at least questionable. Forcing such labels upon SBUs not only leads to suboptimal allocations of funds and personnel, but to dissension where consensus would be needed for success in business.

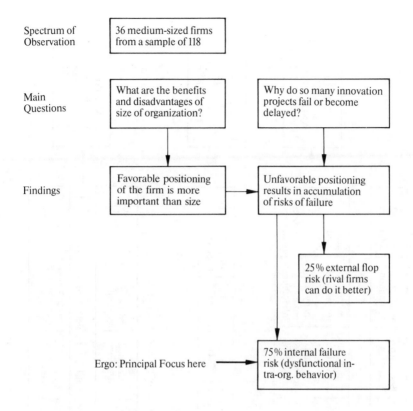

Figure 1: Why are many industrial firms in trouble?
Results from a Seven-Year Field Study on Innovation Management in Small, Medium, and Medium-Large Industrial Firms in the City of Berlin, Germany (population: 3000 industrial firms)

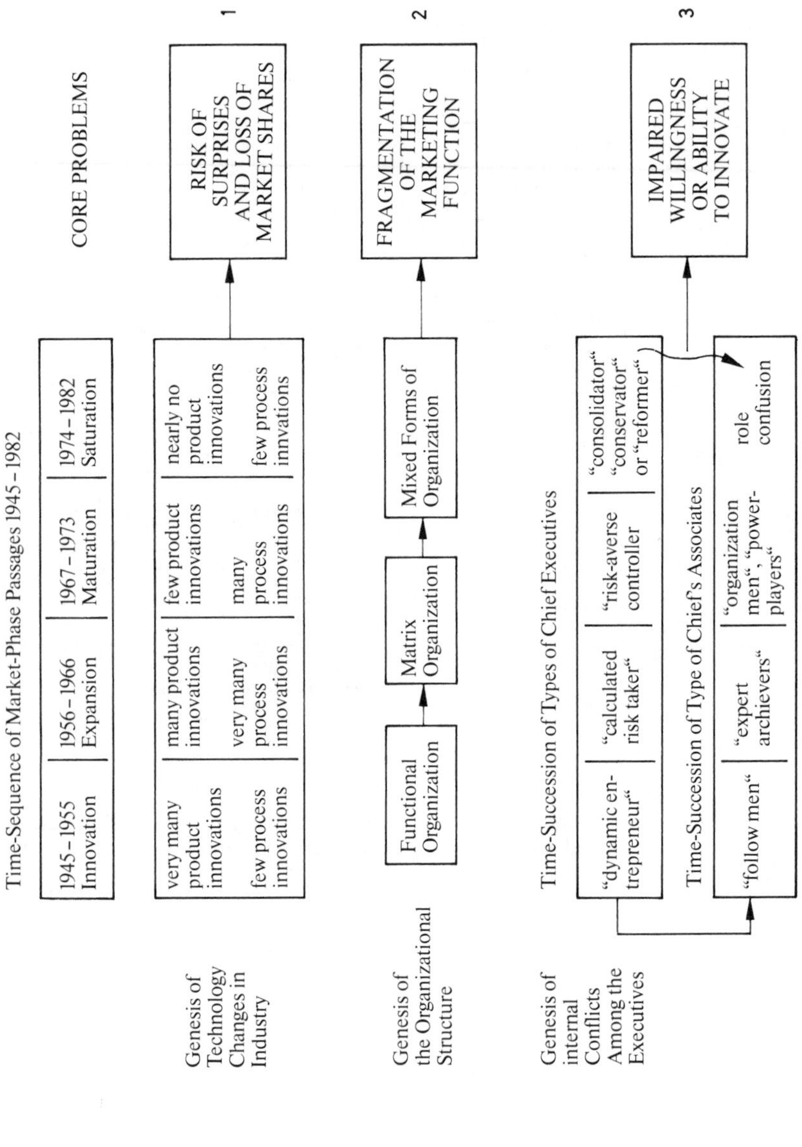

Figure 2: How did the firm's deterioration develop?

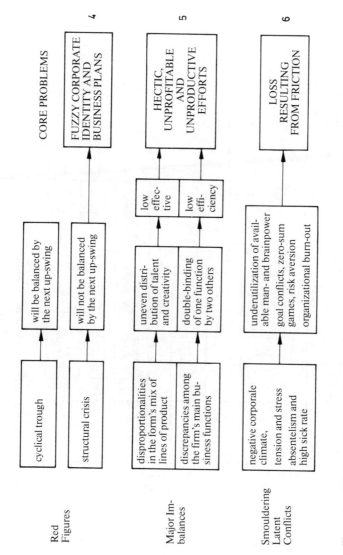

Figure 3: What are the recognizable indicators of the firm's deterioration?

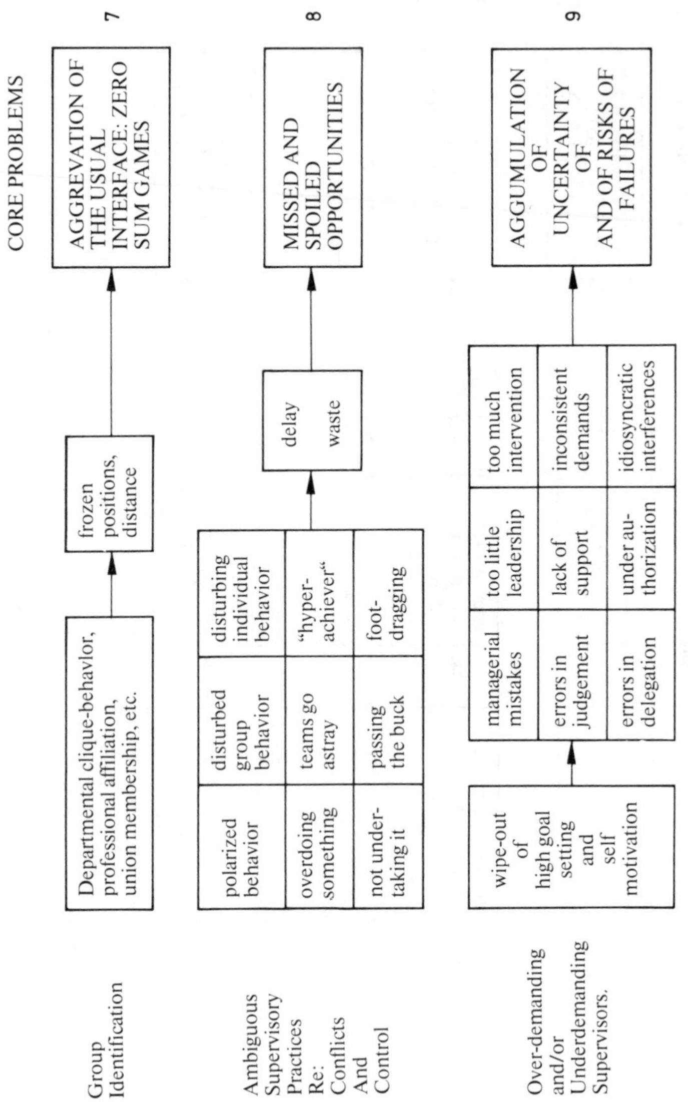

Figure 4:   What debilitating habits lie behind the deterioration?

CORE PROBLEMS

7	AGGREVATION OF THE USUAL INTERFACE: ZERO SUM GAMES	
8	MISSED AND SPOILED OPPORTUNITIES	
9	AGGUMULATION OF UNCERTAINTY OF AND OF RISKS OF FAILURES	

Group Identification — Departmental clique-behavior, professional affiliation, union membership, etc. — frozen positions, distance

Ambiguous Supervisory Practices Re: Conflicts And Control

polarized behavior	disturbed group behavior	disturbing individual behavior
overdoing something	teams go astray	"hyper-achiever"
not under-taking it	passing the buck	foot-dragging

delay / waste

Over-demanding and/or Underdemanding Supervisors.

wipe-out of high goal setting and self motivation	managerial mistakes	too little leadership	too much intervention
	errors in judgement	lack of support	inconsistent demands
	errors in delegation	under au-thorization	idiosyncratic interferences

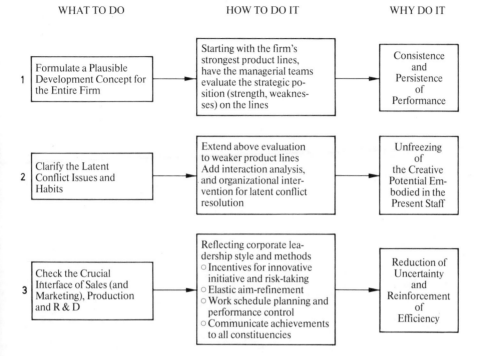

Figure 5:   Three initial steps for remedy

References

Alchian, A., Demsetz, H. (1972) Production Information Costs and Economic Organization. *American Economic Review,* 62.

Burns, T., Stalker, G. M. (1961) The Management of Innovations. London.

Fernelius, W. C., Waldo, W. H. (1980) Role of Basic Research in Industrial Innovation. *Research Management,* 23, pp. 36–40.

Homans, G. C. (1974) Social Behavior. Cambridge, Mass.

Jensen, M., Meckling, W. (1976) Theory of the Firm: Managerial Behavior Agency Costs, and Ownership Structure. *Journal of Financial Economics,* 3, pp. 305–360.

Lawrence, P. R., Lorsch, J. W. (1967) Differentiation and Integration in Complex Organizations. *Administrative Science Quarterly,* 12, pp. 1–47; (1969) Developing Organizations: Diagnosis and Action. Reading, Mass.

Leibenstein, H. (1979) A Branch of Economics is Missing: Micromicro Theory. *Journal of Economic Literature,* 17, pp. 477–502.

March, J. G., Simon, H. A. (1958) Organizations. New York – London.

Roethlisberger, F. J. (1977) The Elusive Phenomena. Cambridge, Mass.

Strategic Planning Institute (1977) *The Limited Information Report.* Cambridge, Mass.

Strategic Product Exit – The Organizing of Product Disinvestment

Ulf Sternhufvud and Rolf Wolff

Disinvestment in the Schumpeterian World

The Schumpeterian world of economic change contains elements of disinvestment and of development. These processes are strongly interrelated (Schumpeter, 1911). While economic and business administration research have concentrated on development problems, the phenomenon of disinvestment first came into the focus of attention as a consequence of the stagnation in growth during the 1970s, Development implies the generation of new activities; new approaches to problem-solving and new technologies emerge. Disinvestment implies the winding down of old activities, problem-solving methods, techniques and products. Disinvestment is either forced upon us by the environment (e.g. the necessary resources are no longer available) or it is a consequence of corporate decisions. Disinvestment is a question of evolution. It promotes development, because resources which have been tied to outworn problem-solving efforts are now released for new techniques and solutions. Without disinvestment, there will be no development. Although this process is essential to economic evolution, development aspects have always attracted far more interest than the process of disinvestment. Such studies of disinvestment as do exist, have been concerned mainly with the disinvestment of technologies or of entire companies. Product disinvestment, as an important element in the life cycle of a product, has been almost completely neglected in both theoretical and empirical research. In practice the disinvestment process is an essential one, and we might expect it to be planned and implemented almost automatically. In fact, however, there are all sorts of obstacles to the decisions and to their implementation, because a lot of people in a company certainly depend on the product in question: in the course of their on-the-job-training and their personal connection with the product, they have been involved in its development. Products often become like old friends, from whom it is difficult to part. Organizing the withdrawal of a product from the market is therefore a very complex affair, which has to be handled with care.

The Schumpeterian entrepreneur should be concerned with development *and* disinvestment. The psychology of disinvestment is probably very specific and therefore requires specific entrepreneurial skills in those who are driving and implementing the process. Because so many people's future will be affected by the process, great sensitivity has to be shown in carrying it out. Apart from the economic aspect to the problem – the product does not generate the resources necessary for its survival – negotiations must be expected about the decision and its implementation. Depending on the possible consequences of the process, there will be product-defenders (or conservationists), there will be product-advocates, and there will be drivers of the disinvestment process. In a mixed economy such as Sweden's, conservationists can always try to obtain subsidies from the public sector to keep the product alive on grounds of employment. Whether or not they actually succeed in this will depend on their skill in negotiating, on whether they can convince the politicians or the public sector that the product is only in a temporary decline and that if it is allowed to "hibernate" for a while, new revenues can be guaranteed. The employment argument is certainly very strong in an economic world characterized by Keynesian economic policies, as Sweden is. The Schumpeterian world favors disinvestment, but Schumpeter explicityly advocated avoiding the social consequences of change with the help of the state's social or labor market policy. In this article we will address some of the problems connected with disinvestment at the company level and exemplify them in three case studies (Sternhufvud, 1982). The strategic-exit problem appears already during the maturation phase in a product's life cycle. We will therefore consider the maturation phase as well as the phase during which the growth rate begins to level off.

The complex problem of disinvestment receives superficial attention only in current strategic planning concepts. And yet because of the bitterness involved, the realization of a disinvestment program is one of the most difficult decisions that a company may have to make. There may be a correlation between the size of the problem and the size of the company. The smaller the firm and the less diversified the product portfolio, the more difficult it will be to introduce disinvestment plans. In our three cases, however, we are concerned with disinvestment in medium-sized and large enterprises.

In the following chapter we present the Andersson case, which serves to illustrate some of the main ingredients of the disinvestment problem. Before discussing the results of the three cases, we will look at some of the theoretical aspects of the problem. In the last chapter we will compare our own findings with those of some other researchers.

The Andersson Corporation

The Andersson Corporation has been successfully producing components for electric ovens for the European market for decades. It sells its products to well-known producers in Europe. Of its workforce, 140 work in the production department and another 30 in administration. The legal form of the enterprise is that of a joint-stock company. Its main product has long been a component which, with only a few modifcations, has been producing and selling since 1953. The idea of producing this component was that of the founder and former manager of the company.

The company used fairly unsophisticated planning routines. Since sales contracts ran for an average of 1–3 years, it was possible to plan on a relatively long-term basis, i.e. on a basis of orders received. The buyers of the product worked to a medium-long planning policy.

In the spring of 1972 some major customers indicated that the price and present technology of the product were no longer competitve. Suddenly, other technically superior components were being launched on the market. Although the Andersson Corporation lost some contracts, its management did not take the decline too seriously. After all, the firm was selling a solid, reliable product: "Quality has its place." Sales efforts were intensified and managers began to renew old business contracts. The sales department was told to try to open up new markets.

Six months passed, and Andersson began to realize that the dip in sales was by no means only a temporary one. The product was no longer competitive and would have to be discontinued within the foreseeable future. The board of directors called an emergency meeting. The trend in the sales figures spoke for itself. What was to be done? There were no alternative products which could be added to the program at short notice.

At an extraordinary board meeting in November the founder-manager was asked to resign. In the spring of 1973, a young largely technically trained manager was appointed and he immediately took radical action. The remaining members of management were dismissed, three new executives were engaged, the staff was put on short time, and part of the factory workforce was laid off. Fortunately the firm still had solid capital at its disposal, so that it was possible to open up a new market.

For another year 40 per cent of the original capacity was still used for the old product. During this period the great efforts that were being made and the large amount of money being spent resulted in the development of an alternative product. A new strategic concept was worked out, as the company wanted to reduce its one-sided dependence on the buyers. In the autumn of 1974, the first prototypes were produced and the company began to recover.

This case is not unusual. A firm which has been selling one product very successfully for a long time is suddenly confronted with the fact that "harvest-time" is over. The absence of long-term concepts, and a management that believes the previous success will continue, lead to a crisis.

What is rather unusual in this case is the fact that the firm survived. Because of its favorable financial situation the firm was able to withstand the slump, to develop a new device, and to launch it successfully. The average firm is hardly ever as lucky as Andersson was. Some of the particular problems that arose there will be discussed below.

Strategic Problems and Decision-Making

The Andersson case shows that a disinvestment process can be divided into several steps. The most important step is propably the first, when the life of the product is called in question. Several studies of business organizations have shown that current crises tend to be ignored, while the hope that the problem will prove to be temporary is firmly nourished (Hedberg et al., 1976). For this reason the period during which disinvestment is being initiated can vary in length. But once there is a commitment to disinvestment, plans should be made about the timing of the end-game, and here some crucial questions have to be answered. How can the opportunities offered by the declining market be exploited? When should exit occur? Which exit barriers will be most devastating in the attempt to escape? (Porter, 1976).

The theory does not provide us with any very differentiated advice. Studies of the "product life cycle" have been inclined to treat product life cycles as homogeneous in their development, something which is contradicted by the empirical findings (Pfeiffer and Bischoff). Further, according to this somewhat undifferentiated theory, industry is also supposed to behave homogeneously in decline. Business strategy research has paid little attention to the problems of declining industries (Harrigan, 1980) or declining products (Sternhufvud, 1982). Such literature as there is treats disinvestment as a strategic problem that is similar in all business firms, thus ignoring any differences in business structure and internal corporate attributes. But research indicates that firms do not act alike in coping with declining business, and that they should not do so. Different customer structures, different types of technology and marketing, different styles of leadership and different political environments will all make for variations in processes and outcomes.

The Phases of Corporate Development

The development of a company often runs parallel to the development of its products. The typical development of a one-product firm corresponds to the typical life cycle of this particular product. Hence, the product and the enterprise pass through various phases simultaneously:

- product development
- market introduction
- economic breakthrough
- growth
- maturation
- ageing.

Each phase calls for different sets of managerial competences. Consequently, the products of a firm should be regarded as projects – and all projects have a beginning and an end.

The situation of the growing firm in an unsaturated market has been discussed at length in economic literature, and innumerable ways of dealing with it have been designed. But how does the marketing department of a declining enterprise behave in a stagnant market? How should R & D activities be organized, in order to develop alternative profit-yielding products? These problems are only taken up occasionally in the literature.

Managements do have visions and ideas about new opportunities and potential openings. But the routines of everyday business life are a major obstacle that prevent management from trying out such ideas or testing their value to the performance of the company. It takes a long time for vague ideas to be transformed into concrete marketing concepts. This dilemma may explain the persistent popularity of concepts devised by strategic management. These concepts help to establish strategic thinking in companies, making it imperative that the feasibility of project ideas be tested time and again. At the very least these concepts call for a certain detachment from business routines and for a reappraisal of positions. They are therefore of vital importance.

In the following pages we will be discussing two phases in the product life cycle: its maturation phase and the subsequent phase of disinvestment. At present two procedural models are available to companies for the handling of these two phases: (1) the product life cycle concept and (2) corporate strategy models which are based on these product life cycles.

The product life cycle is a very general model which describes the development of a product from its start to its end. Every industry and almost every product has its specific life-cycle patterns on the market. The model makes it possible to recognize trends. Above all, however, it proves one thing: products have to "die".

The schematic development of a one-product firm will be roughly as follows: the introduction and development phase is followed by economic break-through, i.e. by a rapid increase in sales turnover. Not until this breakthrough has occurred will productive capacity be established in the firm, to achieve the target production volume. At the same time marketing and distribution requirements are streamlined to exploit the intended market growth. After a while the growth curve will reveal its upper S-bend; the product is approaching maturity. When exactly this occurs will depend on the kind of product and the circumstances of the industry. Recent experience shows, however, that in many industries the maturity phase is being reached increasingly early. Once the product has thus reached maturity, improvements are made so as to turn the growth curve up again.

Companies which have haveloped a new product are not usually the only ones with ideas. At least, they will not be so for long, because imitators will soon be launching modified or even improved variations of the product on the market. Gradually, depending on the industry, competitors will appear who are prepared to fight for a share of the market. The widespread flow of information and imitation accelerates the maturation process of entire industries today, and this in turn forces companies to plan the tactics of the 'end-game' sooner than before.

Stopping in Time – An Entrepreneurial Skill

The problem of disinvestment, however, is a very special one. Our experience shows that it is closely linked with the notion of "success" that dominates firms in a market economy: leaving a market is often misinterpreted as failure, even though doing the right thing at the right time is generally considered to be a distinguishing feature of entrepreneurial behavior. Thus, leaving the market in time should be regarded as an act of successful management. A manager who was asking our advice, told us quite frankly: "What you tell people in and around a firm should sound optimistic. If you draw a realistic picture showing the real risks, most of the workforce will be scared. When you're driving a car, nobody really wants to know how many people lose their lives on the highways every day. The firm's situation is similar. People want to hear good news rather than to be told how risky business really is. If you informed your staff about everything, it would be become very difficult to find any employees at all."

This kind of attitude leads to the serious "de-dramatization" of important changes in the environment, and quite frequently to a real crisis. Acting in a market economy does not only mean taking risks; it also means being aware of these risks. The workforce knows about the risks, and ignoring them does not help to make a company more willing to face up to them.

A willingness to take risks is inherent in planning. Planning means systematically considering the future, creating scenarios, defining standards of control, and including in the planning process continuous adjustments to changes that actually occur. Management must constantly convey this willingness to its workforce in a symbolical way. McKinsey once said: "Planning is the visible proof of a thinking management." When it comes to the systematization of such thinking and the importance of staff participation in it, there is a lot left to be desired.

The Maturation Process

The maturation phase has several distinctive characteristics. At some point after the economic breakthrough of a product, when production technologies and sales methods have been perfected, an industry or a market segment will stabilize. Many customers have been acquired, the growth limit has been reached, and the capacity in the individual company hardly allows for investment in any major new production technologies. Nevertheless, some measure of investment in "rationalizations" continues, because new production facilities of this kind have a positive effect on the cost structure. The consequence is, however, that the overcapacity in the industry persists. This unthinking response, whereby industries retain their overcapacity rather than reducing it during the maturation phase, is a notable feature of this stage of development.

Several attempts have been made over the last few years to "organize industry" in face of this situation. Since individual firms find it difficult or even impossible to solve the problems caused by such overcapacity, action of a more comprehensive kind is taken (e.g. quotas are fixed). Examples of this sort of action have occurred in the steel and textile industries and, in some European countries, in the construction trade.

Of course it is not the overcapacity as such that is the main problem in this phase; rather it is the unfavorable cost structure and the related drop in profits. Apart from the quantitative problems of the mature industry, such as a falling growth rate, constant overcapacity, unsatisfactory profitability and capital-intensive replacement investments, there are also some qualitative aspects.

Quantitative features alone do not define the nature of the maturity phase. Quite often management simply does not want to admit that the era of growth and profitability has gone for good in this particular industry. Instead they speak of "a short-term slump" that will soon be followed by "the recovery" of the market. Only after a long delay in doing anything about the problem is it agreed in the company that the "short-term slump" in fact represents a long-term decline in the market.

The products of a mature market segment are usually very similar. It is therefore difficult to differentiate the products to fit distinct segments of demand. The products are easily definable, i.e. they assume the character of standard products. Moreover, the existing production technology also becomes increasingly standardized in its structure and its functions. And the technology is comparatively easy to obtain on the market, which means that the barriers to entry are lowered and new competitors, perhaps from low-cost countries, will find it easy to enter the segment at little cost. This results in even greater overcapacity.

In the course of these events the industry or the particular segment of it begins to deteriorate. Companies are forced to reduce their production drastically, unless government subsidies are provided, as is the case in some European countries. Such subsidies, too, are signs that a market section is being saturated.

The explanation for a company "slipping into" overmaturity in this way is often that it has gradually been losing essential contacts with the market. Moreover it seems to be almost impossible to change the dominating business ideas of a company, which help to maintain its established patterns. The situation will not change until the beginning of a structural crisis forces the company to take drastic steps.

Even if the company is aware of structural changes, the knowledge may well be interpreted in different ways. The corporate "establishment" protects its position on a basis of previous success and it is therefore not prepared (often at an unconscious level) to accept that earlier achievements have to be succeeded by something new. Consequently, structural changes are regarded not as a call to revise the internal structure of the firm but simply as a short-term slump in the market. "To do as before, but better", then becomes the slogan for the reinforcement of well-known programmes (and, of course, of reliable and tested measures). This will then make the situation even worse, because the resources necessary for development are being invested in exactly the wrong areas of production.

Maturation Myths

Before addressing the problems of disinvestment we should perhaps mention some myths connected with the necessary restructuring of companies which have entered a period of deterioration.

The almost sacred nature of "development work" is one of the most common myths, "because development work is something special carried out by a special sort of person". However, this attitude often generates an aura of tension which blocks the necessary experimentation and weeding out of inferior products that is really needed. Product developers must be able to feel that there is an "internal market" in the firm, and that this market should be promoted. In stages of development which are free of tension, there is a feeling abroad in the company that "the development department uses scarce resources, disturbs the daily work and makes impossible demands." In its turn the development department functions according to the myth that "the company counteracts new ideas and doesn't understand the specific problems of development works." It is essential to avoid such a stalemate, however, and to make appropriate demands on both "sides".

There is also a myth that it is a lack of ideas that prevents companies from making readjustments. Nevertheless, it often seems that ideas are simply collected rather than classified and tested. What is needed are repeated attempts to pursue a few lines of development and to test them for feasibility. In most companies this proves more difficult than creating new development possibilities.

Then there is the myth of the innovation chain, i.e. that we start with the technical solution, which should be followed by a market test, after which the project is passed over to those responsible for current production and distribution. However, this fragmentation causes a loss of knowledge, while responsibility is shifted to the heads of department instead of being delegated to groups of employees with diverse qualifications. It simply seems easier to stick to the established structure of the company even in the case of development work, than to try to find more flexible forms of project planning.

In cases where firms are more or less forced into reorientation, "fantasy development projects" are often thought up, and projects are initiated that are far removed from the present product portfolio. The choice often falls on some high-technology product which suddenly appears to be attractive, although little is known in the company about its market chances.

There are thus certain special features attaching to the maturity phase. Once these become apparent, management should think very carefully about the connection between cause and effect. Some of the characteristics mentioned illustrate the need for readjustment. Recent attempts to find some sort of "early-warning system" should concentrate on this kind of qualitative aspect. Such aspects should be incorporated into the planning process, and should serve to alert companies to the definition and reappraisal of their own situation. Putting this into effect is not a question of formal planning, however; rather it is a question of acting on management's part – management which also has to subject itself to readjustment. In fact this is management's first and most important task.

Preparing Product Termination

The maturity phase of a product prepares for strategic exit. When this disinvestment process should be started is often only a question of time. The problems of the disinvestment phase frequently have their roots in the maturity stage. The sooner the pertinent decisions can be prepared, the less resistance is there likely to be in the company, and this will naturally make it easier to implement decisions at a "more favourable level of cost". This last is mainly a reference to the kind of social cost that occurs in connection with crisis and dramatic change. Disinvestment planning helps to keep these costs as low as possible.

The disinvestment problem becomes acute when some of the company's market segments begin to degenerate, and the disinvestment itself can assume a variety of forms: parts of the firm are sold; restructuring is undertaken; parts of the firm are closed down; the production of an alternative product is successively introduced.

Very little has been written about disinvestment in combination with restructuring in the company. We have chosen to focus on such a case because it has the greatest relevance to all kinds of enterprises: the large, the medium-sized and the small. Some of the more recent studies have suggested that very few enterprises have access to institutionalized forms of disinvestment. Even in innovative industries such as the pharmaceutical industry, it is exceptional to find disinvestment planning as an integral part of a company's overall planning. In general, the disinvestment process is monitored intuitively, without the use of specific disinvestment calculations. Rather, the different products of the company are compared and weighed against each other. Applying the methods of the product portfolio, this weighing-up is formed into a fairly systematic procedure. Products are assessed for their development potential, and strategies are decided accordingly. The analysis of the development is based in this case on the classification of the products in terms of product life cycles.

Only very seldom is a decision taken in the company about preparing for or deciding on disinvestment. Furthermore, it seems that central strategic decision-making is more difficult when the company carries a large number of products. Obviously, these bigger companies have to formalize the planning of their disinvestments in a different way from that applied in small firms. Small firms are at an advantage, since information can be exchanged more quickly; their contact with the market is of a different kind. On the other hand, their insufficient access to planning personnel impedes the implementation of institutionalized forms of disinvestment planning.

The most frequent reasons for the absence of disinvestment procedures are:

– *Lack of time.* Due to its heavy workload the management of a medium-sized enterprise usually has no time to analyse products systematically. The fact that decisions are not delegated so often in smaller companies adds significantly to a management's excessive workload.

– *False feeling of security:* In the initial product analysis executives are convinced that their calculations for covering amortized fixed costs are satisfactory. What is still lacking in medium-sized companies is any kind of differentiated information system providing a broader basis for assessment.

– *Concentration of new products.* Management pays too much attention to new products at the expense of old ones, forgetting the importance of these old products to the enterprise (e.g. as regards costs).

– *Internal organization problems.* Certain people are to be made responsible for reviewing products. Controller departments do not suffice; a product-scrutinizing function is to be established.

– *Opposition to changes.* Those responsible for certain products or groups of products tend to justify the existence of "their" products.

Although disinvestment is a part of entrepreneurial action, the decision to disinvest can be compared psychologically with a decision to part from an old friend. Moreover, managers tend to think that deciding on a disinvestment is tantamount to admitting that a wrong decision had been taken in the past. In many companies disinvestment is associated with mismanagement. It is not therefore suprising that disinvestment receives meager treatment in the literature of corporate planning. All kinds of organizational barriers are raised as a result of this "emotionalization" of the situation. For this reason efforts have to be made to prepare for disinvestment decisions well in advance and to discuss them frankly, thus providing a solid basis for action and minimizing fear and opposition. This approach also makes it less likely that disinvestment will be seen simply as a last way out, and that the decision to disinvest is delayed. Delay only increases the cost, so that resources cannot be made available for development. Added to which, such delays discourage just the kind of creative employees who are particularly needed in difficult situations.

Finally, it is important that companies should reward disinvestment decisions. Although these decisions require a great deal of real managerial thinking and a willingness to take risks, the people who have to take them are rarely specifically rewarded. Instead they are surrounded with an aura of failure, which they naturally find disappointing. To keep on identifying with the company in a situation like this must become increasingly difficult.

Empirical Data

Case A: Delayed Disinvestment

Since the mid-1930s this company has been producing a variety of products which it sells very successfully. During the initial phase the company was largely dependent on one bulk customer. At the beginning of the 1960s this customer suddenly announced that he was going to reduce his volume of purchases significantly. Consequently the company was forced to reappraise its situation and it tried to develop a couple of new products and to sell components to other firms. For the new product, AA, a budget was made available. The new product was by no means comparable to the previous products of the company. The main buyer during the first development phase continued to be the main customer for the product throughout its life. Due to marketing difficulties and because of technical deficiencies, the company failed to attract other customers. To start with, top management still believed in exports to the European market, but attempts in this direction brought no positive results.

At the end of the 1960s a bank took over the majority of the company's shares. Four years passed between development of the first prototype and the final decision to disinvest, by which time the company had already suffered significant losses.

During the 1960s disinvestment was much less usual than it became during the 1970s, with the result that the disinvestment decision met with strong resistance from the unions. Since the problem was still an uncommon one, the union was able to gain the support of local politicians and of the government. The general resistance was quite understandable, as the existence of the whole company was at stake.

The unions knew that product AA was unprofitable. By delaying the disinvestment decision, however, they hoped that the company's problems could be solved. And due to all this resistance, management's decision to disinvest was taken only very reluctantly.

Up to the end of the 1960s the company was able to show a profit, but from the beginning of the 1970s is started to get into the red. Its very existence was in jeopardy. Until then, no product reappraisal had been undertaken. But now the cost of production, market potentials and profitability were all looked into, and it was shown beyond doubt that the product was so unprofitable that the whole company might have to be closed down. Nor could the losses be made good by any alternative product.

Decision-making was highly centralized in this company, and in the initial phase this had a conservative effect. The strong general manager protected the product and planned to expand its production. Once he was replaced, the centralization began to have a positive effect: it was possible to get the disinvestment decision through despite the resistance. The losses provided the necessary stimulus for a speedy disinvestment, and by this time it was generally accepted that radical measures were necessary if the firm was to be saved.

The forces opposed to disinvestment had long dominated. At least, they had dominated as long as the former top executive had been able to exercise his "protective" funktion. Once he had left, the changes necessary to a disinvestment decision took place. The new manager was the promoter of the disinvestment idea, thus paving the way for its implementation. Arguments about the pros and cons of disinvestment went on for about a year, which is a long time to sustain such an unnecessary drain on resources. But the resulting threat to the existence of the company finally led to a radical disinvestment and the elimination of all internal opposition.

Case B: Forced Disinvestment

As a result of government controls two products of this company were at risk. Management therefore decided to open up a new market by introducing product BB. The company undertook development of the product, and large-scale investments were made. For example, new executives were recruited from outside to be responsible for the new product. In BB's market segment there was already a competing product that fulfilled the same function as BB.

If customers wanted to replace the competing product by BB they would have to invest about US $ 50 000 in the conversion of their production facilities.

The company's efforts did not succeed. This was partly because one of its managers left to produce a similar but less expensive product elsewhere, and partly because BB was less efficient than the competing product already on the market.

Quite soon after the product had been launched on the market, some of the staff suggested that BB had little chance of succeeding. Nevertheless several million dollars were invested in improving the product – but, as predicted, without success. Some people in the company had hoped to make the product a bestseller by any means, and so the failure was thoroughly discouraging, particularly when it became obvious that disinvestment was going to be inevitable.

When sales fell far short of their targets the opposition increased, and in order to reduce the friction management established a project group to work exclusively on BB. This decision prolonged the life of the product, but only seemed to postpone the disinvestment decision. All sorts of remedies were tried, ranging from stepping up sales efforts to the printing of expensive promotional material "More of the same" seemed to be the slogan during this phase. At the same time, however, those responsible for the product were replaced several times over.

After all these measures failed, management finally decided to take more radical action. The manager who had left the firm at an early stage and whose product was selling successfully in serious competitor with BB, was contacted with a view to possible cooperation. He turned down the offer.

In the meantime the company had been trying to develop other products, but the necessary resources had been witheld in favour of BB. This resulted in even greater opposition to BB. Finally a foreign company was found to buy BB and the relevant production machinery for a symbolical sum. It was also agreed that Company B should put its know-how at the disposal of the buyer.

The personal prestige of staff members and of the company as a whole was bound up in its products, and this fact helped to prolong the product's life. Time and again costly solutions were sought in order to save face. Most staff members decided in favor or product termination at a relatively early stage, but management could not make up its mind. As a result the whole disinvestment process took 8 years. By delaying the disinvestment decision, the company faced exactly what it had tried to avoid, i.e. a loss of prestige. Only the symbolical purchase and the chance to retain a modicum of dignity smoothed the way for the disinvestment decision.

Case C: Systematic Exit

From its foundation in the 1940s until the mid-1970s Company C was a notably sound family firm. It was run on patriarchal lines. The president was usually a member of the family. The firm was originally established for the production of CC, i.e. the product that long remained its economic pillar. During the same period, however other products started to expand, although CC remained unique until the beginning of the 1950s.

CC was used mainly in food stores. In the mid-1950s the self-service idea was spreading, and the president accepted the inevitability of the new trend. CC was affected by this reorientation and the company began to push other products, thus reducing CC's share of the whole product assortment. The manufacture of the new products called for other raw materials, and the production technology was converted accordingly. CC was still the pride of the company and Company C was in fact its main Scandinavian producer. Nevertheless, the disinvestment decision did not meet any opposition. Management regretted the decision, but had no alternative.

Over a period of 12 years CC had gradually been losing ground. As a result of this gradual process C's employees grew accustomed to the reduction in production volume, until the product was discontinued altogether. The company was anxious to keep its CC customers satisfied. For each model of CC that was terminated, alternative sources of supply were offered. This helped to maintain the good reputation of the company and prevented any damage to the reputation of its other products. What helped to make this gradual disinvestment possible was the extraordinarily slow deterioration of the market. The decision-making structure of this company was highly centralized. The president took both strategic decisions and the more important operatonal decisions as well. Although the decision to disinvest did not meet with an enthusiastic response, it was accepted. And of course the existence of succeeding products guaranteed employment and therefore made acceptance all the easier. The slow decline of the product made for a reasonably smooth transfer of workers to other product lines. In fact the existence of alternative products even generated a kind of enthusiasm – "We are treading new paths!" And the reduction in dependence on a single product also contributed to the positive attitude.

Since no replacement investments had to be made in the final phase, CC managed to cover at least its production costs even at that point.

The patriarchal management style left no room for argument between conservative and progressive forces, nor did C's type of organizational culture favor any questioning of the president's decisions. However, even the president had conflicting feelings about the disinvestment decision. In the final phase he found it hard to scrap the last ten machines, and it was a new owner who brought this decision about.

Systematizing the Case Studies

We can now briefly summarize characteristic features of the three cases described above. We will then suggest some ways of improving disinvestment.

Companies tend to adopt quasi-solutions to their disinvestment-related conflicts. In the case of Company B the quasi-solution was the establishment of a project group. Instead of openly discussing the disturbances on the market, attempts were made to reduce the resulting uncertainties. Acceptance of these disturbances would have been much more constructive. Except in case C, which because of its specific circumstances is an unusually positive example, solutions have always been triggered off by serious crises.

The difference between CC and many other cases of which we have knowledge, is that only a relatively small amount of money had been invested in production facilities (at least compared to A und B), and that CC had already reached maturity. Further, the disinvestment decision was taken in an authoritarian manner by a single person detached from the product itself.

Company	A	B	C
Market	Disturbed relations with the market; product did not meet quality and price requirements	Disturbed market relations; product did not meet price requirements	Disturbed relations with the market due to extensive but slow decline of the market
Former investements	Large, both from an economic and a prestige point of view	Small in economic terms but extensive in terms of prestige	Negligible
Surplus resources	Hardly any	Very large	Large to start with, later gradually shrinking
Spurious conflict resolution	None	Formation of a special project group to reduce the conflict potential	None
Uncertainty avoidance	Uncertainties were perceived, negotiations with external financial sources	Uncertainties were perceived and negotiations took place concerning cooperation in production	Uncertainties were perceived, no outside negotiations; president solved the problem
Crisis as triggering factor	Crisis triggers internal problem-oriented search	Long internal search for solutions – "more of the same"	Immediate search in a new expansive direction
Lessons learnt	Product targets and assessment criteria changed	Sales targets were adjusted	Sales/marketing targets were adjusted
Product's stage in the life cycle	Introductory phase	Introductory phase	Maturity phase
Kind of disinvestment	Delayed disinvestment	Delayed disinvestment forced on by competitors	Systematic, gradual disinvestment

Thus, delay in making a strategic exit usually depends on the prestige of the key people identified with the product, on the identification of the product with the company, and on the total investment in the product. In companies with a sound financial base, prestige and the degree of product-company identification are the main causes of delay.

Prescriptions for Systematic Product Withdrawals

Crucial questions to be asked at the outset of a round of strategic planning are: Where do we stand today? Where do we want to be tomorrow? What are the obstacles? What are the opportunities? What ways and means are available for the achievement of our goals?

In the course of intensive discussions and the gathering of information, it must be borne in mind that certain of today's successful products will not stay profitable for ever. New strategic-management procedures can help companies to establish the position of their own products and that of competing products. These processes are very time-consuming, but they do stimulate strategic thinking and they can reduce opposition and conflict when such planning is being introduced to as many levels in the company as possible.

The advantage of current models of strategic planning is that they are relatively easy to apply. The strengths and weaknesses of a company's own products and hence of the company too, are defined according to various criteria. Thinking in terms of future strategies is also based on this definition of strengths and weaknesses. Frank discussion and a down-to-earth approach involving broad participation on the part of the staff members helps to stimulate cooperation and commitment. Open discussion is a prerequisite of adequate action. No company will be able to achieve all this overnight. Learning processes of this kind can take years, but ultimately only companies which allow for continuous learning will have any chance of surviving.

Can Survival be Learnt Systematically?

Planning does not replace either thinking or acting, but it is a step on the way towards a conscious learning process (Weick, 1979). Planning encourages the systematic analysis of the reasons for change, so that these become part of the basis for future decisions. Strategic planning which is thus based on "futures thinking" recognizes that some sort of "end game" will take place: for every product a time will come when it can no longer be forced. These trends have to be recognized and the conclusions drawn accordingly.

Chaotic or Systematic Disinvestment

The following brief proposals for handling disinvestment problems sum up our own substantial experience of such problems.

– Companies should analyse the market problems without fixing their minds on the most conventional solution: a continuous analysis of the market situation is a prerequisite of strategic exit. If problems arise, many companies tend to look for the "most obvious" solutions, i.e. those that have been applied before. Further, alternative solutions are excluded because acute problems have been mistakenly de-dramatized.

– Surplus resources should not be used as a justification for keeping unprofitable products alive. Products have their supporters in the company, and it is easier to include a product in the program again than to discontinue it. An economically sound company is more tolerant of unprofitable products. Consequently it is easier to justify such products, perhaps quoting the prestige of the company as a reason for going on with them. Products of this kind are thus given a "second" chance over and over again.

– The disinvestment of products while they are still profitable is vital, but preparing profitable products for disinvestment arouses strong opposition. Convincing arguments are thus necessary to justify the decision. In nine cases out of ten the decision is not taken until the problem has already become acute.

– The importance of a product affects the disinvestment decision: readiness to disinvest depends on the product's share of total turnover. In this context is often seems less important whether the product is profitable or not. One cause of resistance may be the number of jobs involved. Also, the greater the importance of the product, the greater the prestige it generates. In such cases disinvestment attracts attention both inside and outside the company. It is therefore necessary to "sell" the exit externally. If this is skilfully managed, the decision may well help to create a dynamic image of a market-oriented company.

– The best employees should work on the worse products. In reality, however, companies often assign their best people to their best-known products. Disinvestment decisions have to be taken by future-oriented people prepared to take risks. Such members of the company should be closely associated with an image of "entrepreneurial thinking and personal courage". If disinvestment decisions are taken instead by people associated with failure, then the decisions are also more likely to fail.

– Thus, employees associated with disinvestment and failure should be rewarded. Indeed, it is one of management's job to perform symbolical actions of this kind, and such rewards often reflect in symbolical terms the general orientation of the management in question.

– Identification with a product is positive only to a limited extend. Products should be handled like projects; they should be expected to have a beginning and an end. The weaker the identification between company and product, the greater is the likelihood that disinvestment will happen in time. Executives must promote an "atmosphere for exit", and must be prepared to take the disinvestment decision themselves rather than delegating it.

– A product should be granted a short rich life . . . instead of a long life full of trouble. From a psychological point of view it is difficult to disinvest products during their development phase. The usual counterargument is then on grounds of investment costs: "We have invested so much that disinvestment is simply impossible." Disinvestment will then not be permitted until the degeneration phase.

– Myths about high-status products should be avoided. There are several indicators of product status: the fluctuations in staff turnover among those concerned with the development and production of the product; the dominant view of the product's importance to profits and to the external corporate image. More often than not this status has irrational grounds; it is, rather, a well-established myth, and one which has to be dealt with when it comes to the elimination of a high-status product. Information about the real significance of the product must be given to all those concerned.

– Disinvestment and product development are interdependent. Timely disinvestment is easier to manage if there are some alternative products. Product development depends in turn on timely disinvestment, i.e. disinvestment implemented at minimum cost.

– The idea that customers will react negatively is often exaggerated. If customers are informed accurately and in good time, they will understand disinvestment decisions. Using "the reaction of the customers" as an argument against exit is often completely irrational.

– An exclusive concentration on hard data should be avoided. A continuous reappraisal of products should be the rule. These examinations should include qualitative data such as developments in the particular branch of industry, developments in the market segment, the technological maturity of production, and the differentiation of the channels of distribution. As a rule disinvestment decisions are subjective in their nature, ased more on qualitative than on quantitative data.

– Minor personnel problems are allowed to become major internal crises. As a result of disinvestment, employees are transferred and given new jobs. This arouses considerable opposition on the part of the staff and the unions. The inclusion of the unions and large sections of the workforce in the decision process does not help to make this decision easier, but it reduces the problems surrounding its implementation.

It would be a mistake to believe that a disinvestment is largely complete once the decision has been taken. The actual work of disinvestment starts after the decision, and should be subject to continuous monitoring. At best, disinvestment processes take 1½ to 2 years, because of the legal and – even more important – the human factors that play an important role alongside the economic.

As used to be said of armies, companies seem to be inspired only by attack. In systems organized according to the laws of the free market economy, the "orderly retreat" is also decisive to the survival or ruin of a company. A pioneering entrepreneur is remarkable not only for the innovation he inspired but also by managing the timely and systematic disinvestment that he supports. And yet companies often postpone disinvestment decisions as though they were not part of business. But, strategic exit is part of the business game.

References

Alexander, R. S. (1964) The Death and Burial of Sick Products. *Journal of Marketing,* 2, pp. 1–7.

Anell, B., Persson, B. (1981) *Avveckling, Utveckling, Omvandling.* Working Paper, Lindköping University.

– (1982) *Avveckling av verksamhet.* Linköping.

Goldberg, Walter (1979) Stagnation and Crisis. *Surviving Failures.* Bo Persson (Ed.), Stockholm: Almquist & Wiksell, pp. 188–195.

Hedberg, B., Nyström, P., Starbuck, W. (1976) Camping on Seesaws: Prescriptions for a Self-Designing Organization. *Administrative Science Quarterly,* 21, pp. 41–65.

Hedley, Harry (1977) Strategy and the Business Portfolio. *Long-Range Planning,* 10, pp. 9–15.

Harrigan, Kathryn Rudie (1980) *Strategies for Declining Business.* Lexington Mass.: Lexington Books.

Kotler, Philip (1965) Phasing out Weak Products. *Harvard Business Review,* March–April.

Nees, Daniella (1979) The Disinvestment Decision Process in Large and Medium-Sized Diversified Companies. *Journal of International Studies of Management and Organization,* January–February.

Persson, Bo (1979) *Surviving Failures: Patterns and Cases of Project Mismanagement.* Stockholm: Almquist and Wiksell International.

Pfeffer, J., Salancik, G. (1978) *The External Control of Organizations. A Resource-Dependence Perspective.* New York: Harper and Row.

Porter, Michael (1976) Please Note Location of Nearest Exit: Exit Barriers and Planning. *California Management Review,* Winter, Vol. XIX, pp. 21–33.

Weick, Karl (1979) *The Social Psychology of Organizing.* Massachusetts: Addison-Wesley.

The Impact of Electronic Communications on Organizations

Herbert A. Simon

Introduction

In the summer of 1969, Walter Goldberg was instrumental in organizing a conference at Aspenås, Sweden, on modern developments in organization and management. For that conference, I prepared a paper that undertook to analyze some of the consequences of the new technologies of computation for the memories, or data banks, of organizations. Now fifteen years have passed, a period during which both the character of computers and the extent of their application to the work of organizations has changed enormously. It is time for a new look at the impact of computers and electronic communications on organizations; and this time, I will not limit my discussion to organizational memories but will address a broader range of questions.

Computers today are orders of magnitude larger (in terms of memory capacity), smaller (in terms of the physical space they occupy and the power they consume), faster, and cheaper (in terms of operations per dollar) than they were fifteen years ago. Even though computers, with all of these changes, retain almost the same von Neumann architecture they have had from the beginning, quantitative changes of these magnitudes cannot fail to have qualitative effects. These qualitative effects, in turn, are vastly multiplied by the concomitant increases in the technical and economic feasibility of wideband information transfer among computers through electronic communications networks.

The quantitative effects to which I refer are the great increases in breadth and sophistication of the applications of computers to the work of business and governmental organizations. What the increases in speed and size and the decreases in cost have meant is that all kinds of information processing capabilities can be, and have been, developed to form the basis for these applications. It is not simply a matter of running faster the programs we had written a decade ago, but of implementing entirely new kinds of programs, and even of programming languages, which we could conceive of at an earlier time but could not implement practically with the technology we then had available. Under this heading come, for example, the graphics capabilities of computers that underlie modern computer-aided design; the list-processing programming languages that are required in the construction of expert systems and other applications of artificial intelligence; powerful systems for understanding spoken language; flexible systems for interactive communication on wide-flung computer networks that link many different kinds of computers; and sensory and motor systems for the robotic devices.

The ubiquity of new applications of this technology is obvious enough. But the applications are mostly of such recent date that we have not had time to accumulate much experience about their implications for the structure and operation of organizations. These implications may even extend far beyond the boundaries of individual organizations. In Paris, for example, there has been founded the Centre Mondiale de Informatique et Ressource Humaine, one of whose missions is to see what contribution computer technologies of these sophisiticated kinds can make to the economic and social development of the Third World nations.

In the absence of extended objective data about the impact that these developments are having, or are about to have, on organizations, we have to rely on anecdote or ethnographic observation.[1]) On a modest scale, some sophisticated computing systems and computer networks have now existed for more than a decade. As a member of the computing community at Carnegie-Mellon University, which, in turn, is a node in the national ARPA communications network, I have lived within such a system for the past dozen years of my professional life. If I do not have data of a systematic sort, I can at least provide my ethnographic report on what life has been like in such a system. Much of the "data" reported in this paper will come from this very personal source. I hope that in time it will be joined by the reports of other observers, as well as by data gathered in a thoroughly systematic way with due attention to the requirements of sampling.

It will not always be easy to interpret the significance of these personal observations. For example, it would be interesting to know what effects, if any, the new computing environments will have upon people's leisure time activities. I can report that, among the graduate students and faculty in my environment there is a very high interest in outdoor activities of many kinds, including hiking, backpacking, spelunking (cave exploration), skiing, hang-gliding, navigating hot-air balloons, and sports. Interest in television appears low (a poor competitor with computer games?).

Now these are rather interesting facts, if they are facts, but it is not clear what they mean for the societies of the future. Perhaps they mean that computing

---

[1]) The more dignified term is "ethnography". Sherry Turkle, in *The Second Self,* New York: Simon and Schuster, 1984, uses the term to characterize her own observations of the computer culture, which differ rather widely from mine. But this would not be the first time that two ethnographers have seen different things in the same culture.

and electronic communications attract people with certain personality traits that predispose them to these kinds of leisure activities. Perhaps all they mean is that computing communities today are inhabited largely by young academic people, who do the things that young academic people like to do. I am afraid that a large part of the information we have at this time about the social systems of computerized environments is of this iffy kind.

The Design of Communications

In order to have a framework for our discussion, it may be well to consider first some of the considerations that need to go into the design of electronic communications systems that are to be installed in organizations. The question to be addressed here is not how such systems actually *are* designed, but rather what considerations *ought* to govern their design. These can sometimes be quite distinct questions.

Capacity Limits

A communication network consists of nodes, or processors, and links, or communications channels. The processors can be human beings or computers; usually there are both kinds in a network. Links transmit messages from one node to another. Nodes input messages, operate upon them, store information extracted from them, and output new messages.

Each node in a communication network is characterized by its capacity to handle the messages that are input to it, and by the volume and characteristics of the messages it outputs. The capacity of a node, in turn, depends on the processing it is expected to do on the messages it receives, and on what messages it is expected to output. When the capacity of a node is exceeded by the load of input messages imposed on it, and/or its responsibilities for producing output messages, the quality of its performance will degrade. The degradation may be graceful or catastrophic. Degradation can take the form of processing incoming and outgoing messages less completely and thoroughly than before, or assigning priorities to tasks and ignoring those of low priority.

For example, laboratory studies of an early-warning station in an air defense organization showed clearcut degradation in the processing of radar information and information received from other nodes in the system whenever the total number of planes under surveillance increased. On a few occasions, in the face of extremely high loads, the degradation was catastrophic: the system simply failed to keep track of flights in its area. In most cases, however, as load increased, the flights associated with the radar blips were classified as safe or potentially dangerous, and only the flights in the latter category were tracked. This particular system had a built-in (human) component that, by application of rules of priority, regulated the amount of information it processed, sometimes successfully, but sometimes at the expense of quality of performance.

On a less formal basis, most of us are aware of priority schemes that we apply to our own everyday agendas. Some kinds of matters are handled immediately; others are set aside to be taken care of "when there is time". Many tasks may be handled with considerable care whenever the total load is light, but in much more cursory fashion as the load increases.

Early management information systems were typically designed in terms of the criterion of "making more information available to the manager". The decisions as to what information was to be provided, and when, largely resided in the hands of the system and its designers. The main filtering device left to the manager was to ignore information received when it exceeded capacity or seemed irrelevant to needs. The idea of balancing the volume of information transmitted against the capacities of recipients to absorb it was not a common feature of such designs; nor were notions of priority as between different kinds of information.

With the development of the information technology, these grave defects in management information systems, while they have not been fully corrected, are being somewhat ameliorated. System design now includes the concept of an information bank that does not shovel information at users, but can be accessed when and if users perceive the need for information. Of course, the indexing of data banks must be sophisticated, so that potential users can know what information is available, and can access it with ease.

As the techniques of artificial intelligence are applied to the architecture of information systems, another possibility emerges that has not yet been much exploited: to provide such systems with the intelligence that will permit them to participate in the filtering process. For example, the system itself, if sufficiently intelligent, may call to the attention of managers information that is of potential relevance to them, and may take over a large part of the task of indexing information automatically, and even of analysing it.

In all such systems, maintaining the balance between the production and consumption of information remains a central design criterion. I have always thought it a good rule of thumb that no new automatic component should be introduced into an information system unless the volume of information it absorbs is at least an order of magnitude greater than the volume it produces.

Networking and Capacity

The same questions of capacity that arise in information systems and data banks arise in the design of electronic communication networks. Design has too often been based on the simple premise that more communication is better than less. That assumption is just as questionable when applied to networks as it is when applied to information systems.

Most human white-collar organizations in developed nations are already networked electronically: the network is a telephone system. To anyone accustomed to a phone system of high reliability and good voice quality, trying to operate in an environment that lacks such a system is highly frustrating. But what implication does the presence of the system have for the loads imposed on its nodes?

The load-creating capabilities of a telephone system are limited by one important feature: placing a call imposes a time-load on the caller that is as heavy as the load placed on the receiver. However, the choice of recipient and of time of calling are entirely in the hands of the caller. For this reason, persons who are likely to be the targets of many calls generally require the protection of a filter – a secretary, or nowadays sometimes an automatic answering device.

Phone communications may also increase loads in another way. Many people find it easier to pick up a phone than to write a letter, and will call on occasions where they would not trouble to write. However, I don't know whether anyone has gathered data to determine whether the recipient of a phone inquiry typically spends more or less effort in responding than the recipient of the same inquity in the form of a letter. Two opposing forces are at work here. On the one hand, people find it far easier to generate an oral stream of words than a written one, hence are likely to answer inquiries in more detail orally than in writing. On the other hand, the oral stream can also be produced much more rapidly than the written one. I should not like to hazard a guess as to where the balance lies.

As experience has accumulated with telephones, a consensus has evidently been reached that they make a net positive contribution to the functioning of an office, for we see phones on virtually every desk, and relatively simple human filtering systems (e.g., secretaries) to manage them. The introduction of automatic calling systems with taped or synthesized messages creates, or will soon create, an entirely new problem, for it is likely to produce a massive, and strongly resented, imbalance between callers and receivers. It will surely call for stronger filtering measures than are now usually employed.

In the electronic communications systems that are now coming into being, the telephone is supplemented with an electronic mail facility. What are its characteristics? Does it differ in any significant respects from the telephone, and if so, what are the implications of the differences? The obvious and important difference is that sender and receiver don't have to be synchronized. The recipient need not be present or available at the time the message is transmitted, nor the original sender at the time of the reply. This provision of a memory to unhitch sender and recipient eliminates, first of all, the frequent sequences of phone calls that must be placed between people who are only intermittently free, hence seldom simultaneously available. At the same time, it hardly delays the message turnaround time (and, in my experience, usually reduces it).

The second important difference between the telephone and the network message system is that the latter does not require real-time response to inquiries or requests, but provides respondents with the opportunity to gather their wits, or even to seek out additional information before replying. One of the most useful pieces of advice that my father gave me was never to sign in the presence of the salesman. That advice is easier, and more gracious to follow with a network mail system than with a telephone system. On the other hand, the message system does not permit the kind of interactive interchange that characterizes human conversation. More cycles may be required to detect and correct errors of interpretation, and context must be regenerated on each round of the discontinuous exchange.

The sound, if bland, conclusion one might draw is that telephone and message systems are complementary rather than competitive commodities, and that organizations possessing both – as will soon be the case for most large organizations – will find message systems gradually playing a larger and larger role in relation to phone systems.

Networks and Hierarchies

Traditional organizations, including those we work in today, are hierarchical in form. Hierarchy has two aspects in organization: the familiar pyramid of authority, and a pattern of communications that matches the pattern of departmentalization. By the latter I mean that if we record the frequency of communication between different nodes, we find that the pattern is not uniform but highly structured. There are clusters of nodes with very high rates of inter-node communication, and much lower rates between clusters than within clusters. There are many levels of such clusters, with a drop in communication rate as we proceed from each level to the next above. In fact, the pattern of communication frequencies reflects, approximately, the pyramid of authority. In the technical literature, communication networks with this hierarchical structure are called "nearly decomposable".

There are some very good reasons why organizations are hierarchical; some of these reasons are discussed in the last chapter of my book, *The Sciences of the Artificial,* Cambridge, Mass.: MIT Press, Second edition, 1981. Above all else, hierarchy has a complexity-reducing effect that vastly simplifies the operation of large systems with multiple, heterogeneous tasks. There is nothing in the new technology of electronic communication that removes these functions and advantages of hierarchy. Hence, when we think about "networking", we should not imagine an even flow of messages from all nodes of the network to all others, but instead the highly patterned flow that is characteristic of nearly decomposable structures. In the design of networks, the pattern of flow that is anticipated will be reflected in the band widths of different linkages. Small work groups will have a high level of internal communication, not necessarily among the human members, but especially with data sources that are access-ible by all members of the group. Other, less frequently accessed common facilities will be shared by larger units of the organization, made up of sets of the first-level groups. The network hierarchy, then, will parallel the hierarchy of organizational units. Up to the present, relatively little research has been done on the design of such hierarchical networks, and the topic is in urgent need of attention.

The Need to Know

The problems of information-processing capacity need also be addressed in making decisions about where information should be stored in organizations. Who needs to know what facts and to have access to what data? To answer these kinds of questions, we must scrutinize the meaning of "to know".

In a non-literate society, people know something when they have that some-thing stored in their heads and can access it on demand. In such societies, there is no place to store information other than in human heads. Of course, even in a non-literate society, knowing can be delegated. The king can dispense with knowing certain things if he can be sure that the knowledge is stored in the head of an accessible advisor. Thus, knowledge can be social as well as individual.

With the introduction of written documents and reference books, the situation changes radically. A great deal of knowledge continues to be carried in human heads, for in literate societies we see even highly skilled and professional personnel carrying on their work with only occasional reference to books. Nevertheless, the books are there, containing most, if not all, of the collective knowledge of the society, and ready to supplement or replace the fallible human memory at the cost of some reduction in speed of access.

The availability of rapid communication networks again tilts the balance between storing in the head and storing in external memories in favor of human storage, for now knowledge becomes available to anyone who has a good index of, and access to, the experts in whose heads the knowledge is stored. When data banks become part of the communication networks, the balance is shifted once more. Now the data bank, adequately indexed, can aspire to the roles of both human memory and reference book. Now we have to re-examine the question of what human beings need to know, but also open the question of what information should exist in "hard copy" rather than in computer memories.

Neither data banks nor networks have yet reached such a stage of development that we have moved much from our traditional attitudes and modes of behavior with respect either to human knowledge or to books. But the questions are being raised more and more frequently. I can cite only a few illustrative examples, mostly pertaining to the so-called "expert systems" that are now being created by research in artificial intelligence.

Several systems have been created that do a credible, professional-level job of medical diagnosis in their domains of competence. One of these is the CADUCEUS system developed by Myers and Pople at the University of Pittsburgh. Another is the MYCIN system developed by Shortliffe and his associates at Stanford University. Most of the information that finds its way into these systems is derived from medical textbooks, with some supplementation from the experience of expert human diagnosticians. Some fraction of this information is also stored in the head of every person who has gone through medical training.

The question we will be asking with increasing urgency and frequency is whether and in what form such information needs to be stored in the heads of the next generation of medical students. (Since the advent of hand-held calculators we have been asking a similar question about the storage of addition and multiplication tables in the heads of schoolchildren.) I do not have an answer to the question, but I am certainly not prepared to predict that the informational content and medical education will be the same in a decade as it is today. Already, we have begun to make minor modifications and adjustments in other curricula. For example, calculus courses place less emphasis than they did a decade ago upon students' learning large numbers of specific integrals.

Computer systems themselves are interesting testbeds for the study of alternative forms of information storage. When does a computer user consult a hard-copy manual, and when an on-line "help" message? Of course the answer depends on some crucial technical details – the relative accessibility and comprehensibility of the two information sources, as well as the problem to be solved. But it is clear that in the Carnegie-Mellon system the balance is swinging steadily and inexorably from hard-copy to on-line information.

Good contemporary examples of such shifts in the realm of business are the on-line systems that provide information on stocks and bonds to security brokers, replacing hard-copy, frequently revised reference sources. Most of the substitution to date has been a replacement of reference books and other hard-copy sources by on-line data banks. There has as yet been no substantial replacement of information that is stored in human memories. If that is to take place on an important scale, it will have to await the further development of expert systems.

One prediction is easy to make: that a larger and larger part of society's information will be stored in electronic memories. As we have seen, it is much harder to predict what changes this implies for the information that will be stored in books and in human heads. The library continues to play its traditional role at Carnegie-Mellon, and members of the community continue to find it more convenient, on many occasions, to consult the local human experts than to use on-line "help" facilities. But it is no new thing for there to be a high level of duplication and redundancy in information sources. For the near future, that redundancy is likely to increase as computer memories duplicate information already available in other memories.

Removing People From the Loop

Thus far we have been proceeding under the assumption that communication takes place ultimately between human beings, the electronic system serving only as some kind of mediator. This assumption must be reexamined.

The following account is not fiction, but a description of actual events. A certain sum of money was to be transferred from an account in a bank in a European city to another person's account in a bank located in a midwestern American city. (That decision was made by human beings.) The decision was communicated to the computer of the European bank, which sent notice of the transaction to the computer of its American correspondent bank. The correspondent bank's computer created a new message, in two parts, which was transmitted to the computer of the New York branch of the midwestern American bank. One part of the message contained the bare fact of the transfer of funds; the other part gave the details of the account in which they were to be deposited. The New York branch bank's computer, receiving the two parts of the message at different times, failed to connect them. It set up an account for the money received, pending the receipt of information about its disposition. After several days, still lacking this information, it notified the correspondent bank's computer that it was returning the funds. An account was set up to hold them, and a message prepared returning them to the originating European bank. The story might have gone much further, but at this point it was interrupted by some humans who, wondering what had become of the money, traced the transactions and put matters back on the track.

This story is not recounted as a piece of evidence for the superiority of human intelligence over computer intelligence. I am sure that such comedies of errors did not originate in the computer era; human beings are fully as capable as computers of creating them. The story's purpose is simply to point out that there are whole realms of business today in which sequences of communications take place wholly within computing systems – or sets of mutually communicating computing systems – without human intervention. That being the case, we must not conceive of the network design problem as one of facilitating communication between human beings, but as one of facilitating decision making and the communication of decisions through networks of nodes, each of which may be a computer or a human being.

The only place where the design of such a network can begin is with an analysis of the decisions that have to be made and the transactions that have to be carried out to do the system's work. Working back from the load of decisions and transactions, we can consider the allocation of that load to people and computers, and the communications that are necessary to implement and support the allocation. This is a quite different design process from taking as given the set of human tasks and creating a system of computers and communication links to support the human actors.

Communications and Human Interaction

A question that constantly arises, and should arise, in relation to the new information technology is the impact of that technology on human life in organizations. In some human minds, the words "machine" and "automation" have strong associations to words like "dehumanization" and "alienation". What precautions must we take to prevent the introduction of electronic systems from causing a deterioration in the human qualities of organizational life?[2])

The Human Workplace

We human beings have very ambivalent attitudes towards the artifacts that we create and among which we live. A few generations past, the ambivalence was

---

[2]) A reader of an earlier draft observes that I do not mention unemployment as one of the dangers to be guarded against. In my *New Science of Management Decision*, Englewood Cliffs, N. J.: Prentice-Hall, Revised edition 1979, Chapter 4, I explain why I do not think there is any particular relation between computerization – or automation in general – and unemployment.

much less: except for a few Thoreau-like outliers, the term "civilized" had positive valence for most people, and the term "primitive" negative valence. Nowadays, the number of people who are aware of the costs associated with the benefits of civilization, is large. Moreover, most of us are able to conjure up vivid pictures – sometimes based on experience – on insults to the environment and of inhuman workplaces that are products of contemporary industrialization.

Our ambivalence will defy analysis until we are able to define with some care, and some degree of operationality, just what we mean by "civilized" and "primitive", and by a human, or humane, work environment; and unless we understand something about the causes of alienation. When we stigmatize the factory assembly line as an inhumane workplace, we seem to have at least four things in mind: the boredom of routine, repetitive work, the subservience of the human worker to the pace and conditions set by machines, the suppression of meaningful human contact and interaction, and the lack of participation of the worker in the decision-making process in the work place. Of course, many of these same stigmata apply to the work of hoeing a potato field or hollowing a dugout canoe, or doing many of the other arduous, and sometimes, repetitive, tasks, that occupy much time and effort in other, simpler societies.

But the question is not whether boredom, isolation, and lack of independence of action are good for human beings. Most of us would agree that they are not. The important question is whether, and to what extent, they are necessary concomitants of work in a modern automated factory or office environment. How can we design jobs for such an environment so that they will not be excessively repetitive, will *not* prevent social interaction, and will not destroy autonomy?[3])

One thing we notice immediately in the automated office and the highly automated factory is that the people who operate the system are mostly not linked to it on a second-to-second basis. In contrast to the traditional, and old-fashioned, assembly line, their work and responses do not have to be synchronized with the movements of machinery. Rather, their interventions are aperiodic, and often associated with assigning tasks to the machines and monitoring output. The environment in which the work is done is usually physically comfortable, and noise levels are low enough to permit conversation. People interact with machines, but they often also interact with each other.

This description fits some environments better than others, and I do not wish to idealize a less-than-ideal reality. But as a generalization, we have been more

---

[3]) In another place, I have discussed the issue of worker participation in decision-making. See my *What is Industrial Democracy? Statsvetenskaplig Tidskrift,* No. 2, 78–86, 1979.

successful in automating the routine than the non-routine components of work, and we have largely released the worker from the moment-to-moment grasp of the machine that characterized the most objectionable forms of the assembly line. What this shows is not that the work environment produced by the introduction of electronic communications will inevitably be a humane environment, but that there are wide possibilities to design it deliberately to be so.

Social Interation by Network

Although our experience with organizations linked by electronic networks is still not extensive, certain phenomena have already emerged in such settings, and have been commented upon. While the evidence is anecdotal, there is considerable consistency in the observations that have been made in different settings.

First, the availability to organization members of a computer with which (whom?) to communicate, does not appear to reduce communication with other human beings. Nor does the interpersonal communication take place mainly through computer messages. The computer science department in which I have lived for many years is a highly "social" group of people. The amount of face-to-face social interaction among its members appears to me at least as great as in any other university department of which I have been a member. There are numerous departmental social affairs, as well as shared hobbies, political interests and what not.

One way in which the network contributes to this interaction is by providing a means for advertising activities to the group, so that they are well informed about opportunities for participation. Sports teams, cave-exploring expeditions, and many other activities are organized by this means. For many years, there has been a cooperative organization for purchasing cheese, the orders being placed through the electronic network.

These interactions are supported by a system of electronic bulletin boards – files to which messages can be sent, and which can be read by members of the system. Each member specifies which of the bulletin boards will be automatically displayed to him or her at each new login to the system. Items are displayed by title, and the viewers can decide for each item whether they wish to read the entire message. There is a general bulletin board, and specialized boards for many different special interest groups. For example, the cognitive science bulletin board transmits messages about seminars and other events of interest in the general domain of cognitive psychology and artificial intelligence.

The bulletin boards exercise a socializing influence not only in keeping people informed about events of many kinds, but also in acquainting them with their fellow members, whose messages they see displayed on the boards. If they read, from time to time, the "opinions" bulletin board, they come to know the views on many subjects of the members who provide messages to that board.

One phenomenon that was not predicted when these systems were installed, but that has been observed in a number of different systems, is "flaming". Members of a system who are angered by something that has occurred (perhaps by some "anti-social" use or misuse of the system) transmit messages of protest, often expressed in quite hostile and extravagant language, to the bulletin board. The messages are considerably more violent in expression than would be messages transmitted in hard-copy writing or in a face-to-face encounter. The "impersonality" of the medium evidently allows expressions of hostility that would be unacceptable under other conditions.

The consequences of flaming for the solidarity of the social groups is hard to assess. It is my impression that, once the phenomenon has become familiar, the violence of expression is discounted (like the rhetoric of political speeches), and has no long-term effects. However, flaming deserves more careful study than it has had. It, in any event, counters the idea that the use of computers for communication will remove emotion from the human interaction.

The mail bulletin board facilities of electronic communications systems create real dangers that members of the system will be overwhelmed with messages. I have already mentioned two kinds of safeguards against those dangers. First, members may choose which bulletin boards they wish to scan. Second, messages on both bulletin boards and mail files are first presented by title, and the recipient may decide whether or not to read the full messages.

Even these safeguards may prove to be insufficient, and may have to be supplemented by more intelligent filters. It is easy for anyone on the system to create small or large mailing lists for messages, so that mail messages can be sent broadcast. On occasion, this capability has led to systems being flooded by messages, and even brought to their knees by the overload. However, networks also develop and enforce norms of "good citizenship". Members who are thought to abuse the system are subject fo "flaming" and other social sanctions imposed by their colleagues. A local culture develops that defines proper and improper communication, and the culture is to a very considerable extent self-enforcing. In our University environment, official administrative interventions have been called for only rarely.

Electronic Communications and Power

There has been much speculation about the implications of electronic communications systems for the distribution of power in organizations. Starting with the unexceptionable proposition that "knowledge is power" much concern has been expressed that those who "control" the electronic systems will control the organizations that they serve. The difficulty with this claim lies in determining who "controls" the electronic system. And the answer to the question of control is surely not independent of the system architecture and mode of operation.

At the outset, I think we can dismiss the ideal that electronic systems will be controlled by programming specialists. Systems programmers are technicians, and as with all technicians, their work must be directed and supervised so that it will be meshed with the goals of the organization. But I am not aware that there are any problems of supervising systems programmers that are different from the problems of supervising other kinds of experts. Their role is much like that of the staffs that maintain and operate the telephone system: they have little to say about the content of the messages that go out over the wires.

The Technical Possibilities

Our task is not to *predict* how electronic communications will affect the distribution of power, but to *design* electronic systems that will deal with power in the ways we think desirable. To oversimplify vastly, we can decentralize power by creating numerous sophisticated work stations with strong capabilities for acquiring and analysing information, or we can centralize power by creating centralized data banks with carefully controlled access.

Undoubtedly, we will want both to centralize and to decentralize. We will want both to provide wide access to information and to control access. The computer science profession has already been addressing for many years the technical issues involved in making this kind of differentiation possible. Personal computers and work stations, combined with networks having capabilities for broad-band information transmission, provide a technology for decentralization. Security systems, involving passwords and other means for restricting access, provide a technology for maintaining control over information and securing personal privacy.

I do not mean that the social and technical problems are easy to solve, or that the solutions will be perfect. But I urge that we not limit our system designs on the supposition that they cannot be solved.

Design Criteria

The balance between centralization and decentralization of information and decision-making must be evaluated in terms of effects on control, on the quality of decisions, and on the costs of information transmission. The question of control is heavily laden with values – with our beliefs as to which organization members should participate significantly in the making of which sets of decisions. There is no technical "right answer" to these questions. In a society like Sweden or the United States, where participation is regarded by many as a desirable social goal, per se, a different answer will be reached than in a totalitarian society.

With respect to the quality of decisions, it is often claimed that cheap means for transmitting information will inevitably make more centralization attractive. There is some historical evidence for this claim – for example in the changed and diminished role of ambassadors after telegraphic communication appeared on the scene.

Cheap information transfer can be interpreted to imply that *all* the relevant information can be transmitted to a central decision point, and that such a central point cannot help but make better decisions than decentralized units that are only partially informed. But the conclusion rests on a dubious technical assumption – that *all* or most of the relevant information can be transmitted through the electronic system, and the even more dubious assumption that the human members of the system have nothing to contribute in the way of analysis. Finally, it rests on the assumption that is easier to transmit information required for decision to central points than to transmit the goals and criteria that are to govern decision to the decentralized locations where the information about immediate circumstances is available.

To justify centralization, it is not enough that all of the information can be centralized; it is necessary that all of the expertise be centralized also. (Ambassadors have been known to point this out when decisions are taken out of their hands.) If cheap communication makes it easier to centralize information, it also makes it easier to transmit centralized information to decentralized decision points. Messages can flow in both directions on the telegraph wire equally well.

Thus, the increasing capabilities of electronic communications systems offer no simple answers to the question of centralization versus decentralization. System designers will have to begin with the nature of the decisions that have to be made; the sources of information and expertise for making them; the relative ease of transmission of the various kinds of relevant information; the kinds of decision-making processes that are available to man and machine. In any foreseeable future, we will surely see in our organizations a distributed decision-making system that will not seem wholly strange to us in terms of our previous experience.

Conclusion

In talking about the future of a technology as radically new and powerful as electronic computers and networking, one is continually torn between the temptation to predict a wholly new (and brave?) world, and the temptation to predict that all will go on exactly as before. The faint image on the crystal ball will hardly refute either prediction. And in any event, all depends upon the time horizon one selects. In a sufficiently short time, nothing will change, and in a sufficiently long time, everything.

For this reason, I have been less concerned in this paper with predictions than I have with proposing points of view that may be helpful in understanding and planning for the new developments. In the first part of the paper, I have pointed out that we must shift from a view that focuses upon the availability of information to a view that focuses upon the availability of capacity for attending to information. That has seemed to me, for some years, to be a very obvious point, but it still does not receive the attention it deserves in the design of information systems.

In the second part of the paper, I asked whether we have reason to expect that the workplaces of the future will be more or less congenial to human beings than those of the present. On balance, I arrived at a rather optimistic answer – again not in the form of a prediction, but in the form of an assertion that we can determine the outcome by the way we design our systems.

Finally, in the last part of the paper, I have asked what implications the new information technology has for the distribution of power in our organizations. My answer to this, as to the previous, question is that the decision lies in our own hands. The technology offers a wide range of possibilities; we must decide how they will be exploited.

In sum, then, I do not see a single future ahead of us that is inexorably determined by technological forces. I see an exciting new technology coming into being, and that technology presenting us with a wide range of options. The past history of our species shows us absorbing a large number of technologies – from stone tools to the steam engine – with results that have been both good and bad. On balance, I do not have any urge to return to the life of the happy savage, and I suspect that most of my readers do not either. So we must hope, with a modicum of historical support for the reasonableness of that hope, that the benefits we will derive from these new electronic possibilities will outweigh their costs. But "hope" is not enough. Technology creates the possibilities, but it is we, through our plans and decisions, who determine which of them will be realized, and what the consequences will be for human welfare.

Third World, Third Wave? On the Information Society as a Model for Developing Countries

Bo Hedberg

Background

Is modern information technology a better base for development in Third World countries than the conventional industrial technologies which are transferred today to set up paper mills, steelworks, clothing factories and other cornerstones of industrialization? Developing countries are often compared with industrialized countries in international statistics and in the development dialogue. The first wave, agricultural, is followed by a second wave, industrial. Then perhaps it is time for a third wave, heralding the information society.

Walter Goldberg triggered my interest in computers and communication technology. He pioneered the early Swedish attempts to teach computer science and to use the computer as a tool for improving managerial decision-making, logistics, the use of decision-support systems and so on in business firms and in public administration. Walter Goldberg had visionary ideas about the use of these new technologies, and he combined his enthusiasm for the technology itself with a profound sense of responsibility for the individual and societal choices connected with computerization.

Development problems in the Third World have been another favorite theme of Dr. Goldberg's. He has served as an advisor to the United Nations and to several governments on issues of this kind.

Selecting a topic at the crossroads between these two interests of Walter Goldberg's, I have focused this chapter on the role of information technology in Third World development strategies. Is the third wave, the information society, a possible development model for countries in the Third World?

Underdeveloped, Developing, and Industrialized Nations

Words imply values. Sometimes they misdirect our attention, and succeed in substituting labels for reality. The phrase "underdeveloped countries" implies the existence of a reference point, the "developed country". Since global resources are limited, there may also be "overdeveloped countries", nations which threaten the globe's carrying capacity. Maybe that is why the expression "the developing countries" is preferred to "the underveloped countries" in the international debate. "Developing countries" carries dynamic overtones. Something is happening! Who could be against development? The phrase "industrialized countries" defines the development vision. Industrialization is the key to wiping out underdevelopment.

But the sad fact is that it is underdevelopment rather than development that is evolving in Third World countries. With the exception of a few newly-rich oil countries and some NICs and free-zones in Asia, the gap between rich and poor countries is still widening. Some observers use the term Fourth World to refer to the seemingly permanent state of poverty and hopelessness that characterizes the lives of the more than one billion people who starve every day. The recent upturn in our Western economies, together with a new fascination for microelectronics, biotechnics, robotics, individualism, and entrepreneurship, have almost made us forget how little success has been achieved by Third World development strategies. The Green Revolution failed, and the Red Revolutions – as manifest in China, Cuba or Mozambique – seem to offer more problems than solutions. The Shah of Iran, who tried to buy and build up an industrial state, has disappeared. And with him went his dreams.

The collapse of conventional development strategies is only too obvious. The New International Economic Order has remained at the blueprint stage. The North-South dialogue ceased. Big paper mills and hospitals today serve as monuments of second wave aid strategies in several countries in Africa and Asia – too big and too complicated for the receiving country; lacking maintenance, professionalism and a matching infrastructure.

In their attempts to industrialize, many developing countries have found themselves facing uncontrolled urbanization, slums, and the rapid decay of villages and rural areas. The late E. F. Schumacher observed:

"In many years of work in or for developing countries, I have come to the conclusion that the problems of economic misery cannot be solved in the cities; if it can be solved at all then only by the revitalisation of life in villages and in small and medium-sized towns. The rural areas cannot hold their people because they are culturally, and (in most cases) economically stagnant, retrogressive, decaying. All over the world it can be observed that the range of activities in these areas is diminishing; nonagricultural activities are dying out; what they used to make themselves they now receive in celophaned packages from the big city; and even agriculture itself tends to become reduced to monoculture.

The forces that move people into the slums of monster cities and conurbations are not found in the attractiveness of the cities but in the decay of life outside them. Unless this process of decay is stopped and reversed, a catastrophic deterioration in the condition of mankind cannot be averted." ("Patterns of human settlement". Unpublished manuscript 1976.)

It is no wonder that people who take a serious interest in a development dialogue have begun to question industrialization as a success formula for developing countries. Instead, there is a need for alternative development models and for appropriate intermediate technologies, allowing for development but avoiding the worst side-effects of traditional industrialization.

Early reactions in the 1970s called for a moratorium on foreign aid and envisioned the development of a self-reliance movement in Third World countries. Other documents called for profound changes in the international trade system. In recent years several OPEC countries have evolved a series of development strategies apparently based on bitter experience of unsuccessful industrialization attempts over the last few decades. Downstream exploitation of national (oil) resources, together with well-designed strategies for technology transfer in other areas, appear to be the basic components. Industrialization follows the major natural resources (down the oil stream). There is no attempt to establish a fully-fledged industrial state on Western lines. Instead technology and know-how is imported to fit in with national development plans. "The real price of oil is the transfer of technology. Modern technology. Technology on our terms", said an OPEC document in 1983.

The Real Price of Oil

The real price of oil is the transfer of technology. When Mr. Ahmed Said, head of the OPEC Secretariat's Research Division opened the Vienna seminar on Cooperation among Developing Countries in March 1983, he described a strategy whereby upstream – and later downstream – oil investments in developing OPEC countries were supplemented by national attempts to create employment, to transfer technology, to substitute for imports, and to develop individual and national self-reliance.

In particular the problem of technology transfer appears to be the subject of considerable re-thinking among OPEC strategists.

Jean-Jacques Servan-Schreiber devoted several chapters of his book "Le Défi Mondial" (1980) to describing these deliberations in OPEC. He quoted Dr. Zaki Yamani describing technology transfer as "the real price of oil". A permanent system for the transfer of technology – advanced technology, intermediate technology, and technology to fit in with national development visions and plans – is called for. "You must admit that oil and time is on our side. It is you in the Western world who ought to be playing your cards". Later in the same book Servan-Schreiber described the rapid evolution from OPEC's first call for development by way of "appropriate technology" transfer in Alger 1975 to the drafting of the Taif document five years later. At least to Servan-Schreiber it is clear that information technology, the raw material of new societal infrastructures, should be a major component of such technology transfer in the future.

The real price of oil: is it the transformation of developing countries into information societies? Is there a short-cut from first wave to third wave societies?

Hardware, Software, Know-Ware... Everywhere!

The chip is really only a very small part of the new information technology. It is not computers alone that make up the information society. The Japanese use the Term C & C – Computers *and* Communications. The French concept of *télématique* has the same connotation. Computer technologies *and* communications networks blend in combinations ranging from highly talkative computers to highly intelligent networks. In addition to C & C we can also note the upgrading of the intelligence incorporated in computerized systems. Artificial intelligence and expert systems are examples of sophisticated knowledge components in modern information technology. Decision-support systems, decision models, and various other management tools widen this range. So computerization is no longer a matter of hardware and software only; know-ware is a third component.

Programmed machines with intelligence link up with other machines in local, national, and global networks ("everywhere", or spreadware). Thus, information technology consists of *hardware, software, know-ware* and *"everywhere"*.

Computerization used to be regarded as a factor geared mainly to changing the mental and physical labour involved in work processes. It is becoming increasingly clear that information technology also affects products and services. Services previously undreamt-of can be produced, and established products can be replaced by similar products with similar or improved functions but based on new technologies and new work skills. Finally, information technology affects the very infrastructure of our societies (Figure 1). Indeed, information technology contains building blocks with which society could be radically restructured or restored.

And if modern information technology provides building blocks, links, and tool kits for changes in industrialized countries, why could not appropriate

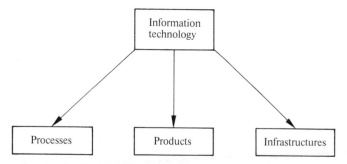

Figure 1:   Information Technology – Impact Areas.

information technology be used to tackle some of the enormous challenges in the development of Third World countries?

Must There be a Second Wave?

Toffler (1980) outlined the sequence whereby the agricultural society (first wave) is gradually taken over by the industrial society (second wave), only to be followed by another, third, wave, the information society. Others have developed fairly detailed descriptions of this coming society. MITI's document (1982) and Yoneji Masuda's "The Information Society as Post-Industrial Society" (1982) are two of the most elaborate examples. Most writers regard the information society as a transformation of the industrial state. Hawken (1982), for example, shows how the mass economy turns into the informative economy, the next economy. And he demonstrates in some detail how materialistic, formative cultures can develop into informative ones, in which values and knowledge, rather than materials and tools, play the central roles. To Hawken two important factors characterize the move from the mass economy to the informative economy:
– an increasing information/mass ratio in goods and services
– disintermediation ... a simplification, or short-cutting, through several links in the chain between producer and customer. This last point particularly brings in the industrial perspective. The often over-complicated industrial society, with its couplings of mediating technologies and its hordes of middlemen, representatives, wholesalers etc., must be simplified. There will be new shortcuts between producers and customers and new and more effective delivery systems for both goods and services. The perspective is clear and distinct: first come the complications of the industrial age, followed by the simplifications:

From Mass Economy		To Informative Economy
Expansive	———————▶	Contractive
Replicative	———————▶	Differentiative
Accretive	———————▶	Mutual
Affluent	———————▶	Influent
Consumptive	———————▶	Conservative
Intermediative	———————▶	Disintermediative
Entropic	———————▶	Information-rich
High wages	———————▶	Lower Wages
Specialization	———————▶	Broad skills

Source: Hawken (1983) "The Next Economy"

Toffler (1980) also described a transition characterized by decentralization, variation, distribution of resources, and growing local activities in the move from second to third wave societies.

There is no point criticizing writers in highly industrialized countries for adopting this perspective. But it should be pointed out that information technology need not necessarily be restricted to postindustrial development.

If third wave information economies in many ways recreate systems characteristics of the first agriculture wave, would it not be possible to avoid the industrial parenthesis and to superimpose the information society, with its public data networks and other immaterial infrastructures, directly on to pre-urbanized, pre-industrialized and pre-centralized economies? Or rather, could not new development models combine downstream industrialization along resource niches with a new kind of "informatization", exploiting the qualities of rural economies, avoiding the uprooting of village people and their transfer to metropolitan slums, and doing less damage to Third World cultures than industrialization and urbanization have done?

Dr. Ayensu, director of the office of biological conservation at the Smithsonian Institute, advocates such strategies: ". . . one of the clearest signs of hope is how well the information society can be superimposed upon the existing rural societies of most developing countries. Computers fit the current settings of developing countries better than people realize", he says. "Decentralized societies are more appropriate for the new technologies than the conquested cities of the 20th century." (International Management, Sept. 1982: 25–31.)

Servan-Schreiber (1980) clearly advocated similar strategies. And if he is right, influential people in OPEC have already blueprinted such development strategies and begun to specify what they will require of the appropriate information technology. The Centre Mondiale de Informatique et Ressource Humaine in Paris is directing its main mission in the same way, studying the potential of information technology for the developing countries. Maybe the third wave is first of all a process of development in the less industrialized countries?

C & C and 3 W

Just as many industrial countries today transfer their near-obsolete and excessively labour-intensive or environmentally hazardous production systems to Third World countries, so computerization in developing countries risks being based on the outgrown information technology of the industrialized world.

Another informatization strategy could be to build up a limited range of specialized production in the electronic field. It appears that the development of a domestic electronics industry is an important part of Rajiv Gandhi's new development strategy for India.

Others advocate computerization in poor countries on the general assumption that "the fundamental reason why there are poor countries today is that they have no access to information" (Edward Ayensu, The Smithsonian Institute, Washington). Simple logic says that information is power, and that access to information will encourage economic growth. "Give them more" and development will follow.

A fourth group emphasizes the educational challenge and the use of information technology to cope with this gigantic task.

I would like to emphasize the very important role that C & C can play in the establishment of new *infrastructures* in Third World countries.

Four major problems face most Third World countries today:

- the *Production* challenge: to create competitive production systems which can feed the people and provide reasonable welfare by way of production for export and for domestic markets
- the *Educational* challenge: covering the whole range from literacy-teaching, conscientization, public schools, trade schools, adult education, and higher education
- the *Environmental* challenge: to raise production and standard of living without destroying the environment or causing health hazards to the population
- the *Social* challenge: to take on the first three challenges without causing

serious damage to established social patterns and infrastructures. The aim should rather be to harmonize social and economic development.

Modern information technology could be used to work towards solutions to all these challenges. However, in a Third World perspective it is probably on the educational and social fronts that modern information technology can provide the most promising approaches.

Let us thus return to the question of the technologies appropriate for transfer to developing countries, and to the rather wild idea of bypassing the industrial development phase.

Using Toffler's (1980) language as a shorthand description of the development of Western countries from rather self-contained, local, agricultural societies to their present move into post-industrialism, we can distinguish the following phases:
– the agricultural society (first wave), with distributed production in local, partly self-contained, economies
– the industrial society (second wave) with concentrated production, trade economies, and massive investment in infrastructures such as roads, railroads, and power systems
– the information society (third wave) with investment in overbridging infrastructures of data networks (international, national, and local) and with the possibility of renewing distributed production, counteracting urbanization, and providing for a better fit between the different spheres (work, family, society etc.) of people's lives.

This model can be illustrated as follows (Figure 2):

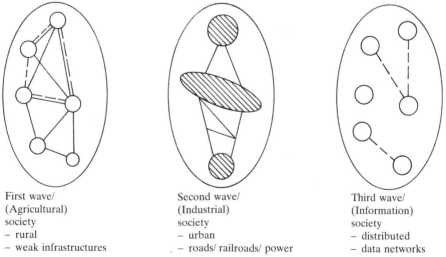

First wave/   Second wave/   Third wave/
(Agricultural)   (Industrial)   (Information)
society   society   society
– rural   – urban   – distributed
– weak infrastructures   – roads/ railroads/ power   – data networks

Figure 2:   Development of Industrialized Countries.

If industrialized countries evolve into information societies with increasing decentralization, local variation and pluralism, they will be returning in some respects to the structure from which industrialization originally took off. The third wave society, according to the scenarios, is a distributed system held together by two very costly infrastructures – the second wave infrastructure consisting of roads, waterways, and railroads and the third wave infrastructure consisting of optocables, radio links and satellite links – the former mainly for the transportation of materials and people, and the latter for the distribution of information.

Merely connecting local farming villages with public data networks and communication links is most unlikely to change Third World countries into information societies. An economy that is growing in the area of advanced service production needs a competitive level of popular and specialist education. But an economy that develops an appropriate local production of goods and basic services might well benefit from an advanced information network that allows for the dissemination of information and the coordination of local production, as well as a much less expensive network for the transportation of goods and people. If Third World countries can maintain a high level of distribution and develop effective systems for the transportation of materials and finished goods, while avoiding the massive investment in infrastructure that is associated with the transportation of people, food supplies and goods in centralized urban societies, they might achieve a good mix between tradition and progress, between roots and visions, and between crafts and skills and competence already available and others that are newly acquired. Passing over the second wave would mean less strain on the publik transportation system. It would hopefully save some countries from the darkest sides of urbanization – from the rapid spread of metropolitan slums where powerless masses live without jobs, without the means of subsistence, and without hope for to-morrow.

Perhaps in this way, third wave economies in the Third World may have a better chance of achieving growth in production and employment based on local and regional economies. Public information networks provide a promising infrastructure for widespread education. Local production, counterforces to urbanization, weaker systems for the transportation of people and a (slowly) growing share of service production – all these together would make it a little easier to handle environmental problems, such as pollution, and the risks and vulnerabilities attendant on concentrated power production. And, finally, the social challenge could be more easily met. Industrial evolution, and the evolution of service and information industries, would be the alternative to the dramatic and revolutionary changes from which most NICs and many mature industrialized countries are still suffering.

The third wave development strategy for the Third World in its simplest form
would imply the following transformation of the infrastructure (Figure 3):

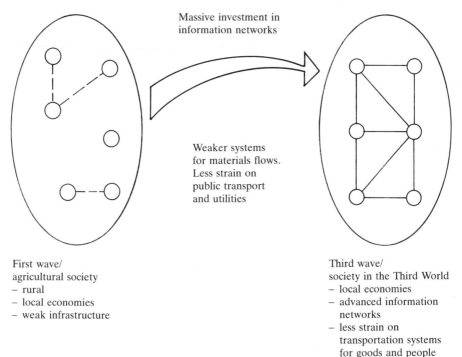

Massive investment in
information networks

Weaker systems
for materials flows.
Less strain on
public transport
and utilities

First wave/
agricultural society
– rural
– local economies
– weak infrastructure

Third wave/
society in the Third World
– local economies
– advanced information
  networks
– less strain on
  transportation systems
  for goods and people

Figure 3:   Third Wave Development Strategy for the Third World

Brave New Third World

Nothing could be easier than to criticize these visions and to dismiss the
strategies as mere paper products, unrealistic dreams, expressions of third
wave imperialism, etc. And people in Third World countries may have little
reason to pay much attention to development recipes prescribed by writers in
Washington, or politicians and scientists in Paris, or researchers in Stockholm.
However, a development dialogue would do no harm. Many of the people who
work with technologies of this kind in highly industrialized countries, and who
help to mould the infrastructural policies of our information societies, have
acquired certain insights which could perhaps be transformed and developed in
the appropriate contexts by policy-makers and scientists in Third World
countries.

C & C technology possesses tremendous development potential. It is by no means self-evident that the new information technologies must be moulded in Western, industrialized forms. On the contrary, information technology opens up promising perspectives to the advocates of the development of local economies, variety in learning, intermediate production technologies, and federalism as a way of coordinating national activities. Likewise, information technology offers interesting prospects to those concerned in the conservation of energy, the problems of pollution and uncontrolled urbanization, and, perhaps, in investment in mass popular education.

And of those who criticize or scorn such visions, we can only ask: what is your alternative? Who could claim that conventional industrialization has proved to be a successful development strategy? Is it really certain that the step from the agricultural to the industrialized society is less drastic, demanding, and unrealistic than the transformation into the appropriate kind of information society?

The advantages as regards social stress are fairly obvious. Fewer people would have to leave their home tracts, their roots, and their social structures. The potential for facing the enormous educational challenges is also evident, even though programmed learning and computer-aided instruction are certainly not ideal educational strategies. And the environmental challenges would also probably be more manageable. The major problems and doubts arise on the production side. Economic growth in the Third World information society is likely to be rather slow, and such a society would have largely to develop its own intermediate production and applications of appropriate technology. There would be very little that could be copied from the industrial nations. The advocates of self-realization, of a moratorium on conventional foreign aid, and of new rules in the economic world order, should not find anything very threatening in such prospects. But the failure of conventional foreign aid strategies does not, of course, ensure the success of their negation.

The potential of modern information technology for changing societal infrastructures must be widely acknowledged and discussed – and soon. So far, discussion and research on computer impacts have focused mainly on ways in which work processes and mental processes can be changed. The focus has been on the individual, sometimes on the group, but rarely on organizations or infrastructures.

But some of the most fundamental changes are likely to occur at these meta-levels. Patterns of human life, material flows, and public transportation are examples of this, as are electronic payment and funds-transfer systems. All are related to society's infrastructure. It seems to me that there is an interesting potential here, that could open up new vistas in the development dialogue, C & C... Computers and Communications... may prove to be a very important building-block in creating a Brave New Third World.

References

Hawken, Paul (1983) *The Next Economy*. New York: Hold, Rinehard and Winston.

Masuda, Yoneji (1981) The Information Society as Post-Industrial Society. Bethesda, Md.: World Future Society.

MITI (Ministry of International Trade and Industry) (1981) Report of the Information Industry Committee. Tokyo: Industrial Structure Council.

Nakajima, Masaki (1981) The Global Infrastructure Fund (GIF). A Progress Report. Tokyo: Mitsubishi Research Institute.

Servan-Schreiber, Jean-Jacques (1980) Le défi mondial. Paris: Librairie Arthime Fayard.

Schumacher, Ernst F. (1976) Patterns of Human Settlement. Unpublished manuscript.

Toffler, Alvin (1980) The Third Wave. London: Collins.

Part IV. Research and Change

How We Decide and How We Act – On the Assumptions of Viking Organization Theory

Barbara Czarniawska and Rolf Wolff

Introduction

The last 15 years or so have witnessed a variety of interesting phenomena in the social sciences: a growing popularity for the reflective and critical orientations, a revival of qualitative studies, and criticism of the Americanization of the social sciences. Non-American researchers have begun to attack the persistent American imperialism in this field.

The implicit assumption is that phenomena which occur in the American civilisation are universal and only sociologists of those countries have the right to use a grand quantifier. Hence probably the conviction that organisations which function in those societies have culture-free contexts. Culture-loaded context applies solely to provinces (Mrela and Kostecki, 1981: 107).

The fact that for a long time American ethnography was mistaken for a universal truth has been severely castigated, especially by European scientists (Kassem, 1976; Graumann, 1976; Mrela and Kostecki, 1981). As the result of such a debate one might have expected to see a switch from ethnocentric generalizations to a well-grounded comparative social theory. But this is not what has happened. There has been a switch in geography but not in methodology.

What we are witnessing now might be called a growing Scandinavization of organization theory, especially where it touches on management processes. The organization research of the last 20 years or so has challenged some of the basic assumptions and models of the classic paradigm, and in particular the assumption that organized actions depend on clear goals, precise plans and measurable outcome criteria. Above all, the rational model of decision-making has been called in question.

Herbert Simon, James G. March and others revolutionized organization theory in the late 1950's by introducing the notion of bounded rationality. The challenge to the classical model continued during the 1960's with the introduction of the "garbage-can" model, largely based on research results from studies of Norwegian educational organizations. During the 1970's the topic was pursued by the next generation of researchers. While most of these are from the USA (William H. Starbuck, John W. Meyer, Brian Rowan, W. Richard Scott and others), there is also a growing number of Swedish researchers who have recently proposed a concept of action rationality to replace the idea of decision rationality.

We are not writing this paper to defend the classical model of decision-making from its attackers. Our question is, do we need another universal model at all? What surprises us is the fact that theories, which are well-grounded in a certain type of organization in a certain social reality, are promoted to constitute a universal theory of organizations.

It is commonly accepted that there is a specifically Scandinavian culture. It is less well attested, but still to some extent recognized that Scandinavian managers possess specific characteristics which distinguish them from their colleagues in multinational corporations. This is widely explained by the fact that their behavior is molded by their culture. However, the possibility that the organization researchers themselves may be influenced both by the culture and by existing practice is somehow being overlooked.

We do not intend to accuse Scandinavian organization theorists of an attempt at usurpation. The worst one can say is that, without being aware of it, they are guilty of "Scandinavianism", i.e. a tendency to base their theory on data derived from their own culture. But nobody is blameless in this respect, and most definitions of culture tell us that a culture is taken for granted by those who live within it. The phenomenon can actually be perceived as a new variation on the Americanization theme ("Besides Americanization, there is no other direct way from the local spheres to the world sphere", Mrela and Kostecki, 1981: 119). If Scandinavians are contributing, it is only in a passive way; they write in English, they use American theory as their frame of reference (who doesn't?) and they do not claim specificity. They are simply luckier, or perhaps better, than other provincial social scientists, and as a reward the label "made in the provinces" has been removed from their research. Were they from Poland, for instance, the situation would be different. They would have to add to every title "...in a centrally planned economy", which really means "exotic trivia; of no relevance to normal organizations".

And yet we continue to believe that more interesting than a universal organization theory would be a *set* of organization theories, which can be compared, exchanged and borrowed from. In this paper we shall discuss the empirical basis of Scandinavian organization studies, their culture-bound generality and their relevance in other cultural contexts. In our attempt we shall be referring to Swedish examples more often than to Norwegian or Danish, partly because Sweden seems to be in the lead, and partly because this is the country in which we live and work. In choosing contrasting cultural examples we may refer to

West Germany and Poland more often that statistical representativeness requires, because these are the two cultures of our own origins.

In undertaking this enterprise we know that we are doomed. Hasty generalizations, superficiality, ethnocentrism, stereotyping, unscientific approach – this is a typical bunch of labels only too readily thrown at those indulging in cross-cultural comparisons. We recognize our sin, but the temptation is too great to resist. We are fascinated by the topic, and on this we rest our plea for mercy.

Managerial Practice

Is there anything that distinguishes Swedish managers from managers in other cultures? We hear a lot about the oddities of Japanese management, the peculiarities of Chinese managers and the idiosyncracies of Arab businessmen. In such an exotic context "Western" managers seem to represent a monolithic bloc of uniformity. However, the growing number of studies of multinational corporations provides an accumulation of data from which a more differentiated picture emerges.

Before we move on to cross-cultural research, we should mention a study which became a classic, providing inspiration for many others (e.g. Mintzberg, 1973; Forsblad, 1980; Kotter, 1982). In the early 1950's and very much against the then prevailing normative tradition, Sune Carlsson decided to go and see what managers were actually doing in their companies (Carlsson, 1949; 1952). This first decriptive study of managerial behavior produced surprising results:

Before we made the study, I always thought of a chief executive as the conductor of the orchestra, standing aloof on his platform. Now I am in some respects inclined to see hin as a puppet in a puppet-show with hundreds of people pulling the strings and forcing him to act in one way or another (Carlsson, 1952: 52).

In their own opinion, most of the directors studied did not take part in so many decisions and it was seldom that they gave orders (ibid., 4, 49).

Carlsson did not consider the possibility that his observations might be culture-bound, but such an idea comes readily to mind when his results are confronted with the observations of foreign managers in Swedish MNCs (Hedlund and Åman, 1980). An attempt to discover a "Swedish style of management" (Forss, Hawk and Hedlund, 1984) produced the following observations:

• The organizational structure of Swedish corporations is perceived by foreign managers as ambiguous. There is a preference for complicated matrix structures; double or triple reporting systems are quite common; and the divisions of responsibilities, the allocation of resources and the role expectations are unclear.

- The decision-making process is long and diffused. This trait is described in several variations: as unclear objectives, indecisiveness, slowness, poor visibility over decision processes. "When decisions are made, it is often difficult for foreigners to recognize that they have indeed been made. Cases when such uncertainty has arisen, in spite of the bewildered foreigner having been present at the meeting where the decision was supposedly taken, are reported" (Forss, Hawk and Hedlund, 1984: 13).
- Relations between foreign subsidiaries and their Swedish headquarters are less formalized than in corporations based in the USA, the UK, Japan and Germany, for example (Hedlund, 1981). The control is informal, implicit, but still very compelling.
- There is a very strong tendency to attain consensus accompanied by a tendency to avoid confrontation. Difficult and embarrassing situation are avoided, neither negative nor positive feed-back is very clear, and corrective action against poor performers is exceptional. "It is rare that authority is exercised solely on the basis of formal power, which would be considered suspect" (Forss, Hawk and Hedlund, 1984). This is why "a good Swedish boss with his ideas of democracy and codetermination would be a catastrophe in Germany" (Ledarskap, No 8–9, 1984).

One would expect Swedish organization theorists to rush to explain these phenomena. But this is not the case. Instead we witness an attempt to build a universal theory. Some authors are more involved in this attempt than others, and we will concentrate in the first place on their works. We will also try to use the above observations as a key to an understanding of the emerging theory.

Decision

The history of decision-making theory can be seen as an evolutionary process, in which consecutive stages of development can be easily distinguished. The formal decision-making model (the classical model) was guided by a focus on the outcomes of rational decisions. The rational design of various steps in a decision-making process was supposed to produce maximized outcomes. The way in which a decision should be made was therefore guided by the objectives (outcomes) adopted by those who designed the process. Less attention was paid to the implementation in the organization of the decisions made. This problem was dealt with by other parts of management science and normative administration theories.

Theories are simplifications of reality. One of these simplifications is the conceptual apparatus provided by formal decision models. This apparatus includes:

- the range of alternative decision
- perceived consequences of alternative problem solutions
- the criteria by which consequences are to be evaluated.
- states of environment that might affect the consequences, and
- algorithms that can produce the "best" decision when applied to the above data (Haberstroh, 1982).

The formal model of decision-making may be adequate for handling situations in which uncertainty and guessing do not play a central role. The model does not apply to situations of decision-making under uncertainty or to market situations with imperfect competition (Simon, 1976).

Since the 1950's various modifications have been introduced into the formal model. Unlike the normative formal model, decision-making was investigated with the help of descriptive analysis. Actual decisions as made by real-life decision-makers were compared with the normative rational model. Herbert Simon (1951) introduced the concept of bounded rationality, and the development of this idea is closely related to the behavioral theory of the firm (Cyert and March, 1963).

In contrast to the positive classical model, the evidence for bounded rationality is negative. It describes what people don't do in decision-making processes (Simon, 1978). The positive classical model with its strong normative implications provides us with knowledge about how people should make decisions in complex problem-solving contexts. Whereas the classical decision-making situation is "simple and beautiful" (Simon, 1978: 7) because of its underlying rationalities and its predictive power, the theory of bounded rationality leaves us with a somewhat more complex and unpredictable reality.

Bounded rationality is a rather comprehensive explanation of human striving to achieve the rational gathering and processing of information. The theory takes into account the cost of intelligence and information processing. Intelligence is selective, the definition of a situation is oversimplified and/or subjective; the choices made are biased, etc. The ways in which information is processed constitute a central focus in this descriptive research. The outcomes of the process have been described in terms of optimal (satisfactory, as opposed to maximal) outcomes, in contrast to the descriptions of the classical model.

Both the classical model and the theory of bounded rationality are still based on decision-making as a sequential process. The stated difference between the two does not therefore challenge the assumption of a logical consequence, which pressupposes certain characteristics of decision-making and choices. There has to be a problem to be decided upon, there has to be an argument for the alternative chosen, and there has to be some kind of implementation following these different steps. Further, the descriptions of bounded rationality still assume a specific rationality on the part of the decision-maker involved. Sequential logic is one element of this, but there are also other elements which make the whole process rational from the decision-maker's point of view. Information-gathering and information-processing costs are evaluated in light of the anticipated benefits. It is assumed that the real-life decision-maker will make a rational evaluation of the information costs, and bounded rationality thus still implies at least quasi-rational decisions.

This development in rational decision-making models was challenged at the beginning of the 1970's, when Cohen, March and Olsen (1972) introduced the notion of the "garbage can" as a model for explaining decision-making in organizations. "Irrationality" was introduced as an important concept in decision-making theory.

While the theory of bounded rationality allows for the limitations of decision rationality due to difficulties in anticipating or evaluating all the alternatives or all the information, the garbage-can model (Cohen, March and Olsen, 1972) describes organizations in terms of "anarchy". "Anarchistic" decision situations consist of four loosely linked elements: choice opportunities, problems, solutions and participants. The theory was based on the computerization of these elements in a process. Most of the empirical research has taken place in Scandinavia (March and Olsen, 1976; Enderud, 1977). Essentially a choice opportunity is an occasion when an organization is expected to produce a type of behavior which could be called a decision. Problems occur inside and outside organizations. They are distinct from choices and "they may not be resolved when choices are made" (March and Olsen, 1976: 26–27). Solutions are answers looking for questions, and in organizations people often don't know what the question is until they know the answer. Participants come and go, because of other demands on their time. In organizational decision-making these elements of decision situations are independent of one another. Even if this independence is not complete, the fact that the elements "flow" in separate streams in the organization, makes any coupling between elements a matter of coincidence. The idea of dependencies – causal or logical sequences – is sacrificed in favour of a somewhat irrational world.

Empirical research on actual organizational decision-making has modified the classical model in two important ways: it has revealed the problem of contingency and complexity and the effects of this on limited rationality, and it has revealed the organizational processes which cannot be interpreted from a rational-model point of view at all. But whereas bounded rationality is seen as a sensible adjustment to reality, the notion of "irrationality" or "anarchy" – which in terms of theory could simply represent a challenge – evidently produces anxiety in both the theoretical and practising advocates of efficient organization.

From this point of view the new wave of research can be seen as an attempt to save the concept of rationality in organizations. In a study of the propensity to change, Brunsson (1976) found that while some decisions are made in a way that resembles a bounded rationality model, most are made in a way that can only be called "impressionistic". Managers first form certain impressions about the issue at hand; they then become publicly committed to their opinions and continue to look for arguments confirming their judgements, disregarding alternatives and avoiding contradictory information. Does this mean that their behavior is irrational?

No, says Brunsson. What might seem irrational from the point of view of decision-making is highly rational from the point of view of action. Finding numerous alternatives and looking for contradictory information weakens commitment, reduces motivation and dilutes responsibility. Once the final choice is made no-one feels enthusiastic enough to take on its implementation, which is left to subordinates and which invariably runs into trouble at some point. Thus important "decisions", or rather important actions, are prepared by building up the kind of enthusiasm and commitment that is hampered by "rational decision-making". The impressionistic decision is used afterwards to interpret the action. Decisions and actions are thus mutually dependent, and the classical separation which imposes a purely cognitive character on decisions is useless. A decision is rational only when it prepares properly for action, not when it fulfills a priori criterion of rationality. Such a conceptualization comes very close to the point of view presented by Weick (1979), and the Scandinavian theorists are in fact often inspired by his theory of loose coupling. Is this model a last attempt to save the concept of rationality in organizations? Or is it a logical consequence of developments in decision-making theory over the last three decades, representing a new stage in organization theory? Finally, to what extent can this model describe all organizations rather than specific organizations in a certain culture? In attempting to answer these questions we now turn to other categories of organizational behavior introduced by the model.

Action

The Scandinavian organization researchers thus found existing organization theory to be insufficiently general: based mainly on examples from private industry, it is not really appropriate to an analysis of the public sector. What is more, they noted that the normative decision-model, a central model in organizational theory, does not even apply to private industry. What is needed, then, is a non-normative model or models of organizational behavior which will help us to analyse and understand what actually happens in many types of organization.

Before proceeding to a discussion of concrete proposals, we should comment on some more general issues. In most Scandinavian studies, de-normatization is applied to the middle level of analysis only, i.e. the functional aspect of organizational behavior: how things are being done. When it comes to *what* is being done and *why,* we are left uninstructed. A few scattered comments give us an indication of the ideological stance of some of the relevant authors:

Political work aims at steering societal development towards something better (Brunsson and Jönsson, 1979: 22).

Such an elite role for planners is obviously democratically unacceptable (ibid.: 26).

It is incompatible with our notion of democracy to allow this responsibility (that of politicians toward the citizens) to disperse in a game played for its own sake (ibid.: 31).

Using Morgan's classification of paradigms in organizational theory (Morgan, 1980), we could say that the authors quoted are steering clear of critical paradigms; they can be placed within the functionalist paradigm, but close to the interpretive. This is in fact where Morgan places the "action frame of reference" himself, but up to now this has been more closely connected with the study of culture, theatre etc. than with "hard" organizational reality.

Their critique of the traditional decision-making model leads the authors to call for a more adequate concept for handling organizational phenomena, and action seems to be such a concept:

The decision-making perspective fails to recognize that practitioners do more than make decisions. Making a decision is only a step towards action. A decision is not an end product. Practitioners get things done, act and induce others to act (Brunsson, 1982: 32).

An action perspective will be more fruitful for understanding large areas of organizational behavior. The action perspective explains behavior within attempts to change and differences in abilities to achieve changes (ibid.: 31).

What, then, is an organizational action?

Action takes place within the objective world and yet it is performed by the individual human subject (. . .)
Action involves deliberation and has a rationality.
Action must find a means of outward manifestation to have an impact on the real world.
Action is motion as opposed to rest.
Action is process as opposed to a sudden event.
Action is behaviour not just connected occurrences.
(Jönsson, 1982: 22–23).

The philosophical grounds for this approach bring us in contact with phenomenologists (Tymieniecka, 1978; Wojtyla, 1979; after Jönsson, 1982), as well as one Polish realist, Tadeusz Kotarbinski, whose works have aroused considerable interest among Scandinavian researchers (Kotarbinski, 1972; Guillet de Monthoux, 1981). Kotarbinski's praxiology (a theory of efficient action) is concerned with making action rational and efficient, without considering political contexts (what action is taken or why). Do these characteristics which allowed non-Marxist praxiology to survive in contemporary Poland, also make it attractive to Swedish organization theorists?

Whatever the philosophical grounds and political connotations, the fact remains that Scandinavian researchers are deeply interested in the theory of action, as an alternative to the theory of decision. And none too soon, according to Guillet de Monthoux (1981):

Those who take a deeper interest in the reason for industrialization will in vain search for an explicit theory of industrial action in economic texts. It seems as if the industrial engineers who organize the world of production, as well as the business economists who control its efficiency, lacked a philosophy of their own. Is there really any philosophy behind efficient action other than economics? (p. 2).

This author shares his colleagues' interest in a theory of action, but not their frame of reference. The interpretive functionalists' lack of interest in values is replaced in his case by a very clear individualistic (as opposed to organizational) perspective, and non-involvement is replaced by a modern version of anarcho-existentialism (Guillet de Monthoux, 1983a, 1983b). He prescribes spontaneous action as an antidote for the bureaucratic control that has been imposed on organizations due to the belief in "objectively rational" decisions.

Using the terminology introduced in Lindblom (1979), we could say that Guillet de Monthoux opts for a "partisan mutual adjustment", whereas others indicate that incrementalism is the main course of action:

Getting things done is particularly problematic in political organizations (...) The ideological differences block radical actions because each prepared action is scrutinized from diverse viewpoints (...). Thus, proposed actions that involve major changes are rejected, and the organizations move in small steps (Brunsson, 1982: 43).

Thus, whether from the point of view of individual happiness or of organizational survival, action acquires a central place in organizational studies: "Organizational action is at the same time the raison d'être of the organization and the cause of its main difficulties" (Brunsson, 1985: 5–6). Namely,

(...) organizations have two problems in relation to action – to find out what to do and to do it. When confronting difficult actions, organizations separate these problems. Organizations solve the problem of choice by forming ideologies, then the activities preceding specific actions focus on creating motivations and commitments (Brunsson, 1982: 43).

Empirical studies show that what can be seen as decision irrationality is actually action rationality (Brunsson, 1985). What is important to action is the creation of commitment and motivation, and it is for this purpose that organizational ideologies exist (Jönsson and Lundin, 1977; Hedberg and Jönsson, 1977; Brunsson, 1982; Jönsson, 1982; Brunsson, 1985). This organizational phenomenon (sometimes referred to as "organizational myths") is then operationalized as "organizational talk" (Brunsson, 1984). Ideology or talk, facilitates action, gives meaning to it and sometimes replaces it.

Does this mean that the concept of decision is useless? Not entirely:

(...) decision processes often comprise some of the process associated with action. Because managers and representatives in political bodies describe part of their work as decision-making, decisions and decision-making should remain important topics for study (Brunsson, 1982: 32).

This can be taken to mean that decisions share some of the characteristics of "talk" and some of "action", and the concept must therefore continue to exist, if only because managers insist on it (but maybe managers are inspired by traditional organizational theorists?). The weakness of the "decision" concept within the "Viking theory" will be further analysed and interpreted below.

Talk

Since talk as a category is still emerging, we cannot simply quote descriptions of it from the various Swedish authors. We shall have to reconstruct it, partly quoting, partly guessing, and partly introducing our own comments and suggestions.

The beginnings of this category can be traced back to Jönsson and Lundin's influential paper on "Myths and Wishful Thinking as Management Tools" (Jönsson and Lundin, 1977). Long before "organizational culture" came into fashion, these writers suggested that managers actually control their organizations by using emotionally loaded ideas and visions which help to carry out actions. This notion was then developed in studies of organizational ideologies, and now flourishes in the study of organizational cultures. Perhaps, though, the simpler category of "talk" will prove more resistant to fashion and the passage of time than the many rather ornamental studies of culture.

Talk is a very common form of organizational behavior, although its content varies not only from one organization to another, but also and more distinctly between cultures.

Daun (1985) tell us more about attitudes towards "talk" in Swedish culture as compared to other cultures. In French, spoken words are regarded as "light-weight".

The consequences of what you say are not very important, because afterwards you are not held to what you have said. Language is extremely important in conversational situations. Words and views are to be played with, and a person can express opinions which he does not really hold, just to liven the conversation. Talking is considered a pleasure in the French culture, not in the Swedish (Daun, 1985: 10).

"Talk" in Swedish implies transmitting important information by means of language. "Talk" as an alternative or complement to organizational decision-making and action therefore implies a specific quality of functional communication in organizational contexts. There should be very few emotional elements in "talk", as Brunsson uses the term (1984). As Daun (1985) points out, Swedish culture is strongly conflict avoiding. Thus talking has no useful role in conflict-resolution, or rather conflict-dissolution, as it has in other organizational settings. "Talk" is not an instrument for ventilating strong emotions. "The strongly held attitude in the Swedish culture and society in favor of objective argument" equates "sensible behavior with maturity or adulthood, in contrast to childish behavior which is ruled by emotions" (Daun, 1985: 11).

What, then, is the function of talk in organizations in general and in Swedish organizations in particular? Brunsson (1984) speaks of two ideal types of organization: *reflecting organizations* (their function in society is to reflect correctly the interests of their constituencies – e.g. political organizations) and *acting organizations* (e.g. business organizations). We therefore suggest that "talk" can be regarded as the main activity of the former type. "Talk" then no longer appears as something inappropriate, a fake or ersatz action, but as an activity proper to a certain kind of organization and quite common in all of them. The popular saying "stop talking, start acting" may not make much sense in certain organizational surroundings.

Talk is also a powerful means of change, due to its capacity for arousing emotions, describing commitment and maintaining involvement.

Talk can also serve as a means of organizational catharsis and as a means of communication. These two functions of talk, however, are severely limited in Swedish organizations. This statement may seem paradoxical. If "talk" is so important in Swedish organizations, does it not mean that communication is also important? Are we saying that communication is faulty in Sweden? Such a statement runs counter to the common view of the country. It is a small society, covered by a dense communications network. It is an open society, because in principle information is accessible to everyone. But as information is primarily task-oriented, so is communication. As Weick (1983) points out, the relationship between talk and communication is far from clear. Talk is not simply communication. What is more, task-oriented communication is functional in a task situation, but in interpersonal settings it may be dysfunctional. These functions melt into one another in organizational settings, and it is not at all clear what is effective communication in what situation. "Talk" is certainly an attempt to communicate, but so are wars, as Vickers (1972) reminds us. In fact, it is very easy to obtain information in Sweden, but it is very difficult to become informed. One is left with a pile of computer printouts, and is none the wiser: Effective communication, as opposed to information delivery, requires not only transmission of information but also a corrective feedback to ensure that the recipient understood the message. This assumes a parity between transmitter and receiver which is prevented from occurring by another institutionalized device: specialization. Specialization is a very important feature of Swedish society, and according to Anton (1980) one that is more highly developed there than in most other countries. The dense networks which we have mentioned are based and maintained on the specialization principle. The communication between specialists and laymen, or even between different specialists, is not on an equal footing; it tends to be a one-way affair. And so common sense often gives way to abstract rationality, supported by the professional authority which specialists so enjoy.

Talk, Decision and Action

Hence, in place of the traditional decision-making model, we have a new model of organizational behavior, composed of three elements loosely linked to one another, as shown in Figure 1.

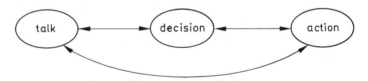

Figure 1:   The New Model of Organizational Behavior.

In our own two countries, Poland and West Germany, talk is highly elaborate as well as being privilege of the higher hierarchic levels. Bottom-level employees do not participate in it, as they know that they exert little or no influence, and they watch only for certain formal attributes which will have important consequences for action. In the meantime they may engage in some spontaneous action, disconnected from talk and motivated by their personal goals or by a sheer will to do something. According to some radical views, it is entirely thanks to these spontaneous actions that organizations actually accomplish anything. Be that as it may, the employees do some acting while waiting for a signal. From the stream of incessant talk signals emerge, in the shape of directives, pieces of information, incentives. These signals are called "decisions", and their origins are rather unclear and comparatively irrelevant – what is important about them is that they indicate a legitimate starting-point for action.

Again, action is only loosely connected with decision: action may consist of the opposite of what a decision proclaims, or it may mean putting a stop to a previous action. A typical remark on the part of a Polish manager who has heard of a debate at central headquarters, is: "I won't move a toe until I see a decision in writing, until they tell me what the decision is".

Action is also loosely connected with talk, and the relation is mainly concerned with the formal characteristics of talk: for example, if several powerful parties are fiercely fighting one another, it may be wiser not to start any action even if a decision has been reached, because there is a good chance that it will soon be changed.

One thing is clear: "talk" (to which planning certainly belongs) has an uncertainty-reducing function for "decision-makers", and "decision" has an uncertainty-reducing function for "executors", whereas action produces un-certainty since it changes reality and thus provides new grounds for subsequent talk and decisions. If action ceased to be, organizations would be perfectly secure places – as Parkinson tried to show us.

So what do the non-Swedish managers mean when they say that Swedes make no decisions? In light of our own experience we have to agree with them: in Swedish organizations talk seems to blend into action and vice versa without any intermediary step.

Several stories are told by foreigners – academics and business people, members of service organizations and various authorities – about Swedish organizational behavior. A meeting has ended and nothing has been decided, and yet nobody asks what action should be taken. Sometimes it is just the reverse: the foreigner is sure that a decision has been reached, and then learns that it hasn't. If we insist on detecting decisions in Swedish organizations, the best way is probably to deduce them from some irreversible action: if the removal trucks have arrived, the office is most likely going to move. Whether or not this is a good thing is hard to say, but for people from other cultures it creates great uncertainty.

This line of reasoning led us to see "uncertainty" as a key concept in explaining specific attributes of Viking organizations and of the Viking theory. Hofstede's monumental work on the consequences of culture (1980) helped us in this endeavour. One of the dimensions which he found in his data he designated as "uncertainty avoidance":

Uncertainty about the future is a basic fact of human life with which we try to cope through domains of technology, law and religion. In organizations these take the form of technology, rules and rituals (p. 153).

It should be added that the avoidance of uncertainty is usually accompanied by a search for it. Uncertainty is a source of anxiety, but also of creativity, the joy of surprise, and many of the pleasures of life. We seek it by placing ourselves in risk situations, by looking for adventure, by abolishing old orders. Thus, it is not uncertainty per se which human beings find threatening, but situations in which the degree of uncertainty exceeds the threshold of tolerance, be it individual or cultural.

Hofstede's collected data showed that the tolerance of uncertainty varies considerably among employees in different countries, and three indicators – rule orientation, employment stability and stress – formed an Uncertainty Avoidance Index (UAI). A comparison of 40 countries placed Sweden third from the bottom as regards UAI and, after controlling for age, in the very bottom position.

That result alone would be enough to account for the fact that Swedes tend to neglect many uncertainty-reducing organizational processes, emphasizing instead such uncertainty-producing process as action. This tendency can also be explained by a stability in the environment, uninterrupted by wars or violent social movements and reinforced by a well-organized welfare state.

There are many temptations to indulge in "whys" and "hows", but being neither historians nor anthropologists we will turn away from them. Our interest is in description, as it serves us to explain the pecularities of organizational studies as we see them, and the organizational life.

If we accept the assumption that Swedish employees are less prone to avoid uncertainty in task situations, than it should be obvious that many uncertainty-reducing mechanisms employed elsewhere will not be used in Swedish organizations, and that those which are used are likely to be of a different kind.

Hofstede says that apart from technology and rules (which can be regarded as typical uncertainty-reducing means in all modern organizations), a whole array of rituals is used:

1. memos and reports with no significant information
2. accounting systems
3. planning systems
4. control systems
5. use of experts.

We do not have enough data on the first and fourth of these, so we shall concentrate on the other three.

Brunsson and Jönsson's "Beslut och handling" (1979) dedicates much space to the role of planning processes. They conclude that:

Planning is excellent employment for those who want to avoid action (p. 32).

Yet, if we accept the three-element model we have been discussing, it becomes clear that planning, loosely connected with action, belongs to the category of "talk" and as such has a very important function to perform: that of uncertainty-reduction. "Having a planning system (...) allows managers to sleep more peacefully, even if it does not really work" (Hofstede, 1980: 160). Action produces uncertainty, whereas planning changes the perception of reality towards a more structured version.

Brunsson and Jönsson (1979) deny this, claiming that:

The above-described properties of the planning processes create great opportunities for producing uncertainty (p. 76).

It is often easier to be certain about a general direction in which some work should be going, or which type of measures are desired, than to be certain about the correctness of all the details connected with a decision concerning a single measure (p. 106).

And the normative prescriptions go even further:

Organizations have many stabilizers but quite often lack proper destabilizers (...) Current information – and accounting – systems do more to stabilize organizations than to destabilize them. They filter away conflicts, ambiguities, overlaps, uncertainty etc. and they suppress many relevant change signals and kill initiatives to act on early warnings (Hedberg and Jönsson, 1978: 47).

What is very interesting, however, is the use of experts in Swedish organizations. According to our line of argument, we would not expect to find any great need for experts. But this is far from being the case: the number of business consultants per capita must be higher than in the U.S. How is this to be explained in a context of low uncertainty-avoidance?

Hofstede says that we cope with uncertainty through technology, law and religion. It is on this last element that we would like to concentrate here. Sweden's dominant religion is rationality (see also Anton, 1975; Gouldner, 1975; Daun, 1985). One could argue that rationality is a general Western religion. To a certain degree this is so, but we claim that the degree is higher in Sweden than elsewhere. It could then be claimed that rationality is the main religion of all organizations, and again we say this is true only up to a certain point. There is a profit religion and an obedience religion, both of which are quite different from the worship of rationality as such.

What are the consequences of this creed? One is that certain elements present in other religions are lacking, particularly those in which esthetic aspects such as myths and ceremonies prevail over functional aspects. In a study of Polish and American managers (Czarniawska, 1985a) evidence was found of strong myths concerning the origin of organizational effectiveness, whereas an extension of the study to Swedish managers revealed a myth which was actually a rationalized version of certain events in Swedish history. When Jönsson and Lundin (1977) speak of "myths as managerial tools", they actually mean situationally created ideologies, concrete projects which serve to guide the performance of organizational members, rather than myths.[1]) There are rituals, but they are stripped of ceremonal. We could say that Swedish rituals are highly rational; ornament, fantasy, coloring and role-playing have no great part in them.

Legitimacy, Rationality and Responsibility

So far we have discussed organizational practice, and theories about this practice, and we have developed some insights concerning the main focus of Scandinavian empirical studies. In this section we shall discuss the phenomena from an analytical point of view. We use the concepts of legitimacy, responsibility and rationality, which are commonly used in Scandinavian organization research as concepts for the interpretation of organizational reality. The Scandinavian authors are not alone in this endeavour; indeed, these notions are widely used by other researchers as well (see e.g. Epstein and Votaw, 1975). There is, however, a certain specificity, both in the way they are understood and the importance assigned to them in the research we are discussing.

The astonishing success of the idea of "legitimacy", borrowed essentially from Weber via Offe (1972) and Habermas (1975), can be seen as a functionalist's half-hearted admission of the existence of a larger value system (see e.g. Dowling and Pfeffer, 1975). So long as we note that organizations try to achieve legitimacy, we are free from the obligation of analysing the values of the larger system, and we can safely focus on studying whatever antics organizations choose to produce.

An alternative or perhaps a complementary explanation would regard the analytical notion of legitimacy as a trademark of public sector research (see e.g. Meyer and Rowan, 1977). As the public sector is the law-giver and law-enforcer, being legitimate is the minimum requirement that its organization have to fulfill.

Both observations can be applied to the Swedish organization research that we have discussed above. The concept of legitimation as used in current Swedish research is based on public sector and political organizations (Brunsson and Rombach, 1982; Brunsson and Wolff, 1984; Brunsson, 1985). There is an additional aspect, however, which makes the concept even more important.

---

[1]) Following Cohen (1979: 337), we understand myth as "a narrative of events; the narrative has a sacred quality; the sacred communication is made in a symbolic form; at least some of the events and objects which occur in the myth neither occur nor exist in the world other than that of myth itself; and the narrative refers in a dramatic form to origins and transformations".

The Scandinavian countries are characterized by a widespread acceptance of and identification with the societal value system. This can be observed both among practitioners (Czarniawska, 1985) and researchers. "Legitimation" then acquires a leading position among the analytical concepts used to explain organizational behavior. At the 7th EGOS Colloquium in Saltsjöbaden in June 1985, a discussion under the heading "Legitimation in organizations" attracted almost exclusively Scandinavian researchers.

What categories of organizational behavior can be explained with the help of the concept of legitimacy? As we have mentioned before, "reflecting" (political) organizations use talk to legitimate their existence, while business organizations use action for the same purpose. Decisions seem to have been dropped. However, in certain contexts they do appear to be the main legitimating device. Retail organizations in Poland cannot be legitimated by their actions, as these are determined by suppliers; talk is not supposed to be their main activity; what else remains but decisions?

For a long time the concept of rationality was connected with decision-making, and Scandinavian research helped to separate the two. We have discussed this at some length above and do not want to repeat ourselves. So let us return to questions formulated in section 3. Does the new idea of "action rationality" announce the death of rationality as a major analytical concept (Brunsson's new book, published in 1985, is called "The irrational organization")? Is it an attempt to save the concept by linking it to the more viable category of action? If it is true that rationality is the main Swedish religion, the first suggestion is very unlikely. We could say, rather, that rationality is being disconnected from "decision", which is regarded as a relatively weak category, and is being linked instead to the more important categories of talk and action.

The concept of responsibility derives from accounting (Olson, 1983). As Jönsson (1985) shows, accounting practice and theory has long guided Swedish business administration, in the same way as it has guided German. Accounting helps to create responsibility centers and coordination among these centers, and it implies the possibility of control (Anthony and Herzlinger, 1975; Olson, 1983).

Generally, the concept of responsibility is strongly connected with decision-making and power. Responsibility is seen as an essential factor in determining both means and ends. The access to decisions about means and ends is asymmetrically distributed in organizations. The right to decide therefore implies power which serves as an important analytical concept of clarification and explanation. This is not the case in Swedish organizational research.[2]) Nevertheless, responsibility is connected with decision-making.

---

[2]) Recently some attempts to re-introduce "power" can be observed (Daudi, 1984; Lundin and Sköldberg, 1985).

The responsibility aspect of decision-making does not only help to explain decision processes but also why formal decisions are made at all, why organizations call certain activities decision-making, why decisions are visible and along what criteria decision-makers are chosen. Organizations can be expected to make formal and visible decisions when they consider responsibility to be an important aspect (Brunsson, 1984: 17).

However, Brunsson (1984) has also noted that by decentralizing budgets, i.e. control over money, organizations are delegating not only responsibility but also influence. The two may go together, but do not have to. Responsibility, understood rationally within the framework of accounting theory (Olson, 1983) fails to explain many phenomena observed in practice.

In traditional organizational research, power (or control) is used as an explanatory concept related to decisions, and in fact we could say that "power" encompasses both responsibility and influence, even if their proportions and relations vary. Czarniawska (1985b), studying the role perceptions of executives in the public service sector in Sweden, found that many respondents said: "I do not have power, I have responsibility". One wonders why the concept of power is not used in the explanatory framework of organization theories in Sweden, in order to elaborate its interconnectedness with decision behavior. We suggest that the fact that decisions are the least important type of organizational behavior induces a translocation of relevant analytical concepts. What we would call "power" is divided into "responsibility" and "influence" (the latter rarely discussed). Thus, the concept of responsibility as socially attributed causality can be linked with talk (talk is necessary to distribute responsibility), whereas the term "influence" relates better to action. Decisions increasingly emerge as the weakest concept in the triangle of orgnizational behavior.

We will disregard the question of links between legitimacy, rationality and responsibility, as this lies outside the acceptable limits of the present paper. We would like to conclude by recommending the use of the Swedish contribution in formulating a general analytical model, which can and should be filled with varying organizational behavior: talk, decision and action in fact provide us with a broader perspective than the former concentration on decision-making. Their characteristics and mutual relationships will vary in different organizations and different cultures. The three categories can also be interpreted with the help of three analytical concepts: legitimacy, rationality and power (embracing both responsibility and influence). Again, the links between the analytical concepts and the categories of behavior can vary; there is no reason not to apply all the analytical concepts to each category of behavior. And, finally, the analytical concepts themselves cannot be seen as ultimate and objective categories of analysis, but must be derived from a given socio-cultural context in which they function. Not only their meaning but also their relative importance probably varies from one context to another.

The model can thus be regarded as being composed of three spheres which can be moved by the researcher at will (Figure 2).

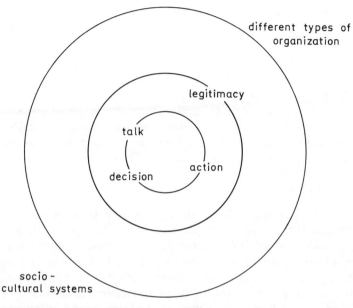

Figure 2:   The Formal Model of Organizational Analysis

By using a common formal model, we facilitate the possibility of comparison and reciprocal learning. However, there is always a danger that the form will dominate the substance. Some of these categories may be irrelevant in non-Western cultures, and some others altogether may prove to be more appropriate. So long as we remember that models are tools for achieving a better understanding and not the end result of the research process, we won't waste our time besieging fortresses which we have built ourselves.

Making Sense of Viking Life

Swedish organization theory as developed during the last decade is a descriptive rather than a prescriptive theory. Brunsson (1982) characterizes the aim of this research as "language building" – researchers provide practitioners with empirically grounded theory. The theories are meant to help them to structure their everyday life by means of a theoretical language. This approach is not explicitly value-avoiding, but it stems from an implicitly functional point of view and perpetuates this functional basis.

We would like to add two comments. First, that a descriptive theory requires empirical research. The absence of such research is not always the result of the researchers' theoretical preferences. The access problems which German students of organization, for example, have to overcome whenever they approach an empirical study, fully explains the number and the sophistication of German theoretical papers. Briefly, this is an appeal to practitioners: if you want a theory which applies to practice, give us the chance to see this practice first.

Secondly, we would like to point out that it is hard to construct a complete explanatory language, without getting involved in phenomena which fall outside the organizational context. And a neutral explanatory language is not much use to practitioners who want change rather than status quo, as the action rationality concept has shown us. Thus, we predict that it will be necessary for Swedish researchers to leave the quiet haven of functionalism for the troubled waters of broader sociopolitical contexts.

The frame of reference of Swedish organization theory has been extended from decision-making to action theory. It now comprises both frames of reference and clarifies their reciprocal relationship. Decisions are to be understood in the light of action and vice versa. This shift or extension of the theoretical perspective implies the existence of different kinds of rationalities: decision rationality, action rationality and the reciprocal rationality of decision and action. But whereas the idea of the garbage-can acknowledges the existence of irrationality in everyday organizational life, the implicitly functional perspective in Swedish organization theory tries to save rationality by explaining irrationalities as rationalities of a different type. To break this vicious circle it would be sufficient to accept the existence of irrationality as an important element in organizational life. "Emotionallity" is perhaps a better term, and one long since proposed by psychologists; it is also the one which makes of rationality a relative rather than an absolute concept.

These are the contributions that Viking organization theory can make, and we believe them to be extremely important. It should be added, however, that the empirical basis of these studies has been mainly provided by municipalities, universities, and public sector organizations. The choice, then is, either to limit the theory to these organizations or to extend it by including business firms to a much greater degree. Otherwise we will find the next generation of critical researchers declaring that the theory of action rationality does not apply to the private sector, just as the classical model was said not to apply to the public sector.

We suggest that the importance of these contributions can be enhanced, not by translating them into universal truths but by placing them in a relevant cultural and societal context. March (1980) reminds us that making sense of organizational life is complicated by the fact that organizations exist on various levels. The first is the level of practice, where organizations cope with the environment and experience and where learned routines are predominant. A second level is that of interpretation, where we fit our history into an understanding of life.

This level is dominated by intellect and metaphors of theory (March, 1980). The distinction between theories-in-use and theoretical interpretations (Argyris, 1974) allows for the fact that managers act *and* reflect, whereas researchers reflect mostly about the theories-in-use. But there is also a third level which is the subject of this paper. Theories-in-use and organization theories are culture-bound. Theories-in-use and academic organization theories both choose similar frames of reference for the interpretation of organizational action and processes, if the doer and the thinker have both been socialized within the same cultural bounds. And these frames of reference, taken for granted by managers and researchers belonging to the same culture, are far from obvious to actors and observers from another culture.

Culture is usually treated as a contingency variable in organization theory (Hofstede, 1980). We argue for a "third-level interpretation", whereby culture is itself a broader context which serves as a frame of reference for interpreting "organizing" and organizations in particular societies.

References

Anthony, R. N., Herzlinger, R. (1975) *Management and Control in Non-profit Organizations*. Homewood, Ill.: Irwin.

Anton, T. J. (1980) *Administered Politics*. Boston: Martinus Nijhoff.

Argyris, Ch. (1977) Organizational Learning and Management Information Systems. *Accounting, Organization and Society*, 2, pp. 113–123.

Brunsson, N. (1976) *Propensity to Change*. Göteborg: BAS.

– (1982) The Irrationality of Action and Action Rationality: Decisions, Ideologies and Organizational Actions. *Journal of Management Studies*, 19, 1, pp. 29–44.

– (1984) *Decision-Making as Responsibility Allocation*. Typescript, Stockholm: EFI.

– (1985) *The Irrational Organization*. New York: Wiley.

– Organizing for Inconsistencies. Forthcoming in Scandinavian Journal of Management Studies.

Brunsson, N., Jönsson, S. (1979) *Beslut och handling*. Falköping: Liber.

Brunsson, N., Rombach, B. (1982) *Går det att spara?* Lund: Doxa.

Brunsson, N., Wolff, R. (1984) *Industripolitisk rationalitet*. Stockholm EFI, School of Economics.

Carlsson, S. (1949) *Företagsledning och företagsledare*. Stockholm: Nordisk Rotogravyr.

– (1952) *Executive Behavior: A Study of the Work Load and the Working Methods of Managing Directors.* Stockholm: Strömbergs.

Cohen, P. S. (1969) Theories of Myth. *Man,* 4, pp. 337–353.

Cohen, M. D., March, J. G., Olsen, J. P. (1972) A Garbage Can Model of Organizational Choice. *Administrative Science Quarterly,* March, pp. 1–25.

Cyert, R. M., March, J. G. (1963) *A Behavioral Theory of the Firm.* Englewood Cliffs, N. J.: Prentice Hall.

Czarniawska, B. (1985a) Controlling Top Management in Large Organisations. Aldershot: Gower.

Czarniawska, B. (1985b) Public Sector Executives: Managers or Leaders? Stockholm: EFI, Stockholm School of Economics.

Daudi, Ph. (1984) *Makt, Diskurs och Handling.* Dissertation, Lund.

Daun, Å. (1985) *Swedishness as an Obstacle in Cross-cultural Interactions.* (forthcoming), Ethnologia Europea, 2.

Dowling, J., Pfeffer, J. (1976) Organizational Legitimacy. *Pacific Sociological Review,* 18, pp. 122–136.

Enderud, H. G. (1977) *Four Faces of Leadership in an Academic Organization.* Copenhagen: Busck.

Epstein, E. M., Votaw, D. (Ed.) (1978) *Rationality, Legitimacy, Responsibility.* Santa Monica, Cal.: Goodyear Publishing Company.

Forsblad, P. (1980) *Företagsledares beslutsinflytande.* Dissertation, Stockholm: EFI, Stockholm School of Economics.

Forss, K., Hawk, D., Hedlund, G. (1984) *Cultural Differences – Swedishness in Legislation, Multinational Corporations and Aid Administration.* Stockholm: Stockholm School of Economics.

Gouldner, A. W. (1975) *Renewal and Critique in Sociology Today.* Harmonworth: Penguin.

Graumann, C. F. (1976) *Modification by Migration: Vicissitudes of Cross-National Communication.* Social Research, Vol. 43, No. 2.

Habermas, J. (1976) *Legitimation Crisis.* London: Heinemann.

Haberstroh, C. J. (1982) *Decision Making.* Working Paper.

Hedberg, B., Jönsson, S. (1979) Designing Semi-Confusing Information Systems for Organizations in Changing Environments. *Accounting, Organization and Society,* Vol. 3, No. 1, pp. 47–64.

Hedlund, G. (1981) Anatomy of Subsidaries and Formalization of Headquarters-Subsidary Relations in Swedish MNCs. *The Management of Headquarters – Subsidary Relationships in Multinational Corporations.* Otterbeck, L. (Ed.) Guildford: Gower.

Hofstede, G. (1980) *Culture's Consequences.* Beverly Hills and London: Sage.

Jönsson, S. (1982) *A City Administration Facing Stagnation.* Stockholm: BFR.

– (1986) Mental Standardization and Industrial Development. *Organizing Industrial Development.* R. Wolff (Ed.) Berlin – New York: De Gruyter.

– Lundin, R. (1977) Myth and Wishful Thinking as Management Tools. *North Holland TIMS Studies in the Management Sciences,* 5, pp. 157–170.

Kassem, M. S. (1976) European vs. American Organization Theory. *European Contributions to Organization Theory.* G. Hofstede and M. S. Kassem (Ed.), Assen.

Kotarbinski, T. (1975) *Traktat o Dobrej Robocie.* Wroclaw: Zaklady im. Ossolinskich.

Kotter, J. P. (1982) *The General Managers*. New York – London: Collier Macmillan.

Lindblom, Ch. E. (1979) Still Muddling, Not Yet Through. *Public Administration Review,* November/December.

Lundin, R., Sköldberger, K. (1985) Power as Process. Paper presented at the 7th EGOS Colloquium. *Challenges to Organizational Authority.* Saltsjöbaden, June.

March, J. G. (1978) Bounded Rationality, Ambiguity, and the Engineering of Choice. *Bell Journal of Economics,* pp. 587–608.

– (1980) How We Talk and How We Act: Administrative Theory and Administrative Life. David D. Henry Lecture on Administration, Urbana-Campaign: University of Illinois. September 25.

March, J. G., Olsen, J. P. (1976) *Ambiguity and Choice in Organizations.* Bergen: Universitetsforlaget.

Meyer, J., Rowan, B. (1977) Institutionalized Organizations: Formal Structure as Myth and Ceremony. *American Journal of Sociology,* 83, pp. 340–363.

Mintzberg, H. (1973) *The Nature of Managerial Work.* New York: Harper & Row.

Monthoux, Pierre Guillet de (1981) *If Walesa was a Work Philosopher?* Studies in Economics and Organization of Action. Lund: University of Lund.

– (1983) *Läran om Företaget: Från Quesnay till Keynes.* Stockholm: Norstedt.

– *Action and Existence: Anarchism for Business Administration.* London: Wiley.

Morgan, G. (1980) Paradigms, Metaphors and Puzzle-Solving in Organization Theory. *Administrative Science Quarterly,* 15, pp. 605–622.

Mrela, K., Kostecki, M. J. (1981) Social Sciences Usurped: Reflections on the Americanization of Sociology. *Barriers and Perspectives.* Warszawa: PAN.

Offe, C. (1972) *Strukturprobleme des kapitalistischen Staates.* Frankfurt: Suhrkamp.

Olson, O. (1983) *Ansvar och Ändamål.* Lund: Doxa.

Simon, H. A. (1978) *Rational Decision-Making in Business Organizations.* The Nobel Foundation, November, 24.

Svensk Chef i Tyskland (1984) *Ledarskap Ekonomen,* Stockholm, No. 8/9, September, pp. 16–19.

Tymieniecka, A. T. (1978) *The Prototype of Action. Ethical or Creative? Annalecta Husserliana,* Vol. VII, Dordrecht: Reidel.

Vickers, G. (1972) *Freedom in a Rocking Boat.* London: Penguin.

Weick, K. E. (1983) Organizational Communication: Toward a Research Agenda. *Communication and Organizations. An Interpretive Approach.* L. Putnam and M. E. Pacanowsky (Eds.), Beverly Hills et al.: Sage.

– (1979) *The Social Psychology of Organizing.* Reading, Mass.: Addison-Wesley.

Wojtyla, K. (1979) *The Acting Person.* Dordrecht: Reidel.

Theories of Choice
and Making Decisions[1]?

James G. March

Actual decision making, particularly in organizations, often contrasts with the visions of decision making implicit in theories of choice. Because our theoretical ideas about choice are partly inconsistent with what we know about human processes of decision, we sometimes fail to understand what is going on in decision making, and consequently sometimes offer less than perfect counsel to decision makers. Behavioral research on how decisions are made does not lead to precise prescriptions for the management of choice. It will not tell the president of the United States, the president of Mitsubishi, or the reigning mafioso how to make decisions. Nor will it tell a headmistress of a private academy what she should do as she decides what new programs to offer, whom to hire, what kinds of staff development to authorize, what uniforms to prescribe, what new rooms to build, what kinds of disciplinary procedures to implement, and what kinds of promises to make to what kinds of patrons. However, the research results may contain a few observations that might – when combined with a headmistress's own knowledge and imagination – provide clues of how to think about decision making. In that spirit, this article attempts to summarize some recent work on how decisions are made in organizations. It draws heavily on work I have done jointly with Michael Cohen, Martha Feldman, Johan Olsen, Guje Sevón, and Zur Shapira.

Rational Choice

Virtually all of modern economics and large parts of anthropology, psychology, political science, and sociology, as well as the applied fields that build upon them, embrace the idea that human action is the result of human choice. Our theories of human behavior, like our ordinary conversations and our pop visions of ethics, present life as choice, comprehensible and justifiable primarily in terms of decisions made by human actors. Moreover, these theories of

---

[1] This article is based on a paper presented at the annual meeting of the American Association for the Advancement of Science. Reprint from: *Society*, Vol. 20, No. 1, Nov./Dec. 1982: 29–39.

choice are theories of willful choice. They presume that choices are made intentionally in the name of individual or collective purpose, and on the basis of expectations about future consequences of current actions. If we wish to understand behavior in such terms, we ask three questions: Who made the decision? What were the decision maker's preferences? What expectations did the decision maker have about the consequences of the alternatives? If we wish to change behavior, we seek to change the decision maker, the preferences, or the expectations.

These two fundamental ideas – that life is choice and that choice is willful – are self-evidently useful ideas. They are as much a part of human history and human culture as the wearing of clothing. To suggest that life is more (or less) than choice and that choice is not always best understood as willful is not to propose the overthrow of Bentham or the restoration of Coleridge, but simply to argue that our ideas of choice, like our clothing, can sometimes get in the way.

Standard theories of choice view decision making as intentional, consequential action based on four things:

- A knowledge of alternatives. Decision makers have a set of alternatives for action. These alternatives are defined by the situation and known unambiguously.
- A knowledge of consequences. Decision makers know the consequences of alternative action, at least up to a probability distribution.
- A consistent preference ordering. Decision makers have objective functions by which alternative consequences of action can be compared in terms of their subjective value.
- A decision rule. Decision makers have rules by which to select a single alternative of action on the basis of its consequences for the preferences.

In the most familiar form of the model, we assume that all alternatives, the probability distribution of consequences conditional on each alternative, and the subjective value of each possible consequence are known; and we assume a choice is made by selecting the alternative with the highest expected value.

The durability of this structure has been impressive. It is also understandable. Simple choice models capture some truth. Demand curves for consumer products generally have negative slopes, and labor unions usually are more resistant to wage cuts than to wage increases. Moreover, the core ideas are flexible. When the model seems not to fit, it is often possible to reinterpret preferences or knowledge and preserve the axioms. Finally, choice is a faith as well as a theory; it is linked to the ideologies of the Enlightenment. The prevalence of willful choice models of behavior in economics, political science, psychology, sociology, linguistics, and anthropology attests to the attractiveness of choice as a vision of human behavior.

The attraction extends to ordinary discourse and journalism. A reading of the leading newspapers or journals of any Western country will show that the primary interpretive model used by individuals in these societies is one of willful choice. The standard explanation provided for the actions of individuals or institutions involves two assertions: Someone decided to have it happen. They decided to have it happen because it was in their self-interest to do so. In cases involving multiple actors, a third assertion may be added: Different people, in their own self-interest, wanted different things and the people with power got what they wanted. Ideas of willful, rational choice are the standard terms of discourse for answering the generic questions: Why did it happen? Why did you do it?

The same basic structure underlies modern decision engineering. Operations analysis, management science, decision theory, and the various other analytical approaches to improving choices are variations on a theme of rational choice, as are standard ideas for determining the value of information and the design of information systems. These efforts at improving the decisions of individuals and organizations have been helpful. Systematic rational analyses of choice alternatives have improved the blending of aviation fuel, the location of warehouses, the choice of energy sources, and the arrangement of bank queues, as well as providing the solutions to many other decision problems. And although it is also possible to cite examples in which the consequences of decision analysis have been less benign, a balanced judgment must conclude that these modern technologies of choice have done more good than harm.

Within such a framework, the advice we give to a headmistress is straightforward: Determine precisely what your alternatives are. Define clearly what your preferences are. Estimate the possible consequences stemming from each alternative and their likelihood of occurrence. Select the alternative that will maximize the expected value.

This basic theory of choice has been considerably elaborated over the past thirty years with the discovery of computational procedures for solving problems and the development of various more specific models within the general frame. At the same time, empirical research on the ways in which decisions are actually made by individuals and organizations has identified some problems in fitting the standard theory of choice to observed decision behavior.

Uncertainty and Ambiguity

Theories of choice presume two improbably precise guesses about the future: a guess about the future consequences of current actions and a guess about future sentiments with respect to those consequences. Actual decision situations often seem to make both guesses problematic.

The first guess – about the uncertain future consequences of current action – has attracted attention from both students of decision making and choice theorists. In fact, some of the earliest efforts to relate studies of decision making and theories of choice raised questions about the informational assumptions of the theories. Even if decisions are made in a way generally consistent with choice theories – that is, that estimates of the consequences of alternative actions are formed and that action is *intendedly* rational – there are informational and computational limits on human choice. There are limits on the number of alternatives that can be considered, and limits on the amount and accuracy of information that is available. Such a set of ideas leads to the conception of limited rationality for which Herbert Simon received the Nobel Prize in 1978.

The core ideas are elementary and by now familiar. Rather than all alternatives or all information about consequences being known, information has to be discovered through search. Search is stimulated by a failure to achieve a goal, and continues until it reveals an alternative that is good enough to satisfy existing, evoked goals. New alternatives are sought in the neighborhood of old ones. Failure focuses search on the problem of attaining goals that have been violated, success allows search resources to move to other domains. The key scarce resource is attention; and theories of limited rationality are, for the most part, theories of the allocation of attention.

They are also theories of slack – that is, unexploited opportunities, undiscovered economies, waste, etc. As long as performance exceeds the goal, search for new alternatives is modest, slack accumulates, and aspirations increase. When performance falls below the goal, search is stimulated, slack is decreased, and aspirations decrease. This classic control system does two things to keep performance and goals close. First, it adapts goals to performance: that is, decision makers learn what they should expect. At the same time, it adapts performance to goals by increasing search and decreasing slack in the face of failure, by decreasing search and increasing slack when faced with success. To the familiar pattern of fire alarm management are added the dynamics of changes in aspirations and slack buffers.

These ideas have been used to explore some features of adaptation to a changing environment. Decision makers appear often to be able to discover new efficiencies in their operations under conditions of adversity. If we assume that decision makers optimize, it is not immediately obvious why new economies can be discovered under conditions of adversity if they could not be discovered during good times. The explanation is natural in the slack version of adaptation. During favorable times, slack accumulates. Such slack becomes a reservoir of search opportunities during subsequent periods of trouble. As a result, environmental fluctuations are dampened by the decision process. Such a description seems to provide a partial understanding of the resilience of human institutions in the face of adversity.

Thus, in the case of our headmistress, we would expect that so long as the academy prospered, slack would accumulate. Control over the pursuit of private pleasures by staff members would be relaxed: search for improvements in existing programs would be lackadaisical: discipline would decline. If, on the other hand, a major patron were dissatisfied, or demand for the product weakened, or a loss in quality recorded, then discipline and control would be tightened and search for refinements in existing techniques would be stimulated. As a result, we would probably expect that refinements of existing techniques in the academy, or more energetic performances, would be more likely during times of adversity, but that, because of the extra slack, experiments with unusual new techniques would be more common during times of success.

Partly as a result of such observations by students of decision making, theories of choice have placed considerable emphasis on ideas of search, attention, and information costs in recent years, and these efforts in combination with concern for the problems of incomplete information and transaction costs have turned substantial parts of recent theories of choice into theories of information and attention – tributes to the proposition that information gathering, information processing, and decision making impose heavy demands on the finite capacity of the human organism. Aspiration levels, incrementalism, slack, and satisfaction have been described as sensible under fairly general circumstances.

The second guess – about the uncertain future preferences for the consequences of current actions – has been less considered, yet poses, if anything, greater difficulties. Consider the following properties of preferences as they appear in standard theories of choice:

- Preferences are *absolute*. Theories of choice assume action in terms of preferences: but they recognize neither discriminations among alternative preferences, nor the possibility that a person reasonably might view his own preferences and action based on them as morally distressing.
- Preferences are *stable*. In theories of choice, current action is taken in terms of current preferences. The implicit assumption is that preferences will be unchanged when the outcomes of current actions are realized.
- Preferences are *consistent* and *precise*. Theories of choice allow inconsistency or ambiguity in preferences only insofar as they do not affect choice (i.e., only insofar as they are made irrelevant by scarcity or the specification of tradeoffs).
- Preferences are *exogenous*. Theories of choice presume that preferences, by whatever process they may be created, are not themselves affected by the choices they control.

Each of these features of preference seems inconsistent with observations of choice behavior among individuals and social institutions: not always, but often enough to be troublesome. Individuals commonly find it possible to express both a preference for something and a recognition that the preference is repugnant to moral standards they accept. Choices are often made without much regard for preferences. Human decision makers routinely ignore their own, fully conscious preferences in making decisions. They follow rules, traditions, hunches, and the advice or actions of others. Preferences change over time in such a way that predicting future preferences is often difficult. Preferences are inconsistent. Individuals and organizations are aware of the extent to which some of their preferences conflict with others: yet they do little to resolve those inconsistencies. Many preferences are stated in forms that lack precision. And while preferences are used to choose among actions, it is also often true that actions and experience with their consequences affect preferences.

Such differences between preferences as they are portrayed in theories of choice and preferences as they appear in decision making can be interpreted as reflecting some ordinary behavioral wisdom that is not always well accommodated within the theory. Human beings seem to recognize in their behavior that there are limits to personal and institutional integration in tastes. As a result, they engage in activites designed to manage preferences. These activities make little sense from the point of view of a theory that assumes decision makers know what they want and will want, or a theory that assumes wants are morally equivalent. But ordinary human actors sense that they might come to want something that they should not, or that they might make unwise choices under the influence of fleeting but powerful desires if they do not act to control the development of unfortunate preferences or to buffer actions from preferences. Like Ulysses, they know the advantages of having their hands tied.

Human beings seem to believe that the theory of choice considerably exaggerates the relative power of a choice based on two guesses compared with a choice that is itself a guess. As observers of the process by which their beliefs have been formed and are consulted, ordinary human beings seem to endorse the good sense in perceptual and moral modesty.

They seem to recognize the extent to which preferences are constructed, or developed, through a confrontation between preferences and actions that are inconsistent with them, and among conflicting preferences. Though they seek some consistency, they appear to see inconsistency as a normal and necessary aspect of the development and clarification of preferences. They sometimes do something for no better reason than that they must, or that someone else is doing it.

Human beings act as though some aspects of their beliefs are important to life without necessarily being consistent with actions, and important to the long-run quality of decision making without controlling it completely in the short run. They accept a degree of personal and social wisdom in simple hypocrisy.

They seem to recognize the political nature of argumentation more clearly and more personally than the theory of choice does. They are unwilling to gamble that God made those people who are good at rational argument uniquely virtuous. They protect themselves from cleverness, in themselves as well as in others, by obscuring the nature of their preferences.

What are the implications for our headmistress? Uncertainty about future consequences (the first guess) and human limitations in dealing with them lead decision makers, intelligently, to techniques of limited rationality. But what can a sensible decision maker learn from observations of preference ambiguity, beyond a reiteration of the importance of clarifying goals and an appreciation of possible human limits in achieving preference orderliness? Considerations of these complications in preferences, in fact, lead to a set of implications for the management of academies and other organizations, as well as for human choice more generally.

To begin with, we need to reexamine the function of decision. One of the primary ways in which individuals and organizations develop goals is by interpreting the actions they take, and one feature of good action is that it leads to the development of new preferences. As a result, decisions should not be seen as flowing directly or strictly from prior objectives. A headmistress might well view the making of decisions somewhat less as a process of deduction, and somewhat more as a process of gently upsetting preconceptions of what she is doing.

In addition, we need a modified view of planning. Planning has many virtues, but a plan can often be more effective as an interpretation of past decisions than as a blueprint for future ones. It can be used as part of our efforts to develop a new, somewhat consistent theory of ourselves that incorporates our recent actions into some moderately comprehensive structure of goals. A headmistress needs to be tolerant of the idea that the meaning of yesterday's action will be discovered in the experiences and interpretations of today.

Finally, we need to accept playfulness in action. Intelligent choice probably needs a dialectic between reason and foolishness, between doing things for no "good" reason and discovering the reasons. Since the theory and ideology of choice are primarily concerned with strengthening reason, a headmistress is likely to overlook the importance of play.

Conflict

Theories of choice either ignore conflict with respect to objectives or assume that the conflict can be resolved by tradeoffs or contracts prior to the making of decisions. Actual decision making frequently involves considerable conflict at all stages.

In standard choice theory, conflict among objectives is treated as a problem in assessing tradeoffs, establishing marginal rates of substitution among goods. The process *within* individuals is mediated by the choice theory analog of the central nervous system: the process *among* individuals is mediated by an explicit or implicit price system. For example, classical theories of the firm assume that markets (particularly labor, capital, and product markets) convert conflicting demands into prices. In this perspective, entrepreneurs are imagined to impose their goals on the organization in exchange for mutually satisfactory wages paid to workers, rent paid to capital, and product quality paid to consumers. Such a process can be treated as yielding a series of contracts by which participants divide decision making into two stages. At the first stage, each individual negotiates the best possible terms for agreeing to pursue another's preferences, or for securing such an agreement from another. In the second stage, individuals execute the contracts. In more sophisticated versions, of course, the contracts are designed so that the terms negotiated at the first stage are self-enforcing at the second.

Seeing participants as having conflicting objectives is a basic feature of political visions of decision making. In political treatments of decision making, however, the emphasis is less on designing a system of contracts between principals and agents, or partners, than it is on understanding a political process that allows decisions to be made without necessarily resolving conflict among the parties. The core ideas are that individuals enter a decision with preferences and resources: each individual uses personal resources to pursue personal gain measured in terms of personal preferences. The usual metaphors are those of politics. There is a metaphor of combat. Disputes are settled by "force," that is, by reference to some measurable property by which individuals can be scaled. Collective decisions are weighted averages of individual desires, where the weights reflect the power distribution among individuals. There is a metaphor of exchange. Disputes are settled by offering or withholding resources and establishing a mutually acceptable structure of prices. Markets facilitate cross-sector trading (e.g., bribery, blackmail) and encourage pursuit of resources with high exchange value (e.g., the taking of hostages). There is a metaphor of alliance. Disputes are settled by forming teams through exchange agreements and side payments and then engaging in combat. Outcomes are (mostly) clear once the coalition structure is given. The coalition structure is problematic.

In a conflict system, information is an instrument of strategic actors. Information may be false; it is always serving a purpose. Actors may provide accurate information about their preferences: normally they will not, except as a possible tactic. They may provide accurate information about the consequences of possible alternative decisions: normally they will not, except as a possible tactic. As a result, information is itself a game. Except insofar as the structure of the game dictates honesty as a necessary tactic, all information is self-serving. Meaning is imputed to messages on the basis of theories of intention that are themselves subject to strategic manipulation. The result is a complicated concatenation of maneuvers in which information has considerably less value than it might be expected to have if strategic considerations were not so pervasive.

Alliances are formed and broken. They represent the heart of many political visions of choice, yet the real world of alliances is unlikely to be as simple as the world of the metaphor. Political alliances involve trades across time in the form of promises and implicit promises. Rarely can the terms of trade be specified with precision. The future occasions are unknown, as are the future sentiments with which individuals will confront them. It is not a world of contracts, but of informal loose understandings and expectations.

Mobilization is important. In order to be active in forming and maintaining a coalition and monitoring agreements within a coalition, it is useful to be present: but attention is a scarce resource, and some potential power in one domain is sacrificed in the name of another. Allies have claims on their time also, and those claims may make their support unreliable at critical moments. To some extent the problems of attention can be managed by making threats of mobilization, or developing fears on the part of others about potential mobilization, or using agents as representatives. However, each of those introduces more uncertainties into the process. The difficulties of mobilization, in fact, are the basis for one of the classic anomalies of organizational behavior – the sequential attention to goals. If all participants were activated fully all of the time, it would not be possible to attend to one problem at one time and another later. Since attention fluctuates, it is possible to sustain a coalition among members who have what appear to be strictly inconsistent objectives.

Political perspectives on organizations emphasize the problems of using self-interested individuals as agents for other self-interested individuals. It is a set of problems familiar to studies of legislators, lawyers, and bureaucrats. If we assume that agents act in their own self-interest, then ensuring that the self-interest of agents coincides with the self-interest of principals becomes a central concern. This has led to extensive discussions of incentive and contractual schemes designed to assure such a coincidence, and to the development of theories of agency. It is clear, however, that principals are not always successful in assuring the reliability of agents. Agents are bribed or coopted. As a result, politics often emphasizes trust and loyalty, in parallel with a widespread belief that they are hard to find. The temptations to revise contracts unilaterally are frequently substantial, and promises of uncertain future support are easily made worthless in the absence of some network of favor giving.

Such complications lead to problems in controlling the implementation of decisions. Decisions unfold through a series of interrelated actions. If all conflicts of interest were settled by the employment contract, the unfolding would present only problems of information and coordination, but such problems are confounded by the complications of unresolved conflict. For example, one complication in control is that the procedures developed to measure performance in compliance with directives involve measures that can be manipulated. Any system of controls involves a system of accounts, and any system of accounts is a roadmap to cheating on them. As a result, control systems can be seen as an infinite game between controllers and the controlled in which advantage lies with relatively full-time players having direct personal interest in the outcomes.

Such features of organizations arise from one very simple modification of classical theories of choice: seeing decisions as being based on unreconciled preferences. It seems hard to avoid the obvious fact that such a description comes closer to the truth in many situations than does one in which we assume a consistent preference function. Somewhat more problematic is the second feature of much of the behavioral study of decision making – the tendency for the political aspects of decision making to be interminable. If it were possible to imagine a two-step decision process in which first we established (through side-payments and formation of coalitions) a set of joint preferences acceptable to a winning coalition and *then* we acted, we could treat the first stage as "politics" and the second as "economics." Such a division has often been tempting (e.g., the distinction between policy making and administration), but it has rarely been satisfactory as a description of decision making. The decisions we observe seem to be infused with strategic actions and politics at every level and at every point.

An academy, like a business firm or government agency, is a political system of partly conflicting interests in which decisions are made through bargaining, power, and coalition formation. In general, there appear to be a few elementary rules for operating in a political system. Power comes from a favorable position for trading favors. Thus it comes from the possession of resources and the idiosyncrasy of preferences, from valuing things that others do not and having things that others value. If you have valued resources, display them. If you don't have them, get them – even if you don't value them yourself. Grab a hostage. Power comes from a reputation for power. Thus it comes from appearing to get what you want, from the trappings of power, and from the interpretations people make of ambiguous historical events.

Power comes from being trustworthy. Politics is trading favors, and trading favors is a risky game. A first principle of politics is that if everyone is rational, no one can be trusted. A second principle is that someone who never trusts anyone will usually lose because although no rational person can be trusted, some people are innocent and *can* be trusted. Those who, by chance or insight, trust those who can be trusted will have an advantage over those who are unconditionally untrusting. A third principle is that all players will try to look trustworthy even though they are not, in order to be trusted by those people who might become winners (by virtue of being willing to trust some people). A fourth principle is that the only reliable way of appearing to be trustworthy is to be, in fact, trustworthy. Thus all rational actors will be trustworthy most of the time. And so on.

These complications of trust in politics are manifest in the use of that most prototypic of procedures for decision making in political systems – the log-roll. Log-rolls combine individuals with complementary interests. We solicit the support of individuals who are indifferent about a current issue by offering subsequent support on another issue. The training director supports the headmistress' project to expand the gymnasium in return for her approval of a new testing program. But log-rolls are invitations to disappointment. Support that is strategic (as most support in a log-roll is) tends to be narrow. It is possible to organize a coalition for a decision: it is less feasible to assure that all coalition members will be willing to invest equally in coping with post-decision complications thay may arise. Perhaps for this reason, studies of coalition formation suggest that log-rolls occur less frequently than would be expected. Although log-rolls among individuals who are indifferent to each other's concerns certainly occur, they appear to be less common than alliances requiring more significant compromises between individuals with overlapping concerns and sentiments of trust. Moreover, when we consider more global understandings over long periods of time and across a wider range of possible agreements, the significance of trustworthiness as a source of power is further enhanced.

Rules

Theories of choice underestimate both the pervasiveness and good sense of an alternative decision logic – the logic of obligation, duty, and rules. Actual decisions seem often to involve finding the "appropriate" rule as much as they do evaluating consequences in terms of preferences.

Much of the decision-making behavior we observe reflects the routine way in which people do what they are supposed to do. For example, most of the time, most people in organizations follow rules even when it is not obviously in their self-interest to do so. The behavior can be viewed as contractual, an implicit agreement to act appropriately in return for being treated appropriately, and to some extent there certainly is such a "contract." But socialization into rules and their appropriateness is ordinarily not a case of willful entry into an explicit contract. It is a set of understandings of the nature of things, of self-conceptions, and of images of proper behavior. It is possible, of course, to treat the word *rule* so broadly as to include any regularity in behavior, and sometimes that is a temptation too great to be resisted. But for the most party, we mean something considerably narrower. We mean regular operating procedures, not necessarily written but certainly standardized, known and understood with sufficient clarity to allow discource about them and action based on them.

The proposition that organizations follow rules – that much of the behavior in an organization is specified by standard operating procedures – is a common one in the bureaucratic and organizational literature. To describe behavior as driven by rules is to see action as a matching of behavior with a position or situation. The criterion is appropriateness. The terminology is one of duties and roles rather than anticipatory decision making. The contrast can be characterized by comparing the conventional litanies for individual behavior:

Consequential action:
(1) What are my alternatives?
(2) What are my values?
(3) What are the consequences of my alternatives for my values?
(4) Choose the alternative that has the best consequences.

Obligatory action:
(1) What kind of situation is this?
(2) What kind of person am I?
(3) What is appropriate for me in a situation likes this?
(4) Do it.

Research on obligatory action emphasizes understanding the kinds of rules that are evoked and used, the ways in which they fit together, and the processes by which they change.

The existence and persistence of rules, combined with their relative independence of idiosyncratic concerns of individuals, make it possible for societies and organizations to function reasonably reliably and reasonably consistently. Current rules store information generated by previous experience and analysis, even though the information cannot easily be retrieved in a form amenable to systematic current evaluation. Seeing rules as coded information invites the questions of the long-run good sense of rule following and its vulnerability to short-run anomalies. In this way, studies of decision making are connected to some classical puzzles of studies of culture and history, as well as population ecology.

Research on rules in decision making has examined the ways in which rules are learned, applied, and broken by individual actors, but the major efforts in studies of organizational decision making have been toward understanding some ways in which rules develop. Within this tradition, three major processes are commonly considered.

First, we can imagine an organization or society learning from its experience, modifying the rules for action incrementally on the basis of feedback from the environment. Most experiential learning models are adaptively rational. They allow decision makers to find good, even optimal, rules for most of the choice situations they are likely to face. However, the process can produce some surprises. Learning can be superstitious, and it can lead to local optimums that are quite distant from the global optimum. If goals adapt rapidly to experience, learning what is likely may inhibit discovery of what is possible. If strategies are learned quickly relative to the development of competence, a decision maker will learn to use strategies that are intelligent given the existing level of competence, but may fail to invest in enough experience with a suboptimal strategy to discover that it would become a dominant choice with additional competence. Although such anomalies are not likely to be frequent, they are important. They are important in practical terms because they are unanticipated by ordinary ideas of learning. They are important in theoretical terms because they make a useful link between sensible learning of rules and surprising results.

Second, we can see action as driven by an evolving collection of invariant rules. As in the case of experiential learning, choice is dependent upon history, but the mechanism is different. Although individual rules are invariant, the population of rules changes over time through differential survival and reproduction. Evolutionary arguments about the development of decision rules were originally made as justification for assuming that decision makers maximize expected utility. The argument was simple: competition for scarce resources resulted in differential survival of decision makers depending on whether the rules produced decisions that were, in fact, optimal. Thus, it was argued, we could assume that surviving rules (whatever their apparent character) were optimal. Although the argument has a certain charm to it, most close students of selection models have suggested that selection will not reliably guarantee a population of rules that is optimal at any arbitrary point in time. Not all rules are necessarily good ones, least of all indefinitely. It has been pointed out, for example, that species that disappear were once survivors, and unless selection processes are instantaneous, some currently "surviving" rules are in the process of disappearing.

Third, decision making can be seen as reflecting rules that spread through a group of organizations like fads or measles. Decision makers copy each other. Contagion is, in fact, much easier to observe than either learning or selection. If we want to account for the adoption of accounting conventions, for example, we normally would look to ways in which standard accounting procedures diffuse through a population of accountants. We would observe that individual accountants adopt those rules of good practice that are certified by professional associations and implemented by opinion leaders.

Insofar as action can be viewed as rule-following, decision making is not willful in the normal sense. It does not stem from the pursuit of interests and the calculation of future consequences of current choices. Rather it comes from matching a changing set of contingent rules to a changing set of situations. The intelligence of the process arises from the way rules store information gained through learning, selection, and contagion, and from the reliability with which rules are followed. The broader intelligence of the adaptation of rules depends on a fairly subtle intermeshing of rates of change, consistency, and foolishness. Good sense is not guaranteed. At the least, it seems to require occasional deviation from the rules, some general consistency between adaptation rates and environmental rates of change, and a reasonable likelihood that networks of imitation are organized in a manner that allows intelligent action to be diffused somewhat more rapidly and more extensively than silliness.

In these terms, decision making in our headmistress's academy involves a logic of appropriateness. The issue is not what the costs and benefits are of an innovative new idea, but what a good headmistress does in a situation like this. The headmistress's role, like other roles, is filled with rules of behavior that have evolved through a history of experience, new year's resolutions, and imitation. These are rules about dress and decorum, rules about the treatment of staff members and guests, rules about dealing with grievances, rules about the kinds of equipment that should be provided and how it should be used. People in the organization follow rules: professional rules, social rules, and standard operating procedures. In such a world, some of the most effective ways of influencing decision outcomes involve the relatively dull business of understanding standard operating procedures and systems of accounting and control and intervening unobtrusively to make a particular decision a routine consequence of following standard rules.

Disorder

Theories of choice underestimate the confusion and complexity surrounding actual decision making. Many things are happening at once: technologies are changing and poorly understood: alliances, preferences, and perceptions are changing; problems, solutions, opportunities, ideas, people, and outcomes are mixed together in a way that makes their interpretation uncertain and their connections unclear.

Decision making ordinarily presumes an ordering of the confusions of life. The classic ideas of order in organizations involve two closely related concepts. The first is that events and activities can be arranged in chains of ends and means. We associate action with its consequence; we participate in making decisions in order to produce intended outcomes. Thus, consequential relevance arranges the relation between solutions and problems and the participation of decision makers. The second is that organizations are hierarchies in which higher levels control lower levels, and policies control implementation. Observations of actual organizations suggest a more confusing picture. Actions in one part of an organization appear to be only loosely coupled to actions in another. Solutions seem to have only a modest connection to problems. Policies are not implemented. Decision makers seem to wander in and out of decision arenas. In *Ambiguity and Choice in Organizations,* Pierre Romelaer and I described the whole process as a funny soccer game: "Consider a round, sloped, multigoal soccer field on which individuals play soccer. Many different people (but not everyone) can join the game (or leave it) at different times. Some people can throw balls into the game or remove them. Individuals while they are in the game try to kick whatever ball comes near them in the direction of goals they like and away from goals they wish to avoid."

The disorderliness of many things that are observed in decision making has led some people to argue that there is very little order to it, that it is best described as bedlam. A more conservative position, however, is that the ways in which organizations bring order to disorder is less hierarchical and less a collection of means-ends chains than is anticipated by conventional theories. There is order, but it is not the conventional order. In particular, it is argued that any decision process involves a collection of individuals and groups who are simultaneously involved in other things. Understanding decisions in one arena requires an understanding of how those decisions fit into the lives of participants.

From this point of view, the loose coupling that is observed in a specific decision situation is a consequence of a shifting intermeshing of the demands on the attention and lives of the whole array of actors. It is possible to examine any particular decision as the seemingly fortuitous consequence of combining different moments of different lives, and some efforts have been made to describe organizations in something like that cross-sectional detail. A more limited version of the same fundamental idea focuses on the allocation of attention. The idea is simple. Individuals attend to some things, and thus do not attend to others. The attention devoted to a particular decision by a particular potential participant depends on the attributes of the decision and alternative claims on attention. Since those alternative claims are not homogeneous across participants and change over time, the attention any particular decision receives can be both quite unstable and remarkably independent of the properties of the decision. The same decision will attract much attention, or little, depending on the other things that possible participants might be doing. The apparently erratic character of attention is made somewhat more explicable by placing it in the context of multiple, changing claims on attention.

Such ideas have been generalized to deal with flows of solutions and problems, as well as participants. In a garbage-can decision process it is assumed that there are exogenous, time-dependent arrivals of choice problems, solutions, and decision makers. Problems and solutions are attached to choices, and thus to each other, not because of their inherent connections in a means-ends sense, but in terms of their temporal proximity. The collection of decision makers, problems, and solutions that comes to be associated with a particular choice opportunity is orderly – but the logic of the ordering is temporal rather than hierarchical or consequential. At the limit, for example, almost any solution can be associated with almost any problem – provided they are contemporaries.

The strategies for a headmistress that can be derived from this feature of decision making are not complicated. First, persist. The disorderliness of decision processes and implementation means that there is no essential consistency between what happens at one time or place and what happens at another, or between policies and actions. Decisions happen as a result of a series of loosely connected episodes involving different people in different settings, and they may be unmade or modified by subsequent episodes. Second, have a rich agenda. There are innumerable ways in which disorderly processes will confound the cleverest behavior with respect to any one proposal, however important or imaginative. What such processes cannot do is frustrate large numbers of projects. Third, provide opportunities for garbage-can decisions. One of the complications in accomplishing things in a disorderly process is the tendency for any particular project to become intertwined with other issues simply by virtue of their simultaneity. The appropriate response is to provide irrelevant choice opportunities for problems and issues: for example, discussions of long-run plans or goals.

Symbols

Theories of choice assume that the primary reason for decision making is to make choices. They ignore the extent to which decision making is a ritual activity closely linked to central Western ideologies of rationality. In actual decision situations, symbolic and ritual aspects are often a major factor.

Most theories of choice assume that a decision process is to be understood in terms of its outcome, that decision makers enter the process in order to affect outcomes, and that the point of life is choice. The emphasis is instrumental: the central conceit is the notion of decision significance. Studies of decision arenas, on the other hand, seem often to describe a set of processes that make little sense in such terms. Information that is ostensibly gathered for a decision is often ignored. Individuals fight for the right to participate in a decision process, but then do not exercise the right. Studies of managerial time persistently indicate very little time spent in making decisions. Rather, managers seem to spend time meeting people and executing managerial performances. Contentiousness over the policies of an organization is often followed by apparent indifference about their implementation.

These anomalous observations appear to reflect, at least in part, the extent to which decision processes are only partly – and often almost incidentally – concerned with making decisions. A choice process provides an occasion:

- for defining virtue and truth, during which decision makers discover or interpret what has happened to them, what they have been doing, what they are going to do, and what justifies their actions.
- for distributing glory or blame for what has happened; and thus an occasion for exercising, challenging, or reaffirming friendship or trust relationships, antagonisms, power or status relationships.
- for socialization, for educating the young.
- for having a good time, for enjoying the pleasures connected with taking part in a choice situation.

In short, decision making is an arena for symbolic action, for developing and enjoying an interpretation of life and one's position in it. The rituals of choice infuse participants with an appreciation of the good sense of life's arrangements. They tie routine events to beliefs about the nature of things. The rituals give meaning, and meaning controls life. From this point of view, understanding decision making involves recognizing that decision outcomes may often be less significant than the ways in which the process provides meaning in an ambiguous world. The meanings involved may be as grand as the central ideology of a society committed to reason and participation. They may be as local as the ego needs of specific individuals or groups.

Some treatments of symbols in decision making portray them as perversions of decision processes. They are presented as ways in which the gullible are misled into acquiescence. In such a portrayal, the witch doctors of symbols use their tricks to confuse the innocent, and the symbolic features of choice are opiates. Although there is no question that symbols are often used strategically, effective decision making depends critically on the legitimacy of the processes of choice and their outcomes, and such legitimacy is problematic in a confusing, ambiguous world. It is hard to imagine a society with modern ideology that would not exhibit a well-elaborated and reinforced myth of choice, both to sustain social orderliness and meaning and to facilitate change.

The orchestration of choice needs to assure an audience of two essential things: first, that the choice has been made intelligently, that it reflects planning, thinking, analysis, and the systematic use of information: second, that the choice is sensitive to the concerns of relevant people, that the right people have had a word in the process. For example, part of the drama of organizational decision making is used to reinforce the idea that managers (and managerial decisions) affect the performance of organizations. Such a belief is, in fact, difficult to confirm using the kinds of data routinely generated in a confusing world. But the belief is important to the functioning of a hierarchical system. Executive compensation schemes and the ritual trappings of executive advancement reassure managers (and others) that an organization is controlled by its leadership, and appropriately so.

Thus, by most reasonable measures, the symbolic consequences of decision processes are as important as the outcome consequences; and we are led to a perspective that challenges the first premise of many theories of choice, the premise that life is choice. Rather, we might observe that life is not primarily choice; it is interpretation. Outcomes are generally less significant – both behaviorally and ethically – than process. It is the process that gives meaning to life, and meaning is the core of life. The reason that people involved in decision making devote so much time so symbols, myths, and rituals is that we (appropriately) care more about them. From this point of view, choice is a construction that finds its justification primarily in its elegance, and organizational decision making can be understood and described in approximately the same way we would understand and describe a painting by Picasso or a poem by T. S. Eliot.

As a result, a headmistress probably needs to see her activities as somewhat more dedicated to elaborating the processes of choice (as opposed to controlling their outcomes), to developing the ritual beauties of decision making in a way that symbolizes the kind of institution her academy might come to be. Just as educational institutions have libraries and archives of manuscripts to symbolize a commitment to scholarship and ideas, so also they have decision processes that express critical values. For example, if an important value of an organization is client satisfaction, then the decision process should be one that displays the eagerness of management to accept and implement client proposals, and one that symbolizes the dedication of staff of principles of availability and service.

Information and Implications

These observations on decision making and theories of choice are not surprising to experienced decision makers. But they have some implications, one set of which can be illustrated by examining a classical problem: the design of an information system in an organization. In the case of our headmistress, there are issues of what information to gather and store, which archives to keep and which to burn, what information to provide to potential contributors, and how to organize the records so they are easily accessible to those who need them.

In most discussions of the design of information systems in organizations, the value of information is ordinarily linked to managerial decision making in a simple way. The value of an information source depends on the decisions to be made, the precision and reliability of the information, and the availability of alternative sources. Although calculating the relevant expected costs and returns is rarely trivial, the framework suggests some very useful rules of thumb. Don't pay for information about something that cannot affect choices you are making. Don't pay for information if the same information will be freely available anyway before you have to make a decision for which it is relevant. Don't pay for information that confirms something you already know. In general, we are led to an entirely plausible stress on the proposition that allocation of resources to information gathering or to information systems should depend on a clear idea of how potential information might affect decisions.

A notable feature of the actual investments in information and information sources that we observe is that they appear to deviate considerably from these conventional canons of information management. Decision makers and organizations gather information and do not use it: ask for more, and ignore it; make decisions first, and look for the relevant information afterwards. In fact, organizations seem to gather a great deal of information that has little or no relevance to decisions. It is, from a decision theory point of view, simply gossip. Were one to ask why organizations treat information in these ways, it would be possible to reply that they are poorly designed, badly managed, or ill-informed. To some extent, many certainly are. But the pervasiveness of the phenomenon suggests that perhaps it is not the decision makers who are inadequate, but our conceptions of information. There are several sensible reasons why decision makers deal with information the way they do.

Decision makers operate in a surveillance mode more than they do in a problem-solving mode. In contrast to a theory of information that assumes that information is gathered to resolve a choice among alternatives, decision makers scan their environments for surprises and solutions. They monitor what is going on. Such scanning calls for gathering a great deal of information that appears to be irrelevant to "decisions." Moreover, insofar as decision makers deal with problems, their procedures are different from those anticipated in standard decision theory. They characteristically do not "solve" problems: they apply rules and copy solutions from others. Indeed, they often do not recognize a "problem" until they have a "solution."

Decision makers seem to know, or at least sense, that most information is tainted by the process by which it is generated. It is typically quite hard to disaggregate social belief, including expert judgment, into its bases. The social process by which confidence in judgment is developed and shared is not overly sensitive to the quality of judgment. Moreover, most information is subject to strategic misrepresentation. It is likely to be presented by someone who is, for personal or subgroup reasons, trying to persuade a decision maker to do something. Our theories of information-based decision making (e.g., statistical decision theory) are, for the most part, theories of decision making with innocent information. Decision information, on the other hand, is rarely innocent, and thus rarely as reliable as an innocent would expect.

Highly regarded advice is often bad advice. It is easy to look at decision making and find instances in which good advice and good information were ignored. It is a common occurrence. Consequently, we sometimes see decision makers as perversely resistant to advice and information. In fact, much highly regarded advice and much generally accepted information is misleading. Even where conflict of interest between advice givers and advice takers is a minor problem, advice givers typically exaggerate the quality of their advice: and information providers typically exaggerate the quality of their information. It would be remarkable if they did not. Decision makers seem to act in a way that recognizes the limitations of "good" advice and "reliable" information.

Information is a signal and symbol of competence in decision making. Gathering and presenting information symbolizes (and demonstrates) the ability and legitimacy of decision makers. A good decision maker is one who makes decisions in a proper way, who exhibits expertise and uses generally accepted information. The competition for reputations among decision makers stimulates the overproduction of information.

As a result of such considerations, information plays both a smaller and a larger role than is anticipated in decision theory-related theories of information. It is smaller in the sense that the information used in decision making is less reliable and more strategic than is conventionally assumed, and is treated as less important for decision making. It is larger in the sense that it contributes not only to the making of decisions but to the execution of other managerial tasks and to the broad symbolic activities of the individual and organization.

If it is possible to imagine that life is not only choice but also interpretation, that they are heavily intertwined, and that the management of life and organizations is probably as much the latter as the former, it is possible to sketch some elements of the requirements for the design of useful management information systems.

We require some notion of the value of alternative information sources that is less tied to a prior specification of a decision (or class of decisions) than to a wide spectrum of possible decisions impossible to anticipate in the absence of the information: less likely to show the consequences of known alternatives for existing goals than to suggest new alternatives and new objectives: less likely to test old ideas than to provoke new ones: less pointed toward anticipating uncertain futures than toward interpreting ambiguous pasts. Such a view of information is associated classically with literature, art, and education: and if there are appropriate models for a management information system of this sort, perhaps they lie in discussions of education and criticism rather than in theories of decison.

To describe information management in such terms is, of course, to glorify it. It suggests that office memoranda might be viewed as forms of poetry and staff meetings as forms of theater, and we may perhaps wonder whether it would be better to admit a distinction between a sales chart and a Van Gogh painting – if only to assure that each may achieve its unique qualities. Yet the vision has a certain amount of charm to it. At least, it seems possible that with a little imagination here and there, educational philosophy and literary criticism might be used to help management information systems achieve a useful level of irrelevance.

More generally, research on how organizations make decisions leads us to a perspective on choice different from that provided by standard theories of choice, and may even provide some hints for an academy headmistress. The ideas are incomplete: the hints are rough. They point toward a vision of decision making that embraces the axioms of choice but acknowledges their limitations: that combines a passion for the technology of choice with an appreciation of its complexities and the beauties of its confusions: and that sees a headmistress as often constrained by sensibility and rules, but sometimes bouncing around a soccer field.

A Philosophy of Rationalization
– The Polish Praxiology of T. Kotarbinski

Pierre Guillet de Monthoux

Introduction

In an industrialized world "action" is often taken to mean the profitable (in money terms) labor of men or machines. The history of ideas tells us that many other human preoccupations have been regarded as "active" in the past. In Antiquity the political discussions among free men in the agora, which today would be discarded from the class of actions as unproductive gossip, were considered the most noble kind of action at the time (Arendt, 1968). Critics of inhuman industrial work have sometimes proposed the revival of such forgotten meanings of "action". *Vita activa* is not only a matter of labor; rather, it includes politics as well as craftsmanship. Referring to Hanna Arendt's famous argument: *Animal Laborans* is not the only actor; *Homo Politicus* and *Homo Faber* are actors too.

Such extended interpretations of "action" are not, however, uncontroversial, as we soon discover when we try to introduce *praxis* in the form of industrial democracy and *poeisis* by way of autonomous craftsmanship in an industrial world where action means labor only in a very mechanistic sense. Is it then impossible to embark on new interpretations of action in an industrial society? So long as *Homo Faber* and *Homo Politicus* pay less than *Animal Laborans,* capitalists in industry will be reluctant to accept action as craftsmanship or political argument. In capitalism, only such human behavior as makes a profit deserves the name of action. In socialistic economics, where such a narrow definition of "action" should be taboo for ideological reasons, we would expect to find a climate adapted to broader definitions of the meaning of action. This is true only in the very specific sense which this paper sets out to show.

The theoreticians of the socialist economies are certainly not ready to turn their industry into a political playground for free men. Nor does the Marxist credo for technological development allow the arts and crafts to be placed unconditionally on an equal footing with labor. Nevertheless, in the absence of the simple definition of profitability, socialism does offer a small niche for inquiries into the technological or engineering interpretation of action. Even here there may be the same stubborn resistance to any totally new concept of action, but whereas industrialists in capitalist systems take the definition of action for granted, socialism does at least provide an opportunity for immanent criticism of the concept. I will elucidate this abstruse statement with the help of a theory of efficient action conceived by the philosopher Tadeusz Kotarbinski – praxiology – and developed in post-war Poland.

Economy Versus Production

Those who take a deeper interest in the reasons for industrialization will search in vain for an explicit theory of industrial action in economic texts. It seems as though the industrial engineers who organize the world of production, as well as the business economists who control its efficiency, lack a philosophy of their own. Is there really any philosophy behind efficient action, other than economics? What is worth doing is simply what pays best, and what pays best is what is valued most highly. Prices are set by the interplay of demand and supply, which in turn reflect the subjective utilities of producers and consumers. In such a theoretical perspective the question of what to do and how to do it becomes essential. In fact, economics has nothing to say about how to perform the profitable actions. G. L. Shackle emphasizes the pure, theoretical and unpractical character of subjective economic "high theory":

To crack crude petroleum into marketable constituents, a large and complex plant is indispensable, and the question whether the distillations should be effected by individuals each using his own handfed still does not arise. The businessman's *production policy questions* will be framed in terms which include an essential reference to technological, viz engineering, chemical and biological, detail; detail of materials science and soil science, of colour esthetics, of pharmacological effects; details of practical arts. Economic theory must appear to the businessman as summary and commentary of his methods, or else a viewing of them in an irrelevant and trivial light. Its real purpose is quite other than to offer him guidance in his individual, peculiar, special situation and affairs, where "marginal cost" is no more than a curious gloss or pale reflection from practical realities. *Economic theory that has elected to be general* in its bearing and interests, and those concerned with human affairs at such a level of generalness are politicians and representatives of large masses of opinion, leaders of parties or trade unions (Shackle, 1972: 41–42).

It seems that the generality of economics has blocked the articulation of a practical philosophy of action in fields covered by economic policies. Early scientific management authors such as Frederick Taylor tell us what we ought to do and how it should be supervised, but say little about why. When such pioneers occasionally find it necessary to give a reason, they to it in the non-argumentative form of a moral judgement, e.g. it is a crime not to work at full capacity. Their modern successors in operations research and systems analysis base their mathematical elaborations on the same grounds. Is there then a hidden philosophy of engineering action? A closer look at what engineers have written about work soon shows that such people do not argue like economists. Instead of constantly referring to "profit maximization" or elaborating subjective utility theories, they have a mode of reasoning of their own based on the minimization of physical waste. The waste philosophy focuses on the "bodily" or physical aspects of the world – a perspective which provides the cornerstone of Tadeusz Kotarbinski's praxiological philosophy of efficient action. In Kotarbinski's work we therefore find a rare expression of the hidden philosophy of production.

What is meant by "the bodily aspects of the world"? This is a problem connected with the question of what language is about. Kotarbinski, writing in the Polish analytical philosophical tradition, conceives a language with two sorts of words only: *concrete statements* about things and persons and *onomatoids*. Talking carefully in "ultimate formulations" means filtering away the meaningless onomatoids so that only nouns or adjectives of the concrete sort are left. Only such ultimate formulations acquire meaning in the sense of being either true or false. Words such as "smoothness", "relationship", "tune" and "shift" are examples of onomatoids which should be avoided because they are not counterparts of particular bodies; they are therefore confusing and lead to meaningless speculation. In essence this is the message of Kotarbinski's "somatic reism" or, as he has also called it, "concretism". According to Kotarbinski this focusing on the bodily aspects of the world is actually an everyday commonsense attitude. Watching a teacher, we will see that he explains words to children in just this way, by telling them stories in which things and persons are the concrete counterparts of the words. The concept of "similarity" is explained in a concrete manner, for example by pointing at two sparrows hopping along together with the same beaks and the same feathers. According to Kotarbinski's "somatism", language is meaningful only when it designates objects, i.e. things or persons. This is because "we can think only of things, since only things are the subject matter of cognition". The "reism" of somatic reism is defined in these terms:

... the reists accepts only one ontological category – namely that which has traditionally been called a category of substances ... they eliminate Aristotelian substances in the secondary sense – that is, general substances, in other words the universals. What remain are only the Aristotelian substances in the primary sense: Socrates, horses, stones – in a word, individual things or persons; the term "thing" becomes modernized and covers everything which is temporal and spatial and physically defined – for instance, physically influencing something else (Kotarbinski, 1966: 426).

Somatism implies that "any psychic being is a physical object". Somatic reism thus appears to be a very materialistic doctrine. However, Kotarbinski emphasizes that his somatic reism is an antimechanistic materialism:

The assumption that every object is a physical object does not in the least mean that a law of mechanics sufficiently explains everything that happens to objects, for it seems that the laws of mechanics do not even explain all that happens to objects in those respects in which physics is concerned with objects. A fortiori, they do not explain those changes with which psychology is concerned (Kotarbinski, 1966: 427).

This remark I think, is, very important to an understanding of the power of praxiology as a doctrine in socialism. Praxiology, being both anti-mechanistic as well as materialistic, can raise lots of problems about action in that materialistic system of thought in which the engineers who influence industrial practice seem to dwell. In the following pages I shall try to show how praxiology forms the basis for an alternative approach, which I shall call *individual materialism*. The socialistic attitude which is immanently criticized by this individual materialism can be dubbed *mechanistic collectivism*. In the introductory chapter to his book *Praxiology* (Kotarbinski, 1965) Kotarbinski not surprisingly refers to Aristotle and Nicomachian ethics. The Aristotelian concept that Kotarbinski seems to have been influenced by is that of "intermediarity", i.e. the idea that optimum action should never be confounded with maximum activity. After paying due respect to Marx, authors in the area of business management and industrial organization are also recognized as having attempted to write such a general "grammar of action", in which "the idea of rationalizing engineer coincides with a philosopher's methodological considerations". To take one example, Frederick Taylor was simply repeating, with special reference to the processing of methods, what Descartes had recommended with regard to the speculative task of the thinker. The same holds for ideas on rationalization such as Fayol's industrial work organization theory, or for the work of those engaged in production scheduling and network planning. However, Kotarbinski, who had himself spent some years studying architecture, remarks that engineers avoid a deeper study of praxiology because they are too interested in the profits of the industrial enterprise. In fact economists often use praxiological concepts, but their dominating economic interests prevent them from pursuing the analysis further. The vocabulary of economists consists of expressions like "raw material", "quotation", "finished products", "productivity" and "cost saving" – of which Kotarbinski comments that only the last two have purely praxiological meaning. Since neither the vocabulary of engineers nor that of economists meets the demands of a theory of efficient action, Kotarbinski sets out to elaborate his own vocabulary in order to be able to name the important elements of "good" work. He claims that economics will then be transformed into a subclass of general praxiology. The concrete basis of praxiology will make it possible to demystify exonomic jargon. Once the praxiological vocabulary has been established, we can address the problem of making objective and concrete statements about actions.

Elements of Efficient Action

Kotarbinski postulates that all work can be reduced to simple acts which, in turn, should be viewed as causal bonds between an agent and the result of his action. The word "result" should be strictly reserved for an event, i.e. a change or a continuation of a certain state of nature. The cause that brings about a result is the agent's free impulse. A free impulse is an objective pressure, muscular or mental, on some concrete material. Impulses may be direct or indirect. The agent may touch the objective material, but he may also, for instance, remove an obstacle so that a train can later pass by. Pressures may not be the only free impulses; it could also be a question of releasing the pressure of an agent. It should be noted that, in line with his somatic reism, Kotarbinski considers mental action on a par with muscular activity.

Praxiology thus has little to do with intentional theories of action. The praxiologist does not attempt to construct syllogisms or to understand intentions behind a given action. A free impulse may well be the cause of an unintended result, and still be of great praxiological interest. Kotarbinski notes that we often become agents "precisely of what we did not intend", simply by being one cause in a dynamic chain of causal relations that ends up in an event. The interest of praxiology is to assess, objectively, the nature of agenthood. For instance, when someone closes the door carefully so that a sleeping person is not woken, the objective result is precisely that the person continues to sleep. The product of action is the physically sleeping state of the person, and this state is independent of the original intention of the careful door-closer. Thus in the case of simple acts it is of no praxiological interest to investigate the concept of responsibility ad administrative justice, "since it is not concerned with the conditions of making any action more effective". Here we find the most important difference between economics and praxiologoy. But as Kotarbinski notes, administrative justice may so influence motivation and the efficiency of action, in the case of collective actions that it becomes a cause of praxiological importance.

Praxiology claims to be anti-mechanistic, and Kotarbinski does not want to call himself a behaviorist. According to his way of thinking there is in general no law that relates the importance of a given result to the intensity of the free impulse that causes it. Only partial relationships can be found when bodies interact, e.g. "the dependence of the distance covered by a javelin on the force with which it was thrown". In other words the praxiologist, unlike the mechanistic engineer, will always be on the alert for changes in the relationship between the cause and its effects, i.e. the specific efficiency of the specific action. In an anti-mechanistic world there are many paradoxes as regards the efficiency of action. Although all living beings from beavers to human carpenters are able to act, the human being also talks and uses intricate instruments designed to increase the pressure of his free impulse or to act in his place. The clear difference between the spider waiting for an insect to get trapped in his web and the fisherman manipulating his net to catch a fish, also suggests that in the case of human action the relation between cause and effect can be subject to the most interesting unlawful variations, i.e. to technological change.

When several simple actions occur together but disconnectedly, they are called "sets of actions". When they are connected, they form "compound acts". Actions may be connected so as to cause, prevent, facilitate or make one another possible. Compound acts may consist of simultaneous actions, such as the violinist's fingering the strings with one hand and handling the bow with the other, or they may be linked consecutively in a chain. It is in the consideration of compound acts that the concept of organization becomes important.

In praxiology the notion of organization does not imply the linking of men and things in certain patterns. Rather, to organize is to arrange sets of actions into compound acts. Organization is a functional not a material task. To organize is in some sense to prepare for action, and preparation consists mainly of two elements; testing and planning. There are different sorts of tests, for instance the simple training of the body, trail-and-error, and diagnostic tests. Planning consists of preparing for future actions by describing them. Plans include several goals, some immediate and others more remote. Sometimes short-run actions are described that seem to counteract the long-run goal, as for instance when someone "steps back in order to gain momentum to jump forwards". Planning can end up as method, i.e. the knowledge of precisely how compound acts should be done according to a certain system of behavior. Methodology is therefore not exclusively a matter of logics; it is a praxiological concern as well.

Compound acts may be performed by one or several agents. In the latter case we have collective actions. Collective actions imply that at least two agents assist or hinder each other in doing something. In the first case it is a question of cooperative helping, in the second of a struggle. To attain cooperation, coordination of leadership ist required. To lead means letting one's own free impulse become the work of others. Leading can also consist of creating compulsory situations, in which others have to act. Leading may also mean giving orders. Leadership involves agenthood, although the leaders do not themselves carry out the actions. Leaders act differently in totalitarian situations, for instance by trying to extend the orders to a maximum number of people by centralizing and pushing the planning to higher hierarchical levels. But the true function of organizing is not fulfilled by way of totalitarianism and centralization. Compound acts are best performed when work groups are organic, i.e. when there is an objective for the actions of the group as a whole and when conflicting objectives and actions contrary to the common product are kept to a minimum. Thus, as we can see, the term "organic" should not be taken literally in praxiology. Kotarbinski criticizes those who regard collectives as individual beings. An institution consisting of people and their apparatus is certainly not the same as a single acting individual. An institution cannot suffer pain, nor does it have a unified mental life. Collectives lack unconditioned responses and have no intuitive memory. On the other hand, institutions have longer lives than individuals and certainly a greater capacity to carry out a number of tasks with the help of several agents. These are the reasons why praxiology criticizes collective anthropomorphism and adopts an individualistic approach.

Up to now we have been considering the elements of efficient action, but why should we act at all? Kotarbinski notes that action may be a compulsory solution, in the sense that a person who does not act faces "serious difficulties". Such difficulties occur when "essential needs" are threatened by some sort of evil, such as "the loss of life and health or difficulties of subsistence and personal freedom, threats to social status, honour, clean conscience and reciprocal feelings in those one loves". Action occuring as a result of such social control is what we usually call "labor". It is this sort of action which should be the subject of praxiology. But praxiology is not primarily about the obligation to work; it is about the practical values that make us work efficiently. The praxiologist's task is thus to articulate the practical values of work, so that:

Man should do willingly what he must do, that he should not do what he must do only because he must do it, that in doing what he must do he should find satisfaction and therefore greatly increase the efficiency of his labour (Kotarbinski, 1965: 152).

Values of Efficient Action

Compulsory situations necessarily demand action and man's own actions create further compulsion to act. Kotarbinski's concrete world is manmade. Its values are human and social, not biological. Still he claims that the ethical values of the humanities are not related to the praxiological values of action. Praxiological values are purely technical. Kotarbinski's examples range from the "good boy-scout who can make a fire with a match split in four" (Kotarbinski, 1965: 83) to the good working guillotine chopping off heads with perfect "sureness". Kotarbinski's ambition is to elaborate a set of objective values, but although we cannot accuse him of simple moralism, many of his praxiological judgements have an ethical slant. Naturally, though, by clinging to concretism praxiologists find it easier to criticize actual practice in socialistic countries without being accused of idealism.

To the praxiologist "good" action is what brings the agent closer to his objective, and this can be assessed in terms of some real or ideal standard. For example, the suit which the tailor has to copy is real, but the plans of a house which is to be built are ideal. In this way the classical problem of economics regarding the definition of utility is avoided. Usefulness is equated with objective facilitation. Kotarbinski certainly indicates all the problems of assessing efficiency in practice, drawing attention to the complex set of values which may be involved.

In evaluating efficiency it is not only the primary aspects of work that must be considered. Values such as "carefulness" and "elegance" are among secondary aspects which are of praxiological importance. It is praxiologically valuable if the florist serves the customer in a charming manner, adding a sprig of greenery to the flowers (Kotarbinski, 1965: 78). Likewise, a product may be judged in terms of "purity", i.e. the level of foreign bodies included in it. The praxiologist dislikes dirty windows in passenger cars and litter on the ground. This is precisely what Kotarbinski means by the concrete costs of action. To behave economically by reducing costs certainly does not mean, in praxiological terms, choosing the best alternative; rather, it means restricting waste and other decrements. The increase in revenue is no longer defined as the maximization of profits on the market, but as increasing the productivity of action. The following ideal types of praxiological economic behavior can illustrate this point:

It is said that a certain author wrote a comprehensive book in ten-minute bursts between his coming home from the office and the moment when the dinner was served. Occasionally we happen to see very small plots where every inch of land is used in the best possible way and which yields astonishingly large crops (Kotarbinski, 1965: 83).

Praxiologically it is also a good thing when an agent exhibits "sureness" and "skills", so that he has perfect knowledge of his own action without observing it. An action may be "correct" when it conforms to methods of behavior developed by experts. "Expertise" is defined in turn as a combination of routines, skills and rationality. These and other concepts may be used to determine whether or not an action should be deemed efficient. At this point Kotarbinski turns to the "how-to-do-it" part of praxiology. This involves a very normative approach, which turns the invisible hand of the economists into visible praxiological standards of industrialization.

Economization of Action

"A good organizer does not do anything. He just watches everything" (Kotarbinski, 1965: 97). But isn't man born active? With a desire to expand his sphere of activities and to keep open the opportunities to act? To Kotarbinski this is a physical fact. Every active human being has an incredible appetite for action, and this produces so much physiological tension that it has to be retained by inner pressure if it is not released. As soon as something happens around us, we long to intervene. At this point Kotarbinski introduces his concept of "economization".

An economic action is an action undertaken with a minimum of intervention A person who minimizes intervention is not lazy or passive. He is not involving himself in all affairs or moving his body to no purpose. He is attentive and watchful. "We fairly often recognize one who is a good manager, because nothing that is important in his duties escapes his attention" (Kotarbinski, 1965: 96). But the bad manager does not mind walking around amongst heaps of machines "out of operation which lie for weeks rusting in the open air" (Kotarbinski, 1965: 96). Minimization of intervention has practical everyday consequences. It leads to the construction of apparatuses and machines which carry out physical actions while man observes and stays ready to intervene. This sort of human action is called "pure invigilation" in Kotarbinski's terminology. Again, it may appear that the invigilator is resting or simply doing nothing. But in fact he is maintaining the inner pressure for action. When someone does not intervene but still participates "by an inner tension internally inhibited" (Kotarbinski, 1965: 100), this is referred to as "interference".

Another important form of economization is the shaping of *"faits accomplis"*. Defense is cheaper than attack. Preservation is less costly than change. To create a *fait accompli* means bringing about at an early stage a state which then spontaneously develops into a desired event. This is the background to praxiological rules such as "act first – ask later" and to expressions like "first-mover advantage". According to this line of reasoning it is also better not to act but to demonstrate instead a readiness to act or a possibility of action. This economization is known as "potentialization". Not only does the agent avoid energy expenditure in this way, but he often also reserves the possibility of acting in the future. Likewise it is economical to "imitate" someone else's behavior, to try to repeat an action, and to do several actions "at one stroke". Sometimes it is more economical to think than to do. But thinking must be practical. In discussing the preparation and planning of actions, Kotarbinski goes into some details on the question of practicality. For instance, preparation may concern our own bodies or knowledge, and it is then a question of mental action or bodily training to acquire certain skills. This demands special training in which the demands together with the individual responsibility are gradually stepped up. With the help of concrete reasoning Kotarbinski sees no problem in treating mental preparation in the same way as the training of our bodies. Although we say that the result of the mental act is a thought, a sheet of paper, or a work of art, Kotarbinski assures us that this is only a metaphorical way of speaking. The real product is always a body, in the case of a mental action as well. Just look at the thinking person, as he

... frowns or knits his brows, his eyeballs move, he sometimes clenches his fists or makes tense movements with his extremities (Kotarbinski, 1965: 176).

Doesn't this clearly indicate that mental action, too, is a form of pressure on some internal organ? To think and plan is therefore another way of exercising a free impulse, of acting on one's own organism. Thus the product of thinking is hardly abstract. The product is the change in the thinker's body from a state of being ignorant to one of knowing – a change no different from starting out thin and becoming fat by eating. The planner "moulds himself" by planning, and he does so only if he makes the practical plan purposive and nonutopian. To want to change the world at a stroke, for instance making everyone rich by giving them bank notes printed in large quantities (Kotarbinski, 1965: 118), is as Utopian as the idea of producing perpetual motion. Planning has to be concrete and it has to pertain to known matters. This does not mean that plans must be accompanied by a lot of documentation, but that they should be "cognitively substantial". To Kotarbinski "documentation" is simply a term for information used to convince evaluating agencies of the merit of the plan. Cognitive substantiation, on the other hand, means a plan is based on scientific research. A cognitively substantiated plan is founded on objective reality outside the agent's own intention. Kotarbinski does not say that this reality is all physical. Some of it consists of regularities established by man-made rules and conventions.

The less the advanced knowledge, the more flexible the plan has to be. Agents should then act according to situational and local knowledge. Future actions should not be unnecessarily constrained by the plan. Kotarbinski then enumerates several other values of "good" plans, but the above presentation is sufficient for our present purpose. Let us now turn to the second group of practical values.

Instruments of Action

Men act, but so do animals. Man, however, is also a toolmaker who incorporates instruments and apparatuses into his institutions. The reason for instrumentation is to minimize intervention. Instruments of various kinds bring reliability, precision and independence to the agents of compound acts. A machine must be operational and the praxiologist's task is to ponder the dangers of, for instance, making machines more dependent on a single component – to consider the dangers of mechanical centralization. Standardization is an important consequence of instrumentalization, but it is not only machines which are standardized. Agents tend to regard their fellow-agents as standardized tools. This is especially true of those "leaders" who treat institutions as means. Greater instrumentalization will sometimes degrade action and skills, and Kotarbinski also notes that unemployment may follow the introduction of new machinery. But these are only some of the negative aspects of instrumentalization, which generally speaking must continue. The process is irreversible and, praxiologically, is largely to the good. It is the task of the praxiologist to handle the negative consequences of the process as well as guiding its further development. In general it seems that the more involved Kotarbinski becomes in the practical implications of praxiology, the more clearly does the role of the praxiologist emerge as a moderator, as an advocate of the Aristotelian intermediate in the realm of industrial development. He frequently repeats that "optimum should not be confused with maximum", emphasizing the importance of the technical efficiency of action rather than the beauty of manmade constructions. This attitude becomes especially clear when he discusses the problems connected with organizing actions.

Organization of Action

It should be noted that Kotarbinski never regards an organization as a product as such. To organize is to plan several actions, to coordinate cooperation. The improvement of one component of a machine does not necessarily lead to an improvement in the whole apparatus. Rather, the opposite is true. This also holds for actions included in compound acts. In an organization, actions should interact, so that the "whole" works. And an organization should not be loaded with unnecessary parts. Ornaments should be abolished. In fact it is tempting to look upon organizations as mere instruments consisting of men. But the praxiologist's task is rather to criticize this kind of view, as we can see when Kotarbinski mentions specialization, and dissatisfaction with specialization. He asks:

Is it a praxiological problem to seek remedies against the satisfaction? My firm reply is, yes. Of course, this is the responsibility primarily of social workers who have public means at their disposal. But this is not their concern only, because the mood in which an individual does his job signally affects the efficiency of his behavior (Kotarbinski, 1965: 140).

Specialization in moderate praxiological form, however, does lead to more intereesting work. Think of the medical specialist who has a lot of patients, or the craftsman who gets to know many people through his skills, or of the worker who becomes a robot instructor. In these cases agents become more active as a result of specialization, and in just these cases the single agent is no longer viewed as an instrument but as a co-agent with the planner. Planning and leading then resemble teaching, and are not to be "understood as merely conveying information, but rather as developing the mind of the pupil" (Kotarbinski, 1965: 151).

Extreme centralization makes many individuals over-dependent upon a single leader. Kotarbinski provides three remedies for restoring the right kind of organization, in which collective action may flourish.

1. Confining the dependence of the individual B on the individual A to certain specified fields, functions or tasks.
2. So arrange the relations that individual B should be in some respects dependent on individual A, and individual A on individual B in certain other respects.
3. So formulating instructions that the executer may display his inventiveness within fairly broad limits (Kotarbinski, 1965: 150).

It is in his discussion of organization that Kotarbinski's critique of mechanistic collectivism emerges most clearly. Again, he criticizes the simple minded collectivism which sees groups and teams as single individual agents. He then proposes the praxiological value system as an alternative to the view which regards agents and groups of agents as functioning according to mechanical laws. Praxiological values which are set to be objective thus provide an intrasocialistic critique of the management of industry and production. But is it really possible to formulate such a criticism, without coming back in some respects to the idea of a market? In conclusion let us look at the meta-values of praxiology, to see whether they actually represent a market approach in philosophically concrete guise.

Meta-Values of Efficient-Action

Even if we accept Kotarbinski's praxiological value system, we may of course ask on what grounds the values are fomulated. Why must action be efficient? Why not the Greek practice? The philosophical literature of ethics is full of discussions on various criteria of goodness, apart from efficiency. Why do we have to cling to technical values? Why do we choose an industrial technological world?

At the superficial level Kotarbinski simply postulates that technological development is an irreversible process. He remarks that

... from time to time (there are) paroxysms of crazy urges to return to old forms of activity, which from a praxiological point of view are quite obsolete. But all planned restoration of technological primitivism is doomed to failure (Kotarbinski, 1965: 140).

At the same time the discussion of praxiological values open up a debate on how to go about developing this irreversible technology. Kotarbinski slips numerous critical points into his text: crowded trams in Warsaw, machines rusting in factories, the dirt on the windows of passenger cars, and signposts giving wrong information. In a world of praxiology, we are told, all this would be otherwise. But why?

Mechanistic collectivism argues that historical development forces us to become more technical. This explanation is alien to Kotarbinski. He also discards biological development models. According to concretism, development is not an immanent matter, but one that depends on external relations. Praxiological values are obvious because they have occurred as a result of external hardship and a struggle for survival in compulsory situations in the past. Compulsory situations are not created by biology alone, but are often manmade. We might now ask how Kotarbinski's "struggle" differs from the economist's "competition"? Do not profitability, money and various forms of market structure provide a more suitable vocabulary for struggle than that developed by Kotarbinski?

Technical development occurs because parties stimulate one another to overcome obstacles. It is in attack and defense that new techniques for efficient action, new praxiological values, develop. This is a fact that is well known to patent-holders, who have also developed a technique for defending their positions. It is also well known to the advocates of free pricing and the abolition of collusion and cartels. They would all agree with Kotarbinski that

... men are like deep sea fish accustomed to strong external pressure; so when they reach shallow water they perish, burst by internal forces (Kotarbinski, 1965: 193).

Mechanistic collectivism, however, is more favorable to collusion than patents and free pricing. When the socialistic work ideology has been freed from mechanistic collectivism, what remains is simply a very libertarian idea of the economy. Perhaps Kotarbinski was trying to launch this dangerous gospel in the shape of his individual materialism? Take the following quotation, for instance, and simply substitute the word "market" for the word "door":

It is only the narrow door of maximum and highly strenuous effort which constitutes an exit from a situation with only one way out. This, in my opinion, is the same door which opens on to the summits of creativeness and mastery (Kotarbinski, 1965: 113).

Is this the incipient voice of the market knocking on the collectivist's door?

References

Arendt, H. (1968) *The Human Condition.* Chicago: The University of Chicago Press

Kotarbinski, T. (1965) *Praxiology, An Introduction to the Sciences of Efficient Action.* Oxford: Pergamon Press

Kotarbinski, T. (1966) *Gnosiology, The Scientific Approach to the Theory of Knowledge.* Oxford: Pergamon Press.

Shackle, G. L. (1972) *Epistemics and Economics, A Critique of Economic Doctrines.* Cambridge: Cambridge University Press.

Towards a Control Theory of the Firm[1]

Richard M. Cyert and Morris DeGroot

Introduction

The theory of the firm in neoclassical theory is simple and clear. The firm is assumed to be maximizing profits and, therefore, follows a single decision rule. That rule tells the firm's management to operate at the point where marginal cost equals marginal revenue. By moving to the demand curve at that point the firm can determine the appropriate price and output. This general rule lies in back of all micro-theory relating to the firm. New models consist of making a behavioral assumption and then showing how the marginal revenue curve can be determined. Once the marginal revenue curve is found, a "solution" is immediately forthcoming. The dominant firm model and the kinked-demand curve model are obvious examples (see Cohen and Cyert). There has been little empirical testing of any of the propositions from the theory of the firm and, where there has, the testing casts doubts on the theory.

Nevertheless, the theory has played a useful role in increasing the understanding, in a general sense, of the way the price system operates. By assuming competitive markets and utilizing the decision rule described above, economists have gained insight into the resource allocation problem within an economy. Little insight, however, is gained about the actual decision-making process of individual firms. This paper is motivated by a desire to develop a theory of the firm that corresponds more closely to the behavior of firms I have observed. My observations has been made as a member of the board of directors of some ten firms for various periods of time over the last ten years. Firms in the real world do function under conditions of uncertainty and the theory we will develop will assume uncertainty. The relationship between the approach that we will take in this paper and neoclassical theory will be explored after the theory is developed.

---

[1] This paper borrows significantly from "The Maximization Process under Uncertainty", Advances in Information Processing in Organizations, Vol. I, 1984, L. S. Sproull and P. Larkey (Ed.), Greenwich, Connecticut: JAI Press by R. M. Cyert and M. H. DeGroot.

The Firm

In neoclassical theory, the firm is viewed as consisting of a single person, an entrepreneur, who makes decisions in accordance with the decision rule given earlier. In fact, all firms have more elaborate organizational structures, and most of these structures are of a decentralized form. The basic unit in each firm is typically a division. Each division is a profit centre and is usually managed as though it were an independent firm. The firm will sell a number of different products and through its divisions, will operate in a number of different market structures in which it will have different market shares.

The manager of each division will usually be a vice-president, although this person's title may range from manager to president depending on the size of the firm. The division vice-president will have the power to make pricing and output decisions as well as some capital expenditure decisions. Furthermore, the division vice-president, along with the chief executive officer of the firm, will constitute the management coalition of the firm, although this coalition may also contain other executives depending on the nature of the business and the characteristics of the individuals involved (see Cyert and March).

The firm in our theory operates under conditions of uncertainty. Thus the chief executive officer and his managers must make decisions about events whose occurrence is uncertain. Uncertainty as we use it might be described by a stochastic model in which the probability distributions of the observable random variables depends on the unknown values of various parameters (see DeGroot). Under these conditions, the true values of the parameters cannot usually be learned with certainty. Thus there will always be uncertainty facing the firm as it makes decisions because of both the stochastic nature of the variables to be observed and the unknown values of the parameters.

The description of the firm that we have presented is appropriate for most corporations regardless of size and, therefore, our theory is meant to be general.

Developing the Plan

Since the concept of maximizing profits has no unique meaning under conditions of uncertainty, the firm cannot derive any operational guidance from the simple desire to maximize profits. Therefore, the management of a firm attempts to develop a plan from which some specific operational steps will follow. The form of the plan consists of a series of target values for certain critical variables. These target values are developed on a monthly as well as annual basis. They are specified for the firm as a whole as well as for the divisions. The targets together with the initial positions of the firm and its divisions enable the firm to develop some specific strategies and tactics to attain the targets. The plan essentially gives structure to an unstructured situation characterized by uncertainty. The firm in neoclassical theory in a perfectly competitive market does not suffer from such a lack of structure and hence does not need a plan. In fact, the situation for the firm in perfect competition is so structured that it does not need a manager.

In order to develop such a plan, the management must be concerned with three sets of conditions: (1) conditions in the economy as a whole, (2) conditions in the industry and, in particular, in competitive firms, and (3) conditions inside the firm.

The initial step in the process of developing target values is to forecast the first set of conditions specified above. The management is particularly interested in the growth expected in the economy as a whole in each of the countries in which it is operating. The aim is the development of the growth factors that can be applied to the specific markets in which the firm sells – the second set of conditions. Out of a more complex framework than that given here, the firm's planners arrive at a specific estimate of the total sales expected in the industry, essentially based on estimated growth rates.

The third step is to take account of the set of conditions inside the firm. The planners must determine the firm's capability of expanding production over the previous period. They must look at such variables as labor negotiations, capital expenditures, and similar items related to the firm's productive capacity. The next step is the establishment of the targets.

Establishing Targets

In the planning process management selects certain key variables, which we shall call target variables, whose actual values during the year reflect the progress of the firm. The firm's management selects specific target values for these variables for the firm as a whole and for each of the divisions. The plan consists of these target values specified for the firm and each division on a monthly basis and for the year. The target values are the goals for the firm. These goals are believed by management to have a reasonable probability of being attained and thus, the plan is a prediction. This predictive process does not lead to unique values for the plan. Predictive probabilities are established for a range of value of the variables, and management, with the approval of the board, must select the values that will constitute the plan.

The target values established are a compromise generated by an interactive process between the board and the management. Management wants to have high prior probabilities of achieving any targets that it selects. The board of directors wants target values that show a significant rate of growth for the firm. Thus, the management tries to establish lower targets and the board tries to establish higher targets.

The target variables will vary somewhat from to firm. We will specify some targets that are generally used in order to illustrate our theory. We shall consider six targets for the firm as a whole: (1) net earnings per share, (2) net dollar sales, (3) cash flow, (4) return on investment, (5) return on stockholders' equity, and (6) new orders received.

1. *Net earnings per share (EPS)* is equal to the net profit divided by the number of shares outstanding, and represents the profit target for the firm. This variable is important because management will be evaluated on the attainment or non-attainment of its target values, and executive compensation plans are frequently tied to the degree of attainment.

2. *Net dollar sales* are important because of their relationship to market share. The firm in our theory does not know its demand curve with certainty and gains information about it through the trend of net sales. Net earnings in the future are a function of this trend as is the long-run survival of the firm. In a period of inflation, the sales figure is examined closely to see if the number of physical units sold has increased or decreased.

3. *Cash flow* is equal to net profit plus depreciation plus deferred taxes, and is crucial to the firm since the ultimate measure of the success of the firm is the amount of cash the firm generates. The flow of cash gives the firm information about the need for short- and long-term borrowing and, thus, becomes another indicator of the firm's overall well-being in the face of uncertainty.

4. *Return on investment* represents the proportion of the money invested in the firm by owners and lenders that is being returned as profit. It gives information to the firm that is important as a measure of quality of performance, and in addition, its value is one criterion of whether the firm should stay in business or not.

5. *Return on stockholders's equity* has many of the same characteristics as .return on investment. By focusing on the return on stockholders' equite the firm's management recognizes its responsibilities to the owners.

6. *New orders received* gives a measure that, like net sales, enables the firm to determine how well it is doing with respect to the future. It is a significant

variable because it gives the firm information about changes in its demand curve.

The monthly target values for variables 1 through 6 are important because they are related to the targets for the year. If the target value for a variable is attained each month, the firm will reach its target for the year. Thus, whenever the actual value for a variable is less than its target value in any month, the firm is concerned.

The division targets are essentially the same as those for the firm as a whole. However, the return on stockholders' equity does not make as much sense for the division as for the firm and is replaced by a target variable representing the ratio of net profit to sales. This variable gives the division a measure of the effectiveness of its pricing policy in producing profits since it shows the amount of profit per dollar of sales revenue.

Thus, from a situation of uncertainty, the firm and its divisions establish a set of target values. Once the plan is completed the firm must choose specific strategies to attain the target values and then wait for feedback to see if changes in strategy are necessary.

Comparison of Actual and Target

This feedback is obtained from the monthly financial statements for the divisions and the firm as a whole. Each month the financial system generates actual values of the target variables. When these are printed, the division managers meet with the CEO and analyze their positions. They examine the actual values for each of the target variables. Each division manager assesses his situation in the light of the three sets of conditions utilized to determine the plan. The objective of the meeting is to develop explanations for discrepancies between the actual values and the target values. The explanations are desired whether the actual values are less than, greater than, or equal to the target values.

If the actual value is less than the target value for one or more of the target variables an explanation must be found. This part of the process is known as the analysis phase.

An explanation must be found for the deficiency of an actual value from its target, whether the target relates to a particular division or to the firm. This explanation must be presented in terms of the present and recent past values of the variables involved in the three sets of conditions on which the plan is based. The search for an explanation depends on the relationship between the particular target variables being considered and the variables in these three sets. If no satisfactory explanation is found, then, as in the other sequential decision processes, the firm takes no new actions but rather waits for more information during the following month. The process of searching for an explanation is essentially a process of making inferences from the body of data consisting of the three sets of conditions and continues until an explanation is found with a high enough probability to warrant acceptance. Once an explanation is accepted the firm enters the next phase of the process, namely, the control phase.

Control Actions

If the explanation indicates that the deficiency in the actual values is due to random factors that are essentially transient in nature, no action will be taken. Frequently, however, even when the explanation lies in the variables relating to the economy as a whole the firm may be able to take internal actions designed to bring the actual values into control, that is, make the actual values equal to or greater than the target values for future months.

The various control actions that might be used by the firm are many and varied. Some actions affect the firm's interactions with the market, such as price changes, marketing policy changes, and mergers and acquisitions. Others relate to the contraction of the firm's operation such as closing a plant, selling a division or reducing the labor force. Basically, the first set is designed to increase revenue and the second to reduce cost.

In the usual control models, a cost function drives the model, but the cost function is usually chosen to have a canonical form, more for its mathematical convenience than its relationship to reality (see DeGroot). The specification of the cost function for the control process in the theory of the firm has the same difficulties. Consider, for example, the total earnings-per-share target. Management sets the target it desires to achieve for a variety of reasons. Some of these may be personal relating to executive compensation plans. Others may be professional, since the achievement of the goal is a measure of the quality of the management. Still others may involve the concept of responsibility to the shareholders. It is difficult, therefore, to give meaning to the notion of the cost of falling short of the target.

On the basis of the explanation the management must decide what actions to take in order to make the actual values meet the targets in future periods. Two aspects of each action that must be considered by management are the length of time required to take the action and the length of time for the effects of the action to become apparent. As examples, we will describe five commonly used control actions: (1) price changes, (2) mergers and acquisitions, (3) contraction, (4) selling some parts of the business, and (5) changing management.

1. *Price change is of course the primary action that has generally been considered in economic theory.* The firm that is considering this action goes through the kind of reasoning that has generally been portrayed in oligopoly theory. The reaction of competitors is of major concern. Of equal importance, however, is a judgment about the position of the demand curve based on the information flow from net sales and new orders. The advantage of a successful price change is that it takes effect quickly and the firm, therefore, can be brought into control relatively soon.

2. *Mergers and acquisitions are part of a longer-run set of actions designed to make actual values equal to or greater than target values.* This form of control action is used when the explanation indicates a structural deficiency that results in the firm's inability to attain its targets.

3. *Contraction as a control action includes such activities as closing plants, reducing the labor force and hence, the output, eliminating certain products completely, and similar actions.* These actions are taken, generally, when the firm believes it cannot affect the market and must respond by internal changes. The aim of the control is to reduce expenses proportionally more than revenues.

4. *Selling parts of the firm that are losing money is a common, longer-run type of control.* Again this method tends to be used when the explanation indicates that fundamental problems in the structure of the firm are preventing it from attaining control. Frequently, these segments of the business have been retained for a period of time while they are losing money because the future prospects are bright. At some point the firm makes a decision to sell. That decision will be made when one or more of the actual values has been less than its target value for a number of months and the explanation leaves the firm with no other action that can be taken to bring the firm into control.

5. *Changing management tends to be a last resort.* Such action, obviously, follows an explanation that leads to the inference that management is at fault. Generally, this action can take place immediately and usually a replacement from within the organization is available. The effects of the change will likely be fast. Thus, this action can have immediate effects in bringing the firm into control. The management changes might be at any level in the firm where the unit involved could have a significant effect on the target variables of the firm.

These control actions are only a subset of the total number of actions that might be taken, but they are the most important, we believe, and the ones most frequently taken. The objective of management is to select a control action that will be effective in bringing the firm into control. It must select that action among all the possible actions that will achieve this objective with the least cost over the entire planning period.

We have discussed being out of control only in terms of some of the actual values being less than the corresponding target values, but there are some control actions that may be taken when the actual is greater than the target. In particular, the firm is sensitive to the amount by which the actual EPS exceeds the target. The primary reason for this caution is that the management wants to show steady growth. This objective is desired because steady growth of a given percentage is an indication of good management, and because it is believed that the stock market places a high value on steady growth. All other things being equal, management would prefer two years of steady growth rather than one of great growth and one of relatively low growth. The firm tries to reduce profits that will push it far beyond its EPS target by putting more funds into contingency reserves of various kinds. A general contingency reserve is not allowed but it is frequently possible to reserve for plant damage or to develop reserves for unemployment insurance or workmen's compensation. Thus rather than allow the actual EPS to be significantly in excess of the target, the firm will increase its reserves and reduce profits in a particular period.

Methological Implications

The control approach to the firm is obviously a significant departure from conventional theory. The new approach was developed because of dissatisfaction with the empirical content of the neoclassical approach, and it therefore seems important to air some of the methodological issues involved.

The basis for arguing that standard microeconomic theory provides a good account of market behavior is weak. It consists chiefly of remarks that refer in a general way to a limited variety of situations where there is a qualitative agreement between what orthodox microeconomic models predict and what goes on in markets. Furthermore, the cases chosen for exhibiting this kind of agreement between theory and reality typically are picked out in the light of careful hindsight. Awkward disagreements between theory and reality tend to be swept under the convenient rug provided by the *ceteris paribus* clause which is a pervasive feature of the theory of the firm.[2]

According to the methodological position we hold, neoclassical micro-economic theory must be replaced by a different theory because its account of

---

[2] Some of this material is taken from Richard M. Cyert and Garrel Pottinger (1979) Towards a Better Microeconomic Theory. *Philosophy of Science,* Vol. 46, No. 2, June.

the behavior of individual firms is at odds with the facts about how firms behave. As we indicated above, the firm develops its plan as a way of making decisions under uncertainty. Profit maximization offers no operational clues to the management. The plan is a specific form of adaptation to the uncertainty facing the firm.

There are a variety of ways in which economic theory can deal with uncertainty. One of these is to retreat from the analysis of the individual units and rely on an analysis of market forces (see Alchian). This approach is related to the use of the environment by the biologists to explain adaptation of species. It has merit and might be used to provide an explanation for certain kinds of behavior in the long run and at an aggregate level. The approach in question, is, however, bound to lead to theories which are deficient in one important respect – such theories will not give an account of the behavior of the individual firms. This deficiency is important for two reasons. First, one must have an account of the behavior of individual firms in order to deal with monopoly and oligopoly. Second, although we are concerned with microeconomics as a positive science, it must be remembered that microeconomic theories are intended to have normative uses and that one of these is to help in the making of public policy decisions. Theories which do not give an account of the behavior of individual firms will not be helpful in policy discussion.

A second method of handling the problem of decision-making under uncertainty, which brings to bear the existing techniques of mathematical analysis, is to assume that the firm can develop subjective probability distributions of profit for decision alternatives. In addition it is necessary to assume that the firm has a utility function that enables it to convert probability distributions of profit into utilities and that the firm makes decisions so as to maximize the utility function. This may well be a useful approach if by empirical work the process by which businessmen establish probability distributions can be determined and if the form of the utility functions used by businessmen can be discovered (see Cyert and DeGroot, 1970).

A third method is to study empirically the way that businessmen make decisions in the face of uncertainty, to embed the decision process into a theory of the firm, and then to construct a theory of market behavior based on the resulting theory of the firm (see Cyert and March). This approach is the behavioral approach. The first problem to be considered is that of constructing the desired theory of the firm. The construction of such a theory will require the making of many observations. "Observation" can be viewed as a process in which a trained scientist watches and records the actual process of making a decision. The observations will include being present at meetings, interviewing relevant participants, analyzing written documents, and any other steps designed to lead to understanding of the criteria being used to make the decision and the goals these criteria are intended to serve. Such an approach requires the cooperation of the firm and the cooperation of the participants in the decision-making process. There are difficulties (e.g., the problem of getting an accurate picture of the process rather than a formalized, polished one developed for external purposes), but it is possible to make such observations (see Cyert, DeGroot, and Holt).

The critical problem involved in constructing the theory of the firm required by the behavioral approach is to determine the goals of the firm and to understand the process by which decision rules are learned and modified in the face of feedback from the environment in the interest of serving these goals. This problem is critical because one of the main ideas behind the approach is that the way to get a better theory of the firm is by viewing it as an adaptive mechanism that can learn from its environment, and it seems clear that the features of this sort of learning which will lend themselves to theoretical treatment are the decision rules used in the firms.

As an adaptive mechanism the firm is able to learn about its environment by taking actions and analyzing the results. The actions it takes – raising price, increasing output, etc. – are selected from a limited number of alternatives. The actions are designed to achieve a goal – a particular level of profit, a certain market share – and the results of the actions are analyzed in terms of achieving the goal. The results of the analysis are then stored within the organization's memory and the demand curve or the cost curve begin to take on certain characteristics as a result. Thus, if price is increased on a number of different occasions and demand does not slacken, it is likely that the demand curve will be characterized as highly inelastic. This example is a simple one and is designed to illustrate what we mean by the firm as an adaptive mechanism. The firm is capable of learning under far more complex conditions and adapting appropriately.

We note there is reason to think that the goals which drive this process are pretty much the same from firm to firm, when considered in general terms, though different firms will consider these goals to have been achieved by quite different levels of performance and a given firm will alter the desired levels of performance over time. This similarity of goals should make it easier to do the job we are projecting, but we also note that we do not intend to rule out the possibility that a firm may acquire new goals and discard old ones in the course of time. If this process of acquiring and discarding goals is found to be an important aspect of the working of firms, then it will have to be studied in detail.

In treating the processes to be studied, careful attention must be given to the fact that the firm (even with computers) has a limited capability to process information and, therefore, may not reach the position that hindsight analysis demonstrates to have been optimum.

We call the decision rules to be studied behavioral rules. The firm develops these rules of thumb as guides for making decisions in a complex environment with uncertainty and incomplete information. Behavioral rules incorporate the decision-makers' assumptions about the nature of the environment and the nature of the firm itself which suffice to allow a decision to be reached in such circumstances. The aim of the behavioral approach to the theory of the firm is to make business judgment susceptible of rational, theoretical treatment by analyzing what is essential to the process of judgment in terms of sets of behavioral rules.

Turning from the theory of the firm to the problem of constructing a micro-economic theory based on the theory of the firm, we note that we are not recommending that the baby be thrown out with the bath water. Indeed, we lay it down as a requirement both for the theory of the firm and for the theory of market behavior that as the behavioral theory is applied to situations in which uncertainty gives way to certainty and knowledge increases without limit, the results derived from the behavioral theory should approximate more and more closely those derived by *a priori* reasoning about the simplified situation treated by the orthodox theory.

A scientific theory is supposed to provide an account of what will happen in a variety of possible worlds, and we acknowledge that the orthodox theory works admirably for an extensive set of worlds which differ from the one that we live in chiefly by not involving decisions made under uncertainty and incomplete information. Clearly, in such a world the firm operating in the framework of the competitive system with market prices, the marginal cost curve, and the average variable cost curve known has no need for behavioral rules other than those derived by the usual marginalist reasoning. In these circumstances the firm must determine prices and output by the intersection of the price and marginal cost curve. It is the firm operating under conditions of ignorance of its demand and cost curves which must find other methods of decision-making. We are aiming at a theory which, both with respect to the behavior of individual firms and with respect to the behavior of markets, will explain what is going on in the latter situation and establish clearly the relations between this and the existing account of what is going on in the former.

The concept of behavioral rules is not new to economics. Every determinate model developed under conditions of some uncertainty utilizes a behavioral rule. In the cobweb model, suppliers are assumed to determine the current period's supply on the basis of the last period's price, $s(t) = f[p(t-1)]$. In the Cournot duopoly model, each firm assumes that it is independent of its rival, in particular that a change in its output will have no effect on its rival. In the kinked-demand curve model, each firm assumes its rival will always behave in the way that will hurt it the most. Thus a price increase will not be followed by rivals but a price decrease will. For other models where uncertainty exists in the situation being modeled but is eliminated in the model, some form of behavioral rule can be shown to be present.

Implications of the Control Approach

This paper has been an attempt to apply some of these methodological considerations. The firm establishes targets and then uses a control approach to attain the targets. In one sense the selection of optimal control techniques replaces profit maximization as the objective of the firm.

We begin by assuming that uncertainty is important and that behavior will be different under uncertainty from that exhibited under certainty. Specifically, we argue that under conditions of uncertainty, the firm proceeds by setting a target profit figure. This figure stretches the management but has some prohability of attainment that seems reasonable by management. The firm's behavior then, we argue, can be better explained by control theory than by the assumption of profit maximization. We are not interested in whether the targets approximate maximization values or satisficing values (see Simon). We argue that the firm regards the targets as critical and selects its actions to attain its targets.

The model is based on empirical observations but we are not prepared to argue that the extent of the observations is so great that the model should be immediately accepted as valid. The observations have been used as a stimulus for theorizing, and we argue that the current model, if followed, has a better potential for yielding explanations about firm behavior than the neoclassical model. It should also be remembered that the latter is based on certainty.

Any attempt to develop a theory, as we have done, that emphasizes process and does not explicitly use profit maximization, immediately raises the "so what" question. In other words, it is incumbent on the proponents of a new approach to demonstrate that the new approach makes a difference. On that question we make the following propositions:

1) Our approach can explain when a firm will take an economically significant action. The conventional approach cannot.
2) Our approach encompasses within itself actions such as price changes, mergers, acquisitions, and sell-offs. The conventional approach deals only with price changes. All other behaviors are explained separately.
3) Within our approach it is also possible to encompass the capital investment decision.

4) Marginal analysis when the data are available is not ruled out by our approach. In fact, the selection of control techniques explicitly uses a marginal approach.
5) Our approach attempts to explain behavior for a firm explicitly organized like the firms responsible for the majority of assets in the economy.
6) Our approach deals directly with decision-making under uncertainty, which is the condition under which most firms must operate.

These are a few of the reasons why we recommend our approach or variants of it that may be developed. It is true that our approach puts a heavy emphasis on the individual firm but there is no difficulty in dealing with markets.

Summary

We are suggesting in this paper that the economists look at control theory as an alternative form of describing the firm to the conventional marginal analysis. The processes within the firm, we believe, can be better described by control theory. The usual cycle that conventional theory describes can also be described by control theory. The control theory of the firm describes the firm as it makes decisions under uncertainty. Critical aspects of behavior involve the control actions that the firm takes when the actual results are below the target. It is these actions which result in price changes, output changes, inventory changes, layoffs, mergers, and acquisition. It is our belief that it is only through understanding the development of the plans, the setting of targets, and the control actions that the decision-making behavior of the firm can be understood. We have tried to make a start on a descriptive theory of decision-making: As Simon has said "We have now lived through three centuries or more of vigorous and highly successful inquiry into the laws of nature. Much of that inquiry has been driven by the simple urge to understand, to find the beauty of order hidden in complexity. Time and again, we have found the 'idle' truths arrived at through the process of inquiry to be of the greatest moment for practical human affairs. I need not take time here to argue the point. Scientists know it, engineers and physicians know it, congressmen and members of parliaments know it, the man in the street knows it.

But I am not sure that this truth is as widely known in economics as it ought to be. I cannot otherwise explain the rather weak and backward development of the descriptive theory of decision-making including the theory of the firm, the sparse and scattered settlement of its terrain, and the fact that many, if not most, of its investigators are drawn from outside economics – from sociology, from psychology, and from political science." (Simon, 1979).

References

Alchian, A. (1950) Uncertainty, Evolution, and Economic Theory. *Journal of Political Economy,* Vol. 58.

Cohen, K. J., Cyert, R. M. (1975) *Theory of the Firm, Resource Allocation in a Market Economy,* Englewood Cliffs, N. J.: Prentice-Hall.

Cyert, R. M., DeGroot, M. H. (1970) Bayesian Analysis and Duopoly Theory. *Journal of Political Economy,* Vol. 78.

Cyert, R. M., DeGroot, M. H., Holt, C. (1979) Capital Allocation within a Firm. *Behavioral Science,* Vol. 24.

Cyert, R. M., March, J. G. (1963) *A Behavioral Theory of the Firm.* Englewood Cliffs, N. J.: Prentice-Hall.

DeGroot, Morris H. (1970) *Optimal Statistical Decision.* New York: McGraw Hill.

Simon, H. A. (1955) A Behavioral Model of Rational Choice. *Quarterly Journal of Economics,* Vol. 69.

– (1979) Rational Decision Making in Business Organization. *The American Economic Review,* Vol. 69, No. 4.

Why the World Needs Organizational Design[1]

William H. Starbuck and Paul C. Nystrom

This world is a representation of our language categories, not vice versa (Leach, 1964: p. 34). We have edited two collections of articles devoted to organizational design. The first of these, "Prescriptive Models of Organizations" (Nystrom and Starbuck, 1977), began with a widespread search for manuscripts. Eighteen journals and newsletters announced that we were seeking manuscripts: ones prescribing properties organizations should have, or ones prescribing how to induce desirable changes in organizations. We received 47 manuscripts in response. In view of the published announcements, the most striking characteristic of these manuscripts was their irrelevance to organizational design. Only a handful paid any attention to prescriptive issues. Had we judged the manuscripts solely for their existing contents, we would have had to cancel the project. Consequently, we looked for ways the manuscripts could be made relevant to design, and we urged the authors of the more promising manuscripts to make revisions of that type. The revised manuscripts showed more relevance; but some still said nothing about prescriptive issues, and several authors tried to prescribe indirectly, without using the words should and ought to. So we asked for revisions again. And sometimes again.

The second collection, the "Handbook of Organizational Design" (Nystrom and Starbuck, 1981) began with rather specific guidelines for chapters. A general memorandum stated that every chapter should address both prescriptive and descriptive questions; and each chapter's domain was demarcated through typical descriptive questions and exemplary prescriptive questions. Quite a few of the first drafts of chapters ignored the prescriptive questions entirely, and many first drafts gave the prescriptive questions little attention. Some authors engendered confusion by prescribing with the same kinds of words that people normally use when describing; others, using the words must and have to, disguised their prescriptions as inescapable necessities. We again found ourselves having to pull prescriptive statements out of authors: although nearly all authors co-operated with us, several said they found prescription difficult, and a few resisted our urgings strenuously.

These experiences dramatised for us the strength of the barriers against prescription. People (like ourselves) who start out optimistically to promote design or to create design prescriptions run into at least three challenges that

---

[1] Reprint from: The Journal of General Management, 1981

can crush optimism. Do organizations need to be designed? Would design benefit science? Is design practical today?

We believe that all three questions call for affirmative answers. But a lot of people disagree with us. This article explains why design arouses strong opposition and why we have chosen to confront that opposition.

One reason we think we understand opposition to design is that some years ago, in the early 1960s, we ourselves would have answered a couple of these questions negatively. There is something to be said for both sides. However, the key issue should not be which view is right, but which view better stimulates beneficial activities. Because a given activity yields different benefits in different situations, the best view should vary from time to time, and perhaps from person to person.

Thus, we neither expect nor desire to persuade everyone of the rightness of design. We hope to learn from those who disagree with us. Conflicts between views help social scientists to discover their biases and implicit premises, and to observe different aspects of reality. Diverse perceivers see diverse phenomena. Prevalent dissension encourages perceivers to look in unorthodox directions and to say what they see (Hedberg, Nyström and Starbuck, 1976; Coser, 1956). The only view that is truly wrong is a claim that one view alone is right.

Do Organization Need to be Designed?

There can be no doubt that a large part of the process of socialization in any society consists of teaching the young that which they must not see, not hear, not think, feel, or say. Without very definite rules about what should remain outside one's awareness, an orderly society would be as unthinkable as one that fails to teach its members what they must be aware of and communicate about. But as always there are limits and there is an opposite extreme which is reached when the reality distortion inherent in avoidance or denial begins to outweigh its advantages (Watzlawick, Weakland and Fisch, 1974: 42).

Some organization theorists perceive organizations as the admirable products of rational analyses, managerial skills, collective efforts, and social evolution. Such people make purely descriptive studies of organizations' structures, and they portray their findings as inexorable natural laws. We conjecture that these are the people who state prescriptions with descriptive verbs on the premise that organizations actually do what they should do, or who phrase prescriptions as compulsory constraints on the premise that organizations should do what they must do. Certainly, such people have reason to doubt the need for explicit design efforts, for they see elegance and virtue in existing organizations.

Other organization theorists perceive organizations as hierarchical structures that enable a few fortunate people to reap benefits from the labor of many unfortunate people, who receive too little pay for performing dull, demeaning and dangerous jobs. Some of these organization theorists report with outrage about organizations' consequences; others protest that empirical research implicitly endorses the status quo by implying that today's organizations will persist with few changes. These organization theorists also challenge the usefulness of design; they argue that the people who dominate organizations will accept only marginal changes that do not significantly improve jobs or render organizations more equitable, and that actually enhance exploitation even when they appear to alleviate misery.

Those who advocate organizational design inhabit a middle ground between these extremes. Designers see defects in today's organizations, and they believe that these defects are not self-correcting, but require explicit remedial efforts. They also accept that modest improvements are worth seeking – possibly because today's organizations have strong assets and weak liabilities, or because drastic changes arouse resistance, or because improvements may benefit tens of millions of people. Designers perceive quite diverse realities. They also disagree with each other about what ought to be. There are those who advocate making organizations more rational, more playful, more efficient, more humane, more useful to societies, more profitable for owners, more satisfying to members, more stable, more flexible, more proactive, more adaptive, more democratic, more obedient to top managers, and so on . . . and on.

We doubt that we, or anyone, knows what changes should be made. Although we have ideas, others disagree with us. We are, however, persuaded that most of today's organizations are poorly designed, and that large improvements can be made. Consider some of the evidence.

Prevalent Deficiencies

Organizations inflict great harm on their members. Each year, 100,000 American workers die of job-produced illnesses and accidents (General Accounting Office, 1977). This is more deaths per annum than the United States has suffered in any declared war. Less severe injuries to mental and physical health are even more prevalent (Kornhauser, 1965). Approximately 400,000 American workers acquire occupational diseases annually (General Accounting Office, 1977). Job strain correlates with exhaustion, depression, pill consumption, sick days, and dissatisfaction with job or life (Karasek, 1979). Factory closings promote heart disease, and both managerial and non-managerial jobs foster heart disease (Bailey, 1976; Kasl, Cobb and Brooks, 1986; Wright, 1975). Most workers judge their jobs to be deficient in meaning (Argyis, 1973; O'Toole et al., 1973). Asked why they might prefer other jobs to those they were currently performing, 50% to 77% of British workers voiced desires for more intrinsic rewards such as variety and autonomy, whereas only 10% to 35% said they wanted higher pay or promotions (Goldhorpe et al., 1968).

Organizations' methods and values yield wrong decisions, illegal and unethical actions, and deceptions. For example, most organizations incur unnecessary turnovers of personnel merely by failing to give realistic information to prospective members (Wanous, 1980). Another dramatic illustration concerns a company's attempt to sell an unsafe aircraft brake (Vandivier, 1972). Two low-level workers assigned to test prototypes discovered that the brake had been incorrectly designed: they tried to persuade their superiors to redesign the brake. Instead, their superiors ordered the workers to sign false reports about the brake's performance, thus making the workers liable. After a test on an actual airplane confirmed the workers' fears, they secretly reported what had been going on to the Federal Bureau of Investigation. Their superiors reacted differently to the field test: they prepared an analysis which argued that the false performance reports constituted a legitimate exercise of engineering discretion. Investigations by three governmental agencies ended in Congressional hearings, but no criminal charges were filed. The company redesigned the brake, fired the two workers who had spoken up, and promoted two of their superiors who had contributed to the deception.

Stakeholders outside of organizations – clients, customers, neighbours, stockholders, suppliers – complain about their treatment. For example, from 26% to 46% of American customers complain about the automobile tyres made by the five major manufacturers (Wall Street Journal, 1978). From 18% to 24% of defaults by consumer debtors result from defective merchandise, price deception, false promises by sellers, or tricks used to obtain signatures on contracts (Caplovitz, 1974). Stockholders complain about control by managers, and they may have good reason: business firms having boards of directors with many members from the firms' managements tend to retain earnings rather than to pay dividends to stockholders (Williamson, 1963). Even organizations with highly educated, professional workers may take advantage of their clients. Architects, dentists, lawyers, nurses and physicians gain economic benefits from occupational licensing, at the expense of their clients or the public (Stigler, 1971). An experiment placed sane people as patients in psychiatric wards (Rosenhan, 1973). Although these sane patients behaved normally, and many of the real patients recognized that the sane patients were sane, the wards' professional staffs uniformly treated the sane patients as if they were insane. The sane patients were rendered quite unhappy by being deprived of power and individuality. In New Zealand, which pioneered in developing a public ombudsman, people complain strongly about the major governmental agencies of their welfare state: these agencies attract 65% of all complaints in urban areas and 49% elsewhere (Hill, 1972). Governmental regulatory agencies may not serve the public. Regulations upon American trucking appear to have arisen because trucking firms sought protection (Stigler, 1971). The US Interstate Commerce Commission has nurtured high profits by railroads, thus benefiting stockholders and large shippers at the expense of general consumers (Kolko, 1965).

Frequent Failures

If people retain those organizations which are performing well, organizations' life spans may indicate their effectiveness. Table 1 shows the half-lives of two kinds of organizations: half-lives are the periods in which half of the organizations disappear through dissolutions, bankruptcies, mergers or drastic reorganizations. Thus, if each year were an average year, half of the newly created corporations would disappear in 3.3 years.

Studies in both Great Britain and the United States imply that halflives do not vary significantly with organizations' sizes for a wide range of sizes (Starbuck and Nystrom, 1981: IX–XXII). Just two size categories differ substantially from the norm: the very largest new corporations and the very smallest organizations – such as small proprietorships – disappear much more quickly than Table 1 implies. Of all American business firms, 85% are not corporations and three-fourths have fewer than four paid employees, and the half-life of newly created business firms is just 21 months (Churchill, 1955).

Half-lives do, however, grow longer as organizations grow older. This may happen because worse ideas get weeded out earlier, or because organizations gradually learn effective operating procedures, or because time enables organizations to develop supportive relations with their environments (such as lines of credit, loyal customers, grateful legislators, or helpful interest groups). For instance, half on the twenty-year-old corporations can be expected to survive at least 12.4 more years, but the twenty-year-old corporations represent only 10% of those initially created. However, even elderly organizations are far from immortal: 30% of the fifty-year-old corporations can be expected to disappear within ten years, as can 26% of the fifty-year-old agencies.

Thus, all organizations are temporary arrangements, and the great majority of organizations last for just a few years. If people are retaining satisfactory organizations, dissatisfaction must be rampant.

Table 1: Survival by Two Kinds of Organizations

Organizations' ages	American Corporations		US Federal Agencies	
	Half-lives	Percentages remaining	Half-lives	Percentages remaining
Newly created	3.3 years	100%	4.6 years	100%
Ten-years-old	8.6 years	21%	10.7 years	29%
Twenty-years-old	12.4 years	10%	15.1 years	15%
Fifty-years-old	21.0 years	2%	25.0 years	4%

This inference conforms with our own studies of organizations facing serious crises (Hedberg et al., 1976; Nystrom, Hedberg and Starbuck, 1976; Starbuck, Greve and Hedberg, 1978). When these studies began, we thought crises were unusual events that afflicted abnormal organizations, and we were searching for the abnormal properties that made some organizations crisis-prone. But what we saw does not fit these hypotheses. Crises confront all organizations at the times they are first created, and some organizations need a decade or longer to work their ways out of these initial crises. The abnormal organizations are the few that manage to survice for several years. Among those which do survive, some encounter crises: yet when one compares the organizations that encounter crises with those which do not, one is hard pressed to see differences. The organizational processes which produce crises are substantially identical with the processes which produce successes. Indeed, successes foster crises by producing self-confidence and complacency and by making organizations want to stabilise their behaviours and environments.

Of those organizations which encounter crises, almost all disappear or reorganize drastically, so the organizations which survice crises constitute an extremely abnormal class. It may be that surviving a crisis gives an organization characteristics that help it avoid or survive future crises; but surviving a crisis may also breed a reckless self-confidence that leads an organization to encounter future crises or to underestimate the risks they pose. Certainly, there are not many organizations that have survived with continuity for, say, 200 years.

Some Inferences

The foregoing observations imply that organization theorists should proceed very cautiously when they infer design prescriptions from observations of today's organizations. Most of today's organizations, including those several years old, are on route to disappearance, crisis or major re-organization; they are also making their members unhealthy and their stakeholders unhappy. Indiscriminate empirical studies are much more likely to reveal practices which are threatening survival than practices which are fostering survival, much more likely to observe transient characteristics than stable characteristics, much more likely to find characteristics which are generating social problems than characteristics which are solving social problems. If some organizations are worth imitating, they are peculiar organizations that have to be chosen carefully from the general population.

But it is debatable that design prescriptions should promote imitation. One reason is that desirable properties may not be imitable. For example, it makes no sense to tell a new organization to act like an old organization: the new organization cannot instantaneously manufacture effective operating procedures, loyal customers, a history of good relations with creditors or legislators, or an influential political constituency. A second reason is that imitation discourages reflection and so undercuts itself by leading organizations to emulate inappropriate characteristics and practices. For instance, labor unions' efforts to bureaucratise are stifling democracy: democracy in Canadian unions correlates negatively with centralisation, formalisation and specialisation (Anderson, 1978). Yet another reason is that the advantages of many organizational characteristics are comparative rather than absolute. Imitating such characteristics can itself be disadvantageous. For example, idiosyncratic practices by one business firm might confer competitive advantages that produce unusually large profits; but if other firms imitate these practices to enlarge their profits, the competitive advantages disappear and no firm obtains unusually large profits. The Glacier Metal Company of London achieved renown by taking on extreme characteristics that fostered exceptional success (Jaques, 1951). Glacier later opened a plant in a Scottish village, and the employees at this plant struck in protest against Glacier's characteristics (Kelly, 1968). Evidently, Glacier's characteristics had succeeded precisely because of their idiosyncracy: London provided a large labor market in which Glacier could attract unusual employees who enjoyed what Glacier offered, so the company gained comparative advantages. But Glacier lacked comparative advantages in the village, where it employed a crossection of the population.

Valid prescriptions arise from speculations and unsystematic observations as well as from the systematic evidence that characterizes average organizations. Indeed, truly innovative designs have to originate in deviant cases or in fantasies rather than in statistical norms; and highly valuable characteristics and practices have to be statistically unusual, because prevalence destroys comparative advantages. Descriptive statements about average organizations can, however, disclose practices that conform to societal norms and values, and they can suggest practices to avoid in competitive industries.

Well designed organizations would differ from most current organizations, and contingency theories say they would differ from each other. Such organizations would probably be seen as suspect deviants by their environments – which appreciate conformity to societal norms and values (Meyer and Rowan, 1977).

For instance, one small company made expensive chemical instruments which it sold by mail order at prices well below its competitors. This company doubled its revenues and profits every six months for a dozen years, eventually attaining a net worth of $40 million (in 1981 dollars). This success attracted the attention of several large firms, one of which bought the company. The new owners were horrified to discover that their subsidiary had only rudimentary paperwork procedures, no cost accounting system, and no sales staff. No modern firm could operate in this fashion! They installed proper procedures and cost accounting, and they hired sales staff. Costs rose, so prices were raised. Demand fell, revenue fell, and profits became losses.

Communes are deviant kinds of organizations in Israel and the United States. When communes in these societies isolate themselves in order to protect their deviant characteristics, they wither for lack of sustenance; and when communes interact with these societies in order to obtain sustenance, they gradually take on conventional characteristics and lose their deviant characteristics (Niv, 1978). This observation probably generalizes to all kinds of deviant organizations. Although Glacier Metal Company and the small instrument company show that deviance can yield exceptional success, to be both deviant and well designed may be as difficult as to be both conventional and well designed.

Evidently, organizational design should involve mass education. A designer who focuses on one organization can achieve very little, and what the designer does achieve is immediately threatened by a hostile environment. Substantial achievements that persist will entail alterations of organizations' environments.

Prevailing norms and values in the industrialised, urbanised societies preach that organizations ought to be efficient, consistent and rational; procedures should be standardized and spelled out in manuals; specialized experts are expected to outperform versatile generalists; organizations should co-ordinate activities, eliminate redundancy, avoid conflict, and keep complete records. However, equally intelligent norms and values state that organizations also should foster dissension, beware of accumulating wealth, tolerate noncomparable and inharmonious goals, invest in flexible resources, and engage in planning but not rely on their plans (Hedberg et al., 1976; Nicholls, 1980). Therefore, the main educational task for organizational designers is probably to persuade societies to tolerate diverse organizational forms.

Would Design Benefit Science?

... if you want to understand something, try to change it.[2]

Many organization theorists perceive themselves as passive observers of events in which they play no parts. Some of these people aspire to describe and understand their environments, but not to change them. Others would like to influence their environments, but believe they would be wrong to attempt this. Some of them argue that one should understand one's environment thoroughly before one tries to alter it, because premature change efforts may create worse problems than the ones they aim to solve. Some people also argue that social scientists should not inject personal values into their work, because scientific observations should be objective, and because public trust in scientists rests upon their objectivity.

These orientations are reinforced by academic status distinctions: the so-called pure scientists bear higher prestige than the impure appliers of knowledge. Chemists and physicists have higher prestige than engineers, abstract mathematicians more than applied mathematicians, sociologists more than social workers, and psychologists more than marketing researchers.

The Costs of Objectivity

Some value issues are illustrated in the case of a social psychologist who studied conflict resolution and who publicly opposed the United States' warfare in Vietnam during the 1960s. Initially, a few of this psychologist's colleagues were worried that his opposition to warfare might contaminate his scientific findings, but their anxieties eased after he pointed out that he had often published findings that contradicted his hypotheses. After the New York Times published a letter from the psychologist, a multimillionaire protested to the university that professors should abstain from debates about foreign policy and should disdain left-wing publications such as the New York Times. Immediately thereafter, university administrators opined that the psychologist had acted unprofessionally insofar as he had published outside his area of expertise, which was social psychology and not foreign affairs. The multi-millionaire and the university administrators obviously thought that they should influence debates about foreign policy.

One of the social psychologist's colleagues, an economist, asserted strongly that social scientists ought to be dispassionate and value-free. This economist studied the structures of competitive markets, and he published articles proposing changed procedures for selling government securities: he and his

---

[1] Walter Fenno Dearborn, as quoted by Bronfenbrenner, 1976: 164.

colleagues looked upon these articles as proper applications of his professional expertise. The economist also accepted without question his discipline's use of monetary aggregates, such as gross national product and personal consumption expenditures, that weight the activities and preferences of wealthy people much more heavily than the activities and preferences of poor people.

Those who demand objectivity of organization theorists are asking for the wrong thing. Like the economist, organization theorists express their values whenever they speak, and those organization theorists who feign objectivity are deceiving both themselves and their audiences.

Subjectivity is inherent in empirical observation. Because empiricists have to study existing organizations, empiricists have to believe that existing organizations deserve study. Although many empiricists strive to keep their minds open – to see faults as well as virtues – one cannot question every premise. Some properties of existing organizations must be taken as stable givens, and stable properties easily become desirable properties. For example, some organizational members are classified as managers, and they allocate resources, choose strategies and supervise other organizational members. Nearly all organization theorists assume that a managerial class will continue to exist and perform activities like those they now do. But there are ambiguous boundaries between predicting that managers will exist and prescribing that managers should exist, between predicting that managers will supervise and prescribing that managers should supervise. Organization theorists nearly always cross those boundaries. Observers of the correlations between organizations' structures and their technologies assume that structures and technologies are not changing rapidly to correct large imbalances. But if there are no large imbalances, organizations must be well designed; and if one judges today's organizations to be well designed, one is implicitly endorsing the values that steer today's organizations. Theorists who perceive harmonies between organizations and their environments, or harmonies among organizational subsystems, are passing their observations through perceptual filters that interpret change as a sign of stress and stability a sign of balance; and conversely, theorists who see adaptations and corrections of imbalances are regarding change as beneficial and stability as dangerous.

Organization theorists are not wrong to admire their societies or to see faults in those societies. Such feelings cannot be avoided. But it is wrong to claim that one's research, writing and teaching do not express one's values and beliefs. One can compensate for the biases one admits but not for the biases one denies, and one's readers and listeners can more easily correct for the biases one makes public. In effect, the doctrine of scientific objectivity impedes research by making it illegitimate for scientists to be self-aware, and it undermines public trust in scientists by preventing scientists from communicating forthrightly.

The Benefits of Subjectivity

The impure realm of design nurtures self-awareness and forthright communication. People accept the relevance and legitimacy of values in discussions of design prescriptions, so designers are not criticized for pursuing goals and stating their values, even when their specific goals attract criticisms. Knowing that different people often endorse the same action for conflicting reasons, people apply their own values, not the designers' values, when they evaluate designers' prescriptions. In fact, stating their goals helps designers to win acceptance of their prescriptions. Statements of the form "An organization should be X" seem to come from arrogant and dogmatic speakers, but not statements of the form "In order to achieve Y, an organization should be X".

Design also raises the costs of holding erroneous beliefs. When erroneous beliefs exact low costs, comparisons among alternative beliefs yield inconclusive results, and scientists have weak incentives to replace erroneous beliefs with better ones. Involvement in design compels organization theorists to correlate their beliefs with pragmatic consequences, and motivates them to innovate theoretically in order to solve important problems (Gordon and Marquis, 1966).

The Impotence of Postdictive Analyses

One reason organization theorists' beliefs incorporate large errors is that they arise through postdictive analyses of spontaneous phenomena (Starbuck, 1976). Spontaneous phenomena intermingle diverse processes in non-random and uncontrolled blends, and they mix logically impossible events together with events that do not occur because they are deviant, foolish, ineffective, undesirable, unthought of, or without precedents. Spontaneous phenomena are also dominated by uneventful events: nearly all behaviors result from non-reflective executions of preexisting routines; nearly all jobs look the same as they did last week; nearly all business firms say they are seeking profits; nearly all organizations create conventional hierarchies of superiors and subordinates. Because the formulators of postdictive theories know what phenomena they should explain, all serious theories are compatible with the important phenomena – at least those phenomena which the formulators consider important. Competing postdictive theories differ more in what phenomena they try to explain than in their abilities to explain.

These postdictive analyses have also spawned theories
(a) that portray organizations as simple and static;
(b) that emphasize organizations' structures, and
(c) that focus on those characteristics which generalise across diverse kinds of organizations (Daft, 1980).
All three of these emphases are unproductive.

Real organizations are complex and changing, so simple, static theories afford poor bases for predicting what will happen in real organizations. The prevailing theories describe how a few phenomena can vary over small ranges of variation, assuming that multitudinous contingencies vary little, and the theories incorporate large errors. Even postdictive correlations rarely account for more than half of the variance. The theories that describe larger variations generally incorporate larger errors. When theories are extrapolated from smaller ranges of variation to larger ones, when theoretical propositions are combined, or when contingencies are assumed to vary substantially, the projection errors cascade and amplify greatly. Consequently, the only dependable way to discover what will happen in a real organization is to become a designer and to try to make it happen.

Study after study has failed to find strong relations between organizational structures and organizations' behaviors, technologies or environments. Organizational size is the only characteristic that correlates strongly with structures. An implication is that organizational structures have little to do with organizational behaviors. Two sociologists have offered an interesting interpretation of the structures of schools (Meyer and Rowan, 1977): schools' administrative structures do not control what occurs in classrooms, but the structures do serve schools by creating the impression that schools conform to societal expectations about how organizations should look; thus, schools have legitimacy which enables them to attract resources, and yet classroom behaviors are left autonomous. This view generalizes beyond schools. Organizational structures may be superficial facades in front of behavioral processes, facades that confer legitimacy and ease interorganizational flows of information, money and people. Outsiders believe, often wrongly, that they know whom to contact and who will speak for an organization. Lenders expect, usually erroneously, that conventional structures signify expert management. New personnel assume, but not for long, that their new associates will behave like former associates having similar job titles. But these beliefs say little about concrete behaviors or the contents of messages. Organizations with similar structures may be creating humanitarian services or plotting mass destruction, going bankrupt or earning large profits.

Studies have also found few, if any, interesting, strong relations among the characteristics that generalize across all kinds of organizations. This vacuum seems to be meaningful, because it has remained despite careful and sophisticated research methods (Starbuck, 1981). We have already pointed out that the characteristics shared by many organizations undercut comparative advantages and promote instability: organizations that have survived may be organizations that did not rely strongly upon the characteristics they shared. Moreover, diverse kinds of organizations exist, and most organizations possess characteristics that compensate for the characteristics of neighboring organizations. Governmental agencies perform activities in which there is no profit; labor unions and professional associations counteract the demands of employers; small manufacturers that produce to order serve customers who are dissatisfied with the standardized outputs from large bureaucracies (Schriesheim, von Glinow and Kerr, 1977; Starbuck and Dutton, 1973).

The Promise of Experimentation With Prediction

In order to create better theories, organization theorists should use methods that highlight the differences between theories and they should treat organizations as distinctive, changing and complex. Probably the most effective method for studying complex, flexible entities is experimentation. Experiments do not have to be explicitly planned: natural experiments occur whenever spontaneous events perturb organizations. Empiricists can watch organizations react to reorganizations, to disruptions of information flows or material flows, to fluctuating inputs or demands, and to natural disasters, to new laws, or to technological innovations. However, natural experiments do incur the liabilities that go with spontaneous events, so organization theorists should instigate experiments as well as observe natural ones. Indeed, explicitly planned experiments have borne more fruits – both theoretical fruits and pragmatic ones – than experiments that just happened to happen (Warner, 1981; Warner 1980).

Prescriptions for experimenting effectively with organizations include: seek instruction rather than control; replicate; observe behavior over long periods; allow for expectation effects; treat each experiment as one step in a sequence; try to create antithetical treatments (Taylor and Vertinsky, 1981; Warner, 1981). Experimenters should adopt a world view that allows for complex interdependencies, because the world does not confine itself to linear and additive behaviors such as are assumed by the experimental designs that are mislabelled rigorous (Bronfenbrenner, 1976).

Designers instigate experiments, and designers are forced to couple their experimentation with prediction. Before organizations will undertake experiments having significant consequences, they demand plausible predictions about consequences, and they evaluate methods and consequences. These predictions create opportunities to be surprised and then to investigate why the predictions went wrong, and the experimenting organizations insist on plausible explanations for wrong predictions. Visible and significant consequences provide incentives to replace misleading theories. Evaluations by organizational members disrupt designers' complacency and help them discover their own values and implicit assumptions.

Thus, organizational design is another domain in which progress derives impetus from collisions between cultures. Interactions with organizational members can help organization theorists attain greater understanding of organizations, and organization theorists can help members improve their organizations. Organization theorists stand to gain as much from this interaction as do organizational members, and societies gain in both dimensions.

Is Design Practical Today?

A well designed organization is not a stable solution to achieve, but a developmental process to keep active' (Starbuck and Nystrom, 1981).

We have already pointed out that some organization theorists believe this is too soon to attempt organizational design. They say organization theorists should achieve thorough understanding of organizations before trying to change them, because prescriptions in the absence of understanding may make organizations worse, not better.

There is, indeed, reason for concern on this point. Because economists' efforts to control economies have been based on incomplete beliefs about how economies work, their control efforts have created economies in which unemployment rises whenever inflation stops accelerating (Hayek, 1974). Similarly, organization theorists' efforts to improve job satisfaction and productivity through good human relations may have inadvertently increased workers' distrust of managers and reduced their willingness to co-operate; and efforts to engender goal commitment through management-by-objectives programs may have heightened subordinates' awareness of their superiors' dominance and reduced the trust between superiors and subordinates.

However, such errors of prescription may result more from self-inflicted ignorance than from unavailable information. Economists have formulated erroneous control policies even though they possessed observations that could have steered them in other directions. Hayek has remarked:

"We know, of course, with regard to the market and similar social structures, a great many facts which we cannot measure (quantitatively) and on which we have only some imprecise and general information. And because the effects of these facts in any particular instance cannot be confirmed by quantitative evidence, they are simply disregarded by those sworn to admit only what they regard as scientific evidence: they thereupon happily proceed on the fiction that the factors which they can measure are the only ones which are relevant" (Hayek, 1974: 2).

Similarly, human-relations programs and management-by-objectives programs may have produced undesirable consequences largely because organization theorists imputed their own values and world views to managers, and thus discounted the information available about managers.

The injunction to understand before prescribing seems inappropriate to the social sciences. This injunction may fit the physical sciences, for the physical sciences inhabit a slowly changing universe, and the relevant part of this universe is small enough to possess uniform laws. Physical scientists can extrapolate their findings from one time to another, and from one situation to another, so the understanding gained through prior study can be applied in subsequent prescription. In particular, physical scientists should comprehend problems clearly and thoroughly before they try to solve them. The social sciences, on the other hand, inhabit a rapidly changing and heterogeneous universe. Different parts of this universe follow disparate laws, and the laws evolve rapidly. Understanding gained in one situation may not extrapolate to another situation or to another time. Not only do most social problems change faster than scientists learn to comprehend them, but non-reflective efforts to make use of prior studies may actually interfere with problem solving.

Whether observation leads to understanding depends on what is observed and how it is observed. Passive observation, as we have already indicated, has produced ineffective theories of organizations, and merely observing organizations in the uneventful situations that predominate will never lead to understanding. The organization theorists who aspire to prescribe after they have gained sufficient understanding through passive observation will likely wait forever; for them, it will always be too soon.

Organizations' flexibility and dynamism imply that understanding can be attained better through instigating changes and watching organizations react. Organization theorists should at least attend to natural experiments, but this strategy alone would afford only temporary and modest improvements. Clearer discriminations among theories, less ambiguous interpretations of phenomena, and faster progress can be gained through instigating experiments and making predictions – which would transform observers into designers. Thus, design is an essential means to understanding, not merely a potential benefit of understanding.

Some design experiments are bound to harm organizations, and most damage cannot be corrected. However, three factors mitigate these risks. Firstly, today's organizations are far from wonderful, and people are already suffering the damage from ineffective organizations, so it would take amazing potency to make things much worse. Yet the potential benefits from better organizations loom large. Secondly, designers can limit damage by closely monitoring their experiments and promptly terminating harmful treatments. Thirdly, both Anglo-Saxon common law and the Nürnberg Trials provide grounds for holding designers liable for damage from their experiments unless the designers can prove:

(a) that their experiments were scientifically sound; and
(b) that participants in their experiments individually and voluntarily gave informed consent (Taylor and Vertinsky, 1981).

Consequently, designers should ask disinterested organization theorists to appraise their plans, they should try to spell out clearly and completely the potential damage as well as the potential benefits, and they should obtain the consent of each participant individually and without coercion. If designers adhere to these norms, expected benefits will outweigh the risks of harm.

Designers should be expected to try to predict experimental outcomes, but they should not be expected to predict accurately, because design cannot wait for understanding. Organizational designers should not, indeed, even rely upon the perceptions of organizational members. Members' perceptions of their organizations' environments correlate virtually zero with the measurable characteristics of those environments (Downey, Hellriegel and Slocum, 1975; Tosi, Aldag and Storey, 1973). Members are able to say whether their organizations are large or small, but otherwise, members' perceptions of their organizations' structures do not correlate consistently with the measurable characteristics of those structures (Payne and Pugh, 1976). Members in different positions in organizational hierarchies have significantly different perceptions of their organizations' structures (Payne and Pugh, 1976).

Designers' initial efforts are unlikely to succeed: these efforts produce bad consequences as well as good ones, and unpredicted consequences as well as predicted ones. While these consequences are altering target organizations, organizations' environments are changing and their members are learning. Thus, design improvements depend on breaking free from initial misconceptions, monitoring the actual consequences of previous design efforts, revising theories and updating observations, and generating new design efforts that are expected to counteract bad relationships while reinforcing good ones. The designers' products should be iterative sequences of design efforts that keep up with environmental changes and gradually improve both organizations and organization theory.

"During the past four and a half years we have pursued with great patience a lot of crackpot, idiotic, half-baked suggestions which have come from armchair critics. We have looked at all of these in great depth, and some of the ideas brought to us have been put into practice." (Otago Daily Times, 1979).

References

Anderson, John C. (1978) A Comparative Analysis of Local Union Democracy. *Industrial Relations*, 17, pp. 278–295.

Argyris, Chris (1973) Personality and Organization Theory Revisited. *Administrative Science Quarterly*, 18, pp. 141–167.

Bailey, Alan (1976) Coronary Disease: The Management Killer. *Journal of General Management*. 3 (4), pp. 72–80.

Bronfenbrenner, Urie (1976) The Experimental Ecology of Education. *Teachers College Record*, 78, pp. 157–204.

Caplovitz, David (1974) *Consumers in Trouble*. New York: Free Press.

Coser, Lewis A. (1956) *The Functions of Social Conflict*. Glencoe, Ill.: Free Press.

Churchhill, Betty C. (1955) Age and Life Expectancy of Business Firms. *Survey of Current Business*, 35 (2), pp. 15–19, p. 24.

Daft, Richard L. (1980) The Evolution of Organization Analysis in ASQ 1959–1979. *Administrative Science Quarterly* 25, pp. 623–636.

Downey, H. Kirk, Hellriegel, D., Slocum, J. W., Jr. (1975) Environmental Uncertainty: The Construct and its Application. *Administrative Science Quarterly*, 20, pp. 613–629.

General Accounting Office (1977) *Delays in Setting Workplace Standards for Cancer-causing and Other Dangerous Substances, Department of Labor, Department of Health, Education and Welfare: Report to Congress by the Controller General of the United States*. Washington, D. C.: General Accounting Office, May 10.

Goldthorpe, John H., Lockwood, D., Bechhofèr, F., Platt, J. (1968) *The Affluent Worker: Industrial Attitudes and Behaviour*. Cambridge, England: Cambridge University Press.

Gordon, Gerald Marquis, Sue Freedom (1966), Visibility of Consequences, and Scientific Innovation. *American Journal of Sociology*, 72, pp. 195–202.

Hayek, Friedrich A. von (1974) *The Pretence of Knowledge*. Stockholm: The Nobel Foundation, Nobel Memorial Prize Lecture delivered on 11 December.

Hedberg, Bo L. T., Nystrom, Paul, C., Starbuck William H. (1976) Camping on Seesaws: Prescriptions for a Self-designing Organization. *Administrative Science Quarterly*, 21, pp. 41–65.

Hill, Larry B. (1972) Complaining to the Ombudsman as an Urban Phenomenon: An Analysis of the New Zealand Ombudsman's Clients. *Urban Affairs Quarterly*, 8, pp. 123–127.

Jaques, Elliott (1951) *The Changing Culture of a Factory*. London: Tavistock.

Karasek, Robert A., Jr. (1979) Job Demands, Job Decision Latitude, and Mental Strain: Implications for Job Redesign. *Administrative Science Quarterly*, 24, pp. 285–308.

Kasl, Stanislav V., Cobb, S., Brooks, G. W. (1968) Changes in Serum Uric Acid and Cholesterol Levels in Men Undergoing Job Loss. *Journal of the American Medical Association*, 206, pp. 1500–1507.

Kelly, Joe (1968) *Is Scientific Management Possible?* London: Faber and Faber.

Kolko, Gabriel (1965) *Railroads and Regulation, 1877–1916*. Princeton, NJ: Princeton University Press.

Kornhauser, Arthur (1965) *Mental Health of the Industrial Worker.* New York: Wiley.

Leach, Edmund (1964) Anthropological Aspects of Language: Animal Categories and Verbal Abuse. *New Directions in the Study of Language,* Lenneberg, Eric H. (Ed.), Cambridge, Mass.: MIT Press, pp. 23–63.

Meyer, John W., Rowan, Brian (1977) Institutionalized Organizations: Formal Structure as Myth and Ceremony. *American Journal of Sociology,* 83, pp. 340–363.

Nicholls, John (1980) The Alloplastic Organisation: Balancing Flexibility and Stability in a Turbulent Environment. *Journal of General Management,* 6 (1), pp. 61–79.

Niv. Amittai (1978) *Survival of Social Innovation.* Working Paper, Jerusalem Institute for Management.

Nystrom, Paul C., Starbuck, William H. (Eds.) (1977) *Prescriptive Models of Organizations.* Amsterdam: North-Holland.

– (1981) *Handbook of Organizational Design, Vol. 1 Adapting Organizations to Their Environments and Vol. 2 Remodeling Organizations and Their Environments.* New York: Oxford University Press.

Nystrom, Paul C., Hedberg, Bo L. T., Starbuck, William H. (1976) Interacting Processes as Organization Designs. *The Management of Organization Design,* Vol. 1, Kilmann, Ralph H., Pondy, Louis R. and Slevin, Dennis P. (Eds.), New York: Elsevier North-Holland, pp. 209–230.

Otago Daily Times, Dunedin, New Zealand, 13 February, 1979.

O'Toole, James, Hansot, E., Herman, W., Herrick, N., Liebow, E., Lusignan, B., Richman, H., Sheppard, H., Staphansky, B., Wright, J. (1973) *Work in America.* Cambridge, Mass: MIT Press.

Payne, Roy Pugh, Derek, S. (1976) Organizational Structure and Climate. *Handbook of Industrial and Organizational Psychology.* Dunnette, Marvin D. (Ed.), Chicago: Rand McNally, pp. 1125–1173.

Rosenhan, David L. (1973) On Being Sane in Insane Places. *Science,* 179 (4070, 19 January), pp. 250–258.

Schriesheim, Janet, Von Glinow, Mary Ann, Kerr, Steven (1977) Professionals in Bureaucracies: A Structural Alternative. *Prescriptive Models of Organizations,* Nystrom, Paul C. and Starbuck, William H. (Eds.), Amsterdam: North-Holland, pp. 55–69.

Starbuck, William H. (1976) Organizations and Their Environments. *Handbook of Industrial and Organizational Psychology,* Dunnette, Marvin D. (Ed.), Chicago: Rand McNally, pp. 1069–1123.

– (1981) A Trip to View the Elephants and Rattlesnakes in the Garden of Aston. *Perspectives on Organization Design and Behavior,* Van de Ven, Andrew H. and Joyce, William F. (Eds.), New York: Wiley-Interscience, pp. 167–198.

Starbuck, William H., Dutton, John M. (1973) Designing Adaptive Organizations. *Journal of Business Policy,* 3 (Summer), pp. 21–28.

Starbuck William H., Nystrom, Paul C. (1981) Designing and Understanding Organizations. *Handbook of Organizational Design, Vol. 1,* Nystrom, Paul C. and Starbuck, William H. (Eds.) New York: Oxford University Press, pp. IX–XXII.

Starbuck, William H., Greve, Arent, Hedberg, Bo L. T. (1978) Responding to Crises. *Journal of Business Administration* 9 (2), pp. 111–137.

Stigler, George J. (1971) The Theory of Economic Regulation. *Bell Journal of Economics and Management Science,* 2, pp. 3–21.

Taylor, Ronald N., Vertinsky, Ilan (1981) Experimenting with Organizational Behavior. *Handbook of Organizational Design, Vol. 1,* Nystrom, Paul C. and Starbuck, William H. (Eds.), New York: Oxford University Press, pp. 139–166.

Tosi, Henry, Aldag, R., Storey, R. (1973) On the Measurement of the Environment: An Assessment of the Lawrence and Lorsch Environmental Uncertainty Subscale. *Administrative Science Quarterly,* 18, pp. 27–36.

Vandivier, Kermit (1972) The Aircraft Brake Scandal. *Harper's Magazine,* 244 (1463, April), pp. 45–52.

Wall Street Journal (1978) Firestone Radios Had Highest Rate of Troubles in Study. *Wall Street Journal,* 191 (64, April 3), p. 17.

Wanous, John P. (1980) *Organizational Entry.* Reading, Mass.: Addison-Wesley.

Warner, Malcolm (1980) Experimenting, Organising and Theorising: A Contingency Approach. *Journal of General Management,* 5 (3), pp. 30–42.

– (1981) Organizational Experiments and Social Innovations. *Handbook of Organizational Design, Vol. 1,* Nystrom, Paul C. and Starbuck, William H. (Eds.), New York: Oxford University Press, pp. 167–184.

Watzlawick, Paul, Weakland, John H., Fisch, R. (1974) *Change.* New York: Norton.

Williamson, Oliver, E. (1963) *The Economics of Discretionary Behavior.* Englewood Cliffs, NJ: Prentice-Hall.

Wright, H. Beric (1975) Health Hazards of Managers. *Journal of General Management,* 2 (2), pp. 9–13.

Walter Goldberg's Biography

Political systems, economic systems, systems of thought – all tend to isolate themselves from each other as they grow and mature. Sometimes stemming from a common root, they separate as they evolve. The inner logic of a system crystallizes and rejects everything which is extrinsic to it; the world becomes divided into an inside and an outside, "us" and "them", believers and heretics. Communication between well-developed and well-differentiated systems becomes first impossible and then inconceivable, and so the ivory towers grow in their separate realities.

But, from time to time, there is somebody who thinks the unthinkable, who seems not to notice the stone barrier, and who finds holes which permit communication, which help people to notice each other again, to cooperate, to learn about one another. What does it take to perform such a function? Perceptiveness and an uncurbed curiosity. An understanding of people, no matter where they come from. An understanding of organizations, no matter what kind. And, perhaps, the life-status of an outsider.

Walter Goldberg was born on March 24, 1924, in a small village in Bohemia. The war cut into his life, and even now he has never ceased to be surprised at his own survival. Rescue brought him to Sweden. He was then 22 years old, 181 cm tall and weighted 46 kig. He started working as a textile worker, as this was a job he had had before. His first discovery was that unless he learned Swedish immediately, nobody would understand him. His family used to speak Czech and German at home, but neither of these languages was much use in Sweden. Even those who knew German refused to speak it. So he took courses in Swedish at Hermods correspondence school: first a course in spelling, then in Swedish grammar. He used to memorize words in time with his loom. As a shift-worker, he was able to work from 5 in the morning until 2 in the afternoon, then sleep for two hours and study till 11 at night. The Hermods courses were very popular in Sweden, because of the size of the country, but they were not meant for foreigners. Goldberg had to learn French via Swedish, for example, as a foreign language was required. In this way he gained his secondary school certificate.

The second discovery which the young émigrée made was that his new friends and fellow-workers were not interested in the plans, and dreams or achievements he had entertained in the past. They related to him purely in terms of his present activities. This was a very useful discovery, as it helped him to forget the past more easily, and forced him to create a new present for himself. A solution came to him by chance. His fellow-workers asked him to become a union steward. Surprised by this choice – there were many older and more experienced men eligible – he learned that it was his skill in handling the slide-rule that had brought him to this honour. The workers knew that every discussion about a wage increase always ended with the engineer producing his slide-rule, performing some mysterious rites, and then declaring: "No, it's impossible". They wanted to have a representative who could show on the same slide-rule that it was possible.

The stewardship made him sensitive to the problems of an ailing industry, as the textile industry was at the time. The workers were constantly aware that the next week might be their last on the job. How can you assess an employer's capacity to secure jobs? This question, born of a practical interest, became a theoretical problem which still concerns Walter Goldberg today. It led him to apply to the Gothenburg Business School though without much hope of being accepted. And, indeed, the School turned him down because of his "strange background", but the Stockholm Business School accepted him, precisely because his background was unusual. However, life in Stockholm proved too expensive and the term fees too high, and on learning that there were some vacancies in Gothenburg, he reapplied and moved back. He obtained his master's degree (civilekonom) there in 1954.

At that time there were no scholarships and many students worked their way through college. Walter Goldberg tried his skills as a correspondent, then as a bank clerk, and later as an export-import trader. This jack-of-all-trades background prepared him well for one of the most important meetings of his life. At the same time as Walter Goldberg began to study there, a new professor was appointed at the Gothenburg Business School, namely Ulf af Trolle. A man with an unconventional life story, af Trolle was looking for an assistant who should fulfill two basic requirements: he should possess a grass-roots knowledge of the textile industry, and a type-writer. Walter Goldberg had both, and found himself with a job. But Ulf af Trolle's interests were not limited to the textile industry. As Walter recalls it, it was af Trolle's custom to dine with a variety of people, collecting their problems and bringing them to the School: "Here's something we should do something about". One of those dining partners was Assar Gabrielsson. At that time Volvo was a very small car manufacturer which was dreaming of entering the international market. Could the School help Volvo with its new enterprise, introducing modern manage-ment methods into the many small supplier firms? Thus Goldberg acquired a task which kept him occupied until 1973.

Af Trolle continued to dine out. At a dinner soon after he met a member of Gothenburg's municipal council, who was worried about growing costs and progressive taxes. So now the professor and his assistant began to take an interest in another kind of ailing organization, and thus resulted in their writing a book together Måste kommunalskatten stiga? (Do municipal taxes have to grow?), and in Walter's promotion to head the public administration section at IDAF (the Institute of Marketing, Economic and Administrative

Research). This task was particularly difficult and also unusual, since at that time the public sector was not considered to be a topic worth studying. The researchers thus needed a new methodology, new methods of comparison, and a whole new approach.

In his doctoral dissertation, preceded by two first-in-Europe collections of organizational case studies (1952, 1954), Walter Goldberg addressed the issue of efficient performance in the public sector: How can we substitute for competition in non-market organizations? How can we compare performances when the outcomes cannot be measured? The dissertation, defended in 1962, opened the way to further studies of the public sector and facilitated subsequent cooperation with researchers from non-market economies.

At this time the Swedish business schools, much like the German, were still geared largely to accounting: accounting *was* business. And, much to the surprise of the ex-textile-worker, this was accepted as a matter of course. The courses taught students what to do with the accounting information once it was available, but nobody cared about its genesis, about how it related to resources, or about how it could be used in resource planning. Operational research came into fashion, and Walter had to orient himself in yet another field, starting another adventure which was to continue far into the future.

There were many things which Walter Goldberg learned from his mentor, especially as they fitted very will into his own way of perceiving the world. One concerned relations between tutor and pupil, allowing for maximum freedom, and continuous encouragement to try to do things that nobody else dared or cared to do. This proved to be a costly habit, but one which Walter has never abandoned. Another was a belief that the best way of learning about organizations was to study those which were sick. Illness exposes the insides of a firm, and reveals the guts behind its performance. This interest in organizational pathology aroused Goldberg's interest in the works of the Polish praxiologist, Tadeusz Kotarbinski, and led him to start a scheme of cooperation with Polish organization students, which has lasted for the last 30 years.

Last but not least was the assumption, shared by professor and student, both of whom had enjoyed years of practical experience; that behind technology and financial controls there is always human behavior, and it was essential to treat the three factors jointly. This aim, to reconcile people with numbers, led to Goldberg's fruitful encounter with the behavioral theory of the firm.

Although accounting was so important in Swedish business schools at the time, the faculty of accounting was not greatly impressed by the development of punch-card systems and computers. However, the new adept of operational research developed an interest in the technology of data processing, and thanks to the encouragement of his superior was able to steer into the direction of the emerging discipline. The first courses in computing were introduced in 1959, when punch-cards were about to give way to extended memories. The first studies of numerical control in production were made, and the grounds for further research firmly established with the computer being cut down to size as a tool for organizational improvement rather than a technological deity to be approached with awe. Quite naturally, a more advanced examples of use of computer in school curricula were looked for, which brought Walter Goldberg to the Carnegie Institute of Technology. He was fascinated by the use of business computer games, and people from Carnegie began visiting Sweden to help to introduce the games here. Both sides found the cooperation equally rewarding. The Carnegie faculty included the eminent scholars concerned with the behavioral theory of the firm, and so in 1969 a meeting came about between Herbert Simon, James March, Richard Cyert, Harry Leavitt, and a group of young Scandinavian researchers, which initiated the influence of this school on Scandinavian research. A two-week meeting on the outskirts of Gothenburg gave many young people an opportunity to come into contact with a group of leading American organizational researchers, and played an important part in reducing the gap between traditional economics and the behavioral sciences, in building the bridge which still remains one of the most important supports of organizational theory.

The use of computer games in the school curriculum and the interest in "bringing together people and numbers" led to several interesting experiments in simulation and modelling, generally intended to provide at the same time material for a dissertation and a practical tool. The 1960's, during which Walter Goldberg was first promoted associate professor (1964) and later appointed full professor (1966), were spent on research into the use of mathematical models in simulation in business education and business management. Most although by no means all of Walter Goldberg's doctoral students worked on this project. As a teacher, professor Goldberg carefully preserves variety, and protects deviants. He also encourages teamwork, and was in fact behind one of the first joint doctoral dissertation in Sweden. This dissertation, concerned with a simulation model of city traffic appeared just at the time when Sweden was switching to righthand traffic, and the city of Gothenburg found the model very handy.

In the late 1960s many new international management institutes were established in Europa, modelled on American models, and Walter Goldberg was offered a position at the Science Center Berlin. This was a time when Gothenburg Business School was being re-organized as part of the University of Gothenburg and Walter Goldberg preferred for various reasons to stay at home. However, when another offer came from Berlin in 1973, together with the news that research would be welcome on the subject of stagnation, now a major interest, Walter Goldberg accepted. Subsequently, during the period

1973–1979 he served as director of the International Institute of Management (IIM) at Science Center Berlin.

At that time Berlin was a city in decline. After the Wall was built, the city lost its headquarter functions, the big industries started to move out, and the feeling grew of being closed in. The Soviet invasion of Czechoslovakia intensified the sense of claustrophobia; Berlin seemed to be doomed. The new city government saw that something must be done and made it their goal to turn Berlin into an innovative city. Very much against the bureaucratic tradition, researchers were asked for help, more specifically the IIM with its interest in stagnation research.

Walter Goldberg's interest in stagnation and decline stems from his belief that these conditions are actually much more dynamic than growth, that they enforce the search for new solutions and are therefore closely related to innovation. Thus the researchers were invited to present their reports to a loosely connected group of people – trade unionists, employers, city administrators – who had one thing in common: the will to start things moving. A list of desired changes was produced as an outcome of this meeting, and after a certain amount of bureaucratic opposition had been overcome the list was implemented, item by item, at very low cost. The results were rewarding to all the parties concerned.

An achievement on this scale depends very much on the people involved, and Walter Goldberg spent a great deal of effort on assembling the right team. He saw his own role as that of organizer, facilitator and protector. The main task was to attract people of high competence, which meant being able make them an attractive offer. The next point was to free the researchers from everyday concerns, to protect them from bureaucratic threats and to facilitate their adaptation to their new surroundings. Once that was achieved, it was possible to build up positive pressure by setting targets.

This personnel policy was something new to most of the researchers, who as a breed are usually harassed by bureaucratic demands, motivated by threats and the promise of vague and remote rewards. The feelings of personal freedom combined with attractive targets activated a huge potential of creativity and satisfaction.

The professional successes of Walter Goldberg's life have not always been accompanied by private happiness. His wife, Birgit, suffered for years from multiple sclerosis. She spent more than twenty years in a wheel chair, still managing to live a very active and rich life. She wrote novels and letters to other handicapped people, and when her paralysis progressed she typed by touching the electric keyboard with a pin held between her teeth. His understanding of the problems which handicapped poeple have to face led Walter Goldberg to write one of the first books to appear on the employment of the handicapped in industry (1957).

In 1977, Goldberg's oldest son died in an accident at the age of 23. Birgit's health deterioated rapidly. She had to be hospitalized and had trouble communicating in a foreign language, as her voice became inaudible. In 1979 the family returned to Sweden, where Birgit spent the last years of her life in an intensive care home, close to where the family lived. She died suddenly in 1984, her mental capacity and her love of life intact to the end.

Walter Goldberg returned to the University of Gothenburg, without administrative duties, so as to be able to give more time to caring for his wife. But he still retained his main interests – his curiosity about ailing organizations, his search for ways of bringing together people and numbers and of combining different disciplines, systems and people. At present he is deeply involved in an international project concerning innovation in the electrotechnological industry. The participating countries are the Soviet Union, East Germany, Hungary, Bulgaria, Yugoslavia, Czechoslovakia, Austria, West Germany, Finland, Sweden and the U.S.A. When he is asked what we can learn from discouraging events in the socialist economies, his answer is still the same: studying ailing organizations is the best way of understanding conditions of health. And his interest in making comparisons is by no means limited to European countries. His position as Scientific Adviser to UNIDO brought him assignments in Indonesia, Thailand, Taiwan, Pakistan and Bangladesh. He firmly believes that the best way of learning about Sweden is to look at other countries.

Asked on his 60th birthday what he thought about his approaching retirement, Walter Goldberg said he intended to go on adding to his list of published works. This is already impressive, even including items in Japanese. His latest book. "Ailing Steel" (Gower, 1984) deals with his favorite topic, and so will the next four or five that he plans to write. Despite or perhaps because of his all-trades background, he perceives himself as essentially obsessed with one question: how to make a good firm out of a bad one? And the final answer has not yet been found. His next book is "Innovation in Large and Vintaged Enterprises: A Comparative East-West Approach to the Case of the Electrotechnology Industry" (the final report from the IIASA project).

No-on should imagine, however, that research and teaching occupy all Walter's time. He rides a bike everyday, claiming that it is essential to have a good supply of oxygen to the brain in order to be able to produce new and startling ideas. He is a keen gardener, because after dealing with intangibles for most of the day, it is necessary to come into contact with concrete things, things which respond to care by growing. Music has always been the refuge of the Goldberg family, resulting in a large personal collection of Slavic music, from medieval Polish church music to Szymanowski, Lutoslawski and Penderecki, and embracing even Shostakovich and Bartók. Finally, arttravelling provides an opportunity to collect galleries like butterflies, while also satisfying a semi-professional interest in the organizations and values of ancient societis.

Thinking back over his life Walter Goldberg finds himself agreeing with John Lennon: life is something that happens to you while you are making other plans. And that is what is best about it.

The Authors

Nils Brunsson

obtained his Ph. D. in Management in 1976 from the University of Göteborg, Sweden. Since then he has held research positions at the universities of Göteborg and Uppsala and at the Stockholm School of Economics. At present he is Professor of Management at the Stockholm School of Economics. He has published several articles and eight books on subjects such as product development, organizational change, decision-making, organizational control, budgeting and research methodology. His latest book is *The Irrational Organization* (Chichester, John Wiley and Sons 1985) in which a theory of organizational action and change is presented. His current research interests include organizational legitimation in institutionalized environments.

Richard M. Cyert

became Carnegie-Mellon's sixth President in 1972, after serving for 10 years as Dean of the Graduate School of Industrial Administration. He first joined the CMU faculty in 1948 as Instructor of Economics. Cyert has earned international recognition for his work in economics, behavioral science and management. Through his leadership, CMU enjoys a growing national reputation, financial solvency, expanding academic and research programs and a resurgence in athletics.

Barbara Czarniawska

has an MA in Social Psychology from the University of Warsaw (1970), and a PH. D. in Economics from the Central School of Planning and Statistics, Warsaw (1976). Until 1981 she was Assistant Professor in the Faculty of Psychology, University of Warsaw. At present she is Associate Professor in Business Administration at the Stockholm School of Economics, Sweden. Books in Polish: *Managing Enterprises Operating in the Consumer Goods Market* (co-author), *Psychosocial Aspects of Decision-making Processes, Decision Making, Motivational Aspects of Management, Managing Cultural Institutions: A path to success* (co-author), *Management Processes from Different Perspectives.* In English: *Controlling Top Management in Large Organizations* (Gower 1985). Her current interests are: decentralization processes in Swedish municipalities and ideological control in non-ideological organizations.

Anders Edström

has an MS in Industrial Administration from Carnegie Mellon University and a DBA from the University of Göteborg. He has taught and done research at the University of Göteborg, INSEAD, Fontainebleau, France, the European Institute for Advanced Studies in Management, Brussels, and the Stockholm School of Economics. He is presently director of a research program on Leadership and Organization at the Swedish Council for Management and Work Life Issues in Stockholm. His research has covered areas such as information systems, organization design and personnel, strategy and leadership. He has published in several international journals for example Administrative Science Quarterly, Management Science, Human Relations, Journal of International Business and Organization Studies.

Bo Hedberg

is Professor of Management with a background in organization theory, computer science, and work life research.

A graduate of the Graduate School of Business Administration (MBA and Ph.D.) at the University of Göteborg, Sweden, Bo Hedberg's academic career includes associate professorships at the GSBA and Chalmers Institute of Technology. He was later Research Fellow at the International Institute of Management, Berlin, Visiting Professor at the University of Wisconsin at Milwaukee and at the London School of Economics. Since 1977 Dr. Hedberg holds a research professorship at the Swedish Center for Worling life, Stockholm. He is now Executive Vice President in charge of coordination and business development in the largest Swedish banking group, the Swedish Savings Banks Association.

Dr. Hedberg has worked as a consultant to Swedish industry and as an adviser to the prime Minister's Office. His research covers areas such as man-computer interaction, organization design, decision-making processes, work organization, and industrial democracy. His published works include six research monographs, contributions to several international books, and numerous articles in various professional journals.

David Hickson

PhD (Hon) (Umeå), Professor of Organizational Analysis at the University of Bradford Management Centre, England, worked in administration and qualified professionally as a company secretary before moving into academic research at the University of Manchester Institute of Science and Technology. His principal research has been at the University of Aston on the structures of organization and managerial roles; at the University of Alberta, Canada, on intraorganizational power; and at Bradford Management Centre on processes of strategic decision making. He has also been extensively concerned with cross-national comparisons of features of organizations. He has published in Administrative Science Quarterly, Organization Studies, Sociology, Occupational Psychology, Journal of Management Studies, Academy of Management Journal, Academy of Management Review, and a variety of other journals and magazines, together with four books and numerous contributions to edited volumes. He retired from the editorial boards of Administrative Science Quarterly and the Journal of Management Studies to become Editor-in-Chief of the new European based journal, Organization Studies. He was a founder of the European association in his field, EGOS (European Group for Organizational Studied). He holds an honorary doctorate from the University of Umeå in Sweden for his contribution to research. He has a Fellow of the Netherlands Institute for Advanced Studies in the Humanities and Social Sciences for the academic year 1982/83.

Bengt Högberg

is Adjunct Professor at the Linköping Institute of Technology, Department of Management and Economics and Chairman of a development company, Connova Invest AB. He received his Ph. D. in 1978. His publications include studies of interfirm cooperation and East-West economic relations. Current research interests are interorganizational analysis and innovation.

Sten A. Jönsson

Ph. D. 1971, Professor of Accounting since 1976 at the University of Göteborg. Research interests have centered round the symbolic and rational use of economic information in organizations; first in business development processes (e.g. *Decentralization and Development* 1973, in Swedish), later in crisis situations (e.g. *Designing Semi-Confusing Information Systems for Organizations in Changing Environments,* with Hedberg 1977). During the last few years the relation of individuals to norms in political organizations (budgets, plans, decisions) and standards in the accounting community, has been the main focus of interest. The setting of norms and standards, a process of great symbolic importance in which only rational arguments are legitimate, has been the object of his research.

Current research is directed towards the use of economic information in making sense of the operative level in decentralized and automated industrial production.

Stig Larsson

is Assistant Professor at the University of Göteborg, Department of Business Administration. He obtained his Ph. D. in 1984. His research, his published work and his teaching all concern political aspects of management and strategic decision-making. He also has many years of experience in management positions in industrial firms.

Rolf A. Lundin

Rolf A. Lundin obtained his Licentiate from the Göteborg School of Economics and Business Administration in Sweden. His thesis was concerned with methodological problems connected with the formulation and application of an urban traffic simulation model. He obtained his Ph. D. from the Graduate School of Business, University of Chicago, in 1973 on a thesis entitled *Planning Horizon Procedures for Production-Inventory Systems with Concave Costs*. He then joined the Department of Business Administration at the University of Göteborg as Associate Professor. In 1978 he was appointed Professor of Business Administration at the University of Umeå, a position which he still holds.

After returning from the US in 1973, Professor Lundin's research interests have gradually shifted from management science to behavioral science areas. The article "Myths and Wishful Thinking as Management Tools" (together with Sten Jönsson) published in Paul C. Nystrom and William H. Starbuck (eds.): *Prescriptive Models of Organizations* (Amsterdam: North Holland) marks that change. Studies involving local government partly inspired the shift in focus.

Present research interests include leadership, especially in the overlapping zone between the private and the public sector.

Professor Lundin is currently editor of the Scandinavian Journal of Management Studies.

James G. March

is Fred H. Merrill Professor of Management. Political Science, and Sociology at Stanford University and Senior Fellow at the Hoover Institution. He is the author of several books on organizations, leadership, and decision making, including Ambiguity and Choice in Organizations and Leadership and Ambiguity. The research for this article was supported by grants from the Spencer Foundation, the Stanford Graduate School of Business, and the Hoover Institution.

Gerhard O. Mensch

is Professor of Management at the Weatherhead School of Management, and Professor of Economics at the Economics Department of Case Western Reserve University. Before that, he directed an innovations research group at the International Institute of Management, Science Center Berlin, for ten years. Prior to this, he was associate professor of management science at Tulane University, visiting professor at Bonn University, and visiting scholar at Harvard, Stanford and Berkely.

He has published and co-authored several books and numerous articles on economic change, and technological innovation in firms and in regions. He is interested in the internal and external conditions of entrepreneurship, innovation and infant industry formation, and the human resource and policy aspects of it. For his work on the clustering of innovations, and the managerial and industrial consequences, he received the Prognos Prize for 1983, and the Humboldt Prize for 1985.

He has been a consultant to industrial corporations and government agencies. At Case in Cleveland, he heads the teaching and research programs in innovations management and industry-base analysis. Dr. Mensch is a member of the board of directors of Nordson Corporation, General Economics Corporation, and Investment in Innovations, Ltd., Inc. Also, he is co-founder of The International Institute of Industrial Innovations, in Cleveland and Munich.

Pierre Guillet de Monthoux

is currently Visiting Professor at the University of Massachusetts, Amherst, and Associate Professor of Technology and Social Change at the University of Linköping, Sweden. A business economist by education, he has published books and articles in Swedish, German and English in the areas of industrial marketing, organizational behavior and the history of ideas in business economics. In his latest English book *Action and Existence – Anarchism for Business Administration* (Wiley 1983) he investigates the philosophy of action and the hermeutics of projects in a vein close to the article published in this volume. He is now working on a two-volume history of managerial thought in political economy: *Concrete and Abstract Economy – the Doctrines of Enterprise and Money*.

Lars Erik Norbäck

is Assistant Professor at the University of Göteborg, Department of Business Administration. He obtained his Ph. D. in 1978. His research, his published work and his teaching all concern interorganizational cooperation, industrial policy, and leadership and management in the service sector.

Paul Nyström

is Research Professor at the School of Business Administration, University of Wisconsin-Milwaukee. He received his Ph. D. in industrial relations from the University of Minnesota, where he also received a B. S. in economics and an M. A. in public administration. He worked in headquarters staff positions at General Mills, the Office of the Secretary of Defense, and ADM before coming to Wisconsin. Professor Nyström's research interests and journal publications span diverse topics in organizational design, managerial behavior, human resources, and business strategy. He has co-edited two books with William Starbuck, the most recent being the award-winning *Handbook of Organizational Design* (Oxford University Press 1981). He has served as an associate editor of *Management Science* and is a member of the Academy of Management, American Psychological Association, Industrial Relations Research Association, and The Institute of Management Sciences.

Bengt Sandkull

is Professor of Industrial Organization at the University of Linköping, Sweden, where he has become involved in managerial and organizational research. He has a primary interest in the role of participation in the industrialization process in non-industrialized countries, and in industrial renewal in Sweden and other industrial countries. For almost ten years he has been investigating the ways in which industrial strategies shape social and technical production relations. An article on this topic appeared in Human Systems Management (September 1980). Before this he was mainly concerned with innovation and product development; the subject of his Ph. D. dissertation was *Innovative Behavior of Organizations: the Case of New Products* (1970).

F. M. Scherer

is Joseph Wharton Professor of Political Economy at Swarthmore College. His undergraduate studies were at the University of Michigan; he received his MBA and PhD from Harvard University. He has also taught at Princeton University, the University of Michigan, and Northwestern University. From 1972–74 he was senior research fellow at the International Institute of Management, Berlin, Germany, and from 1974–76 he was chief economist at the Federal Trade Commission. His research specialites are industrial economics and the economics of technological innovation, leading to numerous articles and the books as for example: Industrial Market Structure and Economic Performance (Rand McNally and Houghton-Mifflin 1970, revised edition 1980). The Economics of Multi-Plant Operation: An International Comparisons Study (Harvard University Press 1975). Innovation and Growth: Schumpeterian Perspectives (MIT Press 1984).

His current research seeks to illuminate a neglected but increasingly important phenomenon: the sell-off of company units into what is often a self-standing new enterprise. The research is supported by a National Science Foundation grant.

Herbert A. Simon

is Richard King Mellon University Professor of Computer Science and Psychology at Carnegie-Mellon University, where he has taught since 1949. During the past thirty years he has been studying decision-making and problem-solving processes, using computers to simulate human thinking. He has published over 500 papers and 20 books and monographs.

Educated at the University of Chicago (Ph. D. 1943), his work has been recognized by honorary degrees from a number of universities.

He was elected to the National Academy of Sciences in 1967. He received the Distinguished Scientific Contribution Award of the American Psychological Association, the A. M. Turing Award of the Association for Computing Machinery, the James Madison Award of the American Political Science Association, and was elected Distinguished Fellow of the American Economic Association. He received the Alfred Nobel Memorial Prize in Economics in 1978.

He has been Chairman of the Board of Directors of the Social Science Research Council, and of the Behavioral Science Division of the National Research Council, and was a member of the President's Science Advisory Committee.

William Starbuck

is the ITT Professor of Creative Management at New York University. He received his M. S. and Ph. D. in industrial administration at Carnegie Institute of Technology, after receiving an A. B. in physics at Harvard. He has held faculty positions at Purdue University, the Johns Hopkins University, Cornell University, and the University of Wisconsin-Milwaukee, as well as visiting position at London Graduate School of Business Studies, Norwegian School of Economics and Business Administration, the University of Gothenberg, and Stockholm School of Economics. He was also a senior research fellow at the International Institute of Management, Berlin. He formerly served as editor of *Administrative Science Quarterly* and on the editorial board of the *Journal of Applied Social Psychology,* and he chaired the screening committee for senior Fulbright awards in business management. He currently serves on the editorial boards of *Administrative Science Quarterly,* the *Academy of Management Review,* the *Journal of Management Studies,* and the *Scandinavian Journal of Management Studies.* He is a fellow of the American Psychological Association and a member of several other professional associations.

He has published numerous articles on human decision making, bargaining, organizational growth and development, social revolutions, computer simulation, computer programming, accounting, business strategy, and organizational design. He has also edited four books, including the *Handbook of Organizational Design,* which was chosen the best book on management published during the year ending May 1982.

Thomas Stenberg

has a Ph. D. in Business Administration. Following some years as a university lecturer and researcher, he has worked mainly on management and company development on a consultant basis.

Stenberg specializes today on business development and financial reconstruction. He is a member of the board of several Scandinavian companies.

Although heavily involved in the development of his own and his client's companies, Stenberg continues to work on research projects. His main research area at present is the role of investment companies.

Ulf Sternhufvud

has an MA in Psychology and an MA in Business Administration. He also has a Ph. D. in Business Administration. He wrote his doctoral thesis on Product Discontinuation in Firms. The research for this degree was carried out at the International Institute of Management, Berlin, and at the Göteborg School of Economics, Sweden.

Dr. Sternhufvud has worked for five years as a top management consultant. At present he is employed by INDEVO AB, the largest Scandinavian top-management consulting firm. He works primarily in the fields of strategic development, business portfolio analysis and human resources. His clients consist mainly of large Scandinavian privately owned companies and a few state agencies. He has also published several articles in Swedish and German professional business journals.

Ilan Vertinsky

is director of the Center for International Business Studies and the Consortium for Strategic Management at the University of British Columbia. He is also professor of Animal Resource Ecology, Management Science, and Policy Analysis at the same university. He has published more than 90 papers covering topics in population ecology, operations research, energy policy, corporate strategy, international trade, decision analysis, psychology, and organizational behavior.

Rolf Wolff

M. A. in Economics from the University of Wuppertal (1977), Master of Social Sciences from the University of Göteborg (1980), Ph. D. in Business Administration from the University of Wuppertal. He has been Assistant Professor at the University of Göteborg and the University of Innsbruck and a Research Fellow at the Swedish Center for Working Life. At present he is Associate Professor of Management at the Stockholm School of Economics and Professor of Management at Nordische Universität Flensburg. His current research interests are industrial development, industrial politics and leadership problems in institutionalized economies.

de Gruyter Studies in Organization

An international series by internationally known authors presenting current research in organization.

European Approaches to International Management

Edited by *Klaus Macharzina* and *Wolfgang H. Staehle*

1985. 15,5 x 23 cm. XIV, 386 pages. Cloth DM 128,-
ISBN 3 11 009827 X

Management Under Differing Value Systems

Political, Social and Economical Perspectives in a Changing World

Edited by *Günter Dlugos* and *Klaus Weiermair*

1981. 17 x 24 cm. XIV, 868 pages. Cloth DM 148,-
ISBN 3 11 008553 4

Studies in Decision Making

Social, Psychological and Socio-Economic Analyses

Edited by *Martin Irle* in collaboration with *Lawrence B. Katz*

1982. 17 x 24 cm. XVI, 917 pages. Cloth DM 176,-
ISBN 3 11 008087 7

The State of the Masses

By *Richard F. Hamilton* and *James D. Wright*

1986. 16,5 x 24,2 cm. XII, 470 pages. Bibliography, indices.
Cloth DM 148,- ISBN 3 11 010819 4
For USA and Canada:
Cloth $39.95 ISBN 0-202-30324-1 (Aldine de Gruyter, New York)

Management Dictionary

By *Werner Sommer* and *Hanns-Martin Schoenfeld*

English-German:
1979. 12,2 x 18,8 cm. 621 pages. Cloth DM 58,- ISBN 3 11 007708 6

German-English:
1978. 12,2 x 18,8 cm. 542 pages. Cloth DM 58,- ISBN 3 11 004863 9

Prices are subject to change without notice

WALTER DE GRUYTER · BERLIN · NEW YORK